D1526339

8/9/21

Augustine on the Will

Augustine on the Will

A Theological Account

HAN-LUEN KANTZER KOMLINE

OXFORD

UNIVERSITY PRESS

OXFORD
UNIVERSITY PRESS

Oxford University Press is a department of the University of Oxford. It furthers
the University's objective of excellence in research, scholarship, and education
by publishing worldwide. Oxford is a registered trade mark of Oxford University
Press in the UK and certain other countries.

Published in the United States of America by Oxford University Press
198 Madison Avenue, New York, NY 10016, United States of America.

© Oxford University Press 2020

Library of Congress Cataloging-in-Publication Data
Names: Komline, Han-luen Kantzer, author.
Title: Augustine on the will : a theological account / Han-luen Kantzer Komline.
Description: New York : Oxford University Press, [2020] |
Includes bibliographic references.
Identifiers: LCCN 2019021281 | ISBN 9780190948801 (hardback) |
ISBN 9780190948818 (updf) | ISBN 9780190948825 (epub)
Subjects: LCSH: Augustine, of Hippo, Saint, 354-430. | Free will and
determinism—Religious aspects—Christianity.
Classification: LCC BR65.A9 K595 2020 | DDC 233/.5—dc23
LC record available at https://lccn.loc.gov/2019021281

To my grandparents,
Yun-wan Chou Lee
Chi-kang Lee
Ruth Forbes Kantzer
Kenneth Sealer Kantzer

Contents

Acknowledgments

Ultimate thanks are due to God for anything good in this book. I am also grateful to many others for their help.

A number of institutions and groups deserve thanks. The University of Notre Dame, the Louisville Institute, and Western Theological Seminary generously supported my research. I am grateful for permission to draw on some of my previous publications: "'*Ut in Illo Uiueremus*': Augustine on the Two Wills of Christ," *Studia Patristica* 70 (2013): 347–355; "The Second Adam in Gethsemane: Augustine on the Human Will of Christ," *Revue d'études augustiniennes et patristiques* 58 (2012): 41–56; and "Grace, Free Will, and the Lord's Prayer: Cyprian's Importance for the 'Augustinian' Doctrine of Grace," *Augustinian Studies* 45, no. 2 (2014): 247–279. I also thank the anonymous reviewers of the latter two articles for their suggestions, which strengthened arguments that have been woven into this work. Fellow participants at workshops at the Oxford Patristics Conference, the Hope-Western Theology Seminar, the Analytic Theology Workshop, and the Zhejiang Workshop on the Research of Augustine shared helpful feedback, and I am grateful to Michael Rea and Daniel Williams for invitations to present at the latter two workshops.

Countless people helped move the project along. For sharing their input at various points, whether on specific issues, drafts, or presentations, I thank especially Todd Billings, Scot Christian Bontrager, Michael Cameron, Michael Cover, Volker Drecoll, Doug Finn, Allan Fitzgerald, John Hesselink, Mirjam Kudella, Winrich Löhr, Peter Martens, Tom McGlothlin, Warren Smith, Tarmo Toom, David Turnbloom, and James Wetzel. For the sheer amount of help she provided in both written and conversational formats, as well as for the constancy of her encouragement, Suzanne McDonald must be singled out. A number of other friends have taken an interest in this project and encouraged me as I worked on it, including Katie Bugyis, Erik Estrada, Jessica Hughes, Kristen Deede Johnson, Sarah Kornfield, Rhonda and Dean Marsman (representing our whole "city group" at Pillar Church), Jeff Morgan, and Xueying Wang. All my colleagues at Western belong in this category, but I would like to name in particular Carol Ann Bailey, Tim

Brown, Ben Conner, Theresa Hamm, Alvin Padilla, Sue Rozeboom, and Leanne Van Dyk, now at Columbia. I thank my former teachers for their continued support as I worked on this project, including John Bowlin, Ellen Charry, George Hunsinger, Mark Husbands, Bruce McCormack, and Dan Treier.

Some patient individuals took the time to share comments on the project as a whole. First among these are the members of my dissertation committee. I thank John Cavadini, Cyril O'Regan, Randall Zachman, and especially my adviser, Brian Daley, for their stimulating feedback, wise counsel, and generous support. Each has been, in his own way, an inspiration as both a scholar and a person. If not for Fr. Daley's teaching, encouragement, and feedback, I doubt I ever would have stumbled onto the topic of the will in Augustine. This is just one example of the profound debt I owe him for shaping and enriching my work and for doing so in a way that blesses me with the coinciding gifts of grace and freedom. Over a period of months, Gregory W. Lee gradually went over the bulk of this book with a fine-tooth comb, saving me from countless errors and helping me see where clarification and other improvements were needed. I am deeply grateful to him as a collaborator and friend. Matthew Levering gave the entire manuscript a rapid-fire read, sharing helpful overarching comments. Richard Muller, editor of the series of which this book is a part, not only took an interest in this project but also made a number of astute suggestions that have improved it. Two anonymous readers from Oxford University Press offered excellent feedback that has contributed to a stronger final version. I would like to express my appreciation for the time and care they put into their comments. I thank each of these wonderful people for their works of supererogation. They have added their insights to this book and subtracted from its errors.

Special thanks go also to my editor, Cynthia Read, for her gentle encouragement to cut down the footnotes for the sake of my readers and for her cheerfulness about publishing what is still a long book; to the indefatigable Allison Van Liere, who expertly tracked down countless sources via interlibrary loan; and to Joseph Bagdanov, my research assistant, who spent hours of his Christmas break helping me revise and format my manuscript with his characteristic verve and excellence.

Finally, I thank my family. As I tackled each part of this project, my husband, David Komline, served as conversation partner, cheerleader, and tireless proofreader, whose incisive editing made this book shorter and clearer.

His companionship is a comfort and a delight. Every word of this book has also passed before the keen editorial eye of my father, Richard Kantzer, who has tactfully alerted me to issues of grammar, style, content, and accuracy of quotation and spelling in Latin, French, and German, as well as in English. I am grateful that he shared his time and expertise so generously, often staying up late and waking up early to read drafts. (I likely introduced any errors that remain after he and my other readers finished their last round of corrections.) My mother, Huai-ching Lee Kantzer, listened with interest to each of my progress reports, gave helpful strategic advice, and encouraged and celebrated each step forward, on countless occasions relieving me of other responsibilities so I could get this book done. She and my father, along with my siblings, Han-wei and Christina, supported me continually from start to finish. My beloved parents-in-law, Judith and Russell Komline, have blessed me with their steadfast encouragement and quietly helped me in ways big and small, more times than I can count. This book is dedicated to my grandparents, with love and gratitude.

Abbreviations

In the body of the book, I tend to give the abbreviation in parentheses when mentioning a work for the first time. Thereafter I tend to use abbreviations, especially for works with long titles. In the footnotes I use abbreviations.

Augustine's Works

Abbreviation	Latin Title	English Title
Acad.	*Contra Academicos*	*Against the Academicians*
an. et or.	*De anima et eius origine*	*On the Soul and Its Origin*
ciu.	*De ciuitate Dei*	*City of God*
conf.	*Confessiones*	*Confessions*
corrept.	*De correptione et gratia*	*Rebuke and Grace*
diu. qu.	*De diuersis quaestionibus octoginta tribus*	*On Eighty-Three Varied Questions*
duab. an.	*De duabus animabus*	*On the Two Souls*
en. Ps.	*Enarrationes in Psalmos*	*Expositions of the Psalms*
ench.	*Enchiridion ad Laurentium de fide spe et caritate*	*The Enchiridion on Faith, Hope, and Charity*
ep.	*Epistulae*	*Letters*
ep. Io. tr.	*In epistulam Iohannis ad Parthos tractatus*	*Tractates on the First Letter of John*
c. ep. Pel.	*Contra duas epistulas Pelagianorum*	*Answer to the Two Letters of the Pelagians*
ep. Rm. inch.	*Epistulae ad Romanos inchoata exposition*	*Unfinished Commentary on the Letter to the Romans*
ex. Gal.	*Expositio Epistulae ad Galatas*	*Commentary on the Letter to the Galatians*
ex. prop. Rm.	*Expositio quarundam propositionum ex epistula Apostoli ad Romanos*	*Commentary on Statements in the Letter to the Romans*
f. et symb.	*De fide et symbol*	*On Faith and the Creed*

c. Fort.	Acta contra Fortunatum Manicheum	Debate with Fortunatus, a Manichee
gest. Pel.	De gestis Pelagii	On the Deeds of Pelagius
Gn. litt.	De Genesi ad litteram	On the Literal Interpretation of Genesis
Gn. litt. imp.	De Genesi ad litteram imperfectus liber	On the Literal Interpretation of Genesis, an Unfinished Book
Gn. adu. Man.	De Genesi aduersus Manicheos	On Genesis, against the Manichees
gr. et lib. arb.	De gratia et libero arbitrio	On Grace and Free Choice
gr. et pecc. or.	De gratia Christi et de peccato originali	On the Grace of Christ and Original Sin
haer.	De haeresibus	On Heresies
Io. eu. tr.	In Iohannis evangelium tractatus	Tractates on the Gospel of John
c. Iul.	Contra Iulianum	Against Julian
c. Iul. imp.	Contra Iulianum opus imperfectum	Against Julian, an Unfinished Book
lib. arb.	De libero arbitrio	On Free Choice
c. Max.	Contra Maximinum Arrianum	Answer to Maximinus, the Arian
mor.	De moribus ecclesiae catholicae et de moribus Manichaeorum	On the Catholic and the Manichean Way of Life
nat. et gr.	De natura et gratia	On Nature and Grace
nupt. et conc.	De nuptiis et concupiscentia	On Marriage and Concupiscence
orig. an.	De origine animae (ep. 166)	On the Origin of the Soul
pecc. mer.	De peccatorum meritis et remissione et de baptism paruulorum	The Punishment and Forgiveness of Sins and the Baptism of Little Ones
perf. iust.	De perfectione iustitiae hominis	On the Perfection of Human Righteousness
perseu.	De dono perseuerantiae	On the Gift of Perseverance
praed. sanct.	De praedestinatione sanctorum	On the Predestination of the Saints
retr.	Retractationes	Reconsiderations

c. s. Ar.	*Contra sermonem Arrianorum*	*Against an Arian Sermon*
s. Dom. mon.	*De sermone Domini in monte*	*On the Lord's Sermon on the Mount*
serm.	*Sermones*	*Sermons*
Simpl.	*Ad Simplicianum*	*To Simplician*
sol.	*Soliloquia*	*The Soliloquies*
spir. et litt.	*De spiritu et littera*	*On the Spirit and the Letter*
trin.	*De Trinitate*	*The Trinity*
uera rel.	*De uera religione*	*On True Religion*

Modern Sources

Abbreviation	Title
AA	*Augustine through the Ages: An Encyclopedia*
A-L	*Augustinus-Lexikon*
AS	*Augustinian Studies*
CCL	Corpus Christianorum, Series Latina
CSEL	Corpus Scriptorum Ecclesiasticorum Latinorum
PL	Patrologiae Cursus Completus, Series Latina
RÉA[P]	*Revue des études augustiniennes [et patristiques]*
SP	*Studia Patristica*
WSA	Works of Saint Augustine (New City Press)

Introduction

Conversions of the Will

Augustine's conception of the will has proven elusive in two ways. On the one hand, it has defied a stable location in the philosophical tradition. Was Augustine the first to employ a unified concept of the will as distinct from both reason and emotion? No consensus has been achieved on this point. The persuasiveness of Augustine's approach to the will, on the other hand, especially in relation to his other theoretical commitments, has prompted perennial debate. Is Augustine's understanding of the will cogent and coherent? Controversy continues.

The idea that pre-Christian philosophy lacked a notion of will has been circulating at least since the eighteenth century. In *An Enquiry concerning the Principles of Morals*, Hume intimated that the distinction between voluntary and involuntary action, absent from ancient thought, arose as an unnatural abstraction to ground morality as theology came to dominate ethical theory.[1] In the following century, Kierkegaard observed that the notion of willful wrongdoing is alien to classical Greek thinking, which does not accord the will moral relevance, as Christianity does.[2] A number of studies from the past fifty years have lent further support to the view that ancient philosophy was bereft of a distinct concept of will, coupling this claim with the thesis that Augustine was the first to articulate such a notion clearly.

While Mary T. Clark stopped short of claiming that no one before Augustine had developed a full-fledged theory of free will, in her 1958 study she deemed the notions of free will in ancient philosophers before

---

[1] David Hume, *An Enquiry concerning the Principles of Morals: A Critical Edition*, ed. Tom L. Beauchamp (New York: Clarendon Press, 2006), 108–109.

[2] Kierkegaard observes, "The Greek spirit had not the courage to assert that a man knowingly does what is wrong, with knowledge of the right does what is wrong; so Socrates comes to its aid and says . . . that he who does not do the right thing has not understood it; but Christianity goes a little further back and says, it is because he will not understand it, and this in turn is because he does not will the right. . . . So then, Christianly understood, sin lies in the will, not in the intellect." Søren Kierkegaard, *The Sickness unto Death*, trans. Walter Lowrie (Princeton, NJ: Princeton University Press, 1941), 2.1.2, 154–155.

Augustine on the Will. Han-luen Kantzer Komline, Oxford University Press (2020). © Oxford University Press.
DOI: 10.1093/oso/9780190948801.001.0001

INTRODUCTION

Augustine "inadequate."[3] Clark presented Augustine as "a pioneer philosopher of freedom"[4] if not as the "the first philosopher of the will." Hannah
Arendt bestowed the latter title on Augustine in *Willing*, the second volume
of her tripartite work, *The Life of the Mind*, whose material came from the
Gifford lectures she had begun in 1974.[5] Contrary to Gilbert Ryle, the latest,
at the time, in a string of philosophers who had questioned the will's existence, Arendt insisted upon the self-evidence of this phenomenon of human
experience and underlined its necessity to any ethical or legal system.[6] The
emergence of the concept of will in the history of philosophy, according to
Arendt, was due to discovery, not invention. With the insight that the will
was "a faculty distinct from desire and reason," Augustine had uncovered it.[7]

In the same year Arendt began her lectures on "willing" at Aberdeen,
Albrecht Dihle delivered the Sather Lectures at Berkeley, which provided
the basis for his book *The Theory of Will in Classical Antiquity*, published
in 1982. Dihle, like Arendt, argued that ancient philosophy lacked a full-
fledged theory of will and that the rise of Christianity played an integral
role in its emergence. While the notion of the will of God was articulated
in the Christological controversies of the fourth century, the notion of the
human will, Dihle contended in the final chapter of his book, originated
with Augustine. By converting the Roman legal concept of *uoluntas* or *uelle*
to an anthropological one, and defining this concept in relation to the will
of God, Augustine arrived at a concept of the will assumed in the Bible but
never articulated in ancient Greek philosophy or earlier Christian theology.[8]

Dihle's seminal work, especially his provocative claim that "St. Augustine
was, in fact, the inventor of our modern notion of will,"[9] has stimulated

---

[3] Her assessment: "It appears to us that freedom was not adequately understood by the great non-
Christian philosophers before Augustine's time." Mary T. Clark, *Augustine, Philosopher of Freedom: A
Study in Comparative Philosophy* (New York: Desclée, 1958), 36.

[4] Clark, *Augustine, Philosopher of Freedom*, 2.

[5] Hannah Arendt, *The Life of the Mind: Volume Two, Willing* (New York: Harcourt Brace
Jovanovich, 1978), 84.

[6] Arendt, *The Life of the Mind*, 5.

[7] Arendt, *The Life of the Mind*, 86.

[8] More specifically, Augustine arrived at his innovative conception of the will by linking the
concept of a *divine* will to the concept of a *human* will via the biblical idea of the *imago Dei* and
by applying the Roman juridical term *uoluntas*, which already seemed to be taking on a sense distinct from either cognition or emotion, directly to the human being. In Dihle's words, "From St.
Augustine's reflection emerged the concept of a human will, prior to and independent of the act of intellectual cognition, yet fundamentally different from sensual and irrational emotion, by which man
can give his reply to the inexplicable utterances of the divine will." Albrecht Dihle, *The Theory of Will
in Classical Antiquity* (Berkeley: University of California Press, 1982), 127.

[9] Dihle, *The Theory of Will in Classical Antiquity*, 144.

a number of further studies. Building on Dihle's thesis, C. H. Kahn offered in 1988 a multifaceted picture of the sources of the notions of will found in Augustine and Aquinas.[10] Kahn supports Dihle's contention that there was something new about the notion of will in Augustine and that the effort to understand the implications of the biblical portrayal of the divine will played an essential role in shaping this notion. He also observes, however, that philosophical, especially Stoic, notions of will, which had not yet coalesced into a single coherent concept to the degree they would in Augustine and much later in Aquinas, were highly influential upon the bishop of Hippo. Augustine derived his notion of will from an eclectic synthesis of theological ideas drawn from the Hebrew and Christian scriptures and Stoic theories of assent.[11]

Whereas Kahn seeks to complicate Dihle's picture of the sources of Augustine's new theory of will, Christoph Horn seeks to clarify the argument that Augustine was the originator of the concept of the will in light of critiques, like that of Christopher Kirwan, which have suggested that Dihle failed to specify adequately the criteria for a bona fide theory of the will.[12] Horn defends Augustine's claim to the title of first philosopher of the will as sustainable when a philosophical concept of the will is defined as a concept that "1) acknowledges a capacity to which fully conscious wrongful actions may be traced and 2) holds that this capacity for which it allows (namely the capacity to choose consciously to do what is wrong) is not reducible to some other cause or explanation."[13] Horn, then, like Arendt, Dihle, and Kahn, seeks to defend the originality of Augustine's understanding of the will but does so by introducing philosophical criteria rather than by analyzing philosophical influences.

Another stream of scholarship has tended to undermine all forms of the "originality thesis" by supporting the conclusion that Augustine's notion of the will did not in fact achieve a genuine advance upon previous theories

---

[10] C. H. Kahn, "Discovering the Will: From Aristotle to Augustine," in *The Question of "Eclecticism": Studies in Later Greek Philosophy*, ed. J. M. Dillon and A. A. Long (Berkeley: University of California Press, 1988), 234–259.

[11] In a similar vein to Kahn, Richard Sorabji has argued for Augustine's originality as a theorist of the will in terms of the synthesis he created from a number of conceptions of the will that had existed separately. See Richard Sorabji, "The Concept of the Will from Plato to Maximus the Confessor," in *The Will and Human Action: From Antiquity to the Present Day*, ed. Thomas Pink and M. W. F. Stone (New York: Routledge, 2003), 6–28.

[12] See Christopher Kirwan, "Review of Albrecht Dihle's *The Theory of the Will in Classical Antiquity*," *Classical Review*, new series, 34, no. 2 (1984): 335–336.

[13] Christoph Horn, "Augustinus und die Entstehung des Philosophischen Willensbegriffs," *Zeitschrift für philosophische Forschung* 50 (1996): 116.

of the will. Since most of these arguments are based on proving that certain ideas were already present in other thinkers, rather than proving that certain ideas are absent in Augustine, it is not necessary to explore all of them at length here. André-Jean Voelke's study of Stoic notions of the will, *L'idée de volonté dans le Stoïcisme*, appeared in 1973.[14] The year 1979 saw the publication of Anthony Kenny's *Aristotle's Theory of the Will*, whose title, like that of Voelke's work, proclaims its incompatibility with the "originality thesis."[15] An article by Japp Mansfeld from 1991 is titled "The Idea of Will in Chrysippus, Posidonius, and Galen."[16] These studies call into question the general consensus that until Augustine ancient philosophy operated without a clear theory of the will.

In his Sather lectures of 1997–1998, Michael Frede presents the most direct challenge to Dihle's thesis. As Dihle had done in his own series, Frede builds to a climactic final chapter that assesses Augustine's originality. Frede concludes, however, that the originator of the concept of "free will" was the late Stoic Epictetus, not Augustine. Augustine's own thinking on free will, Frede seeks to prove from *De libero arbitrio*, was thoroughly Stoic. The sole difference Frede finds is Augustine's elimination of the Stoic distinction between willing, which applies to intentions that may be thwarted, and choosing, which applies to things like mental assent that cannot be thwarted.[17] Due to the strictures of Latin, Augustine was forced to use *uelle* for both. Thus "Augustine's notion of the will is just a version of the more complex Stoic notion of the will."[18]

Like Frede, Sarah Catherine Byers seeks to highlight Augustine's indebtedness to the Stoics for his notion of will (*uoluntas*). In *Perception, Sensibility, and Moral Motivation in Augustine: A Stoic-Platonic Synthesis*, she argues that Augustine uses the term *uoluntas* to refer to the Stoic notion of *hormē*: an impulse to action, which, according to reconstructions of Stoic theories of motivation, is the product of intellectual assent to an interior

[14] André-Jean Voelke, *L'idée de volonté dans le Stoïcisme* (Paris: Presses universitaires de France, 1973).

[15] Anthony Kenny, *Aristotle's Theory of the Will* (New Haven, CT: Yale University Press, 1979). On Aristotle's notion of the will, see also T. H. Irwin, "Who Discovered the Will?," *Philosophical Perspectives* 6 (1992): 453–473.

[16] Japp Mansfeld, "The Idea of Will in Chrysippus, Posidonius, and Galen," *Proceedings of the Boston Area Colloquium in Ancient Philosophy* 7 (1991): 108–110.

[17] As we will see in chapter 8, for Augustine there is in fact a distinction between willing and choosing.

[18] Michael Frede, *A Free Will: Origins of the Notion in Ancient Thought*, ed. A. A. Long (Berkeley: University of California Press, 2011), 159.

self-command. As the subtitle of the volume conveys, however, Byers also, like C. H. Kahn and Richard Sorabji, characterizes Augustine as an eclectic synthesizer. Though his notions of will (*uoluntas*) and free choice (*liberum arbitrium*) find precedents in the Stoic tradition, Byers contends, Augustine's use of these terms fits into a larger theory of moral motivation that creatively combines both Stoic and Platonic elements. The result is an account of moral motivation that advances upon preceding Stoic versions.[19]

The vigor of the debate surrounding the originality thesis regarding Augustine and the will is more than matched by disputes about how to assess Augustine's view of free will. These disputes center on three basic issues that arise in conjunction with the will in Augustine: theodicy; God's knowledge of the future of creation, often referred to as God's "foreknowledge"; and grace. The first issue concerns the sufficiency of Augustine's concept of will for a so-called free-will defense in response to the problem of evil.[20] The second and third issues have to do with the compatibility of Augustine's views about the will with other key elements of his thought. Can free will be reconciled with divine knowledge of events that lie in our future?[21] Can free will be maintained in light of Augustine's mature teaching on the power of grace and predestination?[22]

---

[19] Byers believes, with Frede, however, that any "differences between [Augustine] and the earlier figures Plato and Aristotle on 'will' are not primarily owing to Augustine's Christianity, but to his being a *late ancient* thinker." Sarah Catherine Byers, *Perception, Sensibility, and Moral Motivation in Augustine: A Stoic-Platonic Synthesis* (New York: Cambridge University Press, 2013), 88n168. For her discussion of the meaning of will (*uoluntas*) in Augustine, see especially Appendix II, 217–231, though Byers also discusses the term in the body of her argument, especially 88–99.

[20] For examples of essays on this topic in a more critical vein, see Fred Berthold Jr., "Free Will and Theodicy in Augustine: An Exposition and Critique," *Religious Studies* 17 (1981): 525–535, and William Babcock, "Augustine on Sin and Moral Agency," *Journal of Religious Ethics* 16 (1988): 28–55. Further examples of contributions on the topic are listed in the introduction to Simon Harrison, *Augustine's Way into the Will: The Theological and Philosophical Significance of* De libero arbitrio (New York: Oxford University Press, 2006), 9–11.

[21] William Rowe's negative answer to this question has elicited a number of responses. See William L. Rowe, "Augustine on Foreknowledge and Free Will," *Review of Metaphysics* 18, no. 2 (1964): 356–363; Jasper Hopkins, "Augustine on Foreknowledge and Free Will," *International Journal for Philosophy of Religion* 8, no. 2 (1977): 111–126; William L. Craig, "Augustine on Foreknowledge and Free Will," *AS* 15 (1986): 41–63; and A. A. Pang, "Augustine on Divine Foreknowledge and Human Free Will," *RÉA* 40 (1994): 417–433. For other expositions of Augustine's thought on the relationship between human freedom and God's knowledge of our future, see J. van Gerven, "Liberté humaine et prescience divine d'après Augustin," *Revue philosophique de Louvain* 55 (1957): 317–330; D. Decelles, "Divine Prescience and Human Freedom in Augustine," *AS* 8 (1977): 151–160; and Theodore J. Kondoleon, "Augustine and the Problem of Divine Foreknowledge and Free Will," *AS* 18 (1987): 166–187.

[22] J. M. Rist, Gerard O'Daly and, recently, Lenka Karfíková argue that it cannot. See J. M. Rist, "Augustine on Free Will and Predestination," *Journal of Theological Studies* 20 (1969): 420–447; Gerard O'Daly, "Predestination and Freedom in Augustine's Ethics," in *Philosophy in Christianity*,

David Sedley observes in his foreword to Michael Frede's *A Free Will*, "The origin of the concept of the will, and more specifically free will, has been endlessly debated, and the inconclusiveness of the debate has mirrored the philosophical indeterminacy of the concept itself."[23] The indeterminacy to which Sedley points unfortunately applies not only to the criteria for a general transhistorical theory of will that might serve as the basis for adjudicating the question of when such a theory first emerged but also to particular theories of the will associated with individual figures. This is especially true of Augustine. Behind the "endless" disputes about whether Augustine discovered the will and how his theory of it relates to other issues in his thought lies a more mundane question: How did Augustine actually understand the will?

Among the studies that have tackled this more fundamental problem directly is Simon Harrison's monograph *Augustine's Way into the Will*.[24] Harrison approaches the puzzle by means of a close reading of *De libero arbitrio*, which, he argues, is designed to yield not a definition of the term *uoluntas* but a sense of what willing is that emerges in the process of questioning: Augustine's unique "way into" the concept of the will. Earlier studies include articles by J. Ball, M. Huftier, and N. W. den Bok, who has perhaps done the most to formulate precise definitions of *uoluntas* and *liberum arbitrium*.[25] According to den Bok, it is essential to recognize the

---

ed. Godfrey Norman Agmondisham Vesey (New York: Cambridge University Press, 1989), 85–97; and Lenka Karfíková, *Grace and the Will According to Augustine* (Boston: Brill, 2012). Byers does not deny the compatibility of Augustine's most mature account of grace with free will, but she does adopt a critical stance toward it. See Byers, *Perception, Sensibility, and Moral Motivation in Augustine*, 212–214. The following scholars argue for the compatibility of Augustine's teaching on grace and free will, though they defend Augustine's understanding of free will in different ways: J. Mausbach, *Die Ethik des Heiligen Augustinus. Zweiter Band: Die sittliche Befähigung des Menschen und ihre Verwirklichung* (Freiburg: Herder, 1909); Etienne Gilson, *Introduction à l'étude de saint Augustin* (Paris: Vrin, 1928); John Burnaby, *Amor Dei: A Study of the Religion of St. Augustine. The Hulsean Lectures for 1938* (London: Hodder & Stoughton, 1938); D. J. MacQueen, "Augustine on Free Will and Predestination: A Critique of J. H. Rist," *Museum Africum* 3 (1974): 17–27; Isabelle Bochet, *Saint Augustin et le désir de Dieu* (Paris: Études Augustiniennes, 1982); James Wetzel, *Augustine and the Limits of Virtue* (New York: Cambridge University Press, 1992); and Pierre-Marie Hombert, *Gloria gratiae: Se glorifier en Dieu, principe et fin de la théologie augustinienne de la grâce* (Paris: Institut d'Études Augustiniennes, 1996), 338–339. For a sketch of additional literature in the debate on the compatibility of Augustine's teaching on grace with human freedom up to around 1980, see J. Patout Burns, *The Development of Augustine's Doctrine of Operative Grace* (Paris: Études Augustiniennes, 1980), 9–12.

[23] David Sedley, foreword in *A Free Will: Origins of the Notion in Ancient Thought*, by Michael Frede (Berkeley: University of California Press, 2011), ix.

[24] Harrison, *Augustine's Way into the Will*.

[25] J. Ball, "Les développements de la doctrine de la liberté chez saint Augustin," *Revue philosophique de Louvain* 55 (1957): 404–413; M. Huftier, "Libre arbitre," *Recherches de théologie*

distinction between these two terms, which renders Augustine's mature assessment of the human condition and workings of grace compatible with his affirmation of free will. The reliability of this distinction, however, has been disputed, most recently by Lenka Karfíková.[26] These helpful studies, then, invite further work to test, refine, and identify the larger relevance of their findings in the context of a broader investigation of the significance of the will in Augustine's thought.

Approaching the Augustinian Will

Challenges present themselves to both chronological and thematic approaches to Augustine's conception of the will. On the one hand, a chronological exploration of a single theme in Augustine's thinking on the will would seem at first to have the potential for opening up a vista of larger patterns in his thinking through a narrow cleft. Two problems, however, beset such efforts. First, as will become clear, the distinctive shape of Augustine's view of the will cannot come into view when one considers but a single theme. Multiple themes must be protracted to bring into view the organizing pattern of Augustine's thinking on this subject. Second, not all of Augustine's writings can be dated precisely and reliably. Thus a strictly chronological approach would automatically disqualify certain works that might be of material importance for understanding Augustine's views.[27] On the other hand, one could organize a study of the will thematically by chapter, drawing on Augustine's relevant writings irrespective of chronology. Yet this approach could risk flattening out the important developments that occur in Augustine's thinking on issues such as the relation of grace to the will and combining perspectives that did not relate organically in the context of the unfolding of his thought.[28]

ancienne et médiévale 33 (1966): 187–281; and N. W. den Bok, "Freedom of the Will: A Systematic and Biographical Sounding of Augustine's Thoughts on Human Will," *Augustiniana* 44 (1994): 237–270.

[26] Karfíková, *Grace and the Will According to Augustine*, 19n18.

[27] In Burns's study of Augustine's doctrine of grace, for example, "the materials examined and employed . . . are specified by its genetic methodology. In a developmental study, writings which cannot be located in chronological sequence are of marginal value" (*The Development of Augustine's Doctrine of Operative Grace*, 14).

[28] Augustine himself invites his readers to discover how his thinking has developed over time, and he takes pains to facilitate such inquiries by treating his works in order in his *retr.* In the prologue, he writes, "For whoever reads my works in the order in which they were written will perhaps discover how I have made progress over the course of my writing" (23). Unless otherwise noted, this and subsequent translations of the *retr.* come from the following edition: Augustine, *Revisions*, trans.

This book merges these two approaches in order to have the best of both worlds.[29] Each chapter is devoted to a different theme, ensuring that the most important sources of material significance to the topic can find a structural home in the work despite uncertainty regarding dating. However, each chapter also finds its center of gravity in a certain period of Augustine's thinking, with successive chapters moving forward chronologically. This ensures the book's coherence and allows it to build momentum as chapters elapse. At the same time, the thematic focus of the chapters will allow flexibility to explore how various themes spill over before and beyond each chronological period that serves as a center of gravity, in light of the fact that Augustine does not simply start or stop thinking about certain issues before or after periods when the volume of his writings on them happens to be the greatest. In sum, this kind of hybrid structure simultaneously reflects the integrity[30] and the evolution[31] of Augustine's thinking on the will.[32]

Boniface Ramsey, WSA I/2, (Hyde Park, NY: New City Press, 2010). I use the title *Reconsiderations*, however, in the list of abbreviations for this book and elsewhere. Burns discusses some of the advantages of a "genetic" interpretation, noting that it helps to explain many of the disagreements in the literature on Augustine's doctrine of grace by tracing different perspectives, often taken as representative of Augustine's thought as a whole, to different periods of his thinking (*The Development of Augustine's Doctrine of Operative Grace*, 12–13, 188). See also Hombert's comments on the importance of a chronological approach to Augustine's teaching on grace (*Gloria gratiae*, 5). A genetic approach to Augustine's conception of will recommends itself for parallel reasons.

[29] Hombert's strategy for addressing the challenges posed by purely chronological and purely thematic approaches is to split his book between the two. The first half is dedicated to a "chronological study," and the second part is "synthetic and theological" (*Gloria gratiae*, 5–6).

[30] Though Peter Brown's chapter "A Lost Future" has done much to promote the idea that Augustine's thinking underwent a drastic change in the 390s, he has since stated in an essay accompanying a new edition of his biography, "As a thinker, Augustine was, perhaps, more a man *aus einem Guss*, all of a piece, and less riven by fateful discontinuities than I had thought." Peter Brown, *Augustine of Hippo: A Biography* (Berkeley: University of California Press, 2000), 490. This study demonstrates the coherence of Augustine's thinking, to which Brown's more recent comment attests, even as it takes seriously Brown's original insight, that the 390s saw a crucial turning point in Augustine's thinking.

[31] For a genetic approach that, in contrast to that of this book, tends to underline the discontinuity in Augustine's thinking to the point of positing two separate Augustines, see Gaetano Lettieri, *L'altro Agostino: Ermeneutica e retorica della grazia dalla crisi alla metamorfosi del De doctrina christiana* (Brescia: Morcelliana, 2001).

[32] This approach thus has aims different from those of "problem-based" approaches to Augustine on the will, exemplified in an extreme form, though by no means limited to, Phillip Cary's trilogy on Augustine. Cary consciously approaches intellectual history by seeking to ferret out the philosophical problems found in various traditions, not necessarily in terms of the concerns expressed in these traditions themselves but from a contemporary analytic perspective. He then recounts the history of ideas by seeking to understand how the contributions of each thinker may be construed as attempted solutions to the problems bequeathed by his predecessors. See the preface to Phillip Cary, *Augustine's Invention of the Inner Self: The Legacy of a Christian Platonist* (New York: Oxford University Press, 2000). Cary's problem-based approach yields a highly critical assessment of Augustine's thinking, but problem-based approaches can yield diverse conclusions. For a sympathetic problem-based approach to Augustine, see Wetzel, *Augustine and the Limits of Virtue*.

The structure of Augustine's own thought makes possible the structure of this study. The key to the affirmation of both the continuity and the development of Augustine's conception of will is the thesis that his mature conception of will is "theologically differentiated." In other words, Augustine's conception of the will comes to encompass multiple, often strikingly different accounts of how the human will works, each of which is indexed to theological events in the narratives of scripture. The will works in different ways in different theological contexts. Given its theologically differentiated character, Augustine's perspective on the human will can embrace his previous conceptions even as it continues to evolve.[33]

A Theologically Differentiated Notion of Will

Diagnosing, in different terms, the same ambiguity Sedley observed in conversations about the origins of the will, Kahn makes the point that in order to ascertain when the concept of will was "discovered" one must first determine what this concept is: "If we do not know what we mean by *the will*, we will not know what we are looking for."[34] In response to this quandary, Kahn distinguishes among four different ways of thinking about the will that have held sway during the past two millennia. Each of these, he suggests, has added its own convolutions to the labyrinth from which our contemporary notions of the will have emerged.

Kahn's fourfold schema is instructive, not just because it provides a rubric for participants in the metaquest for the origins of "the will" but also because of what it suggests about the distinctive characteristics of each conception of will he describes. A post-Cartesian conception sees the will as a mental cause of a physical act. Kahn identifies this family of perspectives as the target of Ryle's critique in *The Concept of Mind* and as the one "which has had a bad press in the last generation of Anglo-American philosophy, though it may currently be undergoing a revival."[35] Kantian and post-Kantian approaches see the will as the locus of self-legislation and the inner reality of the self.

---

[33] This interpretation of Augustine's theory of the will helps to explain how there can be such wildly divergent estimations of the continuity—or discontinuity—of Augustine's thinking. For a discussion of some of the literature on each side, see Carol Harrison, *Rethinking Augustine's Early Theology: An Argument for Continuity* (New York: Oxford University Press, 2006), 14–18.

[34] Kahn, "Discovering the Will," 235.

[35] Kahn, "Discovering the Will," 236.

Schopenhauer and Nietzsche find a place in this family line. There is also the perennial issue of free will versus determinism. This debate overlaps each of the other ways of thinking about the will Kahn describes but qualifies as its own major category of approach. Of particular interest in this study is the fourth conception of will Kahn identifies, which he associates with Augustine and his heirs. According to these thinkers, the human will is analyzed in relation to God's will and understood as "modeled on, or responding to, the will of God." Kahn calls this the "theological concept of will."[36]

The idea that Augustine's understanding of will is inherently theological, and perhaps even inherently Christian, has been proposed in various forms not only by Christian theologians but also by philosophers from Kierkegaard to Arendt and Dihle.[37] Many studies of Augustine on the will have sought to locate his view of the will in larger historical trajectories, to utilize his understanding of the will to solve philosophical problems, or to evaluate his conception of the will for theological or philosophical cogency in terms of external criteria. The aim here is to address the more basic question of how Augustine describes the will and to do so by attending to the theological contexts in which *he* articulates and employs it.

Ideas about creation, the triune God, and Christ are not merely incidental to Augustine's notion of will but—at least in his way of talking about things—are essential for understanding what the will is. The moral significance of the will, in turn, depends upon how these theological contexts condition it. In other words, the moral capacities of the will depend on its theological ontology. What the human will can *do* depends on what the human will *is* in relation to God—what it is in light of its creation ex nihilo in the image of God, its plight due to sin, its re-creation in Christ, and its future glorification. How the will functions varies given each of these theological contexts. In this sense, Augustine's notion of the will is "theologically differentiated." It is calibrated to particular theological events, according to which the capacities and character of human willing vary drastically. Taking into account the specific theological and exegetical contexts in which Augustine develops his notion of will throws into relief the distinctively variegated shape of his theory of the will while at the same time

---

[36] Kahn, "Discovering the Will," 235.

[37] For recent arguments against these kinds of characterizations, see Frede, *A Free Will*, especially chapter 9, "A Radically New Notion of a Free Will?" and Byers, *Perception, Sensibility, and Moral Motivation in Augustine*, especially 88–95.

highlighting its coherence. These particular events are tied together in a coherent story: Augustine's retelling of the story of God's relationship with the human race he finds recorded in scripture.

Augustine's biblically indexed and theologically differentiated view of the human will corresponds to, though it is not exhaustively summarized by, the classic idea that human beings exist in four states. In the primitive state of integrity represented by the first parents, human beings could refrain from sin (*posse non peccare*); in their fallen state, they sin necessarily (*non posse non peccare*); redeemed human beings regain the paradisiacal possibility of avoiding sin (*posse non peccare*); glorified human beings will be sinless by blissful necessity (*non posse peccare*). This pattern, often associated with Augustine, served in the later tradition of Augustinian theology to structure theological anthropology and, indeed, to undergird the general tendency of Christian theology as a whole to read scripture as a drama with four acts: creation, fall, redemption, and consummation.[38]

While Augustine nowhere sums up his views in a single systematic statement that enumerates the four states of the human being in exactly these terms, his theology considered from a macro perspective clearly provides a conceptual framework for a fourfold view of the will corresponding to these major epochs.[39] The biblically indexed and theologically differentiated

---

[38] For an example of the use of this scheme as a framework for theological anthropology, see the classic Scottish work by Thomas Boston, *Human Nature in Its Fourfold State* (Falkirk: Patrick Mair, 1787). For a sketch of the historical tendency to read scripture in a parallel fourfold pattern, see David Kelsey, *Eccentric Existence: A Theological Anthropology* (Louisville, KY: Westminster John Knox Press, 2009), chapter 12B. Oddly enough, Boston never mentions Augustine. Kelsey, on the other hand, mentions Augustine as being at the source of more than one stream of fourfold interpretations of the biblical narrative (see 461–468).

[39] Augustine explicitly contrasts the state of original integrity, with which he associates the phrase *posse non peccare*, with the glorified state, characterized as involving *non posse peccare*, to drive home the superiority of the latter. See, for example, *ciu.* 22.30 (CCL 48:863–864); *corrept.* 12.33 (CSEL 92:259); *c. Iul. imp.* 5.56 (CSEL 85.2:264); *c. Iul. imp.* 5.60 (CSEL 85.2:271–274); and *c. Iul imp.* 6.12 (CSEL 851.2:318–321). Contrary to popular opinion, however, Augustine never explicitly applies the phrases *posse non peccare* and *non posse non peccare* to this life. Augustine himself uses the locution *posse non peccare* for only two purposes: to describe the state of created integrity and to describe his opponents' notion of an inalienable ability not to sin that belongs to human beings by nature. Similarly, while the phrase *non posse non peccare* does appear in Augustine's corpus, when it does Augustine is quoting Pelagius. See *nat. et gr.* 57 (CSEL 60:275). Augustine does speak of four states with respect to the law: *prima hominis = ante legem; secunda = sub lege; tertia = sub gratia; quarta = pace plena atque perfecta.* See *ench.* 31.118 (CCL 46:112–113). These states, however, do not map exactly onto the four states with respect to freedom and sin since there is no state corresponding to the state of original integrity.

Nonetheless, Augustine's repeated use of the *posse non peccare / non posse peccare* distinction in his anti-Pelagian writings provides the basic terminology for taking the additional step of labeling the intermediary states clearly present in his thinking on a conceptual level. On the possibility of

perspective on the human will that emerges from a synthetic and genetic reading of his corpus thus vindicates the genuinely Augustinian character of the multiple states view.[40] Moreover it shows how a fourfold structure can serve as a hermeneutical key not only to Augustine's teaching on will but also to his development as a thinker.

Philip Schaff once remarked that "Augustine had in his own life passed through all the earlier stages of the history of the church."[41] This statement can be pushed further following Schaff's own insight that Augustine's renown stems from his "clear development of the Biblical anthropology."[42] In his thinking on the will, Augustine passes through the earlier stages of the history of the church and through the epochs he finds in scripture. Creation, not just the specter of Marcion behind the Manichees, was in play from the beginning; the eschaton, not only Julian, captured his imagination at the end. The four states of human willing were not only progressive in content but also progressively discovered.

For Augustine, the will is a highly complex phenomenon, whose workings and key features vary drastically in different contexts: the character and capacities of human willing depend on when willing occurs in relation to certain key theological events. Augustine's understanding of the significance of these events, in turn, emerges from his efforts to make sense of scripture—both in terms of its larger narrative arc, running from creation to eschaton, and in terms of specific pericopes, especially those from the writings of Paul. In this sense, Augustine's conception of will is not only inherently theological; it is inherently biblical. It does not make sense apart

doing what is right in this life, see question 24 of *diu. qu.*, *Gn. adu. Man.* 1.3.6, and *retr.* 1.26.2 and 1.10.2, where the former two passages are affirmed and reframed by Augustine in his maturity: he remains convinced that doing good (*facere* vs. *perficere*) in this life is possible, with God's gracious help. For details on Augustine's evolving position on the possibility of sinlessness in this life—to be distinguished from the possibility that discrete nonsinful acts might be performed by a person under grace—see chapter 3, part II. Given the inference that the created state has degenerated after the fall into *non posse non peccare* (see chapter 3), one arrives at the four-states view. I thank Gregory Lee for conversation about these matters.

[40] Previous interpreters have recognized the insufficiency of a single, monolithic characterization of Augustine's theological anthropology. Philip Schaff, for example, divides Augustine's anthropology into three basic phases, the last of which—the *status redemptionis*—includes, to map Augustine's own language onto Schaff's final phase, both the human being *sub gratia* in this life and *in pace plena atque perfecta* in the next. See Philip Schaff, *History of the Christian Church*, 8th ed., vol. 3 (New York: Charles Scribner's Sons, 1914), 817. Schaff also underlines the variety in the types of freedom Augustine articulates, noting a stream of scholarship attuned to this diversity as well as a stream that has ignored it (820n3).

[41] Schaff, *History of the Christian Church*, 816.

[42] Schaff, *History of the Christian Church*, 816.

from the story of God's relationship to human beings as recorded in scripture. It is the story of this relationship that holds Augustine's multifaceted conception of will together as one coherent account.

In a way, the idea that the will works differently in its created integrity, after the human race has been mired in sin, given the redemptive work of Christ, and in the context of eternal beatitude, seems unremarkable, even commonplace. Yet Augustine articulated this idea with a kind of clarity, precision, and depth that no one before him had quite achieved. If it seems self-evident today, this only further indicates the importance of his contribution; the very influence of the theological paradigm he developed for thinking about human willing may have served to obscure its novelty.

The idea that Augustine develops a theologically differentiated conception of will has implications for the contested question of locating his view of will in the Western intellectual tradition and its line of philosophies and "philosophers of the will." However, just as interesting as this question is the issue of how Augustine's theory of the will situates him in the history of Christian theology. This book's conclusion will therefore indicate some important theological precursors, both Greek and Latin, to Augustine's thinking on the human will. The resulting overview of Augustine's debts to previous philosophical and theological traditions will help to identify both the similarities of his thinking on the will to previous conceptions and the features that make it unique.

An evaluation of Augustine's place in the tradition intentionally follows, rather than precedes, inquiry into the peculiarities of his own evolving conception of will found in the body of this book. It has become almost standard to approach Augustine's theory of the will by appending him to the end or beginning of a trajectory in the history of philosophy or by injecting him into contemporary philosophical or theological debates. But Augustine's evolving view of the will is more than a philosophical inception or conclusion, a conceptual problem or solution—one page in a much longer story. It tells a story unto itself—it retells the biblical story—of transformation from division to delight.

1

The Created Will

The Hinge of the Soul

Introduction

The Augustine one meets in the *Confessions* seems always to have been thinking about will. As he tells it, it concerned him from the cradle. Long before he could analyze willing, he was absorbed in satisfying it. The desire to express and fulfill his wishes (*uoluntates*) drove Augustine to communicate with those populating his infant world, first through bodily gestures and signs, then with sounds, and finally in intelligible speech.[1] As an adult, Augustine would come full circle, bending these powers of communication to reflection upon the phenomenon that had prompted their development.

Already in the years following his conversion, Augustine penned a number of works that touched on the human will. In these texts he is not interested, however, in explaining the will as an end, or thing, in itself. He discusses the will, rather, as it relates to God, evil, and the human mind. Augustine turns his attention to the will as a beginning, a dynamic beginning with enormous consequences for what follows.

De libero arbitrio (*lib. arb.*), often considered the most important source for understanding the will in Augustine, provides a more direct

---

[1] He writes of the first stage, "Little by little I began to be aware where I was and wanted (*uolebam*) to manifest my wishes (*uoluntates*) to those who could fulfill them as I could not. For my desires were internal; adults were external to me and had no means of entering into my soul. So I threw my limbs about and uttered sounds, signs resembling my wishes (*uoluntatibus*)" (1.6.8; CCL 24:4). Of the second stage he observes, "By groans and various sounds and various movements of parts of my body I would endeavor to express the intentions of my heart to persuade people to bow to my will (*uoluntati*). But I had not the power to express all that I wanted (*uolebam*) nor could I make my wishes understood by everybody" (1.8.13; CCL 27:7). Finally he describes the achievement of learning to speak in terms of the power of articulating his wishes: "I learnt to articulate my wishes (*uoluntates*) by training my mouth to use these signs. In this way I communicated the signs of my wishes (*uoluntatum*) to those around me, and entered more deeply into the stormy society of human life" (1.8.13; CCL 27:7–8). Augustine presents each stage of his acquisition of language and consequent entry further into human society as a product of his infant will. These means of communication are bridges over which Augustine's wishes cross, from their internal source to the external world. Unless otherwise noted, translations of *conf.* come from Augustine, *Confessions*, trans. Henry Chadwick (New York: Oxford University Press, 1992).

Augustine on the Will. Han-luen Kantzer Komline, Oxford University Press (2020). © Oxford University Press.
DOI: 10.1093/oso/9780190948801.001.0001

and extensive treatment of the will than do many of Augustine's other writings.[2] Still, a number of other texts that approach the theme of the will more obliquely also deserve attention: *Soliloquies* (386–387) and the anti-Manichean writings *De moribus ecclesiae catholicae et de moribus Manichaeorum* (387–391), *De Genesi aduersus Manicheos* (388–389), and *De diuersis quaestionibus* (388–395). Precisely because these texts treat the will incidentally in relation to other topics that serve as the primary focus, they highlight the organic connections between Augustine's understanding of will and broader themes in his thinking.[3]

Even in these texts from early in his career, Augustine uses the notion of the human will to make sense of biblical statements and to think about God piously. His thinking about the will also flows from certain basic theological axioms: God is the good creator; his creation is good as created; yet God and creation are different from one another. Augustine's notion of will, then, is theological in terms of both its purposes and its premises.

Yet in this stage, Augustine's ideas about the will do not tend to emerge from his interpretation of specific biblical passages. In fact, Augustine typically proceeds in the reverse order. He uses a rough and ready notion of the will informed by general theological principles to help him interpret the scriptures in a "pious" way. In book 3 of *lib. arb.*, which he probably wrote sometime between 391 and 395, Augustine's readers feel the first tremors of a shift that takes place in how he thinks theologically about the will.[4]

---

[2] Michael Frede, for example, observes, "We get [Augustine's] most detailed and systematic exposition [of his doctrine of freedom and a free will] in the early treatise *De libero arbitrio voluntatis*.... This is also, in a sense, the authoritative exposition of his view." Unsurprisingly given this assessment, Frede bases his evaluation of Augustine's understanding of free will and his answer to the question of the title of his chapter on Augustine, "Augustine: A Radically New Notion of a Free Will?" upon a close reading of *lib. arb*. See Michael Frede, *A Free Will: Origins of the Notion in Ancient Thought*, ed. A. A. Long (University of California Press, 2011), 159. Simon Harrison adopts a similar approach in his monograph, which is entirely devoted to his creative interpretation of *lib. arb*. See Simon Harrison, *Augustine's Way into the Will: The Theological and Philosophical Significance of* De libero arbitrio (New York: Oxford University Press, 2006). As these examples show, *lib. arb*. is often taken as representative not only of Augustine's thinking on will in his early phase but as the key to his thinking on will *simpliciter*.

[3] Since Augustine tends to emphasize similar issues relating to the will across these texts, examining them together allows one to scrutinize various emerging features of his concept of the will from a number of different angles; *lib. arb*. and these other early works are thus mutually illuminating. These works fit each other sufficiently in terms of the period in which they were composed, their polemical context, and the content of their statements about the will to allow integration of material from all four to sketch the basic contours of Augustine's developing concept of the will in the years following his conversion up to around the time of his ordination as a priest in 391.

[4] While book 1 of *lib. arb*. seems to have been composed sometime between the fall of 387 and fall of 388, while Augustine was in Rome after his baptism, books 2 and 3 were composed sometime after his ordination as priest, between 391 and 395. See *retr*. 1.9. Many scholars are convinced that this hiatus in chronology of composition is accompanied by a shift in theological sensibility

Here he begins to present his conception of the will as emerging more directly from his interpretation of scripture, in addition to the reverse pattern observed earlier, and to elaborate what one might call a "theologically differentiated" view of how the will functions.

Part I: Will and Knowledge Together

Sometime in the months preceding his baptism on Easter 387, Augustine began to write the *Soliloquies* on a quiet country estate in Cassiciacum, where he had retreated along with some of his family members and friends for Christian philosophical conversation and to recover his health. It was the kind of place that lent itself to introspection. The *Soliloquies*, which take the form of a dialogue between "Augustine" and "Reason," may record what ran through Augustine's head at night as he lay in bed alone with his thoughts. Augustine tells us in the *Retractationes* that in the two books of the *Soliloquies*, "I questioned myself and responded to myself as though we were two persons, reason and I, despite the fact that I was alone."[5]

Equally as interesting as the logical arguments that find resolution in this dialogue are the questions it raises that remain puzzles. Some of these will continue to fascinate Augustine for a lifetime. At the outset of the dialogue, he names his interlocutor "Reason" but then immediately interrogates Reason's identity in relation to his own. Is reason identical to himself, something within himself, or something outside of himself?[6] Thus, even as Augustine moves to and from various topics in the dialogue, as a whole the work can be seen as a quest to understand the relation of reason (*ratio*) and the human self as represented by Augustine (*ego ipse*).[7] How the will fits

---

between book 1 and the remaining two books. For a discussion and critique of this tendency in the scholarship, see Carol Harrison, *Rethinking Augustine's Early Theology: An Argument for Continuity* (New York: Oxford University Press, 2006), 200–204. This chapter engages books 2 and 3, as well as book 1 of *lib. arb.*, not out of a conviction that there is no change of perspective that takes place in the work but because books 2 and 3 often pick up themes from book 1 that remain consistent throughout the text. When arguments from books 2 and 3 are taken up that depart from Augustine's earlier persuasions, this will be noted.

[5] *Retr.* 1.4.1.

[6] *Sol.* 1.1.1 (*CSEL* 89:3).

[7] On the dangers of importing modern notions of the "self" into interpretations of Augustine, see John C. Cavadini, "The Darkest Enigma: Reconsidering the Self in Augustine's Thought," *AS* 38, no. 1 (2007): 119–32.

into this picture is another question that arises, but does not find resolution, in this provocative dialogue.

Will (*uoluntas*) is first mentioned in a prayer of invocation (1.1.2–6) at the outset of the work. Imploring God's assistance, Augustine affirms in paradoxical language his simultaneous desire to draw near to God, which itself is a kind of approach, and his ignorance of how to take a step in the right direction, which renders him incapable of progress toward God on his own. In Augustine's pithy formulation: "I come to thee, and how to come I ask thee again."[8]

It is in this spirit that Augustine prays, "Teach me how to come to thee. I have nothing else but the will (*uoluntatem*) to come. I know nothing save that transient dying things are to be spurned, certain and eternal things to be sought after. This only I know, O Father, but how to come to thee I know not. Tell me. Show me. Provide for my journey."[9] Though Augustine protests that he does not yet know by what means (*unde*) to come to God, he does not present himself as completely empty-handed. He knows that certain things must be done, while others must not be. Augustine knows nothing else (*nihil aliud*) besides this, but he does know this one thing. Likewise, he possesses one vital provision for his journey, having "nothing else" (*nihil aliud*) besides. The one thing he has is will (*uoluntas*).

What is this one asset Augustine possesses? His unadorned statement that he has nothing other than will (*nihil aliud habeo quam uoluntatem*) leaves it up to the reader to fill in the details based on contextual clues. When he refers to the *uoluntas*, does Augustine mean a capacity or faculty? Does he have in mind a specific wish or desire? If the latter, what is its content? One might turn to the preceding clause for clarification: "Teach me how to come to thee" (*quomodo ad te perueniatur, doce me*).[10] Yet it proves equally reasonable to look to the following clause for interpretive clues: "I know nothing save that transient dying things are to be spurned, certain and eternal things to be sought after" (*nihil aliud scio nisi fluxa et caduca spernenda esse, certa et aeterna requirenda*). Indeed, the parallel structure

---

[8] *Sol.* 1.1.6. Translations of *sol.* come from Augustine, *Augustine: Earlier Writings*, trans. J. H. S. Burleigh (Philadelphia: Westminster Press, 1953), unless otherwise noted.

[9] *Sol.* 1.1.5 (CSEL 89:10).

[10] This is the approach of J. H. S. Burleigh. His English translation adds an infinitive not present in the Latin text to specify Augustine's statement for the reader: "I have nothing else but the will *to come*" (emphasis mine; Burleigh 26). Burleigh seems persuaded that Augustine intends the term *uoluntas* to refer to a specific wish: the wish to draw near to God.

between Augustine's statement about the will and the next clause invites one to read the two together as a cohesive unit: "I have nothing other than the will; I know nothing other than that . . ."[11]

On this reading, Augustine's description of the one thing he knows sheds light on the one thing he wills. Such an interpretation may at first seem to yield an awkward and improbable conclusion. What could it mean for Augustine to say that he has nothing but the will that certain things are to be spurned, while others are to be sought after?

Even if Augustine's "will" does not stand in direct apposition to his description of the knowledge he possesses, he has clearly aligned these two in a parallel structure as the objects of the phrases *nihil aliud habeo* and *nihil aliud scio*. According to this parallel structure, Augustine's *uoluntas*, the only thing he has, corresponds to the only thing he knows: that dying things are to be spurned, certain and eternal things to be sought after. When Augustine says he has nothing but will, he means he has nothing but a will that comports with his knowledge of what he should and should not do. Thus Augustine's further statement, "I know nothing save that transient dying things are to be spurned, certain and eternal things to be sought after," specifies the character of his will. His point is not that he had just any kind of will or a neutral will without any specific orientation, like a car idling at a crossroads, but a will to do the right thing, a will corresponding to his knowledge of how he ought, and ought not, to behave.

Such a reading coheres well with Augustine's statement earlier in the same paragraph: "I desire (*cupio*) to be under thy jurisdiction. Command, I beseech thee, as thou wilt (*quicquid vis*), but heal and open my ears that I may hear thy voice."[12] Just as Augustine desires not only to come to God but more specifically to do so by being in accordance with God's jurisdiction, so also his "will" (*uoluntas*) is not only to come to God but more specifically to do what he ought.

This oft-quoted passage, then, presents a picture of will in which Augustine's will and knowledge are closely related. Even if they do not map onto each other exactly, they correspond to one another, working in tandem to point him in the same direction. This observation helps to explain why the *uoluntas* tends to drop out of the picture in the rest of the dialogue. If

---

[11] My translation of *sol.* 1.1.1 (CSEL 89:3): *nihil aliud habeo quam uoluntatem, nihil aliud scio nisi . . .*

[12] *Sol.* 1.1.5 (CSEL 89:9).

Augustine's *uoluntas* naturally corresponds to knowledge available through reason, mentioning it alongside its constant companion would be redundant. Augustine can describe something like the happy life in very rationalistic terms, even while understanding these terms inherently to include his *uoluntas,* or without its ever occurring to him that he might need to discuss the *uoluntas* separately alongside reason. In the *Soliloquies,* reason is the subject of the happy life: "This is truly perfect virtue, reason (*ratio*) achieving its end, which is the happy life (*beata uita*)."[13] To say the happy life is a rational matter, without making an explicit reference to will, is sufficient.

Even while Augustine presents his will as aligned with knowledge, the dialogue raises questions about how knowledge and will might be distinct. In *City of God* Augustine associates willing and loving.[14] Here in *Soliloquies* he is already beginning to tease loving and knowledge apart. Following the opening prayer of the dialogue, Reason pushes Augustine to explain what kind of knowledge of God he seeks that would satisfy him. Augustine admits his perplexity at this question; given God's dissimilarity to other objects of his knowledge, he is not sure whether his previous experience can be at all useful in teaching him what to expect or hope. Reason asks Augustine, "If you do not yet know God how do you know that you know nothing similar to God?" Augustine replies, "If I knew anything similar to God I would doubtless love it. But I love nothing (*amo*) but God and the soul, and I know (*scio*) neither."[15] Whereas in 1.1.6 Augustine had presented his will as aligned with his knowledge, as corresponding to his knowledge of right and wrong, here his love outstrips his knowledge. Knowing God would entail loving God, Augustine pronounces, but the reverse is not necessarily the case. According to Augustine's explicit statements in *Soliloquies,* it is already possible to love without knowing, though—as evident later in *Confessions*—how this can be is a matter of perplexity.[16]

Just as the dialogue raises questions about the relation of reason and will, the structure of the work, which Augustine casts as an interior dialogue between himself and Reason, also raises questions about the role of "Reason" in relation to "Augustine." Augustine's own statement from the

---

[13] *Sol.* 1.6.13 (CSEL 89:21).

[14] See, for example, *ciu.* 14.7.

[15] *Sol.* 1.3.7 (CSEL 89:12).

[16] In the opening of *conf.,* Augustine observes a similar puzzle: the human being wants (*uult*) to praise God, but how can those desiring God call upon God, without yet knowing him? See *conf.* 1.1.1 (CCL 27:1).

first paragraph of the work makes these questions explicit: where the voice of reason (*ratio*) comes from—"whether it is [him]self or someone else, from without, or within"—is what he "is struggling so hard to know."[17] By presenting "Reason" as a dialogue partner opposite himself, "Augustine," Augustine tests the extent to which reason and the human self can be teased apart. If only in the context of this imagined or reconstructed conversation, which takes place on a self-reflective level, Augustine extricates reason from himself. Reason is one dialogue partner, and he another.

Clearly the Augustine interlocutor thinks too, as well as Reason, yet this character is repeatedly associated with desiring or wanting rather than knowing. While he earnestly pursues knowledge, on a more mundane grammatical level he serves consistently as the subject of desiring and wanting. When "Augustine" mentions knowledge, it is typically as the object of these volitional verbs rather than as a knowledge he possesses. Augustine does not know God and the soul; he *desires* to know God and the soul.[18] Later, Reason rephrases Augustine's earlier comments: "When I asked you what kind of knowledge of God would satisfy you, you replied that you could not explain it because you had grasped nothing as you desired to know God."[19] Reason continues to interrogate Augustine about what he loves: "R.—Is there anything you love besides knowledge of yourself and of God? A.—I could, of course, reply that in my present mood there is nothing that I love more, but it would be safer to say that I do not know."[20] "Augustine" does not know. He would love to know. On the one hand Augustine presents will (*uoluntas*) in this work as synchronized in harmony with his knowledge. On the other hand, the dialogue poses larger questions about the extent to which loving and desiring can be teased apart from knowing and reasoning.

Part II: The Will Emerges

Whereas in *Soliloquies* Augustine had appealed to the will incidentally as something self-evident, assuming an understanding of the will, in a number

[17] My translation; *sol.* 1.1.1.
[18] *Sol.* 1.3.7 (CSEL 89:12): *deum et animam scire cupio.*
[19] *Sol.* 1.4.10.
[20] *Sol.* 1.9.16.

of his early anti-Manichean texts he turns more directly to the question of what the will is, explaining how he views it. In the private luxury of Cassiciacum, Augustine had no reason to come to grips with these thorny issues. Pressed by the Manichees, he must take the will by the thorns. In fact, the will turns out to be a pivotal conceptual asset in Augustine's polemic against his Manichean opponents, one he defines more precisely in the context of this debate than he had previously.

Section A: Free Will as a Good Gift from God

In his earliest works, preceding his ministry as bishop, Augustine tended to regard the will in a strongly positive light. For Augustine in this stage, doing something willingly is inherently superior to doing it by necessity; doing something willingly inherently implies doing it freely; and the capacity to will is a good gift from God, the creator of all good things.[21] Will is good, will is free, and will is from God.

These affirmations come through especially clearly in De diuersis quaestionibus (diu. qu.), a collection of Augustine's responses to questions from the brothers of the monastic community he formed in Thagaste.[22] In question 2, concerning free choice (de libero arbitrio), Augustine offers a normative assessment: "A human being who is good by will (uoluntate) is better than one who is good by necessity (necessitate). Therefore free

---

[21] For a discussion of different types of freedom Augustine attributes to the will, and the distinctions he will eventually make between them, see chapter 8. By the time of the Pelagian controversy, "free choice" (liberum arbitrium), for Augustine, is a species of "freedom" (libertas) of the will consisting in the freedom to will as one pleases. This kind of freedom of the will is inalienable. Augustine will clearly distinguish liberum arbitrium both from the freedom to choose between options (which corresponds to Julian of Eclanum's understanding of free choice) and from the "full freedom" (plena libertas) or "true freedom" that consists in a voluntary delight in the good. For Augustine in his mature period, the will (uoluntas) inherently possesses and exercises freedom in the sense of free choice (liberum arbitrium) but may or may not possess the freedom of choice between options or the freedom of delighting in the good. In the early phase of Augustine's career now under consideration, he believes that the will, as such, possesses the freedom to turn to evil or to the good. Augustine will later argue that this kind of freedom requires grace, and that free choice does not automatically entail it.

[22] These responses were recorded, it seems, from the very earliest days of the community's life together and were collected and made into a book after Augustine became bishop of Hippo in 395. As indicated by its title, the text covers both philosophically oriented questions (1–60) and questions that mostly concern biblical passages (61–83). It is in the former group of questions that Augustine makes comments pertaining to the will. English translations of diu. qu. are Boniface Ramsey's unless otherwise noted. See Augustine, Responses to Miscellaneous Questions, trans. Boniface Ramsey, WSA I/12 (Hyde Park, NY: New City Press, 2008).

will (*uoluntas libera*) had to be given to humanity."[23] For Augustine, then, freedom is inherently built into the concept of will. For human beings to be able to be good "by will" at all required that they be granted a *free* will. Doing something willingly entails doing it freely. Moreover, Augustine makes a clear value judgment about this kind of voluntary or free action. Like others in the Greek tradition before him, he seems to accept as an axiom that what is free is better than what is necessary. Thus the free will conferred upon humanity entailed more than possession of a morally neutral capacity. The *uoluntas* was a good gift that allowed human beings to be better than they could have been otherwise.

In several places, Augustine explicitly identifies God as the giver of the good gift of will. Turning to the issue of "whether the soul is moved by itself" in question 8 of *diu. qu.* Augustine states that the movement of the soul that is the will (*uoluntas*) is "given to it by God" (*ei tributum est a deo*).[24] Likewise at the conclusion of a long discussion in *lib. arb.* of whether free will is good and therefore attributable to God, Augustine writes, "What perversity it is . . . to hesitate to ascribe free will (*libera uoluntate*) to him," to "the Creator of all good things."[25] Given that free will is good, Augustine reasons, it must come from God.

Section B: Will as a Movement of the Mind

What, then, is this good gift of God? Augustine makes a number of observations that answer this question, though how they fit together is not immediately obvious. On the most basic level, the will is something belonging to the mind and characterized by a fundamental neutrality: it can be used for good or for ill. Augustine characterizes this "something" in a highly dynamic way. In some places, he describes the will as turning a person from one thing to another. Elsewhere he describes it as turned by

---

[23] This is my translation (CCL 44A:11).

[24] *Diu. qu.* 8 (CCL 44A:15).

[25] *Lib. arb.* 2.18.49 (CSEL 74:84). This and subsequent English translations of *lib. arb.* are Burleigh's, unless otherwise noted. See Augustine, *Augustine: Earlier Writings*, ed. and trans. J. H. S. Burleigh (Philadelphia: Westminster Press, 1953). The English title used for Burleigh's translation is "On Free Will," but a more accurate translation is *On Free Choice*. I use the latter title in the list of abbreviations for this book.

the mind from one thing to another. Augustine's image of a hinge (*cardo*) offers a means of conceptualizing how these varying descriptions cohere.

In *lib. arb.* 1.11.21, Augustine characterizes the will as something belonging to the mind. Thus far in book 1, Augustine has shown that a perfectly ordered human person is one in whom "the mind is the chief power," and reason dominates the irrational emotions. Since the irrational emotions themselves are weaker and lesser than the mind, they cannot possibly be responsible for getting it off course.[26] When in 1.10.20–1.14.30 Augustine and Evodius, his dialogue partner, attempt to find out what could actually be the culprit for upsetting this proper ordering, the will enters the foreground. Augustine proposes, "Whatever is equal or superior to a ruling mind possessing virtue cannot make it serve lust because of its just character. And whatever is inferior cannot do it by reason of its weakness. So our argument teaches us: Nothing makes the mind (*mens*) a companion of cupidity, except its own will (*propria uoluntas*) and free choice (*liberum arbitrium*)."[27] The will, then, belongs to the mind (*mens*).[28]

A little later in the same text Augustine describes having a good will, which he has defined as "a will to live rightly and honourably and to reach the highest wisdom," as having "something in our souls" (*quiddam in animo*).[29] Materialist interpretations of the notion that the will is something

[26] For background on Augustine's view of the emotions, especially vis-à-vis Stoicism, see chapter 3 of Sarah Catherine Byers, *Perception, Sensibility, and Moral Motivation in Augustine: A Stoic-Platonic Synthesis* (New York: Cambridge University Press, 2013). See also Richard Sorabji, *Emotion and Peace of Mind: From Stoic Agitation to Christian Temptation* (New York: Oxford University Press, 2000), 400–417.

[27] *Lib. arb.* 1.11.21 (CSEL 74:22–23).

[28] According to Byers, Augustine uses the term *mens* (equivalent to the Greek *nous*) to designate the "higher" part of reason and uses *animus* (equivalent to the Greek *dianoētikon*) to refer to the soul's discursive rationality. In terms of the Stoic theory of perception, which, according to Byers, Augustine follows, the activity of the first is required for the evaluation and judgment of impressions, while the second includes the basic "rational ability to have impressions" (*Perception, Sensibility, and Moral Motivation in Augustine*, 66). This distinction, she argues, is the basis for appreciating how Augustine preserves the difference between pre-passions and passions, following Seneca and Gellius, who use these two terms to define this difference. The *mens* must assent to an impression for it to attain the status of an actual passion, as opposed to involuntary impressions perceived by the *animus* that remain at the level of preliminary passions or "first impressions" (123). Gerard O'Daly, however, notes that Augustine can use *animus*, as well as *mens*, to refer to "mind" and *anima rationalis* to refer to the seat of "mind and will." See Gerard O'Daly, *Augustine's Philosophy of Mind* (Berkeley: University of California Press, 1987), 7. Whether or not Augustine consistently maintains a distinction between *mens* and *animus* across his works, it is clear that in addition to speaking of the *uoluntas* as belonging to the *mens*, he also characterizes it as a movement felt in the *anima* and something in the *animus*. See *lib. arb.* 1.11.21; *diu. qu.* 8; and *lib. arb.* 1.12.25, respectively.

[29] *Lib. arb.* 1.12.25 (CSEL 74:25): "Are we, then, to rejoice a little in having something in our souls, I mean a good will (*bonam uoluntatem*), by comparison with which all those things we have mentioned are worthless...?"

in the mind being out of the question, it is possible that Augustine intends this affirmation to convey that the will is within the mind's power. This statement could then be read as a specification of Augustine's claim later in *lib. arb.* that the will is "in our power" (*in nostra potestate*). Thus neither Augustine's pronouncement that the will is "something in the mind" nor his declaration that the will is the mind's own, the *propria uoluntas mentis*, entails that the will refers to some kind of inherent structural feature or faculty of the mind, as opposed to a product produced by its workings. Both statements assert that will belongs to mind while leaving ambiguous the relationship between the two.

As part of his argument for the goodness of free will in *lib. arb.* book 2, however, Augustine uses an analogy that favors a conception of the will as a kind of faculty. Comparing the will as a part of the mind to various limbs, which form parts of the body, Augustine makes the point that the misuse of the will in no way detracts from its inherent goodness. If a hand strikes an innocent in anger, this reflects poorly upon the person who has misused her hand, rather than upon the moral status of the hand itself. In Augustine's words: "Even so ought you to confess that free will (*liberam uoluntatem*), without which no one can live aright, is a good thing (*bonum*) divinely bestowed, and that those are to be condemned who make a bad use of it, rather than to suggest that he who gave it ought not to have done so."[30] As this analogy makes clear, Augustine construes free will as capable of being employed to various ends. Like an arm or a leg, the will has an integrity in and of itself that is not exhausted by the specific activities in which it is put to use.[31] Distinguishing the will itself from specific acts of will is essential

---

[30] *Lib. arb.* 2.18.48 (CSEL 74:83).

[31] Whether Augustine saw the will as a faculty is a matter of debate. Byers objects to attributing such a view to him, which she judges medieval thinkers to have done anachronistically (*Perception, Sensibility, and Moral Motivation in Augustine*, 90). James Wetzel also denies that Augustine maintains the existence of a faculty of will "distinct from desire, which we use to determine our actions." See James Wetzel, *Augustine and the Limits of Virtue* (New York: Cambridge University Press, 1992), 8. T. D. J. Chappell likewise registers his suspicions about interpreting the Augustinian *uoluntas* as a faculty. See T. D. J. Chappell, *Aristotle and Augustine on Freedom: Two Theories of Freedom, Voluntary Action, and Akrasia* (New York: Macmillan, 1995), 127.

Simo Knuuttila, on the other hand, citing Albrecht Dihle as the one who "introduced the concept of will as a psychological faculty that functions as an ultimate and free arbitrator between possible modes of behavior," observes that for Augustine "the will is the controlling faculty, which, even when not initiating things with a particular act, can be regarded as letting all those things happen which it does not prevent." See Simo Knuuttila, *Emotions in Ancient and Medieval Philosophy* (New York: Clarendon Press, 2004), 168–170. See also "Augustine on Free Will and Predestination: A Critique of John M. Rist's Interpretation," in Jasper Hopkins, *Philosophical Criticism: Essays and Reviews* (Minneapolis, MN: Arthur J. Banning Press, 1994), 43–44. O'Daly too sees the Augustinian

to Augustine's case that God is not responsible for the misuse of the will, which was created good.

Fortunately, in the third book of *lib. arb.*, Augustine clarifies his conception of the will. He not only characterizes the will as belonging to or a part of the mind in a general way but also specifies it as a *motion* of the mind. Summarizing the conclusions of *lib. arb.* book 1, he writes:

> No doubt you remember that in the first discussion we discovered that the mind can become the slave of lust only by its own will (*propria uoluntate*). No superior thing and no equal thing compels it to such dishonor, because that would be unjust. And no inferior thing has the power. It remains that it must be the mind's own motion (*proprius iste motus*) when it turns its will (*uoluntatem*) away from enjoyment of the Creator to enjoyment of the creature.[32]

In this digest of ground covered earlier, Augustine's characterization of will gains specificity and directness. Here he describes will as something turned by the motion of the mind; it belongs to the mind in that it is moved by the mind and therefore within the mind's control.

In response to Augustine's summary, his dialogue partner Evodius expresses his own impressions of what the will is. Since Augustine later compliments the vigor of Evodius's speech without correcting anything he has said, there is no reason to assume that Evodius's comments are inaccurate from Augustine's point of view. In addition to describing the will as something that moves him to "enjoy this or that,"[33] Evodius compares it to a hinge: "Unless the movement by which the will is turned here or there be voluntary and placed in our power, a human person is neither to be praised when he turns toward superior things nor to be blamed when he

uoluntas as a "faculty" of the soul, namely, as "an essential motor of sense-perception, memory, imagination and cognition" (*Augustine's Philosophy of Mind*, 6).

Augustine's analogy between the will and the limbs of the body suggests that at this early phase of his thinking he saw the will as a "faculty," at least in the soft sense of an inherent mental or physical ability and perhaps also in the harder sense of a substantial structural feature of human psychology. Augustine viewed the will dynamically, but he did characterize it as a power of the soul responsible for individual acts and admitting various sorts of use. Of course, even if this understanding does overlap some medieval accounts, it in no way entails that interpretations of Augustine's conception of *uoluntas* need be constrained to map on to medieval usage of the term in every case or in every respect.

[32] *Lib. arb.* 3.1.2 (CSEL 74:91).

[33] *Lib. arb.* 3.1.3 (CSEL 74:92): "There is nothing that I feel more certainly (*firme*) and more personally (*intime*) than that I have a will (*uoluntatem*), and that it moves me to enjoy this or that."

turns toward inferior things, using his will like a hinge" (*quasi quendam cardinem uoluntatis*).[34] The use of *quasi* and *quendam* suggests that the speaker is hard-pressed to find the appropriate image for the idea he wants to convey. Even the formulation he finally chooses leaves further ambiguities for the reader. What is the significance of the hinge illustration in the final clause? Is the point that if the turning of the will were *not* voluntary and within our power it would then function like a hinge?[35] Or does the hinge image merely describe how one turns via the will to higher or lower objects in either case (in both the "real" and the "hypothetical" situations Augustine considers—if the will is in our power, and if it were not), the point being that if it were voluntary, this hinge-like turning would incur praise or blame, while if it were involuntary it would not?

This puzzle can be solved by looking to *diu. qu.*, where Augustine uses the same image in a morally neutral sense, showing it illustrates the "mechanics" of the soul's movement of the body as it does in fact function, rather than in the hypothetical case he considers in *lib. arb.* book 3. In *diu. qu.*, Augustine refers to the will as a motion of the mind (*motus animae*), this time appealing to the hinge (*cardo*) image to rule out the idea that this motion is spatial.

Augustine makes a number of important clarifications in this passage. First, he specifies that the *uoluntas* may refer to at least two kinds of movements of the soul: either the soul's movement of itself or the soul's movement of the body. Second, Augustine emphasizes that this movement is not a spatial one (it is not *de loco in locum* or something that happens as bodily movements do, that is, *localiter*). Finally, he makes positive and more precise use of the hinge image from book 3 of *lib. arb.* to illustrate how the soul can move the body via the will without itself being implicated in spatial movement. When the soul moves the body from place to place, it does so by will (*uoluntate*). By using its will like a hinge, the soul can move things from one place to another without itself changing location in space.[36]

---

[34] I have adjusted the translation of Burleigh. *Lib. arb.* 3.1.3 (CSEL 74:92).

[35] This may be the interpretation Thomas Williams prefers, whose translation suggests the image of a hinge "swinging" helplessly out of control: "If the movement of the will by which it turns this way or that were not voluntary and under its own control, a person would not deserve praise for turning to higher things or blame for turning to lower things, as if swinging on the hinge of the will." See Augustine, *On Free Choice of the Will*, trans. Thomas Williams (Indianapolis, IN: Hackett, 1993), 72.

[36] *Diu. qu.* 8 (CCL 44A:15).

Augustine's image of a hinge helps to unite various statements we have considered whose compatibility is not initially apparent. In *lib. arb.* book 3, Augustine had characterized the will as something turned by the mind. In Evodius's speech in the same book, however, a speech complimented and uncorrected by Augustine, the will was described as that by which a person is moved to enjoy one thing or another.[37] In the latter context, will functioned as the means of moving an individual to action. The juxtaposition of these two descriptions of will poses a question: Is will a movement of the soul in that it is moved *by* the soul, or is it a movement of the soul in that it moves the soul? The comparison of will to a hinge helps to capture how the will could serve both of these functions simultaneously: the soul turns the will, which in turn serves as the instrument that turns what is attached to it, be this body, which moves locally, or soul, which does not. In the latter case, the will serves as a mechanism by which the soul "is moved by itself." Thus will is a movement of the mind both in the sense of being a movement of which the mind is subject and in the sense that it moves a human person toward various ends.

Section C: Will as Capable of Both Good and Evil

A key point Augustine wishes to drive home in his early anti-Manichean works is that the will is capable of both good and evil but not inherently disposed toward evil so as to implicate the creator in creaturely wrongdoing. The will is therefore good, but this very created goodness entails its radical openness to either good or evil. Especially in *lib. arb.*, Augustine emphasizes this dual capacity of the will, stating that it is "in the will" (*uoluntate*), that is, within its capabilities, that we might either enjoy or be without the good.[38]

He explains this conclusion by remarking, "For what is so completely within the power of the will (*in uoluntate*) as the will (*uoluntas*) itself?"[39] According to Augustine, then, the will's power of self-determination is an

---

[37] *Lib. arb.* 3.1.3 (CSEL 74:92).

[38] *Lib. arb.* 1.12.26 (CSEL 74:26): "You see, then, I imagine, that it is in the power of our will (*in uoluntate nostra esse constitutum*) to enjoy or to be without so great and so true a good." Similarly, in *mor.* Augustine characterizes human beings as capable of either being corrected from their fallen condition by good will (*bona uoluntate*) or of surrendering to this condition by a bad will (*uoluntate mala*). See *mor.* 1.34.76 (CSEL 90:81).

[39] *Lib. arb.* 1.12.26 (CSEL 74:26): *quid enim tam in uoluntate quam ipsa uoluntas sita est?*

obvious premise, from which one may deduce its capacity to choose either to enjoy or lack the good. Later, in book 2, he juxtaposes descriptions of good and bad wills that explain in greater detail how the will may either pursue or turn away from the good: "The will (*uoluntas*), therefore, which cleaves to the unchangeable good that is common to all, obtains man's first and best good things though it is itself only an intermediate good. But the will which turns from the unchangeable and common good and turns to its own private good or to anything exterior or inferior, sins."[40] Here as well, Augustine clearly assumes the capacity of the will for both good and ill, defining a good will as one that cleaves to the unchangeable and common good, and a will that sins as one that turns from this unchangeable good to seek its own private good or anything exterior or inferior.[41] Like a hinge, the will can turn in different directions. However, as Augustine's comments indicate, far from entailing a propensity for evil inherent in the will, this twofold capacity itself belongs to the good created character of the will as an "intermediate good" (*medium bonum*).

A similar emphasis on the twofold capacity of the will can be found in *diu. qu.* In answering question 24, "whether both committing sin and acting rightly fall under the will's free choice," Augustine reasons to an affirmative answer from a starting point in God's justice. He begins with the premises that (1) God does not allow unjust punishment or reward, and (2) sin deserves punishment, while right action deserves reward. Since the second premise can be the case only if sin and right action can be justly imputed, and (3) sin and right action can be justly imputed only if they are done by a person's own free will, it follows that (4) because of God's just character, both committing sin and acting rightly must happen by virtue of the free choice of the will.[42] In *diu. qu.* 24, then, Augustine arrives at the same affirmation of the twofold capacity of the will for sin and righteousness, but based upon a distinctively theological premise.[43] As we will see, this affirmation will require qualification in Augustine's later writings.

---

[40] *Lib. arb.* 2.19.53 (CSEL 74:86).

[41] This way of describing a good will and a sinful will is quite different from how Augustine will describe these later in texts such as *en. Ps.* There he will define a good and bad will with reference to conformity to the will of God rather than—as here—by reference to a more abstract idea of the "unchangeable good." This difference may not be substantive, since, for the late Augustine also, God is unchangeably good, but it is at least terminological.

[42] *Diu. qu.* 24 (CCL 44A:29–30).

[43] Augustine makes a very similar argument on the basis of God's justice in *lib. arb.* 2.1.3, where he contends that God's punishment of people for using their free will (*uoluntatem liberam*) to sin would

In addition to making statements that attribute the capacity both for good and for evil to the will, Augustine also refers to the will as the cause or as that *by which* (using an ablative of means) good and evil actions are performed. Rephrasing an earlier argument, Augustine states in *lib. arb.* that the good will (*bona uoluntas*) is "that by which (*ea . . . est qua*) we seek to live rightly and honourably."[44] In parallel fashion, he states that the mind's own will (*uoluntas*) and free choice (*liberum arbitrium*) make it a "companion of cupidity."[45] A little later in *lib. arb.*, Evodius affirms as an article of faith (*credamus*) that it is "by the human being's own will" (*propria uoluntate*) that she has fallen to the "miserable condition of this mortal life." Augustine then goes on to offer rational confirmation of this belief.[46] The conclusion of his reasoning is that only the will (*uoluntas*) can "drive the mind from its seat of authority and from the right course."[47] Summarized by Evodius in other words at the end of book 1, the only thing we can say about the "whence" (*unde*) of our evil-doing is that we do it "from the free choice of our will" (*ex libero uoluntatis arbitrio*).[48] Augustine likewise presents the will (*uoluntas*) as the cause of depravity (*causa depravationis*) in *diu. qu.*[49] In *lib. arb.* book 2, Augustine and Evodius, recalling the argument from book 1, again describe the free choice of the will (*liberum uoluntatis arbitrium*) as that "by which" we sin (*eo peccamus; quo nos peccare*).[50]

It is not until *lib. arb.* book 3 that Augustine gives a name to the kind of will by which one sins. In this context, however, he does not begin with the phenomenon of the evil will, seeking to find terms to describe it. Instead, he begins with 1 Timothy 6:10's reference to avarice, and in the process of explicating what this might mean, connects it with the notion of an evil will: "Avarice must be understood as connected not only with silver and money but with everything which is immoderately desired, in every case where a man wants more than is sufficient. Such avarice is cupidity, and

be unjust unless they also had the freedom to live aright. He concludes, "An action would be neither sinful nor righteous unless it were done voluntarily" (CSEL 74:38–39).

[44] *Lib. arb.* 1.13.29 (CSEL 74:29).
[45] *Lib. arb.* 1.11.21 (CSEL 74:22–23).
[46] *Lib. arb.* 1.11.23 (CSEL 74:24).
[47] *Lib. arb.* 1.15.34 (CSEL 74:34).
[48] *Lib. arb.* 1.16.35 (CSEL 74:35).
[49] See *diu. qu.* question four (CCL 44A:13).
[50] *Lib. arb.* 2.1.1 (CSEL 74:37).

cupidity is an evil will (*inproba uoluntas*). An evil will, therefore, is the cause (*causa*) of all evils."[51] In this case Augustine deduces the evil will's causal role from 1 Timothy 6:10.

Section D: Will as a Necessary and Sufficient Condition for Possibility of Good and Bad Actions

In fact Augustine goes beyond asserting that the will *can* be the cause of good or evil actions. In several places in his early anti-Manichean writings he describes the will as that which actually makes it possible for actions to be good or bad: for Augustine it is not possible to live rightly without free will (*libera uoluntate*).[52] Free will is therefore a precondition for an act being praiseworthy or blameworthy.[53] It is also what makes obligation possible. It only makes sense to say someone "should" do something, Augustine contends, if she has the free will (*libera uoluntas*) and capability (*facultas*) to accomplish it.[54] In addition to arguing that free will is an essential precondition for acting rightly or wrongly, Augustine also insists that sin cannot

---

[51] *Lib. arb.* 3.17.48 (CSEL 74:130).

[52] *Lib. arb.* 2.18.49 (CSEL 74:84). Byers argues that "*libera voluntas, arbitrium voluntatis,* and *liberum arbitrium voluntatis* are synonymous, meaning 'rational impulse which is by definition free,'" and that Augustine thus interchanges the phrase *libera uoluntas* with the term *uoluntas* in *lib. arb.* See her discussion of the term *libera uoluntas* on 228–230 of *Perception, Sensibility, and Moral Motivation in Augustine.* While Augustine does regard *uoluntas* as inherently free in this work, with the result that the two terms function as equivalents, his use of these terms does not correspond neatly to "rational impulse" as defined in Stoic terms by Byers. According to her description of the Stoic theory of motivation, it is assent to a proposition (*sunkatathesis*) that introduces moral responsibility, since this assent is "up to" the person granting it and may be deemed true or false. It is assent that makes the ensuing rational impulse (*hormē*), as well as any action that may result from this impulse, good or bad. While a given rational impulse may be designated good or bad on the basis of the assent that produces it, the impulse itself cannot be described as necessary for a person to live rightly or wrongly or as the basis for moral responsibility; these distinctions belong rather to assent. Thus Augustine's notion of *libera uoluntas* in *Lib. arb.*, which he portrays as the ground for moral responsibility, extends beyond the Stoic meaning for *hormē* to include characteristics Byers attributes to the Stoic notion of assent. At the same time, Augustine's *uoluntas* does not extend so far as to correspond to the Stoic idea of the *hegemonikon*, since it does not act as the seat of the five faculties of sense or even as the seat of all four powers attributed directly to the *hegemonikon* in Stoic thought.

[53] Augustine repeats the idea that something cannot be blameworthy if it is not voluntary. For one example, see *lib. arb.* 3.15.42 (CSEL 74:125). Similar arguments can be found in *uera rel.* 14.27, where Augustine states that sin is committed voluntarily, that censuring sin presupposes that sin is committed voluntarily, and that the fact that sins are committed is evidence of free choice of the will.

[54] Augustine writes, "No man is guilty because he has not received this or that power. But because he does not do as he ought he is justly held guilty. Obligation arises if he has received free will and sufficient power" (*lib. arb.* 3.15.45 [CSEL 74:128]).

result from willing that is necessary. He states in no uncertain terms in *lib. arb.*, "Whatever be the cause of willing (*uoluntatis*), if it cannot be resisted no sin results from yielding to it."[55]

As it turns out, not only is free will a necessary criterion for right action, but it is also a sufficient criterion for right or lawful action. In *diu. qu.* question 27, on providence, Augustine underlines the point that the will to do good or ill determines what recompense one receives, not whether good actually results from one's action. The latter is beyond an individual human being's control and depends on God's providence; it is therefore irrelevant to the moral status of an act. For example, when a good person wills to do good to another person, but harm actually results, the good person does not merit punishment. In Augustine's words: "It is not imputed to the good that, when they themselves will to do good, harm befalls someone, but the reward of a good will (*beneuolentiae*) is bestowed upon the good soul."[56] Augustine drives home the same point even more directly when summarizing the conclusion of question 27: "Hence, because we are not aware of everything that the divine order accomplishes profitably in our regard, we act in accordance with the law solely by good will" (*in sola bona uoluntate*).[57]

According to Augustine, then, since we cannot possibly be acquainted with the full network of other events with which our own actions will interact, and since we therefore must remain ignorant of the ultimate impact an intended deed will have in God's providence, all that matters for determining whether a given action is right (in accordance with the law) is whether one performs it "by good will." By this Augustine seems to mean something like "with good intentions." Here we see the moral weight Augustine accords to the orientation of the will: he does not merely say that the will matters, or that the will matters more, or that the will matters most, in determining whether an action fulfills the law. His final assessment is exclusive: the will *alone* matters (*sola bona uoluntate*).[58]

---

[55] *Lib. arb.* 3.18.50 (CSEL 74:131). This quotation illustrates that, at this point in his career, Augustine designates as sin only those types of willing subject to our control. In this sense, as well as insofar as he sees sin as pertaining to what one wills rather than how this will actually plays out in one's actions, his account does not allow for the idea of "involuntary sin." For a contemporary definition and defense of this notion, see Robert Merrihew Adams, "Involuntary Sins," *Philosophical Review* 94 (1985): 3–31.

[56] *Diu. qu.* 27 (CCL 44A:33).

[57] *Diu. qu.* 27 (CCL 44A:34).

[58] It is not clear how Chappell would account for this assessment given his conviction that "when Augustine makes a distinction between *voluntas* and action which expresses that *voluntas* . . . he never says, in Abelardian mode, that what counts for moral assessment is the *voluntas*, and the action is (as good as) immaterial. Rather he says that, if my *voluntas* fails to get actualised in my doings, then this is an insuperable impediment to our being able to speak of me as a voluntary agent at all" (*Aristotle and Augustine on Freedom*, 127).

Section E: The Will and Responsibility

For Augustine, not only is the will alone a necessary and sufficient condition for the possibility of acting rightly, and that *by which* human beings act both rightly and wrongly; it is also the basis upon which a given action can be attributed to an agent as uniquely her responsibility. Since the morality of a person's actions depends on her will, and her will depends on herself, whether a person acts rightly or wrongly is up to her. Augustine makes this point clearly toward the end of *De Genesi aduersus Manicheos* (*Gn. adu. Man.*).[59] In response to the question of whether God should have made the devil, Augustine declares that God "through his justice and providence . . . uses the devil's malice to set many people right." Yet this raises a further question: If God's providence brings good effects out of the devil's malice, then does the devil's usefulness render him good in spite of himself? Augustine answers, "On the contrary, he is bad insofar as he is the devil. But God is good and almighty, able to bring about much goodness and justice from the devil's malice. The only thing, after all, that is credited to the devil is his own will (*non enim diabolo imputatur, nisi uoluntas sua*) by which he strives to work evil; God's providence, which makes good use of him, is not to his credit."[60] Thus Augustine sharply demarcates what is rightly attributed to God—the providential redemption of the devil's malicious acts for good use—from what is rightly attributed to the devil: the will underlying the actions the devil performs. The devil cannot take credit for the good use to which God puts his bad actions; he can only take responsibility for his will.

In the next paragraph of *Gn. adu. Man.*, Augustine explains why determining what should be imputed to whom is so important. In addition to preventing the creature from taking credit that properly belongs to God, attributing creaturely will to the creature also avoids blaming God for things for which God is not responsible. As Augustine drives home in the rhetorically powerful conclusion of *Gn. adu. Man.*, more is at stake in his controversy with the Manichees than how to think rightly about the created world, though this, of course, is a key point of contention between them. Augustine's dispute with the Manichees finally comes down to a dispute

[59] Subsequent translations of this text, unless otherwise noted, come from Augustine, *On Genesis*, ed. John E. Rotelle, trans. Edmund Hill, WSA I/13 (Hyde Park, NY: New City Press, 2002).

[60] *Gn. adu. Man.* 2.28.42 (CSEL 91:170).

about God. Thus Augustine writes, "Finally, what is at issue between the Manichees and ourselves is a question of religion, and *the* religious question is how to think about God in a godly way."[61] Attributing human sin to the human will is important, not chiefly because it helps to define an anthropology that is more accurate in and of itself but because this attribution insulates against impious thinking about God.

After his initial assessment of the primary issue between himself and the Manichees, Augustine lays out a series of comparisons, which illustrate how the Manichean way of thinking leads to impious conclusions about God while the catholic perspective avoids these errors. In the first of these, the will plays a key role. The will is Augustine's alternative to the Manichean explanation of the human condition. As Augustine sees it, the Manichees attribute the human predicament to God, either because of a problem in God's own nature or because of an inherent deficiency in the human nature he created. Augustine counters Manichean arguments by using the "will" as an explanatory category for human action that allows one to "speak of God in a godly way." By pointing to the human "will" as the reason for human sin and the human plight, Augustine avoids attributing human problems to God: "Now since *we* cannot deny that the human race is sunk in the sorry state of sin, *they* say that God's nature is sunk in a sorry state, while *we* deny that and say that the nature which God made out of nothing is sunk in a sorry state and has come to this pass, not by being forced into it but through its will (*uoluntate*) to sin."[62]

Later in this paragraph Augustine again appeals to the will. It is worth quoting the paragraph at length to illustrate how the concept of the will functions in the rhetorical context of Augustine's argument:

> *They* say that God's nature is forced by God himself to repent of sins; *we* deny this, but say instead that the nature which God made out of nothing is obliged after it has sinned to repent of its sins. *They* say that the nature of God receives pardon from God himself; *we* deny this, but say instead that the nature which God made out of nothing, if it turns back to its God from its sins, receives pardon for its sins. *They* say that God's nature is subject to the necessity of change; *we* deny this, but say that the nature which God made out of nothing is changed by its own will (*uoluntate esse*

---

[61] *Gn. adu. Man.* 2.29.43 (CSEL 91:170).
[62] *Gn. adu. Man.* 2.29.43 (CSEL 91:170).

mutatam). *They* say that God's nature is injured by the sins of others; *we* deny this, but say instead that no nature is harmed by any sins except its own; and we say that God is so good, so just, so immune to harm, that he neither sins, nor does any harm to anyone who has refused to sin (*qui peccare noluerit*), and neither does anyone who has decided to sin (*qui peccare uoluerit*) do any harm to him.[63]

Continuing on, after emphasizing that there is "no natural evil," Augustine affirms God's sovereignty over evil: "The one who makes all things good by his will (*uoluntate*) suffers nothing evil by necessity (*necessitate*) seeing that since his will presides over all things, he does not experience anything in any shape or form against his will."[64]

Taken as a whole, this passage shows how Augustine uses the category of the will to provide an alternative to the Manichean explanation for the human experience of sin and evil in the world. Whereas the Manichees explain the human situation by inferring from it God's character, concluding that God's nature must suffer the same plight to which human beings are subject, Augustine's explanation traces the human plight to human agency. This is the most basic contrast Augustine highlights between the Manichean position and his own. But Augustine also underlines the danger of surmising that human entrenchment in sin reflects what human nature is inherently, by force, or by necessity. For to fall into this error would be to succumb to a more subtle form of the same basic mistake of attributing human sin to God since God, as Creator, would bear responsibility for any feature necessary to human being as such.

To avoid this path, Augustine resorts to the notion of *uoluntas*: rather than stemming necessarily from human nature as such, the human condition indicates humanity's "will to sin." Evil is thus a consequence of human beings willing freely, not of God's subjection to necessity. Appealing to *uoluntas* makes it possible to attribute events to human beings without implicating their Creator. It serves as a conceptual tool for distinguishing what should be attributed to God and what should be attributed to creatures. Human will proves human responsibility for what human beings do. On the other hand, God's good will shows that God is *not* responsible for what human beings do. *Uoluntas* has the effect of "stopping the buck"

---

[63] *Gn. adu. Man.* 2.29.43 (CSEL 91:170–171).
[64] *Gn. adu. Man.* 2.29.43 (CSEL 91:171–172). I have modified Hill's translation.

when it comes to moral responsibility because, as shown in the previous section, it is the necessary and sufficient condition for performing good or bad actions.

Augustine situates his appeals to the notion of the will within the context of a basic theological distinction: the distinction between the Creator-God who makes creatures out of nothing (*de nihilo fecit deus*) and the created human being who is made out of nothing (*ea natura quam deus fecit de nihilo*). Augustine's mantra is that human nature is a nature "which God made out of nothing." He underscores this point both when attributing human sin to the human will and when attributing the change that human nature undergoes to its own will. When he speaks of God's good will, Augustine describes this will specifically as it was in effect in God's work as Creator. The will thus also comes into play as a means of appropriately acknowledging the difference between God the Creator and the creatures he makes out of nothing.

In the series of antitheses from *Gn. adu. Man.* 2.29.43, Augustine asserts that the fundamental problem with Manicheism is not just the mistaken belief that human nature was forced to sin, but a misunderstanding of God's nature: the Manichees fail to grasp that God's nature is on an entirely different plane from the human nature God has created. This is why he points out in each sentence that the Manichees have mistakenly attributed to God what ought to be attributed, in corrected form, to creatures.

By contrasting his own position to that of the Manichees in this way, Augustine turns the tables on them. He had observed earlier that the Manichees object to the doctrine of the image of God because it seems to them to implicate God in human corporality. Now Augustine attempts to show that it is actually the Manichees who have confused God and human beings, ascribing exactly the same kind of necessity and weakness to God as they do to human creatures. Perhaps this is why he repeats over and over again the formula "they say...; we deny this, but we say..." (*illi dicunt...; nos negamus, sed dicimus*), sharply juxtaposing the positions he identifies as Manichean against his own. The Manichees are confused not only about what is true of God and what is true of creatures, but also about the more mundane issue of what Augustine says and what they themselves say. They need to get their distinctions right, Augustine intimates. The notion of "will" plays a key role in making the appropriate distinctions between what Augustine says and what his Manichean opponents say, between what is necessary and what is voluntary, between what should be attributed to

God and what should be attributed to human beings, and therefore between what it means to be the Creator and what it means to be a creature.

Section F: What the Will Is Not

Augustine not only uses the notion of will to draw theological distinctions in his early anti-Manichean writings; he also draws distinctions involving the will itself, distinguishing it from other, related notions. For example, whereas in *diu. qu.* Augustine had characterized a good will as the sole ingredient necessary for fulfilling the law, in a discussion of the second great commandment in *De moribus ecclesiae Catholicae et de moribus Manicheorum (mor.)*, he stresses the insufficiency of a good will for helping one's neighbor. Loving one's neighbor and willing the best for him do not necessarily guarantee that one can actually help him; to translate good will into authentic acts of service requires "much thought and prudence, which no one can have unless God, the source of all good things, grant it."[65] Having a good will, Augustine emphasizes, is not the same as knowing how to execute it properly.[66] For insight into how to realize our good will we are dependent upon God.

Augustine does not characterize the orientation of the will as itself a gift of God; rather, he describes God's help (*auxilium*) as a gift that comes alongside the good will.[67] Issuing a final word of caution at the end of book 1, which presents an apology for the catholic way of life, Augustine writes:

[65] *Mor.* 1.26.51 (CSEL 90:55). This and subsequent English translations of *mor.* come from Augustine, "The Catholic Way of Life and the Manichean Way of Life," in *The Manichean Debate*, trans. Roland Teske, WSA I/19 (Hyde Park, NY: New City Press, 2006), unless otherwise noted.

[66] This assertion does not necessarily conflict with Augustine's statement in *diu. qu.* 27, that "we act in accordance with the law solely by good will." In both cases Augustine draws attention to the fact that guaranteeing the result one wills to achieve is impossible for human beings on their own because of the network of contingencies involved. The difference is that here Augustine emphasizes the challenges of executing the will whereas in the passage referred to in *diu. qu.* he had stressed the value of having a good will regardless of such challenges. In fact the emphasis on the importance of intention is common to both works. In *mor.* 1.33.73, for example, Augustine stresses that the intention behind eating or not eating certain foods is what matters: "The power to defile a person is not in the foods that we eat but in the mind." The key is partaking of foods without "shameful desire."

[67] This characterization confirms Wetzel's conclusion that Augustine's introduction of "divine agency into the very heart of human willing is still years away" in *mor.* (*Augustine and the Limits of Virtue*, 72). In *mor.*, Augustine does underline human need for God's help to bring good human willing to fulfillment (1.26.51). He also states that God preserves the love of himself (1.25.46), which is the key to virtue in all of its forms. But Augustine does not yet give any indication of the necessity of God's help for willing the good in the first place or directly connect God's gift of love with the human will. Other characteristic emphases are starting to appear, such as the role of love in virtue, which

Now I warn you at long last to stop speaking ill of the Catholic Church by criticizing the conduct of persons whom she herself condemns and whom she strives daily to correct like bad children. But whoever of them are corrected by good will (*bona uoluntate*) and the help (*auxilio*) of God recover by doing penance what they lost by sinning. Those who out of bad will persevered in their previous sins or even add more serious sins to their earlier ones, however, are allowed to exist in the field of the Lord and to grow with the good seed, but the time will come when the weeds will be separated out.[68]

For Augustine, a good will and the assistance God renders to reform an individual are not the same.

In addition to distinguishing being "full of good will" from being able to execute it, and being corrected "by a good will" from being corrected "by God's help," Augustine also treats what comes from will as something different from what comes from nature. This distinction is an implication of Augustine's argument in *lib. arb.* that human misuse of the will resulting in evil actions is not a necessary outworking of the good created nature of the will. Augustine also alludes to this distinction in passing in *mor.* In a kind of ode to the Catholic Church in which he proclaims that the love of God that heals disease and is the medicine of salvation is found in her, he includes the line "You connect all the relationships of the family and bonds of affinity in mutual love, while preserving all the ties coming from nature (*naturae*) and will (*uoluntatis*)."[69] Perhaps Augustine's allusion to ties from nature and will refers, respectively, to the ties of family, which belong to one by virtue of biological relationships, and to those of friendship, which one may choose for oneself (parallel to "relationships of family" and "bonds of affinity"). In any case, this formulation implies a distinction between the two. The bonds that come from nature and the bonds that come from will may not be mutually exclusive, but they are distinct.

Augustine will eventually combine with an affirmation of the dependence of good human willing upon God's prior initiative. But it is premature to assume that these emphases already entail such dependence. Carol Harrison's conclusion that *mor.* represents the key turning point in Augustine's thinking on the will since in it "the operation of the will is, then, no longer a matter of reason but of love, a love inspired by God's grace, whereby human beings can will/love its source," seems to be the product of this kind of assumption (*Rethinking Augustine's Early Theology*, 229). The same applies to her conclusion that there is an "identification of will with love in *De moribus*" (235). These claims do not appear to derive directly from Augustine's actual statements about will in *mor.*

[68] *Mor.* 1.34.76 (CSEL 90:81).
[69] *Mor.* 1.30.63 (CSEL 90:66).

In several places Augustine also establishes a distinction between the will and understanding. Willing in a certain way neither entails understanding nor is entailed by understanding. In observations he makes about his Manichean opponents, Augustine makes clear that it is possible to understand the truth of a matter yet fail to will in accordance with this truth. Addressing the Manichean error of thinking that evil is a substance, Augustine writes at the beginning of *mor.* book 2, "But what am I to do? I know that there are many among you who cannot understand these ideas at all. I also know that there are some who, though they somehow see these points with their fine minds, still act stubbornly out of bad will (*mala uoluntate*), because of which they will also lose those fine minds."[70]

For Augustine, then, will and intellectual understanding are not the same thing. Nor does the latter automatically produce the former. One can know that something is true and right, yet resist it. Still, Augustine never suggests that will and mind are completely unrelated. To the contrary, he warns that having a bad will can eventually pollute the mind as well. To understand something rightly (*intellegere*) does not entail willing in a corresponding way, but stubbornly willing in a way that is contrary to the truth one has understood can eventually erode one's grasp of that truth, sinking one in delusion.

Faulty willing can distort knowing, but right willing does not necessarily signal the possession of corresponding knowledge. Just as Augustine believes it is possible to understand without willing rightly, he contends that it is possible to will rightly without understanding. In *Gn. adu. Man.* Augustine points to Adam as a case in point. Augustine writes of Adam, "You see, if he were willing (*uellet*) to keep God's command, and persevered in living by faith until he became capable of really understanding the truth, that is, if he worked in paradise and guarded what he had received, he wouldn't come to that deformed state of mind which would lead him, when displeased with the flesh as with his nakedness, to put together worldly, carnal coverings of lies."[71] The error of the first father of the human race consisted in failing to want to obey God's precepts in the absence of a full understanding of the truth. Adam could have willed rightly, Augustine indicates, even given his lack of knowledge, but he failed to do so. Again in this case, willing and knowing are not unrelated. Part of Adam's difficulty

---

[70] *Mor.* 2.2.4 (CSEL 90:90).
[71] *Gn. adu. Man.* 2.26.39 (CSEL 91:165).

was sustaining right desires without a complete knowledge of good and evil. Yet Augustine clearly deems it possible for Adam to have willed obedience despite his ignorance.

It is instructive to compare Augustine's understanding of the relationship between reason and the will to that of Fonteius of Carthage, whose views on the will come up in *diu. qu.*, question 12, which consists of a quotation from "a certain wise man," namely Fonteius.[72] The gist of the quotation is the importance of preserving the purity of the mind against the wiles of the "wicked spirit" so that the mind might perceive God's presence. What is interesting for the purposes of this chapter is how Fonteius characterizes the *uoluntas*, especially in relation to Augustine's distinctions between knowing and willing. Fonteius writes of reason, "And since this is a ray of heavenly light, there is in it also a mirror of the divine presence; for God and a blameless will (*uoluntas innoxia*) and the reward of deeds well done shine forth in it." Whereas for Augustine, knowledge of the good possessed through the operation of reason can be yoked to a will that defies it, Fonteius seems to see reason as inherently shining forth the light of a "blameless will." The image Fonteius uses suggests that the will is in some way embraced by, or naturally flows from, reason; it adds to the natural rays of reason's own light. For Augustine the will is beginning to have a mind of its own.

Section G: The Human Will as a Window into the Divine Will

Whereas Augustine tends to distinguish human willing from human reason, he tends to associate human willing with divine willing. Examining how Augustine characterizes these two types of willing in relationship to one another therefore helps to shed light on his understanding of the workings of the human will. Augustine presents human willing as standing in analogy to divine willing in at least three ways: he applies the principle that will is involved in any act of creative causality to both God and human beings, using the image of a human craftsperson; he portrays the human will to

---

[72] CCL 44A:19. Question 12 is material that comes from Fonteius of Carthage's text *On Purifying the Mind in Order to See God*. This was written before Fonteius became a Christian. See Boniface Ramsey's comments in Augustine, *Responses to Miscellaneous Questions*, trans. Boniface Ramsey, WSA I/12 (Hyde Park, NY: New City Press, 2008), 35n13.

obey as in humanity's power, much in the way that God's ability more generally is commensurate with God's will; and he argues that recognizing God's will, like recognizing the will of a human person, requires friendship. Given this analogical relationship, everyday realities of human willing, Augustine thinks, should be able to shed light on how the divine will works. His explanations of these everyday realities, in turn, illumine for his readers some of his basic assumptions about human willing.

In one particularly interesting case, Augustine appeals to the human will in order to illustrate the reasonableness of a particular exegetical interpretation he is advancing. The Manichees, according to Augustine, try to read the statement of Genesis 1:2, "The Spirit of God was being borne over the water," as if this were a spatial description of the Spirit's movement. In Augustine's view, however, this verse refers to the Spirit's creative power being effected in bringing the water into being. He writes, "The Spirit, you see, was not being borne over the water through a certain distance of space, as the sun is borne over the earth, but through his own sublimely invisible power."[73] By appealing to the notion of the will of a human craftsperson, he helps his readers consider this nonmaterial interpretation of the language used about God's Spirit in Genesis 1:2. He states:

> Let these people tell us, though, how the will (*uoluntas*) of a craftsman is borne over the things that are to be crafted. But if they cannot grasp such human, everyday realities, let them fear God and seek in simplicity of heart what they do not understand, or else while they are bent on chopping up with their sacrilegious words the truth which they cannot see, the axe may slip and chop off their legs.[74]

This verse, Augustine chides his Manichean opponents, should be as easy to comprehend as the scenario of a craftsperson plying his trade. In the Spirit, God's will was being brought to bear in the creation as the will of a craftsperson is brought to bear on the objects he creates. From Augustine's perspective, the Manichees are cutting apart the scriptural text by excising from their interpretive approach what their everyday experience can tell them about how the will of God must function.[75] Augustine chooses the

---

[73] *Gn. adu. Man.* 1.5.8 (CSEL 91:75).

[74] *Gn. adu. Man.* 1.5.8 (CSEL 91:75).

[75] The Trinitarian implications of this comparison are also worth noting. In aligning the Spirit to the *will* of the craftsman, this passage may represent an early form of ideas further developed and elaborated in Augustine's mature work *De trinitate*, which associates the Spirit with the will.

image of God the creator as craftsperson, however, not merely because it is well suited to expose the elementary character of the exegetical error the Manichees are making. It recurs repeatedly in *Gn. adu. Man.*, and in at least one other place Augustine explicitly restates the exact analogy involving the will that he has used here.[76]

The craftsperson image illustrates the role of will in being the *auctor*, the creator or cause, of something, a connection Augustine makes explicit in *diu. qu.* Addressing the question of "whether it is by God's causality that humankind is evil" (*utrum deo auctore sit homo deterior*), Augustine answers, "When someone's causality is spoken of, it is his willing that is meant. It is by a flaw in his will (*uitium uoluntatis*), therefore, that humankind is evil. If this flaw is foreign to the will of God, as reason teaches, where it may be must be inquired after."[77] Augustine's point, in other words, is that when people speak of someone being the author or agent of something they understand this to include the idea that the person in question willed it. Augustine's use of the image of the craftsperson as applied to the Spirit, an *auctor*, thus serves as a practical example of the will's involvement in creative acts of both God and human beings as *auctores*. For both God and human beings, being the cause of something implies the operation of will.

In addition to being convinced that willing is entailed when we speak of God or a human being acting as the cause or the originator of something (of someone being the *auctor*), Augustine seems to regard the notion of willing as inherently involved in action per se. As we have already seen, Augustine reasons from God's justice to the conclusion that both committing sin and acting rightly are up to the free choice of the will.[78] Thus, insofar as any given human action qualifies as either sin or acting rightly, it involves the free choice of the will. *Diu. qu.* 24 confirms this inference: "Whatever is done in the world is done partly by divine action and partly by our will" (*nostra uoluntate*).[79] Augustine arrives at this idea based on the premise that nothing occurs by chance in the world (*nihil igitur casu fit in mundo*). For Augustine, divine and human willing, at work in any act per se as well as in

---

[76] See *Gn. adu. Man.* 1.7.12, 1.8.13, 1.12.18, and 1.16.25. In 1.7.12 (CSEL 91:78), Augustine writes, "He also called the same material water, over which the Spirit of God was borne as the will (*uoluntas*) of the craftsman is borne over things to be crafted."

[77] *Diu. qu.* 3 (CCL 44A:12): *illo autem auctore cum dicitur, illo uolente dicitur.*

[78] See, for example, *diu. qu.* 24.

[79] *Diu. qu.* 24 (CCL 44A:29).

any act of creative causality, together constitute an explanatory alternative to chance.

A second key respect in which the human will stands in analogy to the divine will in Augustine's early anti-Manichean works is with regard to the connections he establishes between willing and ability. With respect to fulfilling God's commands, Augustine ties willingness and ability to obey tightly together, both positively and negatively: willing to obey means ability to do so while not willing to obey means ability not to do so.[80] In *Gn. adu. Man.*, Augustine states that conversion to obedience is something of which all people are capable so long as they will it. Turning "from a love of visible and time-bound things to the fulfillment of his commands . . . is something all people can do, if they wish" (*quod omnes homines possunt si uelint*).[81] If human beings want to obey, they can: *possunt si uelint*. Augustine will later come to see this statement, at least in its unqualified form, as vulnerable to co-option by his critics; in the *Retractationes* he thus recontextualizes it theologically—his earlier statement is true of all people, *insofar as* their wills have been prepared by God. If people will rightly, they can realize their wills, but whether they can will rightly depends on a preceding chapter of the story: God's prior rehabilitation of the will.[82] For now, however, wanting to obey (*uelle*) means being able to obey (*posse*) without this added qualification.[83]

Just as Augustine pairs wanting to obey with the ability to obey, so he pairs not wanting to disobey with the ability to resist disobedience. In *Gn. adu. Man.* this point comes up in response to the question of why God failed to make Adam so that he would not sin. Augustine replies that God did in fact make him this way. Augustine writes, "Well, but that's precisely what he did

---

[80] The claim that willing to obey entails the ability to obey is not the same as the claim that willing to perform a certain act always entails the ability to execute that act. Augustine affirms the former but denies the latter. See previous discussion of *mor.* 1.26.51. Obedience is a special case because all that is required to meet the specifications of obedience is will, whereas performing other actions may rely on external circumstances beyond one's control.

[81] *Gn. adu. Man.* 1.3.6 (CSEL 91:73).

[82] "But regarding my words, '. . . those who believe in God and who turn away from the love of visible and temporal things to the fulfilling of his precepts, which all people are capable of if they will to be,' the recent heretics, the Pelagians, should not think that they were said in agreement with them. For it is entirely true that all people are capable of this if they will to be, but *the will is made ready by the Lord* (Prov 8:35 LXX), and by the gift of charity it is increased so much that they are capable" (*retr.* 1.10.2).

[83] Augustine does, however, connect right willing with the divine light. He argues that even before the creation of light, God dwelt in "another light," from which comes the light of Christ described in John 1:9. It is God's light that feeds the pure hearts of those who turn from sin. See *Gn. adu. Man.* 1.3.6.

do; the man was so made, after all, that if he hadn't wanted to, he wouldn't sin" (*si noluisset, non peccaret*).[84] Augustine repeats this same logic regarding Eve. If the Manichees raise the point that the devil should not have been given access to the woman, Augustine's reply is "On the contrary, it's she who shouldn't have given the devil access to herself. She was so made, after all, that if she hadn't wanted to she wouldn't have done so" (*si noluisset, non admitteret*).[85] In the cases of both Adam and Eve, which the Manichees attempt to use to attribute responsibility for evil and sin to God, Augustine responds by saying that sin is entirely contingent upon what the human person wants. It is not a necessary result of how God has created the human person. Adam and Eve as God created them were completely equipped not only with the ability to obey had they wanted to but also with the ability to resist sin had they not wanted to choose evil. For Adam and Eve before the fall, neither wanting nor not wanting was divorced from the ability to act accordingly.

This characterization of human willing aligns with Augustine's characterization of God's willing. For God, to want something is to be able to do it. *Uelle* is *posse*. Consequently, appealing to God's will is sufficient to explain why God has done something.[86] No further preconditions must be met besides God's own wish to do something for it to become a reality. God's creation of the world out of nothing demonstrates this principle decisively. The fact that God created out of nothing shows that he did not need any help to do what he wanted. God had the power to implement his will in utter independence. If the world was not created ex nihilo, then God's omnipotence would be compromised. He would be reliant on something external to himself in order to create. In Augustine's words: "But Almighty God did not need the help of any kind of thing at all which he himself had not made, in order to carry out what he wished (*ut quod uolebat efficeret*). If, you see, for making the things he wished, he was being assisted by some actual thing which he had not made himself, then he was not almighty; and to think that is sacrilege."[87] It belongs to God's character to have the power to effect that which he wants without assistance. As demonstrated, creating

---

[84] *Gn. adu. Man.* 2.28.42 (CSEL 91:169).

[85] *Gn. adu. Man.* 2.28.42 (CSEL 91:169).

[86] Thus Augustine writes that "anyone who says, 'Why did God make heaven and earth?' is to be given this answer: 'Because he wished to.' It is God's will, you see, that is the cause of heaven and earth, and that is why God's will is greater than heaven and earth. Anyone though who goes on to say, 'Why did he wish to make heaven and earth' is looking for something greater than God's will is; but nothing greater can be found" (*Gn. adu. Man.* 1.2.4).

[87] *Gn. adu. Man.* 1.6.10 (CSEL 91:77).

human beings out of nothing, God grants to them an analogous capacity to act in accordance with their will when it comes to willing obedience or disobedience.

Not only does Augustine connect the human will, as a dimmer reflection of the divine will, with a concomitant power of execution as concerns the willing of obedience or disobedience; he also describes the will itself as within human power. In response to the question in *lib. arb.* book 3 of whether God's foreknowledge makes human willing necessary, he makes the bold statement that "there is nothing so much in our power as the will itself."[88] According to Augustine, for example, having a good will is as simple as willing it.[89] Elsewhere, Augustine makes the further claim that the characteristic of being within our power belongs intrinsically to the will. "Our will (*uoluntas*) would not be will unless it were in our power (*in nostra potestate*). Because it is in our power, it is free (*libera*)."[90] For Augustine at this stage of his thinking, if the will is the will, it is in our power. If it is in our power, it is free. Thus there is no will but free will.

In addition to affirming that the will, by definition, must be within our power (*in nostra potestate*), Augustine in at least one place suggests that the will itself ought to be considered a power of the soul (*potentia animi*).[91] Augustine states in *lib. arb.* 2.19.50 that "the powers of the soul (*potentiae animi*), without which there can be no righteous life, are intermediate goods."[92] Shortly afterward he states that "will is . . . an intermediate good when it cleaves to the unchangeable good as something that is common property and not its own private preserve."[93] Technically speaking, these two statements do not logically entail that the will is a power of the soul. Augustine has merely said that the powers of the soul are intermediate goods,

---

[88] *Lib. arb.* 3.3.7 (CSEL 74:96). See also 3.1.3 (CSEL 74:92).

[89] Augustine writes, "The good will which is incomparably better than these things . . . though it is so great a good, can yet be had simply by willing" (*lib. arb.* 1.12.26 [CSEL 74:26]).

[90] *Lib. arb.* 3.2.8.

[91] While conceding that Augustine does, on rare occasions, refer to the *uoluntas libera* as a power of the soul (she cites *lib. arb.* 2.18.50–2.18.53 and *gr. et lib. arb.* 15.31), Byers suggests that in cases where Augustine speaks of *uoluntas* or *uoluntas libera* as a power of the soul, "something given to man by the creator, which remains in us regardless of whether we use it well or badly," he is using the terms "as shorthand ways of referring to the capacity for having impulse that follows on assent," observing that "the Stoics also spoke of *hormē*," a notion she understands as equivalent to Augustine's term *uoluntas*, "as a power of the rational soul" (*Perception, Sensibility, and Moral Motivation in Augustine*, 230). Thus Byers believes such uses of the terms still reflect Augustine's understanding of *uoluntas* along Stoic lines.

[92] CSEL 74:85.

[93] *Lib. arb.* 2.19.52.

not that all intermediate goods are powers of the soul. However, two reasons present themselves to conclude that the will is in fact a power of the soul for Augustine. First, he specifies the powers in question as "powers *of the soul*." His characterizations of the will in other places within this same work as somehow belonging to the soul, whether as a movement of the soul (*motus animae*) or as a feature of the soul in analogy to the parts of the body or more generally as "something in the soul" (*quiddam in animo*), thus qualify it for consideration as an obvious candidate for inclusion among the powers of the soul to which Augustine now refers. Second, Augustine also describes the powers in question as those "without which there can be no righteous life." As we have seen, Augustine has described the will in exactly this way. Thus everything he tells us about these "powers of the soul"—that they belong to the soul, that they are necessary for a righteous life, and that they are intermediate goods—fits the descriptions he provides of the will in *lib. arb.* There seems to be no reason to rule out that he understands the will to be one of these powers of the soul; in fact, it seems difficult to explain why he would bring up the powers of the soul were the will not one of these powers.

From the optimistic perspective of these early writings, then, the human will is closely associated with notions of power and ability: we have the power to execute what we will for our own will; it is "in our power," and it constitutes a power (*potentia*) of the soul. There seem to be few, if any, obstacles to the straightforward realization of what the human will wills for itself. Augustine accords the will a godlike capacity for self-control. Yet even beyond reflecting the power that belongs most purely and properly to God, the power of the human will is connected to the power of the divine will in another sense. Augustine seems concerned that his interlocutors see God's foreknowledge as compromising the power and freedom of the human will. Does not the causality of God's omnipotent will deprive the human will of its impact? Augustine's answer is no. In fact, precisely the opposite dynamic is at work. Far from undermining the power of the human will, the divine will secures it. In Augustine's words: "Hence God has also foreknowledge of our power to will. My power is not taken from me by God's foreknowledge. Indeed I shall be more certainly in possession of my power because he whose foreknowledge is never mistaken, foreknows that I shall have the power."[94] Thus not only does the power of the human will mirror the power

---

[94] *Lib. arb.* 3.3.8 (CSEL 74:98).

of the divine will, for Augustine, but the divine will as reflected in God's foreknowledge also guarantees the power of the human will.

This affirmation of the human will's dependence on God presages later developments in Augustine's thinking on the will. Though here it is combined with a view of the power of the will that is, for the most part, quite optimistic, there are already some signs in the third book of *lib. arb.*, which marks a departure from Augustine's thinking in his earlier anti-Manichean writings on this issue, of his doubt about the facility of the transition from right willing to obedience. There Augustine acknowledges:

> That it [the soul] cannot instantly fulfill the duty it recognizes as duty, means that that is another gift it has not yet received. Its higher part first perceives the good it ought to do, but the slower and carnal part is not immediately brought over to that opinion. So by that very difficulty it is admonished to implore for its perfecting the aid of him whom it believes to be the author of its beginning. Hence he becomes dearer to it, because it has its existence not from its own resources but from his goodness, and by his mercy it is raised to happiness.[95]

Here the transition between willing and obedience is not as smooth as it has appeared in other descriptions Augustine has provided. "Difficulty" has been introduced. God's aid and mercy become necessary. Thus the relation of divine action to human willing is already taking on a more complex character than straightforward mirroring.

Gn. adu. Man. 1.2.4 gives insight into a third way Augustine's early notion of the human will stands in analogy to his notion of the divine will. Here Augustine again broaches the topic of the human will in order to illustrate the mysterious workings of God's will. As we have already observed, Augustine initially responds to the question of why God created heaven and earth with the simple explanation that God wanted to. But Augustine then goes on to offer some general warnings about how—and how not—to inquire into this issue. He first makes the point that no further cause can be found for God's actions than his own will, and that therefore human beings should "put a curb on their brashness, and not go seeking what doesn't exist,

---

[95] *Lib. arb.* 3.65 (CSEL 74:144).

in case they thereby fail to find what does." But he also gives advice about how to learn more about God's will:

> Those who desire to know God's will (*uoluntatem Dei*) should first set about learning the force of the human will (*uoluntatis humanae*). . . . If anyone desires to know God's will (*uoluntas Dei*), they should first become friends with God, because anyone wishing to know a human person's will (*uoluntas hominis*) without being their friend would find everybody mocking their shameless folly. Nobody, however, becomes a friend of God except by total integrity of life and conduct, and by means of that end of the commandment of which the apostle says: *Now the end of the commandment is love coming from a pure heart and a good conscience and a faith unfeigned* (I Tm. 1:5).[96]

Though Augustine is no doubt making a partly negative and contrastive point, emphasizing how improbable it is to grasp the divine will when one cannot even fathom the human will, this comparative point is coupled with his positive judgment that the human will teaches us about the divine will. Indeed, as observed, Augustine assumes this pedagogical principle in his use of the craftsperson image. Now the lesson he draws from the human will is the importance of becoming a friend (*amicus*) in order to comprehend another's will.

In a way, Augustine does not really communicate anything substantive about God's will with this injunction. Rather, he reveals a method of approaching this mysterious subject. Discerning God's will requires becoming God's friend. Being God's friend requires abiding by God's commandments. The sum of God's commandments is love. Thus getting to know the will of another—human or divine—requires more than the kind of intellectual inquiry whose results can be recorded in books; it is a matter of action and of conduct, and ultimately, of love. It requires, in the words of scripture, "a pure heart, and a good conscience, and a faith unfeigned (I Tm. 1:5)." The polemical thrust of these comments is clear. Augustine is claiming that knowledge of the will of God is unavailable to the Manichees. Understanding the will of God requires right faith. It takes an accurate sense of who a person is, one formed by history with a person and the

---

[96] *Gn. adu. Man.* 1.2.4 (CSEL 91:71).

cultivation of friendship, to discern a person's desires and wants. Likewise, Augustine argues, if one's view of God is distorted by drastic theological error, if it is based upon a misinterpretation of how God has acted in history and a relationship with God that has been poisoned by disobedience rather than deepened by love, this makes knowledge of his will inaccessible. Understanding either the human or the divine will is possible only in the context of friendship, the history of a relationship that gives one a holistic sense of the identity brought to bear in each discrete act of will. This principle is born out in Augustine's own characterizations of human willing, which are best appreciated in the context of the history of God's loving relationship with humanity.

Section H: Will as Final Word

There is a final point of comparison between the human and divine wills that deserves separate treatment. Unlike the analogous features between divine and human willing already mentioned, this area of common ground between the divine and human wills is not explicitly observed as such by Augustine. Furthermore this common feature of Augustine's descriptions of the human and divine wills deserves special attention because of its prominence in his early characterization of the will. In one sense, it is the raison d'être of Augustine's early theory of will. Augustine only bothers to articulate a notion of the divine and human wills for the purposes of theodicy.[97] His theory of will contributes to his theodicy by putting a stop to further questions. Augustine ingeniously builds into his notion of will an irreducibility that forecloses investigation into prior links in the causal chain. The notion of will acts as a kind of causal dam that stems the tide of the problem of infinite regress, putting an end to questioning about anterior causes.

As we observed, Augustine argues in *diu. qu.* that God made the world because God wanted to. No further explanation can be given beyond God's will for anything that God does. To inquire further into the "reasons" for God's action is not only futile but presumptuous, Augustine argues, since to presuppose that there might be a cause for God's will is to presuppose that it could

---

[97] Augustine does not "explain" evil by making it rationally comprehensible. Indeed, for Augustine evil by definition defies such explanations. He does, however, argue *against* the possibility that God could be the author of evil or in any way to blame for it.

be determined by something more powerful than itself.[98] The logic by which Augustine reaches his conclusion can be traced as follows: (1) the cause of God's will must be greater than God's will, (2) but such a thing does not exist, (3) ergo: not only is it impossible to *know* the cause of God's will, but there *is* no further cause of God's will. Thus the will seems to be the furthest one can go in finding the root of a divine act, not only noetically but also ontically. No cause preceding God's will can be known because no such cause exists.

Augustine had reasoned in a very similar way about the cause of human depravity in question 4 of *diu. qu.* In response to the question of "why humankind is evil," Augustine refuses to attribute a person's evil acts to influences operating on her, either by force or by persuasion. Rather, he concludes, "as far as persuasion is concerned, inasmuch as persuasion does not compel the unwilling, the cause of depravity goes back to the will (*ad . . . uoluntatem*) of a given person, and he is depraved whether he has been persuaded by someone else or not."[99] The culprit for human depravity is the human will, and not some antecedent cause.

Can it really be the case that the will is the final explanation for human sin? Is there not some further explanation of the will's turn away from the good to what is evil? Augustine anticipates this very question in *lib. arb.*: "Perhaps you are going to ask what is the cause of the movement of the will when it turns from the immutable to the mutable good." Though this is a natural question to ask, Augustine does not feel compelled to answer it. Indeed, to provide a substantive answer would be impossible. According to his privative view of evil, sin is a defection from the good, and "all defect comes from nothing." Therefore, looking for the cause of the will's defection is a fool's errand: there is literally nothing to see. The will does not turn away from God because of a real good but in pursuit of an illusory good, because of the illusion that it has found a good superior to God. In defecting from the good, the will is not really turning away from God toward something better, but toward nothing. The cause of this turning therefore has no real existence of its own. Augustine's reply to the question of the cause of the will's perversion, then, is that he cannot give one: "If you ask this, and I answer that I do not know, probably you will be saddened. And yet that would be a true answer. That which is nothing cannot be known."[100]

---

[98] *Diu. qu.* 28.
[99] *Diu. qu.* 4.
[100] *Lib. arb.* 2.20.54.

Thus there is a similarity between Augustine's "answers" to questions about the reasons for God's good creation and his "answers" to questions about the reasons for humanity's turn away from the good. In both cases, the most one can do is to point to God's will and the human will, respectively. No further causes for these actions can be known, because no further causes exist. Just as there can be nothing greater than God's own will that might inspire him to act in one way or another, there can be nothing greater than God himself that might provide the basis for a rational account of why human beings turn away from him. Human beings are not really attracted to something greater than God; they are pursuing a chimera. The will serves as a kind of placeholder, then, for describing the mysterious roots of actions that transcend the explanatory power of reason. Just as reason cannot explain God's goodness in wanting to create the earth, so reason is at a loss to account for our folly in turning away from him. Will is what comes into the picture when reason gives out.

Augustine gives this same argument in the third book of *lib. arb.* Here, however, he constructs his case from a different starting point. Evodius is becoming exasperated with Augustine's appeals to the will as the best explanation for why people sin. He wants a reason for the will's error: "I do not want you to reply that it is the will that does it. What I want to know is the cause that lies behind willing." Augustine, however, refuses to satisfy Evodius's demand, observing that his manner of questioning could easily lead to a problem of infinite regress: if he attempts to indulge Evodius's curiosity by specifying a further cause beyond the will, it will then seem necessary to determine the cause of that cause, and so on. As previously, Augustine maintains that the evil will is the most fundamental explanation available for humanity's rejection of the good. Yet here he provides a scriptural argument to establish his case: "You ought not to push your inquiry deeper, for you must beware of imagining that anything can be more truly said than that which is written: 'Avarice is the root of all evils' (1 Tim. 6:10)."[101] "Avarice," Augustine explains, is scripture's word for an evil will.[102] Thus Augustine invokes scripture in support of the finality of "will" as an

---

[101] *Lib. arb.* 3.17.48 (CSEL 74:130).

[102] *Lib. arb.* 3.17.48 (CSEL 74:130): "Avarice must be understood as connected not only with silver and money but with everything which is immoderately desired, in every case where a man wants more than is sufficient. Such avarice is cupidity (*auaritia cupiditas est*), and cupidity is an evil will (*cupiditas porro inproba uoluntas est*). An evil will, therefore, is the cause of all evils."

explanation for evil, citing 1 Timothy 6:10 as an authoritative mandate for stopping inquiries here.

Part III: The Theological and Exegetical Character of Augustine's Early Conception of Will

Whereas Augustine's earlier thinking is often characterized as "philosophical" as opposed to the more "biblical" and "theological" approach of his later thinking, in the case of his approach to the theme of human will, his perspective is theological from the outset, though the sense in which this is the case will change as his career progresses. Most of the writings considered in this chapter stem from the period preceding Augustine's ordination as presbyter in 391. Yet, already in these texts, the question is not whether Augustine's thinking about the will is theological and exegetical but how it is theological and exegetical. The foregoing analysis indicates that Augustine's thinking on the will evinces a theological character in at least five distinct respects.

As becomes clear in the highly rhetorical conclusion to *Gn. adu. Man.*, the notion of "will" is a tool that Augustine employs in order to think about God in a way that resists the conclusions of the Manichees. It enables him to make crucial theological distinctions that bear upon what he identifies as the central question at issue between himself and the Manichees, a question of religion (*quaestio religionis*), the question of how to think about God in a pious way (*quid de deo pie sentiatur*). Thus, in deploying the will as a polemical weapon to refute the Manichees, Augustine uses the concept of will for the distinctively theological ends with which he associates this polemical endeavor. Ultimately the will is a category that aids in making the distinctions necessary to think about God rightly.

Augustine also uses the notion of will to interpret the biblical text. The image of the will of a human craftsperson plays a pivotal role in his exegesis of Genesis 1:2. He appeals to the notion of the human will to illustrate the viability of an interpretation of this verse that corresponds to his understanding of God as immaterial. Thus, in addition to Augustine's direct usage of the concept of will in his efforts to combat Manichean theological errors, he also draws upon the notion of will to strengthen his exegetical anti-Manichean arguments. Insofar as interpreting scripture is an inherently theological task, and insofar as the particular exegetical moves Augustine makes on the basis of his appeal to the will have implications for how to conceive of the activity of the Spirit, his use of the will as an exegetical aid constitutes a second theological dimension of his thinking on the will in this period.

A further theological feature of Augustine's thinking on the will that has emerged in the texts considered in this chapter is his tendency to make inferences about the human will based on what he knows about God. Several examples of this pattern have been observed, including Augustine's argument that the will's free choice is the basis for both sinning and acting rightly in question 24 of *diu. qu.*, which flows from the premises that (1) God is incomparably better than the best imaginable human being, and (2) this good God is always just. In *lib. arb.* 1.11.23, one may observe a similar movement, this time not from a proposition about God's character to a conclusion about the human will, but from a proposition about the will based on faith to the rational confirmation of that proposition based upon reason. Augustine and Evodius begin by accepting the presupposition that the fallen human condition is due to humankind's own willful misdeed as an article of faith (*credamus*) and then seek to confirm this belief for the intelligence. As these examples show, Augustine often arrives at conclusions about the human will based on what he knows about God or what is accepted upon the basis of faith.

The reverse pattern, however, also occurs: in other cases Augustine reasons about the divine will based on what he regards as common knowledge regarding the human will, presenting the human will as a window into its divine counterpart. In addition to employing the image of the will of a human craftsperson, in *Gn. adu. Man.* Augustine also applies commonsense strategies for discerning the will of a human person to inquiry after the divine will. His thinking about the human will, then, is capable of moving both from and toward thinking about the divine will. Augustine's early reflections on human willing prove theological in that, by turns, they both derive from theological starting points and drive toward theological conclusions.

Finally, Augustine's early conception of will is theological in that he repeatedly explains what the will is in the context of a theological relationship, the relationship between God the Creator and human beings as creatures. His arguments about what the will is and how it works make sense only with reference to this relationship. Indeed it would be impossible to offer an account of Augustine's arguments about how the will works, its innate capacities, and its relationship to evil, without appealing to it.

The relationship of God the Creator to human beings, as his creatures, entails, first of all, that the will is made by God. While Augustine does not yet connect the will directly with the created *image* of God in human beings in so many words, the more general created character of the will is of paramount importance for several of its key features that emerge in the anti-Manichean writings considered in the second part of this chapter. If God relates to human beings as their Creator, then as a movement or power of the human soul, the will, and its natural freedom, is a good gift of God (see sections A and B). It is because the will is designed by God the creator that it shows similarities to the divine will (see section G). Augustine's distinction between what comes from nature and what comes from the will follows from the goodness of the will as made by the creator (see section F).

The relationship of God as Creator to human beings also entails that human beings and all that belongs to them, including their will, are other than their creator. More specifically, the human will is good only by participation and can be harmed by defect. This explains the will's ambivalence (see section C). It is on the theological basis of the doctrine of creation and the human soul's difference from God that Augustine explains how it is possible for the will to do both good and evil. Finally, Augustine ties the argument that there is no further explanation for the will's turn away from the good not only to his privative view of evil but also to the idea that the human will is created ex nihilo.[103] The human being, as "created," comes from nothing, whereas God the Creator has no origin. Thus it is conceivable that the human will might incline to nothing while God cannot.

Though Augustine's early writings treat the notion of will theologically in a number of respects, there are also respects in which his early vision of the human will is not yet as theologically precise as it will come to be later in his career. First, though Augustine does consider the will in light of general scriptural principles or ideas, such as creation and its goodness, God's justice, and human responsibility, for the most part he does not tend to derive his understanding of the will from specific passages of the Bible. As we have

---

[103] The connection of human weakness of will to human origins ex nihilo comes out in a more pronounced way in *c. Fort.*, to be treated in the following chapter, and in *ciu.* 14.13. In the latter text, Augustine observes that the defection of the human will from the good was possible only because of its creation out of nothing. Thus the creation of human beings ex nihilo is the condition for the possibility of the perversion of their wills. Harrison takes this connection a step farther, asserting that for Augustine "the will inevitably falls away from God and sins because it is created out of nothing" (*Rethinking Augustine's Early Theology*, 98).

seen, in at least one prominent instance he uses the notion of will to help him interpret scripture, but he does not draw directly on the biblical text to reinterpret the will. One striking example of this approach is found in *diu. qu.* Though the will does appear in this text, Augustine treats it in the more philosophical part of the treatise rather than in the portion of the text dedicated to addressing specific biblical passages. The absence of comments on the will, even from Augustine's extensive treatment of Romans 7, is striking considering the significance this passage is to have later for his thinking on this theme.

Second, Augustine's view of the will is not yet differentiated theologically. At this point, Augustine does not restrict the relevance of his descriptions of the will to certain situations; he describes how the will works in a general way without qualification. Later Augustine will come to see the will not as an unchanging entity whose character and operations are an inviolable and unchanging fixture of human existence, but rather as something whose limits and possibilities vary drastically depending on how the will relates to key events depicted in the biblical narrative and on how these events are brought to bear in the story of a person's life. As his career continues, Augustine will say less and less in a general way about the limits and potential of the will per se without specifying a given theological context that sets the parameters for what the will can and cannot do (pre-fall/post-fall, pre-conversion/post-conversion, etc.) In the sense that it is not yet closely synchronized with the biblical narratives of God's gracious relationship with human beings, Augustine's view of the will is not yet "theologically periodized" or "theologically differentiated" to the degree it will be later.

One can see Augustine moving toward an approach to the will that shows both this kind of "theological differentiation" and stronger connections to specific scriptural passages in *lib. arb.* book 3. As discussed, in *lib. arb.* 3.17.48 Augustine argues for the same idea he defends elsewhere: the will is the cause (*causa*) of all evils for which we can find no antecedent cause. However, in this case, he defends this conclusion on a different basis, by appealing to 1 Timothy 6:10's designation of avarice as the "root of all evils." Augustine thus not only uses the will to interpret scripture but also uses explicitly scriptural arguments to support his view of the will. Though in this case scriptural appeals merely confirm conclusions Augustine had already reached based on other premises, eventually scripture will come to transform and qualify, not merely ratify, his preexisting views.

Also in book 3 of *lib. arb.*, Augustine begins to describe the will in a more theologically differentiated way. As we will discuss further in chapter 2, there Augustine distinguishes between the freedom of will with which human beings were originally endowed and the loss of "freedom of will to choose to do what [one] ought" that results from sin. The former corresponds to "the nature of man as he was created," the latter to the "penalty of man as condemned." Augustine here contextualizes his description of the will according to stages of the biblical narrative: "When we speak of the freedom of the will to do right, we are speaking of the freedom wherein man was created."[104] Now hesitant to attribute freedom to do the good to the will as a generalized abstract concept, Augustine seeks to calibrate his description of the will to concrete theological events.

Conclusion

In *Soliloquies*, which is among the very earliest of Augustine's surviving writings, he treats the will only tangentially, suggesting its close connection with reason. At the same time, however, the dialogue raises questions about the extent to which reason and will can be conceived as distinct entities. Augustine picks up this thread of questioning in his anti-Manichean writings, in which the will takes on a more prominent role and its features become more distinctly delineated. Appealing to the real-life polemical case of the Manichees, Augustine removes all doubt on the issue: it is possible to understand intellectually what the right thing to do is, yet obstinately will to do otherwise. Augustine makes clear that the will is not the same thing as reason, or even reason's inevitable product.

Augustine's positive description of the will at this early stage of his career is multifaceted, but its various elements cohere to constitute a generally unified vision of what the will is and how it works. Against the Manichees, Augustine insists that free will has been given to humankind as a good gift from God, and he presents a vivid and alluring picture of its integrity. In these writings, the will is powerful, autonomous, and active: it has the potential for both good and evil; it mirrors the divine will; and it enjoys complete self-possession. (What is so much in the will's power as the will itself,

---

[104] *Lib. arb.* 3.18.52 (CSEL 74:133).

Augustine asks.)[105] It is free to determine its own orientation, not only as an accidental advantage but also by virtue of what willing as such means; to will means precisely to will freely. Augustine accords human will a significance commensurate with its capacities.

Like a hinge, the will can affect other things without itself being subject to the kind of movement it causes in them. The will is a movement of the mind (*motus mentis*) that remains unmoved by external forces. It looks on tempests and is never shaken. Though God's help may be bestowed upon a will already oriented to the good, even God does not act directly upon the will, inclining it in one way or another. Rather, the will remains active in almost every description Augustine provides; it is therefore the basis for attributing moral responsibility and for distinguishing between those events and situations that result from God and those that result from the free will of God's creatures. Given its active character, Augustine can describe the will as the cause of all evils, which itself can be attributed to no antecedent cause. What preoccupies Augustine is not so much what happens to the will as what happens as a result of the will.

As shown in part III, in numerous cases Augustine articulates his conception of will in the context of inquiry into the doctrine of creation. Though sometimes his understanding of the will seems to emerge more overtly from this context (for example, when he reasons from what he knows about God the creator to descriptions of human will), while in other cases he reasons about the creation narrative using the will as an exegetical tool, in each of these cases his description of the will is articulated in, and therefore informed by, the theological context of creation. Augustine seems to see these investigations into the will as yielding universal principles about its character and possibilities; he is initially content to leave his descriptions of the will unqualified with respect to their relevance subsequent to the fall.

Already in *De libero arbitirio* book 3, however, Augustine observes that the view of the will described in this chapter—the vision of will as powerful, active, and capable of orienting itself toward either evil or good—has limited application. This characterization of the will does not necessarily correspond to the will of any person one might meet on the street. Rather, it

---

[105] Even in this early stage, however, it is not powerful enough to ensure that other agents respond appropriately to a given action so as to guarantee a certain outcome. God's help is needed when it comes to this larger picture.

applies to the will as created.[106] Augustine will also observe later that some of what he has said about the will pertains to the will as rehabilitated by God.[107] In any case, this much becomes clear to him: the vision of the will he has articulated in these earlier writings must be theologically specified; it must be referred to specific theological contexts. There is a disconnect between the powerfully active and self-determining kind of volition he has described in these early anti-Manichean works and the reality of how the will functions practically in his everyday personal experience, in his ministry as a priest and a bishop, and in the Bible's descriptions of how willing works. To this tension we now turn.

---

[106] This is an observation Augustine echoes in *retr.* as well, where he argues that it is unfair to remove his argument in *lib. arb.* from its original context—polemic with the Manichees—and inject it into the foreign environment of his dispute with the Pelagians. Augustine reminds his readers that he was investigating the will from the perspective of creation in order to find out how the will went wrong, not from the perspective of redemption to figure out what was required to make it better. See *retr.* 1.9.2.

[107] For example, commenting on his question 24 of *diu. qu.*, "are both sin and good action in free choice of the will," Augustine writes, "That this is the case is entirely true, but it is by the grace of God that one is free to act uprightly." See *retr.* 1.26.2 (CCL 57:77). See also *retr.* 1.10.2, where he defends his statement in *Gn. adu. Man.* 1.3.6 that all have the power to turn toward God "if they will." This is true, he argues, invoking Proverbs 8:35, given that God first prepares the will.

2

The Fallen Will

A Link in Sin's Chain

Introduction

In the early years of his ministry, first as priest, and then as bishop, Augustine threw himself feverishly into biblical study. Writing to Bishop Valerius of Hippo shortly after his ordination as presbyter, Augustine requested a leave of absence to immerse himself in scripture as preparation for his impending pastoral ministry.[1] This leave was granted, but even after it had elapsed Augustine's intensive inquiry into the Bible continued. Around the year 394 he turned his attention to composing three exegetical works on Paul's writings,[2] texts that, it seems, had exerted a special fascination upon him ever since the events leading up to and surrounding his conversion.[3] As Augustine became more and more immersed in scripture, and especially in the writings of Paul, his account of the will gained depth and complexity. These two developments were not unrelated. As we will see, Augustine's understanding of the fall's impact on human willing was refined in the crucible of his struggle to interpret Paul.

By 394 Augustine had already begun to reflect on the connection between the sin of the first parents and the experience of the rest of the human race. In *De Genesi aduersus Manicheos* (*Gn. adu. Man.*), he had recorded a highly figurative reading of the account of the first sin in Genesis 3.[4]

---

[1] See *ep.* 21 to Valerius.

[2] *Ex. prop. Rm.*, a complete continuous *ex. Gal.*, and *ep. Rm. inch.*

[3] See *conf.* 7.21.27, *conf.* 8.12.29, and *Acad.* 2.2.5. All three accounts use similar language, describing Augustine as "seizing" (*arripere*) upon Paul, and suggest that Paul played a pivotal role in leading to Augustine's conversion of 386. Though Augustine was by no means a newcomer to Paul, even in the period preceding his conversion in Milan, he was, by his own account, powerfully attracted to the apostle in the interval surrounding his conversion. For a discussion of Augustine's encounters with Paul before the 390s, both more immediately leading up to his conversion and during his time as a Manichee, see Carol Harrison, *Rethinking Augustine's Early Theology: An Argument for Continuity* (New York: Oxford University Press, 2006), 115–127.

[4] Though Augustine's unfinished commentary on Genesis, *Gn. litt. imp.*, was written sometime between 393 and 395, a timeframe that falls precisely within the period we are considering, it breaks off with Genesis 1:26. Thus we turn to the earlier *Gn. adu. Man.* (388–389) for Augustine's interpretation

Augustine on the Will. Han-luen Kantzer Komline, Oxford University Press (2020). © Oxford University Press.
DOI: 10.1093/oso/9780190948801.001.0001

What happened between the serpent, the woman, and the man, he wrote, illustrates what occurs "when everyone slips down into sin."[5] The serpent represents the suggestion (*suggestio*) of sin, whether "in the thoughts, or through the body's senses, by seeing or touching or hearing or tasting or smelling something." Eve signifies desire (*cupiditas*), which may be moved to sin, or remain unmoved, in response to such suggestions. Adam stands for reason (*ratio*), which may consent to desire for sin or withhold its consent to a sinful desire. The implication of his consent to Eve in the biblical narrative, expulsion from paradise, illustrates that when reason consents to desire for sin, the human person is "expelled from the entire life of bliss." Giving rational consent to sinful desire has already sealed the deal of sin, according to Augustine, even before the corresponding act is carried out. Augustine writes, "Sin is already put down to his account, you see, even if the actual deed doesn't follow, since the conscience incurs guilt just by consent (*in consensione*)."[6]

Augustine's assessment of the relationship between the sin of the first parents and subsequent human sin in this account of the fall shows some similarities to his depiction of this relationship in *Contra Fortunatum*, in which, as we will see, he portrays each person as reenacting the fall in her own life. At the same time, his treatment of the fall in *Gn. adu. Man.* already contains the rudiments of his mature interpretations. As he will later, Augustine here describes the first sin as pride; pride was the crux of the serpent's crafty suggestion.[7] Again taking a tack similar to that of his future interpretations, Augustine goes on to describe this pride as wrongful willing.[8] It consisted, he writes, in "wishing (*uolunt*) to be God's equals" and being persuaded to act "against God's law, and

of the fall. Augustine also comments on the fall in later writings. See *Gn. litt.* (401–416), book 11, which treats Genesis 2:25–23:24, and *ciu.* 13.13–15 and 14.12–13. While each of these accounts has its own points of emphasis, they are compatible with each other and certain characteristic themes surface consistently.

  [5] *Gn. adu. Man.* 2.14.21 (CSEL 91:142–143), my translation.

  [6] *Gn. adu. Man.* 2.14.21 (CSEL 91:142–143).

  [7] *Gn. adu. Man.* 2.15.22 (CSEL 91:143): In the words of the serpent, Augustine observes, "we can see it was through pride (*per superbiam*) that the sin was put across.... What else is to be understood but a suggestion that they should refuse to be under God any longer, but should be their own masters." Cf. *Gn. litt.* 11.5.7, 11.15.19, 11.30.39 and 11.31.41. See also *ciu.* 14.13.

  [8] Augustine refers to the first human sin as a misuse of will in *Gn. litt.* 11.4.6 and 11.8.12 and to the serpent's evil will and a twisted will precipitating the devil's fall in 11.13.17 and 11.16.21, respectively. He also diagnoses the first sin as a problem of will in *ciu.* 13.15, 14.12 and 14.13.

so forfeit what they had received, while they had wanted (*uoluerunt*) to grab what they had not received," namely "to enjoy . . . bliss independently of God's control."[9] In the years that followed, Augustine's sense of the repercussions of the prideful willing of the first human beings for the functioning of the will in the present would expand. By the time he completed *lib. arb.*, he would come to see their fall as a crucial turning point for the whole human race.[10] Adam and Eve's fall would mark a fateful fault line.

Augustine's reflection would eventually lead him to the conclusion that, due to the fall, the will no longer functions in the powerful way described in chapter 1.[11] Far from being the center of our moral responsibility over which human beings retain absolute control, the will has now spiraled out of control. It has done so in two ways. First, the will eludes and resists a person's commands. Post-fall, human beings are unable to will what they know is right in a consistent or unalloyed way and therefore become subject to a psychological paralysis that prevents them from leaving sin behind. Second, the will itself now fails to keep command of the body and mind as it was designed to. Even when human beings succeed in willing the right thing, body and mind rebel against the dictates of the will. Thus, subsequent to the fall the will can neither be controlled nor exercise control as it should.

This first part of this chapter will trace the emergence of these views by analyzing Augustine's developing thought on human willing as presented in *De duabus animabus* (391–395), *Contra Fortunatum* (392), *De libero arbitrio* book 3 (391–395), and *Ad Simplicianum* (396–398). The first three works

---

[9] *Gn. adu. Man.* 2.15.22 (CSEL 91:143–144).

[10] In the view of the mature Augustine, all of humanity was in Adam, and therefore because of Adam's sin the whole of human nature was changed for the worse (cf. *ciu.* 13.14 and 13.3, respectively). As a result of Adam's misuse of will, free choice (*arbitrium*) was no longer able to maintain control over the body, while desire (*cupiditas*) came to oppose the will (*uoluntas*). See *ciu.* 13.13 (CCL 48:395) and *ciu.* 14.12 (CCL 48:434), respectively.

[11] The question of how the fall impacts the will is not to be confused with the question of how the fall of the will came about. In Augustine's terse formulation from *lib. arb.*, there is not much to say about the latter question because "that which is nothing cannot be known" (*lib. arb.* 2.20.54). (Considering the same question in the following book of *lib. arb.*, Augustine reiterates that nothing besides the will itself can explain the will's deviation from good. Avarice is the root of all evils, so the most that can be said by way of explanation is that the root of evil is the will's desiring more goods than it needs. See *lib. arb.* 3.17.48–49.) The former question, however, is a puzzle that Augustine keeps exploring. How his answer to it changes and becomes more complex over time is the subject of this chapter.

are roughly contemporaneous, stemming from Augustine's period as presbyter. Each, however, illustrates different facets of Augustine's thinking on
will leading up to the benchmark work *Ad Simplicianum* (*Simpl.*), in which
he comes to a more profound appreciation of the dependence of the fallen
will upon God's grace in order to achieve the good. The order in which the
first three works are analyzed reflects how these facets build logically upon
one another to bring Augustine closer to the view he attains in *Simpl.* but
does not necessarily reflect the chronology of their composition, which remains a matter of speculation.

In addition to explaining the impact of the fall on a more abstract generalized level, Augustine also addresses the implications of the fall on a concrete
experiential plane in his *Confessions* (*conf.*), where he adopts the particular
perspective of his own experience of struggle with sin. Augustine's account
of the significance of the fall for the human will from this perspective is
the subject of part II of this chapter, which assesses Augustine's famous description of conflict of will in *conf.* 8.5.10–11 as well as his inquiry into the
causes of this conflict in *conf.* 8.9.21–22.

Both parts of this second chapter demonstrate that Augustine
modulates his understanding of will to accord with the implications of the
fall he finds described in scripture, especially in Paul. Chapter 1 observed
the powerful and autonomous character of the created will according to
Augustine's early writings. This chapter shows how Augustine qualifies his
earlier and more optimistic vision of the will's independent capacity for
good by differentiating between how the will functions prior and subsequent to the fall.

Augustine's assessment of the fall's impact on the human will illustrates
how he develops his conception of will in relation to key theological events.
Just as Augustine thematizes the will in the context of creation, as observed
in chapter 1, he also appraises its capacities soberly in light of the fall. This
approach results in a multifaceted or differentiated conception of the will,
one that accounts for its radically different character in these two different
theological contexts. A comparison of terminology illustrates the magnitude of this differentiation. In the writings treated in chapter 1, Augustine
spoke of the will as a powerful hinge (*cardo*), rotating the mind and body
effortlessly in accord with its direction. In the *conf.* Augustine calls the will a
link in the chain (*ansula catenae*) binding humanity in sin. The created will,
for Augustine, opens doors of possibility. The fallen will imposes chains of
necessity.

Part I: On the Road to Damascus

Section A: Will as "a Movement of the Soul with Nothing Forcing It" in *De duabus animabus* (391–395)

During his time as priest, Augustine transitioned from viewing human willing as free from external constraint by definition to seeing human willing as necessarily subject to external influence subsequent to the fall. *Duab. an.*, an anti-Manichean treatise that Augustine completed sometime while he was a presbyter,[12] gives a thorough presentation of the former view, which overlaps his "early" conception of the will discussed in chapter 1.[13] This treatise is particularly useful for gauging Augustine's evolving understanding of the will both because he provides a formal definition of will, which serves as the centerpiece of the treatise's anti-Manichean argument, and because of the claims he makes about the self-evidence of this definition. *Duab. an.* at once illustrates the content of the earlier conception of will that serves as the starting point of the evolution culminating in *Simpl.* and the conviction with which he held to it, a conviction which makes his subsequent shift in perspective all the more striking.

In *duab. an.*, Augustine launches a critique of Manichean teaching that is strategic both in his selection of a target and in his means of attack. In choosing the Manichean doctrine of two souls,[14] Augustine argues, he is striking at the heart of the Manichean belief system. This doctrine is

---

[12] See *retr.* 1.15.1.

[13] Unless otherwise noted, subsequent English translations of *duab. an.* come from Augustine, "The Two Souls," in *The Manichean Debate*, trans. Roland Teske, WSA I/19 (Hyde Park, NY: New City Press, 2006), 117–134.

[14] Not all scholars agree that the Manichees taught a doctrine of two souls. See Volker Henning Drecoll and Mirjam Kudella, *Augustin und der Manichäismus* (Tübingen: Mohr Siebeck, 2011), 148–149 for an outline of Augustine's attribution, in various works, of this view to the Manichees, which they contrast with the view the Manichees seem actually to have held. Drecoll and Kudella argue that whereas Augustine portrayed the Manichees as tracing responsibility for all the good and all the evil in a person to two contrary souls (*duae animae*), one good soul that was a part of God and one bad soul, associated with the flesh (*caro*), the Manichees in fact taught an opposition between a single good soul (*anima bona*) and the flesh (*caro*). It was the Manichean emphasis on the independent activity of this flesh, and particularly their application of the terms *mens* and *spiritus* to evoke this dynamic, that led to Augustine's accusation that they affirmed two minds (*mentes*) or souls (*animae*) battling within each person. The fact that Augustine mentions a two souls doctrine only when writing about the Manichees, not in direct debate with the Manichees, indicates, according to Drecoll and Kudella, that they did not themselves teach it in the form Augustine attributed to them: the Manichees nowhere refer to an *anima mala* opposite the *anima bona*. For the purposes of the following analysis, Augustine's accusation against the Manichees is relevant insofar as it provides a foil for his own developing views of the will, regardless of the accuracy of his characterization.

the linchpin that connects the dualistic view of the universe held by the Manichees with their anthropology, showing how their teachings matter existentially. To counter the two souls doctrine, Augustine proposes two simple definitions: a definition of the will and a definition of sin. Given these definitions, Augustine argues, the doctrine of two souls disintegrates.

Manichees affirm that sin happens. Since the definition of sin involves will (Augustine defines sin as an orientation of the will to that which is unjust), if the Manichees want to affirm the existence of sin they must acknowledge the will as well. Yet the Manichees are unable to accept the will, defined as a movement of the soul that is not forced, because this definition suggests that evil enters the world not by necessity but by the free choice of the will.[15] In short, Augustine's case is that since (1) it is impossible to give an account of sin and evil without affirming free will, and (2) the Manichees rule out free will by their account of the two souls that are by nature evil and good, it follows that, (3) ironically, though they attempt to take evil seriously by according it an independent existence as a separate soul in human nature, the Manichees are unable to affirm the reality of sin and evil in a coherent way.

Thus, since there can be no sin without will and since the Manichees say that evil souls are evil by nature and not by will, it is clear that they cannot coherently attribute sin to the souls they call "evil." This problem indicates a fundamental mistake of the Manichean perspective: the belief that some souls are evil by nature. According to Augustine, this belief represents a contradiction in terms. If souls evil by nature existed, they would be evil necessarily, and hence sin or evil, which by definition implies a will that is "free," could not actually be attributed to them. It is impossible for something to be evil by nature, because evil and sin belong to the sphere of will, which, in contrast to the sphere of nature, is inherently free from necessity.

---

[15] Augustine's views on sin, evil, and their relationship differ from those of his Manichean interlocutors in a number of respects. For Augustine, sin and evil are not coextensive, since evil can include both natural evil (*malum physicum*) and moral evil (*malum morale*), while "sin" serves as a term for the latter kind of evil, though not for the former. (Cf. *ciu.* 3.1, where Augustine discusses both types of evil.) The category of evil is thus more expansive than the category of sin in terms of the types of realities it labels, though the category of sin has a kind of "priority" over natural evil in that the presence of any kind of evil in the world results from sin. Evil acts of the will constituting sin, however, have no efficient cause insofar as they are evil (cf. *ciu.* 12.7). This follows from the fact that, in Augustine's privative view of evil, evil lacks being; both natural and moral evils are parasitic upon the good, of which they represent privations, not actual goods with an inner order and logic that might be subjected to rational analysis. By failing to grasp the role of sinful willing in bringing evil into the world, the Manichees commit themselves to portraying evil as necessary, inherent in creaturely natures as created, and also therefore having some kind of positive existence of its own, all conclusions Augustine rejects.

As this brief summary of Augustine's argument in *duab. an.* shows, his definition of will is crucial to the case that he makes against the Manichees in this treatise. Insofar as it gave him the occasion to articulate this definition, his engagement with the Manichees was also crucial for prompting him to clarify his understanding of the human will.[16] Both this definition and the context in which it emerges in Augustine's argument deserve closer examination.

Augustine's intensive discussion of will begins in 7.9, where he differentiates between nature and will to show that sin is not inherent in the created nature of things. "All things come from God" with respect to nature, he asserts, appealing to 1 Corinthians 11:12, but not all things come from God with respect to will. Thus scripture does not require the assumption that every act of will performed by creatures, which come from God with respect to nature, must also come from God. He then goes on to show that sin is a matter of will. Sin thus does not, like created natures, necessarily come from God.

---

[16] J. Patout Burns argues that the debate with the Manichees "moved Augustine to a more careful examination of the limitations of human freedom and of the origin of evil in the world." See J. Patout Burns, *The Development of Augustine's Doctrine of Operative Grace* (Paris: Études Augustiniennes, 1980), 22. He also notes later in the same paragraph the importance of Augustine's exegetical writings on Genesis, the Psalms, the Sermon on the Mount, *diu. qu.*, and the Creed in bringing about his consideration of issues not at the forefront in his earliest writings as a Christian, including the issue of the limits on human autonomy. As Burns indicates, the Manichean and scriptural influences upon Augustine's thinking do not always work at cross-purposes. In fact, with respect to the issue of will in particular, the Manichees may themselves have augmented the biblical influence on Augustine's thinking by increasing his exposure to and interest in Paul. Drecoll and Kudella observe that "Betrachtet man die in Augustins Werk und im Kodex von Tebessa überlieferten Aussagen von Manichäern, ist Paulus als wichtigste Bezugsgröße zu nennen" (*Augustin und der Manichäismus*, 45). While North African Manichees were strongly critical of the Old Testament, rejecting most of it along with some parts of the New Testament, they seem to have regarded Paul's letters as an important authority. Drecoll and Kudella note Augustine's observation in *Gn. adu. Man.* 1.3: "Certainly the Manichees themselves have read the apostle Paul and praise and honor him, and have deceived many by interpreting him badly" (cf. Drecoll and Kudella, 122; my trans. of Augustine from the Latin). Faustus seems to have thought that, unlike the gospels, which were in reality based on oral traditions rather than composed by the evangelists with whose names they were associated, Paul's letters were indeed original to him. Drecoll and Kudella regard this as explaining the "unusual importance as bases for arguments" of the Pauline texts and note that Paul, purged of what these Manichees regarded as interpolations, was, "especially for anthropology, a decisive basis for the arguments of Felix and Fortunatus in their disputations [with Augustine]" (52). It seems probable, then, that Manicheism influenced Augustine's reading of Paul both positively and negatively—positively, in that it raised his awareness of the Pauline corpus, possibly providing an occasion for him to develop an interest in it, and negatively, in that, as a young Catholic, Augustine read Paul with an eye to contesting the Manichean way of interpreting the apostle. Thus Drecoll and Kudella point out that whereas Augustine's polemic against the Manichees regarding Genesis involved a defense of the book, his polemic against them regarding Paul was a matter of trying to "wrest Paul from their hands" (122).

To make this case, Augustine discusses various permutations of a concrete scenario, gradually eliminating alternative explanations of what constitutes sin as he proceeds. He begins by asking whether "someone asleep commits a sin if someone else has used his hand to write something sinful."[17] Augustine anticipates the instinctive answer, no, which points to the conclusion that the use of a person's body for a sinful end does not in itself guarantee that he has committed sin. Going through the motions of doing something sinful is different from actually sinning.

Lest his reader then conclude that it is his unconsciousness of the wrongful use to which his limbs have been put that exonerates the sleeping person, and that therefore committing sin is a matter of doing something sinful *consciously*, Augustine proposes another scenario. What if the person whose hand was moved by another is awake while he is bound and forced to write by a stronger person? "Would the bound man be held guilty of a sin because he knew it, although he did not will it at all?"[18] With this question, Augustine introduces and eliminates another possible explanation for what constitutes commission of sin. He assumes his readers will also regard the forced man in this scenario as innocent, despite his awareness of the wrongful use of his hand imposed upon him by another. Even knowing that one is cooperating with wrongdoing, then, absent the will to cooperate, is not enough to constitute commission of sin.

Finally, Augustine proposes the case of a person who intentionally assists someone else to use his hand to write something sinful. Whether the writer makes himself fall asleep so as to be unconscious of what transpires or is willingly bound to create the impression of opposing what occurs, Augustine observes, he commits sin. Thus, just as consciousness of the use of one's body for a sinful end does not constitute complicity in sin absent the will that this event occur, neither does unconsciousness of the same situation, or the use of force, exonerate one from complicity given the will that this event should occur. The same logic applies to going through the motions of sin. Absent the will to sin, going through the motions of sinning does not entail sin.[19] However, given the will to sin, a

---

[17] *Duab. an.* 10.12.

[18] *Duab. an.* 10.12

[19] In *conf.*, Augustine makes the inverse point, that absent the will (*uoluntas*) to do good, going through the motions of doing the right thing does not entail bringing a good deed to fruition. See *conf.* 13.27.42 (CCL 27:267).

person commits it, even should the opportunity to execute this will never arise.[20]

What is decisive, then, in these examples, is not (1) whether a person writes something of his own initiative or someone else uses his hand, (2) whether he is conscious of writing, or even (3) whether he is forced to write. These issues are *adiaphora*. He could sin or avoid sin in either case with respect to all three points. What matters is whether this person writes something sinful "willingly." As Augustine demonstrates using the case of the person whose will to sin is thwarted, the absence or presence of the will to do something sinful is the single necessary and sufficient criterion for whether a sin is committed. Even before issues such as going through the motions, consciousness, or the use of force arise, it is already a foregone conclusion that sin has been committed if the will to sin is present.

Thus, having eliminated top contenders with the will for establishing the conditions necessary for something to qualify as a sin, Augustine concludes that sin exists nowhere else: "Once these points were granted, I would draw the conclusion that sin exists nowhere but in the will, since I would have also received help from the fact that justice holds people to be sinners because of an evil will alone, even though they were unable to carry out what they willed."[21] At this stage in his thought, Augustine is convinced that commonsense intuitions imply sin's existence in the will and only in the will. To his later chagrin, he drives this point home in no uncertain terms: "There is no sinning, then, apart from the will" (*non igitur nisi uoluntate peccatur*).[22] This statement reiterates Augustine's claims in *diu. qu.* and *lib. arb.*, considered in chapter 1, section D. *Duab. an.*, however, represents the most fully developed version of Augustine's early account of will with respect to this claim as well as others. Here he goes so far as to insist that an evil will is not only a necessary and sufficient condition for committing sin, but it is the exclusive condition for committing sin; sin is a matter of "an evil will alone."

---

[20] This is another counterexample (in addition to the one found in *diu. qu.* 27, discussed in chapter 1) to T. D. J. Chappell's conclusion that Augustine "never says, in Abelardian mode, that what counts for moral assessment is the *voluntas*, and the action is (as good as) immaterial. Rather he says that, if my *voluntas* fails to get actualised in my doings, then this is an insuperable impediment to our being able to speak of me as a voluntary agent at all." See T. D. J. Chappell, *Aristotle and Augustine on Freedom: Two Theories of Freedom, Voluntary Action, and Akrasia* (New York: Macmillan, 1995), 127. In his maturity, Augustine continues to insist that the will that precedes a sinful act is itself sinful. See *ciu.* 14.13 (CCL 48:434), where he describes an "evil will" (*uoluntas mala*) as one instance of the "sin" of which pride is the beginning.

[21] *Duab. an.* 10.12.

[22] *Duab. an.* 10.14 (CSEL 25.1:68).

Augustine is convinced that this conclusion should be self-evident. This conviction comes through clearly in his appeal to human nature in the course of his inquiry into the hypothetical scenarios we have discussed: "And if I asked human nature itself in those persons why this was the case, I would easily arrive at what I wanted by asking questions in this way."[23] Augustine thinks he can persuade people to see that sin is a matter of will simply by interrogating them about their natural sense and instincts. He not only has great confidence in the capacities of the human will; he has great confidence in people's abilities to understand how the will works through the unaided power of reason.

Yet it also becomes clear that, having argued for the connection between sin and will with this series of case studies, Augustine believes he needs to defend a more basic premise upon which this connection depends: the idea that there is something called a will at all. Though Augustine insists that the idea of will, like the inseparability of sin from will, should be self-evident, the fact that he deems it necessary to underline and defend its self-evidence suggests that everything is not as it should be.

For his own part, Augustine is convinced that the phenomenon of "willing," like the phenomenon of "living," is available to every human being who engages in introspection.[24] In arguing for the self-evidence of the will, Augustine does not believe he is appealing to a specialized theoretical knowledge available only to a privileged few. When he refers to will he is discussing something down to earth of which everyone should be intuitively aware. He writes:

> I do not want to meet with any animosity on the grounds that I go after slow minds with the goads of subtle arguments. Just allow me to know that I am living. Just allow me to know that I will to live. If the human race

---

[23] *Duab. an.* 10.12.

[24] In *conf.*, Augustine indicates that he himself went through a process of reflection that led him to recognize that he had a will and thence to realize that this will was the cause of his sin. The language he uses in *duab. an.* 10.13 to persuade his Manichean friends is similar to the language he uses in *conf.* to describe this process: "I directed my mind to understand what I was being told, namely that the free choice of the will is the reason (*liberum uoluntatis arbitrium causam esse*) why we do wrong and suffer your just judgment, but I could not get a clear grasp of it. . . . I was brought up into your light by the fact that I knew myself both to have a will and to be alive. Therefore when I willed (*uellem*) or did not will (*nollem*) something, I was utterly certain that none other than myself was willing or not willing. That there lay the cause of my sin I was now coming to recognize. I saw that when I acted against my wishes, I was passive rather than active; and this condition I judged to be not guilt but a punishment" (*conf.* 7.3.5 [CCL 27:94]).

THE FALLEN WILL 69

agrees with these points, our will (*uoluntas*) and our life (*uita*) are already known to us. . . . I do not think that I have introduced anything obscure, and I fear rather that someone may think me worthy of criticism because these points are too obvious.[25]

For Augustine, then, observing one's own activity of willing, "to know that I will to live," itself counts as evidence of "a will" (*uoluntas*). Just as one knows one is alive, knows one's life (*uita*) by living, so one knows one's will (*uoluntas*) by willing. Mere consciousness of the fact of willing conveys certain knowledge of the will. In Augustine's words, "When we profess to have this knowledge, there is no need to fear that someone might prove that we could be mistaken. For no one can be mistaken about this unless he either is not living or wills nothing." Augustine offers a "self-evidence thesis" with respect to the will, a *uolo* whose logic is similar to his versions of the *cogito*-like argument found elsewhere in his writings: I will, therefore I have a will.[26] Thus, in Augustine's mind the idea of a will is anything but "obscure" (*obscuris*) or "abstruse" (*abditis*). The will (*uoluntas*), Augustine claims by explicit comparison, is as quotidian as life itself.

Thus Augustine closes, as well as opens, *duab. an.* 10.13 with the protest that by invoking the will he is not appealing to something questionable and "obscure."[27] And even after going on to remind readers in a quick sentence at the beginning of 10.14 of the main point of this discussion ("There is no

---

[25] *De duabus animabus* 10.13 (CSEL 25:1).

[26] For background on Augustine's *cogito* arguments in *trin.* book 10 in comparison to Descartes's, see Jean-Luc Marion, *Au lieu de soi: L'approche de Saint Augustin* (Paris: Presses universitaires de France, 2008), chapter 2, "L'ego ou l'adonné" (89–148). Marion does not believe that Augustine anticipates the Cartesian *cogito*, but rather that his perspective stands in stark contrast to that of Descartes (93). Constructing an Augustinian critique of the Cartesian *cogito*, Marion argues that, for Augustine, thinking about the self does not lead one closer to oneself and one's own identity. To the contrary, viewing oneself in a purely self-referential and therefore artificial way requires introducing a divide in the self and requires a kind of distancing from the self that actually obscures rather than illuminates it. Whereas for Descartes thinking is the most foundational human activity, one that opens up access to the identity of the self, for Augustine, Marion argues, pointing to the opening line of *City of God*, book 10, desiring happiness is more basic than thinking. According to Marion, whereas Descartes sees the human person as most basically a thinking (*cogitans*) creature, Augustine sees the human being as, at bottom, a creature that loves (*amans*). The fact that Augustine does not appeal only to thinking as evidence of human existence but, as here in *duab. an.*, also sees the activity of living as a proof of one's life, supports Marion's case that Augustine does not accord thought the unique foundational anthropological status that Descartes does.

[27] At the opening of the paragraph he denies the accusation that he is turning to "obscure matters" (*rebus obscuris*), while in the final sentence of the paragraph he reiterates, "I do not think that I have brought up something obscure" (*quicquam obscurum*) (10.13 [CSEL 25.1:68]). Augustine's double use of the adjective *obscurus* makes even his word choice as straightforward and unmistakable as he maintains the concept of will should be.

sinning, then, apart from the will"), he immediately jumps back to his "self-evidence thesis," reiterating, "But our will (*uoluntas*) is very well known to us. After all, I would not know that I willed if I did not know what the will was."[28] It is only after thus again underscoring the obviousness of what he is about to say that Augustine finally presents a formal definition of will to his readers: "The will is a movement of the soul, with nothing forcing it either not to lose something or to acquire something."[29]

Two features of this definition merit attention. First, Augustine defines the will in a highly actualistic way; he describes it as a movement (*motus*), not as a static thing. Second, he attaches a qualification to this initial identification. The will is not just any movement but a specific kind of movement, one "with nothing forcing it" (*cogente nullo*). Augustine makes his definition more precise not by defining the will in relation to other forces that act upon it but rather by insulating it from such forces. The will is, by definition, a movement with a kind of independence, or autonomy. It has integrity, and is what it is, by being immune to outside influences.

In 10.14, then, Augustine transitions from his argument that the will exists to defending a particular view of what the will is. So far he has pushed his readers to see that they must affirm the existence of the will for two reasons: (1) because of their commonsense notions of what constitutes wrongdoing or sin (10.12) and (2) in order to account for their inherent desire to live (10.13). The discussion of 10.12 is explicitly framed in terms of demonstrating the inseparability of sinning from will rather than proving the existence of the will per se. Yet the whole section flows seamlessly into his argument in 10.13 that the will exists, since the upshot of 10.12 is that moral intuitions all depend on such a notion. The first reason for affirming the existence of the will points to the presuppositions of what Augustine presents as commonsense moral conclusions, while the second appeals to his readers' empirical experience of the will. Both approaches to the question aim to show that the will's existence is already implied in their everyday assumptions.

Just as Augustine presents in 10.12 and 10.13 the idea that will exists as self-evident, in 10.14 he insists on the self-evidence of the definition of will

[28] *Duab. an.* 10.14 (CSEL 25.1:68). Augustine uses the superlative *notissima* to emphasize his point.

[29] *Duab. an.* 10.14 (CSEL 25.1:68): *definitur itaque isto modo: uoluntas est animi motus cogente nullo ad aliquid uel non amittendum uel adipiscendum.*

he proposes. He contends that this definition of will should be universally accessible to all simply by considering how human beings were created. To realize that will by definition admits of "nothing forcing it," nature alone— without teaching—is sufficient. Augustine writes, "In all human beings whom we could reasonably question, from boys to old men, from grade school to the chair of the sage, nature herself (*natura ipsa*) proclaims these truths. . . . This is obvious everywhere."[30] Shortly thereafter he makes the point that the other element of his definition of will—the idea that willing is always either a will to acquire or not to lose something—is also universally obvious: "All these points are clearer than daylight . . . and granted by the generosity of truth not merely to my own knowledge but to that of the human race."[31] These resounding statements are all the more remarkable given their immediate context. Both are couched in references to the unlikeliest of counterexamples: Augustine himself.

The irony of this juxtaposition is not lost on Augustine, who cannot seem to contain his incredulity at his blindness to the obvious phenomenon of the will during his own years as a Manichee. Repeatedly he reproaches himself with rhetorical questions, in the last two of which his references in *duab. an.* 10.14 to the self-evidence of his definition of will are embedded. Immediately after stating this definition, he exclaims, "Why, therefore, could I not define it at that time? Was it difficult to see that unwilling is the contrary of willing, as we say that left is contrary to right, not as black is contrary to white?" In this initial question, Augustine seems to have in mind his general failure to deduce the existence of the will from the phenomenon of unwillingness (as opposed to his failure to grasp certain features of it, which he discusses later). Augustine makes the point that just as left and right are relative terms, each implying the other, so it is with willingness and unwillingness: being unwilling to do something means willing that one not have to do it. Grasping what it means to be forced to do something unwillingly, which he did as a Manichee, therefore should have enabled him to arrive at the idea of willing.

Augustine also takes himself to task for failing, as a Manichee, to see the two basic features of the definition of will he has formulated: (1) that will is by definition a movement of the soul with nothing forcing it and that (2) willing is always a willing either not to lose something or to

[30] *Duab. an.* 10.14 (CSEL 25.1:69).
[31] *Duab. an.* 10.14.

acquire something. On the first point, Augustine asks rhetorically, "Since in all human beings whom we could reasonably question, from boys to old men, from grade school to the chair of the sage, nature herself proclaims these truths, why did I then not see that I should have put in the definition of the will the phrase 'with nothing forcing it,' which I have put there now. . . ?"[32] He further laments, "If all these points are clearer than daylight, as they are, and granted by the generosity of the truth not merely to my own knowledge but to that of the human race, why could I not even at that time have stated: Will is a movement of the soul, with nothing forcing it, either not to lose something or to acquire something?"[33] In both of these quotations, Augustine pairs claims about the self-evidence of his definition with exclamations of incredulity that this definition did not dawn on him while he was a Manichee.

Embedding his remarks about the self-evidence of his definition of will in a context of self-reproach for his former narrow-mindedness fits well with the larger rhetorical strategy that Augustine employs in this treatise. From the very outset of *duab. an.*, rather than directly attributing the Manichean views he critiques to the friends he is seeking to lure away from Manicheism, Augustine cloaks his criticisms in the guise of regret, chastising himself for what he should have realized long ago: "For there were many things that I ought to have done so that the seeds of the true religion, which were implanted in me for my salvation from childhood, would not so easily and in a few days have been dug up and driven from my mind by the error or deceit of false and deceitful human beings."[34] Rather than bluntly telling his "dear friends"[35] their views are absurd, Augustine directs his criticisms to his former self; instead of announcing what they ought to do, he states what he should have done. In short, Augustine cleverly sugarcoats his critique and advice with self-deprecation. His exclamations about the obviousness of his definition of the will should be seen as a part of this diplomatic strategy. By railing against his own shortsightedness in 10.14, Augustine at once highlights the absurdity of the Manichean viewpoint and avoids wounding the pride of his friends.

[32] *Duab. an.* 10.14.
[33] *Duab. an.* 10.14.
[34] *Duab. an.* 1.1.
[35] *Duab. an.* 15.24.

Yet the rhetorical expediency of Augustine's attribution of these oversights to his earlier Manichean self does not justify the assumption that what he describes as his earlier persuasions, or lack thereof, were a matter of mere invention.[36] In the absence of a reason to disbelieve his description of his former views it makes sense to accept his account as a plausible one. As a Manichee, Augustine was not in a position to define the will as he does in 10.14. He did not see the will as something free from being forced; he did not see willing as oriented toward gaining or not losing something; and he may not have acknowledged the existence of the will at all. Augustine's repeated denial that the concept of will is "obscure" or "abstruse" in 10.13 raises the question of whether Manichean teaching regarded the will in precisely this way: as a notion difficult to understand and of little relevance to everyday life and piety. Augustine certainly suggests that as a Manichee he failed to acknowledge the existence of the will in its full relevance as the decisive factor in determining the morality of a person's actions.[37] If

[36] At this point the reader may object that in the case of the Manichean teaching on two souls, Augustine seems to have been quite willing to portray the Manichees as holding a doctrine they do not seem to have taught. If Augustine, for the sake of polemical expediency, saw fit to present the Manichees as teaching something they did not, why would he not, on the same grounds, see fit to present them as failing to teach something they did teach (i.e., the existence of the human will)? Two responses are in order. First, whether the Manichees taught a doctrine of two souls is a matter of some dispute (cf. n14). Furthermore, Drecoll and Kudella, while arguing against this assumption, have shown how Augustine's accusation of two souls, if not verifiably founded in explicit Manichean affirmations, likely emerges as an inference from the Manichean application of the terms *mens* and *spiritus* to the conflict between the good soul (*anima bona*) and the flesh (*caro*) (see again n14). Thus Augustine's attribution of a two souls doctrine to the Manichees is not a precedent for pure fabrication. At most it serves to establish that Augustine was capable of drawing logical infererences following from premises explicitly affirmed in Manichean thought. Extrapolating from this precedent, the most one could reasonably say would be that Augustine possibly denied the validity of Manichean affirmations of will, despite their actual affirmation of this notion, because of other elements of their teaching, which, he felt, precluded their making such affirmations coherently. This still would not be a case of pure invention. Second, since the issue under consideration is Augustine's own developing perspective on the will, the question is what—if anything—Augustine himself thought about will as a Manichee. What the Manichees as an overarching group, or even what particular varieties of Manicheism would have tended to think about the subject is not in question. Nor is the claim I am advancing that Augustine incontrovertibly failed to subscribe to the existence of will before his turn away from Manicheism. The point is simply that one need not assume the inaccuracy of Augustine's presentation of his own failure to recognize the will's existence as a Manichee.

In his treatise *On Free Will* against Luther, from 1524, Erasmus repeats the idea that the Manichees lacked a notion of free will, arguing that in completely denying free will Luther stands against the entire known intellectual tradition, with only two exceptions: John Wycliffe and "Manicheus," i.e., Mani, the founder of Manicheism. According to Erasmus, Manicheus "explains good and evil by the two natures in man, but in such a way that we owe the good acts to God on account of his creation, and because we can, despite the power of darkness, implore the creator for help." See Desiderius Erasmus and Martin Luther, *Erasmus-Luther: Discourse on Free Will*, trans. Martin F. Winter (New York: Frederick Ungar, 1961), paragraphs 8, 14–15.

[37] *Duab. an.* 10.12.

Augustine's presentation of his own views on the subject are to be trusted, then, his conception of the will seems to have undergone considerable transformation as he transitioned from Manicheism to more mainstream Christianity.

What sparked this transformation? Augustine points neither to scripture nor to "teaching" but to "nature" as the source of his enlightenment on the issue of will. He has now inserted the phrase "with nothing forcing it" into his definition, he tells us explicitly, "thanks to the great caution that has accompanied my increased experience."[38] Though his repeated insistence on the self-evidence of his definition of the will itself gives some ground for skepticism (is this view of will really as obvious from nature as Augustine thinks given that so many, for example the Manichees, fail to arrive at it?), he claims that this definition of will derives directly from experience and nature. Arriving at this view of the will does not require any special revelation.[39] Given this assessment, Augustine's eventual revision of this initial definition raises interesting questions: Will his new view of will also rely on natural knowledge, or will it derive primarily from some other source? Will the change in perspective to come change his views on the reliability of knowledge derived from nature and experience untested by the teaching of scripture and the church? It is precisely these questions—the gradual transformation of Augustine's initial definition of the will in *duab. an.* and its implications—that the remaining sections of part I address. First, however, the place of Augustine's definition of will in his argument about sin in *duab. an.* must be considered.

Now that Augustine has argued that the will exists and defended a particular conception of what the will is, he has laid the necessary groundwork for defining sin in terms of will. In Augustine's words, "For every mind reads it as something written within itself by God that sin cannot exist without the will. Sin, therefore, is the will to retain or to acquire what justice forbids and from which one is free to hold back. And yet, if it is not free, it is not a will."[40] For Augustine at this point, sin not only implies an act of will; sin is a specific kind of will (*peccatum est uoluntas*).[41] Sin, furthermore, is a kind

---

[38] *Duab. an.* 10.14.

[39] Ironically, the very definition of will that Augustine could not grasp until he became a Christian, he insists, should be evident from reflection upon experience and nature.

[40] *Duab. an.* 11.15.

[41] Here Augustine describes sin as an act of will to retain or acquire something. In *lib. arb.* he had also described sinning as an act of will, but there he used the metaphor of turning: "The will which turns from the unchangeable and common good and turns to its own private good or to anything

of will that is free, though Augustine insists that this specification does not really set a sinful will apart from other kinds of will, since freedom is inherently built into the notion of will per se: "If it is not free, it is not a will."[42]

As with his definition of will, Augustine argues that this definition of sin is engraved in the natural structure of the human mind. In fact, his proofs for the self-evidence of each relies upon the other. Part of his argument for the self-evidence of will is that a notion of will is required to make sense of sin, while part of his argument for the self-evidence of this definition of sin is that sin implies will. As with his definition of will, Augustine stresses the universal obviousness of both aspects of the definition of sin he has articulated:

> Did I have to examine obscure books even on this point in order to learn that no one deserves blame or punishment who either wills what justice does not forbid him to will or does not do what he cannot do? Are not these ideas sung by shepherds in the hills, by poets in the theaters, by the unlearned at street corners, by the learned in libraries, by teachers in schools, by priests in sanctuaries, and by the human race throughout the world?[43]

Augustine is convinced that the definitions of will and sin he has proposed are as vital to right belief as they are central to everyday existence. Properly grasping these definitions, for example, is all that is required to show that the Manichean view of the world is untenable. Given these definitions, the problem of sin cannot be a matter of an inherently evil soul. Rather, the problem of sin indicates an evil will. In 12.16, Augustine invites his readers to consider the payoff of the definitions he has articulated: "Come now, let us see how these points might have helped us."[44]

Augustine begins by once again stressing that these notions of will and sin are available to all by nature via introspection, adding that, as mundane

exterior or inferior, sins" (*lib. arb.* 2.19.53). Later, in *conf.*, Augustine will identify sin as a kind of movement of the will, though there he describes this movement with reference to God rather than with reference to the self. Addressing God, Augustine writes, "The only thing that is not from you is what has no existence. The movement of the will (*motus . . . uoluntatis*) away from you who are, is movement towards that which has less being. A movement of this nature is a fault and a sin" (*conf.* 12.11.11 [CCL 27:221–222]).

[42] *Duab. an.* 11.15.
[43] *Duab. an.* 11.15.
[44] *Duab. an.* 12.16 (CSEL 25.1:71).

as they are, they nevertheless have a profound potential for resisting the "heresy of the Manichees." He writes, "For, if anyone consults the depths of his own conscience and the laws of God, which are deeply embedded in nature, interiorly within his mind where they are clearer and more certain, and concedes that these two definitions of will (*uoluntatis*) and of sin (*peccati*) are true, he can condemn without any hesitation the whole heresy of the Manichees with a very few and very short but utterly invincible arguments."[45]

Augustine makes this case by presenting the Manichees with a dilemma concerning the "evil soul," which they assert is responsible for sin. Either the "evil soul" that does not belong to God had a will and therefore became evil willingly, or it did not have a will. In the first case, it must be acknowledged that the soul was not always evil.[46] In the second, the soul cannot be held culpable for always being evil without the will to be so. In short, then, "evil souls" have to be evil either by nature or by will. If by will, then they possess a free movement of the soul and are not completely bad. If by nature, then they cannot possibly exist because nothing is evil by nature. Furthermore, even were it somehow possible for them to be evil by nature, they could not then justly be held accountable for committing sin, and thus the attribution of "evil" to them would be self-contradictory.

Rather than indicating the presence of two competing souls, one good by nature and the other evil by nature, deliberation is "a sign of one soul, which can be carried to one side and then to the other by free will (*libera . . . uoluntate*). For, when it happens to me, I see that my one self considers both and chooses one of them. But generally the one is attractive and the other is right, and, placed between them, we waver back and forth."[47] Here Augustine portrays free will as hovering between two options

---

[45] *Duab. an.* 12.16 (CSEL 25.1:71).

[46] Augustine notes that if the soul did have a will it wanted either not to lose something or to acquire something and observes that "this something was either good or was thought to be good. For it could not otherwise be desired" (11.15). This is interesting, because it seems to indicate the assumption that one cannot will something perversely, i.e., voluntarily pursue evil. In *mor.* 2.2.4 (387–388), however, Augustine seemed to indicate that it is possible to will badly despite knowing better (as discussed in chapter 1, part II, section F).

[47] *Duab. an.* 13.19 (CSEL 25.1:75). Again in 13.21 Augustine makes the points that (1) the phenomenon of deliberation does not constitute evidence that human beings have two souls, and (2) the definitions of will and sin he has offered are basically sufficient to refute the Manichees. Augustine also makes the argument in 14.22 that the two souls doctrine cannot account for repentance. A soul that is always evil by nature cannot be capable of repenting, and a soul that is always good by nature cannot have turned to evil so as to create an occasion for repentance. Though the Manichees claim, according to Augustine, that nothing evil comes from one soul and nothing good from the other,

and characterized by deliberation. His view of will may still be aptly characterized with the hinge image. Bereft of such a concept of will, he has endeavored to show, the Manichean way of accounting for such a scenario falls prey to incoherence.

The fact that the Manichees can be proved wrong about the issue of allegedly evil souls, argues Augustine, is enough to discredit them entirely. Again, he tactfully instructs his Manichean friends by passing judgment upon his former self: If I had realized that they were wrong about souls, he says, "what reason could have remained why I should have thought that they should be listened to or consulted on any topic?"[48] Augustine's message is clear: if the Manichees are so severely mistaken with respect to this issue, they are not to be trusted about anything. Augustine stresses the absurdity of the Manichean error on the issues of sin and will, arguing that their mistaken conceptions of these two entities undermine not only their credibility but also their entire belief system. A centerpiece of his case is the idea that the will is a movement of the soul "with nothing forcing it." According to the Augustine of *duab. an.*, if the will is not free (i.e., free from force), sin cannot be attributed to it. He is still a long way from his later conviction that the fall limits the freedom of the will. Eventually Augustine will emphasize the idea that sin both implies freedom and restricts it.

Section B: The Will as "Theologically Differentiated" in *Contra Fortunatum*

By the time he writes *Simpl.*, Augustine's notion of will has become "theologically differentiated," that is, modulated to particular situations according to which the characteristics and powers of the will vary. However, even before *Simpl.* one can observe the gradual emergence of such differentiation. *C. Fort.* serves to highlight one aspect of this emergence. Though his identification of the contexts that are determinative for the functioning of the will continues to evolve beyond this work, as does his assessment of the implications of these contexts for human willing, *c. Fort.* shows a kind of

---

neither kind of soul the Manichees describe can commit sin, and therefore neither of them can repent of sin.

[48] *Duab. an.* 13.19.

complexity not found in Augustine's works examined thus far.[49] In *c. Fort.*,
the formation of habit divides an individual's life into two phases. In one
she enjoys a will free from constraint, functioning according to the "self-
evident" rules identified in *duab. an.* In the other she suffers from a will
that has fallen into necessity. This kind of theological differentiation does
not exactly parallel what one finds in *Simpl.*, but it does show Augustine
working out the key insight that human willing functions differently in different contexts.

   C. Fort. records a debate between Augustine and the Manichean priest
Fortunatus that took place on August 28 and 29, 392.[50] Augustine reports
in *Reconsiderations* that stenographers took down the text of *c. Fort.* "as we
were arguing back and forth . . . as though official acts were being composed."[51] Indeed the text that has come down to us is characteristic of a live
debate, preserving moments of immediacy and intensity, as well as moments
of awkwardness and repetition. Augustine repeatedly asks Fortunatus to explain why he believes God sent human souls to be intermingled with evil,
hoping thereby to trap him in a dilemma. One possibility is that God did
not need to resort to this measure. In this case, God is invincible but cruel
for subjecting human beings to this fate unnecessarily. The other possibility
is that God took this action for his own protection. In this case, Fortunatus
must admit he deems God vulnerable to corruption, another conclusion he
wishes to deny. Very early in the debate, Augustine states his central argument, which he proceeds to hammer home repeatedly and which ultimately
causes Fortunatus to capitulate: "My argument, therefore, is short and,
I think, perfectly plain to anyone. If God could not suffer anything from the

[49] While Augustine does position *c. Fort.* after *duab. an.* in the chronological presentation of his
works in *retr.*, he begins his treatment of *c. Fort.* by observing, "At the same period of my priesthood, I argued against a certain Fortunatus," which leaves open the possibility that his debate with
Fortunatus, which occurred on August 28 and 29, 392, may have taken place during his composition
of *duab. an.*, in addition to the possibility that he had already completed *duab. an.* before debating
Fortunatus. As far as a date for *duab. an.*, Augustine tells readers only that he composed *duab. an.*
while a priest, after he wrote *De utilitate credendi*, which indicates a date sometime between 391 and
his ordination as bishop in 395. While it is possible that *duab. an.* was not completed until after *c.
Fort.*, *c. Fort.* clearly moves beyond *duab. an.* in terms of the complexity of the view of will presented
and the degree to which this view overlaps with Augustine's more mature perspective on the will.
Thus it is a more mature work with respect to the issue of will in terms of content if not necessarily
in terms of established chronology. English translations come from the following unless otherwise
noted: Augustine, "A Debate with Fortunatus, a Manichean," in *The Manichean Debate*, trans. Roland
Teske, WSA I/19 (Hyde Park, NY: New City Press, 2006), 145–162.

[50] For background on this debate, see Elke Rutzenhöfer, "Contra Fortunatum Disputatio: Die
Debatte mit Fortunatus," *Augustiniana* 42 (1992): 5–72.

[51] *Retr.* 1.16.1.

nation of darkness because he was inviolable; he sent us here for no purpose so that we might suffer these woes here. But if he could suffer something, he is not inviolable, and you deceive those to whom you say that God is inviolable."[52] Fortunatus too poses questions to Augustine, which Augustine answers. Fortunatus, however, never produces a satisfactory answer to this question. The debate ends with Fortunatus's admission that he has no answer to give.

"Will" is a key concept in the debate, especially in the positions Augustine defends. Augustine uses the notion of will to invoke the sphere of creaturely freedom and agency with which God has endowed human beings in creation but which is entirely "up to them." God is the giver of the will, but he is not responsible for what human beings do with it.[53] These two affirmations hold together since, by Augustine's definition, the will is precisely a gift that allows human persons to do things "on their own," without external influence. Thus, as in *lib. arb.*, the notion of will is the key to Augustine's explanation of how God can be the sovereign creator of everything and yet not be implicated in evil.[54] He thereby sidesteps both the Manichean error of positing powers not created by God and the alternative the Manichees themselves seek to avoid: portraying God as complicit in, or responsible for, evil. Furthermore, in Augustine's debate with Fortunatus, the notion of will proves useful for offense as well as for defense. As in *duab. an.*, Augustine claims in *c. Fort.* that his definitions of will and sin alone are sufficient to undermine the Manichean position.

Fortunatus, for his part, attempts to elicit acknowledgment from Augustine that the soul—insofar as it is enslaved to sins—is not from God, and thus that the soul's misery comes from a source that is neither God nor created by God. At stake is the problem of evil. Fortunatus and Augustine have different strategies for avoiding attributing evil to God. Fortunatus's strategy is to constrict the doctrine of creation so as to locate the source of evil outside of it. Augustine's strategy is to describe more precisely the functioning of the soul that God has created. This is where the will fits in.

---

[52] *C. Fort.* 7.

[53] Augustine at once emphasizes that the soul "is not God" (*c. Fort.* 11) and that it "comes from God as its author because it was made by God" (*c. Fort.* 12).

[54] Chappell observes, "Augustine's interest in voluntariness stems from his concern, as an apologist, with responsibility for evil." Other factors, however, become increasingly important for prompting Augustine to think about human willing in his later works. See Chappell, *Aristotle and Augustine on Freedom*, 122.

As in other works already considered, in *c. Fort.* Augustine asserts that it is impossible to sin without the will and free choice.[55] This time he introduces the argument that forgiveness implies will. Since (1) forgiveness is unnecessary without grounds for forgiveness, namely, sin, and since (2) sin implies will, it follows that (3) forgiveness implies will.[56] Responding with this argument to Fortunatus's quotation of Ephesians 2:1–18, Augustine seeks to show that Fortunatus's argument that sin is a result of "the opposing nature forc[ing] us to do what we do" makes forgiveness—the good news of peace with God and others brought about by Christ and proclaimed in Ephesians—look superfluous. Speaking in the voice of the soul, which was promised forgiveness for sins it was compelled to commit by the "opposing nature," Augustine says, "I have lost my free choice (*liberum arbitrium*). You know the necessity (*necessitate*) that has pressed me down. Why do you blame me for the wounds I received?"[57] Free choice and necessity, in other words, cannot coexist. As we will see, this argument that sin implies will, familiar from chapter 1, stands in tension with new developments in his thinking on the will that surface later in the work.

C. Fort., in which the actual words of one of Augustine's interlocutors are recorded, sheds more light on the Manichean position against which Augustine defines his view of will than did *duab. an.* In that work, though Augustine often contrasted his view with Manichean perspectives, attributing certain positions to the Manichees, he did not cite Manichean sources directly. This work provides more direct exposure to the views against which Augustine seems to have been positioning himself both in *duab. an.* and in his debate with Fortunatus. In both texts, Augustine insists upon the idea that sin presupposes willingness, free will, and free choice of the will. Fortunatus's comments in his debate with Augustine make clear that

---

[55] He affirms both the former and the latter in *c. Fort.* 17: "For someone who is forced by necessity to do something does not sin. But someone who sins sins by free choice. . . . He has done nothing wrong who did not do anything by his will." He affirms the former in *c. Fort.* 20. This latter paragraph includes an interesting series of statements that become progressively more specific. First: *qui non uoluntate peccat, non peccat.* Then: *nisi libera uoluntas esset in nobis, peccata non essent.* Finally: *si manifestum est peccatum non esse, ubi non est liberum uoluntatis arbitrium.* It is almost as if Augustine is going to greater and greater lengths to underline the freedom of the will. Sin not only has to be willing, it has to be by free will, and by free choice of the will, to be sin.

[56] Augustine argues, "But if we receive the forgiveness of sins, it is obvious that we sinned by our will (*uoluntate*). After all, it is quite stupid to forgive someone who did nothing wrong" (*c. Fort.* 17). This argument is similar to Augustine's observation in *duab. an.* 14.22 that the phenomenon of repentance undermines a dualistic two souls theory. Both forgiveness and repentance imply that a single soul is guilty of wrongdoing and capable of good in that it repents of this wrongdoing.

[57] *C. Fort.* 17 (CSEL 25.1:94).

Augustine has not been arguing against a straw man when he presents the opposition as conceiving of sin as something forced or done unwillingly.

Fortunatus is, in fact, convinced that human beings commit sin unwillingly. In his own words, "For we sin unwillingly (*inuiti*) and are forced by the contrary substance that is our enemy, and so we conform ourselves to this knowledge of the way things are."[58] For Fortunatus, sin is a matter of being coerced by a "contrary substance"; it involves precisely the kind of dynamic that Augustine characterizes as inimical to authentic willing in *duab. an.*[59] Augustine's definition of the will from *duab. an.* ("The will is a movement of the soul, with nothing forcing it either not to lose something or to acquire something")[60] and of sin as a kind of willing directly contradict the Manichean conception of how sin and willing relate according to Fortunatus. For Fortunatus, it only makes sense to speak of sin as happening unwillingly, due to an external force; for Augustine, it only makes sense to speak of sin as happening willingly, without the operation of an external force. On Fortunatus's way of thinking, if the soul truly had enjoyed freedom of choice, it would have been absurd for it to choose evil. Rather, he points out to Augustine, "if the soul—to which, as you say, God gave free choice—were situated in the body alone without any opposing nation, it would be without sin and would not make itself subject to sins."[61] For Augustine, however, given that the soul is guilty of sin, to deny that it sins willingly would be absurd; such a denial would undermine the soul's responsibility for the sin attributed to it.

Fortunatus also speaks of the influence of the "contrary substance" as a kind of pseudo-wisdom. Appealing to Romans 8:7, he says, "For the apostle said, *The wisdom of the flesh is opposed to God. For it is not subject to the law of God, for it cannot be.* (Rom 8:7) It is clear from this that the good soul is seen to sin not of its own accord but because of the influence of the wisdom that is not subject to the law of God."[62] Under the power of this false wisdom, rather than "of its own accord," the soul becomes captive to sin and death. The solution to the soul's predicament of unwilling enmeshment

---

[58] *C. Fort.* 20 (CSEL 25.1:99).

[59] See also *c. Fort.* 21, where Fortunatus again emphasizes that the soul sins when the opposing nature forces it.

[60] *Duab. an.* 10.14.

[61] With this statement Fortunatus is not conceding that God did give free choice to the will but considering what would have to be true in a hypothetical situation in which the soul enjoyed the kind of free choice Augustine contends it does in actuality.

[62] *C. Fort.* 21.

in sin, according to Fortunatus, is to acquire knowledge to defeat the false wisdom to which it has been subjected: "Instructed by that knowledge and restored to the memory of its pristine state, the soul recognizes the source from which it takes its origin, the evil in which it is situated, and the goods by which it can correct the sin it committed unwillingly (*quod nolens peccavit*)."[63] Given the insight to recognize its own origins, predicament, and duties for what they are, the soul can escape the sinful condition forced upon it. Thus, for Fortunatus, it does not seem possible for the soul to act contrary to the knowledge or wisdom it possesses. The soul always does what it knows. If for Augustine evil is a problem of will, for Fortunatus it is a problem of ignorance.[64]

In response to Fortunatus, Augustine reiterates what may be the most oft-repeated refrain of the whole debate: "I say that there is no sin if we do not sin by our own will."[65] This principle is the key point of Augustine's case. At stake are two rival explanations of why evil and sin exist in the world. One is that responsibility for sin lies with a force or nation of darkness, which has being independently of God and is outside the realm of God's creation. The other is that responsibility lies with the free will of the souls God has created.

In addition to filling out the contrast between Augustine's view of the will and the Manichean view as represented by Fortunatus, *Contra Fortunatum* reveals new layers of complexity to Augustine's conception of will. These come to light at a point in the debate when Augustine responds to Fortunatus's invocation of Paul. Though earlier in the debate the audience had requested that the debaters refrain from appealing to scripture, the fact that Fortunatus has done so first licenses Augustine to follow suit.[66]

In effect, Augustine's response constitutes an alternative reading of Paul, though he at first avoids referring to Paul directly. Responding to

---

[63] C. Fort. 20 (CSEL 25.1:99).

[64] Thus Fortunatus's view seems to coincide with the view attributed by Kierkegaard to ancient Greek philosophy: no one knowingly and voluntarily chooses evil. See Søren Kierkegaard, *The Sickness unto Death*, trans. Walter Lowrie (Princeton, NJ: Princeton University Press, 1941), 2.1.2, 154–155.

[65] C. Fort. 21 (CSEL 25.1:100): *ego dico peccatum non esse, si non propria uoluntate peccatur.*

[66] See the conclusion of the first day's debate (*c. Fort.* 19). There it is explained that the audience wanted "rational arguments" rather than arguments based on scripture because there was no common basis of agreement between Augustine and Fortunatus about what had to be taken seriously as scripture.

Fortunatus's citation of Romans 7:23–25 and 8:7 and Galatians 5:17 and 6:14, Augustine begins by affirming that he "recognize[s] and embrace[s]" the scriptures and announces that he will explain how they "fit with [his] faith." In what follows he discusses the effect of habit on the will, distinguishes between the freedom of Adam and our freedom, and contrasts the condition of Adam's will and ours.

In many of his works already considered, Augustine attributes free choice of the will to the will per se and states that freedom belongs inherently to the notion of willing as such. Here in *c. Fort.*, however, Augustine introduces an important qualification. He says to Fortunatus, "I say that the free choice of the will (*liberum uoluntatis arbitrium*) existed in the man who was created first. He was created in such a way that nothing at all would have resisted his will (*uoluntati*) if he had chosen to keep the commandments of God. But, after he sinned by free will, we who are descended from his stock were cast down into necessity (*in necessitatem*)."[67] Augustine now suggests that important differences distinguish how the will functioned in Adam and how it functions in us. Adam enjoyed free choice of the will (*liberum uoluntatis arbitrium*), and by free will (*libera uoluntate*) he first sinned. His will was powerful and would have been able to execute its choice for the good, had Adam so chosen. There was "nothing at all" (*nihil omnino*) to stand in its way. Yet Adam's decision to sin by this very free will plunged those to follow him from freedom into necessity. Adam's fall, his sin "by free will," was a turning point; it represented a division between two epochs of the will. Certain conditions pertain to the will of the man created first (*primus*), while others pertain to those who come after (*postquam*). How the human will functions depends on its location in this temporal chronology.[68]

Whereas in *duab. an.* Augustine had repeatedly appealed to everyday experience to substantiate his claim that sin implies free will, here he calls on

---

[67] *C. Fort.* 22 (CSEL 25.1:103–104).

[68] Fascinatingly, Fortunatus too seems to have a theologically differentiated notion of freedom. (While Fortunatus uses the language of freedom, and does sometimes use the language of "unwilling," he consistently avoids the language of "willing" or "will.") At one point he makes the statement, "A commandment is only introduced where there is also opposition. And the ability to live freely only exists as a result of the fall" (*c. Fort.* 16 [CSEL 25.1:92]). He then goes on to quote Ephesians 2:1–18 in support of this view, though how this text corresponds to the conclusions he draws from it is not clear. Perhaps the underlying logic of Fortunatus's view is that having an alternative other than the good is necessary for authentic freedom.

experience to corroborate his point that Adam's sin has attenuated our free will. He continues:

> Each of us can discover after a little reflection that what I say is true. For at present, before we become entangled in some habit, we have in our actions the free choice (*liberum arbitrium*) of doing or not doing something. But after we have done something with this freedom and the deadly sweetness and pleasure of the action has taken hold of the soul, the soul is so entangled in that same habit of its own making that afterwards it cannot conquer what it fashioned for itself by sinning.[69]

As shown clearly in this quotation, Augustine has something specific in mind when he refers to the "necessity" (*necessitas*) from which Adam's offspring suffer: "habit" (*consuetudo*).

Habits take time to develop. Thus Augustine does not claim that the free choice of the will Adam originally enjoyed is always alien to our experience. Rather, he presents the lives of Adam's heirs as a microcosm of the universal transition from freedom to necessity that Adam's sin effected. According to Augustine's remarks in *c. Fort.*, human beings initially enjoy "the free choice (*liberum arbitrium*) of doing or not doing something." At first, it is "up to us to choose what we want" (*quid uelimus*), whether a good will or a bad will.[70] With time, however, obstacles crop up with which Adam did not need to contend before he first chose to sin. It is after we have become enslaved by habit, not from the start, that we do not do what we will.

Augustine presents habit in the life of each person, then, like the fall for the human race, as an important turning point to take into account when evaluating the characteristics and capacity of the will. Just as human beings "after" (*postquam*) Adam have been plunged into necessity, so there is a distinction between the period in a person's life "before" (*antequam*) a bad

---

[69] *C. Fort.* 22 (CSEL 25.1:104).

[70] See *c. Fort.* 22 (CSEL 25.1:105). This idea is reminiscent of Aristotle's notion of "what is up to us" (*eph' hēmin*) to do or not to do, which Charles Kahn identifies as the basis for human responsibility for voluntary action in his thinking, and one of the four component concepts of his theory of action. See Kahn's concise summary of Aristotle's theory of will, C. H. Kahn, "Discovering the Will: From Aristotle to Augustine," in *The Question of "Eclecticism": Studies in Later Greek Philosophy*, ed. J. M. Dillon and A. A. Long (Berkeley: University of California Press, 1988), 239–240. For an in-depth treatment of Aristotle's theory of will, see Anthony Kenny, *Aristotle's Theory of the Will* (New Haven, CT: Yale University Press, 1979). For a comparison of Aristotle's theories of freedom and the voluntary to Augustine's, see Chappell, *Aristotle and Augustine on Freedom*.

habit has been formed and "after" (*postquam*) she has misused her freedom. Beforehand, Augustine asserts, a person has "free choice." Afterward "we experience the necessity of our habit so that we do not do what we will (*quod uolumus*)."[71] Thus—in *Contra Fortunatum*,—for all Augustine's emphasis on a universal plunge into necessity after Adam, there remains a fundamental analogy between our situation and that of the father of the human race. His ancient fall from freedom to necessity corresponds to each person's everyday experience of a fall from freedom into necessity via habit.

Here in his debate with Fortunatus, Augustine allows some rapprochement between his idea of willing and necessity, conceding that our will becomes subject to necessity after the formation of habits. However, Augustine couples this concession with a double safeguard of the freedom of the will. Subjection to necessity comes into the picture for the will only subsequent to two free decisions: Adam's choice, and our own, to eat the forbidden fruit of sin. For Augustine in *c. Fort.*, then, human beings are subject to a kind of necessity, but it is of their own making.

Augustine drives home this point exegetically as well as implicitly in his argument. Whereas Fortunatus had interpreted Paul's reference to "the wisdom of the flesh" as indicating something alien to the human soul that forces it to sin without its accord, an "opposing nature," Augustine concludes that this phrase refers to habit.[72] Though certain actions do become involuntary through habit, habits themselves are established by freely chosen actions. Thus "the wisdom of the flesh" originates in our misdeeds, not from an external source beyond human control. Even when he speaks of necessity, Augustine wants to trace this necessity back to will, not to nature.

Unsurprisingly, then, Augustine's reading of Matthew 12:33 differs from that of Fortunatus, who interprets the two trees as representing two separate natures. According to Augustine, the Lord's commandment to "either make the tree good, or make the tree bad" would make little sense if the two trees were understood as Fortunatus proposes. Instead Augustine concludes that the two trees represent two wills (*uoluntates*). We cannot make natures one way or another, but "it is up to us to choose what we want," he argues.[73] Fortunatus has made a category mistake; the will, not nature, is capable of being made good or bad by our choices.

---

[71] *C. Fort.* 22 (CSEL 25.1:106).
[72] *C. Fort.* 22.
[73] *C. Fort.* 22 (CSEL 25.1:105).

Though Augustine does not dwell on this subject or discuss it explicitly in terms of human will, he does introduce a third kind of theological differentiation in *c. Fort.* In addition to the differentiation between pre- and post-fall conditions, and conditions before and after the formation of a habit, Augustine differentiates between our condition "according to the flesh" and under grace. Commenting on 1 Corinthians 15:21, he observes:

> As long as we bear the image of the earthly man, then, that is, as long as we live according to the flesh, which is also called our old self, we experience the necessity of our habit so that we do not do what we will (*non quod uolumus faciamus*). But the grace of God has poured the love of God into us and made us subject to his will (*suae uoluntati*), since he said to us, *You have been called to freedom* (Gal 5:13) and, *The grace of God has set me free from the law of sin and death* (Rom 8:2).[74]

After the fall, human beings are subject to necessity in the form of habit; in this state "we do not do what we will." After God's grace has been poured into us, we become subject to the divine will (*suae uoluntati*); in this state we do what God wills. The outpouring of grace into our hearts is another theological event of decisive importance for human willing. At this point, Augustine does not explicitly say how grace affects willing. Instead he omits reference to the will after the advent of grace; he does not assert, for example, that our own will actually becomes conformed to God's.[75] Rather, he simply observes that we will be made subject to God's will and, drawing on Romans 8:2, describes our condition under grace as one of freedom in which we are liberated from the domination of our habits.[76]

In *c. Fort.*, Augustine's characterization of the will gains texture. As he contends with Fortunatus over how best to interpret Paul, Augustine describes the functioning of the will with much greater complexity than he had previously. The will functions differently, depending on where one finds oneself in the Christian story. Now the basic parameters of Augustine's

---

[74] *C. Fort.* 22 (CSEL 25.1:106).

[75] This parallels a stage in Augustine's thinking about the human will of Christ where he emphasizes the subjection of Christ to the will of the Father without mentioning the obedience of his human will. See Han-luen Kantzer Komline, "The Second Adam in Gethsemane: Augustine on the Human Will of Christ," *RÉAP* 58 (2012): 41–56.

[76] In addition to Augustine's quotation of Gal. 5:13 in *c. Fort.* 22, see also *c. Fort.* 23.

theologically differentiated conception of the will are in place. Yet his estimation of the radicality of this differentiation will continue to grow.

Section C: Adam's Fall as a Turning Point for Human Willing in *De libero arbitrio* III (391–395)

As Augustine continues developing his theologically differentiated notion of will, he shifts the focal point of this differentiation from the formation of personal habits of sin in each individual's life to Adam's sin that led to the universal fall of humankind. One may observe the latter emphasis coming to the fore in *lib. arb.* III. In *c. Fort.*, which, like *lib. arb.* III, stems from Augustine's time as presbyter, Augustine makes the point that the condition of the will changes significantly before and after Adam. After Adam, free will is constricted given the way it consistently tends to be employed. In *lib. arb.*, Augustine does not allow, as he does in *c. Fort.*, that Adam's descendants enjoy an Adamic state of freedom before they form sinful habits by their own free will. Rather, in *lib. arb.* III, Augustine tends to portray habit as already deeply engrained in the human race, regardless of individual human decisions.[77] The fall strongly disposes Adam's descendants to sin through inherited ignorance and difficulty, even before this disposition is confirmed on an individual level among Adam's posterity. There is not, in *lib. arb.*, as strong a sense of analogy between Adam's situation and our own as there is in *c. Fort.*; rather, the freedom Adam enjoyed is potentially irrevocable and limited more strictly to him: "When we speak of the freedom of the will to do right, we are speaking of the freedom wherein man was created."[78]

This more limited assessment of the scope of free will corresponds to a more expanded assessment of the possible meanings of sin. Though Augustine does not yet affirm inherited guilt, he does affirm inherited ignorance and difficulty[79] and allows for a nontechnical application of the term "sin" "not only to that which is properly called sin, that is, what is committed

---

[77] Augustine writes, "It is not to be wondered at that man, through ignorance, has not the freedom of will to choose to do what he ought; or that he cannot see what he ought to do or fulfill it when he will, in face of carnal custom which, in a sense, has grown as strong, almost, as nature, because of the power of mortal succession" (*lib. arb.* 3.18.52).

[78] *Lib. arb.* 3.18.53.

[79] See also *lib. arb.* 3.22.64, in addition to 3.18.53.

knowingly and with free will, but also to all that follows as the necessary punishment of that first sin."[80] Thus Augustine's estimation of the impact of Adam's sin on the functioning of the will proves more profound in *lib. arb.*

While Augustine stresses how much still lies within the soul's power, stating that God has given the soul "so much dignity as to put within its power the capacity to grow towards happiness if it will,"[81] he also emphasizes the soul's inability to execute what it knows is the right thing to do. Augustine writes, "That it [the soul] cannot instantly fulfill the duty it recognizes as duty, means that that is another gift it has not yet received." According to Augustine, the soul requires God's aid to implement the good. Just as the soul depends for its very existence on God's goodness and mercy, which created it from nothing, so it depends on this same mercy to enable it to carry out its duty.[82] God's mercy stands at the soul's beginning, and God's mercy is required to bring the soul to the happiness of which it is capable, its proper end.

Section D: The Implications of the Fall for Right Willing in *Ad Simplicianum* (396–398)

Upon the death of Valerius, with whom he had been serving as coadjutor bishop for some months, Augustine became sole bishop of Hippo in 396. He began his career as bishop with a more profound sense of the implications of the fall for human willing than had been his as a priest. *Ad Simplicianum*, the first work he wrote as a bishop, provides a series of snapshots of this more chastened view of the condition of the fallen human will, a view that continues to develop even in the work itself.[83]

Simplician, the letter's recipient, was a priest in Milan who had written to Augustine with a number of exegetical questions. Book 1 contains Augustine's replies to two questions on Romans, while book 2 addresses five texts from the "books of the kings," each of which seems to suggest something impious or untrue about God. Augustine's comments in the

---

[80] *Lib. arb.* 3.19.54.
[81] *Lib. arb.* 3.12.65.
[82] *Lib. arb.* 3.12.66.
[83] Augustine states in *retr.* that books 1 and 2 of *Simpl.* were his first two works as bishop (*retr.* 2.1.1). Thus *Simpl.* must have been written at some point after the texts considered thus far, which

Reconsiderations indicate the greater significance of book 1 for his development. Indeed, in this first book one discovers a momentous change in Augustine's thinking about the relationship of grace and the will.[84]

Book 1 offers an in-depth verse-by-verse interpretation of two notoriously thorny passages: chapters 7 and 9 of the book of Romans. In Augustine's interpretation of Romans 7, he explains that this passage concerns the struggles of a person still under the law, who does not yet experience the benefits of grace.[85] His interpretation here is much in line with the views he had expressed in his previous works on Romans. Yet when he moves to interpret Romans 9, Augustine's argument suddenly becomes convoluted, and here the issue of the relation between grace and free will comes to the fore. The reader expects first one resolution, and then another, as Augustine tries various possible readings on for size before rejecting them as unfitting. Why did God choose Jacob and not Esau? Augustine ultimately concludes that the reason cannot be Jacob's works or even his faith and will to do the good. All of these are instances of, not reasons for, God's mercy.

Augustine promises Simplician in the preface of the letter that instead of resting content with his former examinations of the texts about which Simplician has inquired, he has returned to Paul and "investigated with

stem from Augustine's time as a presbyter. English translations of *Simpl.* come from J. H. S. Burleigh, trans., *Augustine: Earlier Writings* (Philadelphia: Westminster Press, 1953), unless otherwise noted.

[84] Cued by Augustine's own retrospective comments in *retr.* 1.1.3, scholars have long recognized *Simpl.* as a crucial turning point in his thinking about grace, though there has been extensive debate as to whether this work marks more of an innovation upon, or an organic unfolding of, his earlier thinking. For a polemical summary in which the author defends and situates his own interpretation with respect to other studies emphasizing the "break" (*Bruch*) in Augustine's thought, as well as with respect to key defenders of versions of the continuity thesis, see Kurt Flasch, *Logik des Schreckens: Augustinus von Hippo, De diversis quaestionibus ad Simplicianum I 2* (Mainz: Dieterich'sche Verlagsbuchhandlung, 1990), 270–276. Pierre-Marie Hombert, in contrast, rejects the idea that *Simpl.* represented a radical "break" (*coupure*) in Augustine's thinking, preferring instead to see it as a "turning point" (*tournant*), which was the culmination of an organic progression that had begun already in 386. See Pierre-Marie Hombert, *Gloria gratiae: Se glorifier en Dieu, principe et fin de la théologie augustinienne de la grâce* (Paris: Institut d'Études Augustiniennes, 1996), 571, where Hombert draws out the implications of his discussion of *Simpl.* on 91–111. Also coming down in favor of seeing *Simpl.* in continuity with Augustine's earlier writings on grace is Harrison, *Rethinking Augustine's Early Theology*, 151–163. For a list that includes more recent publications on both sides of the debate, but not all those cited by Flasch, see Anthony Dupont and Matthew Alan Gaumer, "Gratia Dei, Gratia Sacramenti: Grace in Augustine of Hippo's Anti-Donatist Writings," *Ephemerides Theologicae Lovanienses* 86, no. 4 (2010): 307–308n1. To the extent that the literature has engaged the role of the will in *Simpl.*, it has tended to address it as a subsidiary issue, relevant insofar as it bears upon the development of Augustine's doctrine of grace. The following analysis, however, foregrounds the question of the significance of *Simpl.* for the development of Augustine's conception of will.

[85] Augustine would later come to admit the possibility, and even regard it as likely, that this passage described the spiritual person, the person under grace. See *retr.* 2.1.2.

greater care and attention these same apostolic words and the tenor of his sentences."[86] Augustine depicts himself as returning to the most basic grammatical building blocks of Paul's arguments. He is concerned to attend not only to the big picture of Paul's letter but also to the very words (*verba*) chosen by the apostle and their cohesion on the level of discrete thoughts.[87]

Section D.1: The Problem of Will *sub lege*: Not Doing the Good One Wills to Do

The first question Augustine has been given by Simplician is the request for an interpretation of Romans 7:7–25. True to the exegetical strategy articulated in the preface, Augustine works through this passage virtually line-by-line, beginning with a decisive statement that in this text Paul writes about himself as one under the law.[88] This designation establishes certain chronological parameters that govern his situation: as someone *sub lege*, the subject of this passage is "not yet" (*nondum*) *sub gratia*, with attendant implications.[89] Augustine goes on to explain what this state entails.

The person "under the law" *knows* what the right thing to do is, and he *knows* what he is commanded to do by the law, yet he cannot do the right thing.[90] Here sin is not just a problem of ignorance. Sin is a condition of bondage. A person under the law is captive to his own desires, forced (*cogatur*) to serve them as a slave (*mancipium*). In *duab. an.*, Augustine had clearly defined sin as a kind of willing, which by definition was not subject to force. Sin was voluntary. Here Augustine characterizes wrongdoing as being overmastered by desire.[91]

---

[86] Before composing *Simpl.*, Augustine had already devoted two works to interpreting Romans (*ex. prop. Rm.* and *ep. Rm. inch.*) and responded to questions regarding several passages from Romans in *diu. qu.*

[87] This may be what is suggested by the phrase *tenor sentiarum*—the connection, or course, of his ideas.

[88] *Simpl.* 1.1.1.

[89] *Simpl.* 1.1.7 (CCL 44:13).

[90] See *Simpl.* 1.1.7: "He who knows that an act is prohibited and rightly prohibited, and yet does it, knows that he is the slave of an overmastering desire," and *Simpl.* 1.1.10 (CCL 44:15): "So far as knowledge goes (*ex eo quod scit*) he consents unto law, but so far as action is concerned he yields to sin."

[91] In addition to *Simpl.* 1.1.7, see also *Simpl.* 1.1.9 (CCL 44:14–15): "He is still speaking in the person of a man under the law (*sub lege*) and not yet under grace, who is brought to do wrong by some dominant desire (*concupiscentia dominante*), and by some deceptive sweetness (*fallente dulcedine*) associated with prohibited sin. But he disapproves of this because of his knowledge of the law. 'It is no more I that do it,' he says, because he is overcome when he does it. It is a desire (*cupiditas*) that does it, when we yield to an overmastering (*superanti*) one. Grace brings it about that we do not yield, and that the human mind is strengthened to resist desire (*cupiditatem*)."

When Paul does what is wrong, he is acting not only against what he knows but also against what he wills. Of Paul's statement in Romans 7:16, "If what I would not, that I do, I consent unto the law that it is good," Augustine writes that Paul "does not will (*non vult*) to do what he in fact does. He is overcome because he is not yet free by grace, but he already knows through the law that he is doing wrong, and he does not really want (*nolit*) to do that."[92] Under the law, then, one can both know and will the good without being able to bring oneself to execute it. Augustine here describes wrong-doing differently from the way he had characterized it in *duab. an.* In that work, he had defined sin as an unjust will, which one was free to resist. In *Simpl.*, he does not describe sin first and foremost as a problem in the will's orientation but as a matter of the will's bondage or weakness. It is not the will being unjust but just willing that cannot prevail; that is the crux of Augustine's description of the problem. Here wrongdoing is a matter of doing precisely what one does *not* will to do.[93]

How does this situation of sinning against one's will arise? Augustine explains that two factors combine to bring about the dominion of sin in people's lives.[94] First, nature works against them. Mortality, the penalty Adam's descendents inherit, becomes a kind of "second nature," disposing them to sin. As they sin repeatedly, this problem compounds itself and they form addictions. Custom thus works against them too. By this cooperation, nature and custom strengthen cupidity to the point where it dominates them, even when they know that they should do otherwise and will accordingly.

---

[92] *Simpl.* 1.1.9 (CCL 44:14).

[93] See *Simpl.* 1.1.11: "He who is not yet under grace does not do the good he wills but the evil which he does not will." This view initially seems to stand in tension with the definition of sin Augustine had provided in *duab. an.*, "Sin, therefore, is the will to retain or to acquire what justice forbids and from which one is free to hold back. And yet, if it is not free, it is not a will" (11.15), and his assertion that "there is no sinning . . . apart from the will" (10.14). Augustine's account of his struggle with sin in *conf.* helps to explain how it is possible that one can will what is right yet simultaneously be guilty of sin when sin is understood as a matter of will. In short, the reason is that the sinner does not *merely* or *exclusively* will what is right. For a contemporary defense of the idea that sin can be involuntary, see Robert Merrihew Adams, "Involuntary Sins," *Philosophical Review* 94 (1985): 3–31. For Adams, however, the category of "involuntary" is much more expansive than it is for Augustine, including anything outside an agent's "voluntary control" (7), which, in brief, he construes to mean anything the agent does without aiming to do it. At this stage of his thinking, Augustine sees "involuntary sin" as a product of previous voluntary decisions, whereas Adams wants to push for a stronger notion of involuntary sin that is not limited to such cases. But Adams's argument includes the case for the softer varieties of involuntary sin such as that found in *Simpl.*

[94] See *Simpl.* 1.1.10.

Though, due to this chain of events, fallen human beings are held back from carrying out their good will, Augustine insists, willing rightly is still in their power. Discussing the second half of Romans 7:18 ("for to will is in me, but to do that which is good is not"), Augustine writes, "To those who do not rightly understand these words he seems by them to take away free will. Yet how does he do that when he says 'To will is present with me'? If that is so, actual willing is certainly within our power; that it is not in our power to do that which is good is part of the deserts of original sin."[95] Here, then, Augustine's commitment to free will, which, in his retrospective words, he will "struggle" to maintain in question 2, is on display. Arguing that the inability to execute our will should be distinguished from the inability to will what is right in the first place, Augustine rescues free will by defining it more precisely. "Free will" (*liberum arbitrium*) does not mean the power to do what we will but merely the capacity for "actual willing" (*ipsum uelle*).

Yet it is not as if human beings were created to be free only in this more limited sense. Augustine is careful to insist that our inability to carry out the good we will is not a feature inherent in our created nature. Continuing to comment on Romans 7:18, he observes, "This is not the original nature of man, but the penalty of his guilt, whereby mortality was brought in as a second nature, from which the grace of our Creator sets us free, if we submit ourselves to him by faith."[96] Certain limitations in how human willing is "free" pertain to the fallen will that are not characteristic of the human person in her created nature.

Augustine adds, "These are the words of a man set under the law and not yet under grace. He who is not yet under grace does not do the good he wills but the evil which he does not will."[97] Whether a person can bring her good will to fruition depends on whether she is living *sub lege* or *sub gratia*, as well as on whether her will retains its original natural integrity or is subject to the punishment of original sin. Just as there is a difference

---

[95] *Simpl.* 1.1.11. Augustine begins to employ terminology of original sin (*peccatum orginale*) in the mid-390s, but not until the Pelagian controversy does he fully develop the idea of the inheritance of Adam's guilt (*originalis reatus*). See Harrison, *Rethinking Augustine's Early Theology*, 169–170. As Harrison notes, Sage and Burns disagree with the consensus of most scholars that in *Simpl.* Augustine already understands original sin to have an inherited and direct effect on the operation of the human will. See Athanase Sage, "Péché Originel: Naissance d'un dogme," *RÉA* 13 (1967): 211–248 and Burns, *The Development of Augustine's Doctrine of Operative Grace*. Burns cites Sage on 42n182.

[96] *Simpl.* 1.1.11.

[97] *Simpl.* 1.1.11.

between the will as created and the will as subject to the "penalty of guilt," so how the will works depends on whether a person is living *sub lege* or *sub gratia*. Looking first backward and then forward, Augustine demarcates the workings of the will *sub lege* from both its original state of created integrity and its redeemed state contingent upon faith and the grace of the creator. In addition to the different epochs established by the major events of the Christian story (creation, the subjugation of creation to sin, the reign of grace), there are landmarks in an individual person's life that determine her relation to these larger epochs. Both sets of theological contexts play a role in defining how the will works.

In contrast to the difficulty of carrying out the good one wills, willing the good seems to strike Augustine as a fairly simple matter. Commenting on Romans 7:21, he writes:

> There is nothing easier for a man under the law than to will to do good and yet to do evil. He has no difficulty in willing (*sine difficultate uult*), but it is not so easy to do what he wills. It is easy to do what he hates even against his will; just as a man thrown headlong has no difficulty in reaching the bottom, though he does not want to and indeed hates it. So I interpret the word "is present."[98]

Augustine presents this interpretation of the workings of the will as hinging upon his interpretation of the precise terminology of Paul's argument, the word *adiacet*. When Paul says the will is present, Augustine contends, he is referring to the readiness of the will to do the right thing, its *facilitas*. Thus, on the basis of a specific word from Romans, Augustine arrives at the view that willing is still within our power *sub lege*. Later in life he will read the text differently, reframing the entire passage, so that this and other individual words apply to the Christian's experience *sub gratia*. But long before he explicitly revises his reading of Romans 7 he will reconsider the optimistic assessment of the human power to will what is right that his interpretation here includes.

One might be tempted to interject with a question at this point: If free will consists only in wanting, and not actually in achieving anything, what good does it do? Augustine's answer involves looking beyond the limits of

---

[98] *Simpl.* 1.1.12 (CCL 44:16).

the human person whose will is in question. Though *she* may not be able to do anything with her good will, Augustine replies, *God* can. Free will is worth having because by free will a person can throw herself on the mercy of God. As he is commenting on verse 24, Augustine sums up what free will can and cannot achieve for the person *sub lege*: "In this mortal life one thing remains for free will (*libero arbitrio*), not that a man may fulfill righteousness when he wishes (*cum uoluerit*), but that he may turn with suppliant piety to him who can give the power to fulfill it."[99] In this sense, the freedom to will what is right turns out to be even more—not less—powerful than the freedom to execute one's will. Willing the good allows one to tap into a divine power source, made one's as a gift.

In short, Augustine argues in *Simpl.* question 1 that although, due to the fall, we can no longer fulfill our will to act rightly, we can still will the good. In addition to discussing the difference in the power of our will as created by nature and its powers when subjected to sin, Augustine discusses the will in terms of a new theological periodization: *sub lege* versus *sub gratia*. Though under the law we cannot carry through on the good that we will on our own, we can appeal to God for help. Thus our willing, despite its acknowledged weakness post-fall and under the law, remains an instrument of enormous power upon which God's mercy is contingent.

Section D.2: The Problem of Willing *sub lege* Reconsidered: Calling Must Precede Good Willing (Question 2 of *Ad Simplicianum* I)

Simplician's second question on Romans, like his first, invites Augustine to comment generally on a difficult passage from the book rather than posing a specific predicament. This time the text in question is Romans 9:10–29. Engaging in similar preliminaries to those found in the preface, Augustine begins with some remarks about the exegetical method he will employ before tackling the passage. Whereas in the preface to *Simpl.* he had announced his intention to attend to the specific words and sentences of Paul's argument, now, at the beginning of his interpretation of Romans 9, he states his primary aim as follows: "First I shall try to grasp the apostle's purpose which runs through the whole Epistle, and I shall seek guidance from it."[100] Augustine thus moves from emphasizing the micro-level to directing

---

[99] *Simpl.* 1.1.14 (CCL 44:18).
[100] *Simpl.* 1.2.2.

his attention to the macro-level—from stressing the part (the sense of Paul's individual *verba* and *sententiae*) to prioritizing the whole (the *intentio totae epistulae*). These two statements of his exegetical strategy should not be viewed as incompatible; cultivating a sensitivity to the larger argument and to its individual components are complementary goals. But the difference between the two does suggest an intentional movement in question 2 to consider larger patterns in, and the overall purpose of, Paul's argument. In question 2 Augustine aims to focus on the overall purpose of the book so that it may guide his interpretation of its smaller units rather than the other way around.

Augustine formulates this global purpose without hesitation: "It is that no man should glory in meritorious works, in which the Israelites dared to glory, alleging that they had served the law that had been given to them, and that for that reason they had received evangelical grace as due to their merits."[101] The main point of Romans is to drive home an idea that drives out human boasting: grace is a work of God, not a human work. Augustine quotes Ephesians 2:8–9 to articulate the central message of Romans: "This is the truth [i.e., that good works follow upon grace rather than preceding it] the apostle wanted to urge; just as in another passage he says, 'By the grace of God we are saved, and that not of ourselves. It is the gift of God. It is not of works, lest any man should boast.'"[102] Augustine explains that serving as Paul's proof are the examples of Isaac and Jacob, who were chosen as objects of God's blessing before they had even been born. In Augustine's mind, Paul's discussion of these examples in Romans 9 illustrates the principle from Ephesians that "good works do not produce grace but are produced by grace. . . . No one does good works in order that he may receive grace, but because he has received grace."[103] Thus, not only is Augustine, in this second question of *Simpl.* I, broadening his focus to take explicit stock of the larger scope of Paul's argument in the book of Romans; he is also reading Romans 9 in light of other Pauline writings.

---

[101] *Simpl.* 1.2.2. Hombert regards this statement as a key to the entire treatise, and to its character as a "turning point" (*tournant*) in Augustine's thought (*Gloria gratiae*, 105). Burns cites the view that "Paul's purpose was to refute the presumption of Jewish Christians that they had earned the right to receive the gospel by performing the good works of the law" as one of the three constants in Augustine's interpretation of Romans 9, common as well to his two treatments of the text prior to *Simpl.* (*The Development of Augustine's Doctrine of Operative Grace*, 38). Yet by thinking through the implications of this idea more rigorously in *Simpl.*, Augustine moves beyond his former insights.

[102] *Simpl.* 1.2.3.

[103] *Simpl.* 1.2.3.

Establishing the correct chronology of grace is crucial to Augustine's case for its unmerited character. He writes, "The Jews did not understand that evangelical grace, just because of its very nature, is not given as a due reward for good works. Otherwise grace is not grace. In many passages the apostle frequently bears witness to this, putting the grace of faith before works; not indeed that he wants to put an end to good works, but to show that works do not precede grace but follow from it."[104] By "putting grace before works" (*gratiam praeponens*), Paul shows that grace cannot be attributed to those who perform these works; "works follow rather than precede grace" (*non esse opera praecedentia gratiam sed consequentia*). What events anticipate and what events flow from grace will be a key question in Augustine's interpretation of Romans 9.

In the ensuing argument, Augustine considers possible precursors of grace, potential bases for God's election of Jacob (foreknowledge of Jacob's faith, good works, belief), ultimately concluding that electing Jacob on the basis of any of these things would be tantamount to electing him on the basis of works, something Paul's larger argument in Romans rules out. The question of whether willing is the basis or result of God showing mercy, however, presents a real conundrum. As Augustine struggles with it, he argues first for one perspective and then for another before drawing his final conclusions.

The specific textual provocation for this question is Romans 9:16: "So then it is not of him that willeth, nor of him that runneth, but of God that hath mercy." Quoting this verse Augustine asks, "Does it mean that we cannot even will unless we are called, and that our willing is of no avail unless God give us aid to perform it?"[105]

Initially Augustine considers texts that seem to suggest the answer is no. Verses such as Luke 2:14 ("on earth peace to men of good will") and 1 Corinthians 9:24 ("even so run that you may attain") suggest an element of human initiative and contribution. Our willing and running must matter. Building on the assessment of the human capacity for right willing he had provided in response to Simplician's first question, Augustine presents a nuanced explanation of how this might be the case. As in question 1, he draws a distinction between the power to will what is right and the power

[104] *Simpl.* 1.2.2 (CCL 44:24–25).
[105] *Simpl.* 1.2.10.

to put our good intentions into action, which he now glosses as the difference between the fact "that we will" (*ut uelimus*) and "what we will" (*quod
uoluerimus*): "There are two different things that God gives us, the power to
will (*ut uelimus*) and the things that we actually will (*quod uoluerimus*)."[106]
It is one thing to will that something be the case. It is another actually to
achieve what one wills.

In question 1 Augustine had spoken of this division of labor in rougher
terms. He attributed the first power to us and the second to God.[107] Now
he paints a more complicated picture: "The power to will (*ut uelimus*)
he has willed should be both his and ours, his because he calls us, ours
because we follow when called. But what we actually will (*quod autem
uolerimus*) he alone gives, i.e., the power to do right (*posse bene agere*)
and to live happily forever."[108] The power to do the good that we will still
depends entirely on a gift from God; this is a gift of God alone (*solus*).
Willing the good, however, is no longer "up to us" *simpliciter* but both his
and ours (*et suum . . . et nostrum*), his by virtue of calling (*suum vocando*),
ours by virtue of following (*nostrum sequendo*). It is God who takes the
initiative, Augustine now makes clear, eliciting good will from us by his
calling. Our contribution to willing the good hangs by a thread, our consent to follow when called, a consent upon which God's assistance in carrying out good will is contingent.

Immediately this single thread begins to bother Augustine. He sees a
problem with the solution he has just presented: "But Esau was not yet born
and consequently could be neither willing (*uelle*) nor unwilling (*nolle*) in
all these matters. Why was he rejected when he was still in the womb?"[109]
Jacob was elected when not yet born (*nondum natus*). Yet *in utero* he was
incapable not only of acting in accordance with his will but of willing at
all. How, then, could willing have been the basis of his election? The chronology is awry. Though wearied at the prospect, Augustine must return to
the drawing board.[110]

Augustine quotes Romans 9:16 again, as if mulling it over. This time, instead of reading it through the lens of Luke 2:14 and 1 Corinthians 9:24,

---

[106] *Simpl.* 1.2.10 (CCL 44:35).
[107] See *Simpl.* 1.1.12 and 1.1.14.
[108] *Simpl.* 1.2.10 (CCL 44:35).
[109] *Simpl.* 1.2.10 (CCL 44:35).
[110] *Simpl.* 1.2.10: "We come back to that difficulty, troubled not only by the obscurity of the question but also by our own abundant repetition."

he turns to Philippians 2:12–13 for guidance. Combining the word-based approach he articulated in the preface with the more expansive exegetical perspective that he stated would guide his interpretation of this chapter, Augustine observes:

> If you pay close attention to these words, "Therefore it is not of him that willeth, nor of him that runneth, but of God that hath mercy," you will see that the apostle said that, not only because we attain what we wish by the help of God, but also with the meaning which he expresses in another passage, "Work out your own salvation with fear and trembling; for it is God which worketh in you both to will and to do of his good pleasure" (Phil. 2:12, 13). There he clearly shows that the good will (bonam uoluntatem) itself is wrought (fieri) in us by the working of God.[111]

According to Augustine, Paul does not speak of God working with any preexisting materials. He does not speak of the will being reoriented or reconfigured. He asserts rather that by God's working a good will "is made" (fieri). Augustine presents this conclusion as following from Paul's own verba,[112] considered in light of the larger intention of Paul's other verba.[113] Augustine thus portrays his new insight as emerging through a process of interpreting scripture by scripture.

This method leads him to see that Romans 9:16 ("So then it is not of him that willeth, nor of him that runneth, but of God that hath mercy") proclaims not only the necessity but the sufficiency of God's mercy for willing the good. Augustine points out that if this were not the case, Paul's statement could have been reversed so as to state: It is not of God that had the mercy but of him that runneth. If all Paul intended to communicate were that it is not only of our willing but also of God having mercy, then he equally as well could have said that it is not only of God having

---

[111] Simpl. 1.2.12 (CCL 44:36).

[112] He thus portrays it as the result of his faithful application of the hermeneutical principles articulated in the preface and at the start of question 2. See the preface for Augustine's "word-based" approach. His language in 1.2.12 echoes the language he had used there: compare uerba ... attendas (1.2.12; CCL 44:36) to uerba ... adtentius ... rimatus sum (1.praef.; CCL 44:7).

[113] Cf. Simpl. 1.2.2 (CCL 44:24): et primo intentionem apostoli quae per totam epistulam uiget tenebo quam consulam. Here in 1.2.12 Augustine makes good on his promise to pay attention to the apostle's intentio, drawing on other parts of Paul's corpus to establish Paul's intentio in the whole of the book of Romans.

mercy but *also* of our willing.[114] In reality, however, Paul's statement is not reversible;[115] there is no implied logic of partial contributions. Augustine concludes, "If God has mercy, we also will (*etiam uolumus*), for the power to will is given with the mercy itself."[116] God's mercy, in other words, is in no way contingent upon our consent. Rather, our willing is contingent upon God's mercy.[117] Paul's point is not merely negative, that the will of a human being (*uoluntas hominis*) is insufficient, but also positive: God's grace is sufficient. In this sense, the power to execute our good will is entirely a gift; the calling by which we will what is right is entirely a gift; and even the good will by which we respond to God's calling is entirely a gift.

Again in this case, chronology proves vital to understanding God's role vis-à-vis the human will. "The good will does not precede (*praecedit*) calling, but calling precedes (*praecedit*) the good will."[118] What comes first makes a difference. Since calling comes first, "the fact that we have a good will (*uoluntas bona*) is rightly attributed to God who calls us, and the fact that we are called cannot be attributed to ourselves."[119] Though it is easier to affirm the more general statement that good will is a gift of God, the *order* of having a good will and God's calling invites a sharper formulation. Our good will is rightly attributed to God, *and* the calling that brings about our right willing is not rightly attributed to ourselves. There is thus no parity between God's role and ours in bringing about a right will in us. Since we do not have a good will until God calls us, and his calling is absolutely sufficient for creating this good will in us, there can be no question of what we may have done to earn it. Thus Augustine

---

[114] Cf. *Simpl.* 1.2.12 (CCL 44:36–37): "If he had said, 'It is not of him that willeth, nor of him that runneth, but of God that hath mercy,' simply because a man's will (*uoluntas hominis*) is not sufficient for him to live justly and righteously unless he is aided by the mercy of God, he could have put it the other way round and said, 'It is not of God that hath mercy, but of the man that willeth,' because it is equally true that the mercy of God is not sufficient itself, unless there be in addition the consent of our will" (*consensus nostrae uoluntatis addatur*).

[115] Augustine makes a similar argument in *gr. et lib. arb.* 7.16. Quoting Romans 9:16, he writes, "This statement can in no way also be turned around so that it says, 'It does not depend on God who shows mercy, but on the one who wills and who runs,' for whoever would dare to say this clearly shows that he contradicts the apostle." See Augustine, *Answer to the Pelagians, IV: To the Monks of Hadrumetum and Provence*, trans. Roland Teske, WSA I/26 (Hyde Park, NY: New City Press, 1999). Subsequent English translations of *gr. et lib. arb.* come from this source unless otherwise noted.

[116] *Simpl.* 1.2.12 (CCL 44:37).

[117] Cf. *Simpl.* 1.2.12: Augustine continues, "Clearly it is vain for us to will unless God have mercy. But I do not know how it could be said that it is vain for God to have mercy unless we willingly consent."

[118] *Simpl.* 1.2.12 (CCL 44:37).

[119] Cf. *Simpl.* 1.2.12 (CCL 44:37).

now emphasizes that even willing rightly is something made possible only in response to God's calling; this is the case in such a way that our right willing is contingent upon God's mercy.[120] Augustine characterizes calling as a fundamental cause that explains willing. Calling is the *effectrix* of good will.[121]

However, Augustine wishes to push beyond the claim that God's calling is sufficient for us to respond. For Augustine, God's calling is irresistible. If God wills to aid a person, God calls that person "effectually" (*congruenter*), adapting his calling to her in such a way that it is guaranteed to elicit a positive response.[122] Everyone who is called effectually follows. Romans 9:16, Augustine reasons, requires this conclusion. If it were possible that someone could resist God's call, if someone could have it "in the power of his will not to obey, it could be said correctly that it is not of God who hath mercy, but of the man who willeth and runneth, for the mercy of him that calleth is not sufficient unless the obedience of him who is called follows."[123] According to Augustine, then, God's calling effects a good will such that it is impossible for the will to resist. This idea, that the will can be shaped irresistibly by an outside force, is alien to Augustine's previous descriptions of willing, which had so emphasized that willing of any kind at all must be free in the sense of immunity to outside forces exerted upon it. For Augustine in *Simpl.*, God bestows not only "earnest effort and the power to perform works of fervent charity" but also "voluntary assent" (literally, the nodding of the will, *nutus uoluntatis*).[124]

---

[120] Cf. the statement quoted at n116 from *Simpl.* 1.2.12: "If God has mercy, we also will, for the power to will is given with the mercy itself."

[121] One can find this affirmation embedded in a question Augustine raises in 1.2.13 (CCL 44:37): "But if that calling is the effectual cause of the good will (*effectrix bonae uoluntatis*) so that everyone who is called follows it, how will it be true that 'Many are called but few are chosen'?" For a discussion of Augustine's designation of calling as the *effectrix bonae uoluntatis*, see Volker Henning Drecoll, *Die Entstehung der Gnadenlehre Augustins* (Tübingen: Mohr Siebeck, 1999), 222–230.

[122] Burns emphasizes that at this stage in Augustine, God's congruent calling happens through external circumstances rather than through an interior grace bringing about good will (*The Development of Augustine's Doctrine of Operative Grace*, 41). Yet Augustine's statement that "the good will itself is wrought in us by the working of God" (*ipsam bonam uoluntatem in nobis operante deo fieri*) (*Simpl.* 1.2.12), which portrays God's role in bringing about our right willing as an inward (*in nobis*) work of grace, suggests a broader notion of God's congruent calling. For further evidence that "the manner in which [Augustine] describes the operation of grace in first calling a person, effecting their faith, and then enabling their good actions is most certainly not exclusively an external operation" at the time of *Simpl.*, see Harrison, *Rethinking Augustine's Early Theology*, 150.

[123] *Simpl.* 1.2.13.

[124] Augustine's sentence structure drives home rhetorically the point that, from beginning to end, human advancement toward God is God's work. Neither consent nor industry is procured by human effort. Rather, God imparts these gifts to us by his bountiful grace. My translation: "When, therefore,

Augustine is keenly aware of the questions raised by his proposal that calling is the irresistible *effectrix* of the good will. Has free will been compromised in his theory of God's irresistible calling? Is it not unfair that the free wills of the brothers have no bearing upon who will be the special beneficiary of God's love? Though he does acknowledge the importance of free will, Augustine replies by observing how little there is to lose with respect to free will after the fall rather than denying that God's irresistible calling compromises free will: "Free will is most important. It exists, indeed, but of what value is it in those who are sold under sin?"[125] God's calling, far from depriving humankind of any benefit it might attain via free will under sin, obtains a blessing beyond free will's reach in its sinful state. God's calling does not work at cross-purposes with free will, but heals it.

Whereas in earlier works Augustine had characterized the will as sovereign over its own impulses, he now describes willing as at the mercy of involuntary delight.[126] Earlier he had described the will as a powerful force that moved other things. Now he presents the will as needing to be moved: "Who has it in his power to have such a motive present to his mind that his will (*uoluntas*) shall be influenced to believe" (literally, by which his will may be

---

those things delight us by which we make progress toward God, this is inspired and bestowed by God's grace. It is not obtained by our assent and industry, or the merits of our works, since he imparts and gives bountifully the assent of the will, industry of endeavor, and works of fervent charity" (*Simpl.* 1.2.21 [CCL 44:54]). Augustine uses couplets to underline God's responsibility for making possible our progress toward him. Our delight in the things leading us toward him are "inspired" (*inspiratur*) and "bestowed" (*praebetur*) by God's grace. He "imparts" (*tribuit*) and he "gives bountifully" (*largitur*).

[125] *Simpl.* 1.2.21.

[126] Delight is "voluntary" in the sense that the *uoluntas* is exercised in the act of delighting, but may still be spoken of as "involuntary" in the sense that this delighting itself is not produced by an independent and prior act of will that delighting should occur; it is involuntary, in other words, in the sense of being beyond one's control. Peter Brown identifies Augustine's characterization of delight as a "mainspring of human action" in *Simpl.* as a "psychological discovery" at the heart of the "crucial change" in Augustine's outlook that took place in the 390s. See Peter Brown, *Augustine of Hippo: A Biography* (Berkeley: University of California Press, 2000), 148–149. According to Brown, in *Simpl.* delight becomes, for Augustine, "the only possible source of action, nothing else can move the will," whereas, around the time of his conversion, he tended to view motivation in exclusively intellectual terms (148). "Now, 'feeling' has taken its rightful place as the ally of the intellect," but with an important implication: human motivation becomes something outside a person's control (148). Against this interpretation, Harrison contends that "what Augustine says about the role of love and delight in motivating the will in the second book of *Simpl.* is nothing new in his reflection on Romans and Galatians, except that it is now referred not only to a person's ability to obey the law and to do good works, but also to their choice of faith." She furthermore asserts that "Augustine uses [the idea that it is delight that motivates the will] to describe how grace inspires and motivates the will, through the gift of the Holy Spirit, from Cassiciacum onwards" (*Rethinking Augustine's Early Theology*, 148–149). Harrison addresses Brown's psychology of delight thesis directly on 154. See also her concluding chapter, "Grace" (238–287), which includes a discussion of the role of delight in Augustine's earlier theology.

moved to faith)?[127] For a person to be moved to belief, Augustine explains more specifically, she needs to experience delight. Otherwise she will repel a potential object of belief from herself rather than accepting it. Augustine asks rhetorically, "Who can welcome in his mind something which does not give him delight" (*quod eum non delectat*)?[128] Yet if delight is required for belief, then belief lies beyond the pale of human control, for, Augustine asks, "who has it in his power to ensure that something that will delight him will turn up, or that he will take delight in what turns up?"[129] For human beings to experience the kind of delight that brings them to God, Augustine concludes, something superhuman is required: "If those things delight us which serve our advancement towards God, that is due not to our own whim or industry or meritorious works, but to the inspiration of God and to the grace which he bestows."[130] Augustine thus contrasts human impotence to produce delight with God's power. It is beyond human power to ensure either the presence of a motive that inspires delight or its own response to such an object, but God has the power to address both of these weaknesses, to inspire and bestow this delight by his grace.

Augustine finds in everyday experience ample confirmation of the necessity of divine inspiration to elicit the will's delight. Conversion is bizarre and unpredictable. Unlikely people convert, and they convert suddenly. Sometimes those with impeccable moral credentials go on living contentedly without Christian belief, while those seemingly most unqualified—Augustine mentions "harlots and actors"—are drawn to and transformed by authentic faith. It is impossible to attribute these kinds of developments to the merit of the individuals who have been converted or the demerits of those who have not. It must, Augustine concludes, be a matter of election of the will: "The only possible conclusion is that it is wills that are elected."[131]

Yet Augustine is quick to recognize that this conclusion fails to get to the bottom of the matter, for, as he has just established, "the will itself (*uoluntas ipsa*) can have no motive unless something presents itself to delight and stir the mind. That this should happen is not in any man's power."[132] To support

---

[127] *Simpl.* 1.2.21 (CCL 44:53).
[128] *Simpl.* 1.2.21 (CCL 44:53).
[129] *Simpl.* 1.2.21.
[130] *Simpl.* 1.2.21.
[131] *Simpl.* 1.2.22 (CCL 44:55): *restat ergo ut uoluntates eligantur.*
[132] *Simpl.* 1.2.22 (CCL 44:55). Or, in Augustine's words from the previous paragraph, "We could neither will nor run unless he stirred us and put the motive-power in us" (1.2.21).

this contention, Augustine appeals to the life of the apostle Paul himself. If right willing, without special aid from God, were the basis of election, then God would never have chosen Paul. Augustine writes, "What did Saul will but to attack, seize, bind and slay Christians? What a fierce, savage, blind will was that!"[133] The will that put Paul on the road to Damascus was not merely indifferent but virulently hostile to the Christian faith. He not only took no delight in the Christian faith; he wished to stamp it out.

But Paul's will was transformed in a flash: "He was thrown prostrate by one word from on high, and a vision came to him whereby his mind and will (*uoluntas*) were turned from their fierceness and set on the right way towards faith, so that suddenly out of a marvelous persecutor of the Gospel he was made a still more marvelous preacher of the Gospel."[134] Paul's will was not elected because it was already inclined in the right direction. Rather, hell-bent on persecuting the faith, Paul's will had to be radically reoriented (*retorqueretur*) and corrected (*corrigeretur*). His will was elected not because it already delighted in God but so that he might delight in God. To make Paul the persecutor into Paul the preacher, God had to turn his will around.

To the concluding question of the logic behind God's choice of Paul, or any other person, Augustine's answer is cryptic: "All things have been created each in its own time."[135] The reasons behind this reorientation of Paul's will, he seems to suggest, are as unsearchable as God's purposes in making the world from nothing. Neither divine act emerges continuously from what precedes it. To understand the gratuity of either one requires appreciating it in its own time: as preceding, rather than following, creaturely goodness.

Section D.3: Augustine's "Change of Mind" in *Ad Simplicianum*

Augustine's developing understanding of how the will works as outlined in *Simpl.* entails adjustments to his previous descriptions of the will. Some of these adjustments apply only to the post-fall will, leaving his earlier descriptions intact as applied to the will in its created state. Other adjustments, however, extend to his understanding of the will per se, both pre- and post-fall. All told, a comparison to the vision of human willing

---

[133] *Simpl.* 1.2.22 (CCL 44:55).
[134] *Simpl.* 1.2.22 (CCL 44:55).
[135] *Simpl.* 1.2.22.

from Augustine's earlier works discussed in chapter 1 brings to light significant developments in the vision of human willing he presents in *Simpl.*

Several adjustments to Augustine's conception of the post-fall will are
worth noting. First, after the fall the will is no longer free to withhold its
consent to God's congruent calling.[136] Since God's congruous vocation is
irresistible, the will can no longer be seen as sovereign in the sense of re-
taining an unqualified power to withhold its consent.[137] In cases where the
outside force the will cannot resist is God, this decreased capacity for self-
determination post-fall actually works to its advantage.

The will's inability to resist grace subsequent to the fall entails a second
difference between the post-fallen will and the pre-fallen will: after the fall,
the will loses its status as that upon which attainment of the good hinges.
It no longer enjoys the pivotal importance it did previously. Attainment of
the good is not contingent on the autonomous assent of the will; rather the
will's consent is guaranteed by God's effectual calling. Third, the post-fallen
will is no longer the final causal explanation further than which it is impossible to go, at least not for good acts of will. Rather, after the fall the will is
radically dependent on the intervention of God's grace, which now serves

---

[136] See Burns, *The Development of Augustine's Doctrine of Operative Grace*, 41. Burns notes
that in *Propositions on Romans,* in contrast, "once God calls, a person may accept or refuse the
invitation" (39).

[137] Thus characterizations of Augustine's view of will that take ability to assent or dissent as its primary characteristic do not apply to his understanding of the fallen will in *Simpl.* and beyond, with
the exception of *De spiritu et littera* [*spir. et litt.*]. For a recent example of such characterizations, see
Scott MacDonald, "Augustine and Platonism: The Rejection of Divided-Soul Accounts of Akrasia,"
in *Uses and Abuses of the Classics: Western Interpretations of Greek Philosophy,* ed. Jorge J. E. Gracia
and Jiyuan Yu (Burlington, VT: Ashgate, 2004), 75–88. MacDonald's argument relies on the assumption that for Augustine willing is a matter of rational consent, which he seems to base largely on
Augustine's threefold account of sin in *s. Dom. mon.* His interpretation of Augustine's conception
of will comports well with the general type of solution for reconciling Augustine's doctrine of grace
with free will that Burns attributes to Xavier Léon-Dufour. According to Burns, Léon-Dufour takes
spir. et litt. (412) as the decisive expression of Augustine's teaching on grace and free will. In that work
Augustine states that *consentire uel dissentire propriae uoluntatis est.* Thus Léon-Dufour contends that
for Augustine human beings can reject or accept the grace God offers. See Burns, *The Development
of Augustine's Doctrine of Operative Grace,* 12. Both MacDonald and Léon-Dufour see willing as
necessarily involving the freedom both to consent and to dissent. If Augustine had already come
to see the fallen will as incapable of withholding assent to God's grace in *Simpl.,* why would he state
that *consentire uel dissentire propriae uoluntatis est* in *spir. et litt.,* a mature work? Sarah Catherine
Byers offers one explanation in her account of the development of Augustine's thinking on grace,
whereby, after a hiatus (from 400 to 411) in his intensive engagement with this issue, he returned
to the topic, but only gradually "rediscovered his own characteristically 'Augustinian' position." See
Sarah Catherine Byers, *Perception, Sensibility, and Moral Motivation in Augustine: A Stoic-Platonic
Synthesis* (New York: Cambridge University Press, 2013), 208–212. I agree with Byers's overall thesis
that Augustine recapitulates developments from the 390s in the Pelagian controversy, but offer a
different account of when and how this occurs. We will return to the issue of the development of
Augustine's mature thinking on grace during the Pelagian controversy in subsequent chapters.

as the cause of the good will. Thus, in *Simpl.*, Augustine's conception of the post-fallen will becomes even more profoundly differentiated than it was previously. There is a more dramatic contrast between the character and capacities of the will before and after the fall, and Augustine now gestures toward a third theological period after the fall but under grace in which yet other rules apply to the will.

Some of the new features of the post-fallen will Augustine introduces cannot merely be restricted to the will in a limited phase. Rather they entail a broader reconsideration of his basic understanding of what the will is. Earlier, for example, Augustine had asserted that there is no will but free will, such that freedom is inherently built into the idea of what willing means. Now, however, he proves capable of characterizing the will as in bondage and "sold under sin." Given this characterization, Augustine's original claim about freedom being inherent in the will requires some qualification. The will's inherent freedom can no longer mean freedom of choice between options;[138] clearly the will is susceptible to losing this kind of freedom while still maintaining some kind of ontological integrity. A clue to solving this puzzle may be found in Augustine's growing connection of willing with "delight." If he is moving toward a conception of willing that has less to do with the choice between options and more to do with delight in a certain kind of object, then the lack of freedom of choice no longer necessarily violates freedom of the will.[139]

What prompted Augustine's rethinking of human willing in *Simpl.*? He does not leave us in doubt about his opinions on the matter: it was scripture. He makes this clear in two sets of retrospective comments on the work.

Looking back in *Reconsiderations* on the momentous changes in his understanding of grace that occurred in *Simpl.*, Augustine observes the vital role of scripture in transforming his perspective.[140] His first statement about his treatment of Romans 9:10–29, question 2 of *Simpl.*, book 1, is his famous declaration, "In answering this question I in fact strove on behalf of

---

[138] Indeed, this was the approach of the mature Augustine, who never *denied* the freedom of the will, but did *redefine* it.

[139] For an argument that Augustine's mature perspective on freedom admits certain kinds of necessity, see Jesse Couenhoven, "The Necessities of Perfect Freedom," *International Journal of Systematic Theology* 14, no. 4 (2012): 396–419.

[140] Nor has this point gone unnoticed by scholars. Drecoll and Kudella, for example, observe that Augustine's effort to "follow the details of Paul's argument and to take the wording of his text seriously" leads to the correction of his understanding of *initium fidei* in *Simpl.* 1.2 (*Augustin und der Manichäismus*, 123).

the free choice of the human will, but God's grace conquered."[141] According to Augustine, he had no choice but to prioritize grace in this way because the words of the apostle Paul demanded it: "Otherwise I would have been unable to arrive at understanding what the Apostle said with the most evident truthfulness" (*liquidissima veritate*).[142] Thus Augustine construes his abandonment of "free choice of the human will" in favor of grace in his interpretation of Romans as necessary for reaching a conclusion that would conform to Paul's teachings in 1 Corinthians 4:7.[143] Augustine characterizes his change of mind in composing *Simpl.* as itself a Pauline conversion. A "word from on high" turned him around despite his best efforts to go in the opposite direction.

As in *Reconsiderations,* in *On the Predestination of the Saints*, Augustine attributes the change in his views in *Simpl.* to what he read in Paul. He explicitly observes that his thinking about faith, works, and grace developed as he wrote more and more on the subject, and he describes *Simpl.* as resolving his former problems in understanding their relation "in accord with the truth of the divine scriptures."[144] He credits 1 Corinthians 4:7 specifically with changing his mind: "When I thought otherwise (*aliter*) about this matter, I myself had also been convinced (*convinctum*) in particular by this testimony of the Apostle."[145] As Augustine presents things, his thinking did not merely accord with scripture; scripture itself prompted a change in how he understood grace and faith to relate. Augustine uses strong language to describe this process. In his telling, it represented no less than a revelation from God: "God revealed (*deus . . . reuelauit*) this to me in the answer to the question that, as I said, I was writing to Simplician."[146] Augustine styles

---

[141] *Retr.* 2.1.1.

[142] *Retr.* 2.1.1 (CCL 57: 90).

[143] On the broader significance of this key verse, along with 1 Corinthians 1:31, for Augustine's doctrine of grace, see Hombert, *Gloria gratiae.* Hombert's entire study centers on Augustine's use of these texts, but see especially 16–25 for an overview of their appearance in his corpus.

[144] *Praed. sanct.* 4.8. This and subsequent English translations of this work come from Augustine, "On the Predestination of the Saints," in *Answer to the Pelagians, IV: To the Monks of Hadrumetum and Provence*, ed. John E. Rotelle, trans. Roland Teske, WSA I/26 (Hyde Park, NY: New City Press, 1999). For Augustine's discussion of the development of his view of the relationship of grace and faith, including his "error" of seeing assent to the gospel as from the believer rather than a gift of God, see his comments in *praed. sanct.* 3.7.

[145] *Praed. sanct.* 4.8 (PL 44: 966). Statements such as this pose a problem for Harrison's argument that Augustine himself maintained that "he had never held that the will is free to know or to do the good without grace; that he had always taught, from the very beginning, that it is subject to original sin, ignorance, and difficulty, and that any good action is wholly dependent upon God's grace" (*Rethinking Augustine's Early Theology*, 199).

[146] *Praed. sanct.* 4.8 (PL 44:966).

himself as a new Paul, who, by a revelation of "brightest truth" (*liquidissima veritate*),[147] like Paul's *lux copiosa* (Acts 22:6), gains a new appreciation for God's grace despite his own errant inclinations. According to Augustine's self assessment, then, the changes in his conception of grace and the will in *Simpl.* are not reducible to polemical reactions against Manicheism.[148] Still less would it be true to say that his view of grace and the will took decisive shape only in his struggles against the Pelagians. Augustine insists his mind was changed by his struggle with scripture.[149]

Part II: A Link in Augustine's Chains: His Weakness of Will in *Confessions*

Part I of this chapter traced the development, culminating in *Simpl.*, whereby Augustine came to adopt a new view of the capacities of the fallen human will. Augustine's *Confessions* (*conf.*), which he composed after he became a bishop (397–399), provides a detailed snapshot of this more chastened perspective. While earlier texts we have considered amply demonstrate the inability of the human will to turn toward God without divine

---

[147] *Retr.* 2.1.1.

[148] This is not to say that Manicheism was unimportant for this development. As we have seen from *duab. an.*, Augustine's engagement with Manichean theology goaded him into developing and formulating more fully the basic understanding of will that served as a departure point for his later thinking. For some suggestions as to the influence Augustine's involvement with Manicheism may have had on his thinking on the human soul and will, see Drecoll and Kudella, *Augustin und der Manichäismus*, 210–211. As Drecoll and Kudella point out, "the connection between Augustine's conception of God and his conception of the soul cannot be seen as deriving monocausally from Neoplatonism, but has a Manichean prehistory" (210). This same line of thinking may be extended: the presence of Manichean and Neoplatonic influences on certain developments in Augustine's thinking do not entail that they are exclusive provocations for the changes that take place. Furthermore, given the high regard the Manichees had for Paul's teaching, the influence of Manicheism and Paul on Augustine's anthropological thinking may overlap. Drecoll and Kudella observe that "Paul, purified of interpolations, was a decisive basis of argumentation in the disputations of Felix and Fortunatus, especially for anthropology" (52). See also Erich Feldmann, "Der junge Augustinus und Paulus: Ein Beitrag zur (manichäischen) Paulus-Rezeption," in *Atti del terzo Congresso Internazionale i Studi "Manicheismo e Oriente Cristiano Antico,"* Manichaean Studies 3 (Turnhout: Brepols, 1997), 41–76 and Julien Ries, "La Bible chez Saint Augustine et chez les manichéens," *RÉA* 7 (1961): 231–243.

[149] Despite Augustine's own presentation of the matter, not all scholars agree upon this point. While rightly observing that Augustine's innovative thinking on the will cannot be reduced to a product of his interaction with the Manichees or the Pelagians, Harrison does not tend to attribute a significant role in its emergence to his reading of Paul in the 390s (*Rethinking Augustine's Early Theology*, 198). James Wetzel, in contrast, sees the rereading of Paul recorded in *Simpl.* as revolutionizing Augustine's thinking: "What began as an exegetical exercise for the newly installed bishop of Hippo ended in the quiet revolution of his theology." James Wetzel, *Augustine and the Limits of Virtue* (New York: Cambridge University Press, 1992), 154.

aid, *conf.* shows what it is like to possess a will in this helpless condition.[150] Augustine conveys with poignancy the struggle of living with a fallen will. To have a fallen will is to be in bondage to oneself.

After recounting, in books 1 through 7, many twists and turns in the long spiritual journey by which God was gradually leading Augustine to himself, in book 8 of *conf.* Augustine brings his narrative to a climax. He introduces the story he is about to tell as one of liberation: "'You have broken my chains, I will sacrifice to you the sacrifice of praise' (Ps. 115:16–17). I will tell how you broke them" (8.1.1). One of the strongest links in this chain is Augustine's fallen will.

What is the bondage under which Augustine suffers? He characterizes it in different yet complementary ways. Elaborating on Romans 7:22–23 in book 7, Augustine had interpreted Paul's reference to "captivity under the law of sin" as indicating that "we have been justly handed over to the ancient sinner, the president of death, who has persuaded us to conform our will to his will (*quia persuasit uoluntati nostrae similitudinem uoluntatis suae*) which 'did not remain in your truth.'"[151] Just as Augustine will later characterize doing rightly as aligning one's will with God's, he here characterizes the will's plight before redemption as a captivity in which it takes on the likeness of Satan's will.

Yet in book 8 Augustine both attributes his captivity to sin to the devil's "hard grip" on his will and describes his perverse will as a link in a self-made chain that holds him prisoner. For Augustine, describing his bondage as imposed by the devil yet self-imposed is not a contradiction: "I sighed after . . . freedom, but was bound not by an iron imposed by anyone else but by the iron of my own choice (*uoluntate*). The enemy had a grip on my will and so made a chain for me to hold me a prisoner."[152] The chain holding him, Augustine insists, is made by the enemy, yet exists only because of his own will.

How exactly Augustine's will leads to his bondage becomes clearer when he describes this chain in greater detail. It has four links, each of which leads to the next: a perverse will, passion, habit, and necessity: "The consequence of a distorted will is passion. By servitude to passion, habit is formed, and habit to which there is no resistance becomes necessity. By these links, as it were, connected one to another (hence I have used the term 'chain'), a harsh

---

[150] For an analysis of how Augustine's diagnosis of his weakness of will as a problem of two opposed wills compares to Platonist accounts of *akrasia*, see MacDonald, "Augustine and Platonism."

[151] *Conf.* 7.21.27 (CCL 27:111).

[152] *Conf.* 8.5.10 (CCL 27:119).

bondage held me under restraint."[153] The first link in the chain (*catena*) is a perverse will.[154] From this perverse will (*ex uoluntate peruersa*) the subsequent links emerge so that, because of the chain of events set into motion by the misuse of the will, what begins voluntarily leads to necessity. In earlier days Augustine had described the created will as a hinge opening the door to new opportunities and possibilities. Now he characterizes the fallen will, the will under captivity to sin, as a link in the chain (*ansula catenae*) holding him in the lifestyle of sin he longs to cast off.

Augustine does not portray his enslavement to sin as a matter of inadequate knowledge.[155] He writes, "I no longer had my usual excuse to explain why I did not yet despise the world and serve you, namely, that my perception of truth was uncertain (*incerta*). By now I was indeed quite sure (*certa*) about it."[156] Augustine knows the truth. The problem is that he cannot stir himself to act accordingly. To illustrate his predicament he uses the analogy of a tired person who lingers in bed though he knows he should get up.[157] Though he feebly attempts to rouse himself, Augustine cannot resist sleeping just a little longer.

[153] *Conf.* 8.5.10 (CCL 27:119). I have very slightly tweaked Chadwick's translation.

[154] The term *peruersa uoluntas* appears in a few notable instances in *conf.* When commenting in book 2 on his father's (to his mind unhealthy) delight in his maturation into manhood, Augustine describes his father's will as "perverse." "He was drunk with the invisible wine of his perverse will (*peruersae . . . uoluntatis*) directed downwards to inferior things" (2.3.6 [CCL 27:20]). In book 7 he alludes in a rhetorical question to the *peruersa uoluntas* of the devil as what turned him from angel to devil (7.3.5; CCL 27:95) and defines wickedness as a *peruersitas uoluntatis* (7.16.22; CCL 27:106). Augustine's use of the term implies a turning from superior to inferior things.

[155] He describes his predicament as more than a lack of information even before he recounts, in book 7, the vital role of Platonism in removing intellectual stumbling blocks that were standing between him and the Christian faith. Already in book 4, when discussing his grief at the loss of a dear friend, he observes, "I should have lifted myself to you, Lord, to find a cure. I knew that, but did not wish it (*nec uolebam*) or have the strength for it" (4.7.12; CCL 27:46). Intellectually Augustine was convinced he should have asked God for help. Yet he lacked the will and strength to act accordingly. Likewise, at the conclusion of book 7 and the beginning of book 8, Augustine repeatedly makes clear that his hesitation is not an issue of knowledge. See, for example, his statement "'Assuredly all men are vain in whom there is no knowledge of God; not even from the things which appear good can they find him who is' (Wisd. 13:1). But now I was not in vanity of that kind. I had climbed beyond it, and by the witness of all creation I had found you our Creator and your Word who is God beside you and with you is one God, by whom you created all things (John 1:1–3). . . . Now I had discovered the good pearl. To buy it I had to sell all that I had; and I hesitated" (*conf.* 8.1.2). Knowledge of God is not the missing piece, but the gumption to "hold on to the way that leads there" (*conf.* 7.21.27). Though in book 10 Augustine will also observe that a certain knowledge of the happy life is required to will it with certainty (10.21.31), he does not characterize knowledge as guaranteeing a corresponding kind of willing. Knowledge is necessary but not sufficient for right willing.

[156] 8.5.11 (CCL 27:120).

[157] *Conf.* 8.5.12: Augustine observes, "In this kind of way I was sure it was better for me to render myself up to your love than to surrender to my own cupidity. But while the former course was pleasant to think about and had my notional assent, the latter was more pleasant and overcame me."

He describes his predicament quoting Romans 7:22:

> In vain "I delighted in your law in respect of the inward man; but another law in my members fought against the law of my mind and led me captive in the law of sin which was in my members" (Rom. 7:22). The law of sin is the violence of habit by which even the unwilling mind is dragged down and held, as it deserves to be, since by its own choice it slipped into the habit.[158]

Augustine not only knows what the right thing to do is; he even delights in and wills to obey God's law with respect to his mind. The difficulty is that habit dilutes this will to obey with unwillingness such that he is held fast in sin.

Augustine describes this tension between willingness and unwillingness in terms of two distinct wills in himself. On the one hand, he finds himself in possession of a budding new will (*uoluntas nova*) to serve God. But on the other he recognizes his older will, which, strengthened by habit, prevails over the new. The struggle between these two wills prevents him from taking action. In his words, "So my two wills, one old, the other new (*duae uoluntates meae, una uetus, alia noua*), one carnal, the other spiritual, were in conflict with one another, and their discord robbed my soul of all concentration."[159] Augustine interprets these competing wills as an instantiation in his own experience of the Pauline opposition of flesh and spirit in Galatians 5:17.[160]

These two competing wills create a kind of internal duality following from the fact that Augustine cannot disavow either as his own, even as he sees an asymmetry in his allegiance to the two. He writes, "I was in both, but I was more in that which I approved in myself than in that of which I disapproved in myself."[161] Again using Paul as a lens to interpret his experience, Augustine disassociates his self (his *ego*) with the latter, even while making himself the grammatical subject of both: "In the latter case it was 'no more I (*iam non ego*)' (Rom. 7:17), since in large part I was passive and unwilling rather than active and willing (*uolens*)."[162] Why should the older

---

[158] *Conf.* 8.5.12.
[159] *Conf.* 8.5.10 (CCL 27:120).
[160] *Conf.* 8.5.11.
[161] *Conf.* 8.5.11. I have slightly modified Chadwick's translation.
[162] *Conf.* 8.5.11 (CCL 27:120).

kind of willing be considered "no more I" instead of Augustine's *uoluntas nova*? Augustine reasons that his new will is active, whereas his old will is passive, imposed on him from the outside via habit, even though its existence follows from his own previous acts of will.

Having so described his condition of bondage, Augustine is prepared to begin the story of his climactic struggle to break free. It takes place in a garden.

Part of the agony of this struggle is that its resolution seems so simple and entirely within his power. Entering into a covenant with God, Augustine insists, entails only one thing: willing to do so. He observes, "The one necessary condition, which meant not only going but at once arriving there, was to have the will to go (*uelle ire*)."[163] Thus Augustine hesitates to do something that, unlike performing some physical action, is itself accomplished in the act of willing. Reaching a physical destination requires that one traverse the necessary distance in addition to being willing to move. Like other physical acts, it therefore demands bodily power and the cooperation of external factors. In these cases willing on its own is not enough to achieve the desired end; the will must be executed in an additional step. To will to go (*ire*) is not the same as to arrive (*pervenire*). In the case of willing to serve God, however, willing itself accomplishes the goal, without depending on further powers to perform what the will dictates: "At this point the power to act is identical with the will (*uoluntas*). The willing itself was performative of the action."[164]

The irony is that despite his bone-deep longing for God and the simple solution to satisfying it, Augustine finds it easier to wring his hands as he wishes than to move his will. While his body obeys his soul, his soul refuses to obey itself. What explains his paralysis? In 8.9.21 Augustine inquires after the grounds of this predicament.

Augustine does not approach this problem in the abstract, speculating as to causes in the universal workings of the will that might explain its current conflicted condition. Rather, as he looks into the causes of the "monstrosity" (*monstrum*) of his mind's disobedience to itself, Augustine focuses his attention on a particular situation: that of the "sons of Adam" who suffer

---

[163] *Conf.* 8.8.19 (CCL 27:125).
[164] *Conf.* 8.8.20 (CCL 27:126). As the case of the sleeping writer demonstrates, Augustine regards will or intention as not only necessary but sufficient for doing what is right, though it is not sufficient for ensuring that a willed physical action is successfully performed. See *duab. an.* 10.12.

the punishment of Adam's misdeed.[165] It is in an examination of the human race in light of its condition since Adam, not in a consideration of the general attributes of the will, or even in contemplation of the will in its created integrity, that Augustine hopes to find clues helping him to diagnose his current malady.

Focusing his attention in this way, Augustine works back from the phenomenon under investigation to its cause. If the problem at issue is that the mind orders itself to will something but the will does not obey, the mind must will obedience. Otherwise the mind would not command obedience.[166] Yet the fact that the mind does not perform what is commanded indicates that the command is not wholehearted. The command is not wholehearted (ex toto), Augustine reasons, in turn, because the willing is not wholehearted (ex toto).[167] Thus the problem at the root of the mind's disobedience to itself is a will that is not wholehearted: "The will that commands is incomplete (non plena), and therefore what it commands does not happen."[168]

As Augustine had indicated in 8.8.19, though nothing more is required to enter into covenant with God than willing, willing appropriately is easier said than done. Half-hearted willing will not suffice. To his statement that all that is necessary is will, Augustine had added a proviso: all that was necessary was will, but this meant to will in a way that was "strong (fortiter) and unqualified (integre), not the turning and twisting first this way, then that, of a will (uoluntatem) half-wounded, struggling with one part (parte) rising up and the other part (parte) falling down."[169] Willing to commit his life to God was one thing. Willing this wholeheartedly was quite another. Now in 8.9.21 Augustine makes clear that the mind's rebellion against its own commands stems from willing that fails to achieve this kind of integrity.

In fact, not only does the mind's disobedience to itself indicate *that* there is a will that is not wholehearted, but further, the degree of the mind's disobedience corresponds to the degree to which it lacks the will to obey. In Augustine's words, "To the extent that the mind commands, it wills (uult),

---

[165] *Conf.* 8.9.21. Augustine prays, "May your mercy illuminate me as I ask if perhaps an answer can be found in the hidden punishments and secret tribulations that befall the sons of Adam."

[166] Augustine writes in *conf.* 8.9.21, "Mind commands, I say, that it should will, and would not give the command if it did not will."

[167] *Conf.* 8.9.21 (CCL 27:126).

[168] *Conf.* 8.9.21 (CCL 27:126).

[169] *Conf.* 8.8.19 (CCL 27:126).

and to the extent that what it commands is not done, it does not will, because the will (*uoluntas*) commands that there be a will, not another, but
itself."[170] Thus Augustine shows that the mind's rebellion against itself stems
not from an alien influence but from the fact that its own willingness is only
partial. Willingness and unwillingness are never split apart but always determined in relation to each other. Augustine therefore concludes, "There is
no monstrous split between willing and not willing." "There are two wills,"
but not two unrelated wills: "neither of them is complete, and what is present in the one is lacking to the other."[171] More closely considered, then,
the mind's rebellion against itself stems from its entertaining two opposed,
though organically connected, wills.

Augustine soon makes clear why he is so concerned to avoid the idea
of a monstrously split will: he wants to avoid creating the impression that
the two conflicting wills he has described entail two opposing minds, souls,
or natures, which is the view he attributes to the Manichees. Augustine
denounces those "who from the dividing of the will into two in the process
of deliberation, deduce that there are two minds with two distinct natures,
one good, the other bad."[172] Possessing two wills, Augustine insists, need
not entail possessing two minds with two distinct natures, a view he refuted
in the earlier work, *duab. an.*[173]

Augustine turns to his own experience to illustrate the point, stressing
that the fact that he is both willing and unwilling does not entail that he has
two separate selves. Rather, the selfsame Augustine is both willing and unwilling.[174] Though the lack of integrity in his willing creates internal conflict
for him and causes him to be "dissociated with himself" against his will, he
insists that this internal division does not come from an alien mind. Rather,

---

[170] *Conf.* 8.9.21 (CCL 27:126). My translation.

[171] *Conf.* 8.9.21.

[172] *Conf.* 8.10.22.

[173] To point out the absurdity of assuming, as the Manichees do, that having different wills means
having different minds or natures in oneself, Augustine observes in 8.9.23 that it would be possible
to be torn between many different wills, not just two. In this case, would the Manichees continue to
posit an additional substance, mind and nature to correspond to each additional will? The way out of
this conundrum, according to Augustine, is for the Manichees to accept the view that in such cases a
single soul is wavering between different wills (*conf.* 8.10.22). Augustine makes the related point that
two wills do not entail two substances in 8.10.24. Whereas the Manichees claim that "two conflicting
minds are derived from two rival substances," Augustine characterizes his struggle as an internal one
of self against self, not one of two warring and different minds (8.11.27).

[174] *Conf.* 8.10.22: "In my own case, as I deliberated about serving my Lord God (Jer. 30:9) which
I had long been disposed to do, the self which willed to serve was identical with the self which was
unwilling. It was I."

it is from his own mind, namely from the punishment his own mind suffers as a result of Adam's "more freely chosen sin."[175] Appealing to Romans 7, Augustine concludes that though in this sense he is not directly and actively responsible for this internal division ("not I"), but rather his sin ("sin which dwelt in me"), still, insofar as this sin is a punishment *he* suffers, the division it introduces pertains to himself without implying a second self. Thus Augustine again uses the lens of Romans 7 to interpret his experience, this time applying it to explain how his will to disobey God both is, in a certain sense, "not I" yet at the same time is in no way the product of an alien mind but precisely a punishment suffered in his own.[176] Augustine's own impiety and sin divide him from himself.[177]

Conclusion

In this chapter we have traced Augustine's increasingly radical assessment of the impact of the fall on the will through a number of his writings from the period of his priesthood and the beginning of his ministry as bishop. We began with *duab. an.*, which both gives a detailed snapshot of Augustine's

---

[175] *Conf.* 8.10.22.

[176] MacDonald reads Augustine in *conf.* 8.5.11 as "careful to hedge" Paul's claim that the old self is "no longer I" ("Augustine and Platonism," 80). Augustine's way of framing the matter suggests, however, that to the degree that he does qualify Paul's statement, he is attempting to make sense, as far as possible, of the experience of struggle with sin that Paul describes in Romans 7 (as well as his own similar struggle), rather than to present his interpretation as a qualification of Paul's account. Augustine begins the paragraph by describing himself as coming to understand (*intellegere*) what Paul spoke of in Galatians by means of his own experience; more specifically, his experience helps him grasp in what way (*quomodo*) Paul's statement is the case: "In this way I understood through my own experience what I had read, how 'the flesh lusts against the spirit and the spirit against the flesh' (Gal. 5:17)." Augustine then goes on to describe this experience at further length, incorporating Paul's description of his struggle with sin in Romans 7 into his account. Though MacDonald characterizes Augustine as "hedging" Paul's claim that "it is no longer I" who is sinning, Augustine actually uses Paul's "no more I" claim to qualify his own observation that the "I" is in each—the spirit and the flesh. Augustine continues (I am now using my own translation), "I was in each, *but* I was more in that of which I approved, than in that in me of which I disapproved. In the latter case it was, rather, 'no longer I,' since for the most part I suffered it unwillingly rather than doing it willingly." Thus Augustine's "qualification" of Paul's claims in this passage in the *quia* clause just quoted should be seen as an attempt to carry Paul's claim further by explaining its specific application and meaning, rather than restricting or reversing it.

[177] Augustine makes a similar point in 5.10.8, where he contrasts the Manichean view of sin with the catholic view that acknowledges a person's responsibility for sin. Describing his own stance toward the Manichean perspective while he was in Rome, he writes, "I still thought that it is not we who sin, but some alien nature which sins in us. . . . I liked to excuse myself and to accuse some unidentifiable power which was with me and yet not I. But the whole was myself and what divided me against myself was my impiety."

powerful early conception of will as virtually immune to outside influence and shows how even this early conception marked a dramatic departure from the view of will he had cherished as a Manichee. Not only did Augustine's early view of the will as a movement of the soul with nothing forcing it represent a way of thinking about the will alien to Manicheism; it seems that as a Manichee Augustine was not convinced of the existence of the human will at all. Augustine argues that to acknowledge the will is to acknowledge the incoherence of the Manichean system, and thus his attack on the Manichean doctrine of two souls reads like an apology for the existence of human will. In *duab. an.* Augustine uses the concept of will to expose the weaknesses of the Manichean belief system in an effort to win his Manichean friends to the Christian faith.

In *c. Fort.* we observed Augustine complicating the picture of the will found in *duab. an.* As he contends with Fortunatus over how best to interpret Paul, he portrays sin as mitigating the will's natural created powers and attributes to the will a certain kind of constraint: the necessity of habit. Already in *c. Fort.* Augustine differentiates between how the will works in different situations, though here the basic dividing line is the formation of habit in an individual's life. Before sinful behaviors have become ingrained in a person via habit, she enjoys an Adamic freedom. Once formed, however, sinful habits plunge her into necessity so that she shares the fate that was Adam's because of the fall. Though no such habits threatened to impinge on the will before the fall, demarcating the epoch of creation from the tragic period to follow, in effect, each of Adam's descendants realizes the transition from freedom to necessity of will on an individual level. Thus the differentiation Augustine introduces into his conception of will in this work is not only, or even primarily epochal but also highly individualistic, depending most immediately upon how each person chooses to exercise her will.

Augustine portrays free will as constricted by habit in a more universal sense in *lib. arb.* III. Whether the fall's effects become instantiated in the wills of Adam's descendants no longer depends exclusively on their decisions as individuals. Instead Augustine tends to emphasize Adam's will as having a profound effect on the human race as a whole. Due to Adam's sin, Augustine makes clear in this text, the soul needs God's assistance to carry out the good it knows to be its duty.

In book 1 of *Simpl.* Augustine begins with a similar view to that found in *lib. arb.* As a result of the fall, neither knowing what is right nor willing to do it entails the ability to perform the good. Executing good will, not willing rightly, is the problem. When Augustine begins to interpret Romans 9, however, he finds that he must revise this perspective. Ultimately he comes to affirm that good will itself, not only acting on a good will, is a gift of grace. God's calling precedes good will, not the other way around, and though human will is still free subsequent to the fall, this freedom is of little avail for turning to God.

Thus, in the writings discussed in this chapter, Augustine asserts, to a greater and greater degree with each work, that the fall changed the human will, causing it to function according to a new set of rules. The result is a picture of the will very different from the one Augustine had presented in the writings considered in chapter 1, a vision he ultimately restricted to the will in its created integrity, before Adam's sin. In those writings Augustine presented the created will as a powerful hinge, free to turn a person to good or evil. As shown in this chapter, however, Augustine came to believe that human willing subsequent to Adam's first sin demands a different description. Augustine therefore begins to employ different imagery to describe it. Now the will is a link in the chain that holds human beings in bondage to sin. Far from free to turn people to the good, the will keeps them from turning to God unless God intervenes.

Augustine remarks retrospectively that scripture drove him to this conclusion. Yet even had he not explicitly observed it in *Retractationes* and *On the Predestination of the Saints*, the pivotal role of scripture in the emergence of his new perspective on the will would have been unmistakable. In the preface to *Simpl.*, Augustine presents his findings as the result of a careful engagement with scripture on the level of individual words and sentences. Before addressing the second question of book 1, on Romans 9, Augustine again states his intention to attend to Paul, though this time highlighting his effort to seek guidance from Paul's larger argumentative purpose rather than from the verbal building blocks of Paul's argument. Augustine's argumentation comports with these claims. It is Romans 9:16 that raises the question of whether God's assistance is required for our willing, while other passages, such as Philippians 2:12–13, along with Augustine's assessment of Paul's larger purpose in the letter (which he articulates in terms of yet other texts from scripture), prompt Augustine's conclusions. He presents both the questions he tackles in the work and the solutions upon which he ultimately settles as emerging from the biblical text.

As shown in part II of this chapter, *conf.*, a locus of Augustine's reflections on his experience of a fallen will, complements the more theoretical, abstract perspectives found in the texts considered in part I. Here Augustine characterizes his fallen will as a will in bondage, describing this imprisonment—against the Manichees—as a problem of two opposed wills rather than of two warring souls or natures within the human person. In constructing his argument for the unity of his identity despite this division of his two struggling wills, Augustine again draws on Paul, this time on Romans 7. Interpreting his own experience through the lens of Paul's account of his struggles, Augustine articulates how it is possible that his disobedient will is not his *ego*, "not I," in Paul's words, yet still a product of his own disobedience for which he bears responsibility.

In *duab. an.*, Augustine had contended that "nature itself" proclaims the character of the will as a movement of the soul with nothing forcing it.[178] But in the writings of Paul, Augustine found a proclamation, not only of the human will's created potential for self-movement but also of the profundity of its fallen paralysis. Yet Augustine did not see this biblical revelation[179] as undermining his everyday experience, the same experience that had given him confidence in the optimistic assessment of the will's powers he articulated in *duab. an.* Augustine never rejected the validity of his experience of the will. He did, however, re-present it in terms of scriptural teaching.[180] As we have seen, in book 8 of *conf.* Augustine interprets his own experience of a will in bondage through the lens of Paul's experience as depicted in scripture, drawing repeatedly on Romans 7 to make sense of his predicament.

Thus, just as Augustine uses Romans 9 and other biblical texts to interpret the will more "theoretically," he repeatedly uses Romans 7 to interpret his personal experience of a fallen will. Scripture, reason, and experience are not, for Augustine, three independent or mutually exclusive sources for his conception of the fallen will. Rather, as his familiarity with the biblical texts grows, he runs both his reasoning and his experience through an

---

[178] *Duab. an.* 10.14.

[179] As observed, Augustine himself asserts that when writing *Simpl.* he received a revelation from God through Paul's testimony. See n146 of this chapter.

[180] Harrison argues that "the dramatic contrasts are there from the very beginning [from 388] in Augustine's comparison of our original state *before* the Fall and our subjection to original sin *after* the Fall" (*Rethinking Augustine's Early Theology*, 236). While it is true that Augustine retrospectively reframes some of his earlier discussions of will in terms of this pre- and post-fall contrast, he does not usually discuss the will in terms of these contrasts in works before *Simpl.* In this sense, the "dramatic contrasts" are not present "from the very beginning."

increasingly fine-grained sieve of scriptural interpretation. He uses scripture to sift, shape, and inform the worlds of his intellect and memory.

As Augustine immersed himself in the biblical text during his ministry as priest and his earliest years as bishop of Hippo, his conception of will gained refinement. Indeed it was not simply that Augustine pushed deeper in exploring the same basic patterns and features of the will he had observed in the earliest stages of his thinking. His conception of will acquired more than additional depth; it acquired a new dimension. His insight was that in the fallen world of Adam's descendants new patterns and features have come to punctuate the landscape of volition.

Peter Brown's famous chapter, "The Lost Future," portrays Augustine as transforming, in the 390s, from an ideal classical man, a tranquil philosopher ever progressing toward spiritual and intellectual perfection, to a disillusioned pessimist, a restless romantic always longing for a sense of fulfillment just beyond his reach. For Brown, this transformation corresponds to a change in Augustine's approach to Paul. In the past, Augustine had read "Paul as a Platonist," a proponent of stage-wise "spiritual ascent" and this-worldly achievement:

> Now, he will see in Paul nothing but a single, unresolved tension between "flesh" and "spirit." The only changes he could find were changes in awareness of this tension: ignorance of its existence "before the Law"; helpless realization of the extent of the tension between good and evil "under the Law"; a stage of utter dependence on a Liberator "under grace." Only after this life would tension be resolved "When death is swallowed up in victory." It is a flattened landscape: and in it, the hope of spiritual progress comes increasingly to depend, for Augustine, on the unfathomable will of God.[181]

Certainly Augustine's return to Paul in the 390s altered the landscape of his thought. But if this alteration required a flattening of Platonic progress, the cleared ground it left must not be mistaken for the new landscape that took its place. For, as we have seen, in the case of the will, Augustine posits not merely changes in awareness between the epochs of creation and fall whose effects he traces in Paul, but real changes in the capacities of, and limits

---

[181] Brown, *Augustine of Hippo*, 145.

upon, the will. Augustine's new perspective on the landscape of human moral progress may be clouded by pessimism, but what he sees is anything but level. The topography of Augustine's view of the will now has added dimensions: habit, delight, original sin, unmerited election. These new landmarks push up into view like jagged cliffs of a mountain range running between one territory and another.

The tectonic collision of Augustine's earlier conception of will with the teaching he found in Paul while writing *Simpl.* gave rise to these prominences. It resulted neither in the outright rejection of his earlier views of will nor in continued efforts to read Paul in line with them. Still less was its effect a new one-dimensional concept of will representing an amalgam of Augustine's earlier conception and the description of fallen human willing he found in Paul. Rather the result was a new differentiated perspective, defined by a fundamental division separating the will's functioning before and after the fall, but embracing both arenas of the will's operation in a single overarching perspective: the biblical story of God's will for humankind. How, in this story God, in Christ, through the power of the Holy Spirit, changes the landscape of human willing yet again is the subject of the next chapter, which assesses Augustine's conception of the will under grace.

3

What Is in Our Power

Introduction

Amid the sunny baths, cool nights, and heady philosophical discussions of Cassiciacum, Augustine had found the courage to claim for himself the simplest and most audacious of intellectual ambitions. He wished to know, he protested, but two things and nothing more: God and the soul.[1] Over thirty years later, in Hippo, immersed in the realities of pastoral ministry and embroiled in controversy, Augustine finds these objects of inquiry as pressing and elusive as ever. Hard decades of ministry have only further convinced him of the unreliability of superficial appearances. To achieve authentic knowledge of another, he is persuaded, one must look beyond what first meets the eye. One must tap into the invisible core of one's identity. One must seek the "soul" that Augustine has been striving to understand, and with it, he now specifies, the will. He asks, "Are we ever correct in saying that we have known someone, unless we were able to know the person's soul and will (*uoluntatem*)?" Augustine insists that knowledge of a person's soul, in addition to being necessary to know someone truly, also proves more reliable than knowledge based on external appearances: "Thus we know ourselves more certainly than others, because we know our own conscience and will (*uoluntas*). . . . And so it is clear where one finds the better and truer knowledge of a person."[2] Knowledge of soul and will is both superior to and more accurate than knowledge derived from other quarters.

Not only the exigency but also the difficulty of seeking such knowledge has impressed itself more deeply upon Augustine in the years that have intervened since his preconversion philosophical retreat. He goes so far as

---

[1] *Sol.* 1.3.7 (CSEL 89:11).
[2] *An. et or.* 4.19.30 (CSEL 60:409–410). This and subsequent English translations come, unless otherwise noted, from Augustine, "The Nature and Origin of the Soul," in *Answer to the Pelagians, I*, trans. Roland Teske, WSA I/23 (Hyde Park, NY: New City Press, 1997).

Augustine on the Will. Han-luen Kantzer Komline, Oxford University Press (2020). © Oxford University Press.
DOI: 10.1093/oso/9780190948801.001.0001

to say that grasping the nature of our own souls is more challenging than knowing what God has revealed of God's own identity. "It is more difficult," he argues, "to know some of God's works," including the human soul, "than to know God himself, insofar as he can be known."[3] Our inside perspective on our own persons does not make self-knowledge automatic. In fact, "it is we ourselves who are unable to comprehend ourselves. We ourselves are too high and too mighty and surpass the small measure of our knowledge. We ourselves cannot grasp ourselves, and we are certainly not outside ourselves."[4] The ironic fact of the matter is that self-knowledge, and specifically knowledge of our own soul, is, in some ways, actually more, rather than less, difficult to attain than other types of knowledge.

One example Augustine provides of how we elude our own intellectual grasp is the mystery of our own memory, intelligence, and will: "While we exist, while we are alive, while we know that we are alive, while we are certain that we remember, understand, and will (*uelle*), we boast of having a great knowledge of our nature, but we do not at all know what our memory or intelligence or will (*uoluntas*) is capable of."[5] Despite our existential certainty of the fact that our own willing occurs, in other words, we are hard-pressed to describe what this willing entails. Later Augustine describes our ignorance about our powers of will in closer detail. He asks, "What shall I say about the will (*uoluntas*) where we certainly claim to have free choice?" Then, turning to Peter's threefold denial of Jesus, he observes that the apostle "wanted to lay down his life for the Lord; he clearly willed to do so. He was not trying to deceive the Lord in promising this; rather, he did not know the extent of the power of his will (*uoluntas*). Hence, a man as great as he, who recognized that Jesus was the Son of God, did not know himself." From this example, Augustine concludes, "We know, then, that we will (*uelle*) or do not will something; yet, if we are not mistaken, my dear son, we do not know, even when our will is good (*uoluntas nostra . . . bona est*), what it is capable of, the extent of its powers, what temptations it will give in to or not give in to."[6] It is easy enough to realize that we will something. But the mere recognition that our will is operative in some way is not the same as accurately appraising its powers and limits. Even when we will the right thing, as

---

[3] *An. et or.* 4.5.6 (CSEL 60:385).
[4] *An. et or.* 4.6.8 (CSEL 60:388).
[5] *An. et or.* 4.7.9 (CSEL 60:389).
[6] *An. et or.* 4.7.11 (CSEL 60:390).

Augustine emphasizes with the example of Peter, our will can twist itself out of the hold of our plans and predictions. There is no telling when it will prove strong enough to sustain itself and when it will dissolve in the face of temptation. "Even when our will is good," its workings remain a mystery.

In this quotation we gain a glimpse of a third kind of will that surfaces in our study of Augustine's theology. Chapter 1 focused on the created will, human willing in its original integrity, designed by God to choose freely between good and ill, swinging facilely from one direction to another as easily as a hinge (*cardo*). Chapter 2 examined the fallen will, a devastating link in the chain (*ansula catenae*) of human bondage to sin, whose functioning differed radically from its powerful and free, originally created counterpart. In this chapter we turn to the good will (*uoluntas bona*), redeemed from its fallen condition by God's grace.

Augustine likely penned the comments we find in *On the Soul and Its Origin (De anima et eius origine)* on the importance and elusiveness of knowledge of the will sometime in 421.[7] The difficulty of knowing the capabilities of the "good will" that he here describes is something he had personally experienced, not only in his own struggles with sin as a Christian, so memorably recorded in *Confessions* book 10, but also in his efforts over the previous decade, from 411 to 421, to come to grips intellectually with the capacities of the good will in the crucible of controversy with Pelagius. By the time he writes book 4 of *an. et or.*, Augustine's conception of the nature and powers of the good will redeemed by Christ has undergone considerable transformation. In this work we see Augustine emphasizing the provisionality of human assessments of the good will in a way that both recalls the changes in his own perspective over the previous decade and foreshadows further developments in the next. The will is a mystery; though Augustine has begun to disentangle a new strand, he has not unraveled it yet. How his conception of the good will evolved in the context of the Pelagian controversy is the subject of this chapter.[8]

---

[7] Roland Teske concludes that while the first book of *an. et or.* was probably composed in late 419 or early 420, the third and fourth books were probably written in 421. See WSA I/23, 452.

[8] In moving to the Pelagian controversy, we have bypassed direct treatment of the Donatist controversy. On how Augustine was engaging the Donatists at the time he wrote *Simpl.*, however, see J. Patout Burns, *The Development of Augustine's Doctrine of Operative Grace* (Paris: Études Augustiniennes, 1980), 31n109. A number of scholars have emphasized the importance of the Donatist controversy for Augustine's thinking about grace and its effects on the human person. For Burns's summary of its multifaceted impact, see 186–188. Kurt Flasch inverts a key claim of Burns by arguing that Augustine's doctrine of grace reinforces his advocacy of coercion in the Donatist controversy, and more generally. See Kurt Flasch, *Logik des Schreckens: Augustinus von Hippo, De*

The development, during the Pelagian controversy, of two key features of Augustine's thinking on the will deserves consideration. Chapter 4 addresses Augustine's developing approach to the question of how God impacts the will. The current chapter centers on his estimation of what is within the power of the human will. Augustine's changing appraisal of what lies within the scope of the will lends itself to consideration from two angles. First, to what extent is the will responsible for willing to do what is right? Second, how far do the good will's powers to secure the good actions it targets extend, given that it has been oriented toward the good? These two questions are addressed in parts I and II, respectively, of this chapter.

Augustine had already disentangled these two strands of the powers of will in *Simpl.* as he sought to sort out how grace was woven into each. Commenting in that work upon Romans 7:21, for example, he had observed, "There is nothing easier for a man under the law than to will to do good and yet to do evil. He has no difficulty in willing, but it is not so easy to do what he wills."[9] Later in this work he describes this distinction as obtaining between "two different things that God gives us, the power to will (*ut uelimus*) and the things that we actually will (*quod uoluerimus*)."[10] These two distinct powers, the power to will what is right and the power to put this will into action, continue to structure Augustine's thinking in the

diversis quaestionibus ad Simplicianum I 2 (Mainz: Dieterich'sche Verlagsbuchhandlung, 1990), 116–119. Lenka Karfíková combines aspects of these two perspectives in her argument that Augustine's advocacy of coercion in the Donatist controversy was both influenced by and served to influence his larger understanding of the relationship between grace and the will. See Lenka Karfíková, *Grace and the Will According to Augustine* (Boston: Brill, 2012), 3. For her broader treatment of Augustine's anti-Donatist works, see 133–155. As these scholars have helped to show, aspects of Augustine's thinking in the Donatist controversy resonate with developments in his thinking about the will treated in this chapter, and likely even solidify the groundwork for these developments. Yet it is also easy to overplay the importance of the Donatist controversy post-*Simpl.* and pre–Pelagian controversy for Augustine's thinking on the will. Since the baseline features of Augustine's "anti-Pelagian" perspective on the relationship between grace and the will were already established in his reading of Paul in *Simpl.*, the subsequent period before the outbreak of the Pelagian controversy does not require treatment to demonstrate the overarching trajectory of his thought on this topic. Furthermore, as Sarah Catherine Byers has observed, while absorbed in the Donatist controversy and his pastoral duties from 400 to 411 Augustine does not devote much direct attention to the doctrine of grace and its impact on human motivation. See Sarah Catherine Byers, *Perception, Sensibility, and Moral Motivation in Augustine: A Stoic-Platonic Synthesis* (New York: Cambridge University Press, 2013), 200. Thus, for both qualitative and quantitative reasons, this chapter moves directly to Augustine's explicit claims about the will as redeemed by God as they come to pointed and plentiful expression during the Pelagian controversy.

[9] *Simpl.* 1.1.12 (CCL 44:16).
[10] *Simpl.* 1.2.10 (CCL 44:35).

Pelagian controversy.[11] In *Simpl.*, Augustine had struggled at length with the issue of the degree to which willing rightly is within a person's power. At first, he contended that "actual willing is certainly within our power."[12] He then claimed that "the power to will" (*ut uelimus*) is "both [God's] and ours, his because he calls us, ours because we follow when called."[13] Finally, he concluded that "the good will itself is wrought in us by the working of God"[14] such that refusing to follow when called lies beyond the power of the human will.[15]

Augustine's approach to the issue during the Pelagian controversy mirrors and, to some extent, reprises this earlier struggle.[16] His thinking in this period develops in three major stages. From 411 to 417 he portrays belief as coming from the human will and refers to faith and belief as "in our power."[17] In this period he presents rejecting God's gracious calling as a real possibility. Beginning in late 417, his emphasis shifts. Now he speaks of the will doing "hardly anything." While he never denies the role of the

---

[11] These two lenses for bringing Augustine's assessment of the will's capacities into focus correspond to his description of the twofold effect that sin has upon the will in *Marriage and Desire* (2.7.18). There he points out that sin's effect upon the will goes beyond causing it to be oriented toward disobedience rather than to what is good. This is merely the most obvious manifestation of sin's harmful effects upon our willing, not the only such manifestation. The entry of sin into the world also means that the will cannot command obedience from the parts of soul and body that ought to be subordinate to it. This second consequence of sin for the will is a microcosm of the first; its disobedience to God brings upon it the disobedience of its own erstwhile subordinates. Augustine's increasing awareness of the profundity of the effects of sin upon the will in these two respects and his decreasing estimate of the capacities of human willing in this life are two sides of the same coin. The greater sin's tendency to dispose human beings to disobey God, the less the will's wherewithal to overcome this disposition and convert itself to the good. The more violent an insurrection the human will faces as it strives to obey God, the more limited its progress in realizing the good actions at which it aims. The following analysis considers the second side of the coin but also has implications for the first.

[12] *Simpl.* 1.1.11 (CCL 44:15): *certe enim ipsum uelle in potestate est.*

[13] *Simpl.* 1.2.10 (CCL 44:35).

[14] *Simpl.* 1.2.12 (CCL 44:36).

[15] If it were possible that someone could resist God's call, if someone could have it "in the power of his will not to obey, it could be said correctly that it is not of God who hath mercy, but of the man who willeth and runneth, for the mercy of him that calleth is not sufficient unless the obedience of him who is called follows" (*Simpl.* 1.2.13 [CCL 44:37]).

[16] Byers makes the structurally analogous claim that the development of Augustine's thinking on grace between 411 and 421 parallels changes it had undergone from 394 to 400 (*Perception, Sensibility, and Moral Motivation in Augustine*, 208–212). My contention is that, with respect to Augustine's estimation of the extent to which willing rightly is within human power, there is a parallel between successive statements that surface within a single work, *Simpl.*, and the trajectory of Augustine's thinking on this issue over the entire course of the Pelagian controversy (411–430). Thus despite the overall structural similarity of my suggestion to that of Byers, the material referents are distinct.

[17] Eugene TeSelle notes that *credere* and *fides* are "generally equivalent in Augustine's usage." See Eugene TeSelle, "Faith," in *AA* (Grand Rapids, MI: Eerdmans, 1999), 347–350, and *spir. et litt.* 31.54 (CSEL 60:211) for an example of equivalent usage. I list them here as separate terms to indicate that Augustine uses both.

will in conversion to the good, he insists that we are the children of God because grace "acts upon our wills." In this period Augustine begins to emphasize that the Spirit, rather than "the powers of their own will," "drives" the wills of God's children. He characterizes God's teaching, call, election, and will as efficacious. In the case of infants, he declares in 421, resisting God's will is impossible. But it is not yet clear whether infants, who lack will altogether, represent an exception or a rule. In 426 and the remaining years before Augustine's death, this ambiguity is addressed. He portrays conversion as happening by "the grace of God alone," such that "we do nothing good in our willing," and he states unequivocally that "no choice of human beings" resists when God wills to save. Through these convolutions and clarifications, occasioned by controversy and tested and proven in his own exegetical laboratory, Augustine gradually and painstakingly ekes out the insights at which he had arrived by the conclusion of *Simpl.* Like a scientist who, in a brief flash of intuitive insight, hits upon a groundbreaking hypothesis that can be proven only over a period of years through extensive experimentation, Augustine spends the rest of his life after he writes *Simpl.* questioning, exploring, deepening, and defending a line of thinking he had already expressed *in nuce* in that work.[18]

As we will see, the stages of development in Augustine's thinking during the Pelagian controversy on the topics treated in chapters 3 and 4 correspond. These three stages, in turn, correspond loosely to the major periods into which the Pelagian controversy may be divided according to Augustine's primary dialogue partners in each. In a first phase, from around 411 to 418, Augustine concentrates his energies on the first-generation "Pelagianism" of Rufinus, Pelagius, and Caelestius. After the teaching of the latter two figures is condemned in the Council of Carthage and by Pope Zosimus in 418, a second phase begins in which Augustine's primary interlocutor is Julian of Eclanum, the new champion of the "Pelagian" camp. Last, in 426, Augustine begins to engage the monks of Hadrumetum and Gaul, embarking on a

---

[18] Pierre-Marie Hombert concurs that the key elements of Augustine's mature teaching on grace are already expressed in *Simpl.* In his view, "the doctrine of predestination is exactly the same in *Simpl.* as it is in his latest writings." At the same time, he is reluctant to describe developments that occur in Augustine's doctrine of grace after *Simpl.* as "substantial changes." See Pierre-Marie Hombert, *Gloria gratiae: Se glorifier en Dieu, principe et fin de la théologie augustinienne de la grâce* (Paris: Institut d'Études Augustiniennes, 1996), 371. The thesis that Augustine rediscovers the key ideas of *Simpl.* progressively during the Pelagian controversy helps to explain how his theology of will continues to change substantively in this period, even while leading him to an endpoint that is already expressed in *Simpl.*

final phase of his interaction with "Pelagian" teaching, even as he continues to engage Julian.

Together chapters 3 and 4 yield a tripartite schema for summarizing the major phases of the development of Augustine's notion of the good will in the Pelagian controversy. In a first phase, from around 411 to around 417, Augustine strongly emphasizes that willing rightly is within human power. While he does affirm that God offers twofold help for human willing in this period, he tends to characterize God's assistance as more indirect than he will later: God's assistance comes in the form of knowledge of the good and rendering the revealed good attractive. In the second phase, from around 417 to 426, Augustine begins to shift his emphasis from the human being to God as the primary agent of good human willing. In a final phase, from 426 to the end of his life, Augustine fixes his gaze even more unflinchingly on the divine impact on the human will, portraying it as independent of human agency, insofar as it intrinsically guarantees the accord of the human will.[19] Already before the Pelagian controversy, we saw Augustine situate the created will and the fallen will in relationship to God. During the Pelagian controversy, Augustine develops an understanding of the good will, too, as inextricably bound to its creator; as the controversy goes on, this relationship grows tighter and tighter.

What led to these developments in Augustine's way of talking about the powers of and divine impact upon the human will? Undoubtedly, controversy with various Christian theologians associated with Pelagius provided occasions for him to clarify views whose seeds could already be found in *Simpl.*[20] But thanks to his engagement with Paul, Augustine had already

[19] As with the question of the magnitude of the change that occurred in *Simpl.*, a wide spectrum of interpretations have been proposed with respect to the question of the degree to which Augustine's doctrine of grace develops during the Pelagian controversy. The end of the spectrum emphasizing continuity may be represented by Hombert, who, as noted, sees no "substantial changes" in Augustine's theology of grace during the Pelagian controversy. Burns's monograph on Augustine's doctrine of grace, in contrast, proposes a number of significant developments in Augustine's thinking during this period, with 418 and 426 representing the major turning points. Byers falls between these two more extreme viewpoints in positing that, while significant changes do occur during the Pelagian controversy, these in essence repeat developments that had occurred earlier, in the 390s. I concur with her overarching structural point, while agreeing with Hombert on the singular yet unitive importance of *Simpl.*, which anticipates even his very latest views from 426 to 430. See Hombert, *Gloria gratiae*, 271; Burns, *The Development of Augustine's Doctrine of Operative Grace*, 186–187; and Byers, *Perception, Sensibility, and Moral Motivation in Augustine*, 206–212.

[20] Phillip Cary's observation that the "basic lineaments" of Augustine's doctrine of grace had already been "brought to light" in *Simpl.*, though the Pelagian controversy clarified the implications of this doctrine for both Augustine and others, applies as well to his views on the will. See Phillip Cary, *Inner Grace: Augustine in the Traditions of Plato and Paul* (New York: Oxford University Press, 2008), 70.

established the rudiments of his mature view of grace and the good will before ever he heard of Pelagius. As before the outbreak of the Pelagian controversy, so also during this period Augustine's conception of will took shape as he developed it from distinctively Christian presuppositions. During the Pelagian controversy, Augustine developed his view of the good will in dialogue elicited by Pelagius, Caelestius, and Julian, but its content was also derived from the Christian scriptures, Christian practices of worship, and Christian understandings of the identity of Jesus Christ. We will explore further how this was the case in chapters 5 and 6, which examine the images and characteristics Augustine came to ascribe to the good will during the Pelagian controversy (chapter 5) and the Christological basis for Augustine's view of the good will in the Pelagian controversy (chapter 6).

Pelagius: A Zealot for the Human Will

It was not until around 415, shortly before he wrote *Nature and Grace*, that Augustine finally laid hands on a text written by the zealous British monk after whom the controversy would be named that was to absorb Augustine from around 411 until the end of his life. Well before this point, however, Augustine had heard of Pelagius and begun responding to positions associated with Pelagius's teaching that had been advanced by Pelagius's colleague and disciple Caelestius and by Rufinus the Syrian, who may have been the actual "founder" of the diverse movement best known today as Pelagianism.[21] We first find Augustine writing against a version of Pelagianism in 411 or 412, when he pens *De peccatorum meritis et remissione et de baptismo paruulorum*. Though Caelestius had been condemned at the Council of Carthage in 411 or 412, he had cited Rufinus in support of his teaching, which continued to enjoy a following in Carthage even after Caelestius's departure, leading the tribune Marcellinus to appeal to Augustine for assistance. In response, Augustine wrote *pecc. mer.*, a work that at once responded to Marcellinus's specific questions and implicitly refuted Rufinus's *Liber de fide*.[22] Augustine continued to write

---

[21] Gerald Bonner argues for this view in "Rufinus the Syrian and African Pelagianism," *Augustinian Studies* 1 (1970): 31–47, concluding that "Rufinus of Syria may . . . be given a place, not merely as a founder of Pelagianism but as the Pelagian theologian who first attracted Augustine's attention" (47).

[22] F. Refoulé has shown that "far from being a response to Augustine," Rufinus's work "preceded *De peccatorum meritis* and even constituted one of the sources of this work." See F. Refoulé, "Datation du premier concile de Carthage contre les Pélagiens et du *Libellus fidei* de Rufin," *RÉAP* 9 (1963): 49.

against Caelestius and Pelagius in the years that followed, meeting their vigorous lobbying for their teachings with equally vigorous counterattacks and defenses of his own position. Though Caelestius did manage to convince Pope Zosimus to overturn condemnations that had been pronounced at Diospolis in 415 and Carthage and Milevis in 416, new condemnations of Caelestius and Pelagius by the emperor Honorius and a council of African bishops at Carthage in the spring of 418, which Pope Zosimus then endorsed in his letter *Tractoria*, brought the first stage of the Pelagian controversy to a close.

When Augustine finally received a copy of Pelagius's *Nature*, he found it impossible to postpone reading it. Sent to him by former disciples of Pelagius who likely had received the text as an esoteric teaching for insiders only but were now two-timing Pelagius by submitting it to Augustine for correction, it possessed the added allure of the illicit.[23] Augustine dropped everything to find out what it said. "My dear sons, Timasius and James," he wrote to his informants, "I left aside for the moment other work in progress, and I rapidly, but with considerable attention, read through the book you sent me."[24] In its pages Augustine discovered a man whose religious fervor rivaled his own:[25] "I found in it a man aflame with ardent zeal against those people who ought to lay the blame for their sins upon the human will, but try to excuse themselves by laying the blame on human nature instead."[26] Pelagius's passion was to balance the scales of responsibility for sin. From his perspective, the will was benefiting from a mistake in its favor while nature served as scapegoat. Determined to put this scandal to rights, to vindicate nature and bring the human will to justice, here was a fellow theologian whose obsession with the will rivaled Augustine's.

---

[23] Reflecting on an act of theft he committed as a teenager, Augustine asks in *conf.*, "Was it possible to take pleasure in what was illicit for no reason other than that it was not allowed?" (*Potuitne libere quod non licebat, non ob aliud, nisi quia non licebat?*) See *conf.* 2.6.14 (CCL 27:24). In *Simpl.* 1.1.7, Augustine states that sin is "all the more pleasant the less it is lawful" (*cum tanto magis libet, quanto minus licet*). He would no doubt regard the intended restriction of access to Pelagius's text as an instance of wrongful prohibition, but this would not necessarily detract from its peculiar draw.

[24] *Nat. et gr.* 1.1 (CSEL 60:233). Unless otherwise noted, this and subsequent translations come from Augustine, "Nature and Grace," in *Answer to the Pelagians, I*, trans. Roland Teske, WSA I/23 (Hyde Park, NY: New City Press, 1997).

[25] See Brinley Roderick Rees, *Pelagius: Life and Letters* (Rochester, NY: Boydell Press, 1998).

[26] *Nat et gr.* 1.1 (CSEL 60:233).

But while Pelagius crusaded to restore confidence in the human will's capacity for good, Augustine feared that such confidence would delude people into thinking they could attain righteousness without Christ. Speaking of those who died "in regions where they could not hear the name of Christ," he asked, "Could they become righteous by nature and free choice or could they not? If these people say that they could, then you see what it means to do away with the cross of Christ; it is to maintain that without the cross of Christ a person can become righteous by the natural law and the choice of the will (*uoluntatis arbitrium*)."[27] Pelagius's concern was that attributing too much to nature would compromise will; Augustine's was that attributing too much to either of these would compromise Christ. Rather than seeing the attainment of righteousness by free choice of the will as an independently coherent possibility, whether preceding or following Christ's redeeming work, Augustine saw righteous willing as enabled by and inseparable from Christ's cross. Augustine was ready to modify, and even to constrict, his estimation of the human will's capacities in light of Christ's person and work. His radical claim was that no good will, no choice of the will that leads to righteousness, exists apart from Christ. We will now turn to the long polemical path that wended its way toward this view, whose Christological basis we will examine thoroughly in chapter 5.

Looking back in *Retractationes* (*retr.*) on his younger self, Augustine points out his assumption in the first book of *Simpl.* that Romans 7 described Paul's struggles with sin while still under the law (*sub lege*). Not until much later (*longe enim postea*), he tells his readers, did he come to see this passage as describing the conflict between flesh and spirit that characterizes the Christian's life under grace.[28] The idea that even Christians who possess the good will granted to the faithful in this life continue to struggle with sin, then, was not always self-evident to Augustine. Rather, he became persuaded of this aspect of the good will's radical need of grace gradually. How, when, and why did Augustine change his mind about the extent to which the good will requires the help of grace?

---

[27] *Nat. et gr.* 9.10 (CSEL 60:238–239).
[28] *Retr.* 2.1.1 (CCL 57:89).

Part I: Achieving a Good Will

Around fifteen years after responding to Simplician's questions, Augustine found himself, as he had often in the intervening years of busy ministry as bishop, again responding to a set of inquiries. This time, in late 411 or early 412, a tribune by the name of Marcellinus had written to Augustine from Carthage to seek help in responding to a set of propositions associated with Pelagius and his disciple Caelestius. Both men had passed through the city, and Caelestius had remained for some time, until his condemnation at the Council of Carthage sometime between September 411 and January 412.[29] Caelestius's teachings continued to cause trouble, however, prompting Marcellinus to request Augustine's assistance. In response, Augustine wrote *De peccatorum meritis et remissione et de baptismo paruulorum ad Marcellinum* (*pecc. mer.*), a work in three books, the first dealing with the question of why infants would need to be baptized if not to wash away the stain of original sin (answer: they would not), the second discussing the possibility of avoiding sin in this life, and the third treating Pelagius's arguments concerning Romans 5. Though Augustine had already spoken out against the teachings of Pelagius and his followers,[30] this letter marked the first occasion on which he opposed the "Pelagian heresy" in writing. Augustine could not have foreseen how much time and energy this written altercation would cost him.[31] Such battles of the pen would consume his attention until his life's end, which would interrupt him in the midst of a tome against Pelagius's heir, Julian of Eclanum. With *pecc. mer.* Augustine entered a war of words he would never leave.

Augustine's estimation of the degree to which willing what is right is within the power of the human will evinces one significant change during the Pelagian controversy—whether human beings have the wherewithal to refuse to will what is right given the offer of grace—but this change appears against a background of overarching continuity. From *pecc. mer.* to *c. Iul. imp.*, Augustine remains persuaded that not only putting good willing into

---

[29] On the dating of the Council of Carthage, see Refoulé, "Datation du premier concile de Carthage contre les Pélagiens et du *Libellus fidei* de Rufin."

[30] Augustine tells us in *retr.* 2.33.60, "Earlier we were opposing [the new Pelagian heresy], when there was need, not in writing, but by sermons and conferences, as each of us was able and ought to have."

[31] At this point, Augustine was still hoping for a meeting of minds. He writes in *retr.* that he omitted names for the most part, and spoke well of Pelagius in the text, "in the hope that they could be more easily corrected" (*retr.* 2.33.60).

action but also righteous willing itself is possible only because of God's gracious help. Though one might expect Augustine to adopt a more absolute stance on this question only in the later stages of the controversy, he in fact already maintains in *pecc. mer.* (411–412), written at the very outset of his struggle with Pelagianism, that all that is good in our willing comes from God, that the only source of a good will is God, and that turning to God is possible only with God's help. Augustine is remarkably consistent in declaring independent human willing of the good completely out of the question.[32] Achieving a good will in this sense is decisively beyond human power.

Early in book 2 of *pecc. mer.*, Augustine makes the point that God does even more than help those who turn to him. He turns people to him as well: "God, then, helps those who turn to him, but abandons those who turn away. But he also helps us turn to him."[33] Also in this work, Augustine explains why this help is necessary. In answer to the question of why some people do not will to be without sin, he writes, "Human beings do not will (*nolunt*) to do what is right, either because they do not know whether it is right or because they find no delight in it (*non delectat*)." In short, "Ignorance (*ignorantia*) and weakness (*infirmitas*) . . . are defects which hinder the will (*uoluntatem*) from being moved to do a good deed or to refrain from an evil deed. But it is due to God's grace helping the human will that we come to know what is hidden and find pleasing what was not attractive."[34] Two

---

[32] Augustine, however, did not always hold the view that all good willing comes from God. His interpretation of Romans 7 in *Simpl.* as applying to the human being *sub lege* (*Simpl.* 1.1.1) seems to imply, given Romans 7:18, that the human person under the law can and does will the good. Indeed Augustine writes early in *Simpl.*, "What is easier for the person set under the law than to will what is good and to do what is bad?" (*Simpl.* 1.1.12; my translation). (*Quid enim facilius homini sub lege constituto quam uelle bonum et facere malum?*; CCL 44:16). According to A. F. W. Lekkerkerker, furthermore, *diu. qu.* 66.5 shows a similar pattern. By attributing Romans 7 to a person under the law, Augustine seems to suggest that good willing is possible for a person before grace. See A. F. W. Lekkerkerker, *Römer 7 und Römer 9 bei Augustin* (Amsterdam: H. J. Paris, 1942), 33. Thus Lekkerkerker observes that for Augustine in these works, the person *sub lege* is free to will the good, though not to do it (25). He also points out, however, that Augustine's reading of Romans 7 at this point is incoherent. For example, Augustine says that a person before grace lacks an *interior delectatio*. How then, can Romans 7:22 describe the person *sub lege*? Such tensions were not lost on Augustine and eventually, Lekkerkerker argues, led Augustine to change in his interpretation of the passage (34). By the time of the Pelagian controversy, indeed, already after *Simpl.* and *diu. qu.*, statements attributing good willing to the person *sub lege* are difficult to find.

[33] *Pecc. mer.* 2.5.5 (CSEL 60:75). English translations of the work come from Augustine, "The Punishment and Forgiveness of Sins and the Baptism of Little Ones," in *Answer to the Pelagians, I*, trans. Roland Teske, WSA I/23 (Hyde Park, NY: New City Press, 1997), unless otherwise noted.

[34] *Pecc. mer.* 2.17.26 (CSEL 60:98–99).

things, then, are required to achieve right willing: knowledge of the good and delight in the good. But ignorance and weakness prevent the human will from attaining the knowledge and delight necessary to will what is right. It is God's grace, Augustine claims, revealing and rendering the good attractive, that meets the conditions necessary for human beings to will to be without sin.[35] Again further on in *pecc. mer.*, Augustine confirms that "we have a good will from God" (*bonam uoluntatem habeamus ex deo*) and that this is the gift we receive when God makes us righteous, a point he finds confirmed repeatedly in scripture.[36]

Thus far we have seen that Augustine, in *pecc. mer.*, argues that God helps human beings to turn to him and will the good, attributing good human willing to God. In other places in the work Augustine makes the further point that, in helping in this way, God does something of which human beings on their own are incapable. It is not merely the case that God occasionally assists the human will to do the good, while in other cases the will achieves this good independently. Augustine's claims are more totalizing, ruling out absolutely the possibility that human beings can attain a good will on their own.

Pointing to Christ as paradigm, Augustine rules out the possibility that the will might bring any preceding merits with it that elicit God's grace. Here we see the beginnings of a consistent pattern in the Pelagian controversy: Augustine reasons to conclusions about the human will per se on the basis of Christology. Even in the case of Christ, Augustine contends,

---

[35] Similarly in *spir. et litt.* 3.5 (CSEL 60: 157), written 412–413, Augustine refers to God's assistance to do what is right as twofold. He also discusses the way in which God produces belief in a person, through both internal and external means: "We, on the other hand, say that the human will (*humanam uoluntatem*) is helped to achieve righteousness in this way: Besides the fact that human beings are created with free choice of the will (*libero arbitrio*) and besides the teaching by which they are commanded how they ought to live, they receive the Holy Spirit so that there arises in their minds a delight (*delectatio*) in and a love (*dilectio*) for that highest and immutable good that is God, even now while they walk by faith, not yet by vision. By this [love] given to them like the pledge of a gratuitous gift, they are set afire with the desire to cling to the creator and burn to come to participation in that true light, so that they have their well-being from him from whom they have their being." Unless otherwise indicated, English translations of *spir. et litt.* come from Augustine, "The Spirit and the Letter," in *Answer to the Pelagians, I*, trans. Roland Teske, WSA I/23 (Hyde Park, NY: New City Press, 1997).

[36] *Pecc. mer.* 2.18.30 (CSEL 60:101–102): "If, then, the will is either good or bad and if we certainly do not have a bad will from God, it remains that we have a good will from God. Otherwise, I do not know what other gift of his we ought to rejoice in, when we are made righteous by him. And for this reason, I believe, scripture says, *The will is prepared by the Lord* (Prv 8:35), and in the Psalms it says, *The Lord will guide a man's steps, and he will prosper his way* (Ps 37:23). The apostle also says, *It is God, after all, who produces in you the willing and the action in accord with good will* (Phil 2:13)."

the goodness and merits of human willing followed, rather than preceded, God's grace: "After all, he who was in that way united to the Word of God did not bring it about by any preceding merits of his will (*praecedentibus suae uoluntatis meritis*) that the one Son of God also became the one Son of Man as a result of that union." By how much more, he intimates, is it the case for the rest of the human race that good human willing cannot be achieved independently of grace but comes about only as a result of grace.[37] Later, in *c. ep. Pel.* (421), Augustine will apply this point directly to the human will, stressing that a just will (*uoluntas iusta*) is possible only through grace without any preceding merits.[38] Even in *pecc. mer.*, however, Augustine makes clear that in our case, it is quite impossible to find anything good in our will that is "of us" (*nobis*) and not "from God" (*ex deo*). It is insufficient to say that some of our good willing is from God while, in other cases, good willing is within our power to achieve on our own. We would like this to be the case, but this does not make it true. Try as we might, we cannot identify anything good in our willing that we accomplish independently. Augustine writes, "We human beings strive to find in our will some good that is ours and that we do not have from God, but I do not know how one can find such a good."[39]

---

[37] *Pecc. mer.* 2.17.27 (CSEL 60: 99–100): "The cause of all human failings is, after all, pride (*superbia*). It was to overcome and destroy this pride, that such a remedy came down from heaven; to human beings puffed up with pride, God came humbly out of mercy, revealing his grace with wondrous clarity in the man whom he assumed with such great love before his companions. After all, he who was in that way united to the Word of God did not bring it about by any preceding merits of his will (*praecedentibus suae uoluntatis meritis*) that the one Son of God also became the one Son of Man as a result of that union. It was necessary that there be just one. There would, however, have been two or three or more, if this were something that could be brought about, not by God's gift alone, but by the free choice of a human being (*hominis liberum arbitrium*). This point, therefore, is particularly emphasized: this point especially, as best I can judge, is what we teach and are taught from the treasures of wisdom and knowledge hidden in Christ."

[38] *C. ep. Pel.* 1.3.7 (CSEL 60:429): "None, then, can have a righteous will unless they have received true grace without any preceding merits, that is, grace which has been gratuitously given from on high." Unless otherwise noted, this and subsequent English translations of *c. ep. Pel.* come from Augustine, "Answer to the Two Letters of the Pelagians," in *Answer to the Pelagians, II*, trans. Roland Teske, WSA I/24 (Hyde Park, NY: New City Press, 1998). Similarly, Augustine says in *c. Iul.* (421) that a will that achieves authentic continence needs the grace of God: "'If you genuinely invite persons to the pursuit of continence, you thereby admit that the virtue of continence can be observed by those who will to do so, so that whoever wills it may be holy in body and in spirit.' I reply that I do admit this, but not in the sense you do. For you attribute this to the powers of your own mind, while I attribute it to the will that has been helped by the grace of God" (*c. Iul.* 5.16.65). This and subsequent translations of *c. Iul.* come from Augustine, "Answer to Julian," in *Answer to the Pelagians, II*, trans. Roland Teske, WSA I/24 (Hyde Park, NY: New City Press, 1998), unless otherwise indicated.

[39] *Pecc. mer.* 2.18.28 (CSEL 60:100).

Having made the chronological point that good willing that precedes and merits God's grace is beyond our capacities and the inductive observation that it is impossible to find anything good in our willing that is ours alone, Augustine contends that, a priori, good willing can come to us only from God. Given scripture's indication that human beings have nothing at all that they have not received from God's grace, one must conclude that a good will, and not merely the created capacity for free choice, derives from God. Augustine writes, "Hence, we must maintain not only that the choice of the will, which freely turns this way and that and which belongs to the natural goods which a bad person can misuse, but also that the good will, which already belongs to those goods which cannot be misused, can come to us only from God." Similarly, Augustine states that turning to God, which he identifies as another way of describing what a good will is, is possible only with God's help.[40]

Augustine determines that the good will is from God based on a process of reasoning that begins and ends with the biblical text. This process leads Augustine to believe that scripture not only allows but also requires this conclusion. In his words, "Otherwise, I do not know how we are going to defend the words of scripture, *After all, what do you have that you have not received?* (1 Cor 4:7)."[41] Furthermore, Augustine believes that other biblical passages confirm the conclusion he has drawn from 1 Corinthians 4:7. Hence he states, "It remains that we have a good will from God. . . . And for this reason, I believe, scripture says, *The will is prepared by the Lord* (Prv 8:35), and in the Psalms it says, *The Lord will guide a man's steps, and he will prosper his way* (Ps 37:23). The apostle also says, *It is God, after all, who produces in you the willing and the action in accord with good will* (Phil 2:13)."[42] As we have seen more generally with Augustine's conception of the will, his conclusion that the good will is from God derives from scriptural reasoning. He originally surmises the good will's divine origins based upon 1 Corinthians 4:7, and then confirms his interpretation based on his readings of other passages. Specific verses, as well as the larger scope and narrative trajectory of scripture, are decisive for Augustine's thinking about the will.

[40] *Pecc. mer.* 2.18.31 (CSEL 60:429): "Our turning away from God is our own doing, and this turning is an evil will. But our turning toward God is something we cannot do unless he rouses us and helps us, and this turning is a good will."
[41] *Pecc. mer.* 2.18.30 (CSEL 60:101).
[42] *Pecc. mer.* 2.18.30 (CSEL 60:101–102).

Even in the very first of his formal writings dedicated to combating Pelagianism, Augustine had already made clear that the good will, by which human beings turn to God and do what is right, could not be achieved by independent human effort. He made the descriptive points that God does in fact assist people to turn to him and to will to do what is right, helping the human will by presenting it with knowledge and inspiring it with delight in the good, and that a good will is from God. Even more than this, however, Augustine also made a case that, prescriptively speaking, a good will can come to human beings only from God. The turning to God that is a good will is possible only with God's help. Thus, from the very outset of the Pelagian controversy, Augustine expresses the limits of human power to achieve good willing in no uncertain terms. Willing rightly without God's help is not only difficult but impossible. Augustine regards this conclusion as substantiated by both experiential observation and scriptural reasoning.

Within these parameters, which dictate that a good will does, and can only, come from God and is therefore beyond human power absent divine aid, Augustine gives himself considerable latitude in describing the potential and capacity of the human being to will rightly.[43] He tends to describe these powers as more expansive earlier on, and more limited later in the Pelagian controversy. In a first stage, extending from around 411 to 417, Augustine portrays belief as coming from the human will and describes faith and belief, which he identifies with a good will, as "in our power." For Augustine, however, this portrayal is not at all incompatible with the assertion, which he also makes in this period, that a good will is possible for human beings only with God's help. Willing the good is at once "in our power," in the sense that it is accomplished by our will with God's help, and not in human power operating independently of God. In a second stage, from around 417 to 426, Augustine speaks in contrast of our wills doing "hardly anything."

---

[43] It needs to be borne in mind that Augustine's statements about the powers and potential of the human will presuppose his other statements in the same works about the radical dependence of human beings on God to make good willing possible. Considered unmoored to this larger context, Augustine's statements about the human will's capabilities may seem to suggest a more dramatic retrogression in the development of his thinking on grace and the will than is justified. On the other hand, there is a change of emphasis in his way of talking about the capabilities of the human will that can be overlooked easily if one only considers his statements about the good will's origins in God and does not attend to the powers he ascribes to the will. Augustine's development with respect to the issue of what is in the power of the human will is best approached keeping both trajectories in mind. It is an evolution in which there are changes of emphasis amid an overarching pattern of continuity.

Finally, he speaks of conversion happening by grace alone, and without us, from 426 to 430. These various descriptions of what is in the power of the good will should not be understood as incompatible, however, but rather as changes in emphasis that develop within a larger framework affirming that the good will can be achieved only with God's help.

Section A: Stage 1—411 to 417

In addition to speaking of the good will as coming from God, in *pecc. mer.* Augustine suggests that belief, which for him is a kind of good will, comes "from an individual's will" and is something "within the individual's power." Augustine makes these suggestions in the context of returning to a problem he has considered before. What explains God's choice to grant pardon and salvation to some, while others fail to receive this grace? Have the individuals so blessed done something to merit God's favor? Apparently those in Carthage favorably disposed to the teachings of Pelagius and Caelestius have raised these questions with respect to original sin. If original sin renders everyone guilty, how can it be just that some infants gain eternal life and salvation through baptism, while others do not? Augustine responds not by explaining away this problem but by pointing out that it is much more difficult to escape than these critics of original sin realize. The problem of the diversity of God's judgments does not disappear if one rejects the doctrine of original sin, or even if one looks beyond the special case of infants, who, according to Augustine, in some cases die and face judgment for original sin before having committed any "personal" or "actual" sins of their own. Its paradigmatic instance is found in Romans 9:11–12, which discusses the case of Jacob and Esau, along with the best response to God's sovereign and mysterious choice that human beings can hope to muster: awed exclamation.[44]

Augustine would like to know how these wise critics of original sin would explain the following scenario. Some people upon whom fortune seems to have smiled, who enjoy a disposition to both talent and virtue,

---

[44] "Those who hold this position [preexistence of souls] do not, nonetheless, escape the difficulty of this question; rather, they are trapped by it and are stuck there. And, just as we are, they are forced to exclaim, *O the depth!* (Rom 11:33)" (*pecc. mer.* 22.31).

never hear the preaching of the gospel and thus never enjoy the opportunity to accept it. Others, meanwhile, dimwitted and inclined to crimes
large and small, providentially encounter Christian preaching and receive
its good news. Augustine asks, "Where have these two different kinds [of
people] attained such diverse merits—I do not mean so that the latter believe, while the former do not believe, which comes from the individual
will, but so that the latter hear what they believe while the former do not
hear, for this does not fall within the individual's power."[45] In this particular case, the doctrine of preexistent souls not only fails to stop the gap
but also exacerbates the problem. If souls' merits or demerits in a former
life explain the kind of bodies they receive on earth, the fact that the
latter sort of people can be saved while the former sort can be passed over
would seem to be even more unjust than if only conduct in this life were
taken into consideration.

   Though Augustine's rhetorical question is intended to undermine the
doctrine of the preexistence of souls as a possible explanation of God's
vocation, rather than directly to present his own view, it communicates
at least two assumptions Augustine makes about what is "in our power"
with respect to the will's initial conversion to the good. First, Augustine
describes belief as something that "comes from the individual will."
Insofar as belief always remains a product of will for Augustine, a point
he will make explicit much later, in *Praedestinatio Sanctorum* (427),[46] this
aside is unremarkable, even tautological. What is noteworthy about this
statement is not what Augustine affirms but what he passes over. He does
not mention, in this immediate context, what he established in *Simpl.* as
the most fundamental origin of belief, namely God's call and God's movement of the will. That good willing comes from God is a point Augustine
makes clear in the larger context of the work, but here he is content to
identify the human will as belief's source, without immediately painting
the larger picture of how belief comes about. The point he drives home
here is that belief derives from the will. Thus *pecc. mer.* illustrates how
Augustine carves out a positive role for the will as a source for its own

----

[45] *Pecc. mer.* 1.22.31 (CSEL 60:30).
[46] In *praed. sanct.* 2.5, Augustine defines belief with reference to will. He says that to believe
(*credere*) is to think with assent. Thus there are three components of belief: (1) thought, (2) the will to
believe, and (3) assent to and belief in thought.

orientation toward the good, as in belief, even while presupposing God as the ultimate source of good willing.

When Augustine pronounces that whether one *hears* the gospel "does *not* fall within an individual's power" (emphasis mine), he is contrasting this hearing with believing, with the clear implication that, given a person's opportunity to hear preaching, belief or unbelief falls within her power. In fact, Augustine places the phrases "comes from the individual will" and "fall within the individual's power" in apposition, suggesting that the two expressions function as rough synonyms.[47] These features of Augustine's rhetorical question are not inherently incompatible with his insights from *Simpl.*, since they are susceptible to qualification by pointing to God's call as the ultimate source of the belief that comes from the human will. Indeed, other comments Augustine makes in *pecc. mer.* show that such a qualification is implicit in the work.[48] Nonetheless his emphasis at this point is worth noting; here he underlines the power and potential of the human will to give rise to belief.

Augustine's statement in *De spiritu et littera* (412–413) that assent comes from our will and therefore faith and belief are "in our power" reinforces the positive role he emphatically accords to human beings in achieving a good will in *pecc. mer.* In *De spiritu et littera*, written in response to further questions Marcellinus has raised about Augustine's reply to his inquiries in *pecc. mer.*, Augustine stresses the human will's dependence upon God's help, not only for achieving orientation toward the good but also for moving toward the good in action. He expresses his commitment to this affirmation in strong terms: "But we must fiercely (*acerimme*) and strongly (*vehentissime*) oppose those who think that the power of the human will can by itself, without the help of God, either attain righteousness or make progress in tending toward it."[49] As in *pecc. mer.*, Augustine rules out not only the suggestion that the human will can be turned toward the good on its own but also the notion that it can make any progress toward the good on its own thereafter. However, in the same work Augustine states that the will by which human beings believe in God "arises from the free choice

---

[47] *Pecc. mer.* 1.22.31 (CSEL 60:30).

[48] See, for example, Augustine's citation of Romans 9:11–12, including its reference to God as the "one who calls," in *pecc. mer.* 1.22.23. Clearly Augustine has biblical affirmations of God's calling explicitly in mind as he is composing the work.

[49] *Spir. et litt.* 2.4 (CSEL 60:156).

which they received" in creation[50] and that faith is in our power "because we believe when we will (*uult*), and when we believe, we believe willingly (*uolens*)."[51] Thus here again we find Augustine underlining the necessity of God's help for human beings to achieve right will, even while he stresses that faith and belief originate in the free choice of the will and are within our power. In fact, Augustine seems to regard willing itself as inherently entailing that something is within one's power. He writes, "After all, what is it to believe (*credere*) but to assent that what is said is true? Assent is certainly an act of someone who wills (*uolentis*). Hence, faith (*fides*) is surely in our power."[52] Thus in *spir. et litt.* Augustine's answer to the question of "whether the will by which we believe is itself a gift of God or arises from the free choice belonging to our nature" is to emphasize that both are true.[53] Good human willing comes at once from God and from the free choice of the will.

Augustine is careful to insist, however, that while good willing comes "from" our will in the sense of being effected through our will, good willing cannot strictly be said to happen "because of our will" (*per propriam uoluntatem*). The human will can serve as the instrument of goodness and admits goodness but does not single-handedly set its own goodness into motion. Referring to Romans 3:24, "They have been gratuitously justified by his grace," Augustine says:

> They were not, then, justified by the law; they were not justified by their own will (*per propriam uoluntatem*), but *gratuitously justified by his grace*. It is not that this comes about without our will (*sine uoluntate*); rather, the law shows that our will is weak so that grace may heal (*sanet*) our will and so that a healthy will (*sana uoluntas*) may fulfill the law, without being subject to the law or in need of the law.[54]

---

[50] *Spir. et litt.* 33.58 (CSEL 60:216): "The free choice which the creator has given to the rational soul as part of its nature is a neutral power that can either turn to faith or fall into unbelief. Therefore human beings cannot be said to have this will by which they believe God unless they have received it, when at God's call it arises from the free choice which they received as part of their nature when they were created, but not so that he deprives them of free choice, since they will be judged with perfect justice according to their good or bad use of it."

[51] *Spir. et litt.* 32.55 (CSEL 60:212).

[52] *Spir. et litt.* 31.54 (CSEL 60: 211).

[53] *Spir. et litt.* 33.57 (CSEL 60:215).

[54] *Spir. et litt.* 9.15 (CSEL 60:168).

Against his Pelagian opponents, Augustine is repeatedly concerned to rule out the idea that justification comes about either by the law or by our will. He is determined not to limit grace to the law and the will as is the habit of his interlocutors. But at the same time, he stresses that grace does not override or sideline our will. Grace brings our will along with it, restoring it to health.

Responding a few years later, in *De natura et gratia* (*nat. et gr.*, begun in July 415) to Pelagius's assertion that human beings have by nature the ability to sin or not to sin, Augustine pronounces, "Willing the good is in their power, but doing it is not."[55] His argument drives to the contention that if Pelagius is right that nature suffices for doing the good, then Christ's gracious work is superfluous: "Thus, the grace of Christ is done away with, as though human nature sufficed for its own righteousness."[56] However, he is willing to concede that human beings have the wherewithal to will what is right, even if enacting this good will is beyond their capabilities.

In *De perfectione iustitiae hominis* (*perf. iust.*), written in the same year Augustine began composing *nat. et gr.*, he also characterizes human willing of the good as within human power and significant for salvation.[57] One does not need to look beyond *perf. iust.*, however, for confirmation that Augustine understands this good human willing as itself contingent upon a prior act of God's grace. Only a little later in the work he again makes the point that righteousness is impossible for the unaided human will, referring once more to the "error of believing that without the help of God's grace human beings can be truthful by their own wills alone (*per solam propriam uoluntatem*)."[58] The incapacity of human beings to achieve righteousness by pulling themselves up by their own voluntary boot straps is his constant refrain. But here again, he is careful to qualify. Human beings cannot be

---

[55] *Nat. et gr.* 50.58 (CSEL 60:275–276).

[56] *Nat. et gr.* 50.58 (CSEL 60:276).

[57] Taken out of context, one statement Augustine makes might even seem to suggest that Christ's setting human beings free from bondage to sin depends only on a prior and independent act of human good willing. Augustine writes, "He sets them free from the evil that they brought upon themselves, if they will it, believe, and call upon him." *Perf. iust.* 4.10 (CSEL 42:9): *dum uolentem, credentem, inuocantem liberat a malo, quod sibi ipse fecit.* Though of course Augustine's consistent emphasis that God's grace precedes all that is good "in our will" precludes such an interpretation, this quotation does clearly underline the contingency of Christ's redemptive work upon human willing. Unless otherwise noted, this and subsequent translations of *perf. iust.* come from Augustine, "The Perfection of Human Righteousness," in *Answer to the Pelagians, I*, trans. Roland Teske, WSA I/23 (Hyde Park, NY: New City Press, 1997).

[58] *Perf. iust.* 12.30 (CSEL 42:30).

truthful on the strength of (*per*) their own (*propriam*) wills alone (*solam*), but at the same time, Christ does not set us free without our will's assent. As in *De spiritu et litt*, Augustine presents a balanced view. We achieve righteousness neither on account of our will (*per uoluntatem*) nor without the involvement of our will (*sine uoluntate*). In *perf. iust.* he emphasizes both points: our will is neither sufficient nor superfluous: "We would not be commanded to do them [God's commandments], if our will did nothing at all, and we would not need prayer, if our will alone was sufficient."[59]

Augustine's willingness to affirm that our will is actually at work, "doing something," when we obey the commandments, and to depict Christ's liberation of human beings from evil as hinging upon human willing, is connected to his conviction, in this period, that it is actually possible for human beings to reject an offer of divine grace. This is an issue on which his thinking will experience a bona fide change rather than merely a shift of emphasis, but as of *spir. et litt.* (412–413), as in *pecc. mer.* (411–412), Augustine famously attributes to the will the capacity to assent to or dissent from God's invitation.[60] He writes, "But to assent to God's invitation or to dissent from it is, as I said, in the power of one's will."[61] Thus, in this first stage of his thinking, Augustine speaks not only of faith and belief, instances of "good willing" par excellence, as within our power and coming from our will, but also of the opposite, rejecting belief, as within the "power of one's will."

---

[59] *Perf. iust.* 10.21 (CSEL 42:22).

[60] In an influential article, Xavier Léon-Dufour argued that this affirmation ought to serve as the key to Augustine's account of grace and free will throughout the course of his career. See Xavier Léon-Dufour, "Grâce et libre arbitre chez saint Augustin: A propos de '*consentire vocatione Dei . . . propriae voluntatis est*,'" *Recherches de Science Religieuse* 33 (1946): 129–163. Interpreters who have endorsed versions of Léon-Dufour's conclusions include Eugene TeSelle, *Augustine, the Theologian* (New York: Herder and Herder, 1970); Isabelle Bochet, *Saint Augustin et le désir de Dieu* (Paris: Études Augustiniennes, 1982); N. W. den Bok, "Freedom of the Will: A Systematic and Biographical Sounding of Augustine's Thoughts on Human Will," *Augustiniana* 44 (1994): 237–270; and Scott MacDonald, "Augustine and Platonism: The Rejection of Divided-Soul Accounts of Akrasia," in *Uses and Abuses of the Classics: Western Interpretations of Greek Philosophy*, ed. Jorge J. E. Gracia and Jiyuan Yu (Burlington, VT: Ashgate, 2004), 75–88. For a list of others who defend and assume Léon-Dufour's view, see Burns, *The Development of Augustine's Doctrine of Operative Grace*, 10n3. For a critique of Léon-Dufour's interpretation, see again Burns, who writes, "The principle which Léon-Dufour advanced to generality is here rejected as incompatible with Augustine's fundamental assertion of divine sovereignty, and his proposal is shown to be the consequence of a misinterpretation of the single passage of Augustine in which it occurs" (12; Burns gives his own interpretation of the passage on 129). See also Jim Wetzel's defense of the compatibility of irresistible grace with free will, James Wetzel, *Augustine and the Limits of Virtue* (New York: Cambridge University Press, 1992), 197–206. More recently, Karfíková has interpreted this statement from *spir. et litt.*, adopting a critical stance with respect to Léon-Dufour's thesis (*Grace and the Will According to Augustine*, 185).

[61] *Spir. et litt.* 34.60 (CSEL 60:220): *sed consentire uel dissentire propriae uoluntatis est.*

Section B: Stage 2—417 to 426

In a next broad stage of Augustine's thinking, he tends to downplay the will's power to achieve the good. Whereas he insists in *perf. iust.* that the "will does not do nothing" when human beings obey the commandments, in *On the Deeds of Pelagius* (*gest. Pel.*, late 417) he instead emphasizes that we do "hardly anything" (*aliquid*) so that we act rightly. Rather, Christ acts upon our wills to accomplish this. At a recent synod, Pelagius had been called upon to pronounce upon his former statement (presumably in *The Book of Chapters*) that "all are governed by their own will" (*omnes uoluntate propria regi*).[62] In response to Pelagius's statement, Augustine shifts the focus away from what the human will accomplishes and toward what the will must passively receive to achieve the good. Augustine is concerned not with what the will governs but rather with the will being governed by God. Furthermore, he intensifies the terminology of the initial statement in question, claiming that our wills are not only governed by God but that they are also *driven* by God: "Certainly, to be driven (*agi*) is more than to be governed (*regi*). After all, one who is governed does something and is governed so that he acts correctly, but one who is driven is understood to do hardly anything (*aliquid vix*)." Augustine takes the idea of being driven from the apostle Paul. He writes, "Nonetheless, the grace of the savior acts upon our wills (*uoluntatibus*) to such an extent that the apostle has no hesitation in saying, *All those who are driven by the Spirit of God are the children of God* (Rom 8:14)."[63] Thus Augustine adopts the Pauline terminology of being driven (*agi*), and he takes pains to ensure his readers understand that such terminology leaves less room for attribution of right action to our will. Achieving goodness, he says, depends on God acting upon our will while we ourselves do "hardly anything" to orient our will to the good.

In addition to characterizing willing the good as something that depends on God, in the Spirit, acting upon our will, rather than on the independent initiative of our will, Augustine makes the point that those adopted by God owe this to the work of the Spirit rather than the power of their own will.

---

[62] *Gest. Pel.* 3.5 (CSEL 42: 56). Translations of *gest. Pel.* come from Augustine, "The Deeds of Pelagius," in *Answer to the Pelagians, I*, trans. Roland Teske, WSA I/23 (Hyde Park, NY: New City Press, 1997), unless otherwise noted.

[63] *Gest. pel.* 3.5 (CSEL 42:57).

"After all, those who are children of God are governed and driven by this Spirit, not by the powers of their own will (*uiribus propriae uoluntatis*)," he writes.[64] Here Augustine goes beyond making the point that our will does "hardly anything." He makes the more sweeping claim that we are sons of God by the Spirit and "not" by the powers of our own will. The formulation is exclusive, though again here the point that adoption does not happen by means of the powers of our will does not entail that this adoption occurs without the involvement of our will. Still, what Augustine chooses to emphasize is significant. Whereas in *spir. et litt.* (412–413) he had underscored that faith and belief are "in our power," here his concern is to stress that the adoption does not happen on account of our will, and in this sense is "not by the powers of our own will." The fallen human will is inherently incapable of transforming itself into the good will that becomes ours in adoption.

As Augustine more strongly accentuates that conversion to the good is beyond the pale of the power of our own will, he also drives home the point that God's teaching, call, election, and will are efficacious, a trajectory in his thinking that will ultimately lead to his explicit conclusion that resisting God's offer of grace is impossible. One finds the beginnings of this latter trajectory prominently displayed in *On the Grace of Christ and Original Sin* (*De gratia Christi et de peccato originali; gr. et pecc. or.*, 418), where he describes God's teaching as effective not only in conveying knowledge but even in terms of ensuring a certain outcome in the actions of the person who is the recipient of grace. Because God's teaching by grace through the Spirit targets the human will itself, willing inevitably follows when anyone has learned authentically from God. Commenting on John 6:45, Augustine writes:

> And thus, when God teaches, not by the letter of the law, but by the grace of the Spirit, he teaches not only so that through knowledge people see what they learn, but so that they desire it with the will (*uolendo appetat*) and accomplish it in action (*agendoque perficiat*). In this divine manner of teaching God helps the willing itself (*ipsa uoluntas*) and the acting itself (*ipsa operatio*), not merely the natural ability for willing and acting.[65]

---

[64] *Gest. pel.* 3.6 (CSEL 42:57).

[65] *Gr. et pecc. or.* 1.14.15 (CSEL 42:138). Unless otherwise noted, this and subsequent translations of *gr. et pecc. or.* come from "The Grace of Christ and Original Sin," in *Answer to the Pelagians, I*, trans. Roland Teske, WSA I/23 (Hyde Park, NY: New City Press, 1997).

God's teaching by grace through the Spirit is by definition efficacious in moving the will since it consists precisely in effecting the will's desire. Though this position may logically entail that the will cannot resist God, Augustine does not draw this conclusion explicitly in this context.

A few years later (421), however, Augustine does state that God's omnipotent will cannot be resisted in the case of infants. In response to Julian's teaching, which according to Augustine implies that the reason all are not saved is that "they do not want to ask though God is willing to give; they do not want to seek though God is willing to show them; and they do not want to knock though God is willing to open the door," Augustine points to infants as a counterexample.[66] Since infants are too young to have developed free choice of the will, it cannot be the case that what is decisive for their salvation is whether they will to accept what God wills to offer them. Augustine writes, "But far more infants are not adopted into that grace by him *who wills that all human beings be saved and come to the knowledge of the truth* (1 Tm 2:4). He cannot say to them, *I was willing, but you were not* (Mt 23:37), because, if he has willed, who of those children who do not yet have the choice of their will would have resisted his omnipotent will?"[67] Their example makes clear, Augustine hopes to show, the more general point that the reason people are saved is not because of their own will but because of God's. Augustine does not here take the step of arguing that God's will is irresistible per se, but he does contend that it is irresistible for infants, who as yet lack a will of their own. The fact that infants fail to possess the power of willing such things should make the matter clear, he thinks. He asks, "Or can someone say: God wills this, but they refuse? After all, they do not yet know how to will or refuse these things."[68] In this case there is little room for dispute: "And as everyone agrees, they [infants] cannot oppose his will by a contrary will of their own."[69] At the very least, the case of infants establishes that God's will is decisive for salvation; whether infants are the exception or the rule with respect to the question of whether human beings have the power to resist God's conversion of the will to good remains to be seen.

---

[66] *C. Iul.* 4.8.42 (PL 44:759).
[67] *C. Iul.* 4.8.42 (PL 44:759).
[68] *C. Iul.* 4.8.42 (PL 44: 759).
[69] *C. Iul.* 4.8.43 (PL 44:760).

Section C: Stage 3—426 to 430

In a final stage of his thinking, Augustine makes clear that conversion happens by "grace alone," even speaking of God working "without us" to reorient our will to the good. The emphases of Augustine's view in this stage, as opposed to the previous one, are helpfully highlighted against Julian's understanding, as presented by Augustine, of what is due to us and what is due to God. According to Augustine, Julian believes that good willing is due to human beings, while the translation of this good willing into actual actions is due to God. Augustine says to Julian:

> Why, then, did you believe that, as you do, I too "called heavenly gifts the actions of the human will," as if the will of a human being moved toward something good without the grace of God so that it received its action as a debt owed it by God? Had you forgotten that along with the scripture we said in opposition to you, *The will is prepared by the Lord* (Prv. 8:35 LXX) or that God also produces in you the act of willing?[70]

For Julian, Augustine claims, human beings can want to be good on their own without the aid of God's grace.

In *Answer to the Two Letters of the Pelagians* (*c. ep. Pel.*; 421), Augustine had already expressed a differing, and more complex, view of the division of labor between God and the human being. There, explaining the compatibility of Psalm 81:11 and Exodus 4:12, he had identified at least two distinct moments or aspects involved in the reorientation of the human will toward the good.[71] Augustine wrote, "In that verse, then, in which he says, *Open your mouth, and I shall fill it* (Ps 81:11), the one action seems to pertain to the human being and the other to God, but in the one in which he says, *I shall open your mouth, and I shall teach you* (Ex 4:12), both pertain to God."[72] First, the mouth must be opened; that is, the heart must be prepared to receive God's grace. Second, the mouth must be filled; that is, grace must actually be poured into the mouth of the person receiving it. Augustine's resolution to this exegetical conundrum, expressed

---

[70] *C. Iul.* 4.3.15 (PL 44:744).

[71] Though the verses Augustine discusses do not refer explicitly to the will, he makes it clear that he understands them as pertaining to willing since, "after all, what is it to prepare the heart and open the mouth but to prepare the will?" See *c. ep. Pel.* 2.9.20 (CSEL 60:482).

[72] *C. ep. Pel.* 2.9.20 (CSEL 60:482).

in a rhetorical question, is that God and the human being cooperate in achieving the first aspect of the reorientation of the will to the good, while God alone brings about the second: "Why is it except that in one of these actions he cooperates with the human being who does it, but in the case of the other he does it alone?"[73] Thus Augustine presents, in *c. ep. Pel.* (421), a much more complex picture of how the human will moves toward the good than the one he attributes to Julian in *c. Iul.* (421), crediting God with much more in this process than does Julian. At the same time, however, he does carve out a role for the human being in the conversion of the will toward the good, namely cooperation with God in preparation for receiving grace.

In *On Grace and Free Choice* (*gr. et lib. arb.*, 426), however, a different emphasis comes to light. Here Augustine contends that the initial calling that led to Paul's conversion was due to grace alone, though the subsequent effects of God's grace in him were due both to him and to God: "And for this reason it was neither the grace of God alone nor the apostle alone, but the grace of God with him. But that he received a call from heaven and was converted by such an efficacious calling was the grace of God alone, for his merits were great, but evil ones."[74] Once grace has been given, we gain the ability to accumulate merit through the grace we continue to receive. The initial conversion of the will to grace, however, is accomplished by "the grace of God alone."

Accompanying this accent on the self-sufficiency of God's grace for bringing about good human willing is Augustine's thoroughgoing insistence upon the insufficiency of human effort, without grace, to accomplish anything good whatsoever, even in the realm of will. Without grace, Augustine reports decisively in *Rebuke and Grace* (*corrept.*, 427), we do nothing good in our willing: "For we must understand the grace of God through Jesus Christ our Lord. It alone sets human beings free from evil and without it they do nothing good (*nullum . . . bonum*) whether in thinking, in willing (*uolendo*) and loving, or in acting."[75] In *pecc. mer.*

---

[73] *C. ep. Pel.* 2.9.20 (CSEL 60:482).

[74] *Gr. et lib. arb.* 5.12 (PL 44:889).

[75] *Corrept.* 2.3 (CSEL 92:221). Unless otherwise noted, translations of *corrept.* come from Augustine, "Rebuke and Grace," in *Answer to the Pelagians, IV: To the Monks of Hadrumetum and Provence*, trans. Roland Teske, WSA I/26 (Hyde Park, NY: New City Press, 1999).

(411–412), Augustine had already made a point about the origins of good willing, arguing that one cannot find anything good in our will that is "of us" and not "from God" (*ex deo*). Here the focus is on the act of good willing; Augustine makes the point that our willing cannot have any good object without the assistance of God's grace. Thus, this quotation from *corrept.* brings Augustine full circle, drawing his constant emphasis on the source of good willing in God, expressed already in *pecc. mer.*, back around to the conclusion that the target of good willing falls completely short of goodness without God's gracious assistance. The good will can be such only because it both derives from God's grace and is driven toward its object by God's grace.

Augustine can, at times, be found going beyond even the denial of the sufficiency of human effort for accomplishing the conversion of the human will to the good. In *gr. et lib. arb.* (426), for example, he clarifies that while God does cooperate with us in our actual willing so that this willing might be carried out, meeting the conditions so that we might will what is right in the first place is something God performs unilaterally. This emphasis fits the schema Augustine develops in *gr. et lib. arb.* (426) whereby God is entirely responsible for the will's initial conversion while human beings cooperate with God in the subsequent performance of good works. Augustine writes, "He works, therefore, without us (*sine nobis*) so that we will (*ut uelimus*), but when we will and will so that we do the action, he works along with us; nonetheless, without his either working so that we will or his working along with us when we will, we can do nothing in terms of works of piety."[76] Thus while God assists human beings both by making it the case *that* they will the good and by helping them to do the good they will to do, God does the former "without us." This represents a shift from Augustine's indication in both *c. ep. Pel.* (421) and *Simpl.* that "the power to will (*ut uelimus*) he has willed should be both his and ours, his because he calls us, ours because we follow when called."[77] Thus, in the latest period of his thinking, Augustine not only claims that achieving a good will is something human beings cannot do on their own; he claims it is something that God does on his own without human beings. They are unable to achieve a good will

---

[76] *Gr. et lib. arb.* 17.33 (PL 44:901).
[77] *Simpl.* 1.2.10 (CCL 44:35).

without assistance and, at least in some cases, are unable to bring about the fact that they will rightly at all.

Around the same time as Augustine comes to these conclusions about the human inability to achieve a good will, he explicitly expresses conclusions about the human inability to resist God's grace, conclusions arguably already implied in his teaching about the efficaciousness of God's calling. In *corrept.* (427), he surmises in so many words that God's will is irresistible, not only for infants who yet lack a will with fully developed powers of choice but also for any other human being. On the basis of Old Testament passages in which God moves people's hearts,[78] Augustine asks, "When human beings either come or return to the path of righteousness by means of a rebuke, who produces in their hearts this good health but God . . . whom no choice of human beings resists when he wills to save?" He concludes, "To will or not to will is in the power of the one who wills or does not will in such a way that it does not impede the divine will or surpass its power. He himself does what he wills even with these people who do what he does not will."[79] Thus God's will is irresistible both by human choice[80] and when human choice is absent, as in the case of infants.

Later in the same work Augustine makes the same point in terms of "heart," contending that no heart, however hard, can reject divine generosity.[81] Likewise in *praed. sanct.* (427), Augustine says that the grace by which we come to Christ is irresistible: "This grace, therefore, which the divine generosity gives in a hidden manner to human hearts is not rejected by any hard heart. It is, in fact, given precisely in order that hardness of heart may first of all be removed. When, therefore, the Father is heard interiorly and teaches so that one comes to the Son, he removes the heart of stone and gives a heart of flesh."[82] Thus, just as achieving a good will can never be understood to be "in human power" if this is taken to mean that human beings may accomplish this good will independently of God's help, so also the possibility that human beings might be capable of rejecting God's reorientation of the will is, for Augustine in this latest period, unthinkable. Thus, at this point in

---

[78] He goes on to enumerate these in *corrept.* 14.45.
[79] *Corrept.* 14.43 (CSEL 92:272).
[80] *Corrept.* 14.43 and 14.45.
[81] *Corrept.* 8.13.
[82] *Praed. sanct.* 8.13 (PL 44:971).

Augustine's development, God's reorientation of the will can no longer be seen as contingent upon human acceptance of God's teaching or call. Rather, God's efficacious teaching inherently brings with it a reorientation of the will.

In this first part of the present chapter, we have analyzed the changing emphases in Augustine's description of the extent to which initially attaining a good will is within human power. This analysis has constituted the first half of our answer to the larger question addressed in this chapter: What is within our power, with respect to the good will? We turn next to the second half of the answer to this question, Augustine's teachings on the extent to which it is possible to realize one's good will once one has succeeded in willing the right thing.

Part II: Acting on a Good Will

Constants in Augustine's Case

With respect to the question of the extent of the good will's powers to secure the good actions it targets, as with respect to the question of the extent of our powers to orient our will toward the good, Augustine remains fairly consistent through the course of the Pelagian controversy. From 411 onward he consistently reiterates that human beings, even including believers after baptism, need God's help to see their good willing through to fruition. He never falters on this point. His thinking does develop, however, on two questions related to the human capacity to translate good willing into action: the interpretation of Romans 7 and the possibility of sinlessness in this life. With respect to the issue of what is in our power vis-à-vis making good on our good willing in action, then, the overarching picture remains consistent with insights Augustine had reached in *Simpl.*, even while he further curtails the will's powers to act upon the good as his thinking on these two questions evolves. Augustine always maintains, during the Pelagian controversy, that we can neither achieve a good will nor act upon it independently of God's grace. What changes is his assessment of whether being completely without sin is a possibility in this life, even for Christians.

Impossibility of Enacting One's Good Will, Independently of God's Aid

One of Augustine's complaints about Pelagius's theology is that it does not account for the phenomenon of weakness of will, something confirmed, in Augustine's opinion, not only by everyday commonsense understanding but, even more important, by the testimony of scripture. Augustine attributes to Pelagius the idea that "when human beings will to, they do the action; because they do not will it, they do not do it." Augustine explains Pelagius's reasoning as follows: "After all, if they have an inseparable ability, they cannot have a weakness of will (*uoluntatis infirmatis*), or rather the presence of the will along with the lack of its accomplishment." But Augustine interposes scripture to suppress this line of thinking: "If, then, that is the case, why do we have the words, *I can will the good, but I cannot do it* (Rom 7:18)."[83] In Augustine's view, to think that human good action follows unproblematically from good willing is naive. Though such a description might apply to human willing in its pristine created form, things no longer work this way since the fall.[84] Pelagius, however, Augustine suggests, theologizes blissfully as if the transition between right will and right action is automatic. In his account, once good willing has been achieved, good action inevitably follows. Furthermore, there are no gradations in willing. If one wills something, one does it. If one does not will to do it, one does not do it. Pelagius does not give an account of gray areas between willing and not willing.

Augustine had long left behind the reassuring simplicity of this line of thought. Ever since *Simpl.* he had maintained that the power to will and the power to put one's good will into action were distinct. He had written in that work, "There are two different things that God gives us, the power to will (*ut uelimus*) and the things that we actually will (*quod uoluerimus*)."[85] Rejecting the notion that the first power inherently entailed the second, he had contended that both were given by God. Far from being guaranteed by our natural power of free will, the power to enact our good will by doing the

---

[83] *Nat. et gr.* 51.59 (CSEL 60:276).

[84] "For if the author of this book [Augustine means Pelagius, the author of *Nature*] was speaking of that human nature which was in the beginning created innocent and healthy, his statement would be in some sense acceptable. And yet that nature should not have been said to have an inseparable ability, that is, one that cannot be lost" (*nat. et gr.* 51.59).

[85] *Simpl.* 1.2.10 (CCL 44:35).

right thing, Augustine had maintained even then, was God-given: "But what we actually will (*quod autem uolerimus*) he alone gives, i.e., the power to do right (*posse bene agere*) and to live happily forever."[86] Augustine remains stubbornly insistent on this basic insight throughout the Pelagian controversy.

At the very outset of his written involvement in the Pelagian controversy Augustine definitively rejects the notion that human beings can perform the good independently of God's help once their will has been set free by grace. Arguing that an overestimation of the powers of the unaided human will can lead to an underestimation of the necessity of prayer, he points out that "there are some who rely so heavily on the free choice of the human will that they suppose that we need no help, even from God, in order to avoid sin, after our nature has once and for all received the free choice of the will."[87] Such people are mistaken, Augustine is convinced. Even after the restoration of the free choice of the will accomplished by Christ, human beings require God's continued assistance to resist sin. He is insistent upon this point: "Let us then drive away from our hearing and from our minds those who say that, having received once and for all free choice of the will, we need not pray that God might help us not to sin."[88] God both helps people turn to him, giving them a good will, and helps those who have turned to him, helping them to act on it.[89]

In the coming years, Augustine consistently teaches that having a good will is necessary, but not sufficient, for doing the good. On the one hand, the human will must be involved for human beings to act righteously. Augustine writes in *spir. et litt.* (412–413) that "human righteousness . . . is not attained without the human will"[90] and, a few years later, in *nat. et gr.* (415–416) that "without it we cannot do what is right."[91] On the other hand,

---

[86] *Simpl.* 1.2.10 (CCL 44:35).

[87] *Pecc. mer.* 2.2.2 (CSEL 60:72).

[88] *Pecc. mer.* 2.5.6 (CSEL 60:76).

[89] *Pecc. mer.* 2.5.5 (CSEL 60:75): "God, then, helps those who turn to him, but abandons those who turn away. But he also helps us turn to him."

[90] *Spir. et litt.* 5.7 (CSEL 60:159–160): "Human righteousness itself must be attributed to the action of God, though it is not attained without the human will" (*non fiat sine hominis uoluntate*).

[91] After quoting Philippians 2:12–13 ("With fear and trembling work out your own salvation; it is God, after all, who produces in you the willing and the action in accord with good will"), Augustine writes, "Why should we act with fear and trembling instead of with calm security, if God does this, unless it is on account of our will (*propter uoluntatem nostrum*)? Without it we cannot do what is right." See *nat. et gr.* 27.31 (CSEL 60:256). Here Augustine is making the point that God sometimes withdraws his help so that we remember that we need him to do what is right. When we are left to our will alone, we have reason to fear and tremble because our will is necessary but not sufficient for doing the good.

the human will cannot bring about the good at which it aims without God's assistance. Since "the flesh lusts against the spirit and the spirit against the flesh so that we do not do what we will, and another law in the members resists the law of the mind," Augustine asserts that "we can will the good, but cannot carry it out."[92] He repeats this refrain in *nat. et gr.* (415), asking "What is the reason, then, for that cry, *So that you do not do those things which you will* (Gal 5:17)? What is the reason for this one as well, *For I do not do the good that I want, but I do the evil that I hate* (Rom 7:19)?" Augustine concludes that these statements demonstrate that "human beings do not do the good that they want, but they do the evil that they do not want. Willing the good is in their power, but doing it is not."[93] Willing the good is not the same, for Augustine, as doing it. The first can be in our power, while the second is not.

One problem with our inability to see our good will through to fruition is quantitative. For the baptized, for example, willing the good to some degree is in their power since their will has been converted by God. Yet willing the good strongly enough to do it proves challenging. Augustine stresses in *pecc. mer.* (411–412) that good willing sufficient to overcome temptation cannot be feeble or half-hearted. It must be "great" and in "full strength." Responding to the statement, perhaps from Rufinus's *Liber de fide,* "If we do not will to, we do not sin, and God would not command human beings to do what would be impossible for the human will,"[94] Augustine writes, "In order to overcome temptation in the case of some things which we desire wrongfully or fear wrongfully, we at times need the great (*magnis*) and full strength (*totis uiribus*) of the will (*uoluntatis*). He who willed that the prophet truthfully say, *No living person will be found righteous in your sight* (Ps 143:2), foresaw that we will not in every case fully (*perfecte*) use this power."[95] Fallen wills are turned in the wrong direction, but even the wills of the baptized are only precariously oriented toward the good. They are weak and incomplete. They need help. On this point, Augustine believes scripture is on his side: "We have long known that there is no one who exerts his will as much (*quantum*) as the occasion demands, as the massive testimonies of the scriptures, which I mentioned, declare."[96]

---

[92] *Spir. et litt.* 33.59 (CSEL 60:218): *dum uelle adiacet, perficere autem bonum non.*
[93] *Nat. et gr.* 50.58 (CSEL 60:276): *uelle illi adiacet, perficere autem bonum non adiacet.*
[94] *Pecc. mer.* 2.3.3 (CSEL 60:72). See WSA I/23, 114n3.
[95] *Pecc. mer.* 2.3.3 (CSEL 60:72–73).
[96] *Pecc. mer.* 2.15.22 (CSEL 60:94).

In his latest writings, from the end of the Pelagian controversy, Augustine persists in the belief that the good will in this life suffers from a quantitative insufficiency. In *gr. et lib. arb.* (426), for example, he indicates that after having one's will converted from being evil to being good, one still needs help to obey God's commands. Previously there was a problem of overarching orientation. Now there is a problem of quantity. Citing Sirach 15:16, which he contends describes the will as strengthened by grace, he writes, "For the words of scripture, *If you will to, you will observe the commandments* (Sir 15:16 LXX), amount to this, that someone who wills to observe them and cannot should recognize that he does not yet fully will to observe the commandments and that he should pray that he may have a will great enough (*tantam uoluntatem quanta sufficit*) to observe the commandments."[97] The text Augustine cites would play well into the hands of Pelagius, who propounds that willing straightforwardly translates into obedience. But Augustine sees the "full" (*plene*) willing here described as difficult to attain—indeed achieving it is entirely out of the question without the help of grace. Whether one wills to obey the commandments is a complicated question. It can happen that one wills obedience sufficiently to seek help but insufficiently to achieve obedience. In this case one needs to ask precisely for a stronger will.

Augustine describes the obstacle to acting on one's good will qualitatively as well as quantitatively: "For the flesh lusts against the spirit and the spirit against the flesh so that we do not do what we will, and another law in the members resists the law of the mind. We can will the good, but cannot carry it out. If we make progress with a steady intention, these ills of our old condition are healed, as our new condition increases from day to day, by the faith that works through love."[98] In this case the failure to carry out the good one wills is due to an unstable intention. In *On Marriage and Concupiscence* (*nupt. et conc.*, 418–419), Augustine gives a label to the weakness, both quantitative and qualitative, with which those whose wills have been converted to the good must continue to contend: "concupiscence." Here he explains that while baptism removes the guilt of concupiscence, it does not remove concupiscence itself, making grace essential to carrying through on the good that we will.[99]

---

[97] *Gr. et lib. arb.* 15.31 (PL 44:900).

[98] *Spir. et litt.* 33.59 (CSEL 60:218).

[99] *Nupt. et conc.* 1.25.28. Unless otherwise noted, this and subsequent translations of this work come from Augustine, "Marriage and Desire," in *Answer to the Pelagians, II*, trans. Roland Teske, WSA I/24 (Hyde Park, NY: New City Press, 1998).

In his writings from the latest stage of the Pelagian controversy, Augustine continues to insist that even after the initial gift of grace that brings about our conversion, we continue to need God's grace to help the free choice of the will. It is not as if, once the will has been converted to the good, it can cruise forward toward concrete actions on autopilot. Augustine writes, "But clearly, once grace has been given, our good merits also begin to exist, but through that grace. For, if grace is withdrawn, a human being falls, no longer standing upright, but cast headlong by free choice."[100] Quite to the contrary, fickle free choice can let one down. Thus grace is needed not only for justification but also in order to progress in the life of faith: "Hence, a human being not only needs the grace of God to justify the sinner, that is, to make him righteous from sinful, when he receives good things in return for evil ones. But once a human being has been justified by faith, he needs grace to walk with him so that he may lean on it in order not to fall."[101] As necessary as a good will itself for obeying commands is God's help. Left on its own to carry out the good at which it aims, Augustine asserts, the human will cannot support itself.

In light of the necessity of God's help, even after conversion, to enact the good that one wills, Augustine attributes perseverance to God's aid rather than to the human will. He takes Peter's need of Jesus' prayer on his behalf as one case giving evidence that perseverance in the good is a gift from God rather than accomplished in the independent power of the human will: "If you say that it pertains to the free choice of a human being which you defend, not in accord with the grace of God, but in opposition to it, that anyone perseveres or does not persevere in the good, not because God grants it if he does persevere, but because the human will brings it about (*sed humana uoluntate faciente*), what are you going to devise against the words of the Lord who said, *I have prayed for you, Peter, that your faith may not fail* (Lk 22:32)?"[102] Thus, ultimately, Augustine states his conviction, consistently maintained throughout the Pelagian controversy and initially expressed in *Simpl.*, that acting upon the good one wills requires the help of grace, in terms of perseverance. On their own, human beings can as little assure their perseverance in the good they will as they can bring about the conversion of their will to it.

---

[100] *Gr. et lib. arb.* 6.13 (PL 44:889).
[101] *Gr. et lib. arb.* 6.13 (PL 44:889–890).
[102] *Corrept.* 8.17 (CSEL 92:238).

Weakness of Will after Baptism

In addition to arguing that no one can orient their will toward the good on their own and that it is impossible to achieve obedience that would enact a good will without God's help, Augustine makes explicit that the baptized too struggle with weakness of will.[103] Even these privileged recipients of God's grace, he argues throughout the Pelagian controversy, struggle to bring the good they want to completion. Whereas the fallen will suffers from an inability to will the good, the redeemed will suffers from an inability to perform the good action at which it aims, unless it is enabled to do so by grace.

The argument that baptized believers need grace in order to put their good will into action comes strongly to the fore in *nat. et gr.* (415) in the context of Augustine's argument that Christ's work pertains to the present and future, not only to forgiveness for previous wrongs. Whereas for Pelagius, Christ's help consists in the fact that he "pardons sins committed in the past, not that he helps to avoid future ones,"[104] Augustine's view is that "the flesh is opposed even to the baptized." For Augustine, the notion that the flesh is opposed to the spirit in the baptized clearly follows from reading the assessment of Galatians 5:17, "You do not do those things which you will," in light of Galatians 3:5, "Did he who gave you the Spirit and worked miracles among you do this because of the works of the law or because of the acceptance of the faith?" The latter passage makes clear that Paul's addressees have received the Spirit and accepted the faith, and hence are baptized, while the former informs them that the flesh and spirit are opposed in them.[105] Again leaning on Galatians 5:17, Augustine clarifies what such an opposition involves: "How is it opposed? So that they do not do what they will. See, the will is present in the human beings; where is that ability of nature?"[106] Embroiled in a struggle with "the flesh," the baptized will the good but often fail to act accordingly.

The fact that the good will of the baptized is itself insufficient to help them triumph over temptation is clear from the Lord's Prayer, Augustine asserts.

---

[103] Augustine defines weakness of will as "the presence of the will along with the lack of its accomplishment." See *nat. et gr.* 51.59 (CSEL 60:276): *uoluntatis infirmitas uel potius uoluntatis adiacentia et perfectionis indigentia.*

[104] *Nat. et gr.* 34.39 (CSEL 60:262).

[105] See *nat. et gr.* 53.61 (CSEL 60: 278).

[106] *Nat. et gr.* 53.61 (CSEL 60:278): *et quomodo contraria? ut non quod uolunt faciant. ecce adest uoluntas in homine; ubi est possibilitas illa naturae?*

Unless one is ready to dismiss this prayer as "superfluous" or "shameless," one needs to acknowledge the condition that renders it necessary, namely the weakness of will of the baptized: "But that one should pray so as to be helped not to sin, that is something he [Pelagius] never said, something I have not found here. His silence on this point is utterly astounding, since the Lord's Prayer teaches that we should ask for both of these: both that our debts be forgiven and that we not be led into temptation, the former so that past sins be wiped away, the latter so that future sins be avoided." Augustine directly relates this issue to the will: "Although this does not happen without our willing it, the will alone is not enough to accomplish it (*uoluntas sola non sufficit*). Hence, the prayer offered to the Lord for this purpose is neither superfluous nor shameless."[107] Even the redeemed, "good" will, then, is too weak and insufficient to achieve the good. As we will discuss, at the time he writes *nat. et gr.*, Augustine does not yet read Romans 7 as expressing exclusively the Christian experience under grace.[108] Yet he is already convinced that the faithful suffer weakness of will after baptism on the basis of other scriptural passages. Here again Augustine invokes Galatians 5:17 as evidence against the idea that the baptized "do the good actions they will to do without any opposition from the concupiscence of the flesh."[109] Paul is addressing baptized believers when he observes that "you do not do those things which you will," Augustine argues, and refers in this phrase to the continued struggle with "works which arise from concupiscence of the flesh."[110]

A few years later, now in the second stage of the Pelagian controversy, Augustine once more observes that though the baptized are forgiven for all past sins, they remain weak and vulnerable to temptation. This time he again buttresses his argument with an appeal to the Lord's Prayer.[111] Baptism, he observes, "does not take away the weakness against which those who have been reborn struggle, when they fight the good fight, and to which they

---

[107] *Nat. et gr.* 18.20 (CSEL 60:246).

[108] As Thomas Gerhard Ring observes, *nat. et gr.* (415) belongs to an intermediary phase during which Augustine allows that the "I" of Romans 7:14–25 might represent either a person *sub lege* or a person *sub gratia*. See Thomas Gerhard Ring, "Römer 7 in den Enarrationes in Psalmos," in *Signum Pietatis: Festgabe für Cornelius Petrus Mayer OSA zum 60. Geburtstag*, ed. Adolar Zumkeller (Würzburg: Augustinus-Verlag, 1989), 385n7.

[109] *Nat. et gr.* 56.66 (CSEL 60:283).

[110] *Nat. et gr.* 56.66 (CSEL 60:283).

[111] On Augustine's use of arguments from the Lord's Prayer during the Pelagian controversy, particularly as inspired by Cyprian of Carthage's treatise on the topic, see Han-luen Kantzer Komline, "Grace, Free Will, and the Lord's Prayer: Cyprian's Importance for the 'Augustinian' Doctrine of Grace," *AS* 45, no. 2 (2014): 247–279. Other treatments of Augustine's writings on the Lord's Prayer are listed in 249n8.

consent, when as human beings they are taken by surprise in some sin."[112] It is on account of this vulnerability that they pray "Forgive us our debts."[113]

In the coming years Augustine asserts not only that concupiscence continues to interfere with the baptized bringing their good will to completion but also that what differentiates those with a good will from those without one is precisely that the former recognize the concupiscence that resists them as evil, while the latter lack this self-awareness. He writes in *Against Julian* (*Contra Julianum* [*c. Iul.*], 421), "But we give thanks for the control of concupiscence, because it is conquered though it resists us. But that it does resist the good will is not something good. In fact, who would deny that it is an evil except those who do not have a good will so that they recognize that what resists them is something evil?"[114] Experience of resistance to the good will, Augustine suggests, is so common in the life of the baptized Christian that recognition of its negativity may serve as one of the features that distinguishes her as such.

Augustine continued to defend the bleak doctrine of this worldly weakness of will among the saints in the very last anti-Pelagian work he penned. Leaving no room for misinterpretation, he asks Julian, "What will you reply when you hear that even those whose sins have been forgiven in baptism do what they do not will, that those who the apostle says have received the Holy Spirit through the preaching of the faith do not do what they will, and finally that those who the same teacher of the nations says were called into freedom do not through free will do what they will?"[115] Julian has qualms even about Augustine's contention that sin erodes free choice, but in fact Augustine's claims about the dysfunction sin has wrought upon human willing extend far deeper.[116] Not only fallen humanity at large, but even followers of Christ—whether understood as the baptized, as recipients of the Holy Spirit through the preaching of faith, or those called to freedom (Augustine covers all possible understandings of the phrase from the most narrow to the broadest)—"do not do what they will" (*non ea quae uolunt faciant*). No matter how far one has progressed

---

[112] *C. ep. Pel.* 3.3.5 (CSEL 60:490).

[113] *C. ep. Pel.* 3.3.5 (CSEL 60:490).

[114] *C. Iul.* 4.2.13 (PL 44:742–743).

[115] *C. Iul. imp.* 6.8 (CSEL 85.2:305). Unless otherwise indicated, this and subsequent translations of *c. Iul. imp.* come from Augustine, "Unfinished Work in Answer to Julian," in *Answer to the Pelagians, III*, trans. Roland Teske, WSA I/25 (Hyde Park, NY: New City Press, 1999).

[116] Augustine writes, "You who deny that free choice lost its strength by sinning, that is, by making a bad use of itself, what will you reply here when you hear that, when the flesh has desires opposed to the spirit, even the faithful do not do what they will?" (*c. Iul. imp.* 6.8 [CSEL 85.2:305]).

in receiving God's grace, one never, in this life, escapes the predicament of failing to make good on one's good willing. Unwanted desires of the flesh cling stubbornly, even to the baptized believer. Augustine is confident of this because of the precedent of Paul's teaching. Appealing yet again to Galatians 5:17, he writes, "For the apostle said to those who were already baptized and had already received the Holy Spirit: *The flesh has desires opposed to the spirit, but the spirit has desires opposed to the flesh, for these are opposed to each other so that you do not do what you will* (Gal 5:17) (*non ea quae uultis faciatis*)."[117]

Thus for Augustine, scripture demands the conclusion that the good will of the faithful in no way offers a return to the full Edenic freedom of Adam. The redeemed will, unlike the fallen will, is oriented toward the good. Yet desires continue to crop up that force baptized Christians to do what they do not will. Of Adam, Augustine writes, "But we say that the first human being was so happy before the sin and had such free will (*liberae uoluntatis*) that, while observing the commandment of God by the great strength of his mind, he did not experience anything at all from any desire that he did not will." However, Augustine continues, "his will was first damaged by the poisonous enticement of the serpent so that desire came into being which would rather have followed upon the will than resisted it; but once sin had been committed, concupiscence fought back against the weakened mind as a punishment. And for this reason, if Adam did not first do what he willed by sinning (*faceret peccando quod uellet*), he would not have suffered what he did not will by desiring (*pateretur concupiscendo quod nollet*)."[118] The good will that belongs to the faithful in this life is not the same as the fallen will, but neither is it identical to the created will Adam enjoyed in the garden. It has its own unique character, breathed into being by God's gracious work of redemption, but also marked by the scars of its history of sin.

A New Interpretation of Romans 7

Augustine famously changed his mind about the interpretation of Romans 7, the biblical locus classicus for the theme of weakness

---

[117] *C. Iul. imp.* 6.8 (CSEL 85.2:304).
[118] *C. Iul. imp.* 6.14 (CSEL 85.2:334).

of will.[119] At first he read verses 14–24 rhetorically, as if Paul were adopting the role of a person still under the law.[120] Later he read them biographically, as if Paul were speaking of his own present experience under grace.[121] As late as 415, Augustine still explicitly interprets the passage as applying to a person *sub lege*, but by 418 the latter reading has taken the place of Augustine's earlier interpretation.[122] This change of mind raises the question of whether Augustine's understanding of the postbaptismal powers of the good will experienced a corresponding shift as he came to attribute Paul's description of the struggle to carry through on good willing to the Christian life. The foregoing examination of Augustine's statements about the ability of the faithful to bring their good willing to fulfillment suggests, however, that the basic trajectory of his assessment of their situation had already been set well before 418. Even before he decided that Romans 7:14–24 applied exclusively to the situation of the baptized Christian, Augustine was already convinced that the baptized suffer from an inability to carry their good willing through to completion; he was already arguing that they needed God's grace to enact the good they will; and he had already stated that, even with God's grace, they continue to experience desires in tension with their good willing.[123]

In his study of Augustine's interpretation of Romans 7 and Romans 9, A. F. W. Lekkerkerker rightly acknowledges that Augustine's view of the person's status *sub gratia* does not change on account of his revised reading of Romans 7, according to which reading Romans 7:14–25 refers exclusively to the *homo*

---

[119] See Lekkerkerker, *Römer 7 und Römer 9 bei Augustin*, though some of his claims regarding how Augustine's evolving interpretation of Romans 7 and 9 fit with larger patterns in the Bishop of Hippo's theology require qualification. See also Ring, "Römer 7 in den Enarrationes in Psalmos," 384–387, for a succinct summary of the history of Augustine's interpretation of the chapter.

[120] In *nat. et gr.* 55.66 (CSEL 60:283), written 415–416, for example, Augustine invokes Paul's example to "get these people to grant that those who have not yet been baptized should implore the help of the grace of the savior. . . . After all, he was not self-sufficient who said, *Wretched man that I am! Who will set me free from the body of this death?* (Rom 7:24)." For Augustine at this time, Romans 7:24 describes someone who "seek[s] the sacrament of baptism" (*quaerit baptismatis sacramentum*) (*nat. et gr.* 55.65; CSEL 60:282).

[121] See *nupt. et conc.* 27.30–31.36.

[122] See Lekkerkerker, *Römer 7 und Römer 9 bei Augustin*, 43–55.

[123] However, by the time we find Augustine speaking of weakness of will postbaptism in *nat. et gr.* (415), we also find him allowing for the application of the "I" of Romans 7 to the person *sub gratia*, even though he does not insist on this reading as the only possible one and he also applies the passage to the person *sub lege*. See Ring, "Römer 7 in den Enarrationes in Psalmos," 384–385n7.

sub gratia.[124] Yet Lekkerkerker's account of this status underplays one of the major constants of Augustine's view. In Lekkerkerker's view, "just as, according to Augustine, in the 'status sub gratia' only a struggle between willing and doing, on the one side, and desiring on the other, remains, so Romans 7 is now reinterpreted so that one can speak, along with Jonas, primarily of a sharpening of language: according to Augustine Paul complains here about concupiscence, which still reigns in him; instead of the *doing* of evil his complaints now have to do with *desires.*"[125] While Augustine indeed hesitates to pin an intentional evil act upon the apostle, instead emphasizing that Paul struggles between his consensual willing on the one side and his nonconsensual fleshly desires on the other, this exegetical decision does not entail that Augustine's account of the human condition *sub gratia* identifies "only a struggle between willing and doing, on the one side, and desiring on the other" as remaining in the baptized.[126] For Augustine, the struggles of believers with sin are far less tidy, and more profound, than Lekkerkerker's division suggests. The battle lines are not between "willing and doing" on the one hand and "desiring" on the other. The conflict cuts through each of these categories.

True, there is a categorical distinction between willingly consenting to the good and doing the good on the one hand and desiring only the good on the other, insofar as the first two are possible with the help of grace, while, even under grace, the third, for Augustine in 418 and after, is unattainable in this life.[127] At no point during the Pelagian controversy, however, does

[124] Lekkerkerker, *Römer 7 und Römer 9 bei Augustin*, 52 and 54. He writes, "Grundsätzlich hat sich das Bild des 'status sub gratia' nicht geändert" and "Man würde erwarten, das Bild des 'status sub gratia' bekomme ganz andere Züge, weil R. 7 jetzt auf diesen status gedeutet wird: statt dessen wird, wie wir schon in der Schrift 'de nuptiis et concupiscentia' bemerkt haben, R. 7 nach einer schon vorher feststehenden Anschauung vom Leben unter der Gnade umgedeutet."

[125] Lekkerkerker, *Römer 7 und Römer 9 bei Augustin*, 45.

[126] Augustine's position is that the apostles experienced evil desires but did not consent to them: "The apostles were human beings and carried about the body which is being corrupted and weighs down the soul. But heaven forbid that we should for this reason say, as this fellow falsely claims, that they 'had always been polluted by unbridled passion (*inmoderata libidine*).' We say, rather, that they were free from consent to evil desires (*a consensione prauarum libidinum*), but because of the concupiscence of the flesh (*concupiscentia carnis*) which they reined in through self-control, they groaned with great humility and piety, longing (*optarent*) not to have concupiscence at all rather than to have to control it" (*c. ep. Pel.* 1.11.24 [CSEL 60:444–445]). Note that Augustine is not discussing "willing" per se but consensual willing. Likewise he is not describing "desiring" per se but "immoderate" or "perverse lusts" and "concupiscence of the flesh." Note also Augustine's observation that the apostles "chose or desired" (*optarent*) to be able to resist concupiscence even while experiencing concupiscence.

[127] Augustine writes in *c. ep. Pel.* 1.11.24, "In this mortal flesh only [Christ] could be free of this concupiscence that resists the spirit." Augustine speaks of the difference between being able to do what is good and being immune to concupiscence as the difference between being able to carry out the

Augustine portray doing the good as something believers can accomplish without a struggle. Even Paul, for example, does not do evil insofar as doing evil entails consent, but precisely against his consent.[128] He does indeed do "what I do not want," in the words of Romans 7:15, insofar as some of his actions stem "from the impulse of concupiscence" (*motu concupiscendi*) though never "from having a mind to consent to evil and to do it" (*affectu consentiendi et inplendi*).[129] Paul does not carry the good through to completion *simpliciter* since he experiences concupiscence without his consent. He does not carry evil through to completion *simpliciter* since he does not consent to it.[130] But he does do both evil and good *secundum quid*.

The tension between these two senses of "doing" indicates a struggle that Paul himself experiences. His example shows that even the apostles had to "[rein] in through self control" the concupiscence of the flesh and "groaned with great humility and piety" in the effort. In applying to other Christians Paul's statement "For to will it is available to me, but to carry through with the good is not available (Rom 7:18)," Augustine rules out the notion that this passage indicates the impossibility of actually "carry[ing] out anything" (*facere*) good. It is "carrying through" (*perficere*) with the good rather than "carrying out" (*facere*) the good, Augustine explains, that Paul designates as unattainable. Augustine urges his flock to examine their own experience, which should show their ability to carry out the good (by resisting lust) even if they cannot carry through with the good (since they continue to experience lust):[131] "It isn't the case, after all, that you don't carry out anything. Lust rebels, and you don't consent; you take a fancy to another man's wife,

---

good (*facere*) and carry through the good (*perficere*). See *serm.* 54.12. After the Council of Carthage, Augustine rejected even the theoretical possibility of sinlessness in this life in the latter sense.

[128] Explaining Paul's statement in Romans 7:15, "I do not know what I do," by saying, "He said, *I do not know,* in the sense that I do not do it, since I do it without any consent" (*c. ep. Pel.* 1.11.23).

[129] *C. ep. Pel.* 1.10.18 (CSEL 60:440). I have adjusted Teske's translation, which referred to *affectu* as "the will," to avoid suggesting that Augustine is here contrasting "will" (*uoluntas*) and "desire." Rather, he is contrasting consensual desire with concupiscence.

[130] In Lekkerkerker's succinct summary of Augustine's new interpretation of Romans 7, "Das Böse wird von diesem Menschen nicht vollbracht, weil er den Begierden nicht gehorcht, das Gute nicht, weil die Begierden noch da sind" (*Römer 7 und Römer 9 bei Augustin*, 45).

[131] For Augustine, "carrying out" (*facere*) the good means not giving one's consent to concupiscence while "carrying through with" (*perficere*) the good means no longer experiencing this concupiscence. Earlier in the sermon, Augustine had given descriptions parallel to this distinction: "Not to lust is the mark of the altogether perfect person; not to go after one's lusts marks the person who is fighting, struggling, toiling" (*serm.* 154.8). Unless otherwise noted, this and subsequent translations of Augustine's sermons may be found in *Sermons*, trans. Edmund Hill, WSA III/1–III/11 (Hyde Park, NY: New City Press, 1990–1997). In *c. ep. Pel.* he had defined "carrying through with the good (*perficere*)" by saying that "to bring the good to completion means that one does not even have concupiscence, but the good is incomplete when one has concupiscence, even if one does not consent to

but you don't give your approval."[132] Augustine's claim that Christians do not fail to carry out anything good, however, is different from the claim that Christians carry out the good without a struggle, or that they succeed in carrying out the good in every case.[133] Augustine repeatedly warns against the dangers of overestimating one's capacities to resist temptation, pointing out that petitioning God's aid in this regard, not least in the words of the Lord's Prayer, is a vital practice of Christian piety. He also acknowledges the reality that baptized Christians sometimes fail, not only to carry through with the good, but even to carry it out.[134] Such weakness is endemic in the Christian life.

Despite the fact that consensually willing and carrying out the good are attainable with the help of grace while exclusively desiring it is not, then, without grace and continued reliance on God for help in the struggle against sin, none of the three is possible. In this sense, all three have a more fundamental feature in common, which relativizes differences in the extent to which human beings can carry out each in this earthly life. In terms of "struggle," meanwhile, both doing the good and desiring the good are implicated. Augustine does not speak of doing the good one wills as something automatic or guaranteed, even for the holiest of Christians; rather, he constantly stresses the importance of contending against temptation through prayer and other efforts.[135] Thus the overarching picture he presents of the human capacity for achieving a good will and bringing it to completion in this life, be it in actions or in desires, is one of dependence and struggle, even if it is a struggle in which the baptized tend to triumph in the case of consensual willing and acting.

concupiscence in order to do an evil action" (*c. ep. Pel.* 1.10.19). There he also explains that when Paul says "I do not do it" (in Romans 7:15) he means "I do it without any consent" (*c. ep. Pel.* 1.11.23). Only when our mortal bodies are resurrected will we triumph with respect to concupiscence as well as with respect to consent: "When he has, then, given life to our mortal bodies, not only we will [*sic*] not consent to sin, but we will not even have any concupiscence of the flesh to which we might consent" (*c. ep. Pel.* 1.11.24).

[132] See *serm.* 154.12.

[133] As Augustine observes later in the sermon when commenting on Romans 7:22–23, "The strife is still your business" (*serm.* 154.14).

[134] Baptism, he observes, "does not take away the weakness against which those who have been reborn struggle, when they fight the good fight, and to which they consent, when as human beings they are taken by surprise in some sin" (*c. ep. Pel.* 3.3.5).

[135] Yet at the same time, he stresses the importance of our effort, that we exert our will. "Nor does it follow that we should rely on prayers alone in this matter and not bring to bear the strength of our will (*efficacia uoluntatis*) upon living a good life. After all, God is said to be our helper, and we cannot be helped unless we try to do something ourselves, because God does not produce our salvation in us as if we were mindless rocks or beings in whose nature he did not create reason and will" (*pecc. mer.* 2.5.6; CSEL 60:77).

If Augustine's decisive adoption in 418 of a revised interpretation of Romans 7 did not substantially alter his conception of the status of the human being under grace, does this suggest that biblical statements on this issue were unimportant for his thinking? This conclusion does not follow. First, according to Augustine, Romans 7 was not the only relevant biblical pericope to consider vis-à-vis the question of the ability of baptized believers to enact their good willing. Augustine's preexisting view on this question was not formed in a scripture-free vacuum. It had already been shaped decisively by other biblical passages, especially by Galatians 5:17 and the Lord's Prayer. (We will see further evidence of this in chapter 6.) Thus the fact that Augustine's views about weakness of will postbaptism had already been formed before he resolutely changed his mind about Romans 7 does not indicate the marginality of scripture to his thinking on the baptized person's capacity for good willing. Rather, it represents another instance of his interpreting scripture via scripture, a method we have already seen at work in *Simpl.* in Augustine's reading of Romans 9.[136] Furthermore, as Thomas Gerhard Ring points out, Augustine's new reading of Romans 7 did not surface "over night." The change whereby he came to read Romans 7:14–24 as referring exclusively to the person *sub gratia* was preceded by a period in which he entertained two possible readings of the passage and eventually leaned, even before his final decision, more toward the *sub gratia* reading.[137] Even though he did not decide upon a firm position until 418, then, as early as 411 or 412 with *pecc. mer.* he was already giving serious consideration to an interpretation of Romans 7 that would better accord with his teaching on postbaptismal weakness of will. Thus the date of 418 should not be allowed to disguise the fact that his "new reading" of Romans

---

[136] How Augustine used scripture to interpret scripture in each case is slightly different. Other passages from the Pauline corpus changed his mind about how to interpret Romans 9. As for Romans 7, Lekkerkerker explains, having decided the text referred to Paul's experience *sub gratia*, Augustine used his scripturally shaped understanding of the character of this experience to determine the referents of the "willing" and "doing" of which Paul speaks. Lekkerkerker also argues, however, that the decision to interpret Romans 7 as applying to Christian experience *sub gratia* was itself prompted by scripture, though in this instance by the text of Romans 7 itself rather than other passages from the Pauline corpus. Lekkerkerker argues that neither the authority of other biblical interpreters of the past, nor anti-Pelagian polemic, nor emphasis on the concupiscence of the redeemed prompted the change in Augustine's interpretation of Romans 7. "Augustin selbst nennt andere Motive: *das Wort der Schrift habe ihn zu einer Aenderung der Exegese gezwungen*" (*Römer 7 und Römer 9 bei Augustin*, 52, italics original). See also *c. ep. Pel.* 1.10.22, where Augustine explicitly names Romans 7:17 and Romans 7:22.

[137] Ring, "Römer 7 in den Enarrationes in Psalmos," 384–385n7.

7 was a live option in his thinking before that point and hence capable of interacting with other aspects of his thought.[138]

In short, in 418 Augustine takes a decisive exegetical stance that explains how Romans 7 fits with the evidence he finds elsewhere in scripture for supporting the idea that willing the good is possible for the baptized by grace even while completely fulfilling this good will remains a challenge in this life. His change of mind confirms the importance he accords to passages such as Galatians 5:17, and to pursuing a coherent interpretation of all relevant passages on the topic, rather than the independence of his perspective from the biblical text.

Conclusion

This chapter has traced Augustine's appraisal of what lies within the power of the human will as his views on the issue gain further sharpness and definition over the course of the Pelagian controversy. We approached this topic by addressing two related questions. Part I examined Augustine's answers to the question of the extent to which achieving a good will is in our power, while part II focused on his assessment of the degree to which it is possible to act upon a good will, having once achieved it.

In the first part we observed that, while Augustine insists throughout the Pelagian controversy that right willing is impossible without God's help, there is a shift in emphasis whereby he comes more and more to portray God as the primary agent responsible for producing right human willing in fallen human beings. Around 417, however, Augustine begins not only to emphasize God's role but also to de-emphasize the role of the human will in producing right human willing. In 426 and the years following he becomes even more scrupulous about asserting God's primacy in producing good human willing, now contending that the good will is wrought in us by God alone, without human assistance. These changes are emblematized in Augustine's evolving views on

---

[138] Insofar as the groundwork for the change in Augustine's interpretation of Romans 7 was laid in a multistranded, complex web of thought that he had begun weaving together long before his "new" reading was first introduced, there is a structural parallel to the process Peter Brown has observed at work in the formation of Augustine's mature attitude toward coercion. Sudden symptoms do not warrant the assumption of a short incubation period. As with many aspects of Augustine's thinking, we find "a sudden precipitation, under external pressures, of ideas which, previously, had evolved slowly and imperceptibly over a long time." See Peter Brown, "St. Augustine's Attitude to Religious Coercion," in *Religion and Society in the Age of Augustine* (London: Faber and Faber, 1972), 264.

the resistibility of grace. While in *spir. et litt.* (412), during the first phase of the controversy, Augustine asserts that assenting or dissenting in response to God is proper to the will, in *c. Iul.* (421), written during the second phase of the controversy, he provides infants as an example of the irresistibility of God's omnipotent will. Finally in *corrept.* (427) he explicitly states that human choice per se is incapable of resisting God's will to save.

Part II demonstrated that Augustine's thinking on the extent to which it is possible to enact a good will, once a good will has been attained, evinces even greater continuity. From *Simpl.* on, and throughout the duration of the Pelagian controversy, Augustine consistently affirms that the power actually to perform the good that one wills is God-given. Likewise he maintains through all three major phases of the Pelagian controversy that the baptized suffer from weakness of will. Following the Council of Carthage in 418, Augustine does decisively reject the possibility of sinlessness in this life, and by that same year he has begun to read Romans 7:14–24 as describing Paul's situation *sub gratia* rather than *sub lege*. These new developments in his thinking bring his convictions and interpretation of Romans 7 into alignment with his interpretation of other biblical passages, such as Galatians 5:17 and the Lord's Prayer.

The cumulative picture that emerged from these two sections was one in which Augustine's thinking on the human potential to enact good will remains fairly constant during the Pelagian controversy, while his thinking on human ability to achieve a good will in the first place undergoes considerable development. The latter divides into three major stages, which loosely parallel those outlined by J. Patout Burns in his study of Augustine's doctrine of operative grace. These stages are aptly summarized in a series of statements Augustine had made well over a decade before he became embroiled in the Pelagian controversy, in *Simpl.* There he had not only stated that "actual willing is certainly within our power,"[139] but also that "the power to will" (*ut uelimus*) is "both [God's] and ours, his because he calls us, ours because we follow when called,"[140] and finally that "the good will

---

[139] *Simpl.* 1.1.11 (CCL 44:15): *certe enim ipsum uelle in potestate est.* Of Paul's statement in Romans 7:16, "If what I would not, that I do, I consent unto the law that it is good," Augustine writes that Paul "does not will (*non vult*) to do what he in fact does" (*Simpl.* 1.1.9 [CCL 44:14]).

[140] Augustine concludes in response to Simplician's second question, "The power to will (*ut uelimus*) he has willed should be both his and ours, his because he calls us, ours because we follow when called. But what we actually will (*quod autem uolerimus*) he alone gives, i.e., the power to do right (*posse bene agere*) and to live happily forever." Willing the good, however, is no longer "up to us"

itself is wrought in us by the working of God"[141] such that refusing to follow when called lies beyond the power of the human will.[142] The first claim is well adapted to his allowances in a first stage of the Pelagian controversy, from 411 to 417; the second pronouncement aptly summarizes his transitional, more compromising stance from around 417 to 426, which nonetheless explicitly grants primacy to God's initiative; the last assertion is a point upon which Augustine strongly insists in a final stage in 426 and following. From the very outset of the Pelagian controversy, then, Augustine thought human beings needed drastic assistance in doing the good they willed; over time he insisted more and more vigorously that willing the good at all was just as great a challenge, one requiring equally dramatic levels of divine assistance.

The point that *Simpl.* contains Augustine's mature teaching on our powers of good will *in nuce*, though certainly not in fully developed form, pertains to a question that any consideration of the development of Augustine's thinking inevitably raises: Why did his thinking evolve as it did? The seminal representation of each of Augustine's key mature points of emphasis on this topic in *Simpl.* shows us that the answer cannot be simply that they stemmed from polemical encounters, either with Donatists or Pelagians. Rather their seeds had already been planted in Augustine's struggles to answer the humble inquiries of his colleague Simplician, the bishop of Milan. As we observed in chapter 2, these struggles drew Augustine into a wrestling match with Paul, the true "father," along with other biblical writers, not only of Augustine's teaching on the character of fallen human willing but also, as we have now seen, of his thinking on the possibilities of achieving and acting upon a good will. The Pelagian controversy was the patient midwife, but never the mother, of Augustine's mature thinking on the good will.

Still, thanks to Augustine's labors to clarify his views of good human willing over the course of the Pelagian controversy, we have seen another facet of his theologically differentiated conception of will take on further clarity. Just as Augustine tells a story about the origins of human willing in

---

simpliciter but both his and ours (*et suum . . . et nostrum*), his by virtue of calling (*suum uocando*), ours by virtue of following (*nostrum sequendo*). See *Simpl.* 1.2.10 (CCL 44:35).

[141] *Simpl.* 1.2.12 (CCL 44:36): *ubi satis ostendit etiam ipsam bonam uoluntatem in nobis operante deo fieri.*

[142] If it were possible that someone could resist God's call, if someone could have it "in the power of his will not to obey, it could be said correctly that it is not of God who hath mercy, but of the man who willeth and runneth, for the mercy of him that calleth is not sufficient unless the obedience of him who is called follows" (*Simpl.* 1.2.13 [CCL 44:37]).

its created integrity, a story that explains both its promise and peril, and just as he had a story to tell about how the fall entirely changed the structure of human willing, in the Pelagian controversy he develops a more detailed plot line of the story of its return to goodness. In this chapter we have focused on one of the characters in this story: the human being. What is her part to play? What does she want? Can she change this? Once she wants what is good for her, to what extent can she do it? These familiar questions echo down through every human drama, but they find their complete answer, according to Augustine, only when we consider another character. It is no secret that in Augustine's story, God is the deus ex machina. It is to how God impacts Augustine's story of good human willing that we turn our full attention in chapter 4.

4

God's Gardening

The previous chapter demonstrated that Augustine's thinking on the question of what is within the power of the human will during the Pelagian controversy developed in three major stages corresponding to three key statements already expressed in *Simpl.* From 411 to around 417 Augustine characterized good willing, exemplified in faith and belief, as "in our power." Beginning around 417, however, he shifted emphasis away from the contributions of the human will to its own goodness. Finally, in 426 and following, Augustine asserted that "we do nothing good in our willing" and excluded the possibility of human resistance to the divine will to save.

This chapter is the previous chapter's twin. It addresses the flip side of Augustine's developing treatment of the question of what is within human power with respect to good willing: the question of what must be attributed to God's power. A balanced account of Augustine's developing notion of good human willing during the Pelagian controversy must turn precisely to the question of God's role in this "human" phenomenon since, for Augustine, good human willing is unthinkable, after the fall, without God's intervention to heal and restore it. The vision of good human willing that emerges when God's role is taken into account stands in contrast to descriptions of created and fallen willing Augustine had articulated earlier, but, like Augustine's account of what is in human power, it demonstrates development within a continuous overarching trajectory.

Prayer occupies a central position in Augustine's defense and development of his views about God's impact on the human will over all three of the major phases of the Pelagian controversy: a first phase from around 411 to around 417, a second phase from around 417 to around 426, and a third phase from 426 to the end of Augustine's life. The role of prayer in Augustine's account of God's impact upon the human will is the theme of part I of this chapter. As we will observe, during all three of these periods, the bedrock argument informing Augustine's view of God's impact on the human will is that prayer proves it. According to Augustine, biblical prayers and injunctions to prayer serve as evidence that God helps the will. More

Augustine on the Will. Han-luen Kantzer Komline, Oxford University Press (2020). © Oxford University Press.
DOI: 10.1093/oso/9780190948801.001.0001

specifically, prayer serves as evidence of the need for God's help to over-come temptation (part I, section A) as well as of the fact that God produces good will in conversion (part I, section B). Augustine insists upon the former point from the very beginning of the Pelagian controversy and the latter already in *nat. et gr.* of 416.

The second part of this chapter turns to changes, over the course of the Pelagian controversy, in Augustine's presentation of God's impact upon the will. Throughout the major stages of the Pelagian controversy Augustine describes God as extending a twofold help to humankind with regard to willing the good. His explanation of these two aspects, however, alters over time. Here again, the phases outlined at the outset of chapter 3 will prove useful. In the first phase of the Pelagian controversy, Augustine describes God's twofold help as consisting of bestowing knowledge and making the good attractive (part II, section A). In the controversy's second stage, he describes this twofold help as consisting of a reorientation of the will and of assistance in carrying out the good. During this same period, several other characterizations of how God aids the will surface as well: Augustine speaks of God driving the will, of God granting help for discrete actions, of God pouring love into human wills, and of God's unmediated interior operation on the will. Augustine also begins speaking of God as the author of the good will and to describe the human will as dispensable, language that attributes not only direct agency but also a certain primacy to God over human agents in bringing about good human willing. Thus, in the second stage of the Pelagian controversy, God moves squarely into the limelight of Augustine's account of good human willing (part II, section B). In the last stage of the Pelagian controversy Augustine speaks of God working unilaterally, without human beings, to convert the will from evil to good; of God directing, inclining, and exercising dominion over wills; and of God as the exclusive source of good will, who bestows the love that is neces-sary and sufficient for good will (part II, section C).

In short, this chapter demonstrates that Augustine describes God's im-pact on the will in a variety of ways over the course of the Pelagian con-troversy, but that he always insists on the necessity of God's help for good willing. Part I presents an argument Augustine repeatedly invokes to sup-port according God such a decisive role: prayer, most especially prayer and injunctions to prayer found in the biblical witness. His way of characterizing God's role in good human willing evolves, but the basis for his insistence upon it remains constant. As time goes on, he describes this divine help as increasingly targeted, both in terms of the specific individuals in question and in terms of how God elicits their good willing. By the final phase of Augustine's teachings on the good will in the Pelagian controversy, to ignore God's role in the drama of the redemption of the human will would be to overlook this drama's chief protagonist.

Part I: Prayer and God's Impact on the Will

Augustine consistently draws on biblical prayers, especially the Lord's Prayer, to verify his teaching on God's involvement in good human willing. Prayer for enemies, for example, confirms that God is responsible for converting bad wills to the good. Prayer not to be led into temptation, on the other hand, underlines the need for God's help to carry out the good actions one wills to perform. Again demonstrating development amid over-arching consistency, Augustine reiterates the latter argument throughout the Pelagian controversy, while articulating the former most frequently in the second stage of the conflict.

For Augustine, the Lord's Prayer functions as a mirror (*speculum*) that reflects the life of the just (*uita iustorum*), with all of its shadows and spots. In the images this glass casts back, one may discern the realities of the life of the faithful. The faithful are dependent on God for daily sustenance: they need forgiveness, and they struggle to avoid temptation. Augustine cites Philippians 3:12–15 to sketch the image the prayer reflects: that of a runner straining toward the goal, still far from triumph at the finish line. The prayer Christ taught his disciples paints, for those Christians who honestly con-front the grounds for their petitions, a humbling picture of the Christian life. It is marked by frailty, weakness, and the need for grace.[1]

Given its reflective function, the Lord's Prayer, which was important for the decisions on Pelagianism handed down at the Council of Carthage in 418, served, for Augustine, as a vital source of theological insight. Clearly, he points out in the year 427, God does not need human beings to pray in order to unleash his gracious action in the world.[2] Prayer must have some

---

[1] *Perf. iust.* 8.19 (CSEL 42:17): "If we do not want to be argumentative, we have in that prayer a glass held before us in which we can see the life of the righteous who live from faith and run perfectly, though they are not without sin."

[2] *De dono perseuerantiae* (*perseu.*, 428/429) 7.15: "He could give this to us, even if we did not pray for it, but he wanted us to be reminded by our prayer that we receive these benefits from him." Unless otherwise noted, this and subsequent translations of *perseu.* come from Augustine, "The Gift

other purpose. One reason that God in Christ teaches believers how to pray, Augustine suggests, is so that they might learn their limits and recognize God's grace. The request to be delivered from temptation, for example, indicates that perseverance in the good comes from God: "In this matter the Church does not, of course, await laborious arguments, but pays attention to its daily prayers."[3] If human beings themselves had the wherewithal to secure their perseverance, there would be no need to beseech God for assistance to withstand temptation. For Augustine, the Lord's Prayer provides a theological short-cut. Its obvious implications about grace obviate lengthy argumentative detours.

In Augustine's view, the Pelagians have not only missed this short-cut but also gone astray along a rabbit trail. Far from noticing the implications of the petitions of the Lord's Prayer, Augustine claims, his Pelagian interlocutors go so far as to "say that a petition in the Lord's Prayer is unnecessary for righteous persons in this life," a claim he believes constitutes one of the defining errors of their position.[4] Even if the Pelagians are not in every case ready to admit the implications of their view, their overestimation of the powers of the will entails an underestimation of the necessity of prayer: "These people, however, attribute such power to the will that they remove prayer from a life of piety. For, precisely in order that we may resist the devil and that he may flee from us, we say in prayer, *Bring us not into temptation* (Mt 6:13). Precisely for this reason we have been warned, like soldiers, by our commander who exhorts us with the words, *Watch and pray so that you do not enter into temptation* (Mk 14:38)."[5] Augustine's disagreement with the Pelagians about the scope of the human will comes to a head with the Lord's Prayer. According to Augustine's presentation of the matter, the dilemma is straightforward: Should a preexisting conception of will constrain the practice of prayer, or should the prayers commanded and taught by Christ constrain the church's conception of the nature and needs of the will? For Augustine, this dilemma presents not a complex intellectual

---

of Perseverance," in *Answer to the Pelagians, IV: To the Monks of Hadrumetum and Provence*, trans. Roland Teske, WSA I/26, (Hyde Park, NY: New City Press, 1999).

[3] *Perseu.* 7.15.

[4] Augustine writes, "If anyone does not attribute to the grace of God the freedom to which we are called, or if anyone denies that Christ is the savior of the little ones, or if any say that a petition in the Lord's Prayer is unnecessary for righteous persons in this life on their own account, they receive the name of this error because they share in its crime by their error" (*c. Iul.* 3.1.2 [PL 44:703]).

[5] *Nat. et gr.* 58.68 (CSEL 60:284–285).

puzzle but a simple opportunity to obey Christ's explicit commands and take refuge in God's help.

Section A: Prayer as Evidence of Need for God's Help to Overcome Temptation

Augustine observes at the very outset of the Pelagian controversy that asserting that we can "do what is right, or carry out the commandment of righteousness in every respect" without the help of God is tantamount to declaring that prayers for God's aid to avoid sin are redundant.[6] He writes, "Let us then drive away from our hearing and from our minds those who say that, having received once and for all free choice of the will, we need not pray that God might help us not to sin."[7] While he also warns against presuming that prayer alone can make us righteous without our own effort to "bring to bear the strength of our will upon living a good life," Augustine thinks the unacceptable implications of the notion of the self-sufficiency of the will for Christian prayer clearly demonstrate that the human will needs God's help to do the good.[8] Without a doubt, prayer is both necessary and beneficial, else Christ would not have commanded it. Thus a view of the will that inevitably entails the opposite conclusions about prayer must be mistaken. As the controversy goes on, Augustine repeats this argument in a variety of contexts, appealing to a variety of biblical prayers for aid to avoid sin. Each of these, he is convinced, shows our need for God's aid: "We would not need prayer, if our will alone was sufficient."[9] That God helps believers to overcome temptation follows from scripture and the church's concomitant practice of the prayers contained and commanded therein.[10]

Augustine returns repeatedly to the petitions from the Lord's Prayer "May your will be done on earth as it is in heaven" (Mt 6:10) and "Bring us

---

[6] Pecc. mer. 5.5.

[7] Pecc. mer. 2.5.6.

[8] Pecc. mer. 5.6.

[9] Perf. iust. 10.21.

[10] Perf. iust. 10.21: "After all, we pray, *May my heart become spotless* (Ps 119:80), and *Guide my journeys according to your word, and let not sinfulness lord it over me* (Ps 119:133), and *May your will be done on earth as it is in heaven* (Mt 6:10), and *Bring us not into temptation* (Mt 6:13), and other prayers of this sort, which it would take a long time to mention. By these, we pray precisely for this: that we might carry out God's commandments. We would not be commanded to do them [God's commandments], if our will did nothing at all, and we would not need prayer, if our will alone was sufficient."

not into temptation, but deliver us from evil" (Mt 6:13)[11] as clear evidence that our will's ability "to accomplish what it does" depends on God.[12] To ask for God's will to be done in the world is to seek God's help to enact the good one wills in accordance with God's will.[13] To ask for deliverance from temptation is to seek God's help to resist willing what is evil. Both requests, then, illustrate that "it is not that this is done without our will, but that our will (*uoluntas*) does not accomplish what it does unless it is helped by God."[14]

Augustine regards this conclusion as a matter of "sound faith" (*fidei sanitas*). After observing, "It is not that this is done without our will, but that our will does not accomplish what it does unless it is helped by God," he concludes, "This is the sound faith that leads us to pray." This principle of sound faith not only follows from Christ's teaching of the Lord's Prayer to his disciples as recorded in scripture but also promotes obedience to Christ's general injunctions to seek divine aid.[15] On more than one occasion, then, Christ himself endorsed the idea that the will needs God's help to accomplish the good. Christ did not command that we pray for God's help for his own benefit, moreover, but rather because such prayer promises very real benefits to those who practice it. Thus, Augustine points out, rejecting a "sound faith" in our will's need for God to accomplish the good shuts the door on God's merciful provision.[16] Here again Augustine eschews further

---

[11] See *nat. et gr.* 18.20 (CSEL 60:246): "The Lord's Prayer teaches that we should ask for both of these: both that our debts be forgiven and that we not be led into temptation, the former so that past sins be wiped away, the latter so that future sins be avoided. Although this does not happen without our willing it, the will alone is not enough to accomplish it (*uoluntas sola non sufficit*). Hence, the prayer offered to the Lord for this purpose is neither superfluous nor shameless." See also *nat. et gr.* 67.80. Augustine continues to maintain that the petition not to be led into temptation indicates the will's inability to avoid sin on its own through the very end of his career. In *c. Iul. imp.* 1.108, Augustine points again to the petition in the Lord's Prayer not to be led into temptation as evidence that it is not in the power of our free choice to resist sin on our own in the present. See also *c. Iul. imp.* 3.109.

[12] In *corrept.* (427), Augustine mentions the line "May your name be made holy" as evidence that the faithful need God's help to persevere, noting that Cyprian interprets the text in this way. See *corrept.* 6.10: "Whoever begs from the Lord to persevere in the good admits that such perseverance is his gift."

[13] In making this point in *c. ep. Pel.* (see 4.8.20–4.9.26), Augustine leans on Cyprian's interpretation of the Lord's Prayer, quoting his statement that Christ says "*May your will be done in heaven and on earth* 'not so that God may do what he wills, but so that we can do what God wills. Who, after all, stands in the way of God's doing what he wills? . . . And so that his will may be done in us, we have need of God's will'" (*c. ep. Pel.* 4.9.25).

[14] *Perf. iust.* 19.40 (CSEL 42:43).

[15] *Perf. iust.* 19.40 (CSEL 42:43): "This is the sound faith that leads us to pray: to seek in order that we may find, to beg in order that we may receive, to knock in order that the door may be opened for us."

[16] *Perf. iust.* 19.40 (CSEL 42:43): "One who argues against this faith closes in his own face the door of God's mercy."

argumentation as unnecessary, appealing rather to "the prayerful groans of the faithful."[17] A final reason, then, to embrace the conclusion "It is not that this is done without our will, but that our will (*uoluntas*) does not accomplish what it does unless it is helped by God" is that it corresponds to the lived practice of the faithful who moan and beat their breasts as they recite the Lord's Prayer in worship.[18] For each of these reasons, the affirmation that the human will needs God to enact the good constitutes "such an important thing" (*re tanta*)[19] that it should be regarded as a basic tenet of obedient and salutary faith. Augustine does not think the theological explanation for how a good will is possible needs to be established by argument alone. Rather, this explanation deserves acceptance as a matter of faith.[20]

For Augustine, the Lord's Prayer illuminates but also enables good human willing. In addition to arguing directly from the Lord's Prayer to the notion that perseverance is a divine gift,[21] Augustine draws this same conclusion from the Lord's Prayer on behalf of the fading faith of Peter, who is about to deny Christ, referenced in Luke 22:32. Augustine writes, "If you say that it pertains to the free choice of a human being which you defend, not in accord with the grace of God, but in opposition to it, that anyone perseveres or does not persevere in the good, not because God grants it if he does persevere, but because the human will brings it about,

---

[17] "I do not intend to say anything more on a matter of such importance, because I am better off to entrust it to the prayerful groans of the faithful," he writes (*perf. iust.* 19.40 [CSEL 42:43]).

[18] In addition to citing the faithful's repetition of the Lord's Prayer, Augustine also unpacks the implications of contemporary and spontaneous prayers of Christians. In *gest. Pel.* (417), for example, he points to a prayer of his own, written into a letter he wrote to Pelagius, as itself pointing to the will's need for God's grace to do what is right. His prayer that Pelagius might be pleasing to the Lord, he says (perhaps somewhat circularly), itself implies that God's grace is necessary to make the human will good. Commenting on his letter to Pelagius, which Pelagius used to help establish his credibility at the Synod of Diospolis, Augustine observes, "By my prayer in the closing line, namely, that he might be pleasing to the Lord, I indicated that this lies in God's grace rather than in the human will alone, since I did not exhort or command or teach him this, but uttered a prayer" (29.53). Augustine's point is that his prayer did not endorse Pelagius but rather underlined his theological complaint against him. Though Augustine's intimation that Pelagius should have understood his statement about praying that he might be pleasing to the Lord in this way is far-fetched, his theological point is solid: such prayers are made to no effect if God has no role in helping the will do what is pleasing to him (CSEL 42:106).

[19] *Perf. iust.* 19.40 (CSEL 42:43). My translation.

[20] Augustine clinches the case "from faith" in the concluding lines of *perf. iust.* (415) with another allusion to the Lord's Prayer. See *perf. iust.* 21.44 (CSEL 42:48): "If someone denies that we ought to pray so that we do not enter into temptation—[insisting] that the human will is sufficient (*humanam sufficere uoluntatem*), once the law has been received—I have no doubt that such a person should be banished from everyone's hearing and should be condemned by everyone's lips."

[21] As, for example, in *corrept.* 6.10, where Augustine mentions the line "May your name be made holy" as evidence that the faithful need God's help to persevere. Augustine writes, "Whoever begs from the Lord to persevere in the good admits that such perseverance is his gift."

what are you going to devise against the words of the Lord who said, *I have prayed for you, Peter, that your faith may not fail* (Lk 22:32)?"[22] The Lord himself, Augustine observes, attributes Peter's perseverance not to Peter's willing, or even to Peter's praying, but to his intercession on Peter's behalf. Thus the Lord's Prayer informs Augustine's conception of the capacities of the good human will but also, in the sense of Christ's prayers for his sheep, makes good human willing possible and infallibly guarantees that it comes about. All while maintaining Peter's free will, Christ's prayers on his behalf bestowed upon Peter's willing the permanence and strength it needed to prevail without fail.[23]

Section B: Prayer as Evidence that God Produces Good Will in Conversion

Though Augustine's arguments from the Lord's Prayer and his prayers for his followers that God brings about the conversion of the will collect in the highest concentrations in 418 and following, already in 416, with *Natura et Gratia*, he makes an analogous point. Without using the terminology of "will" or appealing directly to the Lord's Prayer, he nonetheless contends that prayers for conversion recorded in the Bible support the idea that grace enables a person's transition from living under the law to entering the blessing of life under grace. In moving terms, Augustine insists that Pelagius's teachings in effect stifle the cries for help of the unbaptized who plead for grace. Of Paul's entreaties in Romans 7:24 (which Augustine still, at this point, interprets as those of a man under the law), he writes, "Allow him to pray; allow him to demand the help of a most powerful physician. Why oppose him? Why shout him down? Why prevent the wretch from seeking the mercy of Christ? At least, why should Christians do this?" Augustine observes, "There were, after all, companions of Christ who tried to prevent the blind man from crying out and begging to see the light, but even amid the uproar of those who were stopping him, Christ heard his cry.

---

[22] *Corrept.* 8.17 (CSEL 92:238).
[23] *Corrept.* 8.17: "Or will you dare to say that, even though Christ prayed that Peter's faith would not fail, it would have failed if Peter had willed that it fail, that is, if he willed not to persevere up to the end? As if Peter would in any way will something other than Christ prayed that he would will! . . . The human will does not, of course, obtain grace by its freedom; it rather obtains freedom by grace and, in order that it may persevere, it obtains a delightful permanence and an insuperable strength."

Hence, this apostle heard the answer, *The grace of God through Jesus Christ our Lord* (Rom 7:25)."[24] If the natural gift of free choice exhausts God's contribution to good human willing, then even biblical prayers for help such as that of Paul, in Romans 7, or the persistent pleas of Bartimaeus for mercy, recorded in the gospel of Mark, lack a raison d'être. But the fact of the matter is, Augustine observes, these prayers were answered. Paul found grace and Jesus stood still to call Bartimaeus to him. Thus any premise that depicts these prayers as superfluous must be rejected.[25]

Beginning in 418, Augustine advances the more specific claim that Christ's injunction in Matthew 5:44 to pray for one's enemies proves God converts the will.[26] Shifting focus to the prayers of other Christians on Saul's behalf, rather than Paul's own prayers for mercy, he asks, "After all, why does the Lord command us to pray for those who persecute us? Do we pray that they receive the grace of God in return for their good will and not rather that their bad will itself be turned to good?"[27] In Augustine's mind the answer is obvious. Christ commands these prayers, not as an empty exercise or merely for the benefit of the one who prays, but because it truly is in God's power to operate upon the wills of those individuals who are opposed to him, converting them to himself. In his own words, "The will itself, as Saul's was . . . [is] stirred to believe by God, although one is turned away from the faith even to the point of persecuting believers."[28] Christ's injunction to pray for one's enemies, then, illustrates the breadth of the relevant context for considering the causes at work in human willing. It is insufficient to consider the individual whose will is in question as a voluntary universe unto herself. The movements of her willing cannot be charted unless the paths of other celestial bodies are taken into account, which exert their

[24] *Nat. et gr.* 55.65.

[25] Later Augustine's focus will shift from people's own prayers for their conversion to the prayers of believers for the conversion of unbelievers, as, given his increasingly intense insistence that we need God to even begin to will the good, it will make less and less sense to speak of someone calling out to God for help without an antecedent act of grace making this possible. At this point, Augustine thinks that the prayer being made indicates one cannot accomplish what is being prayed for alone, but later he will become persuaded that even being able to make the prayer presupposes grace.

[26] Augustine often repeats this argument in the years following. In 421 he writes, "To no purpose did he command us to pray for our enemies, if it was not up to him to turn back hearts that have turned away and are hostile" (*c. Iul.* 4.8.41). At the very end of his career, he again insists that biblical injunctions to pray for conversion of unbelievers constitute evidence that God converts the will. Among these is the Lord's Prayer, and he alludes to Cyprian's interpretation of it, concluding, "For if God did not make human beings willing from unwilling, we certainly would not pray that those who are unwilling to believe might will to believe" (*c. Iul. imp.* 6.10 [CSEL 85.2:313]).

[27] *C. ep. Pel.* 1.19.37 (CSEL 60:454).

[28] *C. ep. Pel.* 1.19.37

own pull upon her, and, in God's case, possess the power to redirect the trajectory of her willing.

Just as Christ's directive to pray for one's enemies confirms God's conversion of the will, so, according to Augustine, the prayer he taught his disciples, which includes a prayer for enemies, offers further evidence of this very same point. Following Cyprian's lead, Augustine interprets the petition "May your will be done in heaven and on earth" as a metaphorical request for God's will to be done in the lives of both believers and nonbelievers.[29] Though Cyprian himself does not develop this argument with respect to implications for the human will, Augustine reads the request as targeting the transformation of the unwillingness of unbelievers into willingness: "We pray, therefore, not only for those who are unwilling, but even for those who resist and attack. What, then, do we pray for but that they become willing instead of unwilling, that they are made to consent instead of to resist, that they are made lovers instead of attackers."[30] According to this figurative reading of the petition for God's will to be done, then, the Lord's Prayer itself confirms that God converts the wills of unbelievers so that they are transformed from attackers into lovers.[31]

Having interpreted the request for God's will to be done on earth as an instance of prayer for God to convert the enemies of grace so that they turn to the good, Augustine can invoke the prayers of the faithful, as well as scripture and the explicit commands of Christ, as proclaiming in chorus God's power to convert the human will.[32] Augustine frames his appeal to the church's testimony as a question: "Does not the Church pray for her

---

[29] See Han-luen Kantzer Komline, "Grace, Free Will, and the Lord's Prayer: Cyprian's Importance for the 'Augustinian' Doctrine of Grace," *Augustinian Studies* 45, no. 2 (2014): 247–279.

[30] *C. ep. Pel.* 4.9.26

[31] Augustine asks, "By whom will this be done but by him of whom scripture says, *The will is prepared by the Lord* (Prv 8:35 LXX)?" (*c. ep. Pel.* 4.9.26). Augustine often repeats this argument as the Pelagian controversy continues. In *ep.* 215.3 (CSEL 57:390), for example, noting that he has read Cyprian's *The Lord's Prayer* with the monks from Valentine's monastery, he observes, "There we also demonstrated how the same most glorious martyr warned us that we ought to pray, even for our enemies who have not yet believed in Christ, so that they may come to believe. This would, of course, be a pointless act if the Church did not believe that even the evil and unbelieving wills of human beings can be converted to the good by the grace of God." This and subsequent translations of Augustine's letters come from Augustine, *Letters*, trans. Roland Teske, WSA II/1–II/4 (Hyde Park, NY: New City Press, 2001–2005), unless otherwise noted.

[32] Augustine reiterates this argument frequently. In *praed. sanct.* (427), for example, he points to the church's prayer for persecutors and to Paul's prayer for fellow Jews. Both examples illustrate the point Augustine drives home with this rhetorical question: "Why then do we pray for those who do not will to believe if not in order that God might also produce the will in them?" (*praed. sanct.* 8.15 [PL 44:971–972]).

enemies?" He asserts that she does. She prays "that their bad will may be changed into a good will, for *the will is prepared by the Lord* (Prv 8:35 LXX) and, as the apostle says, *It is God, after all, who produces in you the willing as well* (Phil 2:13)."[33] Augustine's interpretation of the Lord's Prayer as including a petition that God convert the wills of unbelievers thus enables him to draw on the testimony of countless faithful who daily pray as taught by the Lord. He calls this ecclesial cloud of witnesses, too, to the stand in developing his case for the conversion of the will to the good by God.

Augustine also interprets the petition "Bring us not into temptation" as providing evidence that God converts the will, in this case, "turning" (*convertere*) a will prone to lapse and redirecting it to himself: "He is, therefore, able to turn wills from evil to good and to turn back to him wills likely to fall away and to direct them into a path pleasing to him." Pointing first to Psalm 85:7, Psalm 66:9, Psalm 140:9, and other biblical petitions, Augustine eventually plays his exegetical trump card: "We do not say in vain, *Bring us not into temptation* (Mt 6:13)."[34] For Augustine, the Lord's Prayer is a powerful, but far from singular, proof of a larger principle demonstrated by many prayers for divine aid recorded in scripture and proceeding from the mouths of the faithful. At stake in the debate with Pelagius about whether God converts the will is not only the validity of the liturgical practice of the church but also the reliability of the scriptures upon which this practice is based.

Augustine sees the church's prayers for the conversion of unbelievers and her prayer for her own perseverance in faith as parallel arrows pointing to her confidence in God's active involvement in producing good human willing:

> For the Church would not pray that faith be given to non-believers unless she believed that God turns to himself the wills of human beings which are turned away and opposed to him, nor would the Church pray to persevere in the faith of Christ, not deceived or overcome by the temptations of this world, unless she believed that the Lord has our heart in his power so that the good which we have by our own will we would not have at all unless God also produces in us the willing.[35]

---

[33] *C. Iul.* 4.3.15 (PL 44:744).
[34] *Perseu.* 6.12 (PL 45:1000).
[35] *Perseu.* 23.63 (PL 45:1031).

Both prayers presuppose that human beings cannot achieve good willing on their own. They need God's help: "Hence, the faith from which we begin and to which there is referred whatever we do temperately, justly, and piously cannot be attributed to the choice of our will, as if it were not given to us by the mercy of God by whom the will itself is prepared, as scripture says." Appealing again to the church's prayers for unbelievers and for perseverance, Augustine continues, "For this reason the holy Church prays by the lips of priests making supplication not only for the faithful so that they persevere in their piety and do not fall away in their belief, but also for unbelievers so that they believe."[36] The common reason for both prayers is the origin of faith and good willing in God, rather than in free choice alone.

God's conversion of unbelieving wills to belief and his maintenance of believers in the good, moreover, are not two drastically different kinds of actions. Rather, in both God is at work producing good willing in human beings. There is a consistency to God's way of interacting with the human will. Just as God must act to bring a good will into being, God must act to preserve the good will in obedience. The church's prayers indicate that God is the source of good willing, whether in the case of the initial gift of a good will by which unbelievers begin to believe, or in the repeated gift whereby believers are preserved in the good.

Part II: Developments during the Pelagian Controversy in Augustine's Presentation of How God Impacts the Will

Section A: Phase 1—411 and Following

God's Twofold Help as Bestowal of Knowledge and Making the Good Attractive

Around 411 and for a few years following, Augustine presents the two basic dimensions of God's help as bestowing knowledge of the good and rendering this revealed good attractive. Even in this initial phase, he does not characterize knowledge of the good as inherently drawing a person to it. Rather, to take delight in the good, people need God to perform an

---

[36] C. Iul. imp. 6.41 (CSEL 85.2:461).

additional act of grace. Just as information hidden from a person does not increase her knowledge, so mere knowledge of something does not automatically render it attractive. God must intervene to connect the human agent with the good, that is, with God, first epistemologically and then volitionally. Without God forging these connections, which have been severed by the fall, the objective reality of the good itself will not be enough to draw a person to it. God must step in to make the good palpable and appealing.

In *pecc. mer.* (411 or 412), for example, Augustine identifies a twofold target of our prayers for God's assistance: "But when we ask him for his help to do and accomplish what is right, what else do we ask for but that he disclose what was hidden and that he make attractive what was not pleasing? By his grace we have learned that we must ask him for this, though it was previously hidden, and we have by his grace come to love it, though we did not previously find it attractive."[37] When we ask for God's help to do the good, we ask for help both to know it and to love it. This request, in turn, indicates for Augustine that both knowing what is right and finding right action attractive come about by God's grace. Again, following the trajectory established in *Simpl.*, chronology is important. God's grace does not further accelerate what is already in motion, or even act as first cause of a chain of events that unfold naturally, one from the other. Rather, God twice creates something that had been missing. What had before (*antea*) been hidden, he makes known. What had before (*antea*) failed to give pleasure, he makes pleasing. There is a consistent pattern in God's gracious actions.[38] God sets into motion what had previously lain still.

Augustine's description of God's twofold help in another treatise written shortly afterward, *De spiritu et littera* (*spir. et litt.*; 412–413), maps onto his account in *pecc. mer.*, which singles out knowledge and delight as the two key components of God's assistance. In this case Augustine identifies the two dimensions of God's gracious assistance as giving the command of how to live and giving the Holy Spirit, who brings about delight in and love for the good. Here, as in *pecc. mer.*, God's assistance cannot be limited to manipulation of circumstantial factors in one's environment. God not only makes knowledge available; God inspires delight.[39] Augustine writes, "We,

---

[37] *Pecc. mer.* 2.19.33 (CSEL 60:103).

[38] Augustine expresses this consistency in elegant parallel phrases: *aperiat quod latebat et suaue faciat quod non delectabat . . . quia et hoc ab illo esse deprecandum eius gratia didicimus, dum antea lateret, eius gratia dileximus, dum antea non delectaret* (CSEL 60:103).

[39] Augustine describes his opponents, in contrast, as believing that God's help is limited to the gift of free choice in creation and giving knowledge of the commandments (*spir. et litt.* 2.4).

on the other hand, say that the human will (*humanam uoluntatem*) is helped to achieve righteousness in this way: Besides the fact that human beings are created with free choice of the will (*libero arbitrio*) and besides the teaching by which they are commanded how they ought to live, they receive the Holy Spirit so that there arises in their minds a delight (*delectatio*) in and a love (*dilectio*) for that highest and immutable good that is God." This love, moreover, is not something given to people indirectly, contingent upon their response to circumstantial options. Rather, "by this [love] given to them like the pledge of a gratuitous gift, they are set afire with the desire to cling to the creator and burn to come to participation in that true light, so that they have their well-being from him from whom they have their being."[40]

A new element of the picture Augustine paints here is the more precise description of how God brings about delight in and love for the good. God helps the human will by creating a delight and a love that stems not from a mere event or new piece of information but from the Holy Spirit. To help the will achieve righteousness, God gives human beings a share in his own being. Thus God makes right willing possible by a direct act of self-giving in the human mind (*in animo*). God does not merely seek to influence human willing from a distance but sets human beings afire with the love of the Holy Spirit.

Section B: Phase 2—417 and Following

God's Twofold Help as Reorienting the Will and Assisting in Carrying Out the Good

As time passes, Augustine both homes in more closely on the issue of how God brings about delight in the good and brings his descriptions of this gracious divine work into sharper focus. This is reflected in his tendency, in 418 and after, to identify God's double help as involving (1) a reorientation of will toward the good and (2) assistance in carrying out this good. Earlier he had identified the two dimensions of divine assistance as knowledge and delight. Though Augustine does not always use the term "delight" to refer to God's double help in 418 and following, cases where he makes the role of delight explicit make clear that God's reorientation of the will

---

[40] *Spir. et litt.* 3.5 (CSEL 60:157).

and assistance to bring this good will to fulfillment in fact represent, for Augustine, more precise descriptions of two ways God brings about delight in a human person, a general fact he had already affirmed in the first stage of the Pelagian controversy. Thus Augustine's tendency to focus on these two "new" aspects represents not a move to replace the two basic components of his earlier accounts (knowledge and delight) but rather an expansion of a particular dimension of his previous treatments of the topic (delight).

A passage in *De gratia Christi et de peccato originali* (*gr. et pecc. or.*) captures Augustine on the cusp of this transition. Commenting on John 6:45, he adds a new item to his list of the ways in which God assists human beings to do the good, but he still retains the two original elements that were his primary focus around 411 and for a few years thereafter: "But who can fail to see that one comes or does not come by the choice of the will? Yet this choice can exist by itself, if one does not come; it must be helped, if one comes—and helped not only so that one knows what to do, but so that one does what one knows one should do." He then specifies the character of this help: "And thus, when God teaches, not by the letter of the law, but by the grace of the Spirit, he teaches not only so that through knowledge people see what they learn, but so that they desire it with the will (*uolendo*) and accomplish (*agendo*) it in action. In this divine manner of teaching God helps the willing itself (*ipsa uoluntas*) and the acting itself (*ipsa operatio*), not merely the natural ability for willing and acting."[41] The three aspects of God's teaching "by the grace of the Spirit" that Augustine identifies here are (1) help with knowing, so that we see the good; (2) help with willing, so that we desire the good; and (3) help with doing, so that we act upon the good. The first and second components correspond to the gifts of knowledge and desire that had previously been at the center of Augustine's attention, but the third component is new. Not only knowing and willing to do the right thing, but also acting accordingly, Augustine now emphasizes, come about only by the grace of the Spirit.

Later in the same work Augustine shifts his focus to God's help with transforming a person from bad to good and then helping that person to act in light of this transformation, two components of God's help that correspond to the second and third elements he had mentioned in *gr. et pecc. or.* 14.15. Discussing the decisive role of whether one has a good or a bad

---

[41] *Gr. et pecc. or.* 1.14.15 (CSEL 42:138).

will for a person's moral character, Augustine writes, "But human beings become good trees, when they receive the grace of God. They do not, after all, by themselves change themselves from bad to good. Rather, they do this from him and through him and in him who is always good." Augustine goes on to describe the work of God the gardener: "And they need to be helped by that same grace, not only to be good trees, but also to produce good fruits, for without that grace they can do nothing good. In the case of good trees he cooperates in producing the fruit, in watering them externally and cultivating them through any minister whatsoever and also by giving them growth internally through himself (per se *dat intrinsecus incrementum*)."[42] Here Augustine does not mention the role of knowledge. His focus is God's role in changing people from bad to good and in assisting them to bear the fruit of good actions.

The change of emphasis that comes to the fore in *gr. et pecc. or.* (418) does not consist in Augustine's willingness to speak of God's internal work upon the human person, if this willingness is taken as a new feature of his thinking that departs from an earlier, more indirect notion of the workings of grace.[43] As we have seen, Augustine was already convinced in the first stage of the Pelagian controversy that God operated directly through the Holy Spirit in the mind of the human person to bring about delight. What has changed is that Augustine now fixes his attention upon God's work in this reorientation and its effects in a more focused and detailed way. He now describes God's help primarily in terms of changing a person from bad to good and providing for the fruitful outworking of this goodness in virtue. Similarly, in *c. ep. Pel.* (421) Augustine identifies two features of God's grace: God's assistance in overcoming resistance to the divine call and God's kindling of the desire (*studium*) for virtue: "The grace of God, in fact, first obtains for a person who resists it the hearing of the divine call, and then the desire for virtue is kindled in that person who no longer resists. But in all the actions which any of us do in accord with God's will, his mercy goes before us."[44]

Starting in 426, Augustine increasingly uses the vocabulary of will to address these two aspects of God's assistance, i.e., reorientation of the will from

---

[42] *Gr. et pecc. or.* 1.19.20 (CSEL 42:141).

[43] J. Patout Burns characterizes this change as a shift from external to internal operation, though James Wetzel and others have pointed out difficulties with this view (cf. n79 of this chapter). See also n78 of this chapter and chapter 2, n122.

[44] *C. ep. Pel.* 4.6.13 (CSEL 60:534).

evil to good and kindling of desire for virtue. Twice in *gr. et lib. arb.* (426) and again in *ep.* 215 (427), he names making an evil will good as the first key component of God's grace before listing the second component as assisting this good will that has been obtained by grace, whether by "making it grow" (*augeatur*)[45] so that it is ample enough to fulfill the divine commandments, by "helping" (*adiuuatur*) it,[46] or by "preserving" (*custodire*) it.[47] In a passage in *corrept.* (427) that does not correspond to this form exactly but nevertheless demonstrates the same two basic components of God's help, Augustine speaks of God producing a good will (*in eis etiam operatur et uelle*), which God makes strong enough to ensure a person's perseverance. Though here these two features of God's help that are superadded to the gift of free will given in creation seem to overlap, Augustine still identifies bringing about a good will and making it sufficiently strong to persevere as two aspects of God's assistance.[48]

Augustine identifies the source of his conviction that God helps the will in these two ways as biblical: "And I think that I have argued so that it is not so much I as it is the divine scripture itself which has spoken with you by the clearest testimonies of the truth."[49] More specifically, Proverbs 8:35, "the will is prepared by the Lord," and Exodus 36:27, "I shall make you walk in my ordinances and observe and carry out my judgments," are among numerous passages Augustine invokes to support God's help for overcoming the resistance of the will and strengthening it to accomplish the good.[50]

[45] *Gr. et lib. arb.* 15.31 (PL 44:899–900): "This grace makes a human being who first had an evil will to have a good will. This grace also makes the good will which has already begun to exist to grow and to become so great that it can observe the divine commandments which it wills to observe since it wills strongly and perfectly."
[46] *Gr. et lib. arb.* 20.41 (PL 44:905): "I have argued enough against those who violently attack the grace of God which does not destroy the human will, but changes it from an evil will to a good will and, once it is good, helps it."
[47] *Ep.* 215.8 (CSEL 57:394–395): "The grace of God is preached in such a way that it is believed and understood to make human wills good from bad and also to preserve the good wills it makes."
[48] *Corrept.* 12.38 (CSEL 92:266): "For he [God] gives them not only the sort of help he gave the first man without which they could not persevere, even if they willed to, but he also produces in them the will as well. For, since they will not persevere unless they both can will to and do will to, they are given the ability and the will to persevere by the generosity of divine grace. Their will is, of course, set afire by the Holy Spirit to the point that they are able because they will to so strongly, but they will to so strongly because God makes them to will."
[49] *Gr. et lib. arb.* 20.41 (PL 44:905–906).
[50] See *gr. et lib. arb.* 16.32 (PL 44:900–901): "For it is certain that we observe the commandments if we will to, but because *the will is prepared by the Lord* (Prv. 8:35 LXX), we must ask him that we may will strongly enough that by willing we observe them," and "It is certain that we do an action when we do it, but he who says, *I shall make you walk in my ordinances and observe and carry out my judgments* (Ex 36:27), makes us do the action by offering fully efficacious strength to the will."

God's help for the will, Augustine stresses in this phase, cannot be left behind after conversion. Human beings, rather, remain in constant need of God's assistance for the preservation and increase of their good willing. This is a conclusion Augustine grounds in scripture, illustrating yet again the reliance of his mature conception of will upon the Bible.

Further Features That Emerge in 417 and Following

While Augustine maintains throughout his career as bishop that God helps the will both in conversion and subsequent to baptism, and that the Lord's Prayer offers evidence of God's assistance to the will in both of these ways, the terminology he uses to describe how God impacts the will varies over time. In 417 and the years following, he begins to speak of God "driving" (*agere*) the human will, to assert that God assists the human will with respect to discrete human actions, to characterize God as pouring love into human wills, and to affirm an interior divine operation upon the will. Together these ways of conceptualizing God's intervention in the process of human willing portray God's involvement in human willing as at once more expansive and more direct than Augustine had indicated previously. This new vision of God's role in human willing thus specifies the scope and clarifies the "mechanics" of some of Augustine's earlier assertions about God's responsibility for good human willing.

God Drives the Will

One of the statements upon which Pelagius had been called upon to pronounce in the Synod of Diospolis (415), which ultimately acquitted him in light of his efforts to distance himself from Caelestius and the statements of Caelestius that were condemend at Carthage in 411 or 412, was his claim that "all are governed by their own will."[51] Pelagius had defended himself at the synod by explaining that he intended this statement to rule out only God's responsibility for the misuse of free choice, not God's assistance of free choice. Commenting in late 417 on the passage of the *Acta* of the synod that he had obtained from Cyril of Alexandria, however, Augustine points out that Pelagius's claim represents at best a misleading half-truth. By coupling it with an affirmation of God's help, a measure he took only under pressure from the bishops deciding his case, Pelagius rendered it innocuous.

---

[51] *Gest. Pel.* 3.5 (CSEL 42:56): *omnes uoluntate propria regi.*

Yet, left on its own, it obscures God's role in governing the human will. In fact, Augustine argues, not only should one affirm that God *governs* the will on the basis of verses such as Psalm 28:9 and Mark 6:34; one needs also to affirm that God *drives* the will on the basis of Romans 8:14: "All those who are driven by the Spirit of God are the children of God." Augustine writes:

> Certainly, to be driven (*agi*) is more than to be governed (*regi*). After all, one who is governed does something and is governed so that he acts correctly, but one who is driven is understood to do hardly anything (*aliquid vix*). Nonetheless, the grace of the savior acts upon our wills to such an extent that the apostle has no hesitation in saying, *All those who are driven by the Spirit of God are the children of God* (Rom 8:14). Nor can our free will do anything better than to offer itself to be driven by that Spirit who cannot act wrongly. And when it has done so, it will have no doubt that it has been helped to do this by him to whom the psalm says, *My God will go before me with his mercy* (Ps 59:11).[52]

For Augustine, then, even affirming that God "governs" the will fails to sum up the full extent of God's involvement in good human willing; Romans 8:14 demands that God's role be recognized as being still more (*plus*) than this verb captures. In fact, God impacts the human will to such a degree (*tantum*) that Paul employs the verb "drive" (*agere*). The difference between the two verbs, according to Augustine, is quantitative—"to be driven is more than (*plus est*) to be governed"—but nonetheless drastic. To say that God governs still allows that the human person does something (*aliquid agit*), whereas the statement that God drives the will attributes so much responsibility for our wills to the Savior that scarcely anything (*aliquid vix*) is left to us. Thus, though human agency is not entirely obliterated, Augustine can say in the following paragraph, "After all, those who are children of God are governed and driven by this Spirit, not by the powers of their own will."[53] The human will is operative, but God governs and drives human willing by the power of the Spirit.[54]

---

[52] *Gest. Pel.* 3.5 (CSEL 42:57).

[53] *Gest. Pel.* 3.6 (CSEL 42:57): *hoc enim spiritu, non uiribus propriae uoluntatis reguntur et aguntur qui filii sunt dei.*

[54] Augustine refers again later to being "driven by the Spirit of God." In *c. ep. Pel.*, for example, he notes that a baptized person has to struggle with concupiscence even "if one is most diligent in making progress and is driven by the Spirit of God" (*c. ep. Pel.* 1.13.27); *et hoc si diligentissime proficit*

God Helps Discrete Actions

Another feature of Augustine's descriptions of how God impacts the will that comes to the fore in 417 and afterward is the idea that God's grace is necessary for each discrete good action an individual performs. Augustine makes clear in this period that God's role in assisting the will is not limited to giving it an initial push whose momentum it can then ride on the way to distinct good acts. Endorsing the view Pelagius accepted under duress at the Synod of Diospolis, Augustine affirms that "the grace or help of God is given for each action (*ad singulos actus*), and it is something apart from free choice or from the law and teaching. Accordingly, we are governed by God in each action (*per singulos actus*), when we act correctly."[55] Pointing to God's role in each action serves, for Augustine, as a way of distinguishing the kind of grace he wishes to affirm from "grace" that refers to God's general gifts of free choice via creation, knowledge of the law via revelation, and forgiveness via Christ's offer of salvation. To point to God's aid in each action is to posit a kind of grace that is not generally or universally available. This grace targets the innermost being of specific individuals in particular situations.[56] By describing God's grace as applying to discrete acts of will, Augustine at the same time posits that grace is inherently personal, enacted in the context of contact established between God and the inner life of an individual.[57] In support of this specific view, as in other arguments about

---

et spiritu dei agitur (CSEL 60:445). In the third book of the same work, he emphasizes that the law is fulfilled only by those who walk in the Spirit, and then he asks, "But who walks according to the Spirit but one who is driven by the Spirit of God?" (*c. ep. Pel.* 3.2.2); *quis autem ambulat secundum spiritum, nisi quisquis agitur dei spiritu?* (CSEL 60:487). Thus, here again, his point is that it is only possible to do good when driven by the Spirit.

[55] *Gest. Pel.* 14.31 (CSEL 42:86). In *c. ep. Pel.* (418), Augustine states that God is involved in both the initiation and the completion of each good action: "That is the way, then, that we should think of the grace of God so that from the start of the change for the good up to its final completion one who boasts may boast in the Lord. For, just as no one can bring to completion a good action without the Lord, so no one can begin one with the Lord" (2.10.23).

[56] See also Augustine's comments later in the same text: "How then can anyone believe that Pelagius—if this letter is in fact his—truthfully acknowledge the grace of God? I do not mean the grace which is equivalent either to nature along with free choice, or to the knowledge of the law, or merely to the forgiveness of sins, but that grace which is necessary for each of our actions" (*gest. Pel.* 31.56).

[57] Phillip Cary argues that Augustine moves more and more toward an "inward" conception of grace during the Pelagian controversy. See Phillip Cary, *Inner Grace: Augustine in the Traditions of Plato and Paul* (New York: Oxford University Press, 2008). In Cary's view, Augustine's Platonist commitments, and his creative way of combining them with Christianity, produce a drive inward that leads the Christian away from external realities like the sacraments and Christ's flesh. This is a central claim in his reading of Augustine, which he also defends in Phillip Cary, *Augustine's Invention of the Inner Self: The Legacy of a Christian Platonist* (New York: Oxford University Press, 2000) and Phillip

God's role in human willing, Augustine invokes a biblical prayer: "And our prayer is not in vain, when we say, *Guide my journeys according to your word so that all sinfulness may not lord it over me* (Ps 119:133)."[58] Particularized intercession presupposes particularized acts of grace.

When Augustine describes God's impact on the will as "driving" it and asserts that God helps discrete actions, he addresses the degree of God's involvement in human willing and action. The issue is quantitative: How much is up to God, and how much is up to us? How frequently does God intervene? In the years following 417, however, Augustine moves beyond these quantitative issues, addressing new qualitative aspects of God's impact upon the will. In answer to the question of how God impacts the will, he emphasizes that God pours love into human wills.

God Pours Love into the Will

In 418 and after, one finds Augustine explaining God's conversion of the *uoluntas* to the good as God's outpouring of love in the will.[59] This explanation surfaces in *gr. et pecc. or.* in the context of a warning Augustine issues regarding Pelagius's affirmation that God is rightly praised, along with human beings, for good human willing and action. This affirmation only seems to endorse the notion that God produces good willing and action in us, Augustine observes; it does not actually do so. In point of fact, Pelagius fails to affirm what, in Augustine's view, is actually the case: "We human beings have the will we do, because God pours into our wills the fire of love (*ardorem dilectionis inspiret*), and . . . we act as we do, because God cooperates with us (*cooperetur*)."[60] For Augustine, God is involved in

---

Cary, *Outward Signs: The Powerlessness of External Things in Augustine's Thought* (New York: Oxford University Press, 2008). While Cary is right that the mature Augustine asserts that grace operates inwardly upon an individual, this does not entail a devaluation of the sacraments or Christ's flesh. In fact, as this chapter has made clear, Augustine sees the internal dimension of grace as mutually reinforcing with the outwardly expressed piety of the faithful, such as prayer and other vital practices of the church. The content of the prayers of the church confirms the reality of grace's direct and internal operation on the will of the human person, and the operation of grace upon the will is part of what makes these prayers possible. In chapter 6 we will also see how Augustine's appreciation of the inward dimension of grace as it impacts the will mutually reinforces, rather than undermines, the saving significance of Christ's flesh.

[58] *Gest. Pel.* 14.31 (CSEL 42:86).

[59] The idea that grace consists in an outpouring of love in human hearts by the Holy Spirit goes back much further in Augustine's thinking. However, he does not strongly emphasize the idea that God converts the will by pouring love out in the *will* specifically until around the second stage of the Pelagian controversy.

[60] *Gr. et pecc. or.* 1.6.7 (CSEL 42:7).

good human willing not merely by endowing human beings with a nature that possesses this capacity but by breathing the fire of love into human wills. Augustine eschews the Pelagian vision of a coldly distant God who sets human beings into motion and then leaves them to their own devices. Augustine's God breathes and burrows his burning presence into the wills of human beings, infusing them with passion for the good.

On occasion Pelagius himself employs ignition imagery to describe how God produces good willing in the human being. Augustine quotes Pelagius as stating, for example, "He produces in us a willing that is good, a willing that is holy, by setting us on fire (*succendit*) with the greatness of the glory to come and with the promise of rewards, while we are given over to earthly desires and, like dumb animals, love only present things." But beneath this superficial terminological commonality lies a theological chasm: Pelagius's explanation of the mechanics of this "setting on fire" is quite different from Augustine's. Elaborating further on how God produces this willing and sets us on fire, Pelagius writes, "[God] does this, by rousing the sluggish will to a desire for God through revealing his wisdom (*reuelatione sapientiae*); he does this, by urging us toward everything that is good."[61] For Pelagius, God sets human beings on fire to will the good by dispensing knowledge, not by a direct outpouring of love in human wills. For Augustine, in contrast, the gift of knowledge is but one aspect of grace's work in human action and willing: "This grace [the grace 'by which virtue is made perfect in weakness' (2 Cor 12: 9)] not only makes us know what we should do, but also makes us do what we know; it not only makes us believe what we should love, but makes us love what we believe."[62]

In addition to using the metaphor of an inspiration of fire in the will to describe God's role in producing good human willing, Augustine also

[61] *Gr. et pecc. or.* 1.10.11 (CSEL 42:134), Augustine quoting Pelagius's *lib. arb.* God's production of a good will in human beings is not one of Pelagius's common themes, but he addresses it in this case in order to explain how his view is compatible with Paul's statement in Philippians 2:13 that God produces both the willing and the accomplishment.

[62] *Gr. et pecc. or.* 1.12.13. Sarah Catherine Byers stresses that love/heart and knowledge/reason should not be pitted against each other in describing Augustine's account of the will. See Sarah Catherine Byers, *Perception, Sensibility, and Moral Motivation in Augustine: A Stoic-Platonic Synthesis* (New York: Cambridge University Press, 2013), 21. This point is fair enough, but, in Byers's account, love tends to be collapsed into knowledge rather than portrayed as mutually interpreting it. This tendency is connected to Byers's efforts to show that Augustine endorses a basically Stoic rationalistic moral framework. Augustine's characterization of the contrast between his own view and that of Pelagius, however, rests on a distinction between the two. Whereas Pelagius sees grace as merely a matter of knowledge, Augustine sees grace as going beyond knowledge to elicit our love.

employs the slightly different image of God producing a good will in the heart.[63] Here the thrust of the imagery is that God brings a good will into being where one did not exist previously, rather than the idea that the will acts as a receptacle for divinely inspired love. Both images, however, highlight God's direct role in creating good willing. In both cases this happens apocalyptically—not gradually or even organically but in a radical, dramatic reversal that happens in the twinkling of an eye.

Already in 412 one finds a precursor of the notion that God produces willing in the heart in Augustine's discussion of the Pauline notion of the heart's circumcision. Augustine observes, "He [the apostle Paul] calls circumcision of the heart a will that is free from every forbidden desire. This is not a result of the teaching and threat of the letter, but of the help and healing of the Spirit."[64] Here Augustine closely connects heart and will, attributing a good human will to the Spirit's work upon the heart. His comments fall short of positing in so many words that the Spirit's help and healing consist in a direct operation upon the will or the production of a good will, but he clearly states that for a good will to be possible implies the Spirit's help and healing of the heart. He does not mention intermediaries and clearly rules out the idea that a good will is achieved by the Spirit's help in the sense of an indirect means of grace such as teaching or the law.

By c. ep. Pel. (421), Augustine is referring consistently to God producing will in the heart. Discussing the sudden, secret conversion that many experience, and bringing this phenomenon into connection with John 6:44, "None can come to me unless the Father who sent me draws them," Augustine concludes that God attracts human beings to himself by working interiorly in their hearts to bring about willingness where people were previously unwilling. Referring to John 6:44, Augustine writes, "He did not, after all, say, 'guides,' so that we might by it somehow understand that the will goes first. Are any people drawn, if they are already willing? And yet, none come unless they are willing." Augustine then explains how this willing comes about: "They are drawn, then, in marvelous ways to willing by the one who

---

[63] In an. et or. 4.6.7 (CSEL 60:388), written 419–421, Augustine will clearly distinguish between the anatomical heart and the heart as a power of the human psyche: "When we hear that we should love God with our whole heart, I know that this does not refer to the part of our flesh that lies behind the ribs, but to the power that produces thoughts. It correctly bears this name, because, as the motion in the heart that carries the pulse through all the veins never stops, so we turn something over in our thought without ceasing."

[64] Spir. et litt. 8.13 (CSEL 60:166).

knows how to work interiorly in the hearts (*cordibus*) of human beings, not so that human beings believe unwillingly—that is impossible—but so that they become people willing to believe from people who were unwilling."[65]

Immediately after giving this description of how God works in people's hearts to make them willing to come to him, Augustine insists that this account of God's impact on the will derives from scripture: "It is not by some human conjecture that we come to suspect that this is true; rather, we discover that it is true by the perfectly clear authority of the divine scriptures."[66] To substantiate his thesis, Augustine cites 2 Chronicles 30:12, which describes God as giving Judah "one heart," and Ezekiel 36:26–27, in which God promises to give his people "a heart of flesh."[67] He also cites Esther 14:13, which refers to God "turning the heart" of the king.[68] Augustine asks, "Why does she say this in prayer to God, if God does not produce (*operatur*) the will (*uoluntatem*) in the hearts of human beings?"[69] Here again Augustine reasons from scripture and the practice of church, in this case the prayers of Queen Esther, to conclusions about how God impacts the will, interpreting references to the changes God effects upon human hearts as shorthand indications that God has produced a good will in them, turning their will to do harm into a will to do good.[70] In the case of the king of Persia, for example,

> divine scripture testifies that God fulfilled [Queen Esther's] request by producing in the king's heart nothing other than the will by which he gave the command and the queen's request was carried out. . . . God changed and transformed the heart of the king by his most hidden and efficacious power from wrath to gentleness, that is, from the will to do harm to the

---

[65] *C. ep. Pel.* 1.19.37 (CSEL 60:454).

[66] *C. ep. Pel.* 1.20.38.

[67] Augustine appeals again to Ezekiel 36:26–27 in *gr. et lib. arb.*, again interpreting its heart language as referring to will: "Can we, then, save with complete absurdity, say that the good merit of a good will comes first in a human being so that the heart of stone is torn out of him? For a heart of stone itself signifies nothing but a will which is most hard and utterly inflexible in opposition to God. For, where a good will is already present, there is, of course, no longer a heart of stone" (14.29 [PL 44:898]). Augustine takes this passage as supporting the idea that "God can convert to the faith even perverse wills which are opposed to the faith" (*etiam peruersas et fidei contrarias uoluntates omnipotentem deum ad credendum posse conuertere*) (*gr. et lib. arb.* 14.29 [PL 44:898]).

[68] Augustine is citing his Latin version of Esther, which included this.

[69] *C. ep. Pel.* 1.20.38 (CSEL 60:455).

[70] Later in the same work, Augustine explicitly states that "heart" and "will" can function as synonyms. Commenting in this case on Proverbs 16:1 he writes, "After all, what is it to prepare the heart and open the mouth but to prepare the will?" (*c. ep. Pel.* 2.9.20 [CSEL 60:482]).

will to grant favors. As the apostle says, *God produces in you even the will* (Phil 2:13).[71]

Using Philippians 2:13 as a hermeneutical key to establish the basic principle that God produces human willing, Augustine unlocks the implications of other passages that speak of God's work on human hearts for how God operates on the human will. His conclusion is that God produces human willing precisely by working "in human hearts" to bring about an internal transformation of will.

In writings from the end of his career, Augustine remains convinced that scripture requires the conclusion that God works in human hearts, inclining wills in accordance with his. In *gr. et lib. arb.* (426), he cites in support of this notion a long litany of texts, including a wide variety from both testaments, some that describe God's working in human hearts to exercise judgment and others in which God works in human hearts to show mercy.[72] Augustine concludes, "By these and such testimonies of the words of God—to mention all of which it would take too long—it is clear enough, I think, that . . . God works in the hearts of human beings to incline their wills to whatever he wills, whether to good actions in accord with his mercy or to evil ones in accord with their merits."[73] Here, as in 418, Augustine understands God to operate on human wills "in human hearts" (*in cordibus hominum*), though now the range of orientations of will in which this may result expands.

Likewise, in *corrept.* (427), citing a number of scripture passages in support of the notion that "human wills cannot resist [God's] will" and that God does "what he wills and when he wills even with the very wills of human beings," Augustine again describes God as working in human hearts to produce human willing.[74] Discussing how the Spirit moved Amisai to join David in 1 Chronicles 11:9, he writes, "Could this man have resisted the will of God and have, instead, not done the will of God who was at work in his heart through his Spirit who came over Amasai so that he willed, said, and did this?"[75] God operated (*operatus est*) in the heart of Amasai, Augustine is

---

[71] *C. ep. Pel.* 1.20.38.

[72] Here he cites 1 Kings 12:15; 2 Chronicles 21:16–17, 25:7–8, 25:19, 25:20; Ezekiel 14:9; Esther 15:7–8; Proverbs 21:1; Psalm 105:25; Romans 1:26, 1:28; 2 Thessalonians 2:9–11.

[73] *Gr. et lib. arb.* 21.43 (PL 44:909).

[74] *Corrept.* 14.45.

[75] *Corrept.* 14.45 (CSEL 92:274).

convinced, so that he willed in accordance with God's will. Also in the case of 1 Chronicles 12:38's description of the hearts of the warriors who were disposed to make David king, Augustine speaks of God producing (*operare*) a will in human hearts (*in cordibus hominum*): "These men, of course, made David king by their own will. Who could fail to see this? Who could deny it? For they did not do insincerely or without good will what they did with a peaceful heart, and he, nonetheless, who does what he wills in the hearts of human beings produced this in them. . . . He worked within; he held their hearts, moved their hearts, and drew them by their wills which he himself produced in them."[76] In *praed. sanct.* (427) Augustine again refers to the indications in Kings and Chronicles "that God acted in the hearts of human beings and brought the wills of those whom he chose to the point that they made Saul or David king."[77] God "guided" (*perducere*) their wills, he writes, by "acting" (*agere*) in "human hearts" (*cordibus hominum*). Thus, in this case also, Augustine uses biblical passages to establish the context of God's impact on the human will. When God moves human wills, Augustine thinks, God is producing an inclination at the core of their being; when moving the will, God is at work in the realm of the human heart.

Unmediated Interior Operation on Will

Accompanying Augustine's increasing tendency, from 418 onward, to describe God's impact on the will in terms of producing human willing in human hearts is an emphasis on the interior character of God's operation upon the will. As we have observed, Augustine characterizes God's grace as operating internally in a person, and even describes it as operating upon the will specifically, well in advance of this date.[78] The key development that

---

[76] *Corrept.* 14.45 (CSEL 92:274–275).

[77] *Praed. sanct.* 20.42. See also *praed. sanct.* 18.37 (PL 44:988). Augustine does not refer to human hearts here, but he does refer to God working "in us" (*in nobis*) so that we will: "But he did this *in accord with the purpose of his will* in order that no one might boast of his own will, but of the will of God toward him; he did this *according to the riches of his grace, in accord with his good will* which he set forth in his beloved Son in whom *we have obtained our lot, predestined according to the plan*, not according to a plan of ours, but *of him who accomplishes all things*, to the point that he himself produces in us even the willing."

[78] In *Simpl.* 1.2.12 Augustine clearly describes a good will as being "made in us by God's working," not merely as being *made effective* by God's working (my translation). See CCL 44:36: *ubi satis ostendit etiam ipsam bonam uoluntatem in nobis operante deo fieri* and the earlier discussion of this text in chapter 2. See also *spir. et litt.* 3.5 (412–413), discussed in chapter 3, n35, where Augustine describes God as producing belief in a person through both internal and external means.

now occurs is that Augustine employs this characterization with greater frequency and emphasis. The actual content of his assertion is not new.[79]

Gr. et pecc. or. articulates Augustine's view of the internal operation of God's grace especially clearly over against the conception of grace found in Pelagius. This is unsurprising insofar as Augustine composed this work "sometime between late July and early September of 418,"[80] in order to prevent misinterpretation of some pronouncements on grace that he believed Pelagius had formulated with intentional ambiguity.

One of the contrasts Augustine identifies between Pelagius's view of grace and his own is the nature of the teaching in which grace consists. The kind of teaching that is authentically called grace, Augustine argues, is distinguished in three ways from the teaching with which Pelagius identifies grace. The true teaching of grace is direct, it is internal, and it is effective. In Augustine's words, "If we are to call this grace 'teaching,' we should certainly mean by it the teaching which we believe God pours out with an ineffable sweetness in the depths and interior of the soul, not merely through those who externally (*extrinsecus*) plant and water, but also through himself (*per se ipsum*) who gives the increase secretly. In that way he not merely reveals the truth, but also imparts love."[81] The teaching of authentic grace, then, involves an interior outpouring of love in the soul. Grace does more than show *veritas*; it bestows *caritas*. Elaborating further, Augustine explains that this interior teaching targets the will: "And thus, when God teaches, not by the letter of the law, but by the grace of the Spirit, he teaches not only so that through knowledge people see what they learn, but so that they desire it (*appetat*) with the will (*uoluntas*) and accomplish it in action. In this divine manner of teaching God helps the willing itself (*ipsa uoluntas*) and the acting itself (*ipsa operatio*), not merely the natural ability for willing and acting."[82]

---

[79] This point is debated. Burns contends that an interior grace causing good will is proper to Augustine's late, anti-Pelagian works. See J. Patout Burns, *The Development of Augustine's Doctrine of Operative Grace* (Paris: Études Augustiniennes, 1980), 41 and 186–187. Harrison and Wetzel disagree with the association of *Simpl.* with an exterior rather than interior operation of grace. See Carol Harrison, *Rethinking Augustine's Early Theology: An Argument for Continuity* (New York: Oxford University Press, 2006), 150; James Wetzel, *Augustine and the Limits of Virtue* (New York: Cambridge University Press, 1992), 191. The discussions of Harrison and Wetzel do not state the point quite sharply enough for our purposes, however, since even Burns allows for a certain kind of "interior grace" in *Simpl.*, a grace that "makes good will effective." The crucial point is that *Simpl.* posits a direct internal operation that causes good will.

[80] Roland Teske, WSA I/23, 374.

[81] *Gr. et pecc. or.* 1.13.14 (*CSEL* 42:136).

[82] *Gr. et pecc. or.* 1.14.15 (*CSEL* 42:138).

Augustine also uses the image of the growth of a tree to convey that God's intervention in assisting the human will goes beyond external measures, including an internal (*intrinsecus*) operation effected in an unmediated manner by God himself: "In the case of good trees he cooperates in producing the fruit, in watering them externally and cultivating them through any minister whatsoever and also by giving them growth internally through himself (per se *dat intrinsecus incrementum*)."[83] Here the characteristic "interiority" and "directness" of the authentic teaching that is grace go hand in hand, just as they did in *gr. et pecc. or.* 1.13.14. When God works externally (*forinsecus*) to prompt human beings to bear fruit, he works through intermediaries, or "ministers." When God works internally (*intrinsecus*), he works through himself (*per se*).

Later in *gr. et pecc. or.*, Augustine points to Peter as a specific example of someone who was granted grace in an interior manner as Christ internally effected a change in him at the level of will. Commenting on Luke 22:61, Augustine observes:

> One cannot say that the Lord looked upon him with bodily eyes, admonishing him in a way that Peter could see. And, for this reason, the action which scripture reports, *The Lord looked upon him* (Lk 22:61), took place interiorly (*intus*); it took place in the mind (*in mente*); it took place in the will (*in uoluntate*). By his mercy the Lord in a hidden manner helped him, touched his heart, awakened his memory, visited the interior human being with his grace (literally: "visited the interior Peter"; *interiorem . . . Petrum*), and stirred up and produced a love in the interior (*interioris*) human being even to the point of exterior tears. See how God is present to help our wills (*uoluntatibus*) and actions. See how he *produces* (*operatur*) *in us the willing* (*uelle*) *and the action* (*operari*) (Phil 2:13).[84]

For Augustine, just as Paul's conversion on the road to Damascus and the king of Assyria's turning from anger to gentleness serve as examples of how God brings about conversion in a will initially bent on opposing him, so Peter's bitter realization of sin and repentance, brought about by a wordless and invisible gaze of his Lord, demonstrates God's assistance in preserving in the good the wills of those who already love him.

---

[83] *Gr. et pecc. or.* 1.19.20 (CSEL 42:141).
[84] *Gr. et pecc. or.* 1.45.49 (CSEL 42:161).

At first, Augustine's interpretation of Luke 22:61 may seem rather eisegetical, as this verse in itself makes no reference to an internal operation of grace. Yet Augustine's conclusion that the evangelist's reference to Christ's gaze must have been figurative rather than literal emerges from concrete observations about the context of the events described in the verse rather than merely from foregone conclusions. Augustine reasons that the gaze of the Lord must refer to something other than a literal glance because of the mundane circumstantial details of the pericope: "The Lord Jesus was indoors at that time when he was being questioned by the chief priests, but the apostle Peter was outdoors and down below in the courtyard, at one point seated, at another standing with the servants at the fire. Hence, one cannot say that the Lord looked upon [Peter] with bodily eyes, admonishing him in a way that Peter could see."[85] It is "for this reason" that Augustine concludes that Christ's gaze "took place interiorly."

In explaining what it might mean for Christ to cast his eyes on Peter in this inward way, Augustine layers several phrases upon each other in apposition: "it took place interiorly (*intus*)," "it took place in the mind (*in mente*)," "it took place in the will (*in uoluntate*)," suggesting that for something to take place "in the will" already inherently implies internality, a suggestion that helps to explain why Augustine's increasing emphasis on God's impact on the will as a production of love in the heart goes hand in hand with a growing emphasis on the interiority of God's assistance with human willing. In this passage, both elements are present. Augustine states both that when Christ operated on (*operatur*) Peter's willing, he was stirring up (*movit*) and producing (*produxit*) love (*affectum*) and that this was an interior process. Augustine drives the latter point home by reiterating the interior context and character of the action three times (*intus, interiorem, interioris*) in addition to describing God's mercy as operating in a "hidden" (*latenter*) manner.

Indeed, also in *gr. et pecc. or.* (418), Augustine links interiority and willing via the motif of interior vision. Responding to Pelagius's statement that "our being able to see with our eyes is not due to us, but our using our sight for good or for bad is due to us" with Psalm 119:37, Augustine develops a notion of the "interior eyes" of the mind, which are responsible for what our bodily eyes do. Exegetically this notion helps to explain why

---

[85] *Gr. et pecc. or.* 1.45.49.

the Psalmist would ask God, "Turn my eyes away so that they do not see vanity." In making this request, the Psalmist is not, of course, asking for God to turn his bodily eyes away. Rather he petitions God's help to choose rightly how to use his sight. Theologically the image of these interior eyes, which are moved by God when God helps the will, helps to illustrate how it is possible to affirm that God helps us use our sight for bad or for good at the same time as these actions come "from ourselves."[86] God's power to direct one's interior vision is a metaphor for God's impact on the will, as shown by Augustine's final rhetorical question: "Why then, do we say to God, *Turn my eyes away so that they do not see vanity?* Why do we ask for what lies in our own power, if God does not help the will?"[87] This metaphor and the interior process to which it refers, then, characterize human willing as taking place at a mysterious interior level on which divine and human causality can overlap such that willing can at once be "in our own power" and happen because of "God's help."[88]

Augustine continues to emphasize God's direct operation upon the will in *Contra duas epistulas Pelagianorum* (*c. ep. Pel.*), a set of four books most likely carried to Pope Boniface in 421, in which he replies to Julian's letter campaign on behalf of the teaching of Pelagius and Caelestius.[89] Augustine had already stated in his writings against Pelagius that "God helps the willing itself (*ipsa uoluntas*) and the acting itself (*ipsa operatio*), not merely the natural ability for willing and acting."[90] Against Julian, Augustine now clarifies that God's help is not something added to our independent willing, as if our willing could already be good without God's aid and only required confirmation or strengthening. Citing the proof texts of Philippians 2:13 ("It is God, after all, who produces in you both the willing and the action in accord with good will") and Proverbs 8:35 ("The will is prepared by the Lord"), Augustine endorses Julian's notion that "none are forced by the

<hr/>

[86] For a maximalist interpretation of the role of interior vision in Augustine's thinking, see Cary's trilogy on Augustine: *Augustine's Invention of the Inner Self; Inner Grace;* and *Outward Signs.*

[87] *Gr. et pecc. or.* 1.15.16 (CSEL 42:139).

[88] Cary contends that Augustine invents a "private, inner space" of the self in order to avoid the ontological continuity between God and the self that elements of the Plotinian philosophical outlook Augustine adopts entail (*Augustine's Invention of the Inner Self*). My contention here is not that Augustine invents a new private inner realm but rather that he draws on figurative language already at work in scripture referring to an interior realm of the heart to describe the context in which God impacts human willing.

[89] See Teske, WSA I/24, 99–100.

[90] *Gr. et pecc. or.* 1.14.15 (CSEL 42:138).

power of God against their will either to do evil or to do good" even while he underlines that free human willing of the good is possible in the first place only because of God: "God helps one even to this point, namely, so that one wills to be [good]."[91] God does this, he further explains, by "stirring the will" (*excitanda uoluntate*) to good action: "You, on the other hand, suppose that human beings are helped by the grace of God in a good action in such a way that you think that grace does nothing to stir their will to do the good action."[92]

To support his case that God stirs the will to good rather than confirming it in an already good orientation, Augustine returns to Paul's example, his classic case study, since *Simpl.*, for showing that the good will results from rather than causes grace: "Tell me, I beg you, what sort of good did Paul will (*uolebat*) when he was still Saul? Did he not, rather, will great evils when, breathing murder, he went about slaying Christians with terrible blindness and fury in his heart? Because of what merits of a good will (*bonae uoluntatis*) did God turn him from these evils to good by a miraculous and sudden call?"[93] For Augustine, Paul's own testimony in Titus 3:5 provides the answer to this question: "He himself cries out, *For he saved us, not because of the works or righteousness which we did, but in accord with his mercy* (Ti 3:5)."[94] Furthermore, Augustine contends, Christ himself supported the notion that belief results from God's action on the human person rather than from the merits of good human willing: "What about the statement of the Lord which I have already mentioned, *None can come to me*—which means: believe in me—*unless it has been given them by my Father* (Jn 6:65)?"[95] In fact, Augustine specifies this "giving" by the Father as involving God's action upon the will: "Is this [to come to and believe in Christ] given to one who already wills to believe because of the merits of a good will, or is the will itself, as Saul's was, rather stirred to believe by God, although one is turned away from the faith even to the point of persecuting believers?"[96] For Augustine, there are only two possible explanations for belief: the "merits of a good will" (*meritis bonae uoluntatis*) or the fact that the "will itself" (*ipsa uoluntas*) is "stirred from above" (*desuper excitatur*) by

[91] *C. ep. Pel.* 1.18.36 (CSEL 60:453).
[92] *C. ep. Pel.* 1.19.37 (CSEL 60:453).
[93] *C. ep. Pel.* 1.19.37 (CSEL 60:453).
[94] *C. ep. Pel.* 1.19.37 (CSEL 60:453).
[95] *C. ep. Pel.* 1.19.37 (CSEL 60:453–454).
[96] *C. ep. Pel.* 1.19.37 (CSEL 60:454).

God. Scripture, according to Augustine, rules out the former, and therefore the latter must be the case: God is responsible for inciting the will.

Augustine points to Christ's commands to pray for one's persecutors as further evidence for this conclusion: "Do we pray that they receive the grace of God in return for their good will and not rather that their bad will itself be turned to good? In the same way we believe that it was not in vain that the saints whom Saul was persecuting prayed for him so that his will might be converted to the faith which he was destroying."[97] Paul's "will was converted" (*uoluntas eius conuerteretur*) by God. Precisely because God affects human wills in this way, Christ commanded his followers to pray for even the seemingly most hopeless of cases. The conversion of Paul's will, Augustine insists, represented a miraculous, but by no means anomalous, divine act:

> How many enemies of Christ are today suddenly and secretly drawn to Christ by grace! . . . Are any people drawn, if they are already willing? And yet, none comes unless they are willing. They are drawn, then, in marvelous ways to willing by the one who knows how to work interiorly (*intus*) in the hearts of human beings, not so that human beings believe unwillingly—that is impossible—but so that they become people willing to believe (*uolentes*) from people who were unwilling (*nolentibus*).[98]

Acting in much the same astonishing way in which he acted on Paul's will, God "works" (*operari*) "within human hearts" (*in ipsis hominum cordibus*) to "make willing people (*uolentes*) from unwilling ones (*nolentibus*)."

This internal divine work, moreover, is not the exception but the rule. Here, as originally in his interpretation of Paul's conversion in *Simpl.*, Augustine views the specific words of scripture as decisive.[99] The *uerbum* "drawn" (*trahuntur*) itself implies the need for one to be coaxed into willing something one does not will on one's own. Hence Augustine asks, "Are any people drawn, if they are already willing?" Those who are drawn, then,

---

[97] *C. ep. Pel.* 1.19.37 (CSEL 60:454).

[98] *C. ep. Pel.* 1.19.37 (CSEL 60:454).

[99] In fact, Augustine suggests that only because he draws this "word" from the biblical text can he be assured that his opponent will not object to its use: "If I had not taken this word 'drawn' from the gospel, how much he would have objected to me on its account, since he even now struggles, not against me, but agains the one who cries out, *None can come to me unless the Father who sent me draws them* (Jn 6:44)" (*c. ep. Pel.* 1.19.37 [CSEL 60:454]).

must by definition be initially unwilling; otherwise "drawing" them would be unnecessary. The words of the "gospel" (*evangelio*) make clear, in turn, that none come to Christ without being drawn. The conclusion is inescapable: God does not fall back on working in people's hearts to reorient their willing only in rare cases when individuals seem particularly immune to grace. Rather, this is God's universal method for saving sinners and drawing them to himself.[100]

Both similarities and differences surface between this account of Paul's conversion and the account Augustine had provided in *Simpl.* In both, Paul's will is turned by God. No less in *Simpl.* than in *c. ep. Pel.*, Augustine portrays the will of Paul the merciless persecutor as passive when it comes to desiring the good. The will must be "turned" (*retorqueretur*) and "corrected" (*corrigeretur*). Paul "is made" (*effectus est*) "from a persecutor of the gospel" (*ex evangelii mirabili persecutore*) into a "preacher" (*praedicator*) of the gospel in *Simpl.*, just as in *c. ep. Pel.* God must "make willing people (*uolentes*) from unwilling ones (*nolentibus*)."[101] In *Simpl.*, just as in *c. ep. Pel.*, God is the agent of this reorientation of the will. In that earlier work, Paul is "thrown prostrate by one word from on high (*una desuper voce*)," just as in *c. ep. Pel.*, Augustine contends that the "will itself" (*ipsa uoluntas*) must be "stirred from above" (*desuper excitatur*). In both cases, Augustine makes clear that human beings alone cannot accomplish this reorientation; a higher power is needed. He also emphasizes in both texts that Paul serves as a paradigmatic example of a more general phenomenon. In *Simpl.*, too, Augustine had pointed to the representative character of Paul's experience: "Don't we see some, men and women, living blamelessly in pure marriage, who are either heretics or pagans or are so luke-warm in the true faith and the true Church that we marvel to see them surpassed not only in patience and temperance but also in faith, hope and charity by harlots and actors who have been suddenly converted?"[102] Paul may have

---

[100] Byers takes the paradigmatic function of the Pauline case to be a hallmark of the third major period of his teaching on grace, beginning in 425. She states that it is not until *gr. et lib. arb.* (426) that Augustine "begins to insist that conversion is God's 'operating through us' (*operari per*) to the exclusion of cooperative grace, and the Pauline case alone is given as the paradigm" (*Perception, Sensibility, and Moral Motivation in Augustine*, 212). An exclusive logic regarding the paradigmatic character of Paul's conversion, however, is already operative in *c. ep. Pel.*

[101] The last phrase is my translation. See *c. ep. Pel.* 1.19.37 (CSEL 60:454): *sed ut uolentes ex nolentibus fiant.*

[102] See *Simpl.* 1.2.22 (CCL 44:55), where Augustine continues: "The only possible conclusion is that it is wills that are elected. But the will itself can have no motive unless something presents itself to delight and stir the mind. That this should happen is not in any man's power. What did Saul will but

been a remarkable persecutor (*mirabili persecutore*) of the gospel, but he was no outlier with respect to the workings of grace. Augustine had already expressed the kind of marvel he would articulate in *c. ep. Pel.*—"How many enemies of Christ are today suddenly and secretly drawn to Christ by grace!"[103]—decades earlier in *Simpl.*

Yet for all these similarities, some differences arise between these two discussions of Paul's example and its significance for human willing. We have already seen that in *c. ep. Pel.*, Augustine describes God's impact on the will as effecting itself through an interior process within human hearts whereby God acts directly upon the will to reorient it to the good.[104] In the description of Paul's conversion in *Simpl.*, in contrast, though Augustine does speak of Paul's "mind" (*mens*) and "will" (*uoluntas*) being "turned and corrected" (*retorqueretur et corrigeretur*), he does not characterize God as bringing this about by working within the human heart and operating directly on the will. Instead he points to a "word from on high" (literally: a voice or call; *una desuper uoce*) and a "vision" (*uiso*) as the means by which (ablative of means: *quo*) God elicits right willing. In *Simpl.*, Augustine describes God as working indirectly through phenomena in the sensible realm, in this case sight and sound, to reorient Paul's will and set it on the right track toward faith.

While *Simpl.* lacks a reference to a direct internal operation with respect to explaining Paul's conversion, *c. ep. Pel.* indicates both that God operates directly on the will and that God uses sensible realities to effect the will's conversion.[105] In addition to speaking of God's inward work upon the will in *c. ep. Pel.*, Augustine describes God as turning Paul from evil to the good "by a miraculous and sudden call (*vocatione*)."[106] Thus in 421 Augustine

---

to attack, seize, bind and slay Christians? What a fierce, savage, blind will was that! Yet he was thrown prostrate by one word from on high, and a vision came to him whereby his mind and will (*uoluntas*) were turned from their fierceness and set on the right way towards faith, so that suddenly out of a marvelous persecutor of the Gospel he was made a still more marvelous preacher of the Gospel."

[103] *C. ep. Pel.* 1.19.37.

[104] In *c. ep. Pel.* Augustine describes God as working "within" (*intus*), "in human hearts" (*in ipsis hominum cordibus*), to "make willing people (*uolentes*) from unwilling ones (*nolentibus*)" (my translations; *c. ep. Pel.* 1.19.37 [CSEL 60:454]).

[105] While Augustine does not describe Paul's *conversion* in terms of a direct internal operation in *Simpl.* (1.2.22), he does assert elsewhere in the work that God brings about good willing through an interior operation of grace (1.2.12; see chapter 2). The difference highlighted here between *Simpl.* and *c. ep. Pel.* is that in the latter Augustine refers to grace functioning both internally and externally in considering the case of Paul's conversion and its larger significance. In other words, the insight of *Simpl.* 1.2.12 has been more thoroughly integrated into Augustine's broader thinking about the will by the time of *c. ep. Pel.*

[106] *C. ep. Pel.* 1.19.37 (CSEL 60:453).

does not hold these two ways of describing God's effect upon the will in conversion (internal and direct on the one hand, and mediated via sensible reality on the other) to be mutually exclusive. His suggestion that God operates directly on the will, then, does not replace but rather supplements and clarifies earlier descriptions of God's indirect impact on the will in conversion through sensible phenomena.

In fact, toward the end of his career, Augustine addresses precisely this issue, the question of how these two perspectives on God's involvement in human willing relate. Does his notion of God's direct operation upon the will render external influences upon it irrelevant, thereby removing the motivation for human actions designed to elicit good willing from others, such as rebuking sin? Augustine addresses this question, posed by a monk at Hadrumetum in response to Augustine's *Grace and Free Choice*, in his work *Rebuke and Grace (corrept.)*. In this latter text, Augustine describes God's internal inspiration, which produces a good will, as maneuvering in tandem with external rebuke: "In that way the pain of the rebuke may give rise to the will for rebirth, if the one rebuked is a child of the promise, so that God may also interiorly by his hidden inspiration produce in him the will when the words of the rebuke sound externally and strike him."[107] The "will to be regenerated" (*uoluntas regenerationis*) arises only if the person in question has been chosen by God as a child of the promise. However, since the given person is elected, two processes occur simultaneously: while "from without" (*forinsecus*) the sound of rebuke falls on a person, "from within" (*intrinsecus*) God's secret inspiration operates (*operetur*) such that this person also wills.

Each of these processes, Augustine's word choice and repetition drive home, has its own integrity and force and takes place on a distinctive causal plane. The first process functions via sensible realities, as Augustine conveys with auditory and tactile terms. He does not refer to "words" falling on a person's ears but rather, almost redundantly, to the "sound" (*strepitu*) of a rebuke "sounding" (*insonante*) and "beating against" (*flagellante*) him.[108] The second process, in contrast, occurs "within" (*intrinsecus*), where inspiration operates "hidden" (*occulta*) from human sense perception. Again here Augustine nearly repeats himself, this time in order to highlight the internal character of this process: it happens *in illo* and *intrinsecus*. He

---

[107] *Corrept.* 6.9 (CSEL 92:227).
[108] These are my translations.

locates human "willing" (*uelle*) on this plane that lies within. God's mysterious operation on the willing of a person through God's "secret inspiration" happens where no eye can see it.

In Augustine's very last anti-Pelagian work, his unfinished tome against Julian (427–430), one finds that his understanding of God's impact on the will as a direct and interior operation in the human heart has remained remarkably consistent with his descriptions from 418 and 421. He writes, "*The will is prepared by the Lord* (Prv 8:35 LXX), not by words that sound in the ears, but as, when the queen prayed and was heard, God changed and transformed the anger of the king into gentleness. For as God acted in the heart of that man in this divine and hidden manner, so *he produces in us both the willing and the action in accord with good will* (Phil 2:13)."[109] Again Augustine uses a biblical paradigm, in this case the conversion of the king of Assyria, to illustrate that God is responsible for the conversion of the will. "Just as" (*sicut*) God "converted" (*convertit*)[110] and "transformed the anger of the king into gentleness," so, in the words of Philippians 2:13, God "produces" (*operator*) good willing, that is, "both the willing (*uelle*) and the action in accord with good will (*operari pro bona uoluntate*)" in believers. Furthermore, Augustine explains, God prepares the will from within. The example of the king of Assyria demonstrates that God effects this preparation "not by words sounding from without" (*forinsecus*)[111] but rather "in the heart" (*in . . . corde*) in a "hidden manner" (*occulto modo*). As in *corrept.*, Augustine locates God's impact on the will in the sphere of the supersensible, in the secret realm of the heart.

Finally, Augustine suggests that this mysterious inward operation in the hearts of human beings involves a gift of love. Commenting on 1 Corinthians 3:7, "And yet neither the one who plants nor who waters is anything, but only God who gives the increase," Augustine writes, "But the increase is that each person obeys the commandments of God, and one does this, when one really does this, only with love (*caritate*). For this reason the Church *produces the increase of the body for building itself up with love* (Eph 4:16). Only God gives this love, for love comes from God." Julian tries to evade acknowledging God's gift of this love, Augustine contends, because doing so would require attributing obedience to God's grace. "You do not want to mention this love

---

[109] *C. Iul. op. imp.* 3.114 (CSEL 85.1:434–435).
[110] Here I have used "converted" instead of Teske's "changed."
[111] I have here used my own translation to highlight the language of externality.

among the helps of grace which you list," Augustine tells him, "so that you do not grant that the very fact that we obey God is due to his grace."[112] He continues, "You, of course, suppose that the choice of the will is removed in this way, though a person can only obey God by the will. But—and here is what you do not want—*the will is prepared by the Lord* (Prv 8:35 LXX)."[113] Julian's reticence to admit the gift of God's love stems from its association with God's preparation of the will, a notion that causes Julian particular discomfort since he fears it undermines the will's free choice. Thus, for Augustine, God's gift of love and preparation of the will are two ways of describing one and the same event. Though God's interior operation upon the human will remains mysterious, it is clear that this operation involves a gift of love by which the will is reoriented, not such that free choice is undermined but such that the person in question genuinely wills obedience. To say that God produces good willing and gives a gracious gift of love is to say that God does more than merely create the opportunity or occasion for human obedience. Rather, God directly effects a change of heart so that human beings themselves want to do what is right. This is a grace that works from the inside out, beginning by changing a person's inner desires and core orientation.

Though not amounting to a turning point in Augustine's way of describing God's impact upon the human will, at least two features do appear in 421 and following that further develop Augustine's view. First, Augustine characterizes God as the author of a good human will. Second, he argues that in baptism, infants receive grace without any involvement of the human will whatsoever. Infants represent a special case, but nonetheless one with larger repercussions for considering the role of will in the reception of grace more generally. Together these two developments in Augustine's thinking highlight a tendency in the trajectory of his thinking about God's impact on the human will over the whole course of his career. The scope of God's role in good human willing increases, while the human contribution decreases.

God as Author (*Auctor*) of Good Human Will

In *De diversis quaestionibus* (*diu. qu.*; 388–395), Augustine had interpreted agency, or being the "doer" or "performer" (*auctor*) of something, as having to do with willing it. He had argued, "When it is said that someone is the cause (*auctor*), this is said since he wills." In that context, Augustine had

---

[112] *C. Iul. imp.* 3.114 (CSEL 85.1:434–435).
[113] *C. Iul. imp.* 3.114 (CSEL 85.1:434–435).

been addressing the question of "whether it is because God is the cause, that humankind is bad."[114] He answered that because being the cause of something necessarily implies the operation of will, and God does not will what is evil, labeling God as the cause of humankind's evil condition is a mistake. Human ills stem from human wills, while evil is alien to the will of God; for this reason, though God is the *auctor* responsible for bringing human beings into existence, they alone are the *auctores* responsible for their own evil acts.[115]

In *diu. qu.* Augustine does not consider the inverse question, which comes to play such an important role in the Pelagian controversy: whether, and if so in what sense, it is because God is the cause that humankind is good. Around three decades later, in *c. Iul.* (421), however, Augustine turns indirectly to this issue. Explaining the proper way to interpret Matthew 7:18, "A good tree does not produce bad fruit," Augustine specifies that this good tree refers to a good will, rather than, as his opponents think, to nature or marriage.[116] He then addresses a possible objection to this interpretation. Does not Augustine's reading imply the superiority of human power to divine power, in that it attributes exclusively good fruit to human causality while God is the creator of all "trees," which may take the form of either good or bad wills?[117]

In response, Augustine presents the contrast between God's role in the origins of a bad will and God's role in the origins of a good will. The claim that God creates evil would be a contradiction in terms since evil is but a deprivation of the good. Thus evil human wills result not because God created them so but from the free defection of good human wills from the good. In this process, human wills, created goods, lose the ability to produce good effects. Insofar as they are good, God has created them; insofar as they are evil, they have defected from, rather than fulfilled, their God-given potential. As in *diu. qu.*, Augustine maintains that God bears no causal responsibility for the fact that some of his creatures have gone astray.

In the case of good wills, however, things function differently. Whereas one errs by designating God as the "cause" (*auctor*) of bad wills, one gives God appropriate credit by acknowledging him as "author of all goods"

---

[114] My translation. *Diu. qu.* 3: *utrum deo auctore sit homo deterior.*
[115] *Diu. qu.* 3: *ergo uitium uoluntatis quo est homo deterior.*
[116] *C. Iul.* 1.19.44.
[117] *C. Iul.* 1.9.45 (PL 44:671).

(*auctor est omnium bonorum*), including the "good will" (*uoluntatis bonae*).[118] Augustine writes, "But the good tree is the good will precisely because a human being is through it turned back to the highest and immutable good and is filled with the good so that it produces good fruit. In that way God is the author of all goods, that is, of good natures and of good wills, for only God, not a human being, produces the good will in a human being since *the will is prepared by the Lord*."[119] According to Augustine, God is the "author of the good will" (*auctor . . . uoluntatis bonae*) because, as indicated in scripture, the will is prepared by the Lord. God serves as author of the good will "through this" (*per hoc*), that he turns human beings back to the good for which they were created, filling the human will with good so that it may in turn bear good fruit. God is rightly called the *auctor* of a good human will since "no one except God works in the human person, the human person does not do it."[120] Augustine designates God as the author of good human willing, then, not to acknowledge God's role in reorienting the human will as a supplementary factor, but because God *rather than* the human person is really the one at work turning the will around. His claim is an exclusive one.

Thus Augustine's interpretation of Matthew 7:18 inverts the distribution of responsibility given in the objection whereby human beings create something (good will) that does not produce bad fruit, while God creates something (human nature) that does produce bad fruit (namely, a bad will or bad tree). Not only is it a mistake to attribute a bad will to God, but it is a mistake to attribute a good will to human beings. God is the *auctor* of good human willing. A good will that does not produce bad fruit is something made by God rather than "something that a human being makes" (*quam facit homo*),[121] as suggested in the objection Augustine addresses.

Infants Receive Baptism without Involvement of Will

In addition to making the argument with respect to bringing about a good will, that "no one except God works in the human person, the human person does not do it," Augustine also says that a good human will is not always

---

[118] Augustine actually uses the singular to refer to the good will God authors, though Teske translates it as a plural.

[119] *C. Iul.* 1.9.45 (PL 44:671).

[120] My translation. *C. Iul.* 1.9.45: *nisi deus in illo operetur, non facit homo.*

[121] My translation.

necessary for a human being's salvation. Not only, then, can God create or make a good human will for the salvation of human beings without any assistance from them, but God can also work the salvation of human beings in the absence of any human willing at all. This latter scenario arises in the case of baptized infants.

The example of infants illustrates the point that God's will, rather than human will, is decisive for whether a person is saved. After quoting John 6:44 and John 6:66, he states:

> All, then, who are saved and come to the knowledge of the truth are saved because he wills it (*eo uolente*), and they come because he wills it (*eo uolente*). For those who, like little ones, do not yet have use of the choice of their will (*uoluntatis arbitrio*) are reborn because he wills it (*eo uolente*), just as they were born because he creates them, and those who do have the choice of their will can only will because he who prepares their will (*uoluntas*) wills this (*eo uolente*) and comes to their help.[122]

The repetition of the phrase *eo uolente* runs through this passage like a red thread securely knotting each of the scenarios he discusses into the larger tapestry of God's sovereign plan. What is decisive for the place human beings have in this artwork is what God wills. Infants offer a compelling demonstration of this point since they lack the capacity to will at all, thereby eliminating the basis for attributing their salvation to the merits of their own willing. Their example provides a knock-down argument that good willing does not need to precede grace "since as yet they have no will."[123]

Augustine employs this argument again five years later in *gr. et lib. arb.* (426). The case of infants shows definitively, he points out, that human beings do not need to merit God's grace. Since, as Augustine had established earlier in his writings, praise or blame implies the presence of will, merit, which depends on the praiseworthiness of an action, is possible only given the exercise of will. Infants, however, lack the ability to will in this

---

[122] *C. Iul.* 4.8.44 (PL 44:760).

[123] *C. Iul.* 4.8.45 (PL 44:760): "I shall reply, 'Why does he not by the bath of rebirth adopt all who are going to die as infants, since as yet they have no will and, hence, no contrary will?'" This passage indicates that, according to Augustine, infants lack a will "for receiving grace" (in the words of *gr. et lib. arb.* 22.44), i.e., the volitional and intellectual apparatus to experience a specific wish directed toward that particular end. However this does not necessarily mean that babies do not have the capacity for other kinds of willing, for example, those "wishes" (*uoluntates*) Augustine attributed to himself as an infant.

way. Hence they cannot exercise it. Yet they still receive grace in baptism. Clearly, then, merits do not need to precede grace. He writes, "About the little ones the Pelagians certainly do not find any answer to make, for the little ones have no will (*uoluntas*) for receiving grace, a will whose merit they might say has come first. . . . Little ones resist with wailing when they are baptized and receive the sacraments. This would be counted against them as a great sin of impiety if they already had the use of free choice."[124] Indeed Augustine pushes his case further. Infants, he believes, illustrate not only that it is possible for grace to precede merits, but also that this is in fact how grace works universally. "But let people imagine some good merits which they think come first in order that they may be made righteous by the grace of God. They do not understand when they say this that they do nothing else but deny the grace of God." Infants highlight the consistency in God's way of relating to human beings in creation and in redemption. Just as God brings creation into existence out of nothing, so he brings about the rebirth of human beings without any preceding merit of their will.[125]

That God can bring about the salvation of infants without their will does not constitute, for Augustine, evidence that, in the case of persons whose wills are capable of an orientation to or away from God, God's grace operates without the human will. Infants illustrate the broader principle that merits of will do not *precede* grace, but they are an exception to the rule insofar as in their case grace does not immediately create and carry a good will along in its wake. In *praed. sanct.* (427), Augustine makes clear that, under normal circumstances, grace brings the will with it. It works in the will, not without it. He writes of Romans 11:7–10, "There you see mercy and judgment: mercy toward the chosen who have obtained the righteousness of God, but judgment for the rest who have been blinded. And yet, the one group believed because they willed to, and the other did not believe because they did not will to. Mercy and judgment, then, were produced in their very wills (*in ipsis uoluntatibus*). Their being chosen is, of course, due to grace, certainly not to their merits."[126] When a human being possesses the power of willing, God always uses the human will and works

---

[124] *Gr. et lib. arb.* 22.44 (PL 44:909).
[125] *C. Iul.* 4.8.45 (PL 44:760): "For those who, like little ones, do not yet have use of the choice of their will (*uoluntatis arbitrio*) are reborn because he wills it (*eo uolente*), just as they were born because he creates them, and those who do have the choice of their will can only will because he who prepares their will (*uoluntas*) wills this (*eo uolente*) and comes to their help."
[126] *Praed. sanct.* 6.11 (PL 44:969).

with it rather than acting against it or obliterating it. By transforming the will itself, God makes it the case that human beings believe willingly, even while belief, like the willing that brings it about, derives, properly speaking, from God's grace rather than human merit. Nonetheless, human existence is possible without the capacity for will, and in this case the lack of this capacity represents no obstacle to God's bestowal of grace. God's impact upon infants shows that God's power over the human will is so great that he not only may work within the will to transform it but even that, in special cases, he may work without it.

Section C: Phase 3—Features That Emerge from 426 to 430

In the final stage of the Pelagian controversy, Augustine's characterization of how God impacts the will continues to develop. Noteworthy elements that appear in this period include his specification that God works "without us" (*sine nobis*) to bring about our good willing but "with us" (*nobiscum*) to enact this good willing; his claim that God "directs" (*dirigit, inclinavit*) human wills; his description of God as "having dominion" (*dominatur*) over human wills; his portrayal of God as the exclusive source of good willing; and his characterization of God's love as necessary and sufficient for good human willing. Thus, in this period, Augustine broadens and deepens his estimation of the character, extent, and significance of God's willing for good human willing.

God Works "without Us"
In *gr. et lib. arb.* (426) Augustine provides a summary statement about how God's role and the human being's role in human willing relate: "He works, therefore, without us (*sine nobis operatur*) so that we will (*ut . . . uelimus*), but when we will (*cum uolumus*) and will so that we do the action (*uolumus ut faciamus*), he works along with us (*nobiscum cooperatur*); nonetheless, without his either working so that we will or his working along with us when we will, we can do nothing in terms of works of piety."[127] Here, as in a strikingly similar passage from *Simpl.*, written thirty years earlier, Augustine breaks down God's help for the human will into two basic divisions. First,

---

[127] *Gr. et lib. arb.* 17.33 (PL 44:901).

God makes it the case that we will the good. Second, God helps us to do what we will to do. The divine aid we receive on each of these accounts entails that we cannot complete works of piety without God. At this point, however, the similarity ends and a striking reversal comes into view.

In *Simpl.*, Augustine offered a statement from which he has retained the basic structural contrast between the two ways in which God helps us. There he had written, "There are two different things that God gives us, the power to will (*ut uelimus*) and the things that we actually will (*quod uolerimus*)."[128] He then went on, however, to give the following explanation of the divine and human contributions in these two areas: "The power to will (*ut uelimus*) he has willed should be both his and ours (*et suum . . . et nostrum*), his because he calls us, ours because we follow when called. But what we actually will (*quod autem uolerimus*) he alone (*solus*) gives, i.e., the power to do right (*posse bene agere*) and to live happily forever."[129] In this passage, Augustine attributed the fact "that we will" (*ut uelimus*) the good to both God and the human being: to God insofar as God contributes by calling and to human beings insofar as they contribute by following in response to God's call. Carrying through on the act of willing (*quod autem uolerimus*), meanwhile, Augustine attributes to God alone.

In *gr. et lib. arb.* Augustine divvies up the divine and human contributions to good willing differently. "That we will" (*ut uelimus*) the good, Augustine attributes to God working "without us," citing Philippians 2:13: "For it is God who produces in you the willing as well." Carrying through on this act of willing is something God does in cooperation "with us." Citing Romans 8:28, he concludes, "But concerning his working along with us (*cooperante*) when we already will, and by willing, do those actions, he says, *We know that God makes all things work together for the good for those who love him.*"[130] Thus, in this late work, Augustine's vision of these two aspects of God's contribution to human willing has undergone a kind of inversion. He reiterates his new conception, leaving no room for mistake: now his view is that God "begins by working in us that we will and works along with our wills in making them perfect,"[131] rather than, as in *Simpl.* 1.2.10, that God

---

128 *Simpl.* 1.2.10 (CCL 44:35).
129 *Simpl.* 1.2.10 (CCL 44:35).
130 Gr. et lib. arb. 17.33 (PL 44:901).
131 *Gr. et lib. arb.* 17.33 (PL 44:901).

works along with human beings in bringing it about *that* they will and alone gives them the ability to bring this good will to fruition.

Juxtaposing these two passages thus dramatically illustrates the development of Augustine's thinking on the issue of God's impact upon the human will. In both, he preserves a role for human willing and cooperation with God. However, whereas he initially locates this cooperation in the actual turning of the will to the good so that subsequent good works are contingent upon both divine and human contributions, he later attributes the initial conversion of the will entirely to God's operation, such that subsequent cooperation is contingent only on this initial divine act. Augustine eventually comes to see the initial conversion of the will as stemming entirely from God's decision. The clarity with which the contrast between Augustine's view in *Simpl.* 1.2.10 and in *Gratia et lib arbitrio* appears, however, does not indicate that this contrast emerged only in 426, when he penned the latter work. In fact, this reversal was already implied, if not formulated in so many words, in *Simpl.*

As discussed in chapter 2, Augustine was not able to rest content with the understanding of the role of human willing in conversion that he articulated in *Simpl.* 1.2.10, deeming revision necessary even before he reached the end of that work. Augustine's position in *Simpl.* 1.2.10 left the conversion of the will up to human beings. Did this really conform to the presentation of the matter in Romans 9? Ultimately Augustine determined that it did not. Rereading Romans 9:16 in light of Philippians 2:12–13, he concluded that Paul saw good willing itself as a divine work: "There he clearly shows that the good will itself is wrought in us by the working of God."[132] Notably Augustine describes God's work as interior, taking place "in us" (*in nobis*), and without specifying mediating realities through which God works, saying only that the good will is made "by God's working" (*operante deo*). Here he uses the language of interiority, leaving room for the kind of direct conception of God's internal operation that resounds decisively in his later anti-Pelagian works. It has become clear to Augustine that the effectiveness of God's calling does not depend upon willing human consent. Rather, God's calling ensures such consent: "But I do not know how it could be said that it is vain for God to have mercy unless we willingly consent. If God has mercy, we also will, for the power to will is given with the mercy itself."[133] Thus God's mercy alone guarantees that human beings will rightly.

[132] *Simpl.* 1.2.12 (CCL 44:36).
[133] *Simpl.* 1.2.12 (CCL 44:37).

In *Simpl.* Augustine does not yet state the implication of this view of God's efficacious mercy in the unflinching terms he employs in *gr. et lib. arb.*, that God works "without us" (*sine nobis*) to bring about our good willing. But such a conclusion follows from the train of thought he develops there. In this respect, the "evolution" of Augustine's explanation of God's role in good human willing after *Simpl.* is less a matter of sheer innovation than of constant and ever-sharpening reformulation of insights he had already attained in that seminal work.

Even Evil Wills Are "Inclined" by God

We have already seen how Augustine began to speak of God "driving" (*agere*) the will in the years following 417 to describe God's gracious action upon the human wills of those who become children of God. In the final stage of the Pelagian controversy, Augustine portrays God as directing and inclining human wills to accord with God's own will, including not only the conversion of evil wills to the good but also the confirmation of evil wills in their preexisting orientations. Though Augustine states that when such a confirmation occurs it serves the greater good of God's overarching plan, and though he does not describe God's influence on good and bad human willing as on a par with one another in terms of God's level of initiative and involvement, the suggestion that God's will may direct human will toward evil represents a new element of his conception of God's impact on the human will.

In *gr. et lib. arb.* (426), Augustine notes that his careful study of the scriptures suggests not only that God converts evil wills to the good but also that other wills, wills that remain in opposition to God, lie within God's power and are inclined by God. He writes:

> If the divine scripture is examined with care, it shows that not only the good wills of human beings which God himself produces out of evil ones (*facit ex malis*) and which, once made good by him, he directs (*dirigit*) toward good acts and toward eternal life, but also those wills which preserve the creature of the world are in the power of God (*in dei potestate*) so that he makes them turn (*faciat inclinari*) where he wills and when he wills, either to offer benefits to some or to impose punishments on others, as he himself judges by his judgment which is, of course, most hidden, but undoubtedly most just.[134]

---

[134] *Gr. et lib. arb.* 20.41 (PL 44:906). The original Latin behind the phrase that has come down to us as "illas quae conseruant saeculi creaturam" is a puzzle, but it is clear from the context that Augustine refers to wills that preserve worldly disobedience so as to merit punishment.

While the purpose of this passage is to point out a commonality between God's impact on wills that turn to the good and wills that persist in evil, namely that both are within God's power and subject to being inclined in accordance with the divine will, the differences between how Augustine describes God's impact on each immediately strike the reader. God's effect on these two types of willing is not symmetrical in every respect.

Augustine describes God's influence upon good wills in three ways. Good wills are something "God himself produces out of evil ones" (*ipse facit ex malis*). Good wills are "made good by [God]" (*a se factas bonas*). After God transforms wills so that they are good, he then "directs (*dirigit*) them toward good acts and toward eternal life." These descriptions paint a picture of God's impact on human willing as pervasive and constant. God not only initially produces the good will but also maintains it in goodness until the goal of eternal life is attained. In a passage from *De dono perseuerantiae* (*perseu.*, 428/429), another work in the final phase of Augustine's endeavors to combat Pelagianism, Augustine also depicts God as assisting from start to finish of the Christian life, initially bending (*flectere*) the will from bad to good, converting (*convertere*) wills prone to wander, and directing (*dirigere*) the will on to the path to God. Augustine connects these modes of impact upon the will to biblical texts: Psalm 85:7, Psalm 66:9, Psalm 140:9 (these three perhaps corresponding respectively to the three modes), and Matthew 6:13.[135]

God's impact on wills that do not turn to the good he describes in other terms. Though characterizing such wills as "in God's power" (*in dei potestate*), Augustine does not claim that God "makes" these wills.[136] Instead of speaking of God "directing" (*dirigere*) wills that persist in disobedience, he uses a different verb: God "makes them be turned" (*faciat inclinari*)[137] at will, in accordance with his just judgment. Indeed to speak of God "directing" (*dirigere*) such wills would be misleading, as by definition such wills are not set on a straight course, as would be implied by the term in its literal sense, but

---

[135] *Perseu.* 6.12 (PL 45:1000): "He is, therefore, able to turn wills from evil to good and to turn back to him wills likely to fall away and to direct them into a path pleasing to him. We do not say to him in vain, *O God, you convert us and give us life* (Ps 85:7); we do not say to him in vain, *Do not allow my foot to be moved* (Ps 66:9); we do not say to him in vain, *Do not hand me over to the sinner in accord with my desire* (Ps 140:9). Finally, in order not to mention too many, since more passages perhaps come to your mind, we do not say in vain, *Bring us not into temptation* (Mt 6:13)."

[136] That Augustine refrains from speaking this way conforms to his position in *c. Iul.* (421) that God "does not make their wills evil, but he makes use of them as he wills, though he cannot will anything unjust" (*c. Iul.* 5.4.15).

[137] This is my translation, overly literal for the sake of preserving the passive voice.

continue diverging from the good. Though these descriptions stress God's absolute sovereignty over abidingly recalcitrant wills, they maintain a certain distance between God and the wills he affects: these wills are decisively in the scope of God's power and entirely subject to God's precise will, inclined according to its precise dictates, but in this passage Augustine does not portray God as operating directly upon them.

Augustine's discussion of a series of concrete biblical examples, however, helps to fill out the picture of the extent of God's influence upon wills that remain inclined to disobedience, betraying a surprising degree of overlap between Augustine's descriptions of God's impact on wills he converts to the good and God's influence on those he does not. The Israelites' flight from Ai recounted in Joshua 7:12, for instance, represents, for Augustine, a case in which God instilled fear in human souls.[138] As God converts an evil will to the good by inspiring love in the human heart, so God is capable of converting a courageous will to cowardice by filling human hearts with fear. Though the Israelites attempted to take a stand against their enemies, Augustine explains, God caused them to fail by acting directly on their will. He asks, "Why did they not stand through free choice, but fled when their will was thrown into confusion through fear, if it was not that the Lord has dominion also over the wills of human beings and throws into fear those he wills when he is angry?"[139] In addressing this concrete scenario, Augustine observes that the Israelites' "will was thrown into confusion through fear" (*per timorem turbata uoluntate*), an assertion that does not specify the origin of this change in willing, but also that the explanation for this change is that "the Lord has dominion also over the wills of human beings" (*dominatur et uoluntatibus hominum*) and "converts (*convertit*)[140] those human beings to fearfulness that he wishes (*quos vult*)."[141]

As he shows in treating the example of the son of Gera who curses David in 2 Samuel 16, God does not move human wills to sin by command. Indeed

---

[138] *Gr. et lib. arb.* 20.41 (PL 44:906): "God produced fear in their heart so that they fled, and he did this in order that their sin might be punished."

[139] *Gr. et lib. arb.* 20.41 (PL 44:906).

[140] Teske translates *per timorem turbata uoluntate* as "thrown into confusion through fear" and *in formidinem convertit* as "throws into fear," but a more literal translation of the latter phrase highlights the change in Augustine's Latin terminology from one phrase to the other.

[141] I have found instances where Augustine speaks of God "inclining" (*inclinare*) wills to evil, but none where he speaks of God "directing" (*dirigere*) wills to evil. If the cases I have considered represent a broader pattern, *dirigere* is restricted to cases where God moves wills to the good, while *inclinare* may describe God's movement of wills toward either good or evil.

obedience to such a commandment would render an otherwise sinful act praiseworthy.[142] Rather, some kind of mysterious operation takes place by God's "hidden judgment": "Scripture said, *The Lord told him to [2 Samuel 16:10]*, because by his just and hidden judgment God inclined (*inclinauit*) toward this sin that man's will (*uoluntatem*) which was evil because of its own sinfulness."[143] However God inclines human wills to sin, Augustine makes clear that God influences the will in this manner only because of the prior sinful orientation of the will. Even in the case of the Israelites at Ai, God turns their wills toward what is bad only in light of their previous disobedience, though in the immediate context of the battle this involves a transition from a more positive kind of willing (viz., courageous willing) to a more negative kind of willing (viz., cowardly willing).

Again in the case of the maltreatment that elicited the clamor of Israel's ten tribes for another king to replace Rehoboam, Augustine refers to the Lord effecting a *conversio* of the will away from the good: God's will was behind King Rehoboam's rejection of wise advice in favor of a decision to treat his people harshly, a decision that precipitated the ten tribes' discontent and, ultimately, the division of God's people. He writes, "All this was, of course, done by the will of the man in such a way that the change (*conversio*), nonetheless, came from the Lord (*esset a domino*)."[144] In this case Augustine derives the term *conversio* directly from the text of 1 Kings 12:15: "And the king did not listen to the people because the Lord produced a change of heart (*quoniam erat conuersio a domino*) in order to accomplish his word."[145] On the strength of this biblical testimony, Augustine portrays God as changing Rehoboam's will for the worse. Yet, as Augustine points out, God's influence did not displace Rehoboam's own willing. Precisely by converting Rehoboam's will, God accomplished his own will without violating Rehoboam's. Furthermore, since Rehoboam had already proven himself to be an "evil" person even before God had prompted him to maltreat his subjects, God's influence upon his willing resulted in punishment he had already merited.[146] Thus, according to Augustine, God can convert wills

---

[142] *Gr. et lib. arb.* 20.41 (PL 44:906): "For, if he had obeyed God commanding him, he ought to have been praised rather than punished."

[143] *Gr. et lib. arb.* 20.41 (PL 44:906).

[144] *Gr. et lib. arb.* 21.42 (PL 44:907).

[145] Teske's translation of Augustine's quotation. *Gr. et lib. arb.* 21.42 (PL 44:907).

[146] Augustine introduces his consideration of Rehoboam's case by stating, "Who would not tremble before these judgments of God by which God does what he wills even in the hearts of evil persons, repaying them, nonetheless, according to their merits?" (*gr. et lib. arb.* 21.42 [PL 44:907]).

to evil as well as to good, though he does not do so in a way that violates justice. Augustine sees human willing, of either good or bad, as entirely compatible with God's interior operation "in the hearts of human beings" (*in cordibus hominum*) to bring about a "movement of their will" (*motum uoluntatis eorum*) that coincides with his own just purposes.[147]

As we have seen, Augustine makes this case on the basis of concrete examples from the story of God's people recorded in scripture. He turns to seemingly mundane incidents, each of which plays a role in the larger scope of God's salvific plan, as case studies for understanding the extent to which God impacts human willing, and the principles according to which this influence works itself out. These examples eventually lead Augustine both to expand and to deepen his conception of God's involvement in human willing. By the latest phase of the Pelagian controversy, Augustine becomes convinced that God converts not only bad wills to the good but also, on occasion, good wills to what is bad. Likewise references to God's mysterious work in "the hearts" of human persons persuade Augustine that God exercises influence on human willing in a direct interior manner: God directs some wills to the good and inclines other wills to evil by bringing about a change in their willing at the secret core of their persons.

In at least a few respects, however, Augustine posits an asymmetry between God's way of "directing" wills to the good and "inclining" wills to evil. First, when God "makes use of the hearts even of evil persons," he does so "for the praise and help of the good."[148] God does not direct some wills to the good for good ends and incline others to evil for evil ends. Rather, his influence on human wills, whether toward what is good or toward what is evil, ultimately serves the good. Second, when God inclines wills to evil, evil merits precede such intervention; when God directs wills to good, this intervention precedes merits. Thus God's inclination of wills to evil is merited, while grace is not.[149] Finally, while God's direction of wills to the good

---

[147] With respect to peoples God "roused up" against Israel, Augustine writes, "They came by their own will and the spirit of the Lord also aroused their spirit. This can also be expressed as follows: The Lord aroused their spirit, and yet they came of their own will. For the almighty produces in the hearts of human beings even the movement of their will in order to do through them what he himself wills to do through them, he who absolutely cannot will anything unjust" (*gr. et lib. arb.* 21:42 [PL 44:908]).

[148] *Gr. et lib. arb.* 20.41.

[149] *Gr. et lib. arb.* 21.43 (PL 44:909): "God works in the hearts of human beings to incline their wills to whatever he wills, whether to good actions in accord with his mercy or to evil ones in accord with their merits. . . . And for this reason, when you read in the words of the truth that God deceives human beings or dulls or hardens their hearts, have no doubt that their evil merits came first so that they suffer these punishments justly."

makes him responsible for the good we will, his inclination of wills to what is evil in no way mitigates our responsibility for failing to will rightly. In Augustine's terse assessment of human and divine responsibility for perseverance, "one . . . who falls falls by his own will, but one who stands stands by the will of God. *For God is able to hold him upright* (Rom 14:4); therefore, it is not he who makes himself stand, but God."[150] Especially in the last case, Augustine may not make entirely clear the correlation between his affirmation of asymmetry and other statements he makes concerning God's impact on human willing.[151] But acknowledging such affirmations is vital to recognizing the complexity—and tensions—in Augustine's view of God's impact upon the human will, both of which result from his attempt to integrate into his account a diverse panoply of biblical statements pertinent to the issue.

God's Gift of Love as an Exclusive, Necessary, and Sufficient Source of Good Will

In Augustine's final, uncompleted work against Julian, one encounters his thinking on God's impact on the human will unfurled in its most seasoned and uncompromising form: God alone can meet the conditions necessary for good human willing, both in the sense that no one but God makes good willing possible and insofar as God's help alone guarantees successful completion of this process once he has set it in motion. More specifically, "only" (*sola*) love that comes from God "wills (*vult*) the beatific good." To suggest that right willing could be achieved on the basis of another kind of love, a love attained by one's own free will rather than received as a divine gift, would be to intimate that human beings surpass God with respect to the kinds of good with which they provide themselves. Even Julian acknowledges that God bestows knowledge by grace. Yet, since love "surpasses knowledge," if human beings achieve without God the love necessary for right willing, then a good greater than the good God gives them derives from themselves. Thus it must be the case, Augustine reasons, that only God, and not human beings, can inspire in people the kind of love necessary for the kind of willing that leads to beatitude. Indeed, Augustine

---

[150] *Perseu.* 8.19 (PL 45:1003).

[151] For example, Augustine elsewhere indicates that both when God turns the will to good and when God turns the will to evil, insofar as the human will itself is turned, it is in play rather than coerced involuntarily, in line with the divine will. There seems, then, to be a symmetry between the two cases insofar as, in both, both divine and human wills are at work.

contends, verses such as Philippians 2:13, Proverbs 8:35 LXX, and I John 4:7 make clear that only God can make good willing possible.[152]

Augustine contends in *Contra Iulianum* that God's gift of love is sufficient, as well as necessary, for right human willing. In response to Julian's statement that a person possesses free choice only if she neither sins nor is righteous by necessity, Augustine characterizes God's gift of love as entirely sufficient for producing a good will, even while defending the notion that this sufficiency does not violate human free choice. He writes:

> If you included among the various kinds of divine grace the love (*dilectionem*) which, as you read most clearly in scripture does not come from us, but from God and which God gives to his children, that love without which no one lives a life of piety and with which no one lives anything but a life of piety, that love without which no one has a good will (*sine qua nullius est bona uoluntas*) and with which no one has anything but good will (*cum qua nullius est nisi bona uoluntas*), you would be defending a truly free choice and not inflating it with pride. If, however, you call that a necessity (*necessitatem*) by which any are compelled against their will (*inuitus*), there is no necessity of righteousness because none are righteous unwillingly (*inuitus*). Rather, the grace of God makes them willing from unwilling (*gratia dei ex nolente uolentem facit*). But if no one sins unwillingly (*inuitus*), scripture would not say, *You have sealed my sins in a sack, and you have noted if I have done anything unwillingly* (Jb 14:17).[153]

Augustine, then, rejoins that authentic free choice is not something human beings already possess, which can then be undermined by the operation of grace. Without God's gracious gift of love, it is impossible to have a good will. Without a good will, one cannot have truly free choice.[154] Therefore

---

[152] *C. Iul. imp.* 1.95 (CSEL 85.1:110): "If grace does not come first to produce the will, but grace works along with the already existing will, how can it be true that *God also produces in you the will* (Phil 2:13)? How can it be true that *the will is prepared by the Lord* (Prv 8:35 LXX)? How can it be true that *love comes from God* (1 Jn 4:7), the love which alone wills the beatific good? Or if knowledge of the law and of God's words produces love in us so that we love, not by a gift of God, but by the choice of our own will, what we know we should love because God teaches us, how can the lesser good come from God and the greater good from ourselves? I mean that we cannot know without God's giving us knowledge, that is, without his teaching us, but we can love without his giving the love which surpasses knowledge. Only the new heretics and fierce enemies of the grace of God think that way."

[153] *C. Iul. imp.* 3.122 (CSEL 85.1:440).

[154] This is a claim we will explore in chapter 8, which is devoted to Augustine's mature conception of "free will."

authentic free choice requires the prior operation of grace even to be possible.

As Augustine's line of argument makes clear, not only is it impossible to have a good will without God's gift of love; it is impossible not to have a good will with God's gift of love. The only possible result of God's inspiration of love in the human heart is the conversion of the will to the good; one cannot genuinely possess God's love and yet fail to want what is right. Though good willing is this love's inevitable result, those who have received this love do not attain righteousness by necessity, if necessity is defined as something that happens against a person's will. Since God's grace operates on human wills precisely by transforming them, making them "willing from unwilling," it inherently avoids such necessity by virtue of the kind of transformation it effects. Thus Augustine argues that God's gift of love is sufficient for producing a good will but also that this sufficiency establishes, rather than compromises, free choice. God never compels a person against her will; instead he ensures the sufficiency of his grace by reorienting the will.[155]

However much Augustine's estimation of the power of God's impact on the will grows over the course of his career, it never crowds out human agency. For the whole of his career, Augustine portrays God as acting so as to preserve the integrity of the relationship between a person's identity and her acts such that her acts really do flow from her will. A key presupposition of such a view of the coincidence of divine and human agency is the notion that something can come "from the will of God" and "from the will of a human being" at the same time. In Augustine's words, "Even if God produces (*operatur*) in a human being a good will (*uoluntas*), he, of course, does this so that the good will comes to be from the one whose will it is (*ab illo . . . cuius est uoluntas*). In the same way he acts so that a human being comes to be from a human being (*ab homine*). For it is not true that, because God creates a human being, a human being is, therefore, not born of a human being (*ex homine*)."[156] For Augustine, the agencies at work in human willing cannot be quantified as parts of a single whole, which together add up to 100%. He instead posits a dual agency at work in human

---

[155] In *c. Iul. imp.* 3.122, Augustine focuses particularly on the issue of whether the "necessity of righteousness" to which Julian refers violates free choice. He pronounces later in the work on the question of the necessity of sin, which Julian also mentions. See *c. Iul. imp.* 5.32.

[156] *C. Iul. imp.* 5.42 (CSEL 85.2:245).

willing, whereby divine and human agents operate upon the will at two different levels. Just as in the birth of the human being God is the agent as creator while the human being is the agent as source, so with respect to establishing a good human will, God "creates" the will, bringing into existence a good will where there was none previously, even while human beings possess this good will as their own and experience it as emerging organically from the heart of their own identities.

Conclusion

In the first part of this chapter we established that, throughout the Pelagian controversy, Augustine relies upon the argument that biblical prayer and injunctions to prayer serve as evidence of God's impact upon the human will. This constant in his teaching on what makes good human willing possible confirms a point we have seen repeatedly in previous chapters. The biblical text serves as the basis upon which Augustine constructs his theologically differentiated view of will. The redeemed human will, the *uoluntas bona*, is not like the created will or the fallen will. Unlike the fallen will, it has been reoriented from evil to the good. But unlike the created will, it continues to suffer from the after-effects of the fall and therefore requires the constant intervention of God's grace. The Bible tells Augustine that this is the reality of how redeemed willing works this side of the eschaton. The prayers and injunctions to prayer recorded in scripture, as put into practice in the distinctive worship of the church, serve as his source for discerning the peculiar rules of the game for the "good will" (*uoluntas bona*) that the faithful possess in this time between the times.

Though the view of the good will that results from the evolutions discussed in this and the previous chapter differs dramatically from the pictures of the created and fallen will that he developed in earlier periods of his thinking, Augustine's convictions about the most basic features of the good will remain consistent throughout the Pelagian controversy. He refines and develops his understanding within these parameters. And he consistently maintains in this period that willing rightly is possible only through grace, that human beings require God's help to put this right willing into action by actually doing the good, and that God impacts the will both externally and internally to orient it toward the good. Thus, throughout the Pelagian controversy, Augustine remains true to the basic insight of *Simpl.*

that the good will is a result of God's grace rather than the reverse. At the same time, however, he deepens and develops the concrete implications of this insight into the good will.

The second part of this chapter has shown that whereas the perimeters of Augustine's assessment of what is "in our power" with respect to good willing contract over the course of the Pelagian controversy (as demonstrated in chapter 3), his estimation of the extent of God's role in bringing about good human willing expands. In the first stage of the Pelagian controversy, he tends to characterize God's help as consisting in the presentation of knowledge and other enticements, to which the will is free to choose how to respond. God "helps" the will indirectly by laying attractive options before it, whether on an internal or an external level. As the controversy progresses, Augustine describes this assistance as more and more direct, potent, and all-encompassing. In the controversy's second stage, the following types of characterizations emerge: Augustine describes God as driving the human will, bringing it to fulfillment in each discrete good action, and filling it with love. He also underlines God's unmediated internal operation upon the good will. Augustine further describes God as the "author" (*auctor*) of good wills[157] and observes on the basis of infants that in special cases God works without the human will to accomplish salvation. In 426 and the years following, during the final stage of the Pelagian controversy, he refers to God working "without" us to convert our wills to the good, not merely as an exceptional case but as the rule. He also speaks of evil wills as inclined by God while he is careful to distinguish this inclination from God's direction of good wills. For Augustine in this final stage, God is the exclusive source of good will. His love is both necessary and sufficient for good human willing. God plants, God waters, God nourishes, God harvests. God gives the growth of the good will from start to finish. This expansion of the divine role in bringing about and fulfilling good human willing corresponds to a diverse but coherent set of descriptions of what the good will is that Augustine provides during the course of the Pelagian controversy. We turn to these in the following chapter.

---

[157] *C. Iul.* 1.9.45 (PL 44:671).

5

The Redeemed Will

A Root of Love

Introduction

The expansion of the divine role in bringing about and fulfilling good
human willing that we observed in chapter 4 corresponds to a diverse but
coherent set of descriptions of what the good will is in Augustine's mature thought. Due to his growing emphasis on God's impact upon human
willing, traced in the previous chapter, God features prominently during the
Pelagian controversy in the images Augustine uses for the good will and
the defining characteristics he attributes to it. Most of these descriptions
do not emerge until the second and third stages of the controversy, as defined in chapter 3, that is, until around 417 or 418, but Augustine uses some
of these descriptions already when he enters the fray against the first-wave
Pelagianism of Rufinus, Pelagius, and Caelestius in 411 and 412.

Over the course of the Pelagian controversy, Augustine describes the
good will as a will in the process of conversion, a will from God, a will
directed to God, a will with faith in God, a will belonging to the believer,
and the one good work necessary for eternal life. For Augustine in this period, God's impact on the good human will is not easy to capture in one
simple description or relationship. Rather, good human willing is bound up
with God's work in numerous ways. It is caught up in a veritable web of
attachments to God: good human willing comes from God, it is directed
to God, its content is faith in God, and, as Augustine pronounces in 418,
it is finally nothing other than *caritas*, the love of God.[1] It is as dependent
on God as a tree on soil and sun to make it grow. Augustine's notion of the
good human will, one might summarize in other words, sinks its roots ever
more deeply, during the Pelagian controversy, into the omnipotent divine
will. Augustine had articulated his notions of the created and fallen human

---

[1] In *gr. et pecc. or.* (418), Augustine writes that a good will is *caritas*, love that comes to us from God
(1.21.22).

Augustine on the Will. Han-luen Kantzer Komline, Oxford University Press (2020). © Oxford
University Press.
DOI: 10.1093/oso/9780190948801.001.0001

wills, too, in theological contexts, but his descriptions of the good will during the Pelagian controversy do not merely relate to God; they center on God.

The contrasts between this strikingly theocentric characterization of the good will and the notions of human willing Augustine had developed earlier are helpfully captured in an image he introduces during the Pelagian controversy to describe the good will. Augustine had spoken of the created will as a hinge (*cardo*) and of the fallen will as a link in a chain (*ansula catenae*). The good will is different. It neither swings neutrally back and forth between good and evil nor holds a person in bondage to sin. Though weak, it grows dynamically in one direction, toward God and, therewith, toward freedom. It is like a root (*radix*), planted and cultivated to bear sweet fruit. The good will of the faithful in this life is destined to become something beautiful but has not quite blossomed yet.

Augustine's descriptions of the good will, emblematized in the image of the will as root, carry implications for his conception of the will at large. As he refines his thinking on human willing in the context of polemic with the Pelagians, he comes to be persuaded that human willing need not be inimical to necessity, as he had once thought. In some cases, willing can be necessary—both for good, as in the necessary goodness of God's own will, and for ill, as exemplified in the subjection of the fallen will to original sin. Human willing, Augustine's thinking during the Pelagian controversy suggests, is radically permeable to outside influences and constraints, including those that impose certain kinds of necessity upon it. Because such influences are always already at work, furthermore, one ought not view the will as a neutral power in the sense of being equally *disposed* to all possibilities. Not only the good will, Augustine comes to believe, but even the created will never enjoyed this kind of neutrality, though it did retain the freedom to *choose* between both good and evil possibilities. The human will had a definite direction from the beginning, though this direction was abruptly reversed. In the Pelagian controversy, Augustine sees various kinds of will functioning more nearly as vectors, pointing decisively in a given direction, than as mathematical points, impartially open to extension in all directions.

Given that human willing always occurs with a concrete orientation, it becomes more difficult to understand what generic willing might entail, if such a notion is coherent at all. It therefore comes as no surprise that, in the Pelagian controversy, Augustine tends to devote more attention to describing instances of the former rather than to theorizing about the latter. Whereas his interlocutors prefer to characterize both good and bad willing as springing from a single source, nature, via a neutral choice of the will, Augustine prefers to see good and bad willing themselves as two radically distinct wellsprings of human action. For Augustine, good and bad willing are not offshoots of the same root. They are, at bottom, different things entirely, with completely different sources, features, and trajectories of growth.

During the Pelagian controversy, then, Augustine does not develop his theologically periodized notion of will on a continuum on which the created, fallen, and good wills gradually give way to one another. Moving from one kind of willing to another does not happen progressively but is a matter of life, death, and rebirth. In this sense, Augustine's overarching conception of will is not gradualistic but apocalpytic. God converts a human will to the good by uprooting and replanting, not merely by sending forth a new shoot from the same volitional trunk.

But the image of a root is not the only image Augustine uses for the good will. Examining his thinking on will is like looking into a kaleidoscope. He does not prioritize conceptual consistency, coherence, or comprehensiveness as ends in themselves in his meditations on human willing. Rather he formulates his thoughts on will as the need arises in response to specific situations involving particular people: a statement from a polemical opponent, a biblical event, a verse in need of clarification, or an episode from his own life. Most often he offers a perspective on human willing that emerges from some creative conglomeration of these provocations, each of which involves its own colorful clusters of human circumstances at issue. What one finds changes from moment to moment. Augustine has bequeathed to us not a systematic theory of the will but a vast array of ad hoc perspectives on how the will works that emerge from accounts of how God has changed lives, above all, from instances and interpretations of such experiences found in the Bible. The overarching picture of the will that emerges enjoys consistency and coherence to the degree that these stories find their place within the larger story told in scripture about the mystery of God's will for humankind. Augustine's account of will holds together in the context of this narrative, not as a system. Fittingly, then, he uses narrative and metaphor to explain what the will is rather than providing technical philosophical definitions. He is concerned with the practical implications of how the will works in real-life stories.

Augustine uses a panoply of different descriptions to shed light on what the human will is. Two key images that fall into place behind the lens of his kaleidoscope during the course of the Pelagian controversy are those of will as root and as eye of the soul. These two images will be discussed in part I of this chapter. In addition to these metaphors for the good will, Augustine identifies a number of other characteristics of the good will as he considers it from various perspectives (discussed in part II). The good will is a will in the process of conversion, comes from God, is directed to God, has faith in God, belongs to the believer, and represents the one good work necessary for eternal life. As this brief list demonstrates, God represents the common link among these diverse descriptions. The good will is unthinkable without reference to its creator and sustainer, from whom it comes, in whom it lives and moves, and toward whom it is directed.

In fact, as we will observe in part III, dedicated to the connections between will and "love" (*caritas*; section A) and will and "heart" (*cor*; section B), the good will not only results from God's love, it is love (*caritas*), participating in God's very being. In this part of the chapter we see that love is the biblical core of Augustine's conception of the redeemed human will. If the created will, in Augustine's early descriptions, is like the movement of a hinge opening doors of possibility, and the fallen will like a link in a chain imposing strictures of necessity, the good, redeemed human will is like a root of love springing up from the soil to the sunshine of divinity.

In part IV we step back to consider the larger picture of Augustine's perspective on will during the Pelagian controversy. These kaleidoscopic reflections on the character of the good will, restored by God from its fallen condition, help to highlight the implications of the conception of good willing that Augustine develops in the Pelagian controversy for his thinking about the will more generally. Specifically, they throw into relief the nonneutral character of human willing, which, Augustine concludes in this phase, always has a definite direction with respect to good and evil.

Part I: Images of the Good Will

Section A: Will as Root (418 and Following)

In 418 and the years following, in the second stage of Augustine's discussion of the good will in the Pelagian controversy, discussed in chapters 3 and 4, the image of the good will as a root comes to the fore. Augustine develops this image in elaborating on texts such as Matthew 7:18, Matthew 12:33, and Luke 6:44, which reference good and corrupt trees bearing good and corrupt fruit, respectively. In the words of Matthew 7:18, "A bad tree does not produce good fruit, and a good tree does not produce bad fruit."[2] Against the Manichees in *Contra Fortunatum*, Augustine had interpreted the two trees Jesus mentions in Matthew 12:33 as referring to two wills, using this text to show that it is "up to us" (*est nobis*) to make our wills good or bad.[3] In this verse Jesus warns, "Either make the tree good, or make the tree bad."[4] In the context of his dispute with the Manichees, Augustine's concern had been to show that free choice, rather than whether one had a good or evil nature, determined the kind of actions a person could perform. In a number of works from the Pelagian controversy, he compares the trees referred to in this and similar texts from the gospels to human beings and describes wills as the roots that determine the form these trees will take, whether bad or good. Thus Augustine still explains the difference between the two trees as a matter of will, but, in the context of anti-Pelagian polemic, he sees the differences between these two kinds of will as more entrenched.

In *gr. et pecc. or.*, Augustine draws on Matthew 7:18 to respond to Pelagius's notion of ability as the single root of both virtue and vice. He writes:

> If, then, the two trees, the good one and the bad one, are two human beings, a good one and a bad one, what is the good human being but one with good will, that is, a tree with a good root? And what is a bad human being but one with a bad will, that is, a tree with a bad root? After all, the fruits of these roots and trees are thoughts, words, and deeds; the good ones come forth from a good will, the evil ones from an evil will.[5]

Rather than, like Pelagius, seeing good and bad actions as stemming directly from a single root, human ability, Augustine construes good and bad

---

[2] This is Teske's translation of Augustine's quotation in *c. Iul.* 1.8.38.
[3] *C. Fort.* 22 (CSEL 25.1:105). "But in order that you may understand that the Lord mentioned these two trees in order to signify free choice, and that those two trees are not our natures but our wills (*uoluntates*) he said in the gospel, *Either make the tree good, or make the tree bad* (Mt 12:33). Who is there who can make a nature? If, then, we are commanded to make a tree good or bad, it is up to us to choose what we want."
[4] This is Teske's translation of Augustine's quotation of the verse in *c. Fort.* 22.
[5] *Gr. et pecc. or.* 1.18.19 (CSEL 42:140).

actions as stemming from two distinct sources: love and covetousness. He calls into question the existence of a generic form of human willing that may produce either good or bad actions. For Augustine, good actions and bad actions are like apples and oranges. They are separate species produced by separate trees that grow from separate roots. In Augustine's words, "That ability, then, is not, as this fellow supposes, the single root of both good and bad actions. In fact, love, the root of good actions, is one thing, and covetousness, the root of bad actions, is something else. They are as different as virtue and vice."[6] Augustine has no interest in a universalized theory of the human will. He concerns himself instead with calling attention to the world of difference between having a good or a bad will.

For Augustine, the decision for virtue or vice takes place far in advance of the moment one performs a given act. At that point, what a person will do is nearly a foregone conclusion. Human beings were created with the ability to be either kind of tree, one that habitually produces good fruit or one that habitually produces bad fruit. But this does not entail the ability to choose spontaneously what kind of tree one will be each time one is tempted to sin. How people live, whether poorly or well, is determined at the level of will, which is a fundamental orientation of the whole person rather than merely a catch-all label for discrete wishes one may have or not.

According to Augustine, the will constitutes an intermediate step between ability and good or bad actions. Human ability, it is true, may be exercised in a twofold way. But ability channels into one of two types of willing before being exercised in discrete actions: "But that ability is clearly able to become each of these roots, because human beings not only can have love by which they are good trees, but also can have covetousness by which they are bad trees."[7] The character of one's willing, then, like a mold, determines the shape human abilities take. Whether ability is processed "through covetousness" or "through love" makes the decisive difference as to what kinds of actions result. What kind of will is at work is not indifferent: "When human beings sin, they do not sin through love; rather, they sin through covetousness."[8] As his use of the image of the root shows, for Augustine, good and bad wills are not available for lighthearted selection from occasion to occasion, like so many varieties of fruit at a market. Rather

[6] *Gr. et pecc. or.* 1.20.21 (CSEL 42:141).
[7] *Gr. et pecc. or.* 1.20.21 (CSEL 42:141).
[8] *Gr. et pecc. or.* 1.21.22 (CSEL 42:142).

they are two fundamentally different ways of being human that well up and spill over from deep inside a person. What kind of will one has depends not only on one's own spontaneous decisions but also on a complex history in which one's own identity takes shape in relation to other human beings and to God.

Augustine alludes to this complex history when he takes up the theme of will as tree/root again in *nupt. et conc.* (418–419), this time in response to Julian's use of Matthew 12:33. Julian uses this text to make the case that Augustine cannot at once maintain that marriage is good and that original sin derives from it.[9] If marriage is good, Julian insists, then its fruits must be good, for: "From its fruits the tree is known."[10] Augustine responds that Julian has misappropriated the gospel text in question, which refers to good and bad wills rather than to marriage: "Was he not rather speaking of the two wills in human beings, namely, the good and the bad, calling this one a good tree and the other one a bad tree, because good works spring from (*nascuntur*) a good will and bad works from a bad will?"[11] Again in this context, Augustine rejects the notion that the cause of something being good or bad can be identified without reference to will. To reason that anything that comes from marriage must be good since marriage is good is as gross an oversimplification as the notion that everything that comes from marriage must be bad: "Marriage is not the cause of the sin which is contracted by the one who is born and wiped away in the one who is reborn; rather, the voluntary sin of the first human being is the cause of original sin."[12] The root of the original sin lies in Adam's voluntary sin, not in marriage. This sin, which poisoned human willing at its very core, introduced a fundamental divide between fallen imprisoned willing and good willing, a divide that proves decisive for whether a person acts well or sinfully.[13] This event gave rise to the phenomenon of a fallen will, and a fallen will, not marriage, gives rise to sin.

A few years later in *Contra Iulianum*, Augustine argues that both the Manichees and the Pelagians have misunderstood the relationship between nature and human action, which has prevented them from appreciating

[9] See Augustine's quotation of Julian's argument in *nupt. et conc.* 26.41.
[10] Quoting Augustine's quotation from Julian.
[11] *Nupt. et conc.* 26.43 (CSEL 42:297).
[12] *Nupt. et conc.* 2.26.43 (CSEL 42:297).
[13] As Augustine has pointed out, "Good works spring from a good will and bad works from a bad will"; *bona uoluntate opera bona nascuntur et mala de mala* (CSEL 42:297).

the significance of the fall and human willing. Julian's misinterpretation of Matthew 7:18, he believes, illustrates these interrelated problems. According to the Manichees, Augustine "reminds" Julian, people do good or bad things because they possess good or bad natures, which the Manichees claim derive from opposed, coeternal principles of good and evil. Thus, on their view, dualism goes all the way down. Some people do what is good while others do what is bad because two ultimate principles give rise to such behavior. These contrary principles determine their nature so that they are good and bad inherently rather than accidentally. Given this view, the Manichees have no use for a notion of falling away from the good: "They say that good and evil are opposed to each other. As a result, they do not say that a nature becomes evil when it falls away from the good and that its very falling away is evil. Rather, they say that the evil is itself a nature."[14] Since they already have a "natural" explanation for the origins of evil, the notion of a fall is superfluous.

The catholic faith gives a much more complex account of the relationship between nature and human action, Augustine explains. On this view, bad actions result not from natures that are inherently evil but from the defects of natures originally created good. Though all natures are good insofar as they are authentic natures, a nature can take on an evil quality if the will that belongs to it falls away, since "wills have sufficient power to determine the character of the natures whose wills they are."[15] In this fashion it comes about that some natures are called evil by virtue of the effect bad willing has upon them: "For, if one asks what is the character of an angel or a human being with an evil will, we answer: evil, taking the name of their character from the evil will (*ex uoluntate mala*) rather than from the good nature (*ex natura bona*)."[16] Thus, for Augustine, how the will is used determines what kind of actions created natures endowed with will produce; their good created character provides no automatic guarantees against defection.

Augustine is convinced that Julian's interpretation of Matthew 7:18 undermines this catholic perspective[17] on the voluntary step between nature and human action, thereby falling into the error of the Manichees.[18] By applying this verse to marriage, Julian suggests that the two trees to which

---

[14] C. Iul. 1.8.38 (PL 44:667).
[15] C. Iul. 1.8.37 (PL 44:667).
[16] C. Iul. 1.8.37 (PL 44:666–667).
[17] Augustine refers repeatedly to the *fides catholica* in c. Iul. 1.8.36.
[18] Augustine makes this argument from c. Iul. 1.8.36–1.8.41.

the Lord refers correspond to natures rather than wills. But such a reading leads to the conclusion that created natures are inherently and unalterably, rather than voluntarily and contingently, good or evil, since the Lord's pronouncement would then translate to a denial that a good nature can bring forth bad actions and that an evil nature can bring forth good actions. This conclusion may seem innocuous enough with respect to explaining good actions, but how does it fare in the case of bad actions? If bad actions stem inevitably from evil natures, Augustine contends, then one is left with two options: either God is responsible for evil, or, as the Manichees believe, some power other than God is. Presumably, Julian realizes the first option is untenable. The principle that evil cannot come from a good nature, which Julian attempts to derive from Matthew 7:18, drives him into the Manichean camp. Eliminating the notion of will from the schema explaining the relationship between nature and action forces Julian into dualism.

Augustine's alternative is to interpret the good tree of Matthew 7:18 as referring precisely to the "good will (*hominis uoluntatem bonam*) of a human being" rather than to "the very work of God, that is, a human marriage or human nature."[19] Given the reasons expressed in Augustine's critique of Julian's interpretation, the two trees in question cannot refer to natures. Rather, they must refer to wills, while the fruit of the trees refers to the works in which these wills result: "For that divine teacher certainly does not want us to understand that the tree from which there comes the fruit about which he was speaking is a nature. Rather, he wants us to understand that the tree is the will (*uoluntatem*), whether good or evil, and that its actions (*opera*) are its fruit."[20] According to this interpretation, good and bad works follow inevitably from good and bad wills, respectively, not from good and bad natures:

> If they [the *opera*] are good, they cannot come from a bad will (*uoluntatis malae*), and if they are bad, they cannot come from a good will (*uoluntatis bonae*). After all, this is what he says: *A bad tree does not produce good fruit, and a good tree does not produce bad fruit* (Mt 7:8 [*sic*: the verse in question is Mt 7:18]). It is as if he said: A bad will (*uoluntas mala*) does not

[19] *C. Iul.* 1.8.39 (PL 44:668): "But you understand the good tree, not as Christ wanted us to understand it, that is, as the good will of a human being, but as the very work of God, that is, as human marriage or human nature."

[20] *C. Iul.* 1.8.38 (PL 44:667).

produce good actions, and a good will (*uoluntas bona*) does not produce bad actions.[21]

Such a reading, Augustine observes, makes possible the affirmation of the common origin of good and bad actions in good natures created by God: "For, if one asks about the origins (*origines*) of these trees, that is, of these wills (*uoluntatum*), what origins are there but the good natures (*naturae*) which God created?"[22] Thus, it avoids suggesting that evil can be traced back to an evil ultimate principle and thereby affirms God's goodness as the single ultimate reality and sole source of all that is. In this way Augustine's proposal that the good and bad trees of Matthew 7:18 designate good and bad wills at once makes it possible to avoid dualism and to explain how good and bad actions stem from an ingrained propensity in human persons. Will serves as a category that helps to interpret this statement of Christ about the two trees in light of what one learns elsewhere in scripture about the original goodness of creation and God's unique sovereignty: that there is no one beside him.

Augustine's explanation of the relationship between human nature and action adds a layer of complexity not present in the accounts he attributes to the Manichees and to Julian. Created human natures do not directly yield works of one kind or another, as if programmed to carry out certain actions like automatons. In Augustine's words, "From the good natures of the angel and of the human being which no evil parents begot, but which the supremely good God made without any parents, there came to be not bad fruit, but bad trees from which bad fruit came to be."[23] From natures come wills. From wills come actions. Will is the intermediate step between the two. The juncture between good and bad occurs with this step of will rather than with an original duality of natures.

Augustine's clever assimilation of Julian's position to the Manichean worldview, even in the face of Julian's own attempt to connect Augustine, and those with whom Augustine aligns himself, with his Manichean past,[24] makes light of Julian's efforts to give an optimistic account of human nature and the decisiveness of human willing. Far from positing the natural

---

[21] C. Iul. 1.8.38 (PL 44:667).
[22] C. Iul. 1.8.38 (PL 44:667).
[23] C. Iul. 1.8.40 (PL 44:669).
[24] See c. Iul. 1.8.36.

inevitability of evil works, Julian in fact underlines the human capacity to resist wrongdoing. Rather than dismissing the will as unimportant, Julian seeks to defend its integrity and power to choose the good.

Nonetheless Augustine puts his finger on a tension between these commitments and Julian's use of the gospel's image of two trees. Augustine quotes Julian as asking him, "Since according to the statement of the Gospel a tree ought to be known from its fruit, should we listen to someone who says that marriage is good, but claims that nothing but evil comes from it?"[25] Julian's point is not even that marriage always produces good things but merely that it would be strange if marriage, something good, produced exclusively evil results. His question nonetheless operates on a questionable presupposition: that the goodness of something like marriage can guarantee good actions at all.

This presupposition rests on a category mistake. The context of Christ's statement in Matthew 7:18 clearly indicates that good fruits refer to good works, to "doing the will of [his] Father in heaven."[26] Thus, by interpreting the good tree of Matthew 7:18 as applicable to marriage, Julian suggests that marriage itself can produce good or bad actions. Marriage, however, is not the kind of thing that does what is right or what is wrong. It is a relationship, not a part of the machinery by which human beings exercise moral agency. Still less could marriage be called a moral agent.

Though at times verging on the melodramatic,[27] then, Augustine's connection of Julian's position with the Manichees rightly pinpoints a significant overlap. Both Julian and the Manichees overliteralize this text so as to imply that certain things per se—be they marriages or natures—guarantee the moral quality of actions that stem from them. By positing instead that the trees of Matthew 7:18 represent wills, Augustine problematizes such generalizations. Everything depends, he suggests, on the particular will in question, and indeed on the larger networks of relationships and histories that influence and constrain this will. Julian's reading of such passages, like the Manichean worldview, promotes an objectivist account of morality. By interpreting references to the two trees in the gospels as referring to will, Augustine calls attention to a factor both his Manichean and his Pelagian

---

[25] C. Iul. 1.8.39 (PL 44:668).

[26] See Matthew 7:21.

[27] As in his prognosis that "if we say that evils come only from evils, the Manichean plague will triumph. It will destroy the universe, and it will violate the nature of God himself" (c. Iul. 1.8.38).

opponents are missing: the decisive role of the psyche of the human subject in shaping right and wrong. Despite further challenges from Julian, he never relinquishes this reading, which he regards as substantiated clearly by scripture itself: "But as to whether the Lord wanted to convey two wills (*duas uoluntates*) by the two trees . . . those who want to know this read the gospel; they do not read you."[28]

Section B: Will as Eye of the Soul

On at least two occasions during the course of the Pelagian controversy, Augustine uses the metaphor of vision for human willing. Whereas the metaphor of will as root serves to highlight the will's importance in giving rise to good or bad actions, and even to determining the qualities a given nature possesses, the metaphor of will as interior eye of the soul serves to highlight human dependence on God to aid the will. This image appears once in *De gestis Pelagii* (*gest. Pel.*, 417) and again in *De gratia Christi et de peccato originali* (*gr. et pecc. or.*), written the following year.

Augustine's use of eye imagery for the will in *gest. Pel.* (417) illustrates by analogy how both God and the human person might be responsible for the same human act of will. He employs this image to help refute one of Pelagius's proofs for the thesis that "all are governed by their own will," an appeal to Sirach 15:16–17: "He set before you water and fire; stretch forth your hand to whichever you want. Before human beings there stand good and evil, life and death. What they choose will be given to them."[29] Augustine interprets this verse as indicating that if human beings make the right choice, "the will (*uoluntas*) does not do that alone; rather, it is helped by God."[30] At this point, Augustine introduces an image to shed light on what legitimately falls within the power of human willing and what does not: "For the eye is sufficient by itself for not seeing, that is, for the dark, but for seeing it is not sufficient by itself with its own light (*non sibi sufficit*), unless the assistance of a bright light is offered from elsewhere (*extrinsecus*)."[31]

---

[28] *Contra Iulianum opus imperfectum* (*c. Iul. imp.*) 5.21.3.
[29] *Gest. Pel.* 3.7.
[30] *Gest. Pel.* 3.7 (CSEL 42:58).
[31] *Gest. Pel.* 3.7 (CSEL 42:58).

This terse image conveys a number of points about the capacities of the human will and the impact God's aid has upon it. First, it rules out conceiving of human willing as either sufficient or insufficient *simpliciter*. Whether the human will can claim self-sufficiency depends on the goal in question. With respect to not seeing (*ad non uidendum*), the eye is entirely self-sufficient; on its own, it can perceive darkness. With respect to seeing (*ad uidendum*), however, the eye's own light does not suffice; to this end, its own powers are insufficient. Just so, the will is sufficient for sinning but insufficient for doing good. Second, the image illustrates where God's aid is necessary and where it is not. Just as the eye requires an external light source, assistance from without (*extrinsecus adiutorium*), if it is to detect anything other than darkness, so God's help is necessary if the will is to attain the good. Third, this image illustrates that what the will can achieve on its own pales in comparison with what it can do with God. The difference between what the eye can perceive with and without a bright light to illumine it is like the difference between day and night. True, the will does have a limited independent capability. But this capability is so restricted that it is hardly worth having. This capability hardly enables the eye to serve a useful purpose. Finally, the image of the eye provides an example of how God can enable and sustain human willing even while leaving the will's own causal operation intact. Though an eye may possess the natural capacity for sight when light is absent, light nonetheless radically alters the eye's de facto possibilities. Yet it effects this alteration without violating the eye's integrity. Rather than forcing the eye into an unnatural function, it enables the eye to fulfill its created purpose.

Augustine utilizes the eye image for human willing again in *gr. et pecc. or.* (418), where he correlates the will with the interior eyes of the mind that must be turned by God to accomplish the good. His larger goal in the part of the work where this discussion appears is to demonstrate that Pelagius's conception of grace is far afield from the view of grace found in the scriptures.[32] Thus, having introduced the overarching contours of Pelagius's doctrine of grace (1.3.4–1.10.11) and put forth his own alternative view of grace (1.10.11–1.14.15), Augustine turns, in this passage, to a number of examples (*exempla*) Pelagius had used in his work *Pro libero arbitrio* (416)

---

[32] This part of the work stretches from 1.3.4 to 1.42.46. Augustine states at the outset of the work that he will show that Pelagius's understanding of grace falls short of grace as portrayed both in scripture and by Catholic authorities.

to elucidate his own views. By means of these, Augustine clarifies Pelagius's position but also finds an opportunity to explain his own views.

The first example Pelagius had offered to illustrate his conception of grace was the functioning of the human eye. Augustine quotes him as stating, "A few examples will make our meaning clearer. Our being able to see with our eyes is not due to us (*nostrum non est*), but our using our sight for good or for bad is due to us (*hoc nostrum est*)." This image serves as a concrete example of Pelagius's view that grace is responsible for the first of the three elements required to accomplish the good: ability (*posse*), a natural endowment; willing (*uelle*), exercised in choice; and being (*esse*), realized when a good work is actually performed.[33] Human beings, Pelagius contends, do not deserve credit for their capacity to see. Nonetheless, how they use this capacity is up to them.

Augustine critiques and then drastically reconfigures Pelagius's analogy of vision by using Psalm 119:37, leading with a citation of the biblical text: "Let our answer to him be the psalm in which we say to God, *Turn my eyes away so that they do not see vanity*."[34] In Augustine's view, Pelagius's conception of grace contradicts the statement of the Psalmist, who credits God with averting his eyes from evil, not merely with giving him the capacity to see. But even more than that, Pelagius's example only touches superficially upon the complex process that gives rise to human action, entirely omitting the dimension of willing from the picture, a dimension that in fact determines the moral status of the actions finally performed.

Augustine's own interpretation of Psalm 119:37 attempts to account for this further dimension. In the text Augustine has adduced, he points out, the Psalmist refers to God's movement of the eyes of the mind, not the eyes of the flesh. It is how God moves these interior eyes that determines the quality of one's literal seeing: "The Psalm is speaking of the eyes of the mind (*oculis mentis*), and it is from those eyes, of course, that these eyes of the flesh (*oculos carnis*) come to see well or badly."[35] This additional set of eyes, Augustine specifies, accounts for the moral quality of one's vision rather than for the physiological condition of one's eyesight. The latter has to do with what one sees; the former with why one chooses to see it. One would see "well" (*bene*) in the moral sense, for example, if one looked

---

[33] Augustine quoting Pelagius's *Pro libero arbitrio* 3 in *gr. et pecc. or.* 1.4.5 (CSEL 42:128).

[34] *Gr. et pecc. or.* 1.15.16 (CSEL 42:138).

[35] *Gr. et pecc. or.* 1.15.16 (CSEL 42:138–139).

at someone "for the purpose of being helpful" (*ad subueniendum*), while one would see "badly" (*male*) if one did so "for the purpose of lusting" (*ad concupiscendum*). Pelagius's example fails to account for what actually determines whether one uses one's sight "for good" or "for bad" in this moral respect, which depends not just on where one directs one's literal eyes but also on one's motivation. Augustine points out, "After all, by these exterior eyes (*exteriores oculos*) we see both a poor person whom we help and a woman for whom we lust, but the mercy or the lust is derived from the interior eyes (*ex interioribus*) so that one sees well or badly."[36] Acting rightly or wrongly, Augustine suggests, concerns the wellspring of the actions one actually carries out, which flows from deep within a human person.

The rhetorical question summing up Augustine's discussion of Pelagius's example makes clear that he interprets this wellspring, the set of interior eyes to which Psalm 119:37 refers, as representing nothing other than the will: "Why then, do we say to God, *Turn my eyes away so that they do not see vanity?* Why do we ask for what lies in our own power, if God does not help the will (*uoluntatem*)?"[37] Augustine then, uses the term *uoluntas* to serve as shorthand for a dimension of human identity and agency for which Pelagius's view of human action does not account. This dimension is one where divine and human doing overlap, one in which God "turns" (*avertere*) human eyes, and yet human beings remain the subject of their seeing. It is a realm in which human beings are not in complete control, but this realm remains irreducible to either natural ability or knowledge, the two areas in which Pelagius acknowledges human need for God's help.[38]

Augustine finds allusions to this mysterious facet of human being all over scripture: in the Psalms' references to changes of heart God brings about, in Paul's more abstract teaching about the character of grace, and in numerous stories in both testaments about God's impact on individual people whereby God brings about a change of heart in a person's inner being. Psalm 119:37, which refers to God's turning the eyes of the Psalmist away from vanity, is just one instance of many such passages. But here we see especially clearly how Augustine uses the terminology of will to refer to a notion he finds assumed in the biblical text. He begins by observing how this passage asserts the human need for God's help. He then concludes that God

---

[36] *Gr. et pecc. or.* 1.15:16 (CSEL 42:139).
[37] *Gr. et pecc. or.* 1.15.16 (CSEL 42:139).
[38] *Gr. et pecc. or.* 1.6.7–1.10.11.

must supply this help. In making this point, he uses the term "will" to refer to that which serves as the object of God's assistance. He appeals to the notion of "will" (*uoluntas*), like the expression "interior eyes" (*oculi interiores*), in the attempt to make sense of what he finds in scripture about God's influence upon human agency.

In both *gest. Pel.* and *gr. et pecc. or.*, then, Augustine uses vision imagery to explain how scripture supports the notion that God helps the will of the human person and to illustrate the significance of God's aid. In *gest. Pel.*, he uses the image of the eye's need for light to illustrate the will's need for God if it is to perform the function for which it is designed. In *gr. et pecc. or.*, he uses the image of interior eyes to characterize human willing as both dependent upon God's help and decisive for the moral quality of an act. In both cases, vision imagery serves to carve out a conceptual space corresponding to a dimension of human identity upon which God acts to enable human beings to do the good. Augustine calls this dimension, which he is convinced Pelagius neglects, "will." Pelagius locates willing in the realm of "choice" (*in arbitrio*), where human autonomy reigns supreme.[39] But for Augustine, willing is much more expansive. It is a way of seeing the world, of relating to what is other than oneself in light of an overarching intentionality. It is an outlook that shapes the moral meaning of every human choice and act. Most significantly, will is susceptible to divine illumination.

Though Augustine does not compare the will to an eye in so many words earlier in his career, he does employ vision imagery in connection with the will in his description of Paul's conversion on the road to Damascus in *Ad Simplicianum*. Augustine describes the will that first put Saul on the road to Damascus, the sinful will to persecute others, as a will suffering from blindness: "What did Saul will but to attack, seize, bind and slay Christians? What a fierce, savage, blind (*caeca*) will (*uoluntas*) was that!"[40] Then, in discussing the transformation of this will, he speaks of a "vision" (*uiso*) that turned Saul's mind and "will" (*uoluntas*) around: he was thrown prostrate by one word from on high, and a vision (*uiso*) came to him whereby his mind and will (*uoluntas*) were turned from their fierceness and set on the

---

[39] Pelagius states, "Ability is found in nature; willing in choice; being in action. The first element, namely, ability, is properly due to God who conferred it upon his creature. The two other elements, namely, willing and being, should be attributed to the human person, because they proceed from choice as their source" (*gr. et pecc. or.* 1.4.5 [CSEL 42:128]). Augustine is quoting Pelagius's *Pro libero arbitrio*.

[40] *Simpl.* 1.2.22 (CCL 44:55).

right way toward faith (*ad fidem*).[41] Thus even in this work from the very beginning of Augustine's ministry as bishop, he implicitly compares the will to an eye, and God's grace as granting this eye the capacity to see in a new way. Again we see that *Simpl.* contains much of Augustine's later thinking on will in seminal form. The image of the eye displays the larger unity of his vision of the will.

Part II: Characteristics of the Good Will
Section A: A Good Will as a Will in the Process of Conversion

In addition to using arboreal and visual metaphors to describe the will during the Pelagian controversy, Augustine also identifies a will in the process of conversion as a "good will." He provides this description in book 2 of *De peccatorum meritis et remissione et de baptismo paruulorum* (*pecc. mer.*, 411 or 412), when addressing the question of whether 1 Corinthians 4:7, "After all, what do you have that you have not received?," portrays God as the author of our good willing because God has created humankind with the natural capacity for willing. If the fact of God's creation of the will is a sufficient basis for attributing responsibility for our good willing to God, Augustine contends, then what prevents us from attributing bad willing to God on the same grounds? Such an interpretation of this text not only underestimates its import for God's involvement in good human willing but also implies God's responsibility for human misuse of the will. In fact, however, Paul is pointing to God's gift of the good will in particular, not merely to God's creation of the conditions for its possibility in creation. His point is that "we have a good will from God" in the sense that "we are made righteous by him."[42]

Indeed Augustine makes his argument even sharper. Not only is it the case that God makes us righteous. It is also the case that our turning to God, which God excites and assists, itself amounts to having a good will: "Our turning away from God is our own doing, and this turning is an evil will (*uoluntas mala*). But our turning toward God (*quod uero ad deum nos conuertimus*) is something we cannot do unless he rouses us and helps us, and this turning

---

[41] *Simpl.* 1.2.22 (CCL 44:55).
[42] *Pecc. mer.* 2.18.30. Augustine cites Proverbs 8:35, Psalm 37:23, and Phillippians 2:13 to substantiate his point.

is a good will (*uoluntas bona*). Hence, what do we have that we have not received?"[43] Thus Augustine affirms not merely that God establishes the preconditions for good willing, either in creation or otherwise, but also that God's assistance, whereby he makes us righteous, intrinsically brings good willing about. Paul refers in 1 Corinthians 4:7 to God serving as author of the good will in this latter direct manner, Augustine contends.

In this passage of *pecc. mer.* Augustine demonstrates both the dynamism and the directionality of his conception of the "good will" (*uoluntas bona*). He resists characterizing the will as a reified substance, instead applying the designation "good will" to the movement by which we turn to God. He describes the good will as an action, not as a static thing. A good will can be a will in the process of becoming, not just one that has already attained perfect goodness. In the dynamism that is good will, there is room for both God and human beings to be engaged in making good will happen. Human beings are the ones turning to God (*ad deum nos conuertimus*), but God also involves himself in this movement, "rousing" (*excitante*) and "helping" (*adiuuante*) us.

Augustine consistently emphasizes the dynamism of the will across his career, but how he characterizes this dynamism changes. In *De duabus animabus* (*duab. an.*, 391–395), for example, he had defined the will as "a movement of the soul, with nothing forcing it either not to lose something or to acquire something."[44] In *pecc. mer.*, however, the turning that is good will drives in a definite direction and is susceptible to outside influence. Whereas Augustine's earlier definition had emphasized neutrality and insulation from external impact, his characterization of good willing in *pecc. mer.* emphasizes directionality and permeability to God's aid.

In this context, Augustine no longer speaks of the will's dynamism in general, unspecified terms. In fact, he does not speak of willing per se at all. Rather, he describes "good willing" and "bad willing" in particular and associates movement headed in a specific direction with each. The turning that constitutes an "evil will" (*uoluntas mala*) veers "away from God" (*a deo*), while the turning Augustine labels "good will" (*uoluntas bona*) turns "toward God" (*ad deum*). These two basic categories of willing correspond to a fundamental divide between two orientations human willing may have. This dynamic conception of willing centers on God, in relation to whom

---

[43] *Pecc. mer.* 2.18.31 (CSEL 60:102).
[44] *Duab. an.* 10.14 (CSEL 25.1:68).

these orientations are defined. Bad willing corresponds to a turning "away from God" while good willing corresponds to a turning "toward God." In both cases, the movement that is willing is defined in relation to God. Augustine's original notion of the created will, in contrast, enjoyed neutrality in that it was capable of moving toward either good or evil without external intervention.

Section B: Good Will Comes from God and Is Directed to God

For the early Augustine, human willing is a single hub from which various spokes radiate outward in different directions.[45] In the Pelagian controversy, Augustine comes to see good and bad human willing as two vectors extending from two origins toward two separate destinations. As discussed in the previous section, Augustine writes in *pecc. mer.*, "Our turning away from God is our own doing, and this turning is an evil will (*uoluntas mala*). But our turning toward God (*quod uero ad deum nos conuertimus*) is something we cannot do unless he rouses us and helps us, and this turning is a good will (*uoluntas bona*)."[46] Bad willing comes from us and swerves away from God. Good willing comes from God and aims at the same.

From the beginning to the end of the Pelagian controversy, Augustine affirms not only that good willing in some cases comes from God but also that good willing comes only from God. As noted, he writes in *pecc. mer.* (411 or 412), "The good will, which already belongs to those goods which cannot be misused, can come to us only from God."[47] In his final uncompleted work against Julian (427–430) it becomes clear that for Augustine, a good will can come only from God because a good will can result only from love that comes from God. He writes:

> If grace does not come first to produce the will, but grace works along with the already existing will, how can it be true that *God also produces in you the will* (Phil 2:13)? How can it be true that *the will is prepared by the*

---

[45] As discussed in chapter 1, he describes it as "a hinge" (*cardo*), from which a door might swing this way or that.

[46] *Pecc. mer.* 2.18.31 (CSEL 60:102).

[47] *Pecc. mer.* 2.18.30.

Lord (Prv 8:35 LXX)? How can it be true that *love comes from God* (1 Jn 4:7), the love which alone (*sola*) wills the beatific good? Or if knowledge of the law and of God's words produces love in us so that we love, not by a gift of God, but by the choice of our own will, what we know we should love because God teaches us, how can the lesser good come from God and the greater good from ourselves? I mean that we cannot know without God's giving us knowledge, that is, without his teaching us, but we can love without his giving the love which surpasses knowledge. Only the new heretics and fierce enemies of the grace of God think that way.[48]

Only love from God "wills (*uult*) the beatific good," and, as Augustine's subsequent rhetorical questions imply, only by God's gift of this love, can one possess it. Thus, for Augustine in the Pelagian controversy, good will comes from God alone (*ex deo*).

In addition to describing a good will as lying at the root of human action, Augustine also identifies good willing as referring to the intention or end of human action, to what motivates one to perform a given activity. This particular view in Augustine's kaleidoscope of perspectives on human willing comes into focus in the work *De nuptiis et concupiscentia* (*nupt. et conc.*, 418–419), where he argues that whether or not the sexual union of male and female is sinful depends on the "intention" (*intentio*) with which a person engages in it: "The union of male and female for the sake of having children is, then, the natural good of marriage. But one makes bad use of this good if one uses it like an animal so that one's intention (*intentio*) is in the pleasure of sexual desire (*in uoluptate libidinis*), not in the will to propagate (*in uoluntate propaginis*)."[49] Here Augustine depicts the good will to propagate as something in which one's intention may consist.

Further elaborating on the character of the intention necessary to avoid sin during sexual union, Augustine explains that even the intention to procreate is not, in itself, sufficient. One must actually intend to procreate

---

[48] *C. Iul. imp.* 1.95 (CSEL 85.1:110).

[49] *Nupt. et conc.* 1.4.5 (CSEL 42:215): *copulatio itaque maris et feminae generandi causa bonum est naturale nuptiarum. sed isto bono male utitur qui bestialiter utitur, ut sit eius intentio in uoluptate libidinis, non in uoluntate propaginis.* Teske translates *ut sit eius intentio in uoluptate libidinis, non in uoluntate propaginis* "so that one's intention is directed toward the pleasure of sexual desire, not toward the will to propagate." That the nouns following "in" take ablative rather than accusative form, however, recommends a locative translation. Translating the prepositional phrases in a locative sense also eliminates the need to insert the verb "be directed," absent from Augustine's Latin. I have adjusted Teske's translation accordingly in the body of the text.

Christians, to bring children into the world so that they can be reborn in baptism. Whereas unbelievers who live in chaste marital fidelity still sin by having sex because they engage in it without faith, believers who have sex with "the intention (*intentionem*) of bringing to birth children to be born again" turn something otherwise sinful "into the practice of righteousness." Augustine concludes, "Hence, those who do not have children with this intention (*hac intentione*), this will (*hac uoluntate*), this goal (*hoc fine*) of transforming them from being members of the first human being into being members of Christ, but who as unbelieving parents boast of their unbelieving offspring, do not have true marital chastity. This is so, even if they so carefully observe the laws of marriage that they have intercourse only for the sake of procreating children."[50] In this final statement Augustine uses the word *uoluntas* in apposition with "intention" (*intentione*) and "end" (*fine*).

This use of the term *uoluntas* as a synonym for intention need not contradict Augustine's indication in *nupt. et conc.* 1.4.5 that it is possible to have an intention "in the will to propagate" (*in uoluntate propaginis*), but it does help to illustrate the significance of the connection he established there between these two terms. If (1) Augustine's reference to an intention *in uoluntate propaginis* is interpreted to mean simply that the intention in question consists "in the will to propagate," and (2) the expression *in uoluntate propaginis* merely identifies propagation as the content of the good intention referenced, with the phrase *in uoluntate* reiterating that this propagation is an object one purposes to attain, then (3) the two ways of relating *intentio* and *uoluntas* may be reconciled. Though, in this case, the locution of an intention being "in the will" (*in uoluntate*) to propagate is redundant with respect to content, the additional phrase *in uoluntate* serves a stylistic purpose, achieving parallelism between the expressions *in uoluptate libidinis* and *in uoluntate propaginis*. Thus there is no compelling reason to reject such an interpretation of the phrase *in uoluntate propaginis*, while accepting it accords better with the larger context of *nupt. et conc.*, resolving the problem of how to read it along with Augustine's suggestion that *uoluntas* and *intentio* may function as synonyms.

The passage where this suggestion is found, in which Augustine uses *uoluntas* in apposition with *intentio*, makes clear that, in at least some contexts, intention and will can be used interchangeably. As Augustine's use

---

[50] *Nupt. et conc.* 1.4.5 (CSEL 42:215–216).

of the term *finis* suggests, both *intentio* and *uoluntas* are teleological notions, referring to the ends for the purpose of which an action is undertaken. The will in this context is a will to something, having a definite orientation and direction. Augustine characterizes a good will that would lead to a good use of sex as following a distinctively Christian trajectory. Such a good will must be oriented not only to procreation but to Christ as ultimate end.

Nupt. et conc. 1.8.9 confirms that *uoluntas* and *intentio* may function interchangeably for Augustine:

> In the marriages of believers this will (*uoluntas*) is not determined by the goal (*eo fine determinatur*) that children destined to pass away should be born into this world (*in saeculo isto*), but that children destined to last should be reborn in Christ (*in Christo*). If this is the result, the marriage will have the reward of a complete happiness; if it is not, the couple will have the peace of their good will (*bonae uoluntatis*). Those who possess their own vessels, that is, their spouses, with this intention (*hac intentione cordis*) certainly do not possess them *in the disease of desire, like pagans who do not know God*, but *in holiness and honor* (I Thes 4:5.4).[51]

Here again Augustine seems to use the terms *intentio* and *uoluntas* synonymously, with "this intention" referring to the "good will" he has just mentioned. Though at first he speaks of a will being "determined by" a certain goal, seeming to suggest a hard distinction between *uoluntas* and *fine*, the rest of the passage points to a functional equivalence of *uoluntas* and *intentio* in this context. Furthermore, Augustine again highlights the distinctively Christian orientation of the good will. Having a right will means not only having a will to perform certain kinds of actions but also performing these actions with a will determined by a specific end (*eo fine determinatur*), in this case, the end of birth in Christ. Having a right will requires a will oriented not only toward this world, determined by an end in earthly time (*in saeculo isto*), but also toward Christ's plan for redeeming it, which takes place in theological time (*in Christo*).[52] A good will comes from God and stretches toward Christ's kingdom.

---

[51] *Nupt. et conc.* 1.8.9 (CSEL 42:220–221).

[52] Insofar as one needs first to have a child born in this world in order to have a child reborn in Christ, this is not a mutually exclusive choice. So the theological goal includes but is not exhausted in the earthly goal of having a child.

As we have seen in this section, Augustine argues throughout the duration of the Pelagian controversy that a good will can come only from God. In addition to characterizing a good will in terms of its origins, moreover, he also speaks of good will in terms of its objectives. The good will is not only from God; it is oriented to God and headed toward God. Examining cases in which Augustine describes the will in the latter sense shows us that he can use intention (*intentio*) as a synonym for will. The interchangeability of these two terms in these contexts highlights both the theological and the teleological character of Augustine's thinking about the good will during the Pelagian controversy. Good will is a will oriented toward the goal of God's work in the world through Christ.

Section C: Good Will as Will of the Believer and as a Will with Faith in God

In the second stage of the Pelagian controversy, Augustine characterizes the good human will as the will of a believer and as a will with faith in God, two attributions that relate closely, since having faith in God describes what belief in God means for Augustine. In Augustine's words, "To believe in Christ belongs to faith, and none can believe in him, that is, come to him, unless this gift has been given to them."[53] In characterizing the good will as the will of the believer in Christ, and a will with faith in God, Augustine broadens the point he made in *nupt. et conc.* in the context of sexuality, that a good will is a will directed toward the distinctly Christian end of procreating Christian children. Just as a good will has a distinctly Christian end, it has distinctly Christian beginnings.[54]

---

[53] *C. ep. Pel.* 1.3.7 (CSEL 60:429).

[54] This is another difference between the *reditus* theme in the Neoplatonists and in Augustine. For Augustine, both the starting point and the end point of the journey of return to God is God's work in Christ. Augustine already saw at the end of book 7 of *conf.* (7.21.27) that the Platonists, despite their crucial role in helping him to recognize fundamental truths about God and all of reality, had not found the heart of the Christian message: Jesus Christ. They had some inkling of the destination Christians seek, namely, God, but they had not recognized how to get there. By the second stage of the Pelagian controversy it is clear that, for Augustine, the Platonists are misconstruing the outset and destination of the journey to God, as well as the path between them, insofar as they fail to appreciate that Christ stands at the beginning and end of this journey. Phillip Cary, however, sees Augustine's commitments to Platonism as encouraging and reinforcing his mature views on grace and free will, rather than as requiring correction in light of them. According to Cary, Augustine's Platonism inherently predisposes him to a doctrine of grace because the Platonic understanding of love as about delight means that the will is already defined as something that is "dependent on

Augustine labels the good will (*bona uoluntas*) as the will "of the believer" (*fidelis est*) in *c. ep. Pel.* as a step in his argument that a righteous will is possible only by grace. Possessing the freedom to sin does not entail possessing the freedom to do what is right, Augustine observes. Rather, "this will (*uoluntas*) which is free (*libera*) for evil actions (*in malis*) because it takes delight in evil is not free for good actions (*in bonis*), because it has not been set free."[55] To attain the latter kind of freedom, Augustine argues, we need Christ, because without faith one can only sin (Romans 14:23), and only Christ can bestow faith. Since the righteous live by faith (Hebrews 2:4; Romans 1:17), and "to believe in Christ belongs to faith," we know that the righteous are believers.[56] Because being righteous, furthermore, requires having good will,[57] and because without faith one can only sin, those who have a good will are believers. In Augustine's words, "And for this reason a good will (*bona uoluntas*), which withdraws from sin, is the will of a believer (*fidelis est*), because *the righteous live from faith* (Heb 2:4; Rom 1:17)." Thus it is clear that human beings need Christ to give faith so that they can have a good will, since only believers have a good will: "None, then, can have a righteous will (*uoluntatem iustam*) unless they have received true grace without any preceding merits, that is, grace which has been gratuitously given from on high."[58] Augustine's characterization of the good will as belonging to the believer emerges from his argumentation on the basis of scripture for the origins of a righteous will in Christ. This biblically informed and Christologically oriented thinking leads him to identify the good will as belonging to someone living "from faith" (*ex fide*), i.e., a believer.

In addition to describing a good will as belonging to a believer, to someone who lives from faith, Augustine also describes faith and belief in terms of will in his writings from the final stage of the Pelagian controversy. In *gr. et lib. arb.* (426), he refers to faith as "the will of the believer," stating,

---

sources of motivation beyond itself" in order to act. See Phillip Cary, *Inner Grace: Augustine in the Traditions of Plato and Paul* (New York: Oxford University Press, 2008), 30. This is a valid point, but what Cary does not appreciate sufficiently is that Augustine's mature conception of will gives an account of the preconditions and origins of this motivation in relation to the God and Father of Jesus Christ, in particular. This specificity entails a critical perspective on Platonism that Cary does not adequately acknowledge.

[55] *C. ep. Pel.* 1.3.7 (CSEL 60:428–429).
[56] *C. ep. Pel.* 1.3.7 (CSEL 60:429).
[57] This is implicit in Augustine's argument, but we know this from his other writings.
[58] *C. ep. Pel.* 1.3.7 (CSEL 60:429).

"I have already, of course, spoken of faith (*de fide*), that is, of the will of the believer (*de uoluntate credentis*), and I showed that it pertains to grace to point out that the apostle did not say, 'I have obtained mercy because I was a believer,' but said, *I have obtained mercy in order that I might be a believer* (1 Cor 7:25)."[59] In *De correptione et gratia* (*corrept.*, 427), Augustine identifies an unfailing faith as a free and firm will to believe: "When, therefore, he prayed that his faith (*fides*) would not fail, what else did he pray for but that he would have a will to believe that is perfectly free, firm, unconquerable, and persevering" (*liberrimam fortissimam inuictissimam perseuerantissimam uoluntatem*)?[60] In *De praedestinatione sanctorum* (*praed. sanct.*; 427), Augustine affirms that belief and faith are found in the will: "It is not that to believe (*credere*) or not to believe does not lie within the choice of the human will (*in arbitrio uoluntatis humanae*), but that in those who have been chosen the will is prepared by the Lord. Hence, the words, *For who has set you apart? But what do you have that you have not received?* also apply to the faith (*ad . . . fidem*) which is found in the will (*quae in uoluntate est*)."[61] Later in the same work, Augustine also takes for granted that God's gift of grace, whereby "hearts are inclined to will" and God "produces in us in a marvelous and ineffable way the willing as well,"[62] refers to the "beginning of faith."[63] In *De dono perseuerantiae* (*perseu.*, 427), he states that faith "cannot exist without the will," making clear that where faith is, there will is inevitably operative: "Grace, therefore, also comes before faith; otherwise, if faith came before grace, the will also came before grace, since faith (*fides*) cannot exist without the will (*sine uoluntate*)."[64] Finally, in *Contra Maximinum*, Augustine states that faith can be called a good will.[65] Thus Augustine's terms "faith" (*fides*) and "will" (*uoluntas*), particularly the good will, mutually define each other.

Such a view of good willing naturally raises questions: Can this view account for the phenomenon of pagan virtue? Julian poses precisely this question in *To Turbantius*: "If a pagan were to clothe the naked, would it be a sin, because it does not come from faith?"[66] Augustine's answer in

---

[59] *Gr. et lib. arb* 14.28 (PL 44:897).
[60] *Corrept.* 8.17 (CSEL 92:238).
[61] *Praed. sanct.* 5.10 (PL 44:968).
[62] *Praed. sanct.* 20.42 (PL 44:990).
[63] See the larger argument of *praed. sanct.* 20.41–20.42 (PL 44:990).
[64] *Perseu.* 16.41 (PL 45:1018).
[65] *C. Max.* 2.23.7.
[66] Augustine quotes Julian in *c. Iul.* 4.3.30.

Contra Iulianum further illuminates his view of the relationship between will and faith. Using the gospel analogy of the two trees, Augustine replies that, while the action of clothing the naked is not itself a sin, it nonetheless remains a sin insofar as it does not come from faith. Parrying Julian's query with a rhetorical question of his own, Augustine writes, "I ask you whether such a person does good actions in a good or a bad manner." He then explains:

> Even though the actions themselves are good, if persons do these actions in a bad manner, you cannot deny that they sin since they do in a bad manner whatever they do. But since you do not want to say that they sin in doing these actions, you are going to say: They do good actions, and they do them in a good manner. A bad tree, then, produces good fruit, though the Truth says this is impossible.[67]

On Augustine's view, the idea that a pagan can avoid sin despite the fact that her actions fail to originate in faith is untenable in light of Christ's teaching on good and bad trees. "Do you claim that a person without faith is a good tree?" he asks Julian.

Augustine's own view is decisive. Without faith, one cannot have a good will and therefore cannot produce the fruit of good works done in a good manner: "Persons, therefore, are bad trees and are unable to produce good fruit, not insofar as they are human beings, but insofar as they have bad wills. See, then, whether you dare to say that a will without faith (*infidelem uoluntatem*) is a good will (*bonam . . . uoluntatem*)."[68] For Augustine then, not only is the good will the will of a believer, a will with faith, but an unfaithful will, the will of someone who does not believe, cannot be a good will. Thus the good will not only does belong to believers but also can belong only to them. A good will is exclusively a believing or faithful will.

Pushing his case even further, Augustine insists that an unbelieving will is not only neutral, failing quite to attain the good that the will of believers does, but also "foolish" and "harmful." He writes:

> The sins, however, by which they [unbelievers] do good actions in a bad manner, belong to them, because they do these actions, not with a

---

[67] *C. Iul.* 4.3.30.
[68] *C. Iul.* 4.3.30 (PL 44:754).

believing (*fideli*), but with an unbelieving (*infideli*) will (*uoluntas*), that is, with a foolish (*stulta*) and harmful (*noxia*) will. No Christian can doubt that such a will is a bad tree which can produce only bad fruit, that is, only sins. *For everything,* whether you like it or not, *which does not come from faith is sin* (Rom 14:23).[69]

An unbelieving will results in unbelievers doing even the good things they do "badly" (*male*) such that it produces only "bad fruit" (*fructus malos*). Thus, the will of those who do not believe not only fails to produce good fruit but also produces bad fruit.

For Augustine, then, there are two types of wills. A good will is a kind of will that believers, and only believers, possess. This good will cannot exist without faith, nor can faith exist without this good will. Only this kind of will can bear the fruit of good works. A bad will is a kind of will that unbelievers and only unbelievers possess. This bad will is without faith (*infidelis*). This kind of will produces exclusively bad fruit.

Section D: Good Will as the One Good Work Necessary for Eternal Life

Given that good willing and faith go hand in hand for Augustine, one always accompanying the other, it comes as no surprise that he depicts a good will as something that can be bestowed only by the one mediator, and as the one good work by which human beings can be brought to eternal life. Given the close connection he establishes between faith and good will, Augustine does not detract from the preeminent role of faith as a gift from God and the basis for eternal life by attributing these distinctions to the good will. Rather, ascribing these characteristics to the good will only further underlines that they belong to faith.

Fittingly, Augustine's discussion of good will as the one good work by which human beings may be brought to eternal life, and as something that can be bestowed only by the one mediator, follows upon the discussion of *c. Iul.* 4.3.32, where he establishes a close connection between will and

---

[69] *C. Iul.* 4.3.32 (PL 44:754–755).

faith.[70] Continuing to drive home his argument that an unbeliever cannot be credited with doing the right thing in the right way, Augustine writes:

> This is what we say: That good of human beings, that good will (*illam uoluntatem bonam*), that good work (*illud opus bonum*) by which alone (*per quod solum*) a human being can be brought to the eternal gift and kingdom of God, can be bestowed on no one without the grace of God (*sine dei gratia*), which is given through the one mediator (*per unum mediatorem*) between God and human beings (*dei et hominum*). Let all the other things that are seen to receive praise from human beings be regarded by you as true virtues, as good works, and as done without any sin. As for me, I know that a good will (*uoluntas bona*) does not produce them and that a faithless (*infidelis*) and unbelieving (*impia*) will is not good. Even if you call wills of this sort good trees, it is enough that in the eyes of God they are barren and are on that account not good.[71]

Here again Augustine makes the point that a faithless and unbelieving will cannot be a good will, drawing a sharp line between good and bad willing. But he also makes several interesting points about the good will. First, a good will is a "good work" (*opus bonum*). Again, then, Augustine defines the will dynamically as a type of doing rather than an inherent reified structural feature of human being. The good will, moreover, claims a special status among other good works. It is the only means of attaining eternal salvation, that "by which alone" (*per quod solum*) a person may be led to the "eternal gift" (*aeternum donum*) and "kingdom" (*regnum*) of God. The good will's destiny, as we will discuss further in chapter 8, on free will, is nothing short of partaking in the eschatological reign of God. As an act of faith, it is the key to the kingdom. Finally, it is impossible to achieve a good will without the grace of Christ. Augustine states in no uncertain terms that he refers not merely to a created or inherent grace but to the grace given through "the one mediator (*per unum mediatorem*) between God and human beings (*dei et hominum*)." Thus the good will, where divine and human agency miraculously overlap, is made possible by Christ's work

---

[70] In this case by referring to a will that produces bad fruit as an "unbelieving," "foolish," and "harmful" will (*c. Iul.* 4.3.32).

[71] *C. Iul.*, 4.3.33 (PL 44:755).

and unique identity as mediator between God and human beings. Christ makes it possible for God and humanity to be united in this special way.

Part III: Love, Heart, and the Will: The Biblical Core of Augustine's Concept of Will
Section A: The *Bona Uoluntas* as *Caritas*

In the second phase of the Pelagian controversy, Augustine begins to describe the good will as *caritas*, love that comes to us from God.[72] This connection between good will and love reinforces the links he forges between will and conversion, will and God, will and faith, and will and the work and kingdom of Christ. Augustine's identification of the good will as love explains how he can coherently describe conversion both as an outpouring of love and the production of good willing in the heart; these are two descriptions of one and the same event. Since God is love, and love comes from God, according to the biblical text, the idea that the will comes from God and goes to God can be specified in terms of love.[73] How can Augustine say that good works flow only from love while he also says that the good will consists in the believer's faith in God, and that this good will is the only tree that produces the fruit of good works? His identification of a good will as *caritas* reconciles these two statements. Finally, the relationship Augustine establishes between good willing and love assimilates the notion that the good will is the one good work necessary for eternal life, and something that can be bestowed only by the work of Christ, into the larger context of his ethics and Christology, in which love plays a central role. Thus Augustine's connection of the motifs of good will and love works like a glue, binding his other characterizations of will securely both to each other and to the larger substance of his thinking.

Augustine virtually identifies good will (*bona uoluntas*) with love (*caritas*) in *gr. et pecc. or.* (418):

---

[72] For further material on the relationship between willing and loving, see Donatella Pagliacci, *Volere e amare: Agostino e la conversione del desiderio* (Roma: Città Nuova, 2003). The discussion here, however, focuses on Augustine's way of relating *uoluntas* and *caritas* rather than on his relation of *uoluntas* and *amor*.

[73] The idea that love comes from God is important to Augustine. He writes in *gr. et pecc. or.* 1.21.22, "But love, which is a virtue, comes to us from God. Scripture bears witness to this, when it says, *Love comes from God, and everyone who loves has been born of God and knows God, because God is love* (1 Jn 4:7–8)."

Since, therefore, scripture says: *love is from God* (1 Jn 4:7) or, what is more, *God is love* (1 Jn 4:8); since the apostle John manifestly exclaims: *Behold what love the Father has given to us, that we should be called children of God* (1 Jn 3:1); why, when this [Pelagius] hears *God is love* (1 Jn 4:8), does he go as far as to contend that of those three major components we have the possibility from God (*ex deo*) but we have the good will and good action from ourselves (*ex nobis*), as if the good will (*bona uoluntas*) were something other than love (*caritas*), which scripture proclaims to us is from God and given by the Father so that we might be children of God?[74]

Pelagius argues "as if" (*quasi*) the good will were something other than the love we receive from God, writes Augustine, despite the fact that they are the same. Since a good will is love, it can come only from God; it cannot, as Pelagius thinks, come from us.

Augustine's designation of a good will as love also coordinates well with his description of the will using tree and root analogies inspired by the gospels to describe the will. Just as Augustine describes a good will and a bad will as two separate trees growing from two separate roots, rather than as two offshoots of the same basic way of behaving, he characterizes love and covetousness, in this passage, as two separate roots, two radically different species of the one good natural ability God created: "When human beings sin, they do not sin through love (*secundum caritatem*); rather, they sin through covetousness (*secundum cupiditatem*), through which they have not been born of God. For that ability, as we have said, is able to become each of these roots (*utriusque radicis est capax*)."[75] This characterization of covetousness and love corresponds to Augustine's earlier presentation of good and bad wills as having distinct characters and trajectories of growth. It is not as if both sin and doing what is right happen through the same type of organic process, love. People "do not sin through love." Instead "they sin through covetousness." By designating the *bona uoluntas* as *caritas*, Augustine further highlights the peculiar characteristics of different kinds of willing that come into view from a theological perspective. He christens the good will with its own name, having no common term with its "counterpart," covetousness.

---

[74] *Gr. et pecc. or.* 1.21.22 (CSEL 42:142). My translation.
[75] *Gr. et pecc. or.* 1.21.22 (CSEL 42:142).

Augustine continues to identify right willing as love in the final stage of the Pelagian controversy. In *gr. et lib. arb.* (426), he equates the two when discussing the martyrs as examples of how God gives and makes perfect the love which makes it possible to obey God's commands.[76] Augustine observes:

> One, then, who wills to carry out a commandment of God and cannot already has, of course (*quidem*), a good will (*uoluntatem bonam*), but a will that is still small and weak. But he will be able to carry it out when he has a great and strong will. For, when the martyrs carried out those great commandments (*magna . . . mandata*), they surely did so with a great will (*magna uoluntate*), that is, with a great love (*hoc est, magna caritate*), the love of which the Lord himself says, *No one has greater love than that he should lay down his life for his friends* (Jn 15:13).[77]

The martyrs, then, possessed a will corresponding to the greatness of the commandments they set out to obey. But this will was not simply "great" (*magnam*) and "strong" (*robustam*) as an absolute quantity, irrespective of content. Rather, their "great will" was also good because it was at the same time a "great love." Though Augustine's statement that a "great will . . . is a great love" may seem at first to suggest that he equates the *uoluntas* per se with *caritas*, context makes clear that he means to identify *caritas* with the good will. He has already specified that anyone who wills to obey has "a good will," a point he reiterates once but, as his use of the term *quidem* suggests, regards as certain and not requiring much further comment. He then goes on to discuss two subtypes of this good will (*uoluntas bona*): a "small and weak" will and a "great and strong" will. Though Augustine does not constantly repeat himself, he clearly presupposes that both types are instances of good will. Throughout it is willing to carry out the commandments that is in question. Though the strength of this willing varies between the two types discussed, the orientation does not. Thus this passage, like *gr. et pecc. or.* 1.21.22, characterizes the good will specifically as *caritas*.

In the next paragraph Augustine again characterizes the "great love" of the martyrs, which is given by God, as a kind of will. Introducing a series of

---

[76] Augustine quotes scripture as saying that "*the fulfillment, therefore, of the law is love* (Rom 13:8–10)" (*gr. et lib. arb.* 17.33).

[77] *Gr. et lib. arb.* 17.33 (PL 44:901).

extensive quotes from scriptural passages on love, beginning with Romans 8:35–39 and 1 Corinthians 12:31–13:8, Augustine writes, "Commending this love (*caritatem*), that is, a will (*uoluntatem*) fully aflame with divine love (*divino amore*), the apostle says. . . ."[78] Here Augustine continues to presuppose that the will in question is the good will referenced at the beginning of the discussion of love in 17.33, thus equating *caritas* with the good will in particular, rather than with willing generally speaking. Here Augustine's previous discussion of "greatness" of will culminates in a citation from 1 Corinthians 13. If, as scripture says, "love never fails," a will "fully aflame with the divine love" is a truly powerful will, "a great will" such as the martyrs possessed. The created will opened doors of possibility before the human race; the fallen will bound humanity in a chain of sin; the good, redeemed will that is *caritas*, Augustine shows here, burns with a divine love (*divino amore*).[79]

Section B: The Will and the Heart

Perhaps unsurprisingly given the close connection we have seen between *uoluntas* and *caritas*, Augustine also sees the human "heart (*cor*)" as closely related to the human will. Consistently through the entire Pelagian controversy (411 through the end of his life), Augustine interprets biblical language concerning the "heart" as applying to will.[80] In this period he sees heart and will as intimately connected, if not as synonyms. Operating on the basis of this connection not only broadens Augustine's base of biblical evidence for his teaching on will but also changes the shape of his teaching. Certainly, establishing a close association between will and heart gives him access to a whole range of further biblical "evidence" he can use to

---

[78] *Gr. et lib. arb.* 17.34 (PL 44:902).

[79] In addition to relating *uoluntas* and *caritas*, Augustine relates *uoluntas* and *dilectio*. In *corrept.* (427), for example, he puts "the inspiration of a good will and action" in apposition to "doing with love": "Grace not merely teaches them so that they know what they should do, but also grants that they do with love what they know. The apostle, of course, asks for this inspiration of a good will and action for those to whom he said, *But we pray to God that you may do no evil, not that we may be seen to have passed the test, but that you may do what is good* (2 Cor 13:7)" (*corrept.* 2.3 [CSEL 92:221]).

[80] Here I will focus on how Augustine relates *cor* and *uoluntas* in his polemical anti-Pelagian writings. However, as we will see in the next chapter's discussion of Christ as modeling the human will, Augustine also relates these closely in his more strictly exegetical writings, such as *Enarrationes in Psalmos*, where he consistently interprets references in the Psalms to a *recta cor* as referring to *uoluntas*.

develop and support his contentions about will against Pelagius, especially from the Old Testament. But it is not simply the case that Augustine has a fixed conception of will for the defense of which he then uses these biblical passages. Rather, interpreting these biblical passages with reference to will actually informs Augustine's understanding of what the will is and how it works. Taking on the features of the biblical notion of "heart" in such passages, the will, as Augustine sees it, becomes more and more permeable to divine influence, and more and more dependent on this influence for becoming good.

A number of references to heart in the first stage of the Pelagian controversy indicate that Augustine understands this term to overlap with *uoluntas*. In *On the Spirit and the Letter* (412–413), Augustine interprets Paul's teaching on the circumcision of the heart as referring to the will: "He [the apostle Paul] calls circumcision of the heart (*circumcisionem cordis*) a will (*uoluntatem*) that is free from every forbidden desire."[81] For Augustine, Paul's description of the state of the heart (*cor*) indicates the state of the will (*uoluntas*); the two function as synonyms such that scriptural pronouncements on the former may be applied to the latter. Both terms, for Augustine, refer to an inner dimension of human identity, determinative for one's moral condition and manifest to God, yet hidden from other human beings.[82] As his discussion continues, Augustine again refers to both the "heart" and the "innermost will" as the seat of one's true preferences, which are often hidden from the view of other people: "It is, after all, possible [to be justified] before human beings, but not before him who sees the heart itself (*cordis ipsius*) and the innermost will (*intimae uolutnatis*). There he sees what one would prefer to do, if it were permitted, even if one who fears the law does something else."[83] God, Augustine indicates, is the *inspector*, the one who may look into the innermost being and inclinations of the human person. Though Augustine names both the "heart itself" and the "innermost will," which could be taken as an indication that they are two distinct things, he also identifies both as referring to that place "where (*ubi*) God sees . . ." again raising the question of whether these two phrases indicate,

---

[81] *Spir. et litt.* 8.13 (CSEL 60:166).

[82] Augustine writes, "And for this reason God did not see in their will [the will of the Jews] what human beings saw in their action; rather, they were held guilty as a result of what God knew that they preferred to do, if only they could have done so with impunity" (*spir. et litt.* 8.13 [CSEL 60:165]).

[83] I have adjusted Teske's translation so that it refers to the "innermost will" rather than the "inner act of the will." *Spir. et litt.* 8.14 (CSEL 60:166).

for Augustine, the same reality. As Teske observes, Augustine's statement here, which refers to God as the "one who looks into (*inspector*)" the heart and the will, is reminiscent of Proverbs 24:12, where God is depicted as the one "who weighs hearts" and knows the soul; Augustine's characterization of heart and will fits with this biblical notion.

Augustine closely relates heart and will again in *gr. et pecc. or.* (418), this time in the context of an explicit interpretation of a biblical passage, Luke 22:61. Analyzing the change of heart that followed upon Peter's denial of Christ, Augustine observes, "By his mercy the Lord in a hidden manner helped him, touched his heart (*cor tetigit*), awakened his memory, visited the interior human being with his grace, and stirred up and produced a love (*affectum*) in the interior human being even to the point of exterior tears." He then draws a conclusion from Peter's experience as recorded in the gospel of Luke: "See how God is present to help our wills (*uoluntatibus*) and actions (*actionibus*). See how he *produces in us the willing and the action* (Phil 2:13)."[84] Though here Augustine does not equate will and heart, he sandwiches his reference to Christ's touching Peter's "heart (*cor*)" between two indicators that this action transpires in a voluntary realm. Before referencing the heart, Augustine states that the divine work described in the verse takes place "in the will (*in uoluntate*)." After describing the "secret" operation of the Lord's mercy, Augustine refers back to his description as showing how God is present "helping our wills (*adiuuando . . . uoluntatibus*)." Thus, while this text falls short of identifying heart and will, it does show that the fields these two terms reference overlap.

Following the pattern he had already established in the first stage of the Pelagian controversy with *spir. et litt.* 8.13, Augustine repeatedly interprets biblical statements about the heart as applying to the will in *c. ep. Pel.* (421), which stems from the second stage of the Pelagian controversy. Immediately after describing how God works in people's hearts to make them willing to come to him, Augustine insists that we know that God works this way on the will because of the Bible: "It is not by some human conjecture that we come to suspect that this is true; rather, we discover that it is true by the perfectly clear authority of the divine scriptures."[85] To substantiate his thesis, Augustine cites 2 Chronicles 30:12, which describes God giving Judah "one heart (*cor unum*)"; Ezekiel 36:26–27, where God promises to

---

[84] *Gr. et pecc. or.* 1.45.49 (CSEL 42:161).
[85] *C. ep. Pel.* 1.20.38 (CSEL 60:454).

give God's people "a heart of flesh (*cor carneum*)"; and Esther 14:13, in which Esther requests that God "turn the heart (*conuerte cor*)" of the king. Importantly, Augustine does not merely portray these passages as incidental echoes of a view of grace's impact on the will he had already held. Rather, he characterizes the "authority of the divine scriptures (*diuinarum scripturarum auctoritate*)" as the means by which one may discern (*dinoscere*) that this view is true in the first place. Augustine believes the idea that God works "interiorly in the hearts of human beings" to turn the human will to belief by "making unwilling people willing" flows smoothly from the biblical text.[86]

Augustine's exposition of Esther 14:13 is an excellent case in point. As in his use of the Lord's Prayer, Augustine works backward from this prayer recorded in scripture to what it presupposes about the will: "Why did Queen Esther pray, *Place in my mouth a pleasing speech, and make my words glorious in the sight of the lion, and turn his heart* (conuerte cor eius) *to hatred of the one who is attacking us* (Est 14:13)? Why does she say this in prayer (*in oratione*) to God, if God does not produce the will (*operatur . . . uoluntatem*) in the hearts (*in cordibus*) of human beings?"[87] Here again, Augustine reasons from scripture to conclusions about how God impacts human willing, from Esther's *oratio* to the will's *conversio*. A vital premise for this position is the notion that biblical statements about the heart may be applied to something Augustine calls the "will."

Though Augustine describes this verse as proving something about the will, the term "will" never actually appears in it. Esther mentions only the king's *heart*. Yet Augustine interprets the change in the king that follows upon Esther's prayer as applying to the will. He argues: "divine scripture testifies that God fulfilled her request by producing in the king's heart (*in corde regis*) nothing other than the will (*uoluntatem*) by which he gave the command and the queen's request was carried out." Heart and will are intimately connected. Augustine continues, "God changed and transformed the heart of the king (*cor regis*) by his most hidden and efficacious power from wrath to gentleness, that is, from the will to do harm (*a uoluntate laedendi*) to the will to grant favors (*ad uoluntatem fauendi*). As the apostle says, *God produces in you even the will* (Phil 2:13)."[88] For Augustine, when

[86] *C. ep. Pel.* 1.19.37.
[87] *C. ep. Pel.* 1.20.38 (CSEL 60:455).
[88] *C. ep. Pel.* 1.20.38 (CSEL 60:455–456).

scripture refers to God bringing about a change in a person's heart, what is meant is that God works precisely by producing will. One might ask, at this point, why Augustine resorts to terminology of will at all. Why not simply stick to Esther's language, speaking only of a change God brings about in the heart? What does Augustine gain by transposing this statement into a voluntary key? Augustine's concluding citation of Philippians 2:13 suggests one answer. By providing a description in terms of will, Augustine can read texts such as this one and New Testament texts that speak of God affecting human will, such as Phil 2:13, as mutually interpreting. In this sense, his effort to relate "heart (*cor*)" and "will (*uoluntas*)" represents more than an abstract exercise. By bringing heart and will together, Augustine highlights the accord between the two testaments and, therewith, the consistency of God's way of changing human lives across the whole story of God's relationship with God's people.

One of Augustine's clearest statements on the relation between heart and will is found further on in *c. ep. Pel.*, where he interprets Proverbs 16:1, *It is up to a human being to prepare the heart*, which seems at first to present a problem for his position on grace.[89] This verse, he argues, depicts a human preparation for grace possible "only with the help of God who touches the heart in such a way that the human being prepares the heart."[90] Continuing to comment on this verse, Augustine poses a rhetorical question that demonstrates clearly that he takes "heart" in this context as equivalent to will: "After all, what is it to prepare the heart (*cor*) and open the mouth but to prepare the will (*uoluntatem*)?"[91] Augustine does not here shed light on the basis on which he applies biblical heart terminology to the will, as he did in *c. ep. Pel.* 1.20.38, but he does express with clarity the hermeneutical premise upon which so many of his proofs for his mature doctrine of grace rest.

In the final stage of the Pelagian controversy, Augustine continues to rely on the connection between heart and will to support his teachings on grace against its detractors. In *gr. et lib. arb.* (426), Augustine again interprets the heart language of Ezekiel, though this time Ezekiel 11:19–20, rather than Ezekiel 36:26–27 as in *c. ep. Pel.*, as referring to will. Augustine takes God's promises to give his people a new heart to replace their heart of stone as

---

[89] Citing Teske's translation of Augustine's quotation.
[90] *C. ep. Pel.* 2.9.19.
[91] *C. ep. Pel.* 2.9.20 (CSEL 60:482).

illustrating that good will does not precede God's gift of faith and conversion. He asks about the text: "Can we, then, save with complete absurdity, say that the good merit of a good will (*bonae uoluntatis*) comes first in a human being so that the heart (*cor*) of stone is torn out of him? For a heart (*cor*) of stone itself signifies (*significat*) nothing but a will (*uoluntatem*) which is most hard and utterly inflexible in opposition to God. For, where a good will (*bona uoluntas*) is already present, there is, of course, no longer a heart of stone (*cor lapideum*)."[92] Again in the context of his exchange with the monks of Hadrumetum in Africa, then, Augustine states clearly that scriptural language of "heart (*cor*) . . . signifies (*significat*) . . . will (*uoluntatem*)."

In *corrept.* (late 426 or 427), in which Augustine responds to an objection raised by one of the monks of Hadrumetum to *gr. et lib. arb.*, he interprets the biblical reference in 1 Samuel 10:25–27 to "men of valor whose hearts (*corda*) the Lord touched" to join Saul as indicating that God enacted his will "to give Saul the kingdom" by acting "through the wills (*per . . . uoluntates*) of human beings."[93] Augustine also brings up scripture passages about the heart to support his case that "human wills (*humanas uoluntates*) cannot resist [God's] will (*uoluntati dei*)" and that God does "what he wills and when he wills even with the very wills (*uoluntatibus*) of human beings."[94] On the basis of 1 Chronicles 12:38, which states that *All these men, warriors in battle formation, came with a peaceful heart* (corde) *to Hebron in order to make David king over all of Israel,*[95] Augustine reasons:

These men [warriors mentioned in 1 Chr 12:38], of course, made David king by their own will. Who could fail to see this? Who could deny it? For they did not do insincerely or without good will (*non ex bona uoluntate*) what they did with a peaceful heart (*corde pacifico*), and he, nonetheless, who does what he wills in the hearts of human beings produced this in them . . . He worked within (*intus egit*); he held their hearts (*corda tenuit*), moved their hearts (*corda mouit*), and drew them by their wills (*uoluntatibus*) which he himself produced in them (*in illis operatus est*). If,

---

[92] *Gr. et lib. arb.* 14.29 (PL 44:898).

[93] "God, nonetheless, did this only through the wills (*uoluntates*) of human beings, since he undoubtedly had omnipotent power over human hearts (*cordium*) to turn them where he pleased. For scripture speaks as follows, *And Samuel dismissed the people, and each went off to his own place. And Saul went off to his home in Gibeah, and the men of valor whose hearts the Lord touched went off with Saul . . .* (1 Sm. 10:25–27)" (*corrept.* 14.45 [CSEL 92:273]).

[94] *Corrept.* 14.45 (CSEL 92:273).

[95] This is Teske's translation of Augustine's citation in *corrept.* 14:45 (CSEL 92:274).

then, when God wills to establish kings on the earth, he has in his control the wills of human beings (*uoluntates hominum*) more than they have in their power their own wills, who else causes a rebuke to be salutary and produces the correction in the heart (*corde*) of the one rebuked in order to bring him to the heavenly kingdom?[96]

Here again, a premise for Augustine's entire argument is that doing something "with a peaceful heart (*corde pacifico*)" entails doing it "from a good will (*ex bona uoluntate*)." Having stated this premise, he can elicit implications for willing from the passage by bouncing back and forth between "heart (*cor*)" and "will (*uoluntas*)" language in his description of God's work "within (*intus*)" the warriors.

Praed. sanct. (427), which Augustine wrote to address difficulties with his doctrine of grace raised by a different group of monks, this time from monasteries in Provence, shows a similar pattern. Toward the end of the work Augustine cites a litany of biblical supports for the idea that God "prepares the wills of human beings (*hominum uoluntates*) and turns them even toward the kingdom of heaven and to eternal life."[97] Of the ten passages he invokes, only one even mentions the will. While two refer to God directing the "steps (*gressus*)" of human beings, one to God putting God's "spirit (*spiritum*)" in God's people and one to people believing as a result of being destined for eternal life, five mention God inclining or otherwise influencing human "heart(s) [*cor(da)*]."[98] Quantitatively speaking, then, the bulk of Augustine's evidence comes from passages that concern the heart. Qualitatively speaking, however, Proverbs 8:35 LXX, *the will is prepared by the Lord*, a locus classicus for Augustine's teaching on grace and the will that explicitly mentions the *uoluntas*, plays the crucial role. Without Proverbs 8:35 and other texts explicitly referencing "will," such as Philippians 2:13, the case for the validity of applying biblical texts about heart to will would be shaky. These verses serve as hermeneutical keys, opening the door to the

---

[96] *Corrept.* 14.45 (CSEL 92:274–275).

[97] *Praed. sanct.* 21.42 (PL 44:991).

[98] The passages Augustine cites include Psalm 119:36 (*cor*), Psalm 37:23 (*gressus*), Proverbs 8:35 LXX (*uoluntas*), 1 Kings 8:57–58 (*corda*), Baruch 2:31 (*cor*), Ezekiel 11:19 (*cor*), Ezekiel 36:27 (*spritum*), Proverbs 20:24 (*gressus*), Proverbs 21:2 (*corda*), Acts 13:48 (*crediderunt quotquot erant ordinati*). Teske actually omits one of the passages citing the heart, Ezekiel 11:19, from his translation. See PL 44:991.

introduction of the category of *uoluntas* into Augustine's canonical reading of scripture.[99]

Some of Augustine's contemporaries may have objected to his hermeneutical move to connect "heart" and "will." After arguing at length in the same work on the basis of a series of New Testament passages that "God, of course, does what he wills in the hearts of human beings,"[100] Augustine observes: "In vain therefore, have they claimed that what we proved by the testimony of scripture from Kings and Chronicles does not pertain to the issue with which we are dealing, namely, that when God wills the accomplishment of something which only willing human beings can do, their hearts (*corda*) are inclined to will this, that is, he inclines their hearts who produces in us in a marvelous and ineffable way the willing (*uelle*) as well."[101] Augustine seems to be referring to a comment from a letter Hilary had written to inform him of opposition in Marseille to Augustine's idea that the will to believe is a gift.[102]

Augustine's critics there argued that if this were the case, then exhortation would be useless. In his letter Hilary had noted: "They think that the testimonies of scripture concerning Saul or David that you quoted do not have to do with the question concerned with exhortation, but they introduce other testimonies which they interpret as commending that grace whereby each person is helped subsequent to his will or toward that calling which is offered to those who are unworthy,"[103] a comment which seems, in turn, to refer to Augustine's discussion of 1 Samuel 10:25–27 and passages from 1 Chronicles in *corrept.* 15.45, whose references to God's work on human hearts Augustine had used to defend the idea that God "has in his control the wills of human beings."[104] Thus, it seems that Augustine's opponents in

---

[99] Canonical, not necessarily in the technical sense described by scholars such as Brevard Childs, but rather in the sense that Augustine tries to interpret the entire canon of scripture as one unified whole, describing in different times, languages, and cultures the same theological reality of God and his way of relating to humankind. Given his "canonical" approach, for example, it is possible to see texts such as Proverbs 8:35 LXX as shedding light on how one might interpret texts such as Psalm 119:36.

[100] *Praed. sanct.* 20.41.

[101] *Praed. sanct.* 20.42 (PL 44:990).

[102] See Teske 187n72, WSA I/26.

[103] *Epistulae* (*ep.*) 226.7.

[104] In the Vulgate (and perhaps in other old Latin versions Augustine would have used during his lifetime—the version he cites in *corrept.* 15.45 is quite different from the Vulgate; he is probably using a *vetus latina* version), the book we now know as the first book of Samuel would have been called the first book of Kings, hence Augustine's reference to testimonies from "Kings and Chronicles" rather than from "Samuel and Chronicles."

Marseille objected that his move to invoke these texts to make his case was somehow invalid. It is tempting to speculate here. What was their more specific concern? Did they balk at his application of passages on the "heart" to the "will"?

While we lack the evidence necessary to determine where exactly the worry of Augustine's opponents lay, his response to their protests about his use of passages dealing with Saul and David sheds light both on his "best hypothesis" as to what bothered his opponents and on his own estimation of the validity of applying scriptural passages on heart to the will. Augustine claims to be perplexed by the objection Hilary mentions: "have they perhaps given you some reason why they had this idea which you preferred to pass over in silence in your letters? But I do not know what that reason could be." Then, he mentions a possible cause, seemingly the only one that occurs to him: "Or, because we showed that God acted in the hearts of human beings and brought the wills of those whom he chose to the point that they made Saul or David king, do they perhaps think that these examples do not suit this issue, because to reign in this world for a time is not the same thing as to reign with God for eternity?" Augustine wonders whether the problem is using passages that concern temporal well being in order to draw conclusions about eternal salvation. Do his critics think it is invalid to reason from God's intervention in favor of establishing earthly kingdoms to God's intervention in human affairs for the purpose of establishing his heavenly kingdom? Augustine never raises the possibility that his detractors in Marseilles questioned his identification of hearts with wills.

Augustine's responses to his detractors' objection, both in the form in which he receives it and in the hypothetical form he has attempted to reconstruct, underlines his holistic scriptural hermeneutic when it comes to the issue of grace's impact on the will. Augustine defends himself against the objection in the latter form not by digging further into the texts from Kings, but rather by introducing his litany of ten texts, which, he contends "were said on account of the kingdom of heaven, not on account of an earthly kingdom."[105] He defends the principle that God "inclines wills" so that people "obtain the heavenly kingdom"[106] by pointing to other texts where, at least in Augustine's view, it finds clearer expression. This response

[105] *Praed. sanct.* 20.42.
[106] *Praed. sanct.* 20.42.

accords with his method of addressing the generalized objection Hilary had reported to him, namely that the testimonies from Kings and Chronicles he adduced seemed irrelevant to the issue in question. Augustine introduces the concern that his scriptural arguments from Kings and Chronicles are irrelevant by alluding to the preceding discussion: "In vain, therefore (*itaque*), have they claimed that what we proved by the testimony of scripture from Kings and Chronicles does not pertain to the issue with which we are dealing . . ."[107] This discussion had focused on another catalog of biblical citations, in this case from the New Testament, which Augustine had used to support the notion that "God, of course, does what he wills in the hearts of human beings."[108] What Augustine portrays as decisive, then, is the overall consensus of scripture on God's role in promoting human faith, whether this be expressed in "will" or "heart" language. Objections to his interpretation of Kings and Chronicles are "in vain," he argues, not because of an inherent feature of these specific texts, but because of the overall consensus of a broad swathe of passages from across the canon pointing to the notion that "when God wills the accomplishment of something which only willing human beings can do, their hearts (*corda*) are inclined to will this, that is, he inclines their hearts who produces in us in a marvelous and ineffable way the willing (*uelle*) as well."[109] Reading these together leads Augustine to use heart and will language interchangeably.

As shown, Augustine relates *uoluntas* and *cor* closely throughout the Pelagian controversy. In its earlier stages, Augustine explains to his readers that "of course," biblical references to heart signify nothing other than will, but does not apply passages on heart to the will with as great a frequency as he does in the final phase of the controversy. Eventually, the connection between heart and will takes on a vital role in his exegetical arguments in defense of his view of God's impact upon the human will. By the time of his exchanges with the monks of Hadrumetum and Gaul, the connection between *cor* and *uoluntas* becomes a stock premise upon which Augustine draws frequently to deploy biblical arguments in defense of his view of grace.

Augustine traverses the bridge between "heart" and "will" to arrive at his exegetical and polemical destinations without preoccupying himself

---

[107] *Praed. sanct.* 20.42 (PL 44:990).
[108] *Praed. sanct.* 20.41.
[109] *Praed. sanct.* 20.42 (PL 44:990).

overmuch with the precise structure of the relationship between these two terms. Sometimes he seems to suggest that the heart is in the will.[110] At others he locates the will in the heart.[111] Often he treats the two terms as interchangeable. In this regard, the tenor of Augustine's comments in *On the Origin of the Soul,* though directed at the question of the corporeal control center for sensation and voluntary movement, rather than the figurative "heart" of the human person, accords with his thinking on the relationship between the figurative heart and will: "With regard to the part of the body which rules over the rest, does it govern from the heart or from the brain? Or does it govern in two ways: from the heart for movements and from the brain for sensations? Or does its governance come from the brain for sensations and voluntary movements, but from the heart for the nonvoluntary pulsations of the veins? And if it produces the former two from the brain, why does it have sensation, even if it does not will to, but only moves its members when it wills?"[112] Augustine is content to be agnostic when it comes to specifying the location of the corporeal control center through which the soul is active in sensation or in willing. For Augustine, this question is a mystery taking its place among those that are too high for human beings to grasp.

Augustine maintains a similar attitude of secure agnosticism with respect to the relationship between the figurative heart and the will. He is not interested in working out a precise philosophical description of this relationship as an end in itself. His concern is rather to use language of "heart" and "will" to shed light on an unmistakable phenomenon that runs through all of scripture like a red thread: God's powerful transformation of human lives. Whether the biblical authors use terminology of heart or of will, the structure is the same. God does not merely help human beings to continue doing what they are doing. In bestowing a good will or a good heart, God turns people around. At key junctures in individual lives and at great turning points of history, God works mysteriously at the very core of

---

[110] In *gr. et pecc. or.* (418), for example, Augustine speaks of Christ's penetrating look at Peter as "taking place in the will" (*in uoluntate actum est*) but also involving the Lord "touching his heart" (*cor tetigit*). See 1.45.49 (CSEL 42:161).

[111] For example, Augustine refers to God as producing will in the heart, asking, "Why does she say this in prayer to God, if God does not produce the will in the hearts of human beings?" (*c. ep Pel* 1.20.38 [CSEL 60: 455]).

[112] *Orig. an.* 4.5.6 (= ep. 166).

a human person to bring about a radical change of heart that seemed other-wise impossible.

"Will (*uoluntas*)" is not a term Augustine invents, but one he finds in bib-lical texts such as Proverbs 8:35 LXX and Philippians 2:13.[113] His creative contribution to the notion consists in his calibration of the term *uoluntas* to the larger story of scripture and to other pericopes found throughout the biblical text. In this latter category, texts referring to God's work on the human heart play a key role. Augustine construes these texts as applying to the realm of the will such that this realm becomes identified, in his mature theology, with that dimension at the center of human identity where God moves and transforms human lives from the inside.

Augustine's characterization of the good will in relation to love and to the "heart (*cor*)," like his characterization of the good will as a will in the process of conversion, as coming from God and directed to God, as a will with faith in God and the will of a believer, and as the one good work necessary for eternal life, shows how, for Augustine, the good will is always defined in relation to God. For Augustine, the good will is not a self-contained concept. Rather, it inherently both depends on God and points beyond itself to God.

What are the implications of this theologically-oriented notion of the good will for assessing the state of Augustine's thinking during the Pelagian controversy on the nature of the human "will" more generally?

Part IV: A Portrait of the Augustinian Will in the Pelagian Controversy

When one steps backs to consider what is new and what is not about Augustine's thinking on will in general (as opposed to his thinking on "the good will," in particular) during the Pelagian controversy, points of conti-nuity and areas of development both come into view. As in earlier periods, Augustine continues to see the will in a highly dynamic way, as an activity of the mind.[114] Yet, at the same time, Augustine becomes less and less

---

[113] In *gr. et lib. arb.* 2.4, Augustine designates around twenty-nine different scriptural passages as addressing "the will by name." He writes, "Moreover, there are so many commandments which ad-dress the will (*uoluntatem*) by name, as it were, such as [then follows a list]."

[114] Interestingly, however, it becomes increasingly difficult to make a case that Augustine sees the will as a reified faculty in his later works. Over time Augustine tends to focus more and more on the will in terms of how it is particularized in specific situations rather than on the will as a fea-ture of the human being with inherent ontological integrity (for comparison see *lib. arb.* 2.18.48,

interested in addressing this activity of willing in abstract, general terms. Augustine has little to say, in this period, about willing per se as a neutral activity. Rather, he is concerned with specific cases of human willing that occur in particular contexts. In these concrete instances, willing, it turns out, always has a very definite orientation. Thus, one of the few safe generalizations to make about Augustine's conception of will during the Pelagian controversy would be that it eludes description in abstract, generalized and neutral terms. Augustine presents the will, in this period, as something that always possesses a definite direction and that demands to be understood in light of the specific context and network of relationships that shape what its orientation will be, if indeed what is most significant about it is to be taken into account.

Augustine makes clear both at the outset of the Pelagian controversy and in his final "Anti-Pelagian" work that will refers to what happens when a certain type of action is performed, rather than to a fixed, static, or reified "thing." In *spir. et litt.* (412–413), Augustine comments that will "takes its name from willing." As *uoluntas* is to *uelle* so *potestas* is to *posse*. Commenting on the etymology of *uoluntas*, Augustine writes: "It is quite clear, and the sound of the words indicates that will (*uoluntas*) takes its name from willing (*uelle*) and power (*potestas*) from being able (*posse*). Hence, as one who wills (*qui uult*) has the will (*uoluntatem*), so one who is able (*qui potest*) has the power (*potestatem*)."[115] As Augustine's last sentence makes clear, "the will" derives not only etymologically but also ontologically from the act of willing. *Uoluntas* is simply a substantive that describes what one who wills possesses by virtue of willing. "The will" is at work whenever "willing" is happening. In *Contra Iulianum opus imperfectum* (*c. Iul. imp.*, 427–430), Augustine specifies that *uoluntas* is itself an "act of the mind." He

discussed in chapter 1). During the Pelagian controversy, he specifically rules out the notion that the will is a substance in *c. Iul.* 1.5.16 (PL 44:641), where he states, "Our nature was not originally created in this [evil] state, and the source of this addition was not a substance (*substantiam*), but a will (*uoluntatem*)." Additionally for Augustine in this period, will cannot be a faculty inherent in human nature in its fully fledged form, as infants lack it. This is a point upon which Augustine and Julian agree. See *c. Iul.* 4.8.45 (PL 44: 760), where Augustine argues that in the case of infants it is easy to prove that human will is not involved before grace "since as yet they have no will and, hence, no contrary will." For Julian's denial that infants possess a will, see *nupt. et conc.* 2.27.44. Augustine writes of Julian, " 'How,' he asks, 'does sin come to be in a little one? From the will? There was no will in the little one' " (2.27.44). While there may be ways of reconciling Augustine's earlier and later statements that pertain to the issue of whether the will is a faculty, perhaps he simply changes his mind on the matter. This would explain the division in the literature.

[115] *Spir. et litt.* 31.53 (CSEL 60:209–210).

writes: "the very act of the mind (*motus animi*) with nothing forcing it is the will (*uoluntas*)."[116]

Augustine's statement in *De gratia et libero arbitrio* (*gr. et lib. arb.* 426) that "both to will to do something and to will not to do something are proper to the will"[117] fits this dynamic understanding of the will. Teske's translation "For to will and not to will are acts which belong to the will" seems to suggest that the absence of willing (as well as willing) belongs to the will such that will would have subsistence apart from specific acts of will, a conclusion that would conflict with Augustine's other more dynamistic descriptions of will. However, this problem disappears in the original Latin, since Augustine attributes "willing not to do something (*nolle*)" rather than "not willing" in the sense of an absence of willing, to the will. Thus, this text in no way implies that the Augustinian will need be conceived as a reified faculty subsisting independently of specific acts of will.

Sarah Byers proposes that will, for Augustine, while not a reified faculty, still functions as a neutral element of a human psychology of motivation. On her view, Augustine's notion of *uoluntas* is equivalent to the Stoic notion of *hormē*, an impulse toward action that is the product of rational assent.[118] While the Augustinian notion of will clearly embraces the capacity to give or withhold assent, however, it can exist without assent and therefore must be distinguished from Stoic *hormē*. In *Contra Iulianum* (*c. Iul.*), for example, Augustine states: "For the desires of the flesh are not brought to completion in evil when the assent of our will (*uoluntatis assensus*) is not given to them, and our will is not brought to completion in good, as long as there remains the movement of those desires to which we do not consent."[119] In this passage, Augustine does indicate that will is the seat of assent, without which desires cannot be carried out. But, at the same time, will cannot be reduced to the product of such assent, since Augustine regards the will itself as imperfect so long as a person experiences sinful desires, even if the will never consents to these. If will were always merely the product of assent, then Augustine would not diagnose the continual experience of desires to which consent was not given as a problem of will. Crucial in this passage is Augustine's consideration

---

[116] *C. Iul. imp.* 5.60 (CSEL 85.2: 273).

[117] My translation. See *gr. et lib. arb.* 3.5: *uelle enim et nolle propriae uoluntatis est.*

[118] See her appendix on *uoluntas*, Sarah Catherine Byers, *Perception, Sensibility, and Moral Motivation in Augustine: A Stoic-Platonic Synthesis* (New York: Cambridge University Press, 2013), 217–231.

[119] *C. Iul.* 3.26.62 (PL 44:734).

of the will in view of what it might take to achieve its perfection "in the good (*in bono*)." This is his main concern, rather than developing a technical and generalizable philosophical conception of the will.

Indeed, the non-neutrality, or even, the non-generalizability, of the will represents, if anything, the single most pronounced new feature of Augustine's conception of the will as such in the Pelagian controversy. Augustine's conception of will as an act or "movement of the soul (*motus animi*)" lends itself to this highly contextualized view of will. As not only something that moves but itself a movement, the will is highly fluid, plastic and malleable; it is capable of assuming many different forms in different circumstances and at different times. Furthermore, Augustine's non-neutral view of will fits well with his theological aims in the Pelagian controversy. Whereas in his earlier writings, especially against the Manichees, the will served the primary purpose of securing moral responsibility and maintaining an appropriate distinction between divine and human agency, now the will serves as a conduit for receiving God's grace and maintaining God's powerful influence on human agency. Accordingly, Augustine focuses in his later descriptions of human willing upon its permeability to outside influence and its orientation toward goals beyond itself.[120]

As we have seen, during the Pelagian controversy Augustine develops a set of definitions and descriptions of the good will that are distinct from those of the bad will.[121] Thus, during the Pelagian controversy, Augustine adds a dimension to his theologically periodized conception of will. Now he develops a unique description, not only of the created and fallen wills, but also of the good will that is restored when sinful human beings receive the grace of Christ. Unlike either the created or the fallen wills, this "good will" is a will that comes into existence when God acts directly upon the sinful human will to reorient it toward himself. But just as the emergence in Augustine's thinking of the distinctive features of the "fallen will" entailed larger implications for his thinking on will, so the development of the notion of the "good will" implies not only an addition to, but a clarification of his earlier thinking in at least one key respect. Whereas in early works

---

[120] Notably, in both controversies the will is a vital conceptual tool for describing the relationship between divine and human action: with respect to the Manichees, in a way that avoids the pitfall of complacency, and with respect to the Pelagians, in a way that avoids the pitfall of pride.

[121] In *pecc. mer.*, for example, we saw that Augustine defines a *uoluntas mala* as a turning away from God, while he defines a *uoluntas bona* as turning toward God. *Pecc. mer.* 2.18.31 (CSEL 60:102): "Our turning away from God is our own doing, and this turning is an evil will. But our turning toward God is something we cannot do unless he rouses us and helps us, and this turning is a good will."

such as *lib. arb.* Augustine had characterized the created will as a *medium bonum* neutrally poised between evil and good, by the latest phase of the Pelagian controversy, Augustine not only portrays the fallen and good wills as non-neutral, but also calls into question the idea that the will ever functioned with absolute neutrality in the first place. Even the created will, he now contends, had a definite orientation from the beginning.

Already in *pecc. mer.* (411–412), even as he describes the difference between a *uoluntas mala* and a *uoluntas bona*, Augustine expresses doubts about the idea that the will might, under any circumstances, adopt a stance of neutrality toward good and evil, maintaining its distance from both at the same time: "Moreover, I would be surprised if the will could stand in between so that it would be neither good nor bad."[122] By *corrept.* (427), Augustine is arguing not only that our wills post fall are never neutral, but also that God did not give Adam a neutral will but a good one: "God, therefore, at that time gave Adam a good will (*bonam uoluntatem*); he, of course, who created him upright created him with that will; he gave him a help without which he could not remain in that will even if he willed to, but he left it up to his free choice to will it."[123]

As may be seen in this quotation, however, even in his maturity, Augustine never goes so far as to say that the created will was non-neutral in a way that would deprive it of the ability to choose between good and evil. The fact of sin in the world clearly proves the contrary, and Augustine affirms explicitly that it was "up to [Adam's]" free choice to use his created will as he saw fit. The image of a hinge for the created will thus continues to be useful to describe Augustine's mature understanding of the created will even amid developments in what he tends to emphasize in characterizing it. The difference is that even the created will is non-neutral in the sense of being always already inclined toward the good in a definitive way. The created will is not just any kind of hinge, but a directed hinge: though deviation is possible, it always has a moral bearing.

Augustine makes the point that God made Adam with a good will, rather than a neutral will, repeatedly in *c. Iul. imp.* (427–430). Whereas Julian subscribes to a deliberative conception of will such that willing requires possessing a set of alternatives,[124] Augustine's view is that the will is always

---

[122] *Pecc. mer.* 2.18.29 (CSEL 60:101–102).

[123] *Corrept.* 11.32 (CSEL 92:257).

[124] Julian's definition of will: "Will then is the movement of the mind which has in its power either to descend toward evil on the left or to strive toward noble things on the right" (*c. Iul. imp.* 1.46 [CSEL 85.1:33]). Note that choice between options is built into Julian's definition.

already inclined in one direction or another. In *c. Iul. imp.* 5.38, Augustine objects to Julian's suggestion that the possibilities of good and evil arising in the garden of Eden were perfectly balanced: "But you say, 'An evil will could arise, just as a good will also could arise.' You say this as if either the angel or the human being were made without a good will. Man was made upright, as scripture said. The question, then, is not how the good will with which he was made, but how the evil will with which he was not made, could have come to be in him."[125] Even in *lib. arb.*, Augustine had characterized the will as good, with the potential for both good and bad use. Without contradicting his earlier description, Augustine now develops a new point of emphasis: that the created will had a definite inclination to the good. Had the will continued in its created goodness there would have been no cause for remark. What is strange, is that it deviated from the good path on which it was originally set.

Later in the same book of *c. Iul. imp.*, Augustine points out that, by working so hard to preserve the neutrality of the will, Julian compromises his affirmation of the goodness of creation. Augustine's accusation is that, on Julian's scheme, human beings, not God, make themselves good, by using their will well: "Why is it, then, that you now say, 'The good God made human beings good,' if they are neither good nor bad by having the free choice which God produced in them, but by using it well (*bene utendo*), that is, when they themselves will in a good way (*bene uult*), not when they have the possibility of willing in a good way?" Augustine continues his questioning: "And how will it be true that *God made human beings upright* (Eccl 7:30)? Or were they upright, though they did not have a good will (*uoluntatem bonam*), but only its possibility?" According to Augustine the implication is clear: "They were, then, evil, though they did not have a bad will, but only its possibility. Then they have from themselves a good will, and scripture was incorrect to say: *The will is prepared by the Lord* (Prv 8:35 LXX), and God *also produces in you the willing* (Phil 2:13)."[126] Augustine wants to credit God with giving them a will that not merely

---

Julian stresses that will is a motion of the mind that is self-generating; it cannot be explained by anything else; it has no antecedents. This is key to maintaining the justice of God, in his view. Julian writes, "This will, then, which is presented with alternatives, received the origin of its ability in free choice. But it receives the existence of the act from itself, and the will does not exist before it wills, nor can it will before it can refuse to will. It has neither, that is, neither willing nor not willing, in the sense of sin, before it acquires the use of reason" (*c. Iul. imp.* 1.47 [CSEL 85.1: 33]). For Julian, then, willing by definition has to involve the possibility of refusal to will. This notion of willing is inherently deliberative. There must be alternatives involved, or there cannot be willing.

[125] *C. Iul. imp.* 5.38 (CSEL 85.2:237).
[126] *C. Iul. imp.* 5.57 (CSEL 85.2:265).

has the possibility of being used well (*habet possibilitatem uolendi bene*), but also actually is good, a *uoluntatem bonam*. Strikingly, Augustine then cites Proverbs 8:35 LXX and Philippians 2:13 as evidence. He does not restrict the application of these verses to God's preparation and production of a good will given the will's fall into sin. Rather, Augustine sees them as describing the consistent pattern of God's relationship to good human willing, in redemption and in the garden.

Yet a third time in *c. Iul. imp.*, Augustine drives home the original goodness of the created will, not only in the sense of possessing the possibility to choose either good or evil, but also in the more robust sense of already inclining toward God:

> That perfection of the nature which was not given by age, but by the hand of God alone [i.e., in the creation of Adam], could not fail to have a will and one that was not bad. Otherwise, scripture would not have said, *God made man upright* (Eccl 7:30). The man was, therefore, made with a good will (*bonae . . . uoluntatis*), ready to obey God and obediently receiving the commandment which he would have kept without any difficulty, as long as he willed to . . .[127]

In *lib. arb.*, Augustine underlined that the goodness of the created will, a *medium bonum*, involved a twofold capacity for both good and evil, without which moral responsibility would be impossible. Here, he places being created with a good will in apposition to being made "ready to obey God" (*paratus ad oboediendum deo*). The created will of the Pelagian controversy is already on a course toward the good rather than merely standing at a crossroads.

From the very dawn of human history, Augustine now contends, God had already established a pattern of giving the good will by grace: "the first good will (*primam uoluntatem bonam*) is the work of God; he, of course, made the human being upright with it. For no one is ever upright except by willing the right things. On this account the good will (*uoluntas bona*), once lost, is not restored except by him who created it."[128] Even as the good will restored by God involves a conversion from opposition to God that reorients a person back toward her creator, a reorientation not required

---

[127] *C. Iul. imp.* 5.61 (CSEL 85.2:275).
[128] *C. Iul. imp.* 5.61 (CSEL 85.2:276).

for the will in its original goodness, both the created good will and the redeemed good will, Augustine underlines, only possess the goodness they enjoy by grace. There is no such thing as good will that human beings accomplish without God's gift.

Conclusion

In this chapter we have seen that Augustine applies a diverse array of images and descriptions to the "good will." For Augustine the good will is a root that gives rise to a whole way of life, bearing good fruit in due season. The good will makes good actions possible; without it one cannot do what is right no matter how righteous one's actions seem to be. But the possibility of attaining a good will is not up to human beings alone. As Augustine illustrates with another image, the will is as dependent on God as an eye on light to see. Indeed, for Augustine, the good will is enmeshed in a web of relations to God so dense that removing it from its tangle of theological ties would rend it asunder. A good will is a will that turns toward God in conversion, it comes from and is directed to God, it belongs to the one who believes and puts her faith in God, it is the one work necessary for eternal life with God, and it is, finally, nothing other than *caritas*, the love that comes from God. The will is at the biblical heart of human identity; it is what scripture means when it talks about God changing human hearts. In short, the good will is unthinkable without God.

This characterization of the good will corresponds both to a major item of continuity with Augustine's earlier understanding of will and to a new emphasis in his conception of will that proves particularly prominent during the Pelagian controversy. As an activity or "movement of the mind (*motus animi*)," rather than a reified substance, the will lends itself to constitution and definition in relationship to God. It does not have a stable independent existence, but by definition is always a movement toward something. Whereas earlier in his career Augustine had drawn attention to the flexibility of the will's movement, comparing it to a hinge upon which the soul might swing freely this way and that, now in the Pelagian controversy he underlines that the will is always already oriented in one direction or another; the will, he contends, never enjoys a position of neutrality over against good and evil. If, for Augustine, the created will was a hinge, and the fallen will a link in the chain of sin, the good will is a root of love, growing in and toward the light from its maker.

Augustine's conception of will, then, takes on a third dimension in the Pelagian controversy whereby it is now structured according to at least three theological periods: creation, fall, and redemption. Indeed, the very fact that Augustine's conception of will demonstrates theological differentiation constitutes a significant point of contrast between his own thinking on will and that of Pelagius or Julian. Augustine's "Pelagian" interlocutors have a single universalized conception of what the will is and how it works. Augustine, however, insists that such a view of human willing naively ignores the fall's radical impact upon the human will and its subsequent need for the redemptive work of Christ. How the fallen and good wills function cannot be understood independently of these events by which the will is reduced to chains and then lovingly implanted in good soil so that it might grow toward God.

Holding true to the contrast he had observed already in *lib. arb.*, Augustine faults Pelagius for failing to distinguish between the capacities of the human will as it was created, and its drastically limited abilities subsequent to the fall. Quoting from *lib. arb.* to clarify his current position against Pelagius, he writes: "But to take what is false for what is true so that one errs against one's will (*inuitus*), and not to be able to refrain from acts of passion, because of the resistance and the biting pain of the flesh's chain (*carnalis uinculi*), is not the nature of human beings as they were created (*natura institutae*), but their punishment after they were condemned."[129] Human beings receiving punishment subsequent to the fall lack the wherewithal to do what they will to do; they are shackled with the chains of sin. But this is not true of created human nature.

Also in *De natura et gratia*, Augustine points out that Pelagius mistakes the capacities of the created will as universal features belonging to the will independent of context, in all times and places. Pelagius thinks that "the ability not to sin is inseparably implanted (*inseparabiliter insitam*)" in human nature such that "when human beings will to, they do the action; because they do not will it, they do not do it. After all, if they have the inseparable ability, they cannot have a weakness of will (*uoluntatis infirmitas*) or rather the presence of the will along with the lack of its accomplishment."[130] But Augustine thinks such an essentialist conception of will is incompatible with scripture, which clearly affirms that the phenomenon of weakness

---

[129] Augustine, *nat. et gr.* 67.81 (CSEL 60:295), citing *lib. arb.* 3.18.51 (CCL 29:305).
[130] *Nat. et gr.* 51.59 (CSEL 60:276).

of will exists: "If, then, that is the case, why do we have the words, *I can will the good, but I cannot do it* (Rom 7:18). For if the author of this book [Pelagius, the author of *Nature*] was speaking of that human nature which was in the beginning created innocent and healthy, his statement would be in some sense acceptable. And yet that nature should not have been said to have an inseparable ability, that is, one that cannot be lost."[131] According to Augustine, Pelagius's failure to recognize the radically contextual character of human willing results both in his dismissal of basic features of human experience and of basic affirmations of scripture. Pelagius's conception of will is overly idealized because it lacks theological differentiation.

Not only, according to Augustine, does Pelagius fail to take into account the difference between the created and fallen wills, he fails to take into account the difference between the will restored to goodness and the eschatological will. Augustine designates the period between baptism and the final perfection of the Church as a "time of prayer (*tempus orationis*)": "Between baptism in which all past stains and wrinkles are removed and the kingdom in which the Church will remain forever without stain and wrinkle, there is the present intervening time of prayer. In this present time the Church must say, *Forgive us our debts* (Mt 6:12)."[132] In this "intermediate time (*medio tempore*)" the church must continue to ask forgiveness for its sins and petition God's aid to do what is right.[133] Within this timeframe, human wills have been reoriented toward the good, but are still subject to weakness and constantly dependent upon God to sustain them in doing what is right. Yet statements of Pelagius such as the claim that "The Church on earth is without stain or wrinkle," discussed at the Synod of Diospolis, indicate his failure to appreciate the contrast between what lies within the power of the human will in this present time, and the perfection that, as yet, lies in its future.

As shown repeatedly in this chapter, and as is the case in *nat. et gr.* 51.59 and *gest. Pel.* 12.28, where Augustine contends with Pelagius with respect to the issue of theological periodization, Augustine constantly refers back to scripture as the basis for characterizing the will as he does. If the fallen will were the same as the created will, why would Paul complain of his will's

---

[131] *Nat. et gr.* 51.59 (CSEL 60:276).

[132] *Gest. Pel.* 12.28 (CSEL 42:81).

[133] *Gest. Pel.* 12.28 (CSEL 42:82): Augustine defines "this intermediate time" as the time "between the remission of sins that takes place in baptism and the permanent state without sin which will be found in the kingdom."

weakness? If the good will were the same as the eschatological will, why would Christ teach us to ask for forgiveness for sins? Augustine's conception of will takes on theological differentiation in order to account in a holistic way for the diversity of scriptural statements bearing upon human ability to do what is right and human need for God's assistance. His conception of will is a theologically differentiated conception of will because it is a scripturally based conception of will.

As Augustine considers the good will through the lens of his kaleidoscope, turning it this way and that, he combines and recombines different scriptural passages, forming new creative combinations, such as the link between heart and will, and the connection of will with the biblical image of root, that bring before his eyes new images to illustrate how the good will might work. Though Augustine does not develop these various images systematically, but rather in an ad hoc fashion as the occasion arises in his pastoral ministry and polemical enterprises, a larger pattern nonetheless emerges, uniting each of his descriptions of good human willing. To see this pattern, however, requires taking in a larger panorama than what is visible within the kaleidoscope of the good will. When this larger picture comes into view, one sees that the "time of prayer," when the root of the good will is planted and begins to grow, marks a vital turning point in the story of human willing, but still makes up but one chapter of a larger narrative. The need for God to assist the good will only makes sense in light of the story of its fall from original goodness, and its current incipient goodness finds fruition only in a final chapter, yet to come. Before considering that last chapter in the story of Augustine's conception of will, however, we turn to the theological underpinnings of the good will. Good human willing, as we have seen in chapter three, is only possible with God's help. But in what precisely does this help consist? As we will see in the following chapters, Augustine explains God's transformation of the human will in terms of the person and work of Christ (chapter six) and the Spirit (chapter seven), further developing his conception of will in a distinctively Christian theological framework.

6

Christ and the Will

Agony in the Garden

Introduction

This chapter continues the analysis, begun in chapter 3, of the views on human willing that Augustine developed over the course of the Pelagian controversy. As we have seen, in this period Augustine is preoccupied with the pressing existential issue of how human beings can once again will what is right given that the human will, good by created nature, has been corrupted in the fall. To what degree, given this state of affairs, is right human willing within our power (chapter 3)? To what extent does God play a role in bringing good willing about (chapter 4)? What are the chief characteristics of good human willing (chapter 5)? Augustine's answers to each of these questions help to fill in the larger picture of his conception of the preconditions and possibilities of the redeemed human will—the *uoluntas bona*, to use his words—a dimension of his theologically differentiated view of the human will that comes to the fore in the Pelagian controversy.

Yet to end our study with these queries would be to shortchange the specificity and theological depth of Augustine's thinking. For Augustine not only deals at length with human willing in relation to God but also has a great deal to say about human willing in relation to Jesus Christ. In fact, Augustine's Christology is a vital source for his thinking on the human will.[1] This chapter, then, turns to Augustine's articulation of the character

---

[1] In a recent essay on Augustine's conception of will, originally entitled "Agony in the Garden: Augustine's Myth of Will," James Wetzel shows via the accounts Augustine gives of his own conversion and of Adam's agony in the garden that Augustine's notion of will emerges in these complex stories about material desires. See James Wetzel, "Augustine on the Will," in *A Companion to Augustine*, ed. Mark Vessey, Blackwell Companions to the Ancient World (Oxford: Wiley-Blackwell, 2012), 339–352. I am in complete agreement with Wetzel's conclusion that Augustine's account of will is "best read as a story." However, more could be said about Christ's role in this story. Gethsemane, as well as Eden and Milan, is a key context for the gradual unfolding of the drama in relation to which Augustine's conception of will takes shape. On the importance of Christ for Augustine's account of human willing, see Brian E. Daley, "Making a Human Will Divine: Augustine and Maximus on Christ and Human Salvation," in *Orthodox Readings of Augustine*, ed. Aristotle Papanikolaou and George E. Demacopoulos (Crestwood, NY: St. Vladimir's Seminary Press, 2008), 101–126. Pierre-Marie

Augustine on the Will. Han-luen Kantzer Komline, Oxford University Press (2020). © Oxford University Press.
DOI: 10.1093/oso/9780190948801.001.0001

of the good will in terms of the personal identity and work of Christ. This Christological aspect of his conception of human willing blossoms in the Pelagian controversy, though the seeds of it may be found even earlier.

In this tripartite chapter, we will first observe that, for Augustine, Christ takes on a human will distinct from his divine will (part I). This basic point, a presupposition for many of Augustine's views about how Christ impacts human willing, is one that has been largely neglected in scholarship on the history of doctrine. Next, this chapter shows how Christ, having assumed a human will, models grace's effect upon the will in the incarnation, in his prioritization of justice over power, and in his struggle in Gethsemane (part II). Finally, we will begin to see how Christ, for the mature Augustine, transforms the will by grace (part III). This work of transformation, however, is incomplete without the work of the Spirit of Christ, and thus a full treatment of it must extend into the following chapter. Even on its own, however, this chapter will show not only how Augustine implements his conception of will in the context of his Christology but also how his understanding of the person and work of Christ informs his conception of the good will and thereby shapes his theologically differentiated conception of the will more generally.

Part I: Christ Takes on a Human Will

Augustine's conception of will deals in particulars and moves from there to larger implications. As we observed in chapter 2, the fallen will came about because of the fateful actions of a single individual. This person's misuse of will brought misery to the whole human race. The redemption of the human will follows a structurally similar trajectory, with the willing of one individual rippling outward to make salvation available to all humanity. "The Christian faith, then, truly consists in the influence of these two men."[2] Augustine contrasts their impact as follows: "By the one we were cast down to death; by the other we are set free for life. The former destroyed us in himself by doing his own will (*faciendo uoluntatem suam*), not the will of

---

Hombert has argued that "Christocentrism is the primary characteristic of the Augustinian theology of grace." See Pierre-Marie Hombert, *Gloria gratiae: Se glorifier en Dieu, principe et fin de la théologie augustinienne de la grâce* (Paris: Institut d'Études Augustiniennes, 1996), 255 and 504–508. The same is true of the Augustinian theology of the redeemed will.

[2] *Gr. et pecc. or.* 2.24.28.

him by whom he was created; the latter saved us in himself, not by doing his own will (*non faciendo uoluntatem suam*), but the will of him by whom he was sent."[3] Here again we see that Augustine declines to develop his conception of will as an abstract theoretical system. Rather, his conception of will takes shape in a concrete theological story where specific individuals play specific roles at specific times. This is a historical conception of the will, insofar as it is modulated according to various epochs depicted in the story of humanity as recounted in scripture.

Section A: The Voluntary Character of Christ's Death

In a number of places, Augustine emphasizes the importance of Christ's willing in this larger story of human redemption. In *Confessions*, he points out the voluntary character of Christ's death, by the righteousness of which he trampled down the death of sinners: "Because the wages of righteousness are life and peace (Rom. 6:23), being united with God by his righteousness he made void the death of justified sinners, a death which it was his will (*uoluit*) to share in common with them."[4] Christ was not forced to die for sinners against his will. Rather Christ "wanted to have death in common" with the impious.[5]

In other works, Augustine rules out explanations for Christ's death that belie its voluntary character. In *nat. et gr.* (415–416), he addresses the notion that Christ died because sin rendered his death necessary. Paraphrasing John 14:30–31, where Jesus states, "*Behold, the prince of this world will come, and he will find nothing in me (Jn. 14:30)*" and "*But in order that all may know . . . that I do the will of my Father, get up, let us leave this place (Jn 14.31),*" Augustine writes, "That is, I do not die by reason of the necessity of sin, but by reason of the will to obey (*oboedientiae uoluntate*)."[6] For Augustine, Christ's will to obey the Father, rather than any necessity

---

[3] *Gr. et pecc. or.* 2.24.28 (CSEL 42:187).

[4] *Conf.* 10.43.68 (CCL 27:192).

[5] This is a theme that also surfaces in Augustine's sermons. Commenting on John 10:17–18, for example, Augustine writes, "And he went off to meet his death, a voluntary death, one not of necessity but of free choice" (*s.* 152.9: *et perrexit ad passionem mortis, mortem uoluntariam, non necessitatis, sed arbitrii*; PL 38:824).

[6] *Nat. et gr.* 24.26 (CSEL 60:253).

sin imposes, explains Christ's death. Augustine reiterates this point with a triple rhetorical emphasis in *trin*: "The spirit of the mediator demonstrated how he did not come to the death of the flesh as any punishment for sin by precisely not forsaking it against his will (*inuitus*), but because he wanted to (*quia uoluit*) and at the time he wanted to (*quando uoluit*) and in the way he wanted to (*quomodo uoluit*)."[7] Christ's will to give himself for human beings not only was the reason that he died but also determined when he died and how he died. His death on the cross was entirely within his voluntary control.

Later in *trin.*, Augustine turns to the question of whether the fact that the Father handed the Son over without sparing him, as indicated in Romans 8:13, betrays an unwillingness in Christ to die on behalf of human beings. Citing Galatians 2:20, Augustine concludes that this cannot possibly be the case. The Father handed the Son over without sparing him, but the Son willed precisely to be handed over in this way. In Augustine's words, "Nor does the Father's not sparing him mean that the Son was handed over for us against his will (*inuitus*), because of him too it is said, Who loved (*dilexit*) me and handed himself over for me (Gal. 2:20)."[8] Christ was not handed over passively by the Father. He handed himself over willingly, out of obedience and love.

Augustine again stresses Christ's voluntary obedience in *c. Iul. imp.* (427–430). In *nupt. et conc.*, he had asserted that Christ did not experience carnal concupiscence. In response to Julian's accusation that such a position revives Apollinarianism, Augustine now makes a clarification: the reason Christ did not experience the desire for sin was not a lack of the appropriate human senses of soul but rather his will not to experience such desires: "For he did not lack the sense by which he would have felt it [*cupiditatem malam*], but he had will (*uoluntas*) by which he did not have it. . . . Christ could have felt this desire, if he had it, and he could have had it, if he had willed to. But heaven forbid that he should have willed to!"[9] Christ was not unable but unwilling to experience sinful desire. He possessed will and all senses proper to human beings; he just did not want to misuse them.

[7] *Trin.* 4.16 (CCL 50:181–182). Unless otherwise noted, this and subsequent translations of *trin.* come from Augustine, *The Trinity*, trans. Edmund Hill, WSA I/5 (Hyde Park, NY: New City Press, 1991).

[8] *Trin.* 13.15 (CCL 50A:402).

[9] *C. Iul. imp.* 4.48 (CSEL 85:2).

Precisely this obedient willingness to abstain from sin and to accept death, Augustine argues repeatedly, made possible our redemption. In *pecc. mer.* (411–412), he contends that Christ's willing obedience served as a remedy for human inability to control disobedience by means of will. Though, as a result of human weakness, disobedience "is not controlled by the will's command (*uoluntate praecipiente*),"[10] Christ provides the cure for this malady of the will because "in the likeness of sinful flesh he willingly (*uoluntate*) and obediently accepted that death which in sinful flesh is the just punishment of disobedience."[11] Christ's voluntary obedience, then, relieved us from our involuntary disobedience. Augustine makes a similar point more minimalistically in *trin.*: "It was surely right that the death of the sinner issuing from the stern necessity of condemnation should be undone by the death of the just man issuing from the voluntary freedom of mercy (*ex misericordiae uoluntate*)."[12] Here Augustine omits reference to obedience and disobedience, concentrating simply on how Christ's voluntary death, issuing from his "merciful will" (*ex misericordiae uoluntate*), undid ours, which results from "damning necessity" (*ex damnationis necessitate*).[13]

At times, too, Augustine speaks of the voluntary character of Christ's death as the reason for his triumph on the cross on our behalf, even without direct reference to the contrast between Christ's powerful willingness and our unwillingness:

> As he was able not to die if he did not wish to (*si nollet*), it follows since he did die that it was because he wished to (*quia uoluit*); and thus He made an example of the principalities and powers, confidently triumphing over them in himself (*semetipso*) (Col 2:15). By his death he offered for us the one truest possible sacrifice, and thereby purged, abolished, and destroyed whatever there was of guilt, for which the principalities and powers had a right to hold us bound to payment of the penalty, and by his resurrection he called to new life us who were predestined, justified us who were called, glorified us who were justified.[14]

---

[10] *Pecc. mer.* 2.29.48 (CSEL 60:119).
[11] *Pecc. mer.* 2.29.48 (CSEL 60:119).
[12] *Trin.* 4.4 (CCL 50:164).
[13] These translations are mine.
[14] *Trin.* 4.17 (CCL 50:183).

Here again Augustine insists that Christ's willingness to die for guilty humankind was vital to his victory on the cross.

Thus from beginning to end of his career as bishop, Augustine regarded
Christ's voluntary obedience in atoning for human sin as an essential factor
in the Christological cure for the human disease of sin. In the texts treated
in this section, Augustine only alludes to Christ's willing in general terms,
without specifying its character in light of Christ's identity as both human
and divine. But if Christ "willingly" accepts death precisely "in the likeness
of sinful flesh in order to destroy the body of sin,"[15] the human character
of his willing would seem to be important. Does Augustine, then, ever explicitly attribute a distinctly human will to Christ? The following section
addresses this question.

Section B: Augustine's Christology and
Anthropology Imply a Human Will in Christ

In combination, Augustine's Christology and human psychology dispose
him to affirm a distinctly human will in Christ.[16] On the Christological
side, he affirms that Christ, being fully human, has a complete human soul
and mind. As he recounts in the *conf.*, he came to this realization early on,
even before he had quite grasped the reality of the incarnation:

> I knew that his flesh was not united to your Word without a soul (*anima*)
> and a human mind (*mente*). Everyone knows this if he knows the immu-
> tability of your Word. I knew it to the best of my understanding, nor had
> I the least doubt on the subject. To move the body's limbs at will at one
> moment, not another (*nunc mouere membra corporis per uoluntatem,
> nunc non mouere*), to be affected by an emotion at one time, not another,
> to utter wise judgment by signs at one moment, at another to keep si-
> lence: these are characteristic marks of the soul and mind with their ca-
> pacity to change.[17]

---

[15] *Pecc. mer.* 2.29.48 (CSEL 60:118).
[16] George C. Berthold makes this observation in "Dyothelite Language in Augustine's Christology,"
Studia Patristica 70 (2013): 357–364.
[17] *Conf.* 7.19.25 (CCL 27:108–109).

Given that these types of actions and experiences are attributed to Christ in scripture, Augustine had reasoned, it follows that Christ possessed the human powers of soul and mind that give rise to them, including a "will" (*uoluntatem*), by which human beings move certain parts of their bodies at certain times and not at others. In Augustine's words, "So because the scriptures are true, I acknowledged the whole man to be in Christ, not only the body of a man or soul and body without a mind, but a fully human person."[18]

Augustine continues to affirm a human soul in Christ after he comes to a more robust understanding of the incarnation.[19] In *an. et or.* he observes that being human entails possessing both a soul and a body: "A human being is not the soul (*anima*) alone or the body alone, but both of them."[20] Here also, however, as in *conf.*, Augustine explains the conclusion that Christ has a human soul as following not merely from his humanity but also from how that humanity is described in scripture: "Many other passages from the holy scriptures show without any ambiguity that there is not only flesh, but also a human, that is, a rational soul (*animam . . . rationalem*), in Christ the man."[21] Augustine affirms Christ's possession of a rational human soul again in *trin.*: "If you go on to ask me how the incarnation itself was done, I say that the very Word of God was made flesh, that is, was made man, without however being turned or changed into that which he was made; that he was of course so made that you would have there not only the Word of God and the flesh of man but also the rational soul (*rationalis hominis anima*) of man as well."[22] In *corrept.*, Augustine speaks of a rational soul (*animam rationalem*) as included in the human nature God assumed in Christ: "God, therefore, assumed our nature, that is, the rational soul and the flesh of Christ the man, and he assumed it in a singularly marvelous and marvelously singular manner."[23] Finally, Augustine insists in *perseu.*, "Nor do we say that he is man in such a way that he lacks something which certainly pertains to human nature, whether the soul (*animam*) or the rational mind (*mentem rationalem*) in the soul (*ipsa anima*) or flesh."[24] Across

---

[18] *Conf.* 7.19.25 (CCL 27:109).
[19] See *haer.* 55 (CCL 46:325) for Augustine's observation that both the Arians and the Apollinarians denied Christ's human soul.
[20] *An. et or.* 2.14.20 (PL 44:507).
[21] *An. et or.* 1.18.31 (PL 44:493).
[22] *Trin.* 4.31 (CCL 50:203–204).
[23] *Corrept.* 11.30 (CSEL 92:254).
[24] *Persev.* 24.67 (PL 45:1034).

a number of texts, then, Augustine emphasizes Christ's possession of a complete human soul (*anima*) and mind (*mens*).

On the anthropological side, Augustine unequivocally teaches that willing constitutes one of the human psyche's three basic and inseparable activities. He develops this theme most famously and fully in *trin.*, but in *conf.* he already writes that people should first attempt to understand the triune structure of "being, knowing, and willing" within themselves before they attempt to understand God's nature as triune.[25] In *trin.*, Augustine makes clear that the activities of remembering, understanding, and loving "always" (*semper*) characterize the life of the mind: "We said toward the end of the tenth book, however, that the mind (*mentem*) always remembers (*meminisse*), always understands (*intellegere*) and loves itself (*amare*), even though it does not always think about itself as distinct from things that are not what it is."[26] Even if the mind is not always conscious of remembering, understanding, or loving itself, it is always engaged in these activities. Augustine makes this point negatively as well as positively. Never for a moment does the mind cease to perform these functions: "The truth of course is that from the moment it [the mind, *mens*] began to be it never stopped remembering (*meminisse*) itself, never stopped understanding (*intellegere*) itself, never stopped loving (*amare*) itself, as we have already shown."[27] And again: "The human mind (*mens humana*), then, is so constructed that it never does not remember (*meminerit*) itself, never does not understand (*intellegat*) itself, never does not love (*diligat*) itself."[28] For Augustine, the human mind not only has these three functions; it is unthinkable without them.[29]

Loving, in turn, inherently implicates will, since loving represents a specific kind of willing. This is a point we have already observed in other Augustinian works, but Augustine makes it explicitly in *trin.*, authorizing

---

[25] "The three aspects I mean are being, knowing, willing. For I am and I know and I will. Knowing and willing I am. I know that I am and I will. I will to be and to know. In these three, therefore, let him who is capable of so doing contemplate how inseparable in life they are: one life, one mind, and one essence, yet ultimately there is distinction, for they are inseparable, yet distinct" (*conf.* 13.11.12 [CCL 27:247]).

[26] *Trin.* 14.9 (CCL 50A:432).

[27] *Trin.* 14.13 (CCL 50A:441).

[28] *Trin.* 14.18 (CCL 50A:445).

[29] In at least one case, Augustine seems to go even further, suggesting that the mind is actually to be identified with these three functions: "So these three [mind, knowledge it knows itself with, love it loves itself with] are what is most eminent in man, but not man himself. And one person (*una persona*), that is any single [human being (*singulus quisque homo*)], has them in his mind, or as his mind" (*trin.* 15.11 [CCL 50A:474]).

an interpretation of other statements he makes as implying that will is one of the three basic activities of the human mind, which, for him, is at the core of the human person. Augustine writes, "But what does loving (*amare*) itself mean but wanting (*uelle*) to be available to itself in order to enjoy itself? And since it wants itself as much as it is, will (*uoluntas*) exactly matches mind here, and love is equal to lover."[30] For Augustine, to love is to the will as to remember is to memory and as to understand is to understanding. The will designates the activity of the mind by means of which one loves: "Again there is this enormous difference [between the image and the Trinity itself], that whether we talk about mind in man and its knowledge and love, or whether about memory, understanding, will, we remember nothing of the mind except through memory, and understand nothing except through understanding, and love (*amamus*) nothing except through will (*per uoluntatem*)."[31] Augustine's tendency to interchange "will" (*uoluntas*) and "love" (*dilectio*) when describing trinities of the human mind confirms that for him the mind's loving of itself is precisely a kind of willing.[32] Just as there can be no mind without loving, there can be no loving without willing.

Stepping back to consider Augustine's anti-Apollinarian Christological affirmation that Christ possesses a fully human psyche, complete with both a "rational human soul" (*rationalis hominis anima*) and a "mind" (*mens*) in conjunction with his anthropological affirmation that the human "mind" (*mens*) necessarily entails the activity of loving and, therewith, willing, we see that for Augustine the incarnation required Christ's human willing. If Christ possessed a human *mens,* he must, given the broader context of Augustine's thinking, have willed as a human being.[33] We can make this claim even stronger, however. In fact, Augustine did more than imply that Christ possessed a distinct human will. He explicitly affirmed this.

---

[30] *Trin.* 9.2 (CCL 50:295).

[31] *Trin.* 15.12 (CCL 50A:475).

[32] For example, Augustine writes, "So here we are then with these three, that is memory, understanding, love or will in that supreme and unchangeable being which God is, and they are not the Father and the Son and the Holy Spirit but the Father alone" (*trin.* 15.12 [CCL 50A:477]). In another example he discusses one of the trinities observable in human beings "with will or love as the third element joining these two [other two elements of this trinity] together as parent and offspring" (*trin.* 15.50: *ista duo scilicet uelut parentem ac prolem tertia uoluntate siue dilectione iungente*; CCL 50A:532).

[33] On this point see also Berthold, who asks, "If the Mediator had *omnia hominis*, everything this man has as man except sin, does this include a will?," answering in the affirmative ("Dyothelite Language in Augustine's Christology," 359).

Section C: The Development of Augustine's
Explicit Attributions of a Human Will to Christ

Though the idea that there were two distinct wills in Christ was articulated most prominently by Maximus the Confessor during the monothelite controversy of the seventh century, earlier Christian theologians had already affirmed this notion,[34] among them Augustine of Hippo.[35] Christ's distinct human will surfaces repeatedly in Augustine's expository writings, where he demonstrates what it means for a human being to be right with God, as well as in his polemical writings against the Homoian Arians of his day, where he underscores Christ's consubstantial unity with the Father. Augustine characterizes the human will of Christ differently in these contexts: by the time of his anti-Arian writings he has developed a new emphasis both on the obedience of Christ's human will and on the distinction between the condition of the human will that was in Christ and the condition of Adam's human will.[36] Thus, despite differences in terminology,

---

[34] Charles Joseph Hefele notes that the *Acta* of Lateran 649 cite the following fathers as ascribing a divine will to Christ's divine nature and a human will to Christ's human nature: Hippolytus, Ambrose, Augustine, Leo, Athanasius, Gregory of Nazianzus, Gregory of Nyssa, Cyril of Alexandria and John Chrysostom, along with his opponents Theophilus of Alexandria and Severian of Gabala. See Charles Joseph Hefele, *A History of the Councils of the Church, from the Original Documents*, trans. William R. Clark (Edinburgh: T. & T. Clark, 1896), vol. 5, 107. On Ambrose's interpretation of the Gethsemane passage, see Giorgio Maschio, "La tristesse de Jésus à Gethsémani: L'exégèse d'Ambroise de Milan," *Communio: Revue Catholique Internationale* 35 (2010): 91–102. Maschio argues that "the position of Ambrose allows him to attribute to the Son of God, having arrived at the hour of his death, a veritable suffering and a true sadness, a fully human will distinct from that of the Father" (100). While he compares Ambrose and Augustine on the issue of the agony of Jesus, specifically his sadness at the moment of his death, Maschio does not address the question of whether—and, if so, how—Augustine, with Ambrose, affirmed a fully human will in Christ distinct from that of the Father.

[35] Daley has argued that just as Augustine understood Christ to exemplify the workings of God's grace toward humanity, so Maximus understood Christ to exemplify the deification of humanity. Both thinkers saw that if Christ reveals the meaning of human salvation in this way, then he needs to have both a divine will and a human will. See Daley, "Making a Human Will Divine." In this section I investigate how the notion of two wills in Christ, which Daley observes in Augustine, may have developed over time in Augustine's thought, drawing on two of my earlier essays, Han-luen Kantzer Komline, "The Second Adam in Gethsemane: Augustine on the Human Will of Christ," *RÉAP* 58 (2012): 41–56 and "*Ut in illo uiueremus*': Augustine on the Two Wills of Christ," *Studia Patristica* 70 (2013): 347–355. On the theme of dyothelitism in Augustine, see also Berthold, "Dyothelite Language in Augustine's Christology," 357–364. For an argument that Maximus, as the author of the *acta* of the Lateran Council of 649 (Rudolf Riedinger's thesis), did in fact know Augustine's *c. Iul.*, see Johannes Börjesson, "Maximus the Confessor's Knowledge of Augustine: An Exploration of Evidence Derived from the Acta of the Lateran Council of 649," *Studia Patristica* 68 (2013): 325–336. All three *Studia Patristica* essays originated as papers delivered at the Oxford Patristics Conference of 2011.

[36] Michael Cameron has noted the importance of Augustine's eventual emphasis on Christ's obedient human will to accept death, although his account of the timing of the emergence of this emphasis, which he finds already in Augustine's *ex. Gal.* (394–395), differs from my own. See Michael Cameron, *Christ Meets Me Everywhere: Augustine's Early Figurative Exegesis* (New York: Oxford University Press, 2012), 152–154. One way of accounting for the difference may be that aspects of

Augustine's *mature* view of Christ's human will shows parallels with that of Maximus the Confessor,[37] and the development of Augustine's thinking on this issue shows some similarities to a development in the history of doctrine often assumed to have happened only over the course of centuries.

Augustine took for granted Christ's sharing in the *divine* will. Since he understood the single divine will to be identical to the divine substance, he necessarily affirmed also that Jesus Christ, God the Son, possessed the will of the Father as his own.[38] For Augustine it is clear that the "will of the Father and of the Son is one" even as there is but "one will, one power and one majesty" of the Trinity.[39] What is unusual about Augustine's affirmation of two wills in Christ is not his affirmation that Christ shared in the one divine will of the Godhead as God the Son but rather his explicit attribution to Christ of a human will.[40]

Augustine's thought drive toward, or even logically demand, the affirmation of an obedient human will to death in *ex. Gal.*, even if he does not explicitly adopt the corresponding terminology until much later. The crucial point is that, whereas we have seen in this book how Augustine's interpretation of scripture shapes his account of will, Cameron shows that the reverse is also the case. The logic of Augustine's understanding of Christ's human volition and action also shaped his Old Testament hermeneutics.

[37] See George C. Berthold, "Did Maximus the Confessor Know Augustine?," *Studia Patristica* 17, part I (1982): 14–17 and Daley, "Making a Human Will Divine."

[38] See *conf.* 12.15.18, where Augustine affirms that the divine will belongs to God's single unvarying *substantia*, and *c. s. Ar.* 7.6, where he affirms that the Father and the Son share one and the same will with respect to the divinity of the Son. Dihle observes that for Augustine "God's will is unchanging and unchangeable and, therefore, identical with His substance (*conf.* 11.10.2 [*sic; recte* 11.10.12], *civ. D.* 22.2 . . .). . . . The will of God is the only structuring and preserving power in the order of being (*civ. D.* 12.23, *c. Faust.* 22.30, *ep.* 140.4, etc.)." See Albrecht Dihle, *The Theory of Will in Classical Antiquity* (Berkeley: University of California Press, 1982), 234.

[39] *Io. eu. tr.* 111.1 (CCL 36:628): *unam uero esse patris et filii uoluntatem, quorum etiam spiritus unus est, quo adiuncto cognoscimus trinitatem, etsi intellegere nondum permittit infirmitas, credit pietas. Io. eu. tr.* 22.15 (CCL 36:232): *faciamus ergo uoluntatem patris, uoluntatem filii, uoluntatem spiritus sancti; quia trinitatis huius una uoluntas, una potestas, una maiestas est.* My translations. See also *trin.* 2.9 (CCL 50:90): "Father and Son have but one will and are indivisible in their working" (*una uoluntas est patris et filii et inseparabilis operatio*).

[40] As Dihle observes, the fourth-century Fathers were forced to refine their understanding of the will of God in the crucible of Christological debate. Origen "had taught . . . that the Son proceeded from the will of the Father," a teaching which had the implication, of which Arius approved, of separating the Son from the Father "like any other creature, by the hypostasis of the divine will" (116). Athanasius countered by proposing that the Son *was* the will of the Father. To preserve the idea that the Father generated the Son freely, rather than by necessity, Gregory of Nazianzus proposed a distinction between God's non-hypostatic will in generating the Son, beyond human understanding because this will is proper to God's substance, and God's hypostatic will as the cause of creation, which is available to human knowing. For Marius Victorinus, "Christ is the *voluntas et potentia Dei*," and as this one divine will he unites the Trinity (118). Thus, though there was some disagreement among Athanasius, the Nazianzen, and Marius Victorinus about how to conceive of the one will of God, they agreed on the assumption that Christ shared in the one will proper to the substance of the Godhead. See Dihle, *The Theory of Will in Classical Antiquity*, 116–118.

Section D: Augustine's Portrait of Christ's Human Will from 395 to 414 in Sermons and Expository Works

Augustine speaks of Christ's human will in a number of his sermons and biblical expositions, whose suggested dates range from his ministry as a priest to the year 414.[41] Most frequently he designates Christ's human will as his *uoluntas humana*, though he also refers to it as the *hominis uoluntas* and *uoluntas filii hominis*.[42] Allusions to Christ's human will surface in Augustine's expositions of the Psalms when he brings up Christ's agony in the garden in order to illustrate what the Psalmist means by the notion of being "right" or "straight" (*rectus*) before God. In his comments on Psalm 100, he describes this kind of rectitude in a passive or negative sense, as having to do with avoiding or correcting a problematic response to God's will. The person who has a right heart is one who does not herself not want all that God wants: "omnia quae uult deus, non ipse non uult." The literal emphasis here is not on achieving something positively or actively but rather on subjecting oneself to the will of God and not resisting this divine will.[43] Jesus Christ's humble submission to God's will as reflected in his prayer in the garden of Gethsemane serves as the preeminent model of what it means to be aligned with God's will in this way.

Augustine's reading in his exposition of Psalm 100 is representative of the tendency in his earlier interpretation of the Gethsemane prayer to associate shrinking from death with Christ's human will. He identifies Jesus' prayer that his passion be averted, "Father, if it is possible, let this cup pass from me," as an instance in which his human will is expressed. The ultimate

---

[41] Among the texts referring to Christ's human will that I have been able to locate, the one with the earliest suggested date is Augustine's exposition of Psalm 100. Augustine's reference to the book of *Wisdom* as *Sapientia Salomonis* in this exposition suggests that it was composed sometime before he penned *On Christian Doctrine* in 396. Cf. *On Christian Doctrine* 2.8, where Augustine calls into question Solomon's authorship of the book of *Wisdom*. For a detailed treatment of Augustine's evolving position on the authorship of the book of *Wisdom* and modes of citing it, see Anne-Marie La Bonnardière, *Le livre de la Sagesse* (Paris: Études Augustiniennes, 1970), 35–57. La Bonnardière concludes that *Enarrationes in Psalmos* 100 and 63, the only two *Enarrationes* that cite the book of *Wisdom* as *Sapientia Salomonis*, belong to the time of Augustine's priesthood (42). If her theory is correct, Augustine's affirmation of a distinct human will in Christ antedates *On Christian Doctrine* and, along with his exposition of Psalm 100, stems from the period of his ministry as a priest.

[42] See *en. Ps.* 100.6, *en. Ps.* 32.2.1–2, *en. Ps.* 31.2.26, and *serm.* 296.8 for references to Christ's human will as his *uoluntas humana*; see *en Ps.* 32.2.1–2 and *en. Ps.* 93.9 for designations of it as the *hominis uoluntas*. *Io. eu. tr.* 19.19 clearly distinguishes the *uoluntas filii hominis* from the divine will, since the *uoluntas filii hominis* is described as a will that resists God.

[43] *En. Ps.* 100.6 (CCL 39:1411).

resolution of Christ's prayer, however, "Yet not what I will, but what you will, Father," shows his right heart.[44] Likewise Augustine observes in his exposition of Psalm 31 that whereas Christ's human will shows through when he prays that, if possible, the cup pass him by, Christ's statement "not what I will" reveals that his heart is right.[45] A similar pattern recurs in *Sermon* 296, probably from the year 413. Augustine quotes the first half of Christ's prayer from Matthew 26:39, "Father, if it is possible, let this cup pass from me," and then interjects, "[See] how he shows his human will," before observing Christ's obedience and quoting the remainder of the prayer: "however, not what I will, but what you will, Father."[46] Yet another example of Augustine's association of the first half of Jesus' Gethsemane prayer with his human will is found in his exposition of Psalm 32. There Augustine writes, "He showed a certain private human will, in which will of his he also represented ours, since he is our head, and, as you know, we assuredly belong to him as members. '*Father*,' he said, '*if it is possible, let this cup pass from me.*' This was his human will, wanting something personal and, so to speak, private."[47] Here again Augustine focuses on the first half of Christ's prayer in Gethsemane as an expression of his human will. In each of these texts, Augustine attributes to Christ's human will his request that the cup pass, while he attributes to Christ's right "heart" (*cor*) or to Christ more generally his obedient submission to the will of the Father.

In some cases Augustine even ventures so far as to associate the human will of Christ with human wills in tension with God's will. Continuing in his exposition of Psalm 32, for example, Augustine writes, "'See yourself in me,' he [Christ] says, 'because you are able to want something personal so that you want something other than what God wants.'"[48] In this passage, Augustine depicts the human will of Christ as reflecting the more general human tendency to will otherwise than God does. While he also points out Christ's positive example of obedience, he does not refer this obedience directly to the human will of Christ. As he draws attention to Christ's human will in his comments on Psalm 32, Augustine is mainly concerned to show how it takes on the weakness of humanity at large, to underline the solidarity of Christ's human will with ours.

---

[44] *En. Ps.* 100.6.
[45] *En. Ps.* 31.2.26.
[46] *Serm.* 296.8.
[47] *En. Ps.* 32.2.2.
[48] *En. Ps.* 32.2.2.

Augustine continues to depict Christ as capable of wanting something other than what the Father wanted even in the very late work *Contra Maximinum* (*c. Max.*): "Nonetheless, in saying, *Not as I want*, he showed that he wanted something other than the Father wanted [*aliud se ostendit uoluisse quam pater*], something that he could only do with his human heart, when he changed our weakness, not into his divine, but into his human love."[49] As I will argue, however, though in *c. Max.* Augustine still associates Christ's human will with the wills of human persons that are in tension with God's will, in *Contra sermonem Arrianorum* (*c. s. Ar.*) and in *c. Max.* the distinction between Christ's human will and the human will of Adam takes on a new importance.

In his exposition of Psalm 93, probably written during the Pelagian controversy, one finds an even more dramatic association of the human will of Christ with human wills that are in tension with God's will. Augustine states that in Gethsemane Christ prefigures in himself those who would come after him in the church who "wanted to do their own will, but afterwards would follow the will of God." He further observes that "if [Christ] had persisted in that will (*ipsa uoluntate*), he would have seemed to show a crooked heart."[50] Augustine does not distinguish clearly here between "Christ's human will" as a constitutive activity of his human mind (*mens*) and "Christ's human will" as a particular wish, or external circumstantial option, that was other than the will of the Father. By *ipsa uoluntate*, he seems to mean the latter. Only a few lines after speaking of the perversity of heart to which Christ's "human will" (*hominis uoluntas*) would have led him had he insisted on it, Augustine uses the phrase *uoluntas humana* as shorthand for sinful desires that oppose God's will: "If a human wish (*uoluntas humana*) should creep up on you—'Oh if only God would kill this enemy of mine, so that he would not persecute me! Oh if only it were possible that I not suffer such things from him!'—now if you persist [in this kind of thinking], and this pleases you, and you see that God does not want this, you are crooked in heart."[51] In this context of pastoral concerns about desires opposed to the will of God, Augustine characterizes Christ's *uoluntas humana* as something he had to resist as he moved forward on the path to the cross.

[49] *C. Max.* 2.20.2 (CCL 87A:621). Roland Teske, trans., *Arianism and Other Heresies*, WSA I/18 (Hyde Park, NY: New City Press, 1995), 301. Subsequent translations in English of Augustine's anti-Arian writings come from this work unless otherwise indicated.
[50] *En. Ps.* 93.19 (CCL 39:1319).
[51] *En. Ps.* 93.19 (CCL 39:1319).

Augustine does take the unity of the two wills of Christ as his starting point for explicating Psalm 93. He opens the discussion of Christ's example by asking, "How did our Lord marry two wills so that they became one in the humanity he bore?"[52] Yet his exposition of Matthew 26:39 in his comments on Psalm 93 never explicitly rules out the possibility that this unity is based on Christ's triumph over his human will rather than on the proper alignment of his human will. Even in treating the human will of Christ, Augustine highlights the tendency of the human will to attempt to compete with the divine will; he does not assert that Christ demonstrated a human will perfectly in sync with the divine will.

Given the perversity of the human will's inclinations, which Augustine underscores in his comments on Psalm 93, a more radical solution than Christ's example alone is required to rectify the will. The ability of the faithful to imitate Christ's surrender of his human will is contingent upon Christ's compassionate and liberating work: "But if he has had compassion on you and is liberating you in himself, imitate what follows, saying, 'yet, not what I will, but what you will, Father.'"[53] The frailty of even Christ's own human will dramatically illustrates the weakness of our human will, underlining its need for Christ's assistance to be made right before God.

In the texts examined thus far, Augustine introduces the human will of Christ in order to set forth what it means to be right before God. Yet in the end, the human will of Christ seems to play a more important role in Augustine's illustration of the tendency of the human heart to stray *away* from God's will, a tendency that must be resisted to be right before God, than in his positive explanation of how to *obey* God's will.[54] The human will of Christ figures prominently in Augustine's sermons when he is describing Jesus' prayer in Gethsemane that the cup might pass from him. When Augustine points to Christ's demonstration of rectitude before God, however, the human will of Christ recedes from view.

---

[52] Here I quote the English translation of Augustine, *Expositions of the Psalms*, trans. Maria Boulding, WSA III/18 (Hyde Park, NY: New City Press, 2000); *En. Ps.* 93.19.

[53] *En. Ps.* 93.19.

[54] In *trin* 1.22, Augustine also implies a human will in Christ in applying John 6:38 to Christ as a human being: "In the form of God, *he and the Father are one* (Jn 10:30); in the form of a servant, he *did not come to do his own will, but the will of him who sent him* (Jn 6:38)." Though the precise date of this passage, stemming from sometime before 416, is difficult to pinpoint, it fits the pattern of the other texts here considered in the period leading up to 414 in which Augustine shies away from attributing obedience directly to Christ's human will. See *trin.* 1.22 (CCL 50:61): *secundum formam dei ipse et pater unum sunt; secundum formam serui non uenit facere uoluntatem suam sed uoluntatem eius qui misit [Io 4,34; Io 6,38] eum.*

Section E: Augustine's Portrait of Christ's Human Will in *Contra sermonem Arrianorum* and *Contra Maximinum*

The portrait of Christ's human will that emerges in Augustine's *c. s. Ar.*, probably written in 419, about five years after he composed his comments on Psalm 93, shows a different set of emphases. In this treatise Augustine responds to an "Arian Sermon" comprising a list of theses representing a Homoian Arianism, a theology whose proponents preferred to speak of a likeness between the Father and the Son rather than a shared substance (*ousia*), even while affirming that the Son was a product of the Father's will different from the creation the Father produced from nothing.[55] As a part of his lengthy reply to the litany of texts where Jesus submits to the will of the Father cited in the *Sermo Arrianorum*, Augustine considers John 6:38: "I came down from heaven, not to do my will, but to do the will of him who sent me." Augustine's main concern is to show that the Son's obedience to the Father does not imply that the divine nature of the Son is different from the nature of God the Father. Yet in considering what implications this verse may have for understanding Jesus' relation to the Father, Augustine's strategy is not to showcase Christ's divine nature while sweeping his human nature under the carpet. Nor does he vindicate the identity of Christ's substance with that of the Father by arguing that Christ's divine nature overrides or suppresses his human nature. Instead Augustine makes a more nuanced argument, using Paul's discussion of the first and second Adam in Romans 5 as a hermeneutical lens for considering this difficult text in John.

Rather than shifting the focus away from the human will of Christ, Augustine uses Romans 5 to establish a distinction between the condition of the human will that was in Christ and the condition of the human will that was in Adam. Adam brought sin into the world by choosing his own will, a will opposed to God. Christ's statement in John 6:38 shows that Christ reversed the pattern Adam had set. Whereas Adam's human will was opposed to God's, Augustine insists, "Christ did not have such a will."[56]

---

[55] For a concise definition of Homoian Ariansim, see Lewis Ayres, *Nicaea and Its Legacy: An Approach to Fourth-Century Trinitarian Theology* (New York: Oxford University Press, 2004), 138–139. For a brief summary of proposed interpretations of the genre and authorship of the *Sermo Arrianorum* as well as an introduction to Augustine's reply, see Hermann-Josef Sieben, ed., *Antiarianische Schriften*, vol. 48, Augustinus Opera-Werke (Munich: Ferdinand Schöningh, 2008), 18–25.

[56] *C. s. Ar.* 7.6.

Rather, Augustine implies, Christ had a human will in perfect accord with God's, since, as is clear from Romans 5:19, "in him, *insofar as he is man*, we are taught the obedience which is just the opposite of the disobedience of the first man."[57] Christ could achieve this obedience only by grace—because his human nature belonged to him as a mediator who was not only man, but God and man.[58] Thus in Augustine's exegesis of John 6:38, the possibility of Christ overcoming the natural human temptation to oppose God autonomously (his capacity to say "not my will") presupposes his divine nature. In the final analysis, Augustine's explanation of how Jesus was able to resist doing his "own will" but nonetheless attain perfect human obedience functions to corroborate Augustine's case that Jesus was *non tantum homo, verum etiam deus*. The obedience of Christ in his humanity becomes, in Augustine's argument, not a reason to object to Christ's full divinity but rather a reason to acknowledge it.

A number of differences arise between Augustine's characterization of the humanity of Christ in *c. s. Ar.* and his characterization of it in earlier texts. First, Augustine's readings of Matthew 26:39 in his expositions of Psalms 31, 32, 93, and 100 and Sermon 296 all explicitly identify Christ's wish to let the cup pass as an expression of his human will. None of these passages attributes his prayer "not what I wish, but what you wish" to his human will. In those earlier writings, Augustine connects Christ's request that the passion be averted, not his obedience to the divine will, with the human will of Christ. In *c. s. Ar.*, however, Augustine writes of John 6:38, "The words, *I came down from heaven*, refer to the excellence of God, but the next words, *not to do my will*, refer to the obedience of the man."[59] Augustine likewise affirms that Christ submits to the will of the Father in his humanity in a series of statements on Christ's "twin substances" that follows soon after in the work:

> Thus we have the same Christ, a twin-substanced giant, in the one obedient, in the other equal to God, in the one the Son of Man, in the other Son of God. In the one he says, *The Father is greater than I* (John 14:28); in the other he says, *The Father and I are one* (John 10:30). In the one he does not do his own will, but the will of the one who sent him; in the other, he

---

[57] *C. s. Ar.* 7.6.
[58] *C. s. Ar.* 7.6 (CCL 87A:194).
[59] *C. s. Ar.* 7.6.

says, *As the Father raises the dead and gives them life, so the Son also gives life to those he wants* (John 5:21).[60]

In *c. s. Ar.*, then, Augustine is concerned to underscore the obedience of Christ in his human nature, which, we have learned from considering Augustine's earlier expository works, was, for Augustine, complete with a human will.

Second, whereas in the sermons and expositions we have discussed on rectitude before God, composed in the period leading up to 414, Augustine associated Christ's human will with the wills of human persons in tension with God's will, in *c. s. Ar.* he dissociates Christ from human wills that are in tension with God's will. Augustine writes, "Adam had such a will [a will opposed to God's] and, as a result, we died in him. Christ did not have such a will so that we might have life in him."[61]

Finally, whereas in earlier texts the human will of Christ receded from view when obedience was in question, here Augustine goes out of his way to underline Christ's obedience in his human nature. In *c. s. Ar.* "the obedience of the *man* [Jesus Christ] on account of Adam who did his own will" is of paramount importance.[62] Christ does not bring life by being less human than was Adam. Rather, we can have life in Christ because Christ did not have a sinful will like Adam, yet still achieved obedience precisely as a human being with a human will.

In the lengthy anti-Arian work *c. Max.*,[63] which he wrote toward the end of his career, Augustine follows further the trajectory along which he had been moving in *c. s. Ar.* He continues to insist upon Christ's human obedience but makes more explicit the obedience of Christ's human *will* in

---

[60] *C. s. Ar.* 8.6. The image of a "twin-substanced giant" is featured in Ambrose's Christmas hymn *Veni, redemptor gentium* and serves as an initial cue for a series of links between Augustine's terminology and argument in *c. s. Ar.* and that of Ambrose in *De fide* and *De incarnationis dominicae sacramento*. See Brian Daley, "The Giant's Twin Substances: Ambrose and the Christology of Augustine's *Contra Sermonem Arianorum*," in *Augustine: Presbyter Factus Sum*, ed. J. T. Lienhard et al. (New York: Peter Lang, 1993): 477–495. As Daley observes on 484–486, "The point of [Augustine's] argument [in *c. s. Ar.*], and the scriptural passages on which he bases it, also resemble closely the argument of Ambrose for the completeness and mutual harmony of two wills in Christ, and for the paradoxical unity of the divine and the human in Christ's single person, which Ambrose developed in *De Fide* II,v,41–ix,73."

[61] *C. s. Ar.* 7.6.

[62] *C. s. Ar.* 7.6.

[63] For an introduction to this work, see Sieben, *Antiarianische Schriften*, 48: 28–31. See also the critical edition and notes by P.-M. Hombert, *Sancti Aurelii Augustini Contra Arrianos Opera*, CCL, 87A (Turnhout: Brepols, 2009), 491–692.

particular, which was implied though not affirmed in so many words in *c. s. Ar.* Augustine refutes an argument hinging on the line "But not as I want, but as you want," from Mark's version of Jesus' prayer in Gethsemane (Mark 14:36). He writes to his opponent, "Why does it help you to add your words and say, 'He showed that his will was truly subject to his Father,' as if we denied that the human will ought to be subject to the will of God? One who looks a bit attentively at this passage of the holy gospel quickly sees that the Lord said this in his human nature."[64] Augustine makes it clear that he does not disagree with the idea that Christ's human will was subject to God's will. Like Maximinus, Augustine affirms this. What differentiates his position from that of Maximinus is not that Maximinus affirms Christ's human will while Augustine does not, but rather that Augustine affirms Christ's divine will in a way that Maximinus does not.[65] In his earlier writings, before his controversy with the Arians, Augustine had emphasized only the direct connection between Christ's shrinking from death and Christ's human will. Here he also connects the fiat with Christ's human will.[66]

Augustine also repeats in *c. Max.* the comparison with Adam found in *c. s. Ar.* He distinguishes the quality of Christ's perfectly obedient will from that of other human wills as represented in Adam[67] even while affirming the unity of Christ's human will with Adam's human will in kind: "The second Adam, who took away the sin of the world, distinguished himself in this way from the first Adam, through whom sin came into the world, because the second Adam did not do his own will, but the will of him who sent him, while the first Adam did his own will, not the will of him who created him."[68] For Augustine, Christ the second Adam has a human will, but he is not a human being like us in every way without exception. Unlike the first Adam, Christ the second Adam makes a new beginning for humanity by obediently subjecting his human will to God's will.

[64] *C. Max.* 2.20.2.

[65] Augustine's characterization of Maximinus's view is that although Father, Son, and Holy Spirit agree in an "incomparable" way in will and charity, they do not share one and the same divine will as they do for Augustine on account of a unity of nature and substance. See *c. Max.* 2.20.1.

[66] Augustine also contends that another verse dealing with Christ's obedient submission to the will of the Father, John 6:38, can be understood as referring to Christ as man. See *c. Max.* 2.20.3.

[67] *C. s. Ar.* 7.6.

[68] *C. Max.* 2.20.3. Augustine does state in *Contra Maximinum* that in saying "Not as I want, [Christ] showed that he wanted something other than the Father wanted [*aliud se ostendit uoluisse quam pater*], something that he could only do with his human heart" (2.20.2). This suggestion that Christ wanted something other than what God wanted, however, is now coupled with an emphasis on the ultimate obedience of Christ's human will and an insistence on its distinction from that of Adam.

As this survey has shown, new developments surface late in Augustine's career when he discusses Christ's will in the context of the Arian debates. In *c. s. Ar.* and *c. Max.*, Augustine presents a much more harmonious vision of the relation between the human and divine wills of Christ, one that clearly attributes obedience to Christ's human will and draws a distinction between the human will of Christ and the human will that has become subject to sin in Adam.

Section F: Augustine's Portrait of the Human Will of Christ in Larger Perspective

In his book *The Byzantine Christ*, Demetrios Bathrellos contends that two basic types of interpretations of Christ's Gethsemane prayer had been articulated before the monothelite controversy of the seventh century, both of which emerged in the context of fourth-century anti-Arian polemics. The first type is exemplified in the writings of Gregory of Nazianzus, who, according to Bathrellos, believed that the "opposition between the will of the Father and the will of the Son merely brings to expression the opposition of our will to the will of God. It is not Christ who has a (*human*) will that opposes the will of the Father, but us." For Gregory, writes Bathrellos, this entails that Christ's will not to die does not belong "essentially to his humanity."[69] Bathrellos finds an alternative view in Athanasius, Marcellus of Ancyra, and Gregory of Nyssa, who, he argues, attribute the "shrinking in the face of the passion to the flesh, [but] the fiat to the Logos."[70] Though Marcellus of Ancyra and Gregory of Nyssa acknowledge two wills in Christ, a human will and a divine will, they seem to oppose them to one another, Bathrellos writes, such that Christ's human will does not become obedient to the divine will. Noting the potentially "satisfactory" interpretations of the prayer in Cyril of Alexandria and John Chrysostom,[71] Bathrellos nonetheless concludes that "Maximus was the first to point out in an unambiguous way that it is the Logos *as man* who addressed the Father in Gethsemane . . . by arguing that both the desire to avoid death and the

---

[69] Demetrios Bathrellos, *The Byzantine Christ: Person, Nature, and Will in the Christology of Saint Maximus the Confessor*, Oxford Early Christian Studies (New York: Oxford University Press, 2004), 141.

[70] Bathrellos, *The Byzantine Christ*, 142.

[71] Bathrellos, *The Byzantine Christ*, 145.

submission to the divine will of the Father have to do with the humanity of Christ and his human will."[72]

Augustine does not fit neatly into the typology Bathrellos provides. Indeed he does not figure into it at all. Yet if one were to try to incorporate Augustine's view into Bathrellos's schema retrospectively, an interesting dilemma would result. Augustine's treatment of the human will of Christ in his earlier sermons and expositions aligns with the interpretation of the Gethsemane prayer espoused by Athanasius, Marcellus, and Gregory of Nyssa. For many years Augustine, like these figures, tended to identify Christ's shrinking from death in the face of the passion, though not the fiat, as a manifestation of his human will. Augustine recognized two wills in Christ, as did Marcellus and Gregory, very early on in his career. Like these two predecessors, he saw these wills as in tension, if not opposed to one another. At this stage, Augustine did not tend to attribute obedience to the human will of Christ.

The late Augustine's anti-Arian writings, however, show him championing a different view of Christ's human will. Ironically it is in his own struggles with Homoian Arianism that Augustine shows he has moved clearly beyond the solutions his forebears had reached in their struggles with the Arianism of their own day. As Maximus the Confessor would two centuries later, Augustine had come to hear the distinctly human voice of Christ not only in the prayer that the passion be avoided but also in Christ's rejection of a course of action opposed to God's will. In a further anticipation of Maximus, Augustine also came to observe an important distinction in quality between Christ's perfectly obedient human will and Adam's human will subsequent to the fall, which was subject to sin.

Augustine's earlier emphasis on the weakness of even Christ's own human will and his later insistence that Christ was obedient precisely in his human will would have dovetailed nicely with Augustine's polemical aims in the Pelagian and Arian controversies, respectively, as he strove first to defend the need for God's grace to reorient the human will and then also to explain why Christ's obedience did not entail a difference in being between the Son and the Father. But it is clear that Augustine's affirmation of Christ's human will was not driven solely by his polemical agenda. Well before the Pelagian

---

[72] Bathrellos, *The Byzantine Christ*, 147.

controversy, Augustine affirmed two distinct wills in Christ, tending to associate Christ's shrinking from death with his human will.

Augustine's treatment of Christ's human will does, however, highlight how he built on insights gained in the Pelagian controversy as he took on the Homoian Arians later in his life. Holding together both Christ's human obedience and the inclination of the human will, since Adam's fall, to resist God's will, ultimately demanded a clear distinction between Christ's human will and Adam's. This distinction, in turn, helped to corroborate Augustine's case against the Homoian Arians with whom he contended. With this distinction in place, Augustine could explain Christ's submission to the Father's will as taking place in his humanity rather than attributing it to a divinity somehow subordinate to that of the Father. How could a perfectly obedient human will, distinct from Adam's fallen will, be possible? In answering this question, Augustine put his Homoian Arian opponents on the defensive. Given the vitiated state of the human will since Adam, the obedience of Christ's human will pointed not only to Christ's humanity but also to the unity of that humanity in one person with Christ's divine nature, a unity that enabled Christ to achieve perfect human obedience by a "marvelous and singular grace."[73] Thus precisely Augustine's mature view of the *humanity* of Christ's will enabled him to make a case for Christ's full *divinity* against his Homoian Arian opponents.

Augustine's eventual affirmation of Christ's graced obedience in his human will is significant, however, beyond the light it sheds on Christ's unique identity as both *deus et homo*. Since Augustine's mature understanding of grace is modeled on his understanding of the grace of Christ, the free graced obedience of Christ's human will also sheds light on how Augustine understands grace to impact the human will of each Christian. Augustine came to see, in Gethsemane, not only the obedience of Christ as the Son of God but also his obedience as the Second Adam, the Light who blazes a new path for those whose human will he shares. We turn next to these aspects of Christ's work, as one who not only takes on but also models and transforms human willing.

---

[73] *C. s. Ar.* 7.6: "But so that the mediator of God and man, the man Jesus Christ, would not do his own will, which is opposed to God, he was not only man, but God and man. And through this marvelous and singular grace human nature could exist in him without any sin."

Part II: Christ Models Grace's Effect on the Human Will

Augustine points to Christ as a model of good human willing in at least three respects. First, Christ's incarnation illustrates the precedence of grace over any merit of the human will. The incarnation serves as the paradigmatic instance of the principle that good willing is contingent upon grace, rather than the reverse. Second, Christ models the prioritization of justice over power that is characteristic of good willing in this life. Though Christ's will was not susceptible to sin, he allowed the fulfillment of his right willing in power to be deferred. He thus shared, albeit briefly, in the humbling experience of the saints in this life, where the good that they will outstrips its own realization, rendering perfect happiness elusive. Finally, Christ's struggle in Gethsemane provides the blueprint for Augustine's depiction of his own struggle of will in a garden in Milan. In each of these ways, Augustine draws on the example of Christ to shed light on the character of good human willing. Yet, as we will see, these examples depreciate themselves. Taken alone, they themselves suggest, they remain insufficient for bringing about the kind of dramatic events they depict. Christ models the need for a radical divine act, for God's supernatural intervention to create and perfect a good human will where only nonexistence, weakness, and agonized indecision anticipated it.

Section A: The Incarnation Models Grace's Independence of the Will's Preceding Merits

As Brian Daley has observed, the mature Augustine came to see Christ, the mediator between God and humanity, "as the personal representation, and the prime instance, of God's victorious and wholly unmerited grace."[74] Augustine sounds this theme in a number of later texts. In *Enchiridion ad Laurentium de fide spe et caritate* (*ench.*; 421–422) he describes the incarnation as the ultimate example of grace, in which the true character of grace is

---

[74] Brian Daley, "Christology," in *Augustine through the Ages*, ed. Allan D. Fitzgerald (Grand Rapids, MI: Eerdmans, 1999), 168. See also Brian Daley, "A Humble Mediator: The Distinctive Elements in Saint Augustine's Christology," *Word and Spirit* 9 (1987): 108–110, where he discusses Augustine's mature teaching on Christ the savior as the paradigm of grace.

shown "abundantly and clearly."[75] He explicitly connects this grace of Christ
with the grace at work in the lives of Christians: "Here the great grace that
is of God alone is shown manifestly (*euidenter*) to those considering it faith-
fully and soberly, so that they might understand that human beings are justified from sins through the same grace itself through which it was that the
man Christ was not able to have any sin."[76] The grace at work in making sin
impossible for the Son of God incarnate is not, then, for Augustine, great in
such a way as to render comparisons to the grace that believers experience
impossible. Rather, the greatness of this grace is shown forth "evidently"
(*evidenter*) so that they might recognize this grace as the very same grace by
which they themselves are justified and thereby better appreciate the profundity of their salvation.

In clarifying the exemplary character of incarnation, Augustine points
out that the humanity of Christ had no existence at all before it was joined
to the Word. A priori, then, it would have been inconceivable for it to do
anything to merit the grace by which it was joined to God. As Augustine
explains, "Without any preceding merits of his own righteousness, Christ
was the Son of God from the first moment he began to be a man in such a
way that he and the Word, which is without beginning, was one person."[77]
In light of this fact, "how could he [the man Christ . . . be joined to God
by any previous merits of his own], since from the very moment he began
to be man he was also God, which is why it said The Word became flesh
(Jn 1:14)"?[78] Just this absence of any preexisting merits explaining the unification of Christ's humanity with his divinity, Augustine argues, reflects
the entirely unmerited character of the grace that the saints have received: "Another point about the incarnation is that in the man Christ it
advertises the grace of God toward us without any previous deserts on our
part, as not even he won the privilege of being joined to the true God in such
a unity that with him he would be one person, Son of God, by any previous

[75] *Ench.* 11:36. Another representative text where Augustine affirms that Christ is the paradigm of
grace is *praed. sanct.* 15.30, in which he refers to Christ as the most brilliant Light of predestination
and grace.
[76] *Ench.* 11:36 (CCL 46:70).
[77] *Corrept.* 11.30 (CSEL 92:254).
[78] *Trin.* 13.22 (CCL 50A:412). Later in *trin.* Augustine makes a similar point, observing that Christ
received the Spirit with no preceding merits: "We must realize that he was anointed with this mystical
and invisible anointing when the Word of God became flesh, that is when a human nature without
any antecedent merits of good works was coupled to the Word of God in the virgin's womb so as to
become one person with him" (*trin.* 15.46).

merits of his own."[79] If even Christ's perfect humanity did not merit union with God, fallen humanity can hardly claim such an accomplishment.

In addition to modeling the unmerited character of grace, the incarnation, for Augustine, illustrates the unmerited character of good human willing in particular.[80] Like the union of Christ's humanity with Christ's divinity, good human willing comes into existence out of nothing, with respect to the human side. This argument emerges at the beginning of the first phase of the Pelagian controversy, while Augustine is still concentrating his efforts against Pelagius and Caelestius, and also appears in *c. Iul. imp.*, Augustine's final anti-Pelagian work, written at the end of his life.

At the beginning of the Pelagian controversy, in around 411–412, we find Augustine pointing to the incarnation as an example of how the beginning of faith in believers comes about without the accrual of merits of will that might earn it. Depicting Christ as destroying the pride that causes failures of will, Augustine observes the humility of the remedy God provides to the problem of sin. In the person of the Son, God stoops to assume a complete human nature into unity with the Godhead, involving himself in an intimate personal union with humanity, who, as his creation, is far below his dignity. But the humility and extent of God's love (it is "such a great love [*tanta . . . caritate*]") are even further demonstrated in that no merits of will in any way anticipate or recommend this union. Augustine writes:

> The cause of all human failings is, after all, pride (*superbia*). It was to overcome and destroy this pride, that such a remedy came down from heaven; to human beings puffed up with pride, God came humbly out of mercy, revealing his grace with wondrous clarity in the man whom he assumed with such great love before his companions. After all, he who was in that way united to the Word of God did not bring it about by any preceding merits of his will (*praecedentibus suae uoluntatis meritis*) that the one Son of God also became the one Son of Man as a result of that union. It was necessary that there be just one. There would, however, have been two or three or more, if this were something that could be brought about, not by

---

[79] *Trin.* 13.22 (CCL 50A: 412).

[80] Harnack rightly observed this point in his *History of Dogma*, though he misunderstood the thrust of this observation in the larger context of Augustine's Christology. He writes, "The Incarnation thus appeared to be parallel to the grace which makes us willing who were unwilling, and is independent of every historical fact." Adolph Harnack, *History of Dogma*, trans. Neil Buchanan, from the 3rd German edition, vol. 5 (Boston: Little, Brown, 1910), 129.

God's gift alone, but by the free choice of a human being (*hominis liberum arbitrium*). This point, therefore, is particularly emphasized: this point especially, as best I can judge, is what we teach and are taught from the treasures of wisdom and knowledge hidden in Christ.[81]

Here Augustine explicitly underlines that rather than resulting from "preceding merits of [Christ's] will" or "the free choice of a human being," the incarnation came about "by God's gift alone." For Augustine, then, Christ's incarnation models not only the unmerited quality of grace as a general principle but also the specific application of this principle in the sphere of will: no preceding merits of the will or its free choice can explain the initial advent of the grace of Christ in a human being's life. Christ's example shows the exercise of divine mercy in a unilateral divine act unanticipated by either human doing or human willing.

Writing to the monks of Gaul much later in the Pelagian controversy (427), Augustine appeals to the example of Christ not only to support the idea that the beginning of faith happens without merit but also to underline the necessity of grace for doing and persevering in the good one wills. As Augustine's conception of our need for grace expands, so does his understanding of how Christ models this need for grace. In the dramatic conclusion of *perseu.*, Augustine appeals to Christ, the most "illustrious example of predestination," to illustrate how grace impacts human willing. Augustine first observes that just as Christ was made a perfectly righteous man despite being the offspring of David, who, at least on occasion, notably failed to preserve his own righteousness, so we are made righteous persons from unrighteous, without any preceding merits of will: "He, therefore, who made Christ a righteous man from the offspring of David, a man who was never not righteous, without any preceding merits of his will, makes righteous persons from unrighteous ones without any preceding merits of their will in order that Christ might be the head and they might be his members."[82] Here again, then, Augustine points out that the incarnation models the beginning of faith in the absence of preceding human merits, specifically with respect to will.

Christ also, however, models the necessity of grace for acting in accordance with the good will God has bestowed. Augustine writes, "He, then,

---

[81] *Pecc. mer.* 2.17.27 (CSEL 60:99–100).
[82] *Persev.* 24.67 (PL 45:1034).

who causes that man, without any preceding merits of that man, neither to contract by his origin nor to commit by his will (*uoluntate perpetrare peccatum*) any sin which might be forgiven him, causes people, without any preceding merits of theirs, to believe in him, and he forgives them every sin."[83] The same gracious God who made Christ righteous "without any preceding merits of his will," then, also prevented his will from deviating from the good. Though the saints do not attain this kind of perfect obedience in this life, according to Augustine's mature views, God's grace is still at work in their lives by assisting the elect to use their will rightly more than they otherwise would, and in that he "forgives them every sin" they commit.

Finally, Augustine finds in Christ a model of God's role in enabling human beings to persevere in the good: "He who makes him such that he never had and never will have an evil will (*uoluntatem malam*) makes a good will from an evil will in his members (*ex mala uoluntate bonam*)."[84] Because of God's gracious union with a full human nature in his very person, Christ not only had a perfectly good human will from the very outset of his existence but never will have anything but a good will.[85] Christ's human will is made righteous from the beginning by God's grace, and it will always remain righteous by God's grace. Just as Christ, then, by virtue of his union with God, is graciously prevented from ever having an evil will, so God continually makes good the wills of the members of Christ's body. The same God responsible for his good will continually turns the wills of those already belonging to his body from evil to good so that they might persevere on the path toward him. Strikingly, Augustine identifies those whose wills God makes "good from bad" as "among his members" (*in membris eius*). God does more than convert the evil wills of those outside the faith; he must make good the wills of saints. Augustine employs the present tense (*facit*) to describe this latter act of grace, as if to emphasize the continual dependence of Christians, even now, upon God to re-create their wills in goodness.

---

[83] *Persev.* 24.67 (PL 45:1034).

[84] *Perseu.* 24.67 (PL 45:1034).

[85] In addition to the passage just cited from *perseu.*, see also, on this point, Augustine's statement "There was no reason to fear that the human nature assumed in this ineffable way into the unity of the person by God the Word would sin by free choice of the will. This assumption, after all, was such that the nature of the man assumed by God in that way would admit in itself no impulse of an evil way" (*Corrept.* 11.30 [CSEL 92:255]).

In the most mature phase of his career, then, Augustine finds in Christ's willing a model for God's gracious role in human willing across the whole breadth of the journey of faith. God is there at the beginning, calling a righteous human will into existence out of nothing. God is there enabling human beings to make good on the good will he has bestowed, to resist sin, and to receive his forgiveness when they fail, even as he kept Christ from ever needing forgiveness in the first place. And God is there continually, making their wills good again and again as they make their way toward their Maker, ensuring that they will persevere in the good, just as God guaranteed that Christ would never falter from the good will initially given to him.

Augustine sees Christ, in his modeling of each of these ways in which God impacts the will, as showing precisely that human beings must draw on more than the innate resources of their human nature to will well. Christ's human nature was perfect, yet his good human willing still derived from, found sustenance in, and reached fulfillment through God's power. By how much more, then, do those whose wills are flawed and fallen need to depend on God's grace to will rightly?

Augustine's contrast of his own perspective against Julian's on the reason for Christ's righteousness, while perhaps caricaturing Julian's Christology, helps to throw into relief Augustine's own view. Julian is keen to emphasize Christ's illustration of the great potential of human nature. In his own words, "Finally, as we read nowhere in the scriptures that Christ fled from a sin that he knew is contracted by the newborn, we are emphatically taught by that clear testimony that the righteousness of the man he assumed came, not from the difference of his nature (*de naturae diuersitate*), but from his voluntary action (*de uoluntaria actione*)."[86] According to Julian, human beings can look to Christ as an example of how to attain righteousness because his righteousness was not a result of a divine nature human beings lack, but rather a product of voluntary action of which they are naturally capable. Christ did not have to be superhuman to attain virtue; he could thus serve as every human person's model of the good will every person has the potential to achieve.

Augustine interprets Julian's position as follows: "That is, he [Christ] did not have a will (*uoluntatem*) of such goodness and greatness because of that union, but arrived at that union by a will (*uoluntate*) of such goodness and

---

[86] *C. Iul.* 4.84 (CSEL 85.2:85).

greatness."[87] In fact, in the quotation Augustine adduces, Julian attributes only Christ's righteousness, not the hypostatic union itself, to the right use of Christ's will. But Augustine's statement does help us to home in on the crux of his own view. For Augustine, Christ could model "a will of such goodness and greatness because of that union," because his divine nature had assumed a human nature. Christ's good human willing resulted from the unique relationship of his human nature with God, and not vice versa. For Augustine, then, the relevance of Christ's example to the remainder of the human race does not hinge on our ability to follow this example by the inherent strength of our nature and will. Rather, Christ's example pertains to the rest of the human race precisely by showing that even the best of human beings requires supernatural assistance to achieve, sustain, and fulfill good will. Christ's example proves the impossibility, not the facility, of following his lead without the aid of grace.

Section B: Christ Models Justice and Augustine's Agony in the Garden

Even with grace, however, enacting a good will by obeying God's will for one's life is not painless. It involves taking up a cross before being crowned with glory. For Augustine, Christ's own prioritization of justice over power models the humility that should characterize a Christian's willing in this life.[88]

Though Christ could have triumphed over the devil by brute power, he instead chose the path of justice, which, for Augustine, "is a property of good will (*uoluntatem bonam*), which is why the angels at Christ's birth said, Glory to God in the highest, and on earth peace to men of good will (*bonae uoluntatis*) (Lk 2:14)."[89] By his good, just, willing, Christ was able to offer himself up as a perfect payment for the debt sinners owed. He overpowered the devil, then, not by flaunting the requirements of justice but by fulfilling them.[90]

---

[87] *C. Iul. imp.* 4.84 (CSEL 85.2:86).

[88] On the role of Christ in establishing a just society, see Robert Dodaro, *Christ and the Just Society in the Thought of Augustine* (New York: Cambridge University Press, 2004), 72–114.

[89] *Trin.* 13.17 (CCL 50A:405). Augustine's formulation is "pertinet autem iustitia ad uoluntatem bonam." One might translate *pertinet ad* more strongly as "refers to."

[90] *Trin.* 13.18.

Christians are called to follow Christ in prioritizing justice over power, to will the right thing before seeking to satisfy their will to power. Augustine explains that the just method of God's deliverance of humankind from sin had a pedagogical aim as well, to drive home this very point: "It pleased God to deliver man from the devil's authority by beating him at the justice game, not the power game, so that men too might imitate Christ by seeking to beat the devil at the justice game, not the power game. Not that power is to be shunned as something bad, but that the right order must be preserved which puts justice first."[91] God chose to deliver humanity by prioritizing justice over power so that human beings might learn to adopt Christ's priorities: "Let mortals hold on to justice; power will be given them when they are immortal."[92]

Christ's priorities carry a cost. Putting justice in first place by self-sacrificially willing the good of the other can sometimes involve deferring one's own personal gratification. As Augustine explains it, happiness involves two components: wanting the right thing and getting what one wants. One can be truly happy only when one achieves both. But in this life, human beings often lack the power to realize a good and just will. A dilemma therefore presents itself. They can will the right thing, even though this will require them to wait for the fulfillment of their desires, or they can set their will upon a lesser good, which will render satisfaction more likely.[93] Christ's example recommends the former choice, for Christ "postponed what he had the power to do, in order to do first what he had to do,"[94] but also shows the high personal cost it sometimes requires. Believers are called to follow his example, prioritizing justice, or right willing, over the immediate gratification of power, even though this involves the short-term sacrifice of their own "self-fulfillment." According to Augustine, Christians should seek happiness as political idealists, not as realists.

Christ's example, then, shows that the restoration of good willing is not the triumphal end of the story of redemption or of the will's initial creation and fall from goodness. Rather, good willing is a first step toward happiness, to be prioritized over power in this life and fulfilled in power in the next. As Augustine expresses it, this time is a "time during which the power

[91] *Trin.* 13.17 (CCL 50A:404).
[92] *Trin.* 13.17 (CCL 50A:404).
[93] *Trin.* 13.17.
[94] *Trin.* 13.18 (CCL 50A:406).

of the people of God is being deferred."[95] The full realization of their good willing, and therefore happiness, must wait until the next life, even as Christ endured crucifixion and death before being resurrected on the third day.

We have noted that Augustine implies, in *conf.*, that Christ takes on a human will. In the same work we can also see how Augustine interprets a key episode in his own life as conforming to the pattern of grace of which Christ is the preeminent model. As discussed in chapter 2, Augustine describes himself in book 8 of *conf.* as undergoing a struggle between two wills. One is carnal, the other spiritual; one is old, the other new. He interprets these two wills in light of the description of conflict between flesh and spirit in Galatians 5:17.[96] They create an internal duality, but Augustine is careful to observe that they do not entail two opposing minds or natures, an idea he attributes to the Manichees. Thus there is an important disanalogy between his own case and Christ's, where Christ's two wills do in fact indicate two distinct natures. Yet at the same time, the struggle of will Augustine undergoes is reminiscent of his descriptions of the relationship between Christ's human and divine wills between 395 and 414, when Augustine tended to emphasize the tension between the two and to depict Christ as needing to overcome the temptations of his human will in favor of his divine will.

Augustine's depiction of himself as experiencing the deepening and, eventually, the cathartic resolution of this struggle in a garden echoes Christ's agonizing struggle in Gethsemane. Of his own experience, he writes, "The tumult of my heart took me out into the garden where no one could interfere with the burning struggle with myself in which I was engaged, until the matter could be settled."[97] As Augustine reflects in *conf.* book 9 upon the problem of will that faced him there, he sets up a further parallel between his own experience and Christ's. Like Christ, Augustine must say no to his own will and accept God's. Looking back, Augustine observes, "The nub of the problem was to reject my will and to desire yours" (*et hoc erat totum nolle, quod uolebam, et uelle, quod uolebas*).[98] The problem before him was the difficulty of accepting Christ's prayer in Gethsemane, as quoted by Augustine in other contexts, as his own: *uerum, non quod ego uolo, sed*

---

[95] *Trin* 13.17 (CCL 50A:405).
[96] "So my two wills, one old, the other new (*duae uoluntates meae, una uetus, alia noua*), one carnal, the other spiritual, were in conflict with one another, and their discord robbed my soul of all concentration" (*conf.* 8.5.10 [CCL 27:120]).
[97] *Conf.* 8.8.19 (CCL 27:125).
[98] *Conf.* 9.1.1 (CCL 27:133).

quod tu uis, pater.[99] Here in the garden in Milan, Augustine was challenged to echo Christ's humble prayer of obedience: Not what I want, but what you want.

Yet in Augustine's telling, Christ was more than a model for his struggle in the garden. Christ was present there, transforming him. Continuing to reflect, he asks, "But where through so many years was my freedom of will? From what deep and hidden recess was it called out in a moment? Thereby I submitted my neck to your easy yoke and my shoulders to your light burden (Matt. 11:30), O Christ Jesus 'my helper and redeemer' (Ps. 18:15)."[100] It is Christ, who himself successfully resisted the pull of autonomous human willing and willed God's will, who is the way out of the problem of divided will. He replaces Augustine's old will with a new one. Augustine goes on to explain that due to Christ's easy yoke, his desires have been transformed. Now obedience is sweet to him; he does not glance back sidelong at old loves. All this is possible because Christ is not only his model but also his "helper" (*adiutor meus*) and "redeemer" (*redemptor meus*), who transforms his willing from the inside out.

Part III: Christ Transforms and Re-creates the Human Will

As Augustine already intimates in book 9 of *conf.*, Christ's involvement in bringing about good human willing extends further than taking on a human will or even setting an example of right human willing. Christ not only experiences and illustrates human willing; he transforms it. The will's sin sickness, Augustine explains in *De perfectione iustitiae hominis* (*perf. iust.*; 415), is much like a lingering limp:

> Persons cannot, nonetheless, be immediately free from their limp, when they want to, but only when they have been healed under the care of a doctor and when some treatment has helped their will. This is done in the interior person with regard to sin, which is analogous to limping, through the grace of the one who came not *to call the righteous, but sinners*

---

[99] *Serm.* 296.8 (MA 1:406).
[100] *Conf.* 9.1.1 (CCL 27:133).

(Mt 9:13), because *it is not those who are in good health who need a physician, but those who are sick* (Mt 9:12).[101]

Seeing the rigorous gait of someone healthy does not, in itself, enable a person to walk properly. People who limp need physicians, not just models. Likewise those seeking to will rightly need not just examples but a healer. It is Christ, according to Augustine, who steps in to provide the requisite medical care.

For Augustine, the grace of God in Christ is not merely one among many possible treatments but the only means of recovering volitional health. Augustine writes, "Nor can a person will something good, unless helped by the one who cannot will evil, that is, by the grace of God through Jesus Christ our Lord."[102] Christ's perfect ability to resist willing evil makes him the perfect helper to assist human beings in willing the good.

Since for Augustine the good will serves, furthermore, as the sine qua non for attaining the kingdom of God, the fact that good willing can come only from Christ, the one mediator, is of no small import. Augustine writes, "This is what we say: That good of human beings, that good will (*illam uoluntatem bonam*), that good work by which alone a human being can be brought to the eternal gift and kingdom of God can be bestowed on no one without the grace of God which is given through the one mediator between God and human beings."[103] For Augustine, then, there is no way to attain human flourishing without a rehabilitation of will. And there is no way to attain good human willing, he insists, except through the one mediator. Thus Augustine's mature notion of human flourishing, along with his mature concept of good human willing, is thoroughly dependent on Christ.

Thanks to Christ, human willing becomes even more fully saturated in God's grace than it was before sin entered the world. By grace Adam enjoyed the possibility of doing the right things he willed to do. The grace we receive now in Christ, however, not only includes this first grace that Adam possessed but also produces the "good willing" itself, which we are at liberty to put into effect: "This help . . . given through Jesus Christ our Lord . . . produces in us not only the ability to do what we will (*posse quod uolumus*), but also the willing of that for which we have the ability (*uelle*

---

[101] *Perf. iust.* 3.5.
[102] *C. ep. Pel.* 1.3.7 (CSEL 60:429).
[103] *C. Iul.* 4.3.33.

quod possumus). This was not the case with the first man, for he had the
first of these helps, but not the second."[104] The help Christ offers the human
will, then, not only makes possible eternal life and participation in God's
kingdom but even improves upon the condition of the human will in Adam.
What is the precise character of this help that Christ offers the human will?
How does he offer assistance in a way that goes beyond the example he sets?

Christ's transformation of the human will as depicted in Augustine's
thinking cannot easily be reduced to a single act or event. Rather, this transformation is an ongoing work that begins with a person's conversion and
continues throughout the Christian life. In a first step, Christ liberates the
will from sin for the good. He then continues to heal the will by delivering
his followers from temptation (helping them to enact their good will) and
enabling them to persevere in the good (helping them to maintain their
good will). Finally, Christ unites the good wills of his followers, fusing them
in the fire of charity so that they become one in the perfect will of God.
From start to finish in the Christian life, good willing depends on Christ.

Section A: Christ Sets the Will Free

Christ's liberating work upon the human will has both negative and positive aspects. The negative aspect is that Christ sets the will free from slavery
to sin. In *perf. iust.* Augustine describes Christ as liberating human beings
from willful vice: "Freedom, after all, is promised to those who believe by
him who sets them free. He says, *If the Son sets you free, then you will truly
be free* (Jn 8:36). For conquered by the vice into which it has fallen by its will,
our nature lacks freedom."[105] Thus Christ promises to throw off the shackles
of bondage to sin in which the fallen will, as discussed in chapter 2, is a
stubborn link.[106] In the quotation just adduced, the human will is responsible for bringing about a fall into vice, but human beings, namely, "those
who believe" (*credentibus*), those who constitute the "you" (*vos*) of John

---

[104] *Corrept.* 11.32 (CSEL 92:258). We will discuss Augustine's contrast between the freedom of will
possible for Adam and the freedom of will made possible by Christ at greater length in chapter 8, on
"free will."

[105] *Perf. iust.* 4.9 (CSEL 42:8).

[106] Indeed, in another work written around the same time, *nat. et grat.*, Augustine uses chain imagery to describe the enslavement from which Christ sets human beings free: "But there is no chain
of necessity when we act correctly, precisely because there is the freedom of love" (*nat. et grat.* 65.78
[CSEL 60:293]).

8:36, serve as the grammatical object of his liberating work. In *c. Iul. imp.*, Augustine similarly emphasizes the necessity for Christ to set the human person free since humanity has lost the "good will" (*bona uoluntas*) with which it was originally endowed. Here again, will factors into the explanation of how freedom was lost but does not serve as the grammatical object of Christ's liberating work.[107] On other occasions in the later stages of the Pelagian controversy, however, Augustine describes the will itself as the object of the liberation Christ effects. In *corrept.*, written in 427, for example, Augustine asserts, "But though the will (*uoluntas*) of the saints was enslaved to sin, it was set free (*liberata est*) by the one who said, *If the Son sets you free, then you will truly be free* (Jn 8:36)."[108] Here Augustine specifies that Christ frees human beings from sin by acting directly upon the will.

In addition to describing Christ's liberating work with respect to the will as bringing about freedom from enslavement to sin, Augustine also attributes to Christ a liberation of the will in the positive sense of setting the will free for good. This characterization of Christ's liberating work comes to the fore in the second stage of the Pelagian controversy, as Julian emerges as the new leader of the Pelagian camp. In *Contra duas epistulas Pelagianorum* (*c. ep. Pel.*; 418), for example, Augustine makes the point that the problem Christ addresses is not merely setting the will free with respect to evil actions. The will already enjoys the freedom to do what is wrong. The problem is that it is neither free to resist what is wrong nor to do what is right. In Augustine's words, "But this will which is free for evil actions because it takes delight in evil is not free for good actions, because it has not been set free."[109] Though it may be free (*libera*) for the bad, the will cannot be free (*libera*) for the good unless it is freed (*liberata*) by Christ. To grant this fuller freedom, Christ puts an end to the will's delight in evil and also instills in it a delight in the good. The result is that the will becomes free for the good (*libera in bonis*) rather than free for what is bad (*libera . . . in malis*). Christ's help is essential, Augustine insists, for the will to exercise this kind of positive freedom: "Nor can a person will (*uelle*) something good, unless helped by the one who cannot will evil, that is, by the grace of God through Jesus Christ our Lord."[110]

---

[107] *C. Iul. imp.*, 1.82 (CSEL 85.1:96).
[108] *Corrept.* 12.35 (CSEL 92:261).
[109] *C. ep. Pel.* 1.3.7 (CSEL 60:428–429).
[110] *C. ep. Pel.* 1.3.7 (CSEL 60:429).

Augustine emphasizes that the grace of Christ is the sine qua non for the will's liberation, both for the good and from the bondage of sin, in his late unfinished tome against Julian:

> No one can have free choice of the will (*liberum uoluntatis arbitrium*) to do the good which one wills or not to do the evil which one hates except by the grace of Christ. This does not mean that the will (*uoluntas*) is carried off as a captive to good in the same way as to evil, but that, once set free from captivity (*a captiuitate liberata*), it may be drawn to its deliverer by the sweet freedom of love, not by the bitter servitude of fear.[111]

Importantly, Christ does not orient the human will to the good by submitting it to a new kind of slavery. Christ sets the will free by "captivating" it with delight.

Section B: The Lord's Prayer as Means and Evidence of Christ's Transformation of the Human Will

Augustine does not leave abstract his claim that Christ liberates the will from bondage to sin and sets it free to delight in the good. Rather he sheds light on how Christ effects this transformation practically in the life of the church. Just as Christ's prayer in Gethsemane is central to Augustine's portrayal of how Christ takes on a human will, the Lord's Prayer is central to Augustine's portrayal of how Christ transforms the human will.

Augustine is already commenting on the role of the Lord's Prayer in the transformation of human willing in 411 or 412, when he pens the first of his anti-Pelagian writings, *pecc. mer.* This issue comes up as Augustine responds to a statement, perhaps from Rufinus's *Liber de fide*, which suggests that not sinning is simply a matter of not willing to sin, and thus clearly within human capacity. In response, Augustine emphasizes that not willing to sin in the first place is a considerable challenge, given that concupiscence abides for the duration of this life. When a person consents to this concupiscence, such consent being "due to one's own will," she can be healed only

---

[111] *C. Iul. imp.* 3.112 (CSEL 85.1:433).

"through the heavenly high priest."[112] Augustine explains that this healing process is much more arduous than the process by which human beings were wounded by sin in the first place.[113] He then points to the Lord's Prayer as part of the difficult procedure by which Christ the heavenly high priest effects healing.

Augustine identifies three distinct ways in which the Lord's Prayer targets the healing of the will. First, he notes, "If, then, we consent to these desires stemming from the concupiscence of the flesh by an illicit turn of the will (*inlicita uoluntatis inclinatione*), we say in order to heal this wound, *Forgive us our debts*. And drawing a remedy from works of mercy, we add, *As we also forgive our debtors* (Mt 6:12)." He then adds, "But so that we do not consent to it, we beg for help with the words, *And bring us not into temptation* (Mt 6:13)." Lastly Augustine explains:

> Finally, we mention what will be accomplished in the end, when what is mortal will be swallowed up by life: *But deliver us from evil* (Mt 6:13). At that time, after all, there will be no concupiscence of the sort that we are commanded to fight and to which we are commanded not to consent. We can, then, briefly ask for this whole cluster of three benefits as follows: "Forgive us those times in which we have been carried off by concupiscence; help us not to be carried off by concupiscence; take concupiscence away from us."[114]

In praying the Lord's Prayer, Christ's followers participate in a healing process he initiates, seeking the forgiveness that Christ's work makes possible.

Part of the process of receiving forgiveness for the healing of one's concupiscent will is to extend, oneself, the kind of forgiveness that Christ offers. Augustine writes:

> In order to overcome temptation in the case of some things which we desire wrongfully or fear wrongfully, we at times need the great (*magnis*) and full strength (*totis uiribus*) of the will (*uoluntatis*). He who willed that

---

[112] *Pecc. mer.* 2.4.4 (CSEL 60:74).

[113] *Pecc. mer.* 2.4.4 (CSEL 60:74): "Evil, indeed, remains in our flesh not by the nature in which human beings are divinely created, but by the defect by which they have fallen voluntarily (*uoluntate*), wherefore, since their strength has been lost, they are not healed with the facility of will (*uoluntatis facilitate*) by which they were wounded." This is my translation.

[114] *Pecc. mer.* 2.4.4 (CSEL 60:74–75).

the prophet truthfully say, *No living person will be found righteous in your sight* (Ps 143:2), foresaw that we will not in every case fully (*perfecte*) use this power. Knowing in advance that we were going to be such persons, the Lord gave us, even after baptism, certain salutary remedies against the guilt and the bonds of sin and willed that they be effective, namely, works of mercy.[115]

Here Augustine depicts "works of mercy" as effective remedies for the guilt and entrapment that result when those who have been baptized fail to overcome temptation because of weakness of will. He goes on to explain that the healing of those who consent to concupiscence takes place "by the medicine of penance and works of mercy through the heavenly priest who makes intercession for us." Here again, the healing effected through penance and works of mercy does not happen independently of Christ's grace. Rather this healing occurs "through the heavenly priest" (*per caelestem sacerdotem*).[116] Penance and works of mercy are not alternatives to reliance on Christ but rather are among the remedies Christ the heavenly priest offers. As summarized and enacted in the petition for forgiveness from debts "as we forgive our debtors," the baptized experience healing through the Word as they both find forgiveness from God and forgive others, participating in Christ's own mercy. In this way, the Lord's Prayer helps to heal a person from the harmful effects of illicit inclinations of will of which she is already guilty.

Praying "Do not lead us into temptation," on the other hand, invites God so to heal the will that it may avoid falling into further illicit willful inclinations in the first place. In this petition, those praying request that God empower them not to be carried away by the temptation of concupiscence and to resist and triumph over it. Finally, in the prayer "Deliver us from evil," believers pray not for strength to overcome temptation but for liberation from experiencing temptation of the will at all. With this prayer they look forward to, and ask God to hasten, the day when the prayer not to be led into temptation will become superfluous, as they will no longer experience concupiscence.

The Lord's Prayer, then, makes clear how God, working in Christ, the "heavenly high priest," transforms the will with respect to past, present, and future. God heals the wound of an illicitly inclined will by extending

---

[115] *Pecc. mer.* 2.3.3 (CSEL 60:72–73).
[116] *Pecc. mer.* 2.4.4 (CSEL 60:74).

forgiveness; God protects the will from its present temptations, giving it victory over concupiscence; and, on the last day, God will so perfect the will that
even temptation cannot touch it. God does all this in Christ. Furthermore,
this prayer is a specific means by which God in Christ transforms the will in
these ways. In addition to his direct role in transforming the will in answer
to these prayers, then, Christ also plays an indirect role in transforming
the will insofar as he teaches his followers the prayer by which they may
request and receive God's "remedy" for its wounds. In praying the Lord's
Prayer, believers echo Christ's words, and in this way participate in Christ's
own prayer as "the heavenly priest who makes intercession for us."[117] Thus
Christ is intimately involved as the agent of the will's transformation as
both primary subject of the Lord's Prayer and its recipient. He transforms
the human will not only by teaching his disciples how to pray for its transformation but also by providing, inseparably with the Father and the Holy
Spirit, the requested remedy. The Lord's Prayer, then, represents another instance in which scripture (the Lord's Prayer) and the liturgical practice of
the church shape Augustine's view of will, in this case, his view of how it is
to be restored to integrity.[118]

Augustine's comments about the impact of prayer upon the will more
generally speaking (rather than in the specific context of his teachings on
the Lord's Prayer) help to fill in the picture of how, in answer to the words
of the Lord's Prayer, God in Christ transforms the will in the present,
protecting it from the temptations of concupiscence. These comments make
it clear that prayer is not simply a means of persuading God to do what we
want. Rather, the point of prayer is to align our wills with what God wants.
Prayer is not a transformation of God's will but rather a transformation of
the human will to fit God's will.[119]

The Lord's Prayer serves to transform the human will not only insofar
as God uses the Lord's Prayer, the prayer Christ taught his disciples, for
this purpose, but also in the sense that Christ's intercession on our behalf
transforms our willing. Augustine further develops this point many years
later in *corrept.* (427), where he uses the example of Peter to show that

---

[117] *Pecc. mer.* 2.4.4 (CSEL 60:74).
[118] Hombert's observation that "the pastoral activity of Augustine and the ecclesial prayer of which
he is the preacher . . . are the veritable site of understanding [*lieu d'intelligence*] for his theology of
grace" thus applies as well to Augustine's doctrine of the redemption of the will (*Gloria gratiae*, 338).
[119] See *ep.* 130.19–21.

the Lord's high priestly intercession on our behalf prevents our wills from falling.

For Augustine, the reference of Luke 22:32 to the Lord's prayer on behalf of Peter to prevent his will from failing constitutes proof that perseverance is not something the human will achieves on its own. Augustine writes:

> If you say that it pertains to the free choice of a human being which you defend, not in accord with the grace of God, but in opposition to it, that anyone perseveres or does not persevere in the good, not because God grants it if he does persevere, but because the human will (*humana uoluntate*) brings it about, what are you going to devise against the words of the Lord who said, *I have prayed for you, Peter, that your faith may not fail* (Lk 22:32)?[120]

Peter's case, far from representing an anomaly, illustrates a basic principle about human willing: perseverance in the good is due to Christ's work, Christ's intercession: it is not achieved on the strength of one's independent human willing.

Augustine continues on to make the point that Christ's prayer that Peter's faith not fail targets Peter's will in particular. Augustine explains, "When, therefore, he prayed that his faith would not fail, what else did he pray for but that he would have a will (*uoluntatem*) to believe that is perfectly free, firm, unconquerable, and persevering?"[121] Peter's example thus illustrates not only a general principle about human dependence on Christ for perseverance but also a general principle about how Christ transforms the will. Through his intercession Christ bestows freedom, stability, victory, and perseverance upon the will by grace, thereby making human faith and adherence to the good possible.

This bestowal is not a mere confirmation of a trajectory of behavior the will has already launched on its own power, however. It is not as if the will obtains this grace based upon its independent exercise of freedom. Rather, Christ so transforms the will as to bring it, as Peter's case so aptly illustrates, from a denial of God's will to delighted conformity with God's will. In Augustine's words, "The human will (*uoluntas*) does not, of course, obtain grace by its freedom; it rather obtains freedom by grace and, in order that

---

[120] *Corrept.* 8.17 (CSEL 92:238).
[121] *Corrept.* 8.17 (CSEL 92:238).

it may persevere, it obtains a delightful permanence and an insuperable strength."[122] Christ transforms the will by taking the initiative, in his intercession, to turn the human will around and thereby set it free.

As Augustine demonstrates both in his explicit remarks about how God in Christ heals the wounded wills of God's people through the prayer Christ taught, and in his treatment of Christ's intercession on behalf of Peter, the Lord's Prayer is one means by which Christ transforms the human will. In addition to serving as an actual vehicle of this transformation, however, the Lord's Prayer also serves an important epistemic function by offering evidence that God must help in order for the human will to be healed. Praying the Lord's Prayer both transforms our wills by Christ's healing and teaches our need of it.

In his later anti-Pelagian writings, when Augustine turns his attention to countering the Pelagianism of Julian of Eclanum, we find him appealing repeatedly to the Lord's Prayer, and particularly to the Lord's Prayer as interpreted by Cyprian in his short work *On the Lord's Prayer* (*domin. orat.*), to undergird the view of grace he defends against his opponent.[123] There are a number of aspects of his doctrine of grace that Augustine connects to precedents in Cyprian's thinking on the Lord's Prayer, but of particular importance for us here are Augustine's assertions that the Lord's Prayer shows that grace is necessary for perseverance, that the Lord's Prayer shows the insufficiency of human willing without God's help, and that this same prayer demonstrates that God makes the unwilling willing. Each of these theses contributes to Augustine's case that the Lord's Prayer proves the human need for God's assistance in Christ in order to be transformed. He thus argues that he is not doing something unprecedented by attributing the transformation of the will as demonstrated in the Lord's Prayer to God's work in Christ; rather, Cyprian had already interpreted the Lord's Prayer in this way.

To support his argument that the Lord's Prayer shows that the faithful need grace to persevere in the good, Augustine appeals to two passages: Cyprian's comments on the petitions for God's name to be made holy and for daily bread. Quoting Cyprian's explicit statement that in the petition *May your*

---

[122] *Corrept.* 8.17 (CSEL 92:238).

[123] For a more detailed presentation of Augustine's reception of Cyprian's *On the Lord's Prayer,* see Han-luen Kantzer Komline, "Grace, Free Will, and the Lord's Prayer: Cyprian's Importance for the 'Augustinian' Doctrine of Grace," *Augustinian Studies* 45, no. 2 (2014): 247–279. The following discussion of Augustine's appeal to Cyprian's treatment of the Lord's Prayer draws from that article.

name be made holy we "pray and ask that we who have been made holy in baptism may persevere in what we have begun to be," Augustine concludes that Cyprian sees perseverance as God's gift.[124] Cyprian says in so many words that in the Lord's Prayer Christians ask for perseverance. And why would they make this request unless perseverance were a gift from God? Augustine argues, "This teacher, therefore, understands that we ask of God perseverance in holiness, that is, that we may persevere in holiness when we say, *May your name be made holy* (Mt. 6:9). What else does it mean to ask for what we have received but that we may also be given the gift of not ceasing to have it?"[125] Pointing to the same text in Cyprian again later, Augustine insists that he is not the first to say that perseverance is God's gift. Cyprian had already pronounced clearly upon this point in his explication of the Lord's Prayer.

> I have not now said this in such a way that no one has said this before me. Blessed Cyprian, as we have already shown, explained our petitions in the Lord's Prayer; he said that we ask for perseverance in the first petition, claiming that we pray for this when we say, May your name be made holy (Mt 6:9), namely, that we may persevere in what we have begun to be, since we were already made holy in baptism.[126]

Augustine denies that his teaching on perseverance is new, or even that he has formulated his teaching on the topic in a new way. He is merely repeating what Cyprian had already stated in *domin. orat.*

Though Augustine typically defends Cyprian's endorsement of perseverance as a gift of grace with recourse to Cyprian's interpretation of the petition *May your name be made holy*, in *perseu.* 4.7 he turns instead to the petition for daily bread. Here Cyprian's figurative interpretations of the Lord's Prayer prove crucial to Augustine's case. Bread "may be understood both spiritually and literally," Cyprian writes, as referring not only to material bread but also to Christ, the "bread of life," and the eucharist.[127] Given

---

[124] *Perseu.* 2.4 (PL 45:996–997), citing Cyprian, *domin. orat.* 12: *id petimus et rogamus, ut qui in baptismo sanctificati sumus, in eo quod esse coepimus perseueremus.*

[125] *Perseu.* 2.4 (PL 45:997).

[126] *Perseu.* 21.55 (PL 45:1027). See also *Corrept.* 6.10 (CSEL 92:230–231), where Augustine cites the same passage in Cyprian, drawing the same conclusion, and *c. ep. Pel.* 4.9.25, where he uses the same passage in Cyprian, though without concluding on its basis that perseverance is God's gift.

[127] Unless otherwise noted, these and subsequent English translations come from Cyprian, "On the Lord's Prayer," in *On the Lord's Prayer: Tertullian, Cyprian, Origen*, trans. Alistair Stewart-Sykes (Crestwood, NY: St. Vladimir's Seminary Press, 2004). Cyprian, *domin. orat.* 18 (CCSL 3A:101).

Cyprian's interpretation of the request for daily bread as a request not to fall into sin so as to be forbidden the eucharist, Augustine concludes that the request for daily bread may also be understood as a request for perseverance in goodness. Thus he finds Cyprian supporting his case even in his interpretation of the fourth petition of the Lord's Prayer.[128]

As we have demonstrated, Augustine understands perseverance not as brought about by the human will but as the gracious gift of a certain kind of will, namely, "a will to believe that is perfectly free, firm, unconquerable, and persevering."[129] In underlining our need for God's help to persevere, the Lord's Prayer also reveals the need for God's work in Christ to transform the will.

Augustine also thinks the Lord's Prayer sheds light on the need for God's transformation of the will in Christ insofar as it presupposes that the human will is insufficient for attaining the good without God's help. Augustine argues for this claim with specific references to Cyprian's exposition of the petition for daily bread. Here again his case hinges on the figurative interpretation of the petition for daily bread as referring to the eucharist and the body of Christ, though the focus is not perseverance. Augustine argues that if, as Cyprian asserts, the prayer for daily bread is a prayer not to fall into sin that might result in excommunication, then this prayer is further evidence that our own will (*nostram . . . uoluntatem*) is insufficient to protect us against doing what is wrong. Thus he concludes that "if blessed Cyprian thought that our will was sufficient to avoid committing these sins, he would not have understood our words in the Lord's Prayer, *Give us today our daily bread* (Mt 6:10), as he did."[130]

In *c. Iul.*, Augustine finds confirmation of the insufficiency of human willing in Cyprian's exposition of the petition for God's will to be done. Here he depends on Cyprian's figurative interpretation of the request for God's will to be done in heaven and on earth as referring to the spirit and the flesh of the baptized. According to Cyprian, Christ's teaching attests to the fact that a conflict between our flesh and spirit requires resolution. Due to this conflict, "we do not do that which we will."[131] From this line of argumentation in Cyprian, Augustine draws the lesson that human powers, of

---

[128] *Perseu.* 4.7 (PL 45:998).
[129] *Corrept.* 8.17 (CSEL 92:238).
[130] *C. ep. Pel.* 4.9.26 (CSEL 60:553), citing Cyprian, *domin. orat.* 18.
[131] *C. Iul.* 2.3.6 (PL 44:676), quoting Cyprian, *domin. orat.* 16: *Non quae uolumus ipsa faciamus.*

willing or otherwise, are insufficient.[132] Only divine grace can resolve the struggle between flesh and spirit that even the faithful continue to experience to some degree in this life.

Citing the same passage in his *c. Iul. imp.*, Augustine warns the opposition, "Cyprian is also against you, because you ascribe to free choice (*libero arbitrio*) what he understands we must ask God to produce in a human being."[133] Thus, for Augustine, the Lord's Prayer also points to the importance of God's work to transform our will insofar as it shows that neither free choice nor the will that might exercise it is up to the task of effecting this kind of transformation on its own.

In addition to underlining the importance of God's transformative work on the will in Christ by indicating that other competitors cannot achieve this, the Lord's Prayer also, according to Augustine, shows that God is the one responsible for transforming human wills from bad to good. As further investigation in his anti-Pelagian writings shows, Augustine believed *domin. orat.* reflected not only the insufficiency of the human will but also God's power to transform people determined to reject the gospel into willing recipients of his grace. Augustine repeatedly drew on the same evidence for this claim: Cyprian's figurative interpretation of the petition that God's will be done in heaven and on earth. One can find appeals to Cyprian along these lines from early in the second stage of the Pelagian controversy on through to *c. Iul. imp.*

Already in *c. ep. Pel.*, Augustine alludes to Cyprian's understanding of this line of the prayer as substantiating the conclusion that, in the words of Proverbs 8:35, "the will is prepared by the Lord."[134] Particularly decisive is

---

[132] Augustine writes, "How vigilant he is against your teaching that leads you to trust in your own power, as he explains this point in his letter on the Lord's Prayer! For he teaches that we should ask the Lord rather than trust in our own powers so that not human strength but divine grace may produce concord between flesh and spirit" (*C. Iul.* 2.3.6 [PL 44:677, trans. Teske, WSA I/24]).

[133] *C. Iul. imp.* 6.6 (CSEL 85.2:300).

[134] Augustine cites the phrase *praeparatur uoluntas a Domino* repeatedly from the outbreak of the Pelagian controversy to the end of his life. See Anne-Marie La Bonnardière, *Le livre des proverbes* (Paris: Études Augustiniennes, 1975), 209–210 for a tabular presentation of his citation of the text and 66–70 for analysis of Augustine's use of it, which occurs exclusively in anti-Pelagian contexts. La Bonnardière observes that in citing heavily from Proverbs, Augustine was following an African tradition established by Tertullian and "surtout Cyprien" (47). A. Sage observes that Ambrose may have drawn Augustine's attention to this particular line. See Athanase Sage, "Praeparatur Voluntas a Domino," *RÉA* 10 (1964): 1–20. According to D. Ogliari, "Pr 8,35 had the advantage of speaking in favour of both grace and free will." See Donato Ogliari, *Gratia et Certamen: The Relationship between Grace and Free Will in the Discussion of Augustine with the So-called Semipelagians*, vol. 169, Bibliotheca Ephemeridum Theologicarum Lovaniensium (Leuven: Leuven University Press, 2003), 30n41.

Cyprian's contention that the petition for God's will to be done on earth may be understood as referring to the conversion of nonbelievers.[135] Cyprian sees this petition as a fulfillment of Christ's command to his disciples to pray for their persecutors as true children of God, who blesses both the just and the unjust (Matthew 5:44–45). This point is not lost on Augustine, who confronts his readers with the radicality of Cyprian's claim. Cyprian suggests that in praying for God's will to be done on earth Christians pray not only for those who lack the will to turn to the faith but also for those who actively resist it—for enemies of the gospel and for those guilty of injustice. In other words, by this petition Christians pray for God to turn wayward wills around.[136]

Augustine repeats similar arguments in *ep.* 215, *ep.* 217, *praed. sanct.*, and *c. Iul. imp.*[137] In teaching that Christians pray for the conversion of their enemies in the Lord's Prayer, Augustine is convinced, Cyprian has in effect endorsed the notion that God can convert the wills of those opposed to the gospel. If God cannot convert unwilling wills, Augustine points out after citing Cyprian in *ep.* 217,

> vainly and perfunctorily rather than truthfully do we pour forth prayers to God for them, so that by believing they may assent to the teaching they oppose, if it does not pertain to his grace to convert to his faith the wills of persons who are opposed to that faith. Uselessly and insincerely rather than truthfully do we thank God in exultation, when some of them come to believe, if he does not cause this in them.[138]

[135] Cyprian explains, "We should pray and intercede as Christ counsels us, and make intercession for the salvation of all, so that just as the will of God is done in heaven, that is in us, through our faith, with the result that we are in heaven, so also the will of God should be done on earth, that is among those who do not believe, so that those who are earthly from their original birth should begin to be heavenly" (*domin. orat.* 17 [CCL 3A:100–101]).

[136] "And yet Cyprian understands our prayer, *May your will be done in heaven and on earth* (Mt 6:10), in the sense that we also pray for those who are for this reason understood to be earth. We pray, therefore, not only for those who are unwilling, but even for those who resist and attack. What, then, do we pray for but that they become willing instead of unwilling, that they are made to consent instead of to resist, that they are made lovers instead of attackers? By whom will this be done but by him of whom scripture says, *The will is prepared by the Lord* (Prv 8:35 LXX)?" (*C. ep. Pel.* 4.9.26 [CSEL 60:553]).

[137] *Ep.* 215.3 (CSEL 57:390); *ep.* 217.6 (CSEL 57:407–408); *praed. sanct.* 8.15 (PL 44: 971–972); *c. Iul. imp.* 6.10 (CSEL 85.2: 312–313).

[138] In the Latin *contrarias* actually modifies *uoluntas*; it is the wills that are opposed. See *ep.* 217.6 (CSEL 57:407–408): *inaniter igitur et perfunctorie potius quam ueraciter pro eis, ut doctrinae, cui aduersantur, credendo consentiant, deo fundimus preces, si ad eius non pertinet gratiam conuertere ad fidem suam ipsi fidei contrarias hominum uoluntates.* Augustine's *conf.*, in which he attributes great importance to Monica's torrents of tearful prayers on his behalf, shows us that personal experience, not just detached observation, informs this argument "from prayer." In *conf.* 3.11.19, for example, he

Cyprian's *domin. orat.* serves here, as in other cases, as a bridge allowing Augustine to call upon the testimony of the whole church. In Augustine's view, Cyprian has merely pointed out in writing a fact confirmed by prayers of Christians everywhere: God is responsible for turning the wills of those who are unbelieving toward himself.

God's responsibility for reorienting the human will implied, for Augustine, that assent to faith could not be seen as the product of independent human willing. Augustine had already explained to Vitalis at the beginning of *ep.* 217 that if assent to the gospel results from "our own will" (*ex propria uoluntate*) rather than grace, the church's prayers for the conversion of nonbelievers are in vain.[139] He further observes that if Vitalis really means to claim that belief is a result of free will rather than grace, he must condemn his fellow Carthaginian Cyprian, since Cyprian had—in his exposition of the Lord's Prayer—presented assent to belief as the gift of God.[140] Thus Augustine also claimed the support of the Lord's Prayer as interpreted by Cyprian for the view that assent to belief could not be understood as brought about by "our own will" operating without God's grace, but rather had to be attributed to the work of God.

As this analysis of Augustine's late appeals to Cyprian's *domin. orat.* has shown, the Lord's Prayer is significant to the will's transformation in at least three ways. First, the prayer Christ taught his followers serves as an instrument by which Christ heals the will, particularly as Christ enables and answers the petitions for forgiveness of debts, triumph over temptation, and deliverance from evil. Second, the Lord's Prayer in the sense of the Lord's intercession on behalf of believers, exemplified in his prayer for Peter, strengthens the will so that it may persevere in faith and in the good. Third,

---

attributes God's deliverance of his soul from deep darkness, not to any willingness on his own part but to God's gracious attention to Monica's insistent prayers on his behalf: "'You put forth your hand from on high' (Ps. 143:7), and from this deep darkness 'you delivered my soul' (Ps. 85:13). For (*cum*) my mother, your faithful servant, wept for me before you more than mothers weep when lamenting their dead children. By the 'faith and spiritual discernment' (Gal. 5:5) which she had from you, she perceived the death which held me, and you heard her, Lord. You heard her and did not despise her tears which poured forth to wet the ground under her eyes in every place where she prayed" (CCL 27:37). This is Henry Chadwick's translation: Augustine, *Confessions*, trans. Henry Chadwick (New York: Oxford University Press, 1991), 49.

[139] If this were the case, the church (the *fideles*) would be praying for "things [that were] not benefits of God's mercy but tasks of the human will" (*ep.* 217.2 [CSEL 57:404]).

[140] To be consistent Vitalis must, "as a learned man in the church of Carthage, condemn as well the book of the most blessed Cyprian on *The Lord's Prayer.* When that teacher explained this prayer, he showed that we petition from God the Father (*a deo patre*) what you say is given to a human being by a human being (*homini ab homine*), that is, by oneself (*a se ipso*)" (*ep.* 217.2 [CSEL 57:404]).

the Lord's Prayer also serves a didactic function, teaching human beings their need for divine aid in order to persevere, showing the insufficiency of human willing without God's assistance, and demonstrating that God makes the unwilling willing to do the good. Both by teaching his followers the Lord's Prayer and by answering the requests therein, then, Christ effects a transformation of the wills of his followers. Furthermore, the content of the Lord's Prayer, as shown from Augustine's appeals to Cyprian's *domin. orat.*, underlines the need for transformation to come from the same source as the prayer itself.

Insofar as the whole church prays together "*our* Father," the context in which Christ effects this transformation is corporate; it is as members of Christ's one body that his followers are transformed. Furthermore, the transformation effected targets not only the wills of each member of this body via acts of worship undertaken in this corporate context, but also the relationships of the various members to one another. A key feature of Christ's transformation of the human will is his work to fuse the wills of his followers together in him.

In *De trinitate*, Augustine describes Christ's transformative work upon the human wills of his followers as bringing about a unity of will that images the perfect unity of will in the Trinity. He characterizes Christ's work in this way based upon John 17:20: "And I have given them the glory that you have given me, that they may be one as we are one." He expands on Christ's statement as follows: "He wants his disciples to be one in him, because they cannot be one in themselves, split as they are from each other by clashing wills (*uoluntates*) and desires (*cupiditates*), and the uncleanness of their sins."[141] For Augustine, then, the impact of the fall on willing extends further than the level of individual will. Given their impurity, and the fact that their wills and desires pull them in different ways, Christ's followers cannot achieve unity independently of their Lord.

Having diagnosed the problem, Augustine then names the solution: "So they are cleansed by the mediator that they may be one in him, not only by virtue of the same nature whereby all of them from the ranks of mortal men are made equal to the angels, but even more by virtue of one and the same wholly harmonious will (*uoluntatem*) reaching out in concert to the same ultimate happiness, and fused somehow into one spirit in the furnace

---

[141] *Trin.* 4.12 (CCL 50:177).

of charity (*caritatis igne*)."[142] To solve the predicament of disunity of will, Christ the mediator must step in to rid his followers of the impurities causing division. Given this purification, they can experience a unity more intimate, even, than that established by their common humanity. This one-ness is not available apart from Christ. Rather, his followers become "one in him" (*in illo unum*).

Augustine also uses the language of "spirit" to describe the unity that Christ effects. The common will on the basis of which believers are united in Christ is also a will that is fused "into one spirit" (*in unum spiritum*). In fact, to express the complete harmony of this common will, Augustine uses the term *conspirantem*. Christ's followers are united by virtue of sharing in a common willing that, literally speaking, breathes together (*conspirantem*), uniting hearts with one another (*concordissimam*), to such an extent that the saints can be described as sharing "the same will." Of course the literal sense of these terms pushes the phrase to a breaking point—How can a single will "breathe together"?—but Augustine is keen to stress precisely the ex-treme character of this unity, hence his layering of adjectives, use of the su-perlative form of *concors*, and repetition of *eadem*. Augustine does not give further details of how this fusion of many wills into one and the same will occurs except by observing that this will has "in some way [been] blown into flame (*conflatam*) by the fire of charity."[143] Thus Augustine repeatedly uses metaphorical language that evokes images with which the Spirit is as-sociated. He not only states that the will is fused into "one spirit" (*in unum spiritum*) but also describes this will as "breathing together" (*conspirantem*) and "blown up or set alight" by the fire of charity. The latter two terms, whose root meanings draw upon images of breath and wind, surround the phrase *in unum spiritum*, unfurling the biblical term of *spiritus* with further biblical images associated with the Holy Spirit. Becoming "one in him" (*in illi unum*), that is, one in Christ, involves the unification of the disciples' will "into one spirit" (*in unum spiritum*).

Augustine observes that the model for this kind of unified willing is, as Christ himself points out, the unity between the Father and the Son: "Just as the Father and Son are one not only by equality of substance but also by

---

[142] *Trin.* 4.12 (CCL 50:177): *unde mundantur per mediatorem ut sint in illo unum non tantum per eandem naturam qua omnes ex hominibus mortalibus aequales angelis fiunt [Lc 20,36] sed etiam per eandem in eandem beatitudinem conspirantem concordissimam uoluntatem in unum spiritum quodam modo caritatis igne conflatam.*

[143] This is my translation of the Latin text cited in n142.

identity of will (*uoluntate unum*), so these men, for whom the Son is mediator with God, might be one not only by being of the same nature, but also by being bound in the fellowship of the same love (*societam dilectionis*)." The relationship between the Father and the Son serves as analogical model for the kind of unity available to Christ's disciples through Christ's mediation. Because Christ cleanses his followers from sin, they are joined together in a bond of common will, in a communion of common love, even as the Father and the Son are united in will and love through the bond of the Holy Spirit.

As shown in this analysis, Christ's transformation of the human will has implications that extend beyond the context of individual human willing. Christ not only sets the will free from slavery to sin and free for the good; heals the illicit inclinations of the will by forgiving debts, saving his followers from temptation, and delivering them from evil; intercedes on behalf of his followers so as to prevent their wills from failing; and teaches his disciples in the Lord's Prayer their need for his healing if their wills are to be transformed. He also takes the disparate wills of his followers, purifies them, and melds them into one and the same will so that his disciples become one in him in a way that images his own unity with the Father. The language Augustine uses to describe the results of and process by which this unity is attained raises the question of the Spirit's role in the will's transformation and unification with the wills of the rest of the body of Christ. Hence we will turn to the Holy Spirit's impact on the will in the following chapter.

Conclusion

This chapter has presented three ways in which Augustine develops his notion of good human willing in relation to Christ. First, we considered how Christ makes willing the good possible by taking on a human will (part I), assuming the experience of human willing along with a fully human mind and body. Here we observed the importance Augustine accords to the voluntary character of Christ's death, noted that Augustine's anti-Apollinarian Christology in combination with his human psychology imply a human will in Christ, and then traced the development of Augustine's explicit affirmations of a human will in Christ over the course of his career. This final task led to the conclusion that not only did Augustine affirm a human will in Christ distinct from his divine will but also that his description of this human will, in his mature period, proved strikingly similar to that of Maximus the Confessor in the seventh century. We next examined Christ's role as a model of grace's effect upon the human will (part II), which involves three key facets: his illustration of the precedence of grace over any merit of the human will in the incarnation; his prioritization of justice over power, a prioritization proper to right willing that he expressed in undergoing the sufferings of the cross before the glory of the resurrection; and his demonstration of a struggle of will in the garden of Gethsemane that choreographs for believers the steps to take in their own struggles to conform their wills to the will of God. In the third and final part of the chapter, we turned to Christ's direct involvement in bringing about a good will in believers, not merely as an external example but as one who effects inner transformation. Part III analyzed Christ's liberation of the will from sin for the good; the multiple methods of healing the will summarized by, petitioned through, and fulfilled in response to the Lord's Prayer; and Christ's work in unifying the disparate and distracted wills of his followers into one and the same "wholly harmonious will" in him.

Christ, according to Augustine, was one particular human being who partook in the universal human experience of possessing and exercising a human will. Yet, as Augustine came to emphasize with increasing clarity as his career advanced, Christ's voluntary assumption of a human will, and his manner of using it in his everyday life, set him radically apart from all other human beings. Christ's perfectly good human willing made him the ideal model of the kind of willing for which humankind was created, but away from which it had fallen due to the missteps of its ancestors in the garden of Eden. Christ thus entered into the world of fallen human willing but was not of it. Furthermore, his life and actions pointed toward and inaugurated a new world of will. Precisely because of his uniqueness as not only man but God and man, Christ was able to will in a blameless way that was universally significant for the human race. His perfect human willing made possible the liberation and transformation of the fallen will of the rest of humanity.

As reflected in the Lord's Prayer, his perfect human willing did this by making possible the redemption of human willing of the past, present, and future. It was in his concrete particularity, in his difference from the rest of humanity, that Christ was able to unite the diverse wills of all his followers into one universal will of one human mind and one body: his own. Augustine's account of good human willing post-fall does not derive from a set of general abstract principles but rather from a set of particular concrete observations about the person and work of Jesus Christ. Insofar as this person is the same person at the heart of the Christian faith, one is justified in identifying Augustine's conception of the good will as a distinctively Christian conception.

Augustine did not arrive at this Christocentric conception of good human willing at the start of his career. He developed it over time as he struggled to interpret the Bible. His earlier conception of will is monochrome, though it too is developed in theological context. For the early Augustine, the human will per se illumines the workings of the divine will. As we have seen in this chapter, for the mature Augustine, in contrast, Christ's will illuminates how our will should function once redeemed by him. Thus Augustine's thought about the correspondence of the human will with God's will evinces increasing specificity. He moves from underlining the similarity between the divine will and the human will *simpliciter* to characterizing the human will of Christ as having some commonality with both the fallen and the redeemed human wills, to emphasizing the parallels between the human will of Christ and the human will as restored by him.

As noted, the biblical story played a crucial role in bringing Augustine to his mature view about the necessary preconditions for and peculiar features of right, or good, human willing. In chapter 1, we observed how Augustine approached the will in the earlier part of his career in relation to the biblical theme of creation; this eventually led to his mature understanding of the created will. Chapter 2 showed how his ideas about the fallen will were shaped by his reading of Romans. Chapters 3 and 4 demonstrated that the biblical testimony, including but not limited to biblical prayers and injunctions to prayer, was central for Augustine's thinking about good human willing with respect to both human power and the divine impact upon the will. In this chapter we have seen how Augustine's ideas about how God brings about a good will in us in Christ were shaped by his expositions of the Psalms, of Christ's agony in Gethsemane, and of the Lord's Prayer.

In Augustine's discussions of this last biblical text, a peculiar implication of his Christological view of good human willing comes to the fore. On the one hand, his thematization of the good will fits straightforwardly into the pattern of increasing complexity that characterizes his developing notion of the human will. As time has gone on, Augustine has added yet another chronological dimension to his vision of human willing. During the Manichean controversy, he developed an overarching and unidimensional picture of human willing. As he delved further into Paul he complexified this picture, pointing to a distinction between how the will functioned before the fall, in its created integrity, and after sin entered the world. His view of will now involved two distinct characterizations corresponding to two distinct periods: the created will functioned in one way and the fallen will in another. In this chapter (and chapters 3–5) we have seen Augustine adding yet another layer to this understanding: the redeemed will, made possible by Christ's life, death, and resurrection on the cross. This redeemed will is different both from the created will and the fallen will. Unlike the created will, it has a checkered history. Unlike the fallen will, it is free from sin.

On the other hand, the theological period of the redemption of the will by Christ is not just one period among others. Not all of the various dimensions of Augustine's theologically periodized notion of will carry equal weight. The righteous human willing of Christ and the epoch of good willing it inaugurates is not content to operate within the temporal bounds of Christ's short life on earth. Rather, Christ's righteous willing has a magnetic effect whereby it draws other periods within the scheme of Augustine's theological periodization of the will into its field of influence. We see this reflected in his discussion of the Lord's Prayer, wherein he observes that Christ invites his followers to request God's transformation of the will not only with respect to the present but also with respect to the past and the future as they request forgiveness to heal the wound caused by "the concupiscence of the flesh by an illicit turn of the will" and petition God for future deliverance from experiencing concupiscence in the first place.[144] The redemption wrought by Christ does belong to one particular time in the larger story of the workings of the will, but this particular time is also the heart of theological time, from which life-giving blood is pumped into the rest of the complex history of the human will.

Once again the Apostle Paul provides a powerful demonstration of the radical changes in human willing that occur from period to theological period in Augustine's mature scheme. Paul's life is a microcosm of the story of how Christ redeems humanity, including the human will; he illustrates the difference between fallen and redeemed willing. Augustine observes that before receiving Christ's grace "in his interior acts the apostle knew that he was such a man [one who 'holds back from sin, not because of the will, but

---

[144] See *pecc. mer.* 2.4.4.

because of fear'] before receiving the grace of God which is given through Jesus Christ our Lord, and he elsewhere openly admits this."[145] Augustine then cites Ephesians 2:1–5, observing that in Titus 3:4–7, Paul shows "that he was changed and freed from these evils [those described in Titus 3:3] only by the grace of the savior (*per gratiam saluatoris*)."[146] Thus, according to Augustine, Paul attributes his ability to hold back from sin by his will (rather than out of fear) to the grace of Christ. Christ ushers in a new and different stage in Paul's life that has implications for his willing: before Christ he does not will what is right; after Christ's grace enters his life he can do the good voluntarily. Christ's grace ushers in a new period of Paul's life wherein his will functions differently. According to Augustine, Adam's influence on the rest of the human race went far beyond setting an example: he was not just "an example for those who sin by their will" but also "the origin of those born with sin." In the same way, Christ impacts human willing in a way that includes but goes beyond the example he sets for others, rewriting again the rules that govern human willing. When looking closely at this Christological rewriting one sees the fingerprints of the Holy Spirit. It is to the Holy Spirit's role in the transformation of the fallen will into a good will by the grace of Christ that we turn in the following chapter.

---

[145] *C. ep. Pel.* 1.9.15 (CSEL 60:436).
[146] *C. ep. Pel.* 1.9.15 (CSEL 60:437).

7

The Holy Spirit and the Will

Intervention and Analogy

Though Augustine most famously connects the Holy Spirit with the human will in *De Trinitate* (*trin.*), his mature masterpiece of Trinitarian theology, he had in fact linked the two before he became a priest.[1] As we observed in chapter 1, in the early work *De Genesi aduersus Manicheos* (*Gn. adu. Man.*), Augustine had used the everyday image of the will of a human craftsperson to illustrate how to interpret Genesis 1:2 in a nonmaterial way.[2] Just as the will of an artisan is "borne over" the objects of her handiwork without being physically localized in them, so—in the person of the Spirit—the invisible, immaterial power of God was "borne over" the waters of creation in a nonspatial way. Both the will of the craftsperson and the Holy Spirit refer to the immaterial activity by which the creative purposes of a maker are directed toward and brought to bear upon what is made.[3]

During the Pelagian controversy, Augustine's descriptions of how the Holy Spirit and the human will relate become far more frequent, diverse, and complex.[4] Most significantly, he no longer speaks only of the analogy

---

[1] For a concise sketch of the patristic background of Augustine's views on the Holy Spirit, see Robert Louis Wilken, "*Spiritus sanctus secundum scripturas sanctas*: Exegetical Considerations of Augustine on the Holy Spirit," *AS* 31, no. 1 (2000): 5–9. For literature on the topic, see also the bibliographies in Chad Tyler Gerber, *The Spirit of Augustine's Early Theology: Contextualizing Augustine's Pneumatology*, Ashgate Studies in Philosophy & Theology in Late Antiquity (Burlington, VT: Ashgate, 2012), 211–215 and Nello Cipriani, *Lo Spirito Santo, Amore che unisce: pneumatologia e spiritualità in Agostino* (Roma: Città nuova, 2011), 197–198.

[2] See *Gn. adu. Man.* 1.5.8 and 1.7.12.

[3] For recent discussions of Augustine's treatment of the Holy Spirit in *Gn. adu. Man.*, see Cipriani, *Lo Spirito Santo, Amore che unisce*, 25–29 and Gerber, *The Spirit of Augustine's Early Theology*, 156–162. Cipriani endorses O. Du Roy's suggestion that in comparing the Spirit to the will of a craftsperson, Augustine is already associating the Spirit with *caritas*. See Cipriani, 26, where he cites Olivier Du Roy, *L'Intelligence de la foi en la Trinité selon saint Augustin, genèse de sa théologie trinitaire jusqu'en 391* (Paris: Études augustiniennes, 1966), 272. Gerber, however, does not discuss, or even allude to, the connection Augustine establishes between the Spirit and will in *Gn. adu. Man.*

[4] In his thorough, and still classic, study of the Holy Spirit in Augustine's writings, Jacques Verhees observes that the Holy Spirit's role in awakening faith becomes more expansive over time. For his interpretation of the stages of this development, see Jacques Verhees, *God in beweging: Een onderzoek naar de pneumatologie van Augustinus* (Wageningen: H. Veenman, 1968), chapters 4 and 5. In

Augustine on the Will. Han-luen Kantzer Komline, Oxford University Press (2020). © Oxford University Press.
DOI: 10.1093/oso/9780190948801.001.0001

between the Holy Spirit and the human will. He now has an added concern: how these two entities interact. In the comparison from *Gn. adu. Man.*, the Holy Spirit and the human will were on parallel tracks that never intersected. Now Augustine is convinced that the engine of the Holy Spirit, the divine will, propels the good human will forward along its divinely predestined yet freely chosen course. The Holy Spirit and the human will are connected causally, as well as analogically.

This causality extends only in one direction. The Holy Spirit enables right human willing, but Augustine never speaks of right human willing as determining the divine will. Nonetheless, as I will argue in this chapter, Augustine's conception of human willing and his views about the Holy Spirit are mutually interpreting on a noetic level. Our understanding of each contributes to our understanding of the other, even while, on the level of being, the Holy Spirit impacts the human will in a way that is irreversible. The Holy Spirit helps us to understand how the human will is intended to function and indeed is the very power by which the human will is freed from its fallen state to run as it was intended to. The human will, on the other hand, when considered in the organic context of its relationship to other elements of Augustine's theological anthropology, sheds light on the way in which the members of the Trinity relate and therefore on the identity of the Holy Spirit. Augustine's conception of the good human will both takes shape in the context of and helps to express his Trinitarian understanding of God.

As we observed in chapter 6, Christ affects human willing in at least three ways: by taking on a human will, by modeling right human willing, and by transforming human willing. In this chapter we will see how the Holy Spirit brings Christ's transforming work to fulfillment by enabling right human willing (part I) and how this good human willing images the Holy Spirit (part II). Augustine, then, does not merely articulate his view of will in relation to God in general; he develops an understanding of the human will in relation to the triune God of the Christian faith, the God who is three in one:—Father, Son, and Holy Spirit. In this sense, Augustine's mature account of good human willing has a distinctively Christian character.

---

particular, observes Verhees, the help of the Holy Spirit, in addition to Christ's work as mediator, becomes more prominent during the Pelagian controversy (353).

Part I: The Holy Spirit Enables Right Willing

The Holy Spirit enables right human willing, in Augustine's mature account of the good human will, neither by performing a work separate from
the redeeming work of Christ in a human person nor by doing something
identical to what Christ does for human willing. Rather, the Holy Spirit
cooperates inseparably with Christ. The Holy Spirit brings Christ's work
to redeem the human will to fruition by bringing about three distinctive
effects in us (section A) via three distinctive means (section B). By bringing
about these particular effects in these particular ways, the Holy Spirit plays
a vital role in making right human willing a reality—a role distinct, yet inseparable, from that of Christ.

The initial point that must be made about the Holy Spirit's work to enable
right willing, then, is that the Holy Spirit assists human willing by following
through on Christ's work in us, not by beginning a new independent work
subsequent to that of Christ. At the same time, however, the assistance the
Holy Spirit provides is more than an optional victory lap in celebration of
what Christ has already done, as if this work were already complete without
the Holy Spirit. The Holy Spirit does not enable right human willing independently of Christ. Nor, however, does Christ enable right human willing
without the Holy Spirit.[5]

From the very outset of his involvement in the Pelagian controversy,
Augustine consistently refers to the Holy Spirit when describing how it
is that Christ's work goes beyond the provision of an external model, or
example, of good willing that a person might imitate. Augustine explains

[5] On the complementary roles of Christ and the Holy Spirit in mediating the virtues to Christians,
a mediation that includes the renovation of human willing, see Robert Dodaro, "Augustine on the
Roles of Christ and the Holy Spirit in the Mediation of the Virtues," *AS* 41, no. 1 (2010): 145–163.
Dodaro intervenes in debates about whether the Holy Spirit or Christ should be seen as primarily
responsible for mediating the virtues to Christians by pointing out the importance of the principle
of the interpenetration of the divine persons and operations, in addition to the principle of the
distinctions between the divine persons and operations, for understanding how the work of the Holy
Spirit and the work of Christ relate. Given this principle, the pressure to determine precisely which
activities ought to be assigned to Christ, which to the Holy Spirit, and how exactly their roles inter-
sect, diminishes. Dodaro's work issues an important reminder of the inseparability of the work of
Christ and the Holy Spirit and of not conceiving of these as locked into the competition of a zero-sum
game, a problematic tendency he points out in previous research on the issue (see his summary of the
debate on 145–155). In this chapter, our chief concern is to show that Augustine does indeed attribute
the work of transforming the human will to the Spirit, as well as to Christ, rather than to draw a sharp
boundary between the work of one person and the other or to demonstrate that Augustine gives primacy to either Christ or the Holy Spirit in a way that would contradict the principle of the interpenetration of divine operations.

in *pecc. mer.,* for instance, that the justification "by which Christ makes the sinner righteous" is a justification that is more than "an example to be imitated." Human beings cannot follow Christ's example of justice on their own; justification is something "that he [Christ] alone can do."[6] But Christ alone, and not any merely human person, accomplishes justification precisely through his Holy Spirit. As Augustine goes on to explain, "Christ is the one in whom all are justified, because it is not merely imitation of him that makes persons righteous, but the grace that gives them rebirth through the Spirit."[7] What sets the kind of justification Christ provides apart from other, merely human examples of justice and what sets the grace of Christ apart from the grace of creation, law, or teaching, is that human beings are made righteous through a regenerating grace that works "through the Spirit" (*per spiritum*). When Augustine refers to what "Christ alone" accomplishes in the human person, he means what Christ does in and with his Holy Spirit.

Augustine applies this general pattern, whereby the Holy Spirit makes the grace of Christ effective in believers, to the predicament of the fallen human will in particular. Continuing on in *pecc. mer.,* he notes that the sin that human beings have "added to original sin by their own will (*propria uoluntate*)" is "taken away and healed through Christ" along with the original sin they inherit from Adam.[8] Again, however, Christ's role in the removal and healing of voluntary sin is not in competition with that of the Spirit. Paul adds the phrase "through Jesus Christ our Lord" in Romans 5:21, Augustine explains, because, while original sin "is contracted through birth in the flesh . . . through rebirth in the Spirit we have forgiveness, not only of original sin, but also of voluntary (*uoluntariorum*) sins."[9] Augustine contrasts and opposes spiritual rebirth, "regeneration in the Spirit" (*regenerante . . . spiritu*) with carnal birth, "generation in the flesh" (*generante carne*), but not with rebirth "through Jesus Christ our Lord." His attribution to Christ of the "taking away" and "healing" of voluntary sin is of a piece with his insistence that forgiveness of voluntary sins is obtained through rebirth in the Spirit. The work of the latter more fully explains and completes, rather than detracts from, the work of the former.

---

[6] *Pecc. mer.* 1.14.18 (CSEL 60:18).
[7] *Pecc. mer.* 1.15.19 (CSEL 60:19).
[8] *Pecc. mer.* 1.15.20 (CSEL 60:20).
[9] *Pecc. mer.* 1.15.20 (CSEL 60:20).

One can find the pattern of cooperation between Christ and the Holy Spirit in renovating the human will at work already in Augustine's eighth homily on First John, likely composed in 407.[10] Augustine begins this homily with the frank pronouncement that "love (*dilectio*) is a sweet word but a sweeter deed."[11] He then proceeds to describe how Christ enables us to act with love by directing us in virtue. The elaborate analogy he employs in this description illustrates that for Augustine, even before the Pelagian controversy, the roles of Christ, the good will, and the Holy Spirit are intimately interwoven in the life of virtue. How he describes the relations between these roles, however, will gain depth and specificity during the Pelagian controversy, over the course of which certain basic patterns emerge.

Here in his eighth homily on First John, Augustine characterizes the good will as soldiering for Christ, whom he depicts as a general:

> For, just as a general (*imperator*) does through his army whatever pleases him, so the Lord Jesus Christ, when he begins to dwell in our inner man (that is, in our mind through faith), uses these virtues as his ministers. And through these virtues, which cannot be seen by the eyes and are nonetheless praised when they are named . . . through these invisible virtues our members are moved visibly. The feet for walking: but where? Where a good will (*bona uoluntas*), which soldiers for a good general (*quae militat bono imperatori*), moves them. The hands for working: but for what? For what charity (*caritas*), which has been inspired by the Holy Spirit (*a spiritu sancto*), commands.[12]

In this passage, as in others we examined in chapter 5, Augustine places a "good will" (*bona uoluntas*) and "charity" (*caritas*), in apposition; just as the good will moves the feet in accord with virtue, so charity moves the hands in accord with virtue. The good will, then, together with charity, is presented as the object of two types of divine action, as well as the subject of actions of its own. First, the good will fights in the command of the good general. It is subject to the direction of Christ. Second, the charity in which

---

[10] The current consensus is that Augustine's ten homilies on First John were preached in 407 rather than in the 410s, as previously thought. See Augustine, *Homilies on the First Epistle of John*, trans. Boniface Ramsey, WSA III/14 (Hyde Park, NY: New City Press, 2008), 9. Unless otherwise noted, translations of *In epistulam Iohannis ad Parthos tractatus* (*ep. Io. tr.*) come from this source.

[11] *Ep. Io. tr.* 8.1 (PL 35:2035).

[12] *Ep. Io. tr.* 8.1 (PL 35:2036).

the good will consists is "inspired inwardly by the Holy Spirit" (*inspirata est intus a spiritu sancto*).[13] Given that it serves as the object of these two distinct divine actions, of the agency of Christ and the Holy Spirit, the good will possesses the power to exert its own impact. In the form of charity, the good will invisibly commands the visible members of the body to carry out what Christ has purposed and the Holy Spirit has inspired. Here in this passage again, then, we see that Christ and the Holy Spirit work in tandem to command and inspire a good will in the human person.

As Augustine provides further descriptions of the work of the Holy Spirit to enable right human willing, he constantly presupposes its indivisibility from the work of Christ, which we have seen clearly displayed as early as 407. Keeping this central presupposition in mind, we can proceed with considering the distinctive work of the Holy Spirit to make the good will possible. First, we will turn our attention to what the Holy Spirit accomplishes in the human person to enable right willing (section A). We will observe that, for Augustine, the Holy Spirit follows through on Christ's redeeming work upon the will by pouring out the love of Christ in our hearts, thereby setting our wills afire to delight in and love God, to freely choose the good, and to obey God's commandments. Next we will focus on Augustine's descriptions of how the Holy Spirit acts upon the will (section B). We will see that the Holy Spirit acts upon the will by the Spirit's very presence, by "driving" the human will, and by the power of the Spirit's own will. From a bird's-eye perspective, then, this part of the chapter will serve to answer the question of how the Holy Spirit enables right willing from the angles of both the effects in us (section A) and the agency of the Holy Spirit (section B).

Section A: What the Holy Spirit Accomplishes in the Human Person to Enable Right Willing

It is clear that for Augustine, the Holy Spirit brings about charity in the believer. Augustine is convinced of this on the basis of Romans 5:5, which he uses as a hermeneutical key to interpret Romans 8:26–27 in his sixth homily on First John.[14] He writes, "What does *the Spirit himself asks on behalf of the*

---

[13] My translation. Ramsey does not translate *intus*.

[14] According to Wilken, this verse plays a pivotal role more generally in Augustine's doctrine of the Holy Spirit: it was a "pillar for Augustine's thinking" ("*Spiritus sanctus secundum scripturas sanctas*," 7).

saints refer to if not to that very charity (*caritas*) which was brought about in you through the Spirit (*per spiritum*)? For that is why the same Apostle says, *The charity of God has been poured out in our hearts through the Holy Spirit, who has been given to us* (Rom 5:5)."[15] But how does the outpouring of charity in a person affect the human will, making right willing possible?

A first observation to make in answering this question is that in pouring out charity in our hearts, the Holy Spirit sets our wills afire to delight in and love God. This point, like the two further points to be treated in this section, comes through especially clearly in one of the earliest works Augustine wrote during the Pelagian controversy, *De spiritu et littera* (*spir. et litt.*, 412–413), which addresses the question of what it means to be righteous before God and how human beings are to achieve such righteousness. Since Augustine's response to the latter question is that righteousness is possible only by the Spirit's outpouring of love in human hearts, *spir. et litt.* explains and explores the Spirit's outpouring of love at length. Augustine reiterates each of the points to be treated in this section, however, in writings from much later during the controversy, showing that his teaching on the Holy Spirit's effects on good human willing follows the trajectory set in *spir. et litt.*, even during the controversy's subsequent phases. His comments show repeatedly that Romans 5:5 has a powerful impact on his Pneumatology. His further comments about the work of the Holy Spirit ripple outward from this central scriptural text.

At the outset of *spir. et litt.*, Augustine takes a decisive stance against "those who think that the power of the human will can by itself (*per se ipsam uim uoluntatis humanae*), without the help of God, either attain righteousness or make progress in tending toward it."[16] To this opinion he opposes his own view: "We, on the other hand, say that the human will (*humanam uoluntatem*) is helped to achieve righteousness."[17] Augustine's explanation of how exactly the human will is helped in this way continues at length, but in these initial phrases he has already put his finger on the crux of the difference, as he sees it, between his position and that of the Pelagian Christians whose views he rejects. They think that the human will can attain righteousness "on its own" (*per se ipsam*). Augustine is convinced, in contrast, that to attain righteousness the human will must "be helped" (*adiuuari*).

---

[15] *Ep. Io. tr.* 6.8 (PL 35:2024).
[16] *Spir. et litt.* 2.4 (CSEL 60:156).
[17] *Spir. et litt.* 3.5 (CSEL 60:157).

Furthermore, not just any help will do: the human will must be helped "by divine influence" (*diuinitus*).[18]

Going on to specify the character of this divine aid more narrowly, Augustine explains that human beings are given an additional gift over and above the free choice with which they were created and the teaching by which they are commanded: "They receive the Holy Spirit so that there arises in their minds a delight (*delectatio*) in and a love (*dilectio*) for that highest and immutable good that is God, even now while they walk by faith, not yet by vision."[19] Divine help for the human will so that it might do what is right, then, comes not only in the forms of natural ability and knowledge but also in the form of the Holy Spirit. The Holy Spirit then inspires in the mind both "delight" (*delectatio*) in and "love" (*dilectio*) for God. As Augustine explains, these gifts of delight and love are essential if one is actually to live righteously. Knowing the right thing to do is necessary but not sufficient for righteousness, since even "when what we should do and the goal we should strive for begins to be clear, unless we find delight in it (*delectet*) and love it (*ametur*), we do not act, do not begin, do not live good lives."[20] Mere knowledge of the good can leave a person aloof and unmoved. Delight and love must be present to spur her on to perform the actions she knows are right.

Augustine uses dramatic imagery to unfurl further the effect such a gift of the Holy Spirit has on the willing of a person: "By this [love] given to them like the pledge of a gratuitous gift, they are set afire with the desire to cling to the creator and burn to come to participation in that true light, so that they have their well-being from him from whom they have their being."[21] Twice Augustine employs terms that portray the human person as being set ablaze by the love (*dilectio*) she receives through the Holy Spirit. This love makes her catch fire (*inardescat*)[22] so that she is inflamed (*inflammetur*).

She does not burn, however, with a capricious conflagration. She is set on fire to be welded (*inhaerere*) to her creator. She is inflamed to draw near (*accedere*) to her God, for the sake of participation (*ad participationem*) in the source of her burning love. The fire the Holy Spirit ignites so that she

---

[18] Teske leaves out the adverb *diuinitus* in his rendering.

[19] *Spir. et litt.* 3.5 (CSEL 60:157).

[20] *Spir. et litt.* 3.5 (CSEL 60:157).

[21] *Spir. et litt.* 3.5 (CSEL 60:157).

[22] This term is used in poetry up to Augustine's time and in prose after Augustine. See Charlton T. Lewis, *A Latin Dictionary* (New York: Oxford University Press, 1879), 916.I.

may will rightly rages back toward God. God is the one who made her will, and God is the one who remakes it to return to its Maker. As if to make this point unmistakable, Augustine closes his explanation of how the "human will is helped to achieve righteousness" by returning explicitly to the Holy Spirit, reiterating that the third person of the Trinity provides the requisite aid: "But so that we may love (*diligatur*) [the good we should do], *the love of God* is poured out *in our hearts,* not by free choice (*arbitrium liberum*) which comes from ourselves, but *by the Holy Spirit who has been given to us* (Rom 5:5)."[23] Drawing again on Romans 5:5, Augustine ends his explanation of how God enables the human will to achieve righteousness with the same person with whom he had begun it, no human person, but a divine person: the Holy Spirit.

Augustine uses similar language about the work of the Holy Spirit to enable human beings to will rightly in the late work *De correptione et gratia* (*corrept.*), when contrasting the grace God originally bestowed upon Adam and the grace God gives to the faithful. The first kind of grace, he explains, enabled Adam to persevere given the will to do so. The second, however, goes further: God "also produces in them the will (*uelle*) as well."[24] Thus, after the fall, God gives his people both "the ability and the will (*uoluntas*) to persevere by the generosity of divine grace."[25] As in *spir. et litt.*, Augustine appeals to the Spirit to elucidate this divine work of enabling right willing, which in this case ultimately produces a will to persevere: "Their will (*uoluntas*) is, of course, set afire (*accenditur*) by the Holy Spirit to the point that they are able because they will to so strongly, but they will to so strongly because God makes them to will."[26] In *spir. et litt.* Augustine had characterized the Spirit's assistance of the human will as involving the implanting of delight and love in the human mind and setting the human person (*homo*) ablaze with that love. Augustine here continues to describe the Spirit's assistance of the will using imagery of burning but now puts an even finer point on his description by characterizing the will itself as "set afire by the Holy Spirit."

In *Contra Iulianum opus imperfectum* (*c. Iul. imp.*), which was still in progress at the time of Augustine's death, he continues to hold firmly to

---

[23] *Spir. et litt.* 3.5 (CSEL 60:157).
[24] *Corrept.* 12.38 (CSEL 92:266).
[25] *Corrept.* 12.38 (CSEL 92:266).
[26] *Corrept.* 12.38 (CSEL 92:266).

the notion that the Holy Spirit is responsible for producing the love in human hearts that makes willing the good possible. Furthermore, in this work Augustine argues not only that a good will can result from love that comes from God, that is, from the *caritas* poured out by the Holy Spirit, but also that a good will can result only from love that comes from God. There are two steps involved in this argument. First, Augustine contends that only *caritas* can will what is good. Even a good as great as the law cannot, on its own, help human beings to achieve right willing. The letter of the law admonishes people to fling themselves on grace, but on its own it only adds to their guilt. Without love, the letter of the law is of no assistance. Only *caritas* can solve the problem of fallen human willing because *caritas* "alone wills what is good."[27] Second, Augustine argues that only God can give us *caritas*. We cannot love, Augustine explains, "without his giving the love (*caritatem*) which surpasses knowledge."[28] If (1) only *caritas* can will what is good and (2) only God can give us *caritas*, it follows that (3) only given God's gift can we will what is good. We are given this gift, Augustine explains, through the Holy Spirit. He condenses his whole argument in this sentence: "Love (*caritas*) wills what is good, and love comes from God, not through the letter of the law, but through the Spirit of grace."[29] As Augustine makes clear here, the love of God poured out in our hearts by the Holy Spirit is not just *a* means by which we may will the good. The work of the Spirit to fill us with *caritas* is the only means by which we may will the good. From *spir. et litt.* on through to *c. Iul. imp.*, then, Augustine portrays the Holy Spirit as enabling right willing by setting human wills afire with delight in and love for God, the true Good.

Further elaborating on the Holy Spirit's impact on the human will in *spir. et litt.* after summarizing what occurs "through the Holy Spirit" (*per spiritum sanctum*) to make human beings delight in the good,[30] Augustine voices a question his readers may be asking themselves: "Are we then doing away with (*euacuamus*) free choice through grace?"[31] Does the Spirit diffuse love (*caritas eius . . . diffusa*) in such a way as to evacuate the human

---

[27] *C. Iul. imp.* (CSEL 85.1:109–110).

[28] Augustine argues that to believe that "we cannot know without God's giving us knowledge, that is without his teaching us, but we can love without his giving the love which surpasses knowledge" would be ludicrous. "Only the new heretics and fierce enemies of the grace of God think that way" (*c. Iul. imp.* 1.95 [CSEL 85.1:110]).

[29] *C. Iul. imp.* 1.94 (CSEL 85.1:109).

[30] *Spir. et litt.* 29.51 (CSEL 60:208).

[31] *Spir. et litt.* 30.52 (CSEL 60:208).

will of free choice? Augustine goes to great lengths to show that far from undermining free choice, the Holy Spirit's work in fact strengthens and undergirds it. Increasing human freedom, then, is another effect in us of the Holy Spirit's work to enable right human willing.

To show how this is the case, Augustine engages in theological chemistry, analyzing the components of a chain reaction that illustrates how the work of the Holy Spirit and free choice are related. Whereas in the *Confessions* he had traced the links of the chain binding fallen human beings in sin, he now turns his attention to a different kind of chain. The chain he described in the *Confessions* ended in bondage; this chain reaction ends in freedom. Both, however, are based on the Bible, according to Augustine. Of the second, Augustine writes, "All these items which I linked together like a chain have their own expression in scripture."[32]

Augustine introduces each component of this chain with the preposition "through" (*per*), showing how one element catalyzes another: "through the law there is knowledge of sin, through faith there is the obtaining by entreaty of grace against sin, through grace there is the health of the soul from the defect of sin, through the health of the soul we obtain the freedom of choice, through the freedom of choice there is delight in justice, through justice there is delight in the doing of the law."[33] Though Augustine does not mention the Holy Spirit directly in his characterization of each of these components, the Holy Spirit's work is clearly implied since it is a description of this work that has prompted him to address the concern he is now addressing, namely, whether grace undermines free will.

This sequence clearly implies at least two things about the relationship of the work of the Holy Spirit and free choice. First, it implies that the work of the Holy Spirit gives people access to free choice of the good. In this sequence, grace, presumably referring to no other grace than "the sweetness of grace through the Holy Spirit" to which Augustine has just referred, leads to a health of soul that promotes freedom of choice (*libertas arbitrium*). Furthermore, precisely through the free choice (*liberum arbitrium*) made possible by this grace, one is able to "delight in justice," another gift Augustine has ascribed to the Holy Spirit. Second, then, the infusion of delight through the Holy Spirit follows this free will. Thus the work of the Holy Spirit, in this account, fully embraces free choice. Free choice

---

[32] *Spir. et litt.* 30.52 (CSEL 60:208–209).
[33] *Spir. et litt.* 30.52 (CSEL 60:208). I have adapted Teske's translation.

presupposes the healing of the will accomplished by the Holy Spirit and the delight in justice that the Holy Spirit introduces happens precisely "through the freedom of choice." The resulting picture of the relationship between the Holy Spirit and free choice is not that the former hems in the latter. Rather this entire sequence is designed to show that "free choice (*liberum arbitrium*) is not done away with by grace, but strengthened, because grace heals the will (*uoluntatem*) by which we freely (*libere*) love righteousness."[34] Already here in *spir. et litt.*, then, Augustine is depicting the Holy Spirit as acting directly upon the will for its liberation.

In uncovering the scriptural framework that orders the causal links he has just summarized, Augustine affirms the positive relationship not only between the work of the Holy Spirit and free choice but also between the Holy Spirit and freedom. After invoking a number of scriptural excerpts, he writes, "Why then do wretched human beings dare to be proud of their free choice (*libero arbitrio*), before they are set free, or of their own powers, if they have already been set free? They do not notice that in the very name for free choice (*nomine liberi arbitrii*) we hear freedom (*libertatem*); *but where the Spirit of the Lord is, there is freedom (libertas)* (2 Cor 3:17)."[35] True enough, Augustine admits, fallen human beings do possess free choice, no matter how wretchedly in need of God's grace they may be. But not until God has freed them does that free choice actually accrue to their benefit, such that they might be at all justified in taking pride in it. Before God's grace breaks in, they are free only to choose evil. Human beings can have "free choice (*liberum arbitrium*), before they are set free (*liberentur*)," but it is not until God liberates them that they become truly "free" (*liberati*). Thus the term "free choice" (*liberum arbitrium*) seems to imply freedom (*libertas*) but does not guarantee the genuine freedom consisting in freedom for the good. This genuine freedom (*libertas*) comes from the presence of the Holy Spirit. Thus, Augustine concludes on the basis of 2 Corinthians 3:17, the Holy Spirit augments rather than contracts the positive potential of "free choice" (*liberum arbitrium*) by bestowing a genuine freedom (*libertas*) for the good on a human person.

As the Pelagian controversy progresses, Augustine continues to affirm that the Holy Spirit sets the will free to will what is right. Pointing to the "Spirit of grace" (*spiritu gratiae*) as making possible human fulfillment of

---

[34] *Spir. et litt.* 30.52 (CSEL 60:208).
[35] *Spir. et litt.* 30.52 (CSEL 60:209).

the law in *Contra duas epistulas Pelagianorum* (*c. ep. Pel.*), likely written in 421, he explains, "The righteousness of the law is not fulfilled when the law commands and human beings observe it as if by their own powers, but when the Spirit provides help (*adiuuat*) and the human will (*uoluntas*) observes it, not a free will, but a will set free by the grace of God."[36] Here again Augustine connects the assistance of the Holy Spirit with the will's free performance of the good. Furthermore, by insisting on the distinction between a "free" (*libera*) will and this "freed" (*liberata*) will, Augustine drives home the point that the will does not inherently enjoy the kind of freedom the Spirit makes possible. To apply the adjective "free" (*libera*) to the will that the Holy Spirit helps to fulfill the law is misleading if construed to suggest that such freedom is the will's inalienable possession, unable to be diminished or increased by external forces, or already within the person's power before the intervention of the Holy Spirit. This "freed will" that is the will redeemed by the work of the Holy Spirit is different from the "created will," which was inherently free to choose good or evil. It is also different from the fallen will, which was free to choose evil, but not truly "free" for the good. Rather the redeemed will is a third kind of will: it is a "freed" (*liberata*) will, one whose freedom for the good is entirely derivative from the work of the Holy Spirit. The redeemed will is a passively free will; it must be liberated to enjoy liberty. The Holy Spirit performs this work of liberation.

For Augustine, then, in addition to setting us afire with delight and love for God, the Holy Spirit enables right human willing by healing the will so that it may love and delight in the good freely. A third effect of the Holy Spirit's work to enable right human willing, one also on display in the passage just considered from *c. ep. Pel.*, is that human beings become capable of obeying God's commands. We have seen that in *c. ep. Pel.* human beings fulfill the law precisely "when the Spirit (*spiritus*) provides help" so that "the human will (*uoluntas*) observes it." But, as with the other two effects of the Spirit's enabling of right human willing we have considered, Augustine already sounds a decisive note of emphasis on the Holy Spirit in *spir. et litt.* This note resounds in works written later during the Pelagian controversy.

In *spir. et litt.*, Augustine makes clear that only a love (*caritas*) that drives out all other preferences from the will makes it possible to achieve the

---

[36] *C. ep. Pel.* 3.7.20 (CSEL 60:510).

"righteousness of God." Fear (*timor*) of punishment, too, can be a powerful motivator. It can obtain certain kinds of results. But even if fear produces the right kinds of actions, it presupposes the wrong kind of will. For fear leads to a situation in which one does what one ought because one is forced, while one would really prefer to be doing something else. The crucial difference between love and fear is that love "only finds pleasing what is permitted," while fear "is forced to do what is permitted" and therefore still "has something else in its will (*in uoluntate*) by which it would prefer, if it were possible, that what is not permitted be permitted."[37] Love purifies the will: it results in a person willing only one thing (*non libet nisi quod licet*). Fear adulterates the will: it leaves a trace of a competing preference in the will (*aliud habeat in uoluntate*). However contained, contingent, and secondary this preference, it remains what it is: something one would rather do than do the good. The righteousness of God (*dei iustitiam*), however, sets the bar high. It does not admit this kind of double-mindedness. Unlike one's "own righteousness" (*iustitiam suam*), God's righteousness requires and consists of the singleminded willing that love makes possible.

What is the source of this love, which alone can produce genuine good works? Posing this question himself, Augustine then answers it in the words of Romans 5:5: "It (*caritas*) would not be in us, however much there is in us, if it were not poured out in our hearts by the Holy Spirit (*per spiritum sanctum*) who has been given to us."[38] Thus, just as the Holy Spirit enables right human willing by enduing the human will with delight in and love for the good, and heals the human will so that it may freely delight in and love the good, so he also purifies human willing by providing the kind of love necessary to make obedience of God's commandments genuine on the level of will. This purifying love, which the Holy Spirit infuses, Augustine explains, is nothing other than a love for God. Certainly, God loves us. But the love poured out in our hearts is different from the divine love for human beings: "The love of God said to be poured out in our hearts is not that by which he loves us, but that by which he makes us love him."[39] While the freedom the Holy Spirit bestows upon human willing by grace is a

---

[37] "Those people who are under the law try to achieve their own righteousness out of fear of punishment and do not, for this reason, achieve the righteousness of God. Only love does that, love which only finds pleasing what is permitted, not fear which is forced to do what is permitted, while it has something else in its will by which it would prefer, if it were possible, that what is not permitted be permitted" (*Spir. et litt.* 32.56 [CSEL 60:213]).

[38] *Spir. et litt.* 32.56 (CSEL 60:215).

[39] *Spir. et litt.* 32.56 (CSEL 60:215).

passive freedom insofar as it is entirely derivative from the work of God in the human person, the love the Holy Spirit diffuses in human hearts gives them the purity of will to have an active, and not merely passive, love and righteousness. Again drawing on the pivotal text of Romans 5:5, Augustine makes clear that the source of this transforming love, which drives out all other preferences from the will and thereby makes it possible for human beings to "achieve" the righteousness of God, is none other than the Holy Spirit.

One finds Augustine making a similar point a few years later in *De perfectione iustitiae hominis* (*perf. iust.*; 415), again using Romans 5:5. Here he argues that the commandment of God is able to be fulfilled only by the Holy Spirit, not by the choice of the human will, because the Holy Spirit pours out a love in human hearts that makes obedience "light and sweet" rather than onerous and bitter. This love, he reminds them, has to be given by the Holy Spirit: "It, of course, *is poured out in our hearts*, not by ourselves, but *by the Holy Spirit who has been given to us* (Rom 5:5)."[40] For the purposes of being raised up on the "wings" (*pinnae*) of this love without divine aid, he warns, "the choice of our will (*uoluntatis arbitrium*) is of little use."[41] Reiterating this point shortly afterward with yet another appeal to Romans 5:5, Augustine writes, "They ought to be admonished by it that the commandment of God is not burdensome for the love of God, which is only *poured out in our hearts by the Holy Spirit* (Rom 5:5), not by the choice of the human will (*non per arbitrium humanae uoluntatis*). By attributing more than they ought to the human will, they fail to know the righteousness of God."[42] In this instance, however, Augustine qualifies his contrast of the powerlessness of the choice of will against the power of the Spirit's love. Augustine presents the Holy Spirit as making possible a kind of loving that the choice of the "human will" (*humanae uoluntatis*), in particular, cannot.[43] Certainly the use of the adjective "human" fits well with the contrasts Augustine sets up between divine and human action,

---

[40] *Perf. iust.* 10.21 (CSEL 42:21).

[41] *Perf. iust.* 10.21 (CSEL 42:21).

[42] *Perf. iust.* 10.22 (CSEL 42:23).

[43] Elsewhere Augustine contrasts the power by which the Spirit pours out love in our hearts with the "powers of the nature or of the will (*uoluntatis*) which are found in us." The full quotation reads: "But wherever or whenever it [righteousness] is so complete that no addition to it is possible, it is, nonetheless, not *poured out in our hearts* by the powers of nature or of the will which are found in us, but *by the Holy Spirit who has been given to us* (Rom 5:5). He comes to the aid of our weakness and along with us restores our good health. For this love is *the grace of God through Jesus Christ, our Lord* (Rom 7:25)" (*nat. et grat.* 70.84 [CSEL 60:298–299]).

especially those between divine action and human action in its vitiated state subsequent to the fall. But this qualifier also raises the question of whether Augustine is already beginning to associate the Holy Spirit with the divine will. Given such an association, attributing causality to the love of the Spirit would not entail denying the same causality to choice of the will per se, but only to the choice of the "human will."[44] In any case, Augustine's main concern is to attribute to the Holy Spirit a transformative love that is not available on the basis of the independent operation of the human will. Working through this transformative love to liberate the human will, the Spirit makes it possible for human beings to obey God's commandments.

In *De gratia et libero arbitrio* (*gr. et lib. arb.*), Augustine continues to maintain that the Holy Spirit's work upon the will has the effect of making people capable of obeying God's commands. Here he argues that the Spirit must help the person suffering from weakness of will[45] if she is to achieve obedience, for "unless the spirit of grace provides help, the prohibitions of the law increase concupiscence and give it strength."[46] In this late stage of the Pelagian controversy, too, the Holy Spirit, for Augustine, helps to explain how "a human being is . . . helped by grace in such a way that his will (*uoluntas*) does not receive the commandments to no purpose."[47] Thanks to the Holy Spirit's work in the human person to enable right willing, she is now able to obey God's commands.

Section B: How the Holy Spirit Acts upon the Will to Enable Right Willing

As we have seen, Augustine provides detailed descriptions, in his anti-Pelagian writings, of the effect that the Holy Spirit has upon the human will. During the Pelagian controversy, he also homes in more narrowly on the character of the Holy Spirit's agency—he is interested in describing the cause as well as the effect of the Holy Spirit's work on the will. Whereas three major aspects of Augustine's teaching on the effects of the Holy Spirit

---

[44] In the second part of this chapter we will address the question of the correspondence between the Holy Spirit and the divine will.

[45] In this case, Augustine describes this weakness of will as expressed in the statement "I will (*uolo*) to observe them, but I am conquered by my concupiscence" (*Gr. et lib. arb.* 4.8 [PL 44:887]).

[46] *Gr. et lib. arb.* 4.8 (PL 44:887).

[47] *Gr. et lib. arb.* 4.9 (PL 44:887).

on the will are already apparent in *spir. et litt.*, his elaboration on the identity of the Holy Spirit as the cause of the renovation of human willing tends to be concentrated more heavily in other works, stemming from both before and after *spir. et litt.* was written. Yet across this broad temporal swath, a coherent picture emerges from a consideration of all of Augustine's comments on the means by which the Holy Spirit acts upon the will. Augustine argues that the Holy Spirit operates on the will by his very presence, by driving the will, and by means of the divine will. We will now consider each of these characterizations.

Willing rightly, Augustine makes clear in *spir. et litt.* (412), is not just about receiving a gift from the Holy Spirit that is a *tertium quid*. Rather, the writing of the law on our hearts and the outpouring of love in our hearts that sets into motion our right willing are possible by virtue of the very finger of God: "What then are the laws of God that are written by God himself on our hearts but the very presence (*praesentia*) of the Holy Spirit? He is the finger of God; by his presence (*quo praesente*) love is poured out in our hearts, the love which is the fulfillment of the law and the goal of the commandment."[48] The Holy Spirit's *presence* in us makes possible right willing. The Holy Spirit does not send an emissary to do the dirty work of sweeping clean the human heart and filling it with fresh air and light. Nor does the Spirit use some kind of instrument external to and distinct from the Spirit's own being to pour out love in human hearts. Instead he serves as both giver and gift. He pours out his love by his own presence because he is this gift of love.

In fact, Augustine had already laid the groundwork for identifying the love poured out in human hearts as the Holy Spirit before writing *spir. et litt.* He had already said in *ep. Io. tr.* that the Holy Spirit is "in love" (*in dilectione*) in general, not just in the love poured out in our hearts. Commenting on the statement "God is love," Augustine writes, "But when you hear *from God*, either the Son or the Holy Spirit is understood. But, because the Apostle says, *The charity of God has been poured out in our hearts through the Holy Spirit, who has been given to us* (Rom 5:5), we should understand that in love there is the Holy Spirit."[49] Given this general principle, the outpouring of love in our hearts already entails that the Holy Spirit is poured out in our hearts in some sense. Here again we see the crucial role of Romans 5:5, in

---

[48] *Spir. et litt.* 21.36 (CSEL 60:189).
[49] *Ep. Io. tr.* 7.6 (PL 35:2032).

this case not for connecting the Holy Spirit with the love by which our wills are reoriented in particular, but for establishing a tight association between the Holy Spirit and love (here: *dilectio*) that will later be brought to bear in Augustine's teachings on the will.

We have already seen in chapter 3 that Augustine's attribution of agency to God in bringing about good human willing expands in the second stage of the Pelagian controversy. One of the ways Augustine describes God's involvement in bringing about good human willing, we noticed, is by characterizing God as driving the human will. Now we observe that Augustine tends to attribute this driving to the third person of the Trinity in particular. Drawing on Romans 8:14 in *De gestis Pelagii* (*gest. Pel.*; 417), "*All those who are driven* (aguntur) *by the Spirit of God* (spiritu dei) *are the children of God* (Rom 8:14)," Augustine concludes that "our free will" (*nobis libera uoluntas*) cannot "do anything better than to offer itself to be driven by that Spirit who cannot act wrongly." Interestingly, Augustine glosses this interpretation of Romans 8:14 as an explanation of how "the grace of the savior acts upon our wills (*uoluntatibus nostris*)."[50] For Augustine, then, the Holy Spirit completes Christ's transformation of the human will by driving the human will, that is by bearing the lion's share of the load of agency in good human action.[51]

The motif of being driven by the Spirit of God in particular surfaces again in *c. ep. Pel.* (418), though not in connection with explicit language of will. Augustine notes that a baptized person has to struggle with concupiscence even "if one is most diligent in making progress and is driven by the Spirit of God"[52] and later that whoever "walks according to the Spirit" (in the words of Romans 8:3–4) is one "who is driven by the Spirit of God."[53] Immediately following the latter point, Augustine again cites Romans 8:14, clearly a crucial text for convincing him that the Holy Spirit drives the human being, a way of describing the Holy Spirit's work which he then applies, as we have seen, to the human will in particular.

---

[50] "Nonetheless, the grace of the savior acts upon our wills to such an extent that the apostle has no hesitation in saying, *All those who are driven by the Spirit of God are the children of God* (Rom 8:14)" (*gest. Pel.* 3.5 [CSEL 42:57]).

[51] Augustine explains, "Certainly, to be driven (*agi*) is more than to be governed (*regi*). After all, one who is governed does something and is governed so that he acts correctly, but one who is driven is understood to do hardly anything (*aliquid vix*)" (*gest. Pel.* 3.5 [CSEL 42:56–57]).

[52] *C. ep. Pel.* 1.13.27 (CSEL 60:445).

[53] *C. ep. Pel.* 3.2.2 (CSEL 60:487).

Intriguingly, though in *ep. Io. tr.* (407) Augustine had referred to a charioteer driving the soul who would guide her to good works, he there characterized this charioteer as charity rather than as the Holy Spirit. Pointing
out the superficial similarities between good works that stem from pride
and good works that stem from charity, Augustine had observed, "All the
good works that love (*caritas*) wants to do and does, pride does likewise, as
if directing its horses. But love is deeper within: it takes the place of badly
driven pride; not badly driving, but badly driven. Woe to the person whose
charioteer (*auriga*) is pride; he will inevitably fall headlong."[54] This image of
a charioteer driving a chariot pulled by two horses is reminiscent of Plato's
analogy of the soul, in which the intellect drives the spirited and appetitive
elements of the soul.[55] Augustine puts his own unique spin on this image.
Insofar as the dominion of pride is a function of the soul's captivity to sin,
when pride drives the chariot of the soul it is "badly driven" more than
"badly driving." But Augustine still attributes the role of charioteer to pride.
In a person under the law, pride is in control, driving (*agitare*) a person to
do what she does, whether seemingly "good works" or bad. In a believer, in
contrast, charity usurps control from pride. Charity then becomes the charioteer who "drives" the human person to do good works. For Augustine,
this is the ideal scenario, rather than Plato's preference that reason take
the reins.

Based on the connection Augustine has already made in this series of
homilies between charity and the Holy Spirit,[56] one might infer that his
characterization of charity as charioteer implies that the Holy Spirit drives
the human person to do good works, though he does not make this point
explicitly in *ep. Io. tr.* As we have seen, however, Augustine does make the
Spirit's role in driving the human will explicit in his later writings. Thus,
while in 407 there are already marked differences between Augustine's vision of what ought to be determinative in the functioning of the human
soul and that of Plato, later on, as we have seen in our examination of *gest.
Pel.*, his view of how human motivation works becomes more explicitly

---

[54] I have modified the translation of Boniface Ramsey. *Ep. Io. tr.* 8.9 (PL 35:2040–2041).

[55] See *Phaedrus* 246a–254e.

[56] See the discussion of the previous homily, homily 7. There Augustine concludes on the basis
of Romans 5:5, which refers to the outpouring of charity (*caritas*) in human hearts, that "in love (*in
dilectione*) there is the Holy Spirit." Though Augustine does not in so many words affirm that "in
caritas there is the Holy Spirit," the fact that he is reasoning on the basis of Romans 5:5 warrants the
conclusion that he is using *dilectio* and *caritas* interchangeably in this context.

Trinitarian, and hence even more distinctively Christian, as he contends that our free will is driven by the Spirit.

In addition to portraying the Holy Spirit as acting upon the will to enable right willing by his very presence and by virtue of driving our wills, Augustine also characterizes the Holy Spirit as enabling right human willing by virtue of "the will of the Spirit." In *corrept.* 11.31 (427), Augustine draws a contrast between the first grace of Adam and the second grace of Christ and the effect each had upon the will. While the first grace was contingent upon human willing, he explains, the second depends on the will of the Spirit. In his words, "For the first grace brought it about that the man had righteousness if he willed to (*si uelit*); the second, therefore, is more powerful, for it makes one even to will (*ut uelit*) and to will so strongly and to love with such ardor that by the will of the spirit (*uoluntate spiritus*) one conquers the pleasure of the flesh which has contrary desires."[57] Thus Augustine not only ties right human willing to the presence and direction of the Spirit but also relates right human willing directly to the Spirit's work as the divine will.[58] What differentiates the second, "more powerful" (*potentior*) grace from the first grace whereby Adam could have remained good had he willed it, is that the second grace helps the human will itself. Augustine now adds the information that God assists on the level of human willing through God's own will. The human will gains the orientation, strength, and intensity to achieve the good precisely by drawing on the power of the divine will, the will of the Spirit.

In this section, we have observed that the Holy Spirit acts upon the human will through three distinct means, though, as we have seen, these means cannot be separated from the Spirit's own person. These means include the Spirit's presence, since the love poured out in our hearts is the very presence of the Holy Spirit who is both giver and gift; the Holy Spirit's driving of our wills, as the Holy Spirit acts as a kind of charioteer who guides us in the way we should go; and the Spirit's own will, which enables us so to will and so to love that we may conquer the pleasures of the flesh, not only having a good will but acting upon it with integrity. This examination of the

[57] *Corrept.* 11.31 (CSEL 92:256).
[58] The fact that Augustine elsewhere associates the Holy Spirit with the divine will favors reading the phrase *uoluntate spiritus* as a genitive of material rather than a possessive genitive. This phrase would then designate the will "consisting in" the Spirit, rather than some kind of will belonging to the Holy Spirit distinct from the divine will with which Augustine associates the Holy Spirit as such. For a discussion of this association, see part II section A.

means by which the Holy Spirit enables right human willing (section B), combined with our investigation of three distinctive effects the Holy Spirit's work has upon human willing (section A), filled out an answer to the question of how the Holy Spirit enables right human willing that accounts for both the subjective and objective poles of this process. We considered, in other words, both how Augustine described the identity and role of the agent of this transforming work, the Holy Spirit, and how he described the effects of this transforming work in the human person. Having considered how the Holy Spirit and the good, transformed, human will relate causally, we are now in a position to turn to the question of how the human will and the Holy Spirit are related on an analogical level. We have already noted that Augustine connects the human will not only to the Holy Spirit but also to the *will* of the Spirit in particular. This raises the question of the precise nature of the analogical relationship between the human will and the Spirit. Is this to be construed in terms of the Spirit's will or even the Spirit as will? How does the human will image the Holy Spirit? To answer these questions, we turn to the analogical relation of good human willing to the Holy Spirit as developed in the Trinitarian context of *De trinitate*.

Part II: Human Willing Images the Holy Spirit

Unlike Christ, the Holy Spirit did not assume humanity and become incarnate. Therefore the Holy Spirit does not take on a human will as Christ does, who possesses a human will as part of a complete human nature hypostatically united to his divine person. But the Holy Spirit does, like Christ, both model and redeem the human will. Just as Augustine points to Christ as not only exemplifying grace's effect on the will but also enabling right human willing by transforming human willing by grace, so he points to the Spirit as both standing in analogy to the human will and as enabling right human willing by transforming the human will. However, the Holy Spirit does not offer an analogy to the human will as Christ does, by possessing a will that is itself human, but rather through his correspondence to the human will in his one divine nature.

This correspondence between the Holy Spirit and the human will comes most clearly to light in *trin*. Tellingly, however, in reflecting upon the human will in the context of meditating upon the doctrine of the Trinity, Augustine not only clarifies the relationship of the human will to the Holy

Spirit but also expresses his mature view of the defining characteristics of the human will with a clarity unmatched by any other text in his corpus. He finally deals with key ambiguities in his thinking on the human will not in a treatise on the human person per se, not by focusing myopically on human psychology or anthropology as a discrete silo, but—of all things— in an essay on the doctrine of the Trinity. Thus *trin.* serves as yet another example of how Augustine's distinctive views about the human will stem from his theology. In *trin.* it becomes clear that for Augustine, the will is not a substance or a reified faculty that might subsist in isolation but rather a dynamic activity of relation. The will is a spiritual reality that connects the human psyche with the external world, with itself, and with its maker. We will explore Augustine's articulation of the nature of the human will in the context of its imaging of the Holy Spirit by turning first to his charac- terization of the Holy Spirit as the divine will in *trin.* (section A) and then to the ways in which he deepens his thinking on the human will in partic- ular in this work (section B). This approach will enable us to examine the contributions of this seminal work to Augustine's theory of will in the larger context of his thinking on the Trinity, and particularly on the Holy Spirit.

Section A: The Holy Spirit as the Divine Will in *De Trinitate*

Three observations arise from a consideration of Augustine's characteriza- tion of the Holy Spirit in relation to the divine will in *trin.* First, he states that it is proper that the Holy Spirit is distinctively called the "will of God" (*uoluntas dei*) though all three members of the Trinity have will "in their own substance." Second, he states that it is proper that the Holy Spirit is distinctively called charity, a virtue that, as we saw in chapter 5, Augustine regards as intimately connected with willing on the human plane. Finally, Augustine identifies divine charity with the divine will just as he identifies charity as good human willing. Each of these points demonstrates the ana- logical connection between Augustine's views about the Holy Spirit and his views about the human will.

We turn first to Augustine's association of the Holy Spirit, as opposed to either of the two other members of the Trinity, with the divine will. He has made this association familiar to us. But it was not a given in his time. In fact, Augustine was heir to a complex debate about the relationship of the divine will to the three persons of the Trinity whose upshot had turned out to be that Christ, rather than the Holy Spirit, should be associated distinctively with the divine will.[59] The role of the Holy Spirit had not yet featured prominently in this debate.

This debate, like so many others in the history of Christian theology, began with Origen, who, in an effort to underline the free and undetermined character of the salvation God offered humankind in the Son, had taught that the Son came into existence by an act of will of the Father.[60] Origen's teaching later proved useful to Arius, since it seemed to imply that the Son was to be classed with the rest of creation insofar as his substance was but a product of the divine will. Athanasius avoided Arius's conclusion with the bold proposal that the Son *was* the will of the Father. This solution differentiated the Son fundamentally from creation, which was a product of the divine will, but also explained how Christ served as a kind of intermediary between God and creation.

According to Gregory of Nazianzus, however, Athanasius's suggestion posed problems of its own. Given the Plotinian principle that the product of a free choice (*prohairesis*) was inherently preferable to the product of natural necessity, Gregory was persuaded that Athanasius's theory implied a lack of divine choice in the generation of the Son that smacked of inferiority. Gregory thus rejected Athanasius's identification of the Son with the divine will, preferring a return to Origen's notion that the Son was the product of the divine will. He rescued this idea from problematic Christological implications, however, by means of a distinction between God's non-hypostatic will in generating the Son, beyond human understanding

[59] For a summary of this debate, see Albrecht Dihle, *The Theory of Will in Classical Antiquity* (Berkeley: University of California Press, 1982), 116–119. The following summary draws upon his sketch of the key figures and issues.

[60] According to Origen, "For if 'all things that the Father doeth, these also doeth the Son likewise,' then in this very fact that the Son does all things just as the Father does, the Father's image is reproduced in the Son, whose birth from the Father is as it were an act of his will proceeding from the mind. And on this account my own opinion is that an act of the Father's will ought to be sufficient to ensure the existence of what he wills; for in willing he uses no other means than that which is produced by the deliberations of his will. It is in this way, then, that the existence of the Son also is begotten by him [Latin]." See *de principiis* 1.2.6 in Origen, *On First Principles: Being Koetschau's Text of the De Principiis*, trans. G. W. Butterworth (New York: Harper & Row, 1966), 19. Later in *de principiis* he writes, "We say that the Word and Wisdom was begotten of the invisible and incorporeal God apart from any bodily feeling, like an act of will proceeding from the mind. Nor will it appear absurd, seeing that he is called the 'Son of his love,' that he should also be regarded in this way as the 'Son of his will' [Latin]" and "Now this Son was begotten of the Father's will, for he is the 'image of the invisible God' and the 'effulgence of his glory and the impress of his substance,' 'the firstborn of all creation' . . . [Greek]" (*de principiis* 4.4.1; Butterworth, 314).

because this will is proper to God's substance, and God's hypostatic will as the cause of creation, which is available to human knowing. This approach allowed Gregory to affirm the freely chosen character of the generation of the Son, even while he made clear that the Son was not a product of the same kind of divine will that produced creation. Meanwhile, in the West, Marius Victorinus mapped out a course for himself different from that chosen by his Cappadocian contemporary; he followed Athanasius in identifying Christ as the divine will. For Marius Victorinus, "Christ is the *voluntas et potentia Dei*," and as this one divine will he unites the Trinity.[61]

Though precise positions varied, then, the fourth century saw a flurry of interest in the Son's peculiar relationship to the divine will. This was not a coincidental association, according to Dihle, but one forged in the crucible of theological tumult. The Christological controversies of the fourth century finally pushed Christian theologians to articulate a "clear-cut notion of the divine will," though they left the puzzle of the human will for subsequent generations to unravel.[62] How does Augustine's association of the divine will with the Spirit fit into, or diverge from, the trajectory of this conversation?

Dihle recognizes that Augustine's view of the divine will differs significantly from that of his role model in the faith, Marius Victorinus. Indeed, he observes that Augustine does not see the Logos as "the principle of Life, Motion, or Will" but rather sees "motion or will that brings about creation [as] represented by the Spirit." But Dihle attributes the differences between the views of these two Latin thinkers to Augustine's introspective approach. According to Dihle, "the key role attributed to will (*uoluntas*) in St. Augustine's corresponding systems of psychology and theology results mainly from self-examination." Dihle rightly points out that Augustine's anthropological and theological notion of will "exactly corresponded to the indistinct but persistent voluntarism that permeates the Biblical tradition," yet he does not show the full extent of the contributions of the biblical text to actually shaping Augustine's views.[63] Augustine's notion of the divine will did not just happen to coincide with parts of the Bible; it derived in large measure from his interpretation of the Bible.[64]

---

[61] Dihle, *The Theory of Will in Classical Antiquity*, 118.

[62] Dihle, *The Theory of Will in Classical Antiquity*, 119.

[63] Dihle, *The Theory of Will in Classical Antiquity*, 127.

[64] Verhees comes to the conclusion that not only Augustine's association of the Holy Spirit with the will but also his entire thinking on the distinctive characteristics of the Holy Spirit takes the Bible, and the salvific action of the Spirit depicted therein, as its starting point. Augustine's doctrine of the

A critique Augustine mounts of Eunomius in book 15 of *trin.* illustrates his awareness of past trajectories in Christian thinking about how the divine will relates to the persons of the Trinity. Augustine is familiar both with Eunomius's use of the notion of the divine will to argue for a distinction between the divinity of the Son (by will) and the divinity of the Father (by nature) and with previous efforts to respond to Eunomius. But neither Eunomius's views nor the attempts others have made to correct him entirely satisfy the bishop of Hippo.

According to Augustine, Eunomius's reluctance to admit that the Word of God was the Son of God by nature led him to assert that "he is not the Son of the nature or substance or being of God but the Son of his will (*uoluntatis dei*)."[65] In Eunomius's view, God's will was to be sharply differentiated from God's essence since "the will by which God begot the Son is something accidental to him."[66] Eunomius inferred the accidental quality of the divine will, Augustine argues, from his observation of human beings; he formed his conclusions about the divine will "on the grounds apparently that we sometimes will something that we were not willing before—as though this were not proof of the changeableness of our nature, a thing we could not possibly believe to be the case in God."[67] More fundamentally problematic, even, than his identification of the Son as a product of the Father's will was Eunomius's failure to see a crucial difference between divine and human willing, one of which is unchangeable and essential to personal identity in each of its concrete expressions and one of which is changeable and accidental to personal identity in some of its concrete expressions. Given this misstep, he was bound to be in error no matter with which member of the Trinity he chose to associate the divine will.

Augustine also knows of attempts to avoid Eunomius's problematic conclusion that the Son of God, as a product of the divine will, possesses a divinity inferior to that of the Father. Though he does not list any such persons by name, he is aware that "to avoid saying that the only-begotten Word

---

Holy Spirit thus belies caricatures that pit his allegedly essentialist Trinitarianism, focusing on the essential unity of the immanent Trinity, against versions of the Trinity associated with the Greek fathers, which supposedly focus more on the economy of salvation, and hence on the distinctions between the three persons. See Verhees, *God in beweging*, 348–349. Verhees specifically points out the biblical roots of the connection Augustine establishes between the "place of the Holy Spirit in the Trinity" and "the place of the will in the human triad of *memoria—intellegentia—uoluntas*" on 349.

[65] *Trin.* 15.38 (CCL 50A:515).
[66] *Trin.* 15.38 (CCL 50A:515).
[67] *Trin.* 15.38 (CCL 50A:515).

is the Son of the Father's counsel or will (*uoluntatis*), some have said that
this Word simply is the counsel or will (*uoluntatem*) of the Father."[68] As we
observed in the overview of pre-Augustinian debates on Christology and
the divine will, this view is found in Athanasius and Marius Victorinus. But
this proposal too has its problems, particularly if the identity of the Son
with the will of the Father is understood to indicate that the Son is accidentally related to the Father and to the Spirit.

It is a grave error, Augustine is convinced, to associate any member of
the Trinity with the divine will in such a way that might suggest that the
other members of the Trinity do not have "counsel or will" in their "own
substance." To affirm such an association would be to fall into Eunomius's
fundamental pitfall of thinking that the divine will, like the human will,
could be changeable or accidental to divine personhood. Instead, divine
willing is perfectly integrated into the one divine substance. The divine
will is an entirely consistent and accurate expression of the one eternal
being of God. Thus all three members of the Trinity possess will in their
"own substance," that is, in the one substance shared by all three members
of the Trinity. Augustine therefore concludes, "I consider it better to
call him [the Son] counsel from counsel and will from will (*uoluntas de
uoluntate*), just as he is substance from substance, wisdom from wisdom;
or we shall find ourselves in the absurdity we have often refuted of saying
that the Son makes the Father wise or willing (*uolentem*), if the Father
does not have counsel or will (*uoluntatem*) in his own substance."[69] Well
aware of the role will has played in the history of Trinitarian thinking,
Augustine is convinced that neither Arius nor Athanasius had things exactly right: in fact all three members of the Trinity possess and even are
to be identified with the divine will on the level of their "own substance"
(*substantia sua*).

Still, Augustine thinks that if any of the three Trinitarian persons is properly to be called the will of God it should be the Spirit: "But if any person
in the Trinity is to be distinctively called the will of God (*uoluntas dei*), this
name like charity fits the Holy Spirit more than the others."[70] Though this
was a new idea in the history of Christian theology, Augustine downplays
his innovation, portraying the association of the will of God with the Spirit

[68] *Trin.* 15.38 (CCL 50A:515).
[69] *Trin.* 15.38 (CCL 50A:515).
[70] *Trin.* 15.38 (CCL 50A:516).

as almost self-evident.[71] As already indicated, in associating the Holy Spirit with the divine will he points immediately to charity (*caritas*) and its association with the Holy Spirit. Having observed this, he deems hardly any further explanation necessary, adding only a rhetorical question: "What else after all is charity but the will?" (*Quid est aliud caritas quam uoluntas?*)[72] Given that Augustine has already identified "charity" as an appropriate name for the Holy Spirit and defined *caritas* as a kind of *uoluntas*, it is but a small step to the conclusion that the Holy Spirit is more properly called the *uoluntas dei* than the other two members of the Trinity. Augustine has done a lot of work to arrive at this conclusion, but this work has been distributed mainly between the two presuppositions on the basis of which he reaches it rather than on the final logical step from them to their implication; that the Holy Spirit should be called "the will of God" follows tautologically from the premises that the Holy Spirit is rightly called "charity" and that "charity" is a form of will.

We have already seen in chapter 5 how Augustine connects charity and will on an anthropological level in works other than *trin*. Now let us examine how he establishes a connection between the Holy Spirit and charity in *trin*. This examination sheds light on the basis of Augustine's identification of the Holy Spirit as the member of the Trinity most properly called the "will of God." Augustine had already identified the Holy Spirit as the friendship or "charity" between the Father and the Son in book 6 of *trin*. There he had observed that "the Holy Spirit is something common to Father and Son, whatever it is, or is their very commonness or communion, consubstantial and coeternal. Call this friendship, if it helps, but a better word for it is charity (*caritas*)."[73] We find a much more extended discussion of the

---

[71] This is not to imply, of course, that Augustine's assertion that the Holy Spirit should be distinctively called the will of God emerged ex nihilo. As Gerber observes, Augustine's reflections on the Holy Spirit's "distinctive character" were not "wholly Augustine's ideas" in the sense of being entirely free of debts to earlier thinkers. Yet, as Augustine observes in *de fide et symbolo* (*f. et symb.*) 9.19, the topic of the *proprium* of the Spirit had not been dealt with extensively by previous Christian writers, and Augustine's Pneumatology represented one of the "most distinctive" aspects of his thought. See Gerber, *The Spirit of Augustine's Early Theology*, 2 and 1, respectively. While Hilary of Poitiers, Didymus the Blind, and Ambrose of Milan had begun to address the issue of the *proprium* of the Holy Spirit, this topic came to the fore in early Christian thinking on the Holy Spirit only after an initial phase focused on proving the Holy Spirit's existence and divinity. Augustine's thinking on the *proprium* of the Holy Spirit builds on, but goes beyond, what one finds in Hilary, Didymus, and Ambrose. See Wilken, "*Spiritus sanctus secundum scripturas sanctas*," especially 6–9. On the originality of Augustine's thinking on the *proprium* of the Spirit, see Rowan Williams, "*Sapientia*: Wisdom and the Trinitarian Relations," in *On Augustine* (New York: Bloomsbury, 2016), 182–185 and "*De Trinitate*," in *AA*, ed. Allan D. Fitzgerald (Grand Rapids, MI: Eerdmans, 1999), 845.

[72] *Trin.* 15.38 (CCL 50A:516).

[73] *Trin.* 6.7 (CCL 50:235).

basis for the connection between the Holy Spirit and charity, however, in *trin.* book 15.

Whereas Augustine de-emphasizes the labor of reaching the conclusion that the Holy Spirit is to be called the "will of God" in a distinctive way, he calls attention to the challenges of understanding why it is uniquely appropriate to call the Holy Spirit "charity."[74] From the very outset of the discussion, he makes clear that the "holy scriptures" serve as the basis for this conclusion,[75] but he also acknowledges the arduous nature of the task: "The divine word (*sermo diuinus*) has made us search with greater diligence into things that are not set out in open display, but have to be explored in obscurity and dragged out of obscurity."[76] Things would have been much easier, Augustine observes, had scripture simply indicated in so many words that "the Holy Spirit is charity" (*spiritus sanctus caritas est*).[77] Instead, he contends, the Bible leaves puzzle pieces strewn about, which summon the reader to ponder how they fit together.

Beginning with the statement from 1 John 4:8 and 16 that "God is love" (*deus caritas est*),[78] Augustine first reminds the reader that each member of the Trinity has and is charity in the one unchangeable and simple substance of the Godhead.[79] Insofar as this is the case, God the Father and God

---

[74] Wilken observes that by the time Augustine wrote *trin.* Didymus the Blind had already highlighted the significance of Romans 5:5, which refers to the *caritas Dei* being shed abroad in human hearts through the Holy Spirit, though Didymus did not, as would Ambrose, single out the term *caritas* and characterize the Holy Spirit as the "fount of divine love." Augustine's teaching on the Holy Spirit as love distinguished itself from that of Ambrose in that he characterized this *proprium* of the Holy Spirit in relation to the Father and the Son, not just in relation to humankind. See Wilken, "*Spiritus sanctus secundum scripturas sanctas*," 8–9. Peter Widdicombe has argued that while Athanasius nowhere directly characterizes the Spirit as the bond of love between the Father and the Son, one can find "seeds of just such a belief in his writings" in his association of the Holy Spirit with God's love for believers. See Peter Widdicombe, "Athanasius and the Making of the Doctrine of the Trinity," *Pro Ecclesia* 6, no. 4 (1997): 472–473.

[75] *Trin.* 15.27 (CCL 50A:501): "According to the holy scriptures this Holy Spirit is not just the Father's alone nor the Son's alone, but the Spirit of them both, and thus he suggests to us the common charity by which the Father and the Son love each other."

[76] *Trin.* 15.27 (CCL 50A:501–502).

[77] *Trin.* 15.27 (CCL 50A:502).

[78] *Trin.* 15.27 (CCL 50A:502). Interestingly, while acknowledging that scripture nowhere says "Spiritus sanctus caritas est," Augustine attributes to scripture the statement "Deus caritas est," which statement, as becomes clear, he finds in 1 John 4:8 and 16. Later, however, Augustine quotes these verses as indicating that "deus dilectio est" (*trin.* 15.31). This fact, a specific instance of his general approach of defending the claim that the Holy Spirit is distinctively to be called "charity" (*caritas*) on the basis of verses that refer to *dilectio*, indicates that he regards the two terms as synonymous in the context of this argument. Indeed Augustine explicitly says in *trin.* 15.32 (CCL 50A:507) that "this love or charity (*dilectio siue caritas*) . . . are two names for one thing."

[79] *Trin.* 15.28. As Dodaro points out with reference to *serm.* 71.29, the love that the Holy Spirit sheds abroad in human hearts is none other than the love of the Father and the Son ("Augustine on the Roles of Christ and the Holy Spirit in the Mediation of the Virtues," 160).

the Son, as well as God the Holy Spirit, can be called charity. Nonetheless, Augustine thinks, one can see that "the Holy Spirit is distinctively called by the term charity"[80] if one more closely inspects the context of 1 John 4:8 by taking the previous verse into one's purview as well.[81] Before pronouncing that God is love, the biblical writer had instructed, "Beloved, let us love each other because love is from God" (1 John 4:7). This injunction provides a vital clue: if the love in question is both God (1 John 4:8) and a love that is from God (1 John 4:7), it must refer distinctively to either the Son or the Spirit, as both Son and Spirit proceed from the Father while the Father is unoriginate. The process of elimination leaves only Son and Spirit in contention for being properly (*proprie*) or distinctively called love (*caritas*).

To determine which of these two persons is meant, Augustine turns not to speculation or to psychology or even to "self-examination." Rather, he forges on in 1 John 4, arriving eventually at verse 13, where he finds the missing puzzle piece: "In this we know that we abide in him and he in us, because he has given us of his Spirit."[82] Since, Augustine argues, this mutual abiding is precisely what it means to love, this verse indicates that "the gift of God who is love"[83] refers to none other than the Holy Spirit. Augustine concludes, "So it is God the Holy Spirit proceeding from God who fires man to the love of God and neighbor when he has been given to him, and he himself is love (*dilectio*)."[84] As added confirmation, Augustine also cites Romans 5:5, his stock verse on the Holy Spirit as the gift of love poured out in human hearts: "The love (*dilectio*) of God has been poured out in our hearts through the Holy Spirit which has been given to us."[85] For Augustine, scriptural descriptions of the nature of the gift of love that has been poured out in our hearts serve as the basis for concluding that the Holy Spirit should be distinctively called charity.[86]

---

[80] *Trin.* 15.31 (CCL 50A:505).

[81] *Trin.* 15.31 (CCL 50A:505): "We can however find where the Holy Spirit is called charity if we carefully examine the words of the apostle John."

[82] Here and previously in this paragraph I am using Edmund Hill's translations of Augustine's Latin quotations from the biblical text.

[83] *Trin.* 15.31 (CCL 50A:506): *ipse est igitur deus dilectio.*

[84] *Trin.* 15.31 (CCL 50A:506).

[85] *Trin.* 15.31 (CCL 50A:507).

[86] In the words of Cipriani, Augustine's demonstration that the Spirit is properly called charity, which Cipriani rates as one of the most original achievements of his theology (74), is "totally based on scripture [*totalmente fondata sulla Scrittura*]" (*Lo Spirito Santo, Amore che unisce*, 77). See *trin.* 15.37 (CCL 50A:513–514) for Augustine's summary of the reasons for concluding that though "the Holy Spirit is not alone in that triad in being charity . . . there is a good reason for distinctively calling him charity."

Thus, in that Augustine's argument that the Holy Spirit is appropriately called "the will of God" rests on his case that it is appropriate to refer distinctively to the Holy Spirit by the name of "charity," and in that he executes this latter case by means of exegetical argumentation, his association of the Holy Spirit with "the will of God" also rests on exegetical arguments. For this reason, it is unsurprising that immediately after linking the issues of the distinctive fit with the Holy Spirit of the names "will of God" and "charity"[87] Augustine adds, "I see that in this book I have been arguing about the Holy Spirit according to the scriptures (secundum scripturas sanctas)."[88]

This avowal of his scriptural method matches the line with which Augustine had opened his inquiry into the Holy Spirit, and the Spirit's associations with both "charity" and "the will of God," in trin. 15.27. There he had pronounced, "According to the holy scriptures (secundum scripturas sanctas) this Holy Spirit is not just the Father's alone nor the Son's alone, but the Spirit of them both, and thus he suggests to us the common charity by which the Father and the Son love each other."[89] He then proceeded to point out the challenges of discovering the Holy Spirit's biblical relationship to charity, characterizing the "divine word" (sermo diuinus) as actively "driving the reader on" (exerceret) to peer into its darker corners, offering up its obscurity as an enticement to draw the reader in. He thus characterizes the word of God as living and active in his account of the Holy Spirit. In his presentation of the matter, this divine word drives him to reach the conclusions at which he arrives. Even structurally speaking, Augustine's treatment of the Holy Spirit's relationship to charity and to the divine will is flanked by the phrase "according to the holy scriptures" (secundum scripturas sanctas) as if to suggest that the word of God as communicated in these texts represents

[87] Augustine writes, "If any person in the Trinity is to be distinctively called the will of God, this name like charity fits the Holy Spirit more than the others. What else after all is charity but the will?" (Trin. 15.38).

[88] Trin. 15.39: uideo me de spiritu sancto in isto libro secundum scripturas sanctas hoc disputasse. Wilken has observed that the relative lack of philosophical resources for thinking about the Holy Spirit, as compared with those available for thinking about the Father and the Son, drove early Christian theologians to look to scripture for inspiration on the former topic. See Wilken, "Spiritus sanctus secundum scripturas sanctas," 3–5. Augustine himself points out in conf. 7.21.27 (CCL 27:111) that he can find little on the "guarantee of the Holy Spirit" (arram spiritus) in the Platonist books. Wilken observes that Augustine's double use of the phrase secundum scripturas sanctas with respect to his discussion of the Holy Spirit in de trinitate (cf. trin. 15.27) expresses the early Christian imperative of turning to biblical exegesis to better understand the Spirit (5). For Wilken's treatment of the scriptural sources of Augustine's reflections in trin. 15 on the Holy Spirit, sources Augustine interpreted through the lenses of the commentators who had preceded him and his experience of Christian worship, see 12–17.

[89] Trin. 15.27 (CCL 50A:501).

the starting point for, and outer limits of, his thinking on the Holy Spirit's identity.

To emphasize the scriptural sources of Augustine's thinking on the Holy Spirit as divine will, however, is not to indicate that his thinking about issues of will on an anthropological level remains segregated from his Trinitarian thinking on this issue. Quite to the contrary, as we have observed, Augustine's association of the Holy Spirit, rather than the Son, with the divine will is informed by two crucial premises: (1) that the Holy Spirit is rightly called charity and (2) that charity is a form of will. We have just seen how Augustine derives the first premise from scripture, particularly from a close reading of 1 John 4:7–16. The second premise, however, is one that coincides with a presupposition Augustine also accepted on the anthropological level, as detailed in part III of chapter 5 of this book. Augustine's association of the Holy Spirit with the divine will, then, is informed both by scripture and by a presupposition about the relationship between love and will that is also basic to his anthropological thinking.

For Augustine, scripture itself prescribes a theological method that draws upon God's visible creation for reflection upon the invisible things of God. After observing that his argumentation has proceeded "according to the scriptures," Augustine expresses the relevance of creation for the course of his thinking about the Trinity, alluding to Romans 1:20: "As far as we could, we have also used the creation which God made to remind those who ask for reasons in such matters that as far as they can they should descry his invisible things by understanding them through the things that are made." Most "especially" (*maxime*) one catches a glimpse of the invisible things of God "through the rational or intellectual creature which is made to the image of God (*ad imaginem dei*); so that through this, as a kind of mirror (*speculum*), as far as they can and if they can, they might perceive in our memory (*memoria*), understanding (*intellegentia*) and will (*uoluntate*) that God is a Trinity."[90] Thus, for Augustine, scripture itself invites one to look into the mirror of human memory, intellect, and will for indications of God's triunity. We have seen how Augustine takes this tack, in addition to drawing inspiration directly from biblical statements, with respect to arriving at the identification of the Holy Spirit as the member of the Trinity distinctively called the "will of God." Looking onto the reflective surface of

---

[90] *Trin.* 15.39 (CCL 50A:516–517).

human willing, Augustine sees a connection between charity and will that corresponds to the convergence of divine iterations of these two features in the Holy Spirit.

Indeed, just as Augustine uses the terms "love" (*caritas*) and "good will" (*bona uoluntas*) interchangeably with respect to the human being, a practice of his we observed in chapter 5 part III of this book, in *trin.* he uses terms for "love" and "will" interchangeably with respect to God. Just after observing that we may perceive a trinity in our "memory (*memoria*), understanding (*intellegentia*) and will (*uoluntate*)," for example, Augustine goes on to refer to "these three" (*quae tria*) as "memory" (*memoria*), "understanding" (*intellegentia*), and "love" (*dilectio*).[91] A similar pattern surfaces in his use of the terms *caritas* and *uoluntas*; he substitutes one for the other without missing a beat. When describing God's essence in the prologue to book 4, for example, Augustine writes, "For God's essence, by which he is, has absolutely nothing changeable about its eternity or its truth or its will (*uoluntate*); there truth is eternal and love (*caritas*) is eternal; there love (*caritas*) is true and eternity true; there eternity is lovely (*cara*) and truth is lovely too."[92] Though initially he highlights eternity, truth, and will as the triad of divine attributes in question, when he explains the relationships between these three, "love" (*caritas*) assumes the place of "will" (*uoluntas*). For Augustine the terms "love" (*caritas* or *dilectio*) and "will" (*uoluntas*) are interchangeable. Their interchangeability, moreover, is self-evident; it does not warrant comment.

There is a difference, however, between how love and will are related on the plane of divine being and how they are related on the plane of human being.[93] Augustine matches *caritas* with good human willing, not automatically with any kind of willing. *Caritas* is a way of referring to redeemed human willing but does not accurately describe fallen human willing or even, necessarily, human willing that enjoys the original created gift of choice between good and evil. Augustine treats divine willing per se, however, as equivalent to love (*caritas* or *dilectio*). Divine willing, unlike human

---

[91] *Trin.* 15.39 (CCL 50A:517). For another example of Augustine using the terms *dilectio* and *uoluntas* interchangeably with respect to the Trinity, see *trin.* 15.12, where he observes, "So here we are then with these three, that is memory, understanding, love or will in that supreme and unchangeable being which God is" (CCL 50A: 477).

[92] *Trin.* 4.1 (CCL 50:160).

[93] John Rist is right to suggest that while in God "*amor* and *uoluntas* must be identical," this is not necessarily the case in sinful human beings. See J. M. Rist, *Augustine: Ancient Thought Baptized* (New York: Cambridge University Press, 1994), 177.

willing, always remains constant. It does not differ across time as human willing does, functioning differently in different contexts. It is the same yesterday and today and forever. This is why it is possible for Augustine to treat the divine will and love as synonyms without introducing qualifications. There is only one kind of divine will, and that will is love. Thus a stronger analogy exists between divine willing and redeemed human willing than between divine willing and fallen or even created willing. Redeemed willing becomes identical to loving by grace, whereas the simple divine will is so by nature.

In this section, we have examined Augustine's characterization of the Holy Spirit as the divine will in *trin.*, looking first at his claim that the Holy Spirit is distinctively called the "will of God" (*uoluntas dei*), then at how he bases this claim on the further claim that the Holy Spirit is distinctively called charity, and finally at his equation of divine charity and the divine will. As a whole this section illuminates how the Holy Spirit does and does not stand in analogical relation to the human will. There is a basic level of correspondence between the human will and the Holy Spirit insofar as the Holy Spirit is associated with the divine will. A consideration of how the Holy Spirit relates to charity, however, helps not only to show the scriptural underpinnings of the association of the Spirit with will but also to illustrate the limits of this analogical relationship. The degree of clarity with which the human will reflects the character of the divine will as charity varies drastically, depending on what type of human will is in question: created, fallen, redeemed, or, as we will see in chapter 8, eschatological. As we turn to Augustine's portrayal of the human will in *trin.*, we will observe further ways in which it stands in analogy to the Holy Spirit and also how Augustine's development of his notion of the human will in the context of Trinitarian theology helps to deepen and clarify the insights on human willing at which he arrives in other works.

Section B: The Human Will in *De Trinitate*

In addition to allowing readers to compare Augustine's conclusions about the Holy Spirit with his statements about human willing in other works, *trin.* also itself serves as a rich resource for understanding his mature conception of the human will. In particular, four aspects of Augustine's thinking on human willing in this work stand out. These aspects in turn help to illumine how the will stands in analogy to the Holy Spirit: Augustine once again links human loving and human willing, a link we saw him establishing in other works in chapter 5 part III; he associates will with the notions of intention and attention; he characterizes will as a connecting link; and he points to the dynamism of the will. We will examine each of these aspects in turn.

In chapter 5 part III, we observed how Augustine identifies the good, redeemed will as *caritas*. In *trin.*, one learns more about this relationship between human willing and loving, as well as about the relationship between divine willing and loving just examined. More specifically, one observes in *trin.* that human loving is a specific species of the genus of human willing, that there is human willing that does not consist of loving, and, finally, that while not all willing is loving, all loving is willing.[94]

As observed in chapter 3, in the late work *gr. et lib. arb.* (426–427) Augustine described love (*caritas*) as "a will (*uoluntatem*) fully aflame with divine love (*diuino amore*)."[95] In *trin.* he also speaks of human loving as a certain kind of "wanting" or "willing." When examining the image of the Trinity in the human mind, self-knowledge, and self-love, for example, he pauses to ask, "But what does loving itself (*amare se*) mean but wanting (*uelle*) to be available to itself in order to enjoy itself?"[96] The human mind's love for itself, Augustine explains, is a specific type of "willing" (*uelle*), namely, a willing to be present to and enjoy itself. Augustine also defines the terms *amor* and *dilectio* as referring to a specific type of will. He writes, "As far as the Holy Spirit is concerned, the only thing I pointed to in this puzzle as seeming to be like him is our will (*uoluntatem*), or love (*amorem*) or esteem (*dilectionem*), which is will (*uoluntas*) at its most effective (*ualentior*)."[97] Here Augustine indicates that what sets apart *amor* and *dilectio* from other kinds of willing is the strength or power of the willing that is at work in these kinds of loving. Love (*amor* or *dilectio*) figures as a particularly potent form of will. However, Augustine goes on to suggest that there are other kinds of will too, since "our will, which is implanted in us by nature, has various moods (*affectiones*) according as it is involved with,

---

[94] While Rist sees a "near-identification" of "will" and "love" as Augustine's "powerful and transforming thesis," he would, if anything, reverse all of these statements insofar as for him will is "an accepted set of loves" (*Augustine*, 186–188).

[95] *Gr. et lib. arb.* 17.34 (PL 44:902).

[96] *Trin.* 9.2 (CCL 50:295).

[97] *Trin.* 15.41 (CCL 50A:518).

or comes up against, things that either attract or repel us."⁹⁸ Thus *amor* and *dilectio* are among the dispositions toward other things of which the will is capable by created nature, though will may include weaker dispositions and dispositions of repulsion as well as dispositions of attraction.⁹⁹ The will is the seat of "various affections" (*uarias affectiones*),¹⁰⁰ including, but not limited to love: *caritas, amor,* and *dilectio.*¹⁰¹

Clearly, then, there are species of human willing that do not consist of loving. These include, presumably, forms of will other than the emotions (*motus*) and affections (*affectiones*), repulsion qua repulsion,¹⁰² but also dispositions of attraction that are too weak to be designated as a full-fledged "love." Augustine points to inquisitiveness, or "the appetite for finding out," as an example of this latter case.¹⁰³ "This appetite, that is inquisitiveness," he explains, "does not indeed appear to be the love (*amor*) with which what is known is loved (this is still busy getting known), yet it is something of the same kind (*ex eodem genere*). It can already be called will (*uoluntas*)

---

⁹⁸ *Trin.* 15.41 (CCL 50A:518). For Augustine, all of the emotions are forms of will, including both right, rational emotions and perverse, irrational emotions: "The will is engaged in all [the emotions (*motus*)]; in fact they are all essentially acts of will." See *ciu.* 14.6 (CCL 48:421): *uoluntas est quippe in omnibus; immo omnes nihil aliud quam uoluntates sunt.* On how Augustine uses the quality of the will to distinguish between "passions," which are distorted emotions, and "emotions" and "feelings," which can be good, see John C. Cavadini, "Feeling Right: Augustine on the Passions and Sexual Desire," *Augustinian Studies* 36, no. 1 (2005): 199–202.

⁹⁹ Augustine's comments in *ciu.* 14.7 (CCL 48:422) do suggest that repulsion, as well as attraction, may be reframed as a matter of love: "The love [*amor*] that shuns what opposes it is fear, while the love that feels that opposition when it happens is grief." However, this still does not require that will and love be coextensive given Augustine's comment in *trin.* that what distinguishes willing that is love from other kinds of willing is relative strength. Love is stronger (*ualentior*).

¹⁰⁰ See also *trin.* 3.5, where Augustine, observing that angels know more about us than we do about ourselves, states, "Indeed, they [angels] even know better than I do how my body changes according to the feelings or moods of my will, which is something I have experienced in myself and observed in others." CCL 50:131: *et magis ea norunt quam ego noui quatenus mutetur corpus meum in affectu uoluntatis meae siue quod in me siue quod ex aliis expertus sum.* Here too Augustine attributes "affection" (*affectus*) to the will.

¹⁰¹ In *ciu.* 14.7 (CCL 48:422), Augustine indicates that the Bible tends to use the terms *caritas, amor,* and *dilectio* interchangeably: "The Scriptures of our religion, whose authority we rank above all other writings, do not distinguish between 'love (*amorem*)' and 'fondness (*dilectionem*)' or 'charity (*caritatem*).'"

¹⁰² As noted, Augustine points out that repulsion, as well as attraction, can be reframed as love. But on a commonsense, colloquial, and practical level, even if this reframing is possible, there is an experiential primacy to repulsion qua repulsion that makes it only secondarily a form of love. For example, fear of death is, from another angle, love of life. But in terms of conscious experience and linguistic habit, the former description has primacy. If I wanted to refer to fear of death in an unmistakable way, I would call it fear of death, not love of life. Hence I include repulsion in this list as a nod to certain intuitive understandings of the meaning of "love," while acknowledging that these may be narrower than Augustine's technical understanding of what counts as "love" as articulated in *ciu.* 14.7.

¹⁰³ *Trin.* 9.18 (CCL 50:310).

because everyone who inquires wants (*uult*) to find out." Thus, while inquisitiveness has not attained the intensity or strength of love (*amor*), it belongs to the same genus to which love belongs, namely, the genus of will, which Augustine here indicates is in play anytime there is willing (*uelle*) at work. This explanation of the relationship of inquisitiveness to love and will fits with Augustine's earlier comment that *amor* and *dilectio* refer to particularly potent forms of will. Some types of will are too weak to qualify as love.

Though not all willing consists of loving, all loving consists of willing, for love is produced by the activity of the will and hence inherently volitional. Explaining a key contrast between the divine Trinity of understanding, memory, and love and the human psychological trinity of understanding, memory, and love, Augustine writes, "Again there is this enormous difference, that whether we talk about mind in man and its knowledge and love, or whether about memory, understanding, will (*uoluntatem*), we remember nothing of the mind except through memory, and understand nothing except through understanding, and love (*amamus*) nothing except through will (*per uoluntatem*)."[104] Augustine's point is that while Father, Son, and Holy Spirit each possess understanding, memory, and love by virtue of being each of these things in their unchanging eternal divine substance, things are different with respect to the image of the Trinity in the human mind. Memory, intellect, and will are not all able to remember, understand, and love by virtue of their own being. Remembering, understanding, and loving can happen only through the corresponding feature of human psychology responsible for each of these functions. One example of this principle is that a human being can love only through the will, otherwise loving is not possible. In the process of clarifying a difference between one of the trinities he has identified in the human mind and the triune relationships of the Godhead, Augustine makes a key clarification about the relationship of human willing and loving as well. Loving can happen only through the will; it is inherently voluntary.

Also in the course of seeking greater understanding of the Trinity, Augustine makes comments that shed light on the relationship of will to intention (*intentio*) and attention (*aciem*). These comments indicate that intention, along with love, inquisitiveness, and various other types and degrees of affections of attraction and repulsion, also represent a variety of will. Attention, on the other hand, is a mental or physical act of vision that

104 *Trin.* 15.12 (CCL 50A:475).

the will can then intentionally apply in one way or another. Augustine treats the will's relationship to the phenomena of intention and attention in book 11 of *trin*. In this book he examines Trinitarian analogies in the "outer" human being, the human being as endowed with sensation, whom he distinguishes from the "inner" human being, the human being as endowed with understanding.

First, we turn to the relationship of intention (*intentio*) to the human will. Augustine begins his analysis in book 11 by identifying a trinity involved in sight. Initially he labels its constituent parts as (1) the thing seen (*res quam uidemus*), (2) the sight or vision of it (*uisio*), and (3) conscious intention (*animi intentio*).[105] Later, however, he describes this same trinity as consisting in the "form of the body which is seen, and its image imprinted on the sense which is sight or formed sense, and the conscious will (*uoluntas animi*) which applies the sense to the sensible thing and holds the sight on it."[106] Intention, then, is a type of will, one that—in the context of literal vision—applies the sense of sight to a sensible thing, fixing a person's vision upon the thing seen. It is a kind of willing that connects a person's capacities for perception with a given object of perception.

In addition to substituting the phrase *uoluntas animi* for the phrase *intentio*, Augustine also utilizes the phrase *intentio uoluntatis*. Explaining a parallel between the Trinities of sensible sight and intellectual vision, whereby "the sight of thought is formed from the internal memory,"[107] he observes:

> What the intention of the will (*intentio uoluntatis*) is to the coupling of a body seen to the sight, so that a kind of unity of three is produced even though they are of such different natures, that the same intention of the will (*intentio uoluntatis*) is to the coupling of the image of a body in the memory to the sight of the one thinking about it, which is the form grasped by the conscious attention as it goes back to the memory.[108]

The phrase *intentio uoluntatis* further confirms the close relationship of intention and willing for Augustine. Considered independently, the precise

---

[105] *Trin*. 11.2.
[106] *Trin*. 11.5 (CCL 50:338).
[107] *Trin*. 11.16.
[108] *Trin*. 11.7 (CCL 50:342–343).

significance of this genitive would be ambiguous, but the previous texts we have examined allow us to specify the nature of the relationship it indicates. Intention belongs to the will in that intention is one possible mode in which "willing" or "wanting" may occur.

Augustine also relates the term "attention" (*aciem*) to will in *trin.* But whereas intention constitutes one form willing may take, attention represents something other than will, which the will may direct in one way or another. When discussing the trinity of internal vision that corresponds to the trinity of external vision, Augustine observes that "the same will (*uoluntas*) . . . now turns the conscious attention (*aciem recordantis*) to the memory in an act of recollection for it to be formed from what the memory has retained, and there is produced in thought something like sight."[109] In the realms of sense perception and memory, then, the will still sits in the driver's seat, directing (*conuertire*) its conscious attention in one way or another. Though, due to the fall, it spins out of control, losing the ability to turn the human person toward the good as it once could, or to convert the human person from evil to good, it retains the basic functionality of being able to fix its attention in different directions insofar as this is necessary for the tasks of beholding the external world and using one's memory. Augustine sees these basic physiological and intellectual functions, as well as the establishing of a person's moral course, as part of the basic operations of human willing, which of course may be applied to diverse moral effects.

The will's operation in the form of intention, including its ability to focus the mind's attention on one object or another, is one instance of a larger pattern in the functioning of the will that Augustine observes in *trin.* whereby the human will serves as a connecting link. This connective or conjoining function represents another way in which the human will stands in analogy to the Holy Spirit, thereby also showing how the relationship between will and intention is of a piece with the analogical relationship between the Holy Spirit and the human will. This connective role of the human will manifest itself in a wide variety of ways. First, one sees the connective role of will in various trinities Augustine identifies in the psychology of the human person: in the relationship of attention to memory, true word to awareness, and other examples. Augustine also speaks of the good human will as

---

[109] *Trin.* 11.6 (CCL 50:340). On the relationship between attention and will, see also Augustine's statement "The will, then, turns the attention (*aciem*) here and there and back again to be formed, and once formed keeps it joined to the image in the memory" (*Trin.* 11.7 [CCL 50: 341]).

connecting a person to God. In a multiplicity of ways, then, the human will performs a function that places it in analogy to the Holy Spirit, who power-fully binds the persons of the Trinity, as well as God and humanity, in love.

In book 11 of *trin.*, Augustine points to two trinities in the human person, to which we have already alluded. Will performs a connective function in each of these trinities, as well as in relating the two trinities to each other. As a member of a first trinity, the will (*uoluntas*) or intention (*intentio*) of the mind, connects the thing seen with sight or vision. As a member of a second, it connects memory and the attention, or internal sight, of the mind. Augustine speaks of this as a "coupling" (*copulare*) or a "yoking together" (*coniungere*).[110] The will also binds these two trinities to-gether, allowing sight that is produced through the collaboration of the con-stituent components of the first trinity to enter the memory. As Augustine summarizes, the will ends up performing a "coupling" function on multiple levels: "So the will couples (*copulat*) quasi-parent with its offspring three times: first the look of the body with the one it begets in the sense of the body; next this with the one that is produced from it in the memory; and then a third time this with the one that is brought forth from it in the gaze of thought."[111]

Although the connective or unifying function of will is especially pervasive in Augustine's discussion of trinities in the "outer" human being in book 11 of *trin.*, Augustine also points to the coupling function of the will when treating trinities in the human being which he connects more directly to the image of the triune God. For example, he identifies a trinity in the human person consisting of knowledge, the true word by which this knowledge is uttered, and will. He states that these are "three things in yourself, in which you can recognize yourself as the image of that supreme Trinity on which you are not yet capable of fixing your eyes in contemplation." He then highlights the third element, "will or love" (*uoluntate siue dilectione*), which serves the purpose of "joining (*iungente*) these two [the other two elements of this trinity] together

---

[110] Augustine speaks of the will coupling memory and internal sight in *trin.* 11.6 (CCL 50:340): "And so one gets another trinity, out of the memory and internal sight and the will (*uoluntas*) which couples (*copulat*) them together; and when these three are coagitated into a unity the result is called cogitation or thought, from the very act of coagitation." He refers to the will conjoining atten-tion and memory in *trin.* 11.7 (CCL 50:341): "The will (*uoluntas*), then, turns the attention here and there and back again to be formed, and once formed keeps it joined (*coniungit*) to the image in the memory."

[111] *Trin.* 11.16 (CCL 50:353).

as parent and offspring."[112] Thus, precisely in its connective function, the human will serves to show forth the image of its creator, and particularly the role of the Holy Spirit who unites Father and Son in love.

Along with its power to connect, the will also possesses, at least in theory, a power to disconnect. In Augustine's words, "Just as it is the will (*uoluntas*) which fastens (*adiunget*) sense to body, so it is the will which fastens memory to sense and the thinking attention to memory. And what fastens them together (*coniungit*) and assembles (*conciliat*) them also unfastens (*disiungit*) and separates (*separat*) them, namely the will (*uoluntas*) again."[113] This power, however, has been mitigated given the mortal human condition subsequent to the fall: "Thus it is by moving the body that the will avoids coupling the senses of the body to sensible things. And it does it as far as it can. When it suffers difficulty in this respect because of our condition of servile mortality, the result is torment, and nothing is left to the will but endurance."[114] Thus even while discussing a rather idealized form of human willing— as it was created to function fully in the image of God— Augustine pauses to register that the fall interferes with the workings of the will, making it more difficult to carry out its most basic activities. The will should serve as a powerful link—coupling and uncoupling effortlessly in accordance with the good. In reality, however, the human condition of servile mortality renders the will weak such that it seems merely to persist or endure rather than to work powerfully to change circumstances, whether by coupling or uncoupling, for the better.

At the conclusion of book 11, a book shot through with descriptions of the connective function the will serves in the routine psychological processes of human life, Augustine associates will with the term "weight" in Wisdom 11:20, providing a striking analogy for its connective function: "But the will (*uoluntas*) which joins and arranges these pairs and couples them in a kind of unity . . . is like weight (*pondus*)."[115] Will, like the mass of a body of matter, both exerts a force pulling other things toward the body in which it itself inheres and makes this body susceptible to the gravitational force of other things. Just as weight "draws everything to itself to rest and stability," as Augustine observes in another place, so will serves as the quality

---

[112] *Trin.* 15.50 (CCL 50A:532): See also *trin.* 14.10.
[113] *Trin.* 11.15 (CCL 50:351–352).
[114] *Trin.* 11.15 (CCL 50:352).
[115] *Trin.* 11.18 (CCL 50:355).

that drives attraction and union.[116] The will thus has something in common with the Holy Spirit, who joins and couples Father and Son in unity. Will makes possible attraction, repulsion, union, and rest and, as weight inheres in a physical object, it shoots through every part of human being, making its pull and influence felt.

In addition to describing the human will's connective role in various trinities internal to the human person, a role nicely illustrated by Augustine's connection of will with weight (*pondus*), he also identifies the human will as serving as a connective link between the human being and God.[117] As Augustine explains it, "For no really holy being takes pleasure in his own power, but rather in the power of him from whom he receives the power to do whatever he appropriately can do; and he knows it is far more effective to be bound to the almighty by a devout and dutiful will (*uoluntate*) than by his own will (*propria uoluntate*) to be able to do things that overawe those who cannot do them."[118] At first this statement seems to suggest that Augustine here attributes far greater potential to the human will than he accords it subsequent to the fall in other writings from this period. Yet a number of factors call into question this initial impression. First, the quotation itself makes clear that the connecting human will to which Augustine refers is not intended to represent something a person accomplishes in her "own power" (*potestate sua*). Quite to the contrary, Augustine emphasizes that this "devout will" (*pia uoluntate*) is distinct from her "own will" (*propria uoluntate*), the kind of will that would attempt to operate independently of God's help, and derives from the power of God. The will in question by which a person is "bound (*coniungi*) to the almighty" is received from God in humility. Furthermore, immediately following this statement, Augustine goes on to refer to the work of Christ, whose work is necessary to "convert [human beings] to eternal realities."[119] Thus the kind of devout

---

[116] See *Gn. litt.* 4.3.7 (CSEL 28:1), where Augustine points out the similarity between created weight and God as the "weight which guides all things." Augustine famously describes love as weight in *conf.* 13.9.10 (CCL 27:246): "My weight is my love" (*pondus meum amor meus*). Notably, he also aligns will with both the Holy Spirit and love: "Love lifts us there" (*amor illuc attollit nos*); the Holy Spirit "exalts" us in our lowly condition (*spiritus tuus . . . exaltat humilitatem nostram*); and "We will be brought to our place [the house of the Lord] by a good will" (*nos conlocabit uoluntas bona*) (CCL 27:246–247).

[117] It should be noted, however, that whereas the will's connective role in the trinities involved in human being is a repeated theme, which we have been able only to suggest—not exhaustively describe—through a number of representative examples, the human will's connecting function between God and humanity is an infrequent topic.

[118] *Trin.* 8.11 (CCL 50:285–286).

[119] *Trin.* 8.11 (CCL 50:286).

372 AUGUSTINE ON THE WILL

will that binds a person to God is precisely not a will that relies on its own power or wisdom but one that submits itself to God, following the example of Christ in Gethsemane, who preferred a "devout and dutiful will" to following "his own will."

By identifying a good will, a "devout and dutiful will," as binding a person to the almighty, Augustine does not so much point to it as a cause as he points to it as a figurative place in the human person. The human will does not enable human connection to God. God's power does that. But the human will is the locus at which human beings receive and embrace God's love.[120] God makes humble willing possible, but he does so precisely at the site of the will; this is where human beings "receive the power . . . to be bound to the almighty."[121]

Augustine uses a variety of terms to express the connective function of will (*copulare, coniungere, iungere, conciliare*) and describes the will as connecting diverse things. Yet all of this language, and each of these descriptions, have something in common. During the period of time when he pens *trin.*, Augustine portrays the will, not as the first and last word that can be spoken about human motivation, not as the most fundamental explanation one can provide for human action, but rather as fundamentally derivative. Human willing inherently implies other entities to which it can respond and with which it may interact. It is not the first link in the causal chain as it was in Augustine's early thinking on the created will. Rather, in every case Augustine describes, it conjoins itself to an existing link in order to connect it to another. Logically, if not chronologically, willing proceeds from prior entities. As will be immediately obvious, this feature of human willing that emerges so clearly in *trin.* matches Augustine's portrayal of the Holy Spirit as proceeding from the Father and thereby connecting the Father and the Son. Augustine highlights this parallel for his readers: "In every instance, however, the will only appears as coupling quasi-parent with its offspring. And for this reason, wherever it proceeds from, it cannot itself be called either parent or offspring."[122] The human will always proceeds from some

---

[120] Dihle makes a similar point when he observes that the human will, for Augustine, is defined as that "by which man can give his reply to the inexplicable utterances of the divine will" (*The Theory of Will in Classical Antiquity*, 127).

[121] *Trin.* 8.11 (CCL 50:285–286).

[122] *Trin.* 11.16 (CCL 50:353).

other source and drives toward an end beyond itself. It is reactive, re-
sponsive, and relational.

Like the phenomenon he is here describing, Augustine's reflections on
will always have a source too. In this case, the clarity with which he expresses
his insight about the derivative quality of will proceeds from the Trinitarian
context in light of which he is considering it. The emphasis produced by
this Trinitarian perspective is far removed from that of his earliest writings
relating to the will: then he had showcased the will as the most fundamental
explanation that could be provided for an action; now he draws attention to
deeper wellsprings of the will.

A final feature of the human will that emerges in *trin.* is the dynamism
of human willing. Augustine describes the will not as a reified faculty in the
human psyche but as designating concrete wishes one may have. Describing
the intuitive understanding of willing shared by all human minds, for example, he writes, "Again they know that they will, and they know likewise
that no one can do this who is not and lives not, and again they relate this
will (*uoluntatem*) to something that they want with this will (*ea uoluntate*)."[123]
This definition may be circular, but it does convey that in the kind of universal human experience Augustine is attempting to express, the will is associated with particular acts of willing oriented toward particular ends.

For the purposes of considering the Trinitarian analogy in the mind toward which Augustine is moving in this material, this is a useful aspect of
supposedly intuitive understandings of the will to express, since Augustine
wants eventually to portray will as coextensive with memory and understanding and the mind itself. If (1) will refers to the object of one's wanting,
and (2) the mind wants itself, and the whole of itself, then (3) will is coextensive with the whole *substantia* of the mind, contributing to the result
that memory, understanding, and will "are each and all wholly contained by
each . . . each and all equal to each and all, and each and all equal to all of
them together, and these three are one."[124] Thus Augustine's search for an
image of the divine Trinity in the human mind encourages him to portray
the will as inseparable from concrete expressions of will since such a portrayal, in turn, allows for will to be characterized as subsisting in irreducible
relationship to the objects of its wanting. Thinking through the psychological function of the human will from the standpoint of the Trinity leads

---

[123] *Trin.* 10.13 (CCL 50:327). I have made a slight adjustment to Hill's translation.
[124] *Trin.* 10.18.

Augustine to approach it as a particularized, concrete activity rather than as a reified, abstract faculty. The noun "will" comes from the verb.

Conclusion

In this chapter we have observed how Augustine's teaching about the Holy Spirit illumines his understanding of the human will.[125] As we saw in part I, Augustine does not limit the Holy Spirit's relationship to human willing to the arena of analogy. The Holy Spirit, in Augustine's account, reaches across the analogical chasm between God and human being. The third person of the Trinity is, for Augustine, the "finger of God" who writes on human hearts and touches human wills. As in Michelangelo's masterpiece in the Sistine Chapel, the Holy Spirit self-extends to electrify the languid human person with life-giving power. More than serving as the divine analogue for human willing, the Holy Spirit actually changes human willing, completing the transforming work begun in Christ.

According to Augustine, the Holy Spirit enables right human willing by bringing about three effects in the human person: setting her will afire to delight in and love God, healing her from sin so that in a free act of will she may choose and delight in the good, and liberating her for obedience to

---

[125] The most important book-length studies of Augustine's conception of human willing produced to date have not, as a general rule, given much attention to the significance of the Holy Spirit for understanding Augustine's thinking on will. Jim Wetzel's groundbreaking volume twice mentions the Holy Spirit, but in both of these cases he is quoting Augustine. See James Wetzel, *Augustine and the Limits of Virtue* (New York: Cambridge University Press, 1992), 152 and 179n41. Sarah Catherine Byers mentions the Holy Spirit on four occasions in her monograph: to explain Jerome's use of the term *suggere*; in alluding to the angel's announcement to Mary that the Holy Spirit would be the Father of her child; in noting the "traditional distinction between gifts . . . and fruits . . . of the Holy Spirit"; and when quoting Augustine. See Sarah Catherine Byers, *Perception, Sensibility, and Moral Motivation in Augustine: A Stoic-Platonic Synthesis* (New York: Cambridge University Press, 2013), 36n81, 137, 182n43, and 187, respectively. Neither author comments on how the Holy Spirit acts upon the human will to change it or on how the Holy Spirit stands in analogy to the human will in Augustine's thought. Lenka Karfíková, to be commended for constantly adhering to Augustine's own descriptions of the human will, refers often to the Holy Spirit (over forty-five times, including quotes from Augustine). Despite laying vital groundwork for the present investigation by addressing the Holy Spirit in relevant texts as they emerge chronologically in Augustine's corpus, however, she does not take the step of drawing together Augustine's disparate observations to present the cumulative picture of the significance of the Holy Spirit for Augustine's thinking on the will in terms of both intervention and analogy. See Lenka Karfíková, *Grace and the Will According to Augustine* (Boston: Brill, 2012), especially 23–25 and 242–245. Taking stock of the Holy Spirit's importance for Augustine's thinking on the human will, which we have endeavored to do in this chapter, not only adds to the available perspectives on Augustine's thought on human willing but also brings into focus its distinctively Christian character.

God's commandments. We discussed these features of the Holy Spirit's work in section A of part I. In section B we explored how Augustine characterizes the Holy Spirit's agency as the Holy Spirit produces these effects in the human will. Augustine describes the Holy Spirit as enabling right willing by the Spirit's very presence, by driving human wills, and by virtue of the Holy Spirit's identity as the divine will. This inquiry into how the Holy Spirit enables right human willing in these two sections of part I sheds further light both on the human will and on the Holy Spirit, giving a clearer idea of the mechanisms needed to rehabilitate the will and clarifying the character of the Holy Spirit's distinctive work in the human person. The Holy Spirit and the human will proved, in part I, to be mutually illuminating in Augustine's mature theology due to their direct interaction.

Having examined in part I the way in which Augustine characterizes the Holy Spirit as interacting with the human will, we turned in part II to analogies between the human will and the Holy Spirit that emerge in *trin.* We found in section A that Augustine's characterization of the Holy Spirit in *trin.* stands in analogy to his descriptions of the human will in at least three ways. First, he characterizes the Holy Spirit in terms of "will" in *trin.* In fact, in this work it becomes very clear that the Holy Spirit does not just *have* a divine will; the Holy Spirit is distinctively *called* the "divine will." Second, Augustine states that the Holy Spirit is also distinctively called "charity," a term he connects in texts outside of *trin.* with good human willing. Finally, he explicitly relates these two terms with which he has associated the Holy Spirit, identifying the divine will as charity, much as he had identified good human willing as charity. As a whole, this section serves to illuminate how the Holy Spirit does and does not stand in analogy to human willing.

In section B of part II, we turned to Augustine's characterization of the human will in *trin.*, which is developed in the context of exploring analogies for the Trinity in the human person. Augustine's descriptions of the human will in *trin.* not only illumine the analogical relationship between the Holy Spirit and the human will but also help to deepen and clarify features of his mature conception of human willing expressed in other works. In chapter 5 we learned that Augustine equates the good will (*bona uoluntas*) with love (*caritas*). Analyzing his connection of human loving and willing in *trin.*, however, allowed us to fill out the relationship between love and will in greater detail. For example, our previous investigation left open the questions of whether other kinds of will besides good will might be identical to love and whether there might be types of love that were not instances of will. Our inquiry into *trin.* showed love is a species of will, though willing includes a wide variety of affections. Some kinds of willing do not always qualify as love, whether for qualitative or quantitative reasons. All loves, however, are forms of will. Though will is not always a matter of love, love is always a matter of will. Intention, we learned, is one kind of will that is not love.

Furthermore, we observed that the will serves as a connecting link in *trin.* Thus will is inherently relational. It connects or disconnects, attracts or repels; it relates other entities and presupposes other entities that it relates. The will cannot exist on its own. It must have an object in relation to which it can experience attraction or repulsion as it pushes for either unity or separation in various degrees. The examination of Augustine's characterization of will as a connecting force already set us well on our way to a fourth key observation about the human will as developed in *trin.* In this work, the human will appears as a dynamic concrete activity rather than as an abstract reified faculty. Will is always on the move toward or away from something else; it always relates to a specific object; and it always refers to something that the mind does rather than simply possesses as unrealized theoretical potential.

In sum, our examination of the human will in *trin.* showed that there are some overarching features of human willing that Augustine does not qualify as belonging only to one period of the set of theological periods in which he tends to contextualize his characterizations of willing. At the same time, however, these features were precisely such as to allow for a diversity of types of will, which, for Augustine's purposes, it proves most practical to classify according to the theological schema of created, fallen, redeemed, and consummated human willing. Human will always involves affections whereby one is attracted or repelled toward various objects, but the precise character of these affections varies depending on context. Human will always has a relational structure, but what entities the will relates and how it relates them depends not just on voluntary whims but also on factors beyond the will itself. The will is a movement of the soul, but where it is headed depends on the kind of willing in question. Thus certain universal structural or formal features of human willing emerge in *trin.*, but these are minimally developed. They are sufficient to help us to identify willing as a certain kind of activity, but not sufficient to help us identify what willing is in terms that enable any kind of evaluative judgment about the significance of this activity. Human acts of will are tied, in one way or another, to the affections, but this does not yet tell us whether we are dealing with love or hate. To learn what will "is" in practical terms requires the added contexts supplied by Augustine's theologically differentiated notions of will.

Even as Augustine supplies more information about the universal or general functioning of the human will in *trin.* than he does in other mature works, this in no way suggests a relaxing of the strictly theological reins with which he has been keeping his thinking about human willing in check since *Ad Simplicianum.* Far from it. *De trinitate* is no treatise on human psychology for its own sake in which the horses of Augustine's anthropological imagination run wild. In fact, he makes the crucial clarifications to his theory of human willing precisely in the context of an investigation into the doctrine of the Trinity. His clarifications about willing, a central feature of his anthropology, find greater clarity in this theological and distinctively Trinitarian context. Yet again Augustine's view of will is here seen to emerge from the contexts of his theology. In the chariot of Augustine's thinking on will, theology is the charioteer.

One striking illustration of the theological driving force behind Augustine's creative use of the term "will" in *trin.* is his reception of Cicero in *trin.* 14.14. As Lewis Ayres has recently discussed at some length, Augustine's triad of *memoria, intellegentia,* and *uoluntas* "finds its origins in Cicero."[126] Augustine makes a crucial adjustment, however, to Cicero's identification of the three activities of wisdom (*prudentia*). For, as it happens, Cicero designates these not as *memoria, intellegentia,* and *uoluntas* but as *memoria, intellegentia,* and *prouidentia.*[127] *Prouidentia,* Augustine argues, cannot be one of the triad making up the image of God in the human person, since "no one has certainty in this last quality except those who have foreknowledge of the future, and this is not a gift enjoyed by men unless they are given it from above, like the prophets."[128] Scripture makes clear that *prouidentia* does not belong naturally to human beings: "So the book of Wisdom, talking about men, says, *The thoughts of mortals are timid and*

---

[126] See Lewis Ayres, *Augustine and the Trinity* (New York: Cambridge University Press, 2010), 308. Ayres observes that this connection, which he treats on 308–315, has been acknowledged but rarely explored.

[127] See Cicero's *De Inventione* 2.53. Augustine refers to Cicero's triad of *memoria, intellegentia,* and *prouidentia* in *diu. qu.* 31.1 (CCL 44A:41). Augustine's introduction of willing into a triad along with "being and knowing" in *conf.* 13.11 is also a distinctive contribution, notes Rowan Williams. While Marius Victorinus had referred to a triad of "being, living, and understanding," Augustine's inclusion of will was "entirely characteristic of Augustine" (Williams, "*De Trinitate,*" 846).

[128] *Trin.* 14.14 (CCL 50A:441–442).

our foresight unsure (Wis 9:14)."[129] Thus a theological consideration (the ontological difference between human beings and God) as corroborated in scripture (the book of Wisdom) prompts Augustine to introduce a substitution. *Uoluntas* thus takes the place of *prouidentia* in Augustine's famous triad of memory, intellect, and will. He here cites theology and scripture as motivating him to utilize the term *uoluntas* in this creative new way.

As a whole, this chapter helps to throw into relief the dynamic crystallized in Augustine's modification of Cicero: theology, though of course not exclusively theology, shapes and informs his use of the term "will" (*uoluntas*). In chapter 6 it was shown that Augustine's thinking about Christ plays a vital role in his account of the good human will since Christ not only assumes a human will and models right human willing but also transforms the human will by grace. In this chapter we have seen how Augustine's thought on the Holy Spirit, too, affects his account of human willing. As in the case of Christ, the Holy Spirit shows forth what human willing ought to be all about. But whereas Christ does this in and through his distinct human will, the Holy Spirit does so on an infinitely higher divine plane than that upon which human willing occurs; human willing at its best is analogically reflected in the perfect, loving, divine will that is distinctively called the Holy Spirit (as shown in part II). Furthermore, like Christ, the Holy Spirit actually intervenes in the process whereby the fallen human will is transformed for the better (as shown in part I). In the cases of both Christ and the Holy Spirit, theology clearly serves to explain and inform Augustine's views about the human will.

Insofar as Augustine's Christology and Pneumatology help give rise to his theory of human willing, Augustine's conception of the human will gains clarity in the context of his Trinitarian theology. He describes the will not just in theologically abstract terms but also in relation to the particulars of the economy of God's salvific plan. The Augustinian will takes shape in the story whereby the Father sends the Son to bring health and wholeness to humankind through the Holy Spirit. In this sense, Augustine's account of the will is not only theologically driven but also distinctively Christian. The will is what it is in relation to the being and activity of the Christian God: Father, Son, and Holy Spirit.

---

[129] *Trin.* 14.14 (CCL 50A:442).

The intersections of Augustine's thinking on human willing with his thought on Christ and the Holy Spirit mark particularly creative and fruitful areas of his thought. On the one hand, pondering the mysterious realities of Christ and the Holy Spirit in relation to will leads Augustine down unfamiliar Christological and Pneumatological trails that would become the broad avenues of subsequent mainstream Western theology. His affirmation of a distinct human will in Christ and his connection of the divine will with the Holy Spirit, as opposed to the Son, would both prove as fruitful for the subsequent tradition as they were surprising in Augustine's own historical milieu. While the former is not always recognized as coming to expression in the works of the bishop of Hippo, it has become regarded as a standard feature of Christological orthodoxy in all major branches of the church; while the latter may not enjoy the universal acceptance of the former, it is a move for which Augustine's Trinitarian theology has become famous. Thinking about Christ and the Holy Spirit through the lens of will led Augustine to conclusions as influential for the subsequent tradition as they were unusual in his own day.

As we have endeavored to show in this chapter, however, the reverse was also true. Thinking about the human will through the lenses of Christ and the Holy Spirit led Augustine in surprising and important new directions. His Christology, Pneumatology, and account of will were mutually influencing. The conception of willing that he deployed in his Christology and Pneumatology was not something he adopted wholesale from existing accounts in preceding pagan rhetorical or philosophical traditions and applied to Christian theology unmodified. Rather the meaning of *uoluntas* was transformed and reframed in the process of being appropriated for theological ends. By connecting the Holy Spirit with the will, Augustine introduces new ideas about the Spirit into the history of doctrine, but he also introduces new ideas about the will into the history of Western thought. We will take up the question of the place of Augustine's thinking in the larger intellectual history of the Western tradition, and in the history of Christianity in particular, in the conclusion. But first we must turn to the final facet of Augustine's theologically periodized notion of will, the eschatological, genuinely free will made possible by the full fruition of the work of the Holy Spirit that we have begun to discuss in this chapter.

8

The Eschatological Will

Full Freedom at Last

Chapters 6 and 7 treated the work of Christ and the Holy Spirit in making good human willing possible in this life. This chapter addresses the kind of human willing that results from the perfection of this divine work of redemption, which, Augustine tells us, will be accomplished only in the next life. This is the fourth overarching type of human willing Augustine treats in his account of the will as created, fallen, redeemed, and perfected in the eschaton. The eschatological will represents the purposeful culmination, not just the arbitrary arrest, of the various transformations Augustine depicts; it is the flower to the seed of the will's previous phases. Yet it is also the type of willing about which he has the least to say.

The reason for Augustine's reserve is simple: he lacks information. The eschatological will, unlike the other three types of will he describes, lies in the future, outside the compass of common human experience. Furthermore, while the Bible does give some indications of what eschatological willing shall be like, the particulars it provides about the realm of the next life remain minimal in comparison to the volume of material it makes available on previous stages of the saga of human salvation. As a result, Augustine has limited data to inform his account of eschatological willing.

In the *City of God* (*ciu.*), Augustine identifies both qualitative and quantitative boundaries of our knowledge of the final perfection, which he finds delineated in scripture. The peace of God we will enjoy, he emphasizes, citing Paul in Philippians 4:7, "is beyond all understanding"—not only beyond human understanding but also beyond the understanding of the angels. God's peace is divine and therefore qualitatively beyond the ken of creatures. Only God himself can comprehend it.[1] Quantitatively speaking, human beings can begin to know this peace to a certain extent, with the

---

[1] *Ciu.* 22.29 (CCL 48:856). Unless otherwise noted, this and subsequent translations come from Augustine, *City of God*, trans. Henry Bettenson (London: Penguin, 2003).

Augustine on the Will. Han-luen Kantzer Komline, Oxford University Press (2020). © Oxford University Press.
DOI: 10.1093/oso/9780190948801.001.0001

qualification that they participate in it on a human plane, though, even so, "human beings in their present state know it in a far lower degree [than the degree in which the angels know it], however highly developed may be their intellectual powers." Drawing again on Paul, this time pointing to 1 Corinthians 13:9 and 12, Augustine urges his readers, "We must remember what a great man it was who said, 'Our knowledge is partial, and our prophesying is partial, until the perfection comes,' and, 'We now see a dim reflection in a mirror; but then we shall see face to face.' "[2] Knowledge of the final heavenly peace in which the saints will share in the next life is, for the moment, incomplete at best.

The indirect and partial knowledge we have of our future heavenly existence, according to Augustine, however paltry it may be compared to the reality we have yet to experience, does allow us to surmise at least three things about the eschatological will. First, the eschatological will is a fully free will, whose full freedom goes beyond freedom of choice. It is distinct from the human will in its originally created, fallen, and even redeemed conditions. Second, the eschatological will enjoys the inability to sin. Augustine defends the good, appropriate, and advantageous character of this "inability" by setting it in theological context. Third, there is a rich panoply of positive characteristics of the free willing that will be enjoyed in the eschaton.

As we will see, the eschatological will possesses unique features differentiating it from the will in its created, fallen, and redeemed states. But even the eschatological will, the pinnacle of human willing, does not transcend the memory of the forms of will that precede it as if they should, or even could, ever be consigned to the realm of forgetfulness. The eschatological will possesses a profile distinct from those of the will as created, fallen, and redeemed, but could never be what it is without these earlier permutations. The joy and perfection of this final, fully free will lies precisely in praising God as the author of a story that began before ever this full freedom came to be.

Part I: A Fully Free Will

As the role of grace in Augustine's theology expands, freedom comes increasingly to the fore as he explains how this expansion avoids encroaching

---

[2] *Ciu.* 22.29 (CCL 48:857).

on human freedom.[3] Providing such an explanation leads Augustine, in the late stages of his thinking, to devise a highly sophisticated account of human freedom. "We . . . always have free will," he contends, in the baseline sense of being free from one external influence or another.[4] This minimalistic meaning of "free will," however, is far from the only type of freedom Augustine describes. For the late Augustine, freedom is complex. There are not only different kinds of freedom but also different degrees of freedom.[5] The idea of freedom becomes more, not less, developed in Augustine's theology over time. His doctrine of grace is like a catalyst that precipitates his multifaceted mature views on freedom.

As the quantity of Augustine's reflections on freedom increases, the methodology of these reflections also changes: his thinking on this theme becomes more and more scriptural. The contrast between his early work *De libero arbitrio* (*lib. arb.*), on the one hand, written while he was still a presbyter and treated in chapters 1 and 2, and the late text *Gratia et libero arbitrio* (*gr. et lib. arb.*), written as a part of his exchange with the monks of Hadrumetum, on the other, illustrates this development. In the latter work, Augustine's arguments become overwhelmingly dependent upon the biblical text.[6]

In a way, *lib. arb.* and *gr. et lib. arb.* set out to accomplish similar tasks. Each approaches free choice from the angle of some other pressing reality with which it is connected: evil (in the former case) and grace (in the latter). In both cases, Augustine presents free choice as illuminating an enigmatic question, whether that question is "Whence evil?," as in *lib. arb.*, or "How can grace and human freedom coexist?," the central question of *gr. et lib. arb.* Both works end up arguing that there is such a thing as free choice

---

[3] For literature pertaining to free will in Augustine, see the notes in the introduction to this book. For another recent study of Augustine's conception of freedom, see Gerald Bonner, *Freedom and Necessity: St. Augustine's Teaching on Divine Power and Human Freedom* (Washington, DC: Catholic University of America Press, 2007). While Bonner stresses the tensions in Augustine's mature view (see especially 97–117), I will argue that Augustine's conception of free will is securely, though subtly, woven into the weft and warp of other central threads of his theology (such as creation, fall, redemption, and eschaton).

[4] *Gr. et lib. arb.* 15.31 (PL 44:899).

[5] In *corrept.*, for example, Augustine argues that free choice will be "more free" (*liberius*) when it is no longer a slave to sin. See *corrept.* 11.32 (CSEL 92:259).

[6] See, for example, *gr. et lib. arb.* 2.4 and 4.7. In 2.4, Augustine argues for free choice (*liberum arbitrium*) by citing scriptural passages that presuppose it. For him, such passages would include any that express a commandment requiring an act of will in response. The sheer quantity of biblical texts he cites is staggering; he quotes at least twenty-eight in paragraph 4 alone. In the latter passage, he again points to God's commands in scripture as evidence of free choice (*liberum uoluntatis arbitrium*).

of the will, and that it is vitally important to understanding these other themes to the greatest degree that human beings can; free choice is not only compatible with the existence of evil and of grace, it also helps to explain a mechanism through which these realities become instantiated in the world. Yet the method according to which Augustine generally operates in these works is drastically different, though we can see him taking a step toward a more scriptural approach in *lib. arb.* book 3. References to scripture are sparse in *lib. arb.*, which has become a classic text of the Western theological tradition. *Gr. et lib. arb.* is rife with biblical quotations. These two works on free choice, a central theme within the larger field of Augustine's thinking on freedom, stand like bookends at the beginning and end of his career. They show, and ensure, that his thinking holds together, but also mark the distance between "early" and "late." The central concerns are the same, but how Augustine tackles the topic is different.

Into the complex matrix of his late teaching on freedom fits Augustine's notion of "full" or perfect freedom, *plena libertas*, the freedom that, he teaches, belongs to the human will exclusively in its eschatological state. To better appreciate what exactly this freedom entails, we will compare and contrast it to various other types of freedom Augustine describes. First, we will contrast eschatological free will with the types of free will that belong to human beings in other periods of the story of human salvation (section A). The freedom of the eschatological will is different not only from the "slavish freedom" of a fallen will but also from redeemed freedom and even created freedom. Second, we will turn to the distinction between the eschatological freedom promised to the saints and mere freedom of choice (section B). In order to show that eschatological freedom includes but is not limited to freedom of choice, we will first clarify in what freedom of choice consists before addressing its limitations and how various types of Christian freedom extend beyond free choice.

Section A: Eschatological Freedom in Contrast to Fallen, Redeemed, and Created Freedoms

In Augustine's view, even sinful actions are performed by exercising a certain kind of freedom, though he designates such freedom "servile." He writes in *trin.*, "Even in their very sins, you see, souls are pursuing nothing but a kind of likeness to God with a proud and topsy-turvy and, if I may so put it, a slavish freedom (*seruili libertate*)."[7] As this quotation shows, the noun "freedom" is susceptible to drastic qualification in Augustine's thinking. Unsurprisingly, the "slavish" or "servile" freedom characteristic of the fallen will and the sinful actions to which it leads stands in contrast to the eschatological freedom the saints are destined to enjoy in the next life. As we will see, whereas Augustine calls the former kind of freedom "slavish," he names the latter type "full freedom."

Augustine also differentiates eschatological freedom of the will from the freedom that belongs to the redeemed, which, though genuine rather than slavish, remains a work in progress.[8] Though the healing of the will is under way in this life, "if we are thinking correctly," he contends, "just as we ought to give thanks for the healing our members have received, we ought to pray for the future healing of our members so that we may enjoy an absolute good health (*absolutissima sanitate*) to which nothing can be added, the perfect sweetness of God, and complete freedom (*plena libertate*)."[9] The freedom we enjoy in this life is partial. That promised to us in the next is complete. At that point the will shall be not only "right" but "pure," not only a work in progress but fully perfected.[10]

Furthermore, the freedom to be enjoyed in the eschaton differs from created freedom. As Augustine explains in *corrept.*, and as we will explore further in part II of this chapter, the key contrast between these two freedoms is that "the first freedom of the will (*libertas uoluntatis*) . . . was the ability not to sin (*posse non peccare*)," whereas "the final freedom (*nouissima*) will be much greater, namely, the inability to sin (*non posse peccare*)."[11] The difference between the freedom of the will as originally created and eschatological freedom of the will, Augustine here tells us, is not slight. Rather, the "latest" or "newest" freedom of the will we are to enjoy in the eschaton makes a significant advance upon the freedom of will human beings enjoyed by virtue of their creation: it is "much greater" (*multo maior*).

---

[7] *Trin.* 11.8 (CCL 50:344).

[8] Though Augustine sometimes describes the redeemed in this life as slaves to righteousness, their freedom is not properly designated slavish since their actions are motivated by love rather than compelled.

[9] *Nat. et grat.* 58.68 (CSEL 60:284).

[10] As we have seen in chapter 5, for Augustine the terms "heart" (*cor*) and "will" (*uoluntas*) are closely related. In *perf. iust.* he sets up a distinction with respect to heart that parallels the distinction he makes between freedom and full freedom in *nat. et gr.* In Augustine's terse words: "But I think there is a difference between one who is upright of heart and one who is pure of heart. . . . The one is making progress; the other has arrived at the goal" (*perf. iust.* 15.36 [CSEL 42:37]).

[11] *Corrept.* 12.33 (CSEL 92:259).

The eschatological freedom of the will, then, is different from the types of freedom of will human beings enjoy in each of the three other "theological periods" discussed thus far in this book. The fully free will that will be ours in the eschaton differs not only from the "slavishly free" fallen will, which is fettered to sin, but also from the "redeemed" will, which is in the process of being freed, and from the created will, which enjoyed the freedom to resist or to yield to sin. The "full freedom" of the eschatological will entails a liberation from sin so complete that resisting sin is a guarantee rather than a mere possibility; sin cannot touch willing in the resurrection.

Section B: Eschatological Freedom of Will versus Free Choice

In addition to possessing a freedom that goes beyond that of the created, fallen, and redeemed iterations of the human will, the eschatological will possesses a freedom that extends beyond free choice. To see how this is the case for Augustine, we will first examine the meaning of free choice and its limitations before addressing the way in which both Christian freedom in this life and eschatological freedom transcend mere freedom of choice. Augustine is convinced that human free choice is inviolable. It is never effaced, even in the eschaton. Full eschatological freedom includes, but is not limited to, free choice.

For Augustine, free choice is the ability to choose as one pleases. Significantly, it does not require the ability to choose between a number of alternatives.[12] All it requires is the ability to choose what one wants. Free choice is a freedom to prefer the object of one's desires rather than the freedom to choose one option over against another. Thus the fall, which made it impossible for people to delight in the good without grace, did not obliterate free choice. In Augustine's words, "It is far from being true that free choice (*liberum arbitrium*) perished in the sinner." To the contrary, "all

---

[12] The question of whether free choice requires the ability to choose between alternatives becomes a bone of contention between Augustine and Julian during the latter stages of the Pelagian controversy. In Julian's view, a person must have both the ability to sin and the ability not to sin for free will to be achieved. According to his (in!)famous definition, "freedom of choice (*libertas arbitrii*) by which a human being has received emancipation from God (*qua a deo emancipatus homo est*) consists in the possibility of committing sin and of refraining from sin" (*c. Iul. imp.* 1.78 [CSEL 85.1:93]). Elsewhere he offers a similar definition: "Freedom of choice, then, is the capability of committing or of avoiding

people sin by free choice, but in particular all those who sin with a delight in and with a love (*cum delectatione . . . et amore*) for the sin and who choose to do what pleases them."[13] As shown in the example of fallen willing absent the influence of grace, free choice does not require the ability to select an alternative (in this case the good) but merely the ability to select that in which one delights (in this case evil).[14] One has "free choice" if one is "free for (*in*)" something by virtue of taking delight in it.[15]

At a baseline level, free choice means being able to choose what one thinks will make one happy, even if the intermediate objects of willing by which one seeks to achieve this goal in fact serve to undermine one's happiness. According to Augustine, this makes free choice per se inalienable, even though one may gain or lose the freedom to choose various types of ends. He explains, "If we look for the free choice (*liberum arbitrium*) of a human being that is inborn and absolutely unable to be lost, it is that by which all will to be happy, even those who do not will those things which lead to happiness."[16] Since free choice as such is the freedom to will to be happy, and since Augustine is convinced that the will to be happy is an inherent feature of human being, all human beings possess free choice innately. Free choice is a species of freedom of the will that all human beings possess at all times in all places; not even sin can deprive them of it.[17] It is

sin, immune from compelling necessity; it has in its own power which path it will follow of the two that suggest themselves, that is, either the arduous and difficult paths of the virtues or the low and swampy paths of the pleasures" (*c. Iul. imp.* 1.82). For Julian, free choice is inherently deliberative; it always involves adjudicating between alternatives. For Augustine, free choice is simply voluntary; all that free choice requires is one possibility, so long as one wills it. Julian finds this Augustinian view ludicrous; Augustine is being "no less stupid than sacrilegious" when he calls "free . . . that which . . . can only will one thing" (*c. Iul. imp.* 1.100). Augustine's rejoinder is "If only that is free which is able to will two things, that is, good and evil, God is not free since he cannot will evil" (*c. Iul. imp.* 1.100).

[13] *C. ep. Pel.* 1.2.5 (CSEL 60:426).

[14] Augustine writes in *c. ep. Pel.* 1.3.6 (CSEL 60:428), "But people have free choice for what is evil, if either secretly or openly the deceiver has sown in them a delight in evil or if they have persuaded themselves to it."

[15] This is again demonstrated by the example of the evil will, "which is free for evil actions because it takes delight in evil," though it "is not free for good actions, because it has not been set free" (*c. ep. Pel.* 1.3.7 [CSEL 60:428–429]).

[16] *C. Iul. imp.* 6.11 (CSEL 85.2:316). This statement helps to interpret Augustine's seeming indication shortly thereafter in the same work that free choice can be lost. He writes to Julian, "Even you admit that free choice (*liberum arbitrium*) can be lost by being used badly" (*c. Iul. imp.* 6.12 [CSEL 85.2:321]). Augustine thinks that the free choice "by which all will to be happy" (*c. Iul. imp.* 6.11) can never be lost even while the "free choice of the man by which he could have and ought to have acted rightly" was lost (*c. Iul. imp.* 6.12).

[17] See *c. Iul. imp.* 6.12 (CSEL 85.2:321). There Augustine states, "That freedom of will, however, with which human beings were created and are created, remains unchangeable, for by it we all will to be happy, and we cannot not will this. . . . The freedom is inborn by which one wills to be happy, something that all will, even those who are unwilling to act rightly."

right to affirm that human beings always have "free will" (*uoluntas libera*), according to Augustine, in the sense, and only in the sense, that they always enjoy free choice (*liberum arbitrium*).[18]

Given Augustine's understanding of free choice as the freedom to choose as one pleases, the freedom to will in such a way as to make oneself happy, it is unsurprising that he sometimes writes as if any act of willing inherently implies free choice. Indeed, given that willing involves a disposition toward some object of will that pleases one, free choice, as defined by Augustine, is implicated in willing by definition. Augustine accordingly concludes in *gr. et lib. arb.* that "where, of course, it says, 'Do not do this,' and 'Do not do that,' and where in God's counsels the act of the will (*opus uoluntatis*) is required for doing or for not doing something, the existence of free choice (*liberum arbitrium*) is sufficiently proven."[19] For Augustine an act of will as such automatically implies the operation of free choice. Thus any passage of scripture that refers to or implies will offers confirmation that free choice exists.[20]

On Augustine's view, then, willing as such implies free choice. This lends free choice an expansive range; it is involved in all sorts of voluntary action. But free choice also has serious limitations. Achieving free choice is easy; guiding it to the good is hard. Free choice falls short of what one might hope for it in at least three ways: it is sufficient for evil but not for the good; it can subsist in the mode of slavery to sin; and, without grace, one can have free choice without being "truly free."

During the Pelagian controversy, Augustine makes clear that free choice does not guarantee freedom for the good. For Augustine, it is possible to have freedom of choice without enjoying this particular variety of

[18] The qualification is important because it explains how Augustine can suggest that freedom of will can be lost by misuse (see, for example, *c. Iul. imp.* 6.14) without contradicting statements such as the following: "We, however, always have free will (*uoluntas libera*), but it is not always good. For it is either free from righteousness when it is enslaved to sin, and then it is evil, or it is free from sin when it is enslaved to righteousness, and then it is good" (*gr. et lib. arb.* 15.31). In *c. Iul. imp.* 6.14 (CSEL 85.2:330), Augustine writes, "Here you admit for the moment what you do not want to admit, namely, that freedom of the will could be lost by its own misuse, because by doing something evil it became less suited to do something good."

[19] *Gr. et lib. arb.* 2.4 (PL 44:884).

[20] A little later in the same work, Augustine reiterates that he regards free choice as amply demonstrated by commandments that call forth a response of will from the human being. He points out, "Do the very many things which are commanded in the law of God against the commission of fornication and adultery point to anything but free choice (*liberum arbitrium*)? For such commands would not be given unless a man had a will (*uoluntatem*) of his own by which he might obey the divine commandments" (*gr. et lib. arb.* 4.8 [PL 44:886]).

freedom.[21] As he clarifies in his debate with Pelagius, both he and Pelagius agree that free choice exists. The difference is that Pelagius believes in the sufficiency of this free choice to do good without God's help (*adiutorio dei*), whereas Augustine rejects this notion.[22] According to Augustine, to be free for the good we need to be set free by the deliverer, to receive a divine gift. This gift cannot come from the human power of free choice (*ex libero arbitrio*). It can only be given by God (*a deo*).[23] Without grace, then, free choice is insufficient for the good. On its own, free choice is capable only of sin.[24]

It is clear from the very start of the Pelagian controversy that this is Augustine's chastened view of the limits upon free choice after the fall. But he eventually comes to believe that free choice was subject to radical limitations not only subsequent to the sin of Adam and Eve but even in the blessedness of Eden. Free choice, he eventually asserts, never possessed the strength to attain the good on its own. It always required a gift of grace, divine "help" (*adiutorium*), to assist it to choose rightly. Even in the garden, free choice on its own was capable only of evil. By the time he writes *corrept.* (427), Augustine has become persuaded that both before and after the fall "free choice (*liberum arbitrium*) is sufficient for evil, but not sufficient for good, unless it is helped by the omnipotent good."[25]

Subsequent to the fall, however, the strictures on free choice prove so severe, in Augustine's view, as to warrant its designation as in thrall to sin,

---

[21] Jesse Couenhoven rightly emphasizes that according to Augustine free choice persists after the fall even though we are no longer free for the good and it is therefore enfeebled. See Jesse Couenhoven, *Stricken by Sin, Cured by Christ: Agency, Necessity, and Culpability in Augustinian Theology* (New York: Oxford University Press, 2013), 84.

[22] See *nupt. et conc.* 2.3.8 (CSEL 42:260): "We both, therefore, say that human beings have free choice (*liberum arbitrium*) and that God is the creator of the newborn; this is not the reason you are Caelestians or Pelagians. But you say that anyone is free to do good without the help of God and that little ones are not rescued from the power of darkness and in that way transferred into the kingdom of God; this is the reason that you are Caelestians or Pelagians."

[23] See *c. ep. Pel.* 1.3.6 (CSEL 60:428): "The power, then, by which those who believe in him become children of God is a gift, since the very fact that they believe in him is a gift. Unless this power is given by God, it cannot arise from free choice, because it will not be free for what is good if the deliverer has not set it free."

[24] See *spir. et litt.* 3.5 (CSEL 60: 157) "For free choice (*liberum arbitrium*) is capable only of sinning, if the way of truth remains hidden." Considered independently, this statement might lead one to conclude that what differentiates free choice capable only of sinning and free choice capable of the good is knowledge, apart from a supernatural gift of grace. This misunderstanding is avoided, however, if we bear in mind Augustine's insistence in the immediately preceding sentences that people can participate in the truth only if God gives them delight, by a gratuitous gift of grace. See also *spir. et litt.* 3.5.

[25] *Corrept.* 11.31 (CSEL 92: 256). Augustine goes on to explain that Adam was given a help or "grace" sufficient to will the good, but not a help that guaranteed he would will the good.

not just as insufficient for the good. In *c. Iul.* (421), Augustine describes the free choice of the will after the fall as "enslaved," calling it a *servo arbitrio uoluntatis*.[26] Then again, in the final stage of the Pelagian controversy, having referred to sinning "by free choice," he explains, "I mean: a choice (*arbitrium*) that is free (*liberum*), but not set free (*liberatum*), a choice free of righteousness, but enslaved (*seruum*) to sin."[27] In language that anticipates Luther's eleven centuries later, Augustine contends that "free choice" can, and does post-fall and pre-grace, subsist in the mode of slavery to sin.

Thus the peculiar limitations of free choice entail that one can possess it while failing to be "truly free." In *nupt. et conc.* book 2 (420 or 421), Augustine concedes that human beings have free choice but denies that this free choice qualifies as true freedom. Responding to Pelagius's accusation that he denies free choice, Augustine contrasts free choice with authentic Christian freedom based on an appeal to John 8:36: "We do not deny free choice (*liberum arbitrium*). Rather, *If the Son sets you free*, the truth says, *then you will truly be free* (Jn 8:36)." He continues, "You begrudge the deliverer to those captives to whom you attribute a false freedom (*uanam libertatem*). *After all, one becomes a slave*, as scripture says, *to one's conqueror* (2 Pt 2:19). And no one is set free from this chain of slavery, from which no human being is exempt, except by the grace of the deliverer."[28] Pelagius, Augustine contends, attributes to fallen human beings a kind of freedom they do not in fact possess. His claims about it are therefore as "false" or "vacuous" as the notion of "liberty" upon whose existence he insists. In fact, the free choice fallen people enjoy fails to measure up to the standard of authentic freedom from the oppression of sin. Free choice is helpless to unshackle the fallen human being from her bonds; it therefore gives no guarantees of genuine freedom.

Augustine makes a similar point in *corrept.* (427). Discussing those "whom the grace of God is leading to the kingdom," he explains that this number includes both "those who do not as yet have any free choice of their will" (presumably he has in mind infants baptized and thereby receiving grace before any merits of their own) and "those with a choice of the will

---

[26] See *c. Iul.* 2.8.23 (PL 44:689). Augustine says to Julian, "You want human beings to attain perfection in this life, and I wish you wanted this from God's gift and not from the free—or rather enslaved—choice of their own will."

[27] *Corrept.* 13.42 (CSEL 92:271).

[28] *Nupt. et conc.* 2.3.8 (CSEL 42:259).

which is truly free (*uere libero*), because it has been set free (*liberato*)."[29] The implication is that free choice that has not been liberated in this way is less than truly free. For Augustine, then, free choice is sufficient for evil but not for the good, can subsist in the mode of slavery to sin, and does not entail being "truly free."

In Augustine's view, the true freedom for which God must set human beings free by grace goes beyond free choice; it consists in a willing delight in obedience. Citing Romans 7:22–23, Augustine explains that grace makes us able to delight in the law of the Lord, and that this delight, as opposed to mere free choice, amounts to genuine freedom. Quoting Paul, he writes, "*For I take delight, he says, in the law of God according to the interior self, but I see another law in my members that resists the law of my mind and holds me captive under the law of sin which is in my members* (Rom 7:22–23)." He then elaborates, "This taking delight in the law of God in the interior self comes to us by a great grace of God. . . . After all, it is not fear that twists our arm, but love that makes us eager. There we are truly free (*ueraciter liberi*) where we willingly take delight."[30] Whereas choosing the good out of servile fear, the only thing that can motivate a person to do the good under sin, in no way mitigates free choice's enslavement, delight in the good inspired by God makes one truly free. Drawing once more on John 8:36 a few years later, Augustine again distinguishes the authentic freedom brought by Christ from inferior versions: "On account of that sin human nature needs God's grace, for the Lord says, *If the Son sets you free, then you will truly be free* (*uere liberi*) (Jn 8:36), free (*liberi*), that is, to live good and righteous lives."[31] Given the work of the Son, human beings can experience the genuine freedom of delighting in the good, and thereby be capable of genuine wholehearted obedience.

This true freedom, available given the liberating work of Christ in and through the Holy Spirit, belongs to the redeemed will. But Augustine also attributes another kind of authentic freedom, freedom in the sense of possessing "complete righteousness with immortality," to Adam and Eve before the fall. While sin's entry into the world did not result in the loss of free choice, Augustine observes, "freedom (*libertas*) did indeed perish through sin, but it was that freedom which existed in paradise and which

---

[29] *Corrept.* 13.42 (CSEL 92:271).
[30] *Nupt. et conc.* 1.33 (CSEL 42:245).
[31] *C. ep. Pel.* 1.2.5 (CSEL 60:426).

consisted in having complete righteousness with immortality (*plenam cum inmortalitate iustitiam*)."³² Though more genuinely free than bare "free" choice, the freedom possible for the saints subsequent to the fall still remains incomplete. With flesh that remains "subject to corruption," those under grace are still held "captive under the law of sin in my members," Augustine asserts, using the words of Paul.³³ Though they do not give consent to concupiscence, they still experience it in their flesh, with the result that the genuine freedom they enjoy remains less than fully perfected.

The full freedom of the eschatological will, however, exceeds not only the freedom of "free choice" but also both the type of "true freedom" made ours in this life through redemption by Christ and the type of "true freedom" with which Adam and Eve were endowed in the garden. To see how this is the case, we turn to parts II and III of this chapter.

Part II: A Will Unable to Sin

As we observed in part I, the eschatological will is, for Augustine, a will whose full freedom is distinct not only from the human will in its originally created, fallen, and redeemed conditions, but also from the power of free choice. For Augustine, free choice is inalienable but has serious limitations; it fails to meet the criteria for "truly free" willing, falling short of both the true freedom that belongs to the redeemed will and of that which belongs to the created will. The freedom of the eschatological will, as we will see, outranks all of these differing types of freedom (created freedom, fallen freedom, redeemed freedom, and freedom of choice) for

---

³² "Who of us would say that free choice was removed from the human race by the sin of the first human being? Freedom did indeed perish through sin, but it was that freedom which existed in paradise and which consisted in having complete righteousness with immortality" (*c. ep. Pel.* 1.2.5 [CSEL 60:425–426]). In *ciu.* 22.30 (CCL 48:864), Augustine does distinguish between the first (*prima*) and final (*nouissima*) immortality of human beings: to be able not to die (*posse non mori*) and to be unable to die (*non posse mori*), respectively. This suggests, by analogy, that complete righteousness, like complete immortality, is a distinguishing feature of the eschatological state as opposed to the created state. The contrast for Augustine between the created and the eschatological will become sharper over time. Still, the point he makes here in *c. ep. Pel.* continues to hold: the authentic freedom of created willing is distinct from the authentic freedom of redeemed willing, not least of all because immortality has been lost and therefore no longer constitutes the type of freedom enjoyed by the redeemed. What the quote from *ciu.* highlights is that the authentic freedom of the created will is distinct, yet again, from the genuine freedom of the eschaton. While eschatological freedom involves *plena iustitia* in the sense of being invulnerable, created freedom before the fall involves *plena iustitia* in the sense of being as yet inviolate.

³³ See *c. ep. Pel.* 1.10.20.

a surprising reason. A peculiar inability, rather than unlimited capability, explains the superiority of the eschatological will's freedom. As Augustine explains in the late work *corrept.* (427), whereas "the first freedom of the will (*prima . . . libertas uoluntatis*), then, was the ability not to sin; the final freedom (*nouissima*) will be much greater, namely, the inability to sin."[34] This inability (*non posse*), Augustine tells his readers, makes the final freedom of the eschatological will "much greater" (*multo maior*), as befits the general tendency of the final goods available to glorified humankind to be "more powerful" (*potiora*) and "better" (*meliora*) than their precursors.[35] The inability to sin makes eschatological freedom superior to other kinds of freedom that precede it.

This unusual claim was at least as counterintuitive in Augustine's own day as it is for us today. After establishing the characteristics of this inability (section A), we will proceed to consider how Augustine constructs a theological defense of it by appealing to the freedom of Christ in particular, and to the freedom of God more generally speaking (section B). In so doing, we will see that Augustine develops his characterization of the eschatological will in theological context and justifies it on theological grounds.

Section A: Characteristics of the Inability to Sin

Augustine characterizes the inability to sin as a reward granted to the saints in the next life, as a gift that brings our will to completion in the good, and as entailing the subjection of the will to a "blessed necessity." Yet this necessity does not signal that the eschatological will is forced to do what it does or that its free choice has been compromised. Rather, the inability to sin augments both "free choice" and the "freedom" of the will in the eschaton.[36] We will examine Augustine's articulation of each of these claims.

---

[34] *Corrept.* 12.33 (CSEL 92:259).

[35] These include the final freedom of the will (inability to sin), the final immortality (inability to die), and the final perseverance (inability to abandon the good). Augustine asks a rhetorical question to show that the superiority of these goods does not detract from the goodness of the gifts of original creation that preceded them, but his question also reflects the superiority of these final goods: "Were those first goods either little or nothing because the final ones are more powerful and better?" (*corrept.* 12.33 [CSEL 92:259]).

[36] For a constructive philosophical and theological defense of an "Augustinian normative conception of freedom" over against libertarian conceptions of freedom, see Jesse Couenhoven, "The Necessities of Perfect Freedom," *International Journal of Systematic Theology* 14, no. 4

As we have seen, in the garden Adam and Eve were able not to sin but were not guaranteed immunity from sin. Those whose wills have been redeemed subsequent to the fall, on the other hand, enjoy freedom from sin in that their wills are no longer bound to consent to it, even though they may experience concupiscence. Freedom in the sense of inability to sin, in contrast to these other types of freedoms, is deferred to the hereafter. Augustine writes, "If, then, you ask where or when the inability to sin (*non posse peccare*) is granted to human beings, look for the rewards of the saints which it is right that they receive after this life."[37] Unlike these other types of freedom, one granted gratuitously in creation, another granted gratuitously in the re-creation of redemption, the inability to sin is a reward God graciously deigns to bestow on those people he has enabled to be obedient.

This reward, Augustine indicates, will bring the human will "to completion in the good" by protecting the saints not only from ever giving consent to wrongful desires but also from ever experiencing such desires in the first place. Already in this life, grace enables us to resist giving our consent to desires of the flesh. In the next, "our will is . . . brought to completion in good (*uoluntas perficitur in bono*)" such that we experience no such desires to resist.[38] An important implication of this promised perfection of will is that the meaning of the term *uoluntas* in Augustine's thinking must be understood to be more expansive than an impulse toward action generated by consent or refusal to consent.[39] If, for Augustine, the perfection of the will (*uoluntas*) remains incomplete until desires of the flesh (*conupiscentiae carnis*) are eliminated, then the term *uoluntas* also includes what we today might call "involuntary desires," tendencies to action we experience even without our consent. While the semantic range of the term "will" certainly extends beyond that of "desire" (*concupiscentia*) since will is responsible for consenting or withholding consent to such desire, it cannot be cordoned off

(2012): 396–419. For Couenhoven's presentation of Augustine's mature views on freedom and its compatibility with a "blessed necessity," see chapter 3 of *Stricken by Sin, Cured by Christ*, 59–106.

[37] See *c. Iul. imp.* 6.12 (CSEL 85.2:321). See also *c. Iul. imp.* 5.61, where Augustine writes that the "necessity of the good" is "reserved for the saints as their reward."

[38] See *c. Iul.* 3.26.62 (PL 44: 734): "For the desires of the flesh are not brought to completion in evil when the assent of our will is not given to them, and our will is not brought to completion in good, as long as there remains the movement of those desires to which we do not consent."

[39] *Pace* Sarah Catherine Byers, *Perception, Sensibility, and Moral Motivation in Augustine: A Stoic-Platonic Synthesis* (New York: Cambridge University Press, 2013), 26 and 217–231, and J. M. Rist, who describes uoluntas as "a love which has been accepted or consented to" in *Augustine: Ancient Thought Baptized* (New York: Cambridge University Press, 1994), 177. See Couenhoven, *Stricken by Sin, Cured by Christ*, 78, in contrast, for further reasons for skepticism about seeing Augustine's notion of *uoluntas* as requiring "conscious consent."

from such desire either. So long as evil desires remain, Augustine teaches, the will has not attained perfection.

Augustine describes the inability to sin, or even to experience sinful desires, that the will shall enjoy in the eschaton as a "voluntary and blessed necessity." In chapter 3 of this book, we noted Augustine's affirmation of the necessity of some voluntary acts, such as sin subsequent to the fall and before liberation by Christ. For Augustine, in contrast to what holds true for two of his most prominent Pelagian opponents, the notion of "voluntary necessity" is not an oxymoron.[40] As we observed, Augustine argues on the basis of Psalm 25:17, "Deliver me from my necessities," that the fallen will is subject to the "hard necessity" (dura necessitas) of remaining mired in sinfulness.[41] But just as the human will is subject to a "hard necessity" (dura necessitas) in its fallen condition, so it is subject to a "happy necessity" (felix . . . necessitas) in its fully transformed condition in the eschaton. When the human will (uoluntas) is "wholly healed and it has received freedom (libertas) . . . that freedom will be so great that, just as there necessarily remains the will to live happily, so there will exist the voluntary and blessed necessity (uoluntaria felixque necessitas) of living well and never sinning."[42] Whereas the "hard necessity" of the fallen will downgrades its freedom (libertas), the "happy and voluntary necessity" of the eschatological will marks the greatness of its freedom (tanta libertas).

The happy and voluntary necessity of the eschatological will's inability to sin, however, does not entail that the eschatological will is forced to stay aloof from sin. Augustine makes this point earlier in his career and he repeats it in works from the final stage of the Pelagian controversy. In c. ep. Pel. (421), he emphasizes that God does not force the unwilling but rather

---

[40] Augustine observes in nat. et grat. 51.59 that for Pelagius willing and necessity are inimical, but Augustine resists this assumption (nat. et gr. 46.54). In c. Iul. imp. 5.55 (CSEL 85.2:262) Julian separates the "necessary" (necessaria) and the "voluntary" (uoluntaria) into two separate groups: "Those things, then, which are necessary are natural, but those which are possible are voluntary." Augustine rejoins that the categories of the "voluntary" and the "necessary" can overlap: "There are also voluntary acts which are necessary; for example, we will to be happy, and it is necessary that we will this." CSEL 85.2:262: sunt et uoluntaria necessaria, sicut beati esse uolumus, et necesse est ut uelimus.

[41] See perf. iust. 4.9.

[42] Preceding this statement, Augustine writes, "But because the will sinned, there came upon the sinner the hard necessity of having sin until its will is . . ." (perf. iust. 4.9 [CSEL 42:9]). See also c. Iul. imp. 5.62 (CSEL 85.2:280), where Augustine refers to the "blessed necessity of virtue (necessitas felix), when our nature will be filled with such great grace and God will be all things in all, so that our nature will not be able to will anything wrongly."

makes the unwilling willing.[43] Even later in his career, in *c. Iul. imp.* (427–430), Augustine denies that grace makes obedience necessary in the sense of compelling people against their will. Although people do sin unwillingly, a point he regards as clear based on Job 14:17, one cannot be righteous unwillingly. Indeed, to be righteous is impossible if one obeys merely out of servile fear rather than out of willing love. God's justifying grace makes people "willing from unwilling" (*ex nolente uolentem*) and hence does not involve "a necessity by which any are compelled against their will (*inuitus opprimitur*)."[44] No one is forced against her will to receive this love by which the saints will be made perfectly righteous in the eschaton because this gift of love itself includes a reorientation of will.

Augustine makes this same point positively by underlining that free choice persists, even in the eschaton when the will shall be unable to sin. Free choice, he contends, becomes more free when it cannot sin than it is when it can: "But what will be more free (*liberius*) than free choice (*libero arbitrio*) when it will no longer be able to be a slave to sin? For this freedom would also have been for Adam the reward of his merit, as it has become that of the holy angels."[45] Not only is it the case that inability to be "a slave to sin" does nothing to mitigate the free choice of the saints in beatitude; it is also the case that the "limitation" of being unable to sin at all does nothing to mitigate free choice. Augustine makes this point explicitly in *ciu.*: "Now the fact that they will be unable to delight in sin does not entail that they will have no free choice (*liberum arbitrium*)."[46]

As it turns out, Augustine argues, the will's inability to sin in the eschaton promises to augment both human "freedom" and "free choice." Not only will the eschatological will be "free" despite this inability, but it will also "freer" because of it: "In fact, the will will be the freer (*magis . . . liberum*) in that it is freed from a delight in sin and immovably fixed in delight in not

---

[43] *C. ep. Pel.* 2.8.17.

[44] See *c. Iul. imp.* 3.122 (CSEL 85.1:440): "If you included among the various kinds of divine grace the love which, as you read most clearly in scripture does not come from us, but from God and which God gives to his children, that love without which no one lives a life of piety and with which no one lives anything but a life of piety, that love without which no one has a good will and with which no one has anything but good will, you would be defending a truly free choice and not inflating it with pride. If, however, you call that a necessity by which any are compelled against their will, there is no necessity of righteousness because none are righteous unwillingly. Rather, the grace of God makes them willing from unwilling. But if no one sins unwillingly, scripture would not say, *You have sealed my sins in a sack, and you have noted if I have done anything unwillingly* (Jb 14:17)."

[45] *Corrept.* 11.32 (CSEL 92:258–259).

[46] *Ciu.* 22.30 (CCL 48:863). I have modified Bettenson's translation to clarify that Augustine is discussing "free choice" rather than "free will."

sinning."[47] Furthermore, free choice in the eschaton will be "more potent" (*potentius*) than created free choice. Augustine writes, "The first free choice (*liberum arbitrium*), given to man when he was created upright at the beginning, was an ability not to sin, combined with the possibility of sinning. But this last free choice (*nouissimum*) will be more potent, for it will bring the impossibility of sinning."[48] For Augustine, the inability to sin, far from entailing a loss of freedom or free choice for the eschatological will, in fact explains the nature of the "liberty" (*libertas*) the human will is to enjoy in its finally exalted state.[49]

Augustine further specifies the character of the inability to sin that will belong to the saints in the next life by locating it in various theological contexts. First, he relates the eschatological will's inability to sin to the distinction between God the creator and his creatures. Does not the inability to sin erode the boundary between these two types of beings, granting to creaturely entities a kind of immunity to sin that belongs only to their Maker? To ward off such implications, Augustine is careful to insist on the point that the eschatological will's freedom from sin, as absolute as it is, remains distinct from God's freedom from sin, which is of a different caliber. Only God enjoys immunity to sin by nature; human beings, on the other hand, will one day possess this immunity by grace, by virtue of participation in God.[50] This distinction entails that, even in the eschaton, the final perfection and power of human willing is something human beings must receive from God. It is not something they inherently possess. At this mature stage of his thinking on human will, then, Augustine continues to construct his account of how human willing works (and, in this case, how willing will work) based on certain basic theological presuppositions. More specifically, as in the earliest stage of his thinking about the human will, he is still allowing the distinction between creator and creature to inform

[47] Ciu. 22.30 (CCL 48:863).

[48] Here again I have adjusted Bettenson's translation to make clear that "free choice" (*liberum arbitrium*) is at issue rather than "freedom of will" more generally speaking. See *ciu.* 22.30 (CCL 48:863).

[49] Augustine writes in *ciu.* 22.30 (CCL 48:864), "But because human nature sinned when it had the power to sin it is set free by a more abundant gift of grace so that it may be brought to that condition of liberty in which it is incapable of sin."

[50] See *ciu.* 22.30 (CCL 48:863): "Yet this also will be the result of God's gift, not of some inherent quality of nature. For to be a partaker of God is not the same thing as to be God; the inability to sin belongs to God's nature, while he who partakes of God's nature receives the impossibility of sinning as a gift from God."

his conclusions about what characteristics are appropriate to attribute to the human will and what characteristics are not.

Second, Augustine distinguishes eschatological free choice, the inability to sin, from the first free choice, the free choice of creation, characterizing the two as distinct "stages" of God's gracious work on behalf of humankind. The inability to sin does not descend on humankind out of nowhere as if it were a discrete act of God having nothing to do with the will in previous epochs or with the grace of God in the creation, fall, and redemption. Rather, the "last gift" of free choice whereby the wills of the saints become unable to sin finds a place in the broader economy of God's saving plan for the world. Explaining this broader context of the inability to sin in *ciu.*, Augustine writes, "Moreover, the stages of the divine gift had to be preserved. Free choice (*liberum arbitrium*) was given first, with the ability not to sin; and the last gift was the inability to sin. The first free choice was designed for acquiring merit; the last was concerned with the reception of a reward."[51] The inability to sin, while constituting a variety of "free choice" drastically different from the variety given in creation, follows logically from the first free choice. They are designed to fit together to form one coherent progression: the first free choice was supposed to prepare the way for and anticipate the last, while the last was intended to complete and reward the first. Though, due to the vagaries of human sin, this logical progression was interrupted and complicated, the organic connection between the first and last stages still holds together in the redemptive purposes of God.

Strikingly, Augustine refers to the "first" (*primum*) and "last" (*nouissimum*) versions of free choice, rather than to the first and second: "The first free choice (*primum liberum arbitrium*) was the ability not to sin, the last (*nouissimum*) the inability to sin."[52] This characterization of the free choice of the eschatological will in relation to the free choice of the created will, then, does not refer explicitly to the intervening stages of the fallen will and the redeemed will, but does use terminology that allows for the complexity of Augustine's multistage account, which includes not only the created and eschatological wills but also the fallen and redeemed wills. It was always part of God's plan for the free choice of the created will to culminate in the fully perfected free choice of the eschatological will,

---

[51] Once again I have modified Bettenson's translation, lest Augustine's reference to "free choice" (*liberum arbitrium*) be mistaken for a reference to "free will" (*ciu.* 22.30 [CCL 48:863]).

[52] *Ciu.* 22.30 (CCL 48:864). My translation.

but this plan has been realized such that two further versions of free choice come alongside these two versions to amount to four distinct stages on the way to the accomplishment of God's will for humanity. Of these four stages, the eschatological will's inability to sin is the last or "newest."

Section B: Augustine's Theological Defense of the Compatibility of Freedom with Inability to Sin

As we have seen in the preceding section, Augustine's description of the eschatological will as possessing the inability to sin demonstrates how this new kind of human willing is at once distinct from previous types of human willing and also stands in coherent connection to them such that together they find their place in the larger patterns of God's ongoing relationship to creation and the economy of salvation. The inability to sin is a reward graciously granted to saints in the next life on the basis of the good willing God has enabled in this one. It represents the completion of God's redeeming work on the human will whereby the will shall be permanently released not only from sinful actions but also from sinful desires. Whereas the fallen will was subject to a "hard necessity," the eschatological will exhibits a "blessed necessity" that does not suffer compulsion in the same way the fallen will did. The inability to sin of the eschatological will means that, even as it represents the culmination and purgation of previous manifestations of human will, it attains a level of freedom unprecedented in any previous stage in Augustine's account of human willing. His description of the eschatological will's inability to sin further demonstrates both its connection to previous types of human willing and its superiority to them.

We now turn to Augustine's theological defense of this superiority. How can the eschatological will be more free than other types of human willing given that fewer alternatives stand open to it? Augustine provides two impressive case studies that challenge the assumption behind this question: the cases of Christ and God. In articulating this defense, as in developing his description of the specific characteristics of the inability to sin that belong to the eschatological will, Augustine further enmeshes his account of the eschatological will in theological context. He uses theological contexts to explain what this kind of willing entails, and he uses theological notions to defend the coherence of the explanations he has provided.

On more than one occasion, Augustine points out an unusual feature of Christ's humanity. Christ's human nature was fully possessed of a distinct human will by which he exercised free choice (as we have seen in chapter 5), but whereas even redeemed human beings always run the risk, in this life, of succumbing to sin, there "was no reason to fear that the human nature assumed in this ineffable way into the unity of the person by God the Word would sin by free choice of the will (*liberum uoluntatis . . . arbitrium*)."[53] For Christ to have used the free choice of his will to sin would have been unthinkable. Indeed the hypostatic union of Christ's human and divine natures assured that sin could never really threaten to hijack the free choice of his will. The assumption of his human nature into union with his divine nature "was such that the nature of the man (*natura hominis*) assumed by God in that way would admit in itself no impulse of an evil will (*motum malae uoluntatis admitteret*)."[54] By virtue of his unique personal identity as not only man but God and man, Christ's human nature always possessed a will like the eschatological human will rather than an "evil will" fitting the mold of the fallen human will, or even a created or redeemed human will: Christ's human will was, from the very beginning of his human existence, unable to sin.[55] It thus offers the one available human example of what our eschatological willing will be like.

Just as Augustine contends that the inability to sin will make our willing in the eschaton more, rather than less, free, so he argues that Christ's inability to sin augmented, rather than constricted, his freedom. He conveys the latter point in *praed. sanct.* by means of a series of rhetorical questions: "Was there any need to fear that, as he grew up, that man would sin by free choice (*libero arbitrio*)? Or did he for this reason lack free will (*libera uoluntas*)? And did he not rather have it to a greater degree to the extent that he was more unable to be a slave to sin?"[56] The first question conveys clearly that no, there was no need to fear that Christ would sin by free choice. As we have seen, such a fear would have been preposterous, according to Augustine, given the grace of the hypostatic union. The second question affirms the compatibility of Christ's inability to sin with free will. The third presses the argumentative point even further. Christ's inability to

---

[53] *Corrept.* 11.30 (CSEL 92:255).

[54] *Corrept.* 11.30 (CSEL 92:255).

[55] See also *Enchiridion ad Laurentium de fide spe et caritate* (*ench.*), 11.40: "the Son of God was Son of Man and the Son of Man Son of God, and thus in the assumption of human nature grace itself, which cannot allow any sin, became in some way natural to that man."

[56] *Praed. sanct.* 15.30 (PL 44:982).

subject himself to sin didn't merely avoid detracting from his free will; it was in fact positively related to his free will. The greater (*magis*) his incapability of sin, the greater (*magis*) his free will.

Though Augustine does not explicitly connect Christ's example to the eschatological will, explicit statements he does make about Christ's inability to become enslaved to sin and this inability's augmentation of his free will show us at least one key respect in which Christ's human will resembles the kind of willing promised to the saints in the eschaton more than any other kind of human willing we have thus far investigated. Yet Augustine does forge an implicit link between Christ and his argument for the compatibility of free will with inability to sin in that he explicitly invokes God as an example to support his case. For, as we have seen, Christ's immunity to sin in his human nature stems not from some intrinsic quality of his human will but from the union of his whole human nature with his incorruptible divine nature. Thus the case study of God, to which Augustine does explicitly connect the inability to sin of the eschatological will, in some sense includes the case of Christ, to which he does not establish such an explicit connection.

Augustine's appeal to God's inability to sin features most prominently in his enormous uncompleted work against Julian. We have observed that for Julian freedom of choice entails the possibility both of "committing sin and of refraining from sin."[57] As Augustine will repeat numerous times throughout the work, however, an insurmountable problem for Julian is that according to this definition of free choice "God then is not free (*liber*)." Why should this conclusion follow? Augustine explains by pointing to scripture, adding immediately, "Scripture says of him, *He cannot deny himself* (2 Tm 2:13)."[58] Given the biblical presupposition that there are certain things that God cannot do (*non potest*), including evils that would involve a denial of his own character, it follows that even God cannot measure up to the standard Julian sets for free choice. Augustine, then, uses a biblically informed theological argument to show why God represents a counterexample that disproves Julian's deliberative understanding of free choice. If Julian is right that free choice requires the ability to select from among multiple alternatives, then God lacks it.[59]

---

[57] C. Iul. imp. 1.78.
[58] C. Iul. imp. 1.81 (CSEL 85.1:95).
[59] See also c. Iul. imp. 5.38 (CSEL 85.2:237), where Augustine repeats a similar argument: "And you suppose that this belongs to the nature of free choice, namely, that it can will both, that is, both

According to Augustine, Julian denies God freedom and free will, as well as free choice, by setting up requirements for freedom and free will according to this same deliberative logic. "If only that is free (*liberum*) which is able to will two things, that is, good and evil," Augustine argues, "God is not free (*liber*), since he cannot will evil (*non potest uelle*)."[60] He later adds, "You define free will (*liberam uoluntatem*) so that it could not be free (*libera*) if it could not do both, that is, both do good and do evil. And for this reason, you must remove freedom (*libertatem*) from God who can have only a good will, but cannot have a bad will (*malam uoluntatem*)."[61] Neither free choice nor freedom nor free will can pertain to God, Augustine maintains, according to Julian's deliberative understandings of these notions.

The dilemma created by relating Julian's views of freedom to God, Augustine explicitly points out, rears its head again when it comes to thinking through the implications of the eschatological will's inability to sin. Augustine writes, "For you said, 'Free choice is nothing but the possibility of sinning and of not sinning.' By this definition you first of all took from God himself free choice, though you do not deny that he cannot sin, for you often say this too, and it is true. Next, the saints themselves will lose free choice in his kingdom where they will not be able to sin."[62] For Augustine, the saints' inability to sin parallels God's inability to sin insofar as in both cases this inability proves compatible with free choice.

God serves as an example, for Augustine, not only of the compatibility of freedom with inability to sin but also of the kind of "blessed necessity" this inability entails. In support of his claim against Julian that Julian's claims about the incompatibility of necessity and will are "not universally true" (*universaliter uerum*), Augustine cites "a certain blessed necessity" (*beata necessitas*) by which "it is necessary that God always lives both immutably and most happily."[63] Augustine is wary of making absolutist claims

---

to sin and not to sin. And you think that man was made to the image of God in this respect, though God himself cannot will both." Augustine also points to God as enjoying free choice despite the inability to sin outside the context of direct polemical debate with Julian, asking in *ciu.* 22.30 (CCL 48:864), "Certainly God himself cannot sin; are we therefore to say that God has no free choice (*liberum arbitrium*)?" I have adjusted Bettenson's translation to reflect that "free choice" rather than "free will" is in question.

[60] *C. Iul. imp.* 1.100 (CSEL 85.1:118). See also *c. Iul. imp.* 6.11 (CSEL 85.2: 316), where he states, "If, as you say, freedom (*libertas*) is only the possibility of voluntary good and evil, God does not have freedom (*libertatem*) since this possibility is not found in him."

[61] See *c. Iul. imp.* 3.120 (CSEL 85.1:439).

[62] *C. Iul. imp.* 6.10 (CSEL 85.2:312).

[63] Augustine's complete statement reads, "If, then, you say that the will cannot be attributed to necessity, even this is not universally true. For at times we will something which is necessary, as it is

about the functioning of the human will. In his conception of will, how the will works is contextually dependent. While there may be some cases and senses in which the will cannot be driven by necessity, there are other cases in which it can. There are "certain necessities so foreign to the will that there is necessity where there is no will and that there is will where there is no necessity," but there are also, as we have seen, necessities with which the will is all too familiar, such as the "hard necessity" of bondage to sin. As we have observed in this chapter, over and above the hard necessity of the "fallen will," there is also a necessity as yet unfamiliar but promised to the saints: the "blessed necessity" of their inability to sin in the eschaton. The "blessed necessity" of God's immutability and happiness corroborates Augustine's case that Julian's universal claims about the incompatibility of willing and necessity must be contextually qualified.

Furthermore, Augustine directly connects the necessity that God wills what is virtuous with the necessity of willing the good conferred upon the saints as their heavenly reward. Augustine first chides Julian that by dismissing the possibility that necessary virtue could also be voluntary, "you completely forgot about God, whose virtue is the more necessary to the degree that he wills it in such a way that he cannot not will it."[64] He then points out another example Julian's dismissal ignores: the "necessity of the good (*necessitatem boni*)" is "reserved for the saints as their reward; you forgot about them too, as you forgot about God."[65] Forgetting or overlooking the necessity of the saints' inability to sin in the eschaton follows, in Julian's case, from a similar theological forgetfulness. According to Augustine, the "blessed necessity" the saints are to enjoy in the eschaton when their will shall be completely insusceptible to sin parallels, and is therefore confirmed by, the "blessed necessity" of God's virtue. Theologically speaking, there are grounds not only for confidence in the possibility of such a voluntary

---

necessary that those who persevere in living good lives become blessed. At times it is also necessary that we will something, as it is necessary that we will happiness. Hence, there is even a certain blessed necessity (*beata necessitas*), because it is necessary that God always lives both immutably and most happily. But since there are also certain necessities so foreign to the will that there is necessity where there is no will and that there is will where there is no necessity, the statement is at least partially true that the will cannot be attributed to necessity" (*c. Iul. imp.* 5.53 [CSEL 85.2:259]).

[64] The full quotation from Augustine reads, "In your statement, 'This good which is called virtue would not have been voluntary if it had had the necessity for the good. It would, rather, have suffered under the necessity of the good if it had not had the possibility of evil,' you completely forgot about God, whose virtue is the more necessary to the degree that he wills it in such a way that he cannot not will it" (*c. Iul. imp.* 5.61 [CSEL 85.2:277]).

[65] See *c. Iul. imp.* 5.61 (CSEL 85.2:277).

necessity but also for desiring it. Augustine observes, "Virtue will be given us as a reward so that we do not have an evil will and also could not have such a will." He then exclaims, "O necessity that we should long for!"[66] The necessity of the eschatological will's inability to sin is nothing short of divine, and therefore worthy of our desire.

Augustine's characterization of the eschatological will's inability to sin, then, is embedded in theological contexts. Not only does he locate this inability to sin in relation to the creator-creature distinction and in the context of the various stages of the divine gift of free choice, corresponding to the various faces of his multifaceted view of will presented in this book. The inability of the eschatological will to sin also corresponds to and coheres with Augustine's description of the divine inability to sin, both as manifest in the perfect human willing of Jesus Christ made possible through the hypostatic union and in the eternally perfect and virtuous nature of the one triune God. In the following part of this chapter, we turn to a discussion of other descriptions Augustine provides of the eschatological will, which supplement in positive terms the information he has already provided in his negative description of it as a will unable to sin.

Part III: Willing in the Heavenly City

In addition to characterizing the eschatological will as a fully free will and a will unable to sin, Augustine provides a number of other positive descriptions of the eschatological will. He describes it as a will that has attained happiness and, as we shall see through a close reading of the conclusion of *ciu.*, as a will in complete harmony with the body, an inalienable will for piety and justice, a "free will" partaking in a common universal freedom, and a will with a history. We turn now to investigating these additional characterizations of the eschatological will. Cumulatively, they help to show that the reduced "options" of the eschatological will in no way exhaustively sum up Augustine's views on the character of human willing in the eschaton. Augustine develops a rich positive account of the eschatological will, one that coheres with his broader account of the entire story of human willing.

---

[66] *C. Iul. imp.* 5.61 (CSEL 85.2:278).

Everyone wills to be happy.[67] But not everyone actually is happy since this will does not suffice itself. What does happiness require, according to Augustine? In book 13 of *trin.*, he lists two necessary conditions for happiness: willing the right thing and obtaining what one wills. A bad will, he observes, is enough to make a person unhappy.[68] Unfortunately the converse does not hold true: a good will fails to guarantee happiness. Happiness requires not only having a good will[69] but also having this good will satisfied: "Thus no one is happy but the man who has everything he wants and wants nothing wrongly."[70]

Augustine calls happiness the final end (*finis*) of the will.[71] A priori, then, the eschatological will must be a happy one. But this is also a point he makes explicitly. In the next life and only in the next life, Augustine writes, will it really be possible for good people to live as they will to: "And only when a man who is faithful and good in these unhappy conditions passes from this life to the happy life, will there really and truly be what now cannot possibly be, namely that a man lives as he would (*quomodo uult*)."[72] All the necessary conditions for happiness will then be met: "He will not want (*uolet*) to live a bad life in that bliss, nor will he want (*uolet*) anything he lacks, nor will he lack anything that he wants (*quod uoluerit*)."[73] In the eschaton, the saints will not only will what is good but enjoy the good they will. In the presence of God, the will's thirst for happiness will finally be satisfied: "Everything that is there will be good, and the most high God will be the most high

[67] For one example where Augustine makes this point, see *c. Iul. imp.* 6.12 (CSEL 85.2:321). There he writes, "We all will to be happy, and we cannot not will this," before reiterating again that "to be happy" is "something that all will, even those who are unwilling to act rightly." The will to be happy, Augustine explains in *trin.* 13.11 (CCL 50A:398), is implanted in human beings by their creator: "The truth cries out that they do [want to be happy; *uolunt*] and nature . . . compels them to, having this will implanted in it by the supremely good and unchangeably happy creator." Augustine repeats in *ciu.* 22.30 (CCL 48:864) that even sin cannot disrupt the desire for happiness: "By sinning we lose our hold on piety and happiness; and yet in losing our happiness we do not lose the will to happiness (*uoluntatem felicitates*)." For an overview of Augustine's treatment of the theme of happiness from Cassiciacum to the *City of God*, see Ellen T. Charry, *God and the Art of Happiness* (Grand Rapids, MI: Eerdmans, 2010), 25–62. Charry points out the surprising dearth of literature on this topic in Augustine, but notes important studies (25n2).

[68] *Trin.* 13.8 (CCL 50A:392): "A man is made unhappy just by having a bad will alone, but much more so by the power to fulfill the desires of his bad will."

[69] See also *c. Iul. imp.* 6.12 (CSEL 85.2:321): "To live rightly . . . is the means to becoming happy."

[70] *Trin.* 13.8 (CCL 50A:393).

[71] See *trin.* 11.10 (CCL 50:346): "The will of man as such (*ipsa uoluntas hominis*) . . . has no other final end but happiness (*finis non est nisi beatitudo*)." By this Augustine means that all "wishes or willings . . . have their own proper ends which are referred to the end of that wish or will by which we wish to live happily and come to that life which is not to be referred to anything else but will be all-sufficient to the lover in itself."

[72] *Trin.* 13.10 (CCL 50A:394).

[73] *Trin.* 13.10 (CCL 50A:394).

good, and will be available for the enjoyment of his lovers, and thus total happiness will be forever assured."[74] The "free will" (*uoluntas libera*) of the heavenly city, Augustine pronounces at the conclusion of *ciu.*, will therefore "be freed from all evil and filled with all good, enjoying unfailingly the delight of eternal joys."[75] There the will shall reach its goal at last.

City of God culminates with a vision of this heavenly felicity.[76] Put in the proper frame of mind by the saying and the hearing of biblical words of praise,[77] Augustine himself tells out his praise for the glory of the city whose occupation shall be endless "praises of God, who will be all in all." This vision fills out the picture of the happiness of human willing in the eschaton. In the eschaton, Augustine writes, the body will immediately obey the dictates of the will, and the will shall will exclusively what promotes the benefit of spirit and body: "And we may be sure that where the spirit wills (*uolet*) there the body will straightaway be; and the spirit will never will (*uolet*) anything but what is to bring new beauty to the spirit and the body."[78] In short, complete harmony will prevail between will and body so that each works for the other's benefit.

Moreover, harmony will prevail in the content of the saints' willing itself, for there will be no more struggles with a divided will, torn between the option to choose good or evil, or a weak will, unable to realize in action the good at which it aims. Augustine reiterates again that by ensuring this kind of harmony and strength of will, the eschatological will's inability to sin will do nothing to interfere with its free choice. In fact, having been "freed" in this way will only increase the freedom of the eschatological free choice of the will, which "will be the freer in that it is . . . immovably fixed in a delight in not sinning."[79] Glossed in negative terms, the eschatological will's inability to sin does foreclose some options. But, viewed in positive terms, the inability to sin also guarantees gifts hitherto unavailable: imperturbable harmony and unshakable strength of will.

[74] *Trin.* 13.10 (CCL 50A:394).

[75] *Ciu.* 22.30 (CCL 48:864).

[76] *Ciu.* 22.30 (CCL 48:852): "How great will be that felicity, where there will be no evil, where no good will be withheld, where there will be leisure for the praises of God, who will be all in all!"

[77] Augustine prefaces the description that follows by explaining, "And this is the picture suggested to my mind by the sacred canticle, when I read or hear the words, 'Blessed are those who dwell in your house; they will praise you for ever and ever'" (*ciu.* 22.30 [CCL 48:852]).

[78] *Ciu.* 22.30 (CCL 48:862).

[79] The full quotation reads: "Now the fact that they will be unable to delight in sin does not entail that they will have no free choice (*liberum arbitrium*). In fact, free choice will be the freer (*magis . . . liberum*) in that it is freed (*liberatum*) from a delight in sin and immovably fixed in a delight in not sinning" (*ciu.* 22.30 [CCL 48:863]).

As we have seen in material already covered in this chapter, Augustine affirms that we do indeed have not just freedom but "free choice" (*liberum arbitrium*) in the eschaton. Still, in his vision of the heavenly will at the close of *City of God*, Augustine contrasts the first "free choice" (*liberum arbitrium*) given to Adam with the "freedom" (*libertas*) and "free will" (*uoluntas libera*) promised in the eschaton. So, though freedom of choice does exist in the eschaton, Augustine does not regard this freedom of choice as the key distinguishing feature of our will in the eschaton. Rather, our will shall have a freedom deeper than choice.

In further describing the freedom that will belong uniquely to the eschatological will, Augustine observes that whereas God granted Adam and Eve an inalienable will to happiness, he grants the saints in beatitude an inalienable "will to piety and justice" (*uoluntas pietatis et aequitatis*).[80] The saints, then, receive not only the longing for happiness but also the means to satisfy it. The created will is needy by nature; the eschatological will is gratified with goodness by grace. This is the positive flip side of the eschatological will's freedom from sin.

The "free will" (*uoluntas libera*) that is to belong to those in the heavenly city, Augustine continues, will not be possessed in different forms and to different degrees by various citizens, hoarded as a private possession. Rather, "it will be one and the same freedom in all, and indivisible in the separate individuals."[81] This unity and inseparability of will is best understood in terms of the common object of the wills of the saints.[82] Since this heavenly freedom will consist precisely in the perfectly harmonious and powerful "will to piety and justice," one may surmise that the citizens of the heavenly city will be united in willing piety and justice, and thereby in loving the one triune God. Distinctions between each person will not be effaced, but each person shall will in solidarity with the rest of the company of saints.

[80] "As man cannot lose the will to happiness, so he will not be able to lose the will to piety and justice" (*ciu.* 22.30 [CCL 48:864]).

[81] CCL 48:864: *erit ergo illius ciuitatis et una in omnibus et inseparabilis in singulis uoluntas libera.*

[82] Augustine's comments on the one faith and will of believers as common yet personal in *trin.* are instructive here. He points out that the Christian faith is common to all believers since they all share a faith of the same kind, even though "everyone actually has his own." The decisive point is that the object of their belief is the same, "what is believed is one thing," while "the faith it is believed with is another" (*trin.* 13.5). Similarly, in this case, what is willed is the same, while the human will in each person is distinct. See also Augustine's comments on the parallel case of the united will of the angels who are "fused into one will by a kind of spiritual fire of charity" in *trin.* 3.8.

This commonly shared eschatological "free will" (*uoluntas libera*), then, will be bound in unity to God and to the free will of the other residents of the heavenly city, but it will also, Augustine declares, be bound to the memory of its own story. While "forgetting all offences, forgetting all punishments . . . it will not forget its own liberation, nor be ungrateful to its liberator."[83] The eschatological will shall forget the past in the sense that the past will no longer be experienced as a present reality.[84] But it will still be able to recall the past intellectually. Both its forgetfulness and its mindfulness, then, will promote its freedom: the eschatological will will be set free from the suffering of the past while also set free to glorify God for the past. We will no longer experience the created will's freedom to choose between good and evil, but we will remember this original freedom, now brought to fruition in a full freedom for the good. We will no longer experience the fallen will's bondage to sin, but we will remember our fallen will, recalling the story of how its shackles fell off. We will no longer experience the struggle of good willing in this life, but we will remember the story of how, over time, our will was healed and liberated more and more until it was fully perfected in the last day. Now beyond the immediate experience of former forms of willing, the free will of the heavenly city will yet recall that the story of the human will contains more than its own blissful perfection. Free will in the eschaton will never "forget its own liberation."

In the synecdoche of this passage Augustine does something peculiar. He ascribes to the *uoluntas libera* attributes that extend beyond the expected domain. It is not only freed (*liberata*) and filled (*impleta*); it does not only enjoy (*fruens*). It can be mindful (*memor*) or forgetful (*immemor*) of things gone by. The will secures or severs a person's bonds to her past; it bequeaths to her a history.

Why think of the past amid such a glorious future? Augustine's answer is that we will remember not in spite of but because of the perfection of our eschatological freedom. For the citizens of the heavenly city will be free precisely to delight in praising God. They will remember their liberation because of the liberator who accomplished it, a liberator whose praises will be their joyful occupation. In Augustine's words, "Otherwise, if they were to lose the knowledge of their past misery how will they, as the psalm says,

---

[83] *Ciu.* 22.30 (CCL 48:864).

[84] *Ciu.* 22.30 (CCL 48:864): "It will remember even its past evils as far as intellectual knowledge is concerned; but it will utterly forget them as far as sense experience is concerned."

'sing the mercies of the Lord for all eternity'? Nothing will give more joy to that City than this song to the glory of the grace of Christ by whose blood we have been set free."[85] Part of enjoying freedom of will in the eschaton will be remembering how one has been set free. The eschatological will does not efface previous forms of human willing, but embraces them, in the memory of the liberation accomplished by Christ and in its endless songs of praise.

The purpose of this remembering, it turns out, sheds light not only on the purpose of the freedom the will shall enjoy in the eschaton but also on the goal of human willing more generally. This remembering of their liberation does help human beings to know themselves better. The larger story of which each individual person is a part—the biblical story of creation, fall, redemption, and final perfection—explains who human beings are, increasing their self knowledge. But this story of the liberation of the human will is eccentric because, despite the adjective "human," its protagonist is divine. The story begins not with the human will itself but with God, who created it. When the human will falls into bondage, it is God who converts it back to the good and grows it by his good gardening. When the will blossoms in full freedom in the eschaton, it is in the freedom of piously worshipping and justly serving its liberator. Knowing the story of the liberation of the human will helps human beings better grasp who God is, as well as who they are. It teaches them to know more and more "the glory of the grace of Christ by whose blood we have been set free." Perhaps for this reason Augustine adds that in the singing of our songs of praise for our liberation "that precept will find fulfillment: 'Be still, and know that I am God.'"[86] Endlessly retelling the story of the liberation of the will is an exercise in growing in knowledge of God, as well as in knowledge of self. Ceaselessly singing this story, and thereby drawing near to God in joyful praise, is the purpose of the freedom of the eschatological will, and the ultimate rest for which the human will longs, according to Augustine, in all of its forms.

Conclusion

In this chapter we have explored Augustine's characterization of the eschatological will in three areas: his description of it as a fully free will (part I),

---

[85] *Ciu.* 22.30 (CCL 48:864).
[86] *Ciu.* 22.30 (CCL 48:864).

his description of it as involving the inability to sin (part II), and other positive descriptions he provides of it, especially in *ciu.* 22.30 (part III). In part I, we observed the contrast between the eschatological will and the freedom of will in other periods of the story of human willing as well as the distinction between eschatological free will and free choice, a type of freedom of will included in but not coextensive with free will in its fullest sense. This part demonstrated that free willing in the eschaton, for Augustine, cannot simply be equated with the other types of human willing described in previous chapters of this book. Nor can the freedom of the eschatological will be reduced to mere free choice, though, importantly, it embraces free choice. Rather, eschatological willing makes up a unique subtype of human willing, possessing its own peculiar limitations and capacities.

Part II presented an analysis of the defining "limitation" of the eschatological will, one that distinguishes it from all other types of willing we have hitherto discussed: the inability to sin. We observed a number of defining characteristics of this inability: for Augustine, the inability to sin is a reward to be granted in the next life; it signifies the cessation of sinful desires as well as the cessation of consent to such desires; it entails a "blessed necessity" that is nonetheless incompatible with being forced against one's will; it increases free choice and it augments human freedom. Furthermore, it was demonstrated that Augustine delineates and defends the eschatological will's inability to sin in theological terms. He specifies the character of this inability to sin in relation to the distinction between creator and creature and in relation to other stages of the divine gift of free choice, and he shows its plausibility as a feature of free human willing by appealing to God's own freedom and inability to sin. This theological contextualization of the inability to sin helped to bring out that, far from representing an unfortunate shortcoming of the eschatological will, this "inability" really represents one of the key advances, if not the single most important advance, that eschatological willing makes upon willing in previous periods. The inability to sin is nothing short of God-like, though Augustine is careful to explain that human inability to sin in the eschaton must be distinguished from God's in that it always remains a product of grace rather than a given feature of human nature.

Continuing on to explore other positive aspects of Augustine's characterization of the eschatological will, part III examined his characterization of it as a will that has attained happiness. The bulk of this part was dedicated to a close reading of *ciu.* 22.30, where Augustine presents a vision of the felicity of willing in the heavenly city. There we learn that, as Augustine imagines it, the eschatological will shall be in complete harmony with the body; it will consist in a will for piety and justice; and it will be a "free will" sharing in a common freedom ensured by the common object of its love. Finally, we observed that *ciu.* 22.30 characterizes the eschatological will as a will with a remembered history of liberation, whose pages render the saints' praise more eloquent and their knowledge of God more profound.

As we observed at the outset of this chapter, Augustine faces a dearth of experiential and biblical material when it comes to characterizing the eschatological will. In this sense, there is much less to say, for the time being, about eschatological willing, than about any other kind of human willing we have investigated thus far. It is hard to tell the story of the eschatological will because this part of the story has not happened to us yet. Still, as we saw in part III, eschatological willing is the most expansive kind of human willing Augustine describes. The eschatological will does not float off into eternal bliss, leaving its history behind. Rather, its very freedom includes an awareness of this history, and the occupation of the saints in the heavenly city will be the endless singing of the story of the will's liberation to the praise of God. Thus free eschatological willing, exercised in endless worship, will embrace and transmute into praise all previous stages of human willing. The last chapter of the story of the human will itself contains the whole of the story, whereby the saints proclaim, "Great are you Lord, and greatly to be praised."

Conclusion

The Story of Augustine's Development as a Thinker

This book has told the story of Augustine's evolving thinking on the human will, an element of human experience that, on his telling, preoccupied him from infancy to old age. Our story began with the sunny scene of Cassiciacum, where, with the leisure to devote himself to philosophical inquiry, Augustine the new Christian articulated a highly optimistic view of the human will, even while already gently pushing the envelope of common assumptions about the relationship of will to reason. In the years between his baptism and his ordination as priest in 391, he continued to develop this hopeful perspective on human willing. In his dialogue with the Manichees, affirming the freedom and the goodness of the will proved vital. Augustine's notion of the will in this period served as a polemical sieve allowing him to separate matters that he believed his opponents confused: what should be attributed to God and what should be attributed to human beings; the necessary and the voluntary; and the identity of God the creator, who makes out of nothing, and the identity of human beings, made out of nothing. Thus, even while Augustine did not tend to corroborate his statements on the will with explicit appeals to specific biblical texts to the degree that he would later, he was already developing his notion of the will in theological context. In addition to deploying the concept of will to make theological distinctions in polemic against the Manichees, he also used the notion of will to interpret the biblical text, reasoned about the human will based on theological presuppositions, and utilized his notions of divine and human wills for mutual interpretation. Finally, Augustine situated his entire thinking on the human will in the context of the relationship between God the Creator and human beings as creatures. If not yet theologically differentiated, Augustine's thinking on the human will was already theological.

As he embarked on his priestly ministry, Augustine's notion of will gained a new dimension. Increasingly he became convinced that the fall had disrupted the power and goodness of the will as God had created it. Initially, in the work *Contra Fortunatum* (392), Augustine described this disruption as realizing itself on an individualized timeline in each person's life as she formed sinful habits; the formation of these sinful patterns of

Augustine on the Will. Han-luen Kantzer Komline, Oxford University Press (2020). © Oxford University Press.
DOI: 10.1093/oso/9780190948801.001.0001

behavior in her life demarcated her enjoyment of Adamic freedom from her participation in the implications of Adam's fall. Each person experienced Adam's fall of will, so to speak, at her own pace. In book 3 of *De libero arbitrio* (391–395), Augustine portrayed the effects of Adam's sin as more universal and immediate. Here he argued that Adam's sin exerted an instantaneous effect on humanity as a whole such that, because of Adam's sin, all people, at all times, need God's help to carry out what they know is right. The landmark work of this period, however, was *Ad Simplicianum* (396–398). This famous text opened with a similar position to that found in *lib. arb.* book 3. Augustine acknowledged a universal impact of the fall upon human willing but regarded this impact as restricted to the level of implementation. Willing the good was not a problem; the problem was performing the good one willed to do. But in interpreting Romans 9 in the second question of the first book of *Ad Simplicianum*, Augustine was compelled to extend his skepticism about the capacities of fallen human willing even further. After a great struggle, he finally gave in to the grace of God, as he recounts the story; the biblical text left him no option but to conclude that the good will itself, not merely enacting it, could be possible only by a gift of divine grace. The fallen will, Augustine had now become convinced, was starkly different from the human will in its created power and integrity; it would not avail to turn a person to God and stand in radical need of God's grace. Augustine had now added a distinct layer to his earliest conception of the human will: a new and distinct characterization of the will as fallen.

During the Pelagian controversy, Augustine chiseled away at yet another facet of his multisided view of human will: the good will, the new kind of human will that results when the fallen will, bound to sin, is set free by God's grace. Augustine's estimation of the extent to which human beings have the wherewithal to orient their wills to the good develops, over the course of the Pelagian controversy, in a way that mirrors the earlier development of his thinking in *Simpl*. From around 411 to 417, he refers to faith and belief as "in our power" and designates the rejection of God's gracious calling as a real possibility. In 417 and following, however, he refers to the will as doing "hardly anything" and points to grace as what "acts upon our wills"; describes God's teaching, call, election, and will as efficacious; and declares that, at least for infants, resisting God's will is impossible. In 426 and following Augustine makes clear that conversion of the will to the good happens "by the grace of God alone" such that "we do nothing good in our willing," while no human choice can resist God's will to save. On the extent of the good will's power to do the good it wills, his thinking is fairly constant during the Pelagian controversy: from *Simpl.* on Augustine teaches that God must grant human beings the power to enact the good they will. Yet another type of human will, willing whose goodness in no way stems from the will's autonomous capacities but rather must be effected, and then re-effected again and again from the outside, has taken shape in Augustine's thought.

Over the course of the Pelagian controversy, Augustine's thinking also developed on the question of God's contribution to the growth of the good will. Informed by arguments from biblical prayers and injunctions to prayer, the evolution of his thought on God's role in good human willing followed a similar trajectory to his thinking on the extent to which good willing was within human power. Throughout the Pelagian controversy, Augustine described God as offering a twofold help to enable good human willing. But whereas initially Augustine identified this twin assistance as bestowing knowledge and making the good attractive, in the controversy's second stage he characterized this help as reorienting the will and assisting people to carry out the good they willed. Also in the second stage of the Pelagian controversy (417–425), Augustine described God as "driving the will," assisting with discrete actions, pouring love into human wills, and operating on the human will in an interior and unmediated fashion. For Augustine in this period, God was the "author" of the good human will. In the controversy's final stage (426–430), the emphasis on God's agency in accomplishing good human willing became even more pronounced. Augustine now referred to God converting human beings to the good unilaterally, without the assistance of human beings. He characterized God as directing, inclining, and exercising dominion over human wills, as the only source of good human willing, and as bestowing a love necessary and sufficient for establishing good human willing. In the epoch of the good human will God takes center stage, and not merely as a creator responsible for hardwiring human willing such that it routinely functions in certain ways. Rather, like an electrical current, God must constantly shoot through the human being to rouse her from her sin-induced stupor and empower her to function well as she was intended to.

Augustine used a number of striking images and descriptions to characterize this new form of human willing, distinct from both created and fallen human willing. He called this good will a "root" and an "eye of the soul." He also described it as a will in the process of conversion, a will derived from God, a will directed to God, a will with faith in God, a will proper to the believer, and the one good work necessary for eternal life. Most important, Augustine not only characterized the good will as resulting from God's love but also identified it as "love" (*caritas*), a participation in God's very being. Love became the biblical core of Augustine's understanding of the redeemed human will.

More and more over the course of his career, and especially during the Pelagian controversy, Augustine saw the incarnation, whereby God demonstrated the extent of the divine love for the world, as illustrating good human willing. For, though this aspect of Augustine's Christology is not always recognized, he affirmed a human will in Christ distinct from Christ's divine will, eventually coming to anticipate, in his late anti-Arian writings, Maximus the Confessor's characterization of Christ's human will. By this time, Augustine saw Christ's human will as perfectly obedient and in harmony with the divine will, and therefore as distinct from the fallen human will, with its inveterate disposition to sin. In addition to coming to see Christ as taking on a distinct, perfectly obedient human will, Augustine also pointed to Christ as a model of grace's effect on the human will and as bringing about the transformation of the human will by grace. Augustine's Christology, then, shaped his account of good human willing from multiple angles.

Along with Augustine's growing emphasis on the importance of Christ's human will and Christ's person and work for the human will came a more highly developed account of the Holy Spirit's significance for the human will. Though Augustine had already connected the Holy Spirit with the human will in *De Genesi aduersus Manicheos* (*Gn. adu. Man.*), a work stemming from before his ordination to the priesthood, he described this relationship at much greater length and depth during the Pelagian controversy. Whereas earlier he had observed an analogy between the Holy Spirit and the human will, later in his career Augustine became persuaded that the Holy Spirit also intervened directly in human willing so as to enable fallen human beings to will the good. In the mature stages of his thinking, then, Augustine not only developed a more sophisticated account of the way in which the human will reflected the image of the Holy Spirit in relation to Father and Son, as recorded in *De trinitate*, but also emphasized the necessity of the Holy Spirit's work to set a person's will afire to delight in and love God, to heal her from sin so that she might freely choose the good, and to liberate her for obedience to God's commandments. For Augustine, the

Holy Spirit accomplished these effects in the human person by the Spirit's very presence, as the divine will that drives human wills. As Augustine developed this account of the Holy Spirit's relationship to human willing, both his understanding of the Holy Spirit and his understanding of the human will gained greater clarity.

The work of Christ and the Holy Spirit, Augustine taught during the Pelagian controversy, was constantly required to sustain believers in the good in this life, yet not brought to full fruition until the next. With the completion of this process of transformation in the resurrection, Augustine asserted, the will would enter a mode of existence distinct from its previous conditions as originally created, fallen, or even redeemed, enjoying a full freedom superior to the freedom the will possessed in any of these other periods. Furthermore, the eschatological will would be unable to sin. In the vision of willing in the heavenly city with which he concluded *De ciuitate Dei*, Augustine described the eschatological will as a will whose happiness would include complete harmony with the body, a will of piety and justice, a will partaking in a common freedom deriving from the single object of its love, and a will free from its former experience of suffering but secured to the memory of its liberation. Thus, at the conclusion of this magisterial work, Augustine brought his "theory of will" full circle. He had reached the "end" of the story of the human will, perfect happiness in praise of God, but in so doing he also returned to the beginning. For the eschatological will, Augustine made clear, would never cut itself loose from the historical account of its liberation. Instead, the saints would glory in this story, which proclaimed the greatness of their creator. The story of Augustine's developing thinking on the human will, then, ends with the completion, and endless repetition, of another story: the biblical story of human liberation from division for delight.

Images of the Will

How might one visualize the basic shape of Augustine's mature view of the human will, drawing together the diverse strands he gradually wove into his account over time: distinct yet linked descriptions of the will as created, fallen, redeemed, and fully perfected in the eschaton? Augustine conveniently provided images that evoke the peculiar character of the will in each of these contexts. He described the created will as a hinge (*cardo*), the fallen will as a link in a chain (*ansula catenae*), and the redeemed will as a root (*radix*). After this life is over, he wrote, the root planted in our redemption would reach perfect maturity, blossoming into a fully free will. We can visualize Augustine's conception of the will in this glorified, eschatological context as a flower in full bloom. As these images already begin to suggest, these types of human willing follow upon each other chronologically; none of them displaces another in the story of human willing, but neither do these forms of willing coexist in the same person simultaneously. Rather, these various types of willing represent successive stages in the story of human salvation.

Defining the Augustinian Will

The foregoing presentation of the key features of Augustine's view of the human will illustrates one of the difficulties of lining up his account of the will with previous accounts from the philosophical tradition. The difficulty is that Augustine does not have "an" account of will as a monolithic entity whose defining characteristics and capacities remain constant. Instead he develops at least four different accounts of human willing, corresponding to the theological contexts of creation, fall, redemption, and the final peace to be attained in the next life.

Baseline features do remain constant in Augustine's thinking about the will across all the phases of his development and across each of the four basic stages of human willing that combine to make up his mature view. He never abandons his earliest dynamic definition of human willing, from his days as a presbyter: it is a "movement of the soul (*motus mentis*) with nothing forcing it."[1] Our examination of *De trinitate* enabled us to fill out this basic definition with some further detail. The will is a movement of attraction or repulsion by which the human person relates to other entities, whether physical or spiritual. The genus of "willing" includes a wide variety of affections. All forms of love are species of will, but not all instances of will merit the designation of "love." As is clear from this brief description, Augustine's generalized notion of what the will is remains minimal, even with the added clarifications from *trin*. What the will is concretely—for

---

[1] *Duab. an.* 10.14 (CSEL 25.1.68): *definitur itaque isto modo: uoluntas est animi motus cogente nullo ad aliquid uel non amittendum uel adipiscendum.*

example, whether it is what we call love or hate—all depends on context: the entities being related, who is exercising the act of will in question, and under what conditions. Augustine's generalized conception of will is fairly useless for determining what a given instance of human willing "is" for practical purposes, for answering questions as basic as whether it is good or evil, say, or enslaved or free. Finding out Augustine's answers to these kinds of questions, questions of existential significance, requires bringing his multi-stage story of the human will within our purview.

To answer the question of whether Augustine's view of will represented a genuine innovation upon the views expressed by his philosophical predecessors, we need not attempt to distill from his thought an abstract philosophical definition of the human will. Indeed, such an attempt is doomed to miss what is most characteristic of his account, since Augustine, while constantly making use of philosophical conceptual tools, never thinks only as a philosopher. He is always thinking as a Christian and as a pastor.[2] And this means he is thinking in the concrete particular terms of God's revelation to his chosen people, culminating in God's taking on human flesh in the person of Jesus Christ. Augustine's perspectives on the will serve as one illustration of how his most original and profound contributions to the history of philosophy, to the Christian tradition, and to the intellectual heritage of the West result not from philosophical finesse but from reconsidering all of life from the ground up in light of the biblical narrative. Augustine's originality stems from his theology.

Sources of Augustine's Thinking on Will

In what, precisely, does the novelty of Augustine's theory of will consist? To discern how Augustine's conception of will is new and how it is not, it is helpful to consider how it relates to at least three groups of sources that shaped his own perspective: philosophical sources from outside the Christian tradition, earlier Christian writings, and crucial verses and pericopes from scripture. According to the work of Sarah Byers, a

---

[2] Pierre-Marie Hombert has made similar observations in considering Augustine's theology of grace, emphasizing its "pastoral" intent: "Behind the manifold writings of Augustine, there is the believer, there is the pastor." See Pierre-Marie Hombert, *Gloria gratiae: Se glorifier en Dieu, principe et fin de la théologie augustinienne de la grâce* (Paris: Institut d'Études Augustiniennes, 1996), 7 and 1.

comparison to the Stoic notion of *hormē* suggests that Augustine's conception of *uoluntas* offered little that was new.[3] As has been shown, there are reasons to question the exchangeability of Augustine's notion of *uoluntas* and Stoic *hormē*. Furthermore, even were Stoic *hormē* equivalent to Augustine's generalized, bare-bones notion of *uoluntas*, the Stoic account of *hormē* would still fail to represent an analogue to Augustine's multistage account of will indexed to the biblical events of creation, fall, redemption, and eschaton. Yet Augustine was clearly developing a notion of *uoluntas* in conversation with the philosophical sources prevalent in his time. Tellingly, however, his application of the term *uoluntas* could and did serve—as we saw in the example of his reception of Cicero's triad of *memoria, intellegentia,* and *prouidentia*—to revise and replace classic Stoic patterns of thought, in addition to repeating them.

Whereas the debts of Augustine's notion of *uoluntas* to Stoic thought have been overestimated, its inheritance from earlier Christian thinkers has been underestimated. Augustine built his understanding of the will upon a venerable tradition of Christian thinking about human freedom and responsibility, spanning East and West, and going back to the early apologists.[4] Origen of Alexandria, the most influential member of this group, will serve as an example. At a time when Christianity was still coming under fire as just one of many religious options in the Greco-Roman world, Origen, writing in the third century, developed the idea of human freedom as a key tenet of the Christian faith, one that distinguished it from other, more deterministic accounts of the human condition. Origen emphasized that the suffering and sinfulness of human life as we know it results from the free choice of each human being rather than from a cosmic clash between the powers of good and evil or the decree of the fates, over which human beings have no control. For Origen, free will referred to the capacity of human reason to choose between good and evil, and therefore served as the basis for human responsibility. Along with other early Christian apologists, he saw free will as presupposed in biblical injunctions to human beings to choose what is good as well as in the biblical notion of human responsibility for sin.[5]

---

[3] See Sarah Catherine Byers, *Perception, Sensibility, and Moral Motivation in Augustine: A Stoic-Platonic Synthesis* (New York: Cambridge University Press, 2013), 217.

[4] In addition to passages from Origen's *de principiis* on the importance of free will (see n5), see also Justin Martyr's first *Apology* 43, Athenagoras's *A Plea for the Christians* 2, Irenaeus's *Against Heresies* 4.37–39, and Tertullian's *de anima* 21.

[5] See Origen's *de principiis* 3.1.1–3.1.22; 3.4.3–3.4.4.

The fourth-century theologian Gregory of Nyssa illustrates how some of the key ideas of the apologists were carried forward into Augustine's time. Like Origen, Gregory viewed human freedom as essential for maintaining that people are responsible for what they do. Gregory therefore concluded that human freedom accounts for whether human beings receive or do not receive grace.[6] Taking on the Manichees, the early Augustine found himself in a polemical situation reminiscent of that in which the early apologists pioneered Christian thinking on freedom and free will. In this phase of his thought, he followed suit in the tradition they had shaped.

But Augustine also drew upon other Christian thinkers even closer to his own cultural and linguistic milieu in developing his unique perspective on the human will. Chief among these were Cyprian of Carthage, the North African martyr bishop, and Ambrose of Milan, Augustine's father in the Christian faith, at whose feet he had learned to appreciate the profundity of the Christian scriptures. Like twin buttresses, these towering figures support Augustine's thought on the will as it joins itself to the larger edifice of his inherited Christian tradition.

Though Cyprian died nearly a century before Augustine's death, his presence on the scene of North African ecclesial politics and theology was still palpable in Augustine's own time, and the great Carthaginian made his presence felt in the bishop of Hippo's written corpus as well as in his daily life.[7] Augustine appealed to Cyprian repeatedly to support his teaching on the limits and capacities of human willing, contending that Cyprian affirmed free choice and the insufficiency of human will without God's help, and that God can and does make the unwilling willing. A comparison with Cyprian's *On the Lord's Prayer* vindicates these claims to his support to a surprising degree. Though Cyprian does not refer to free choice in this treatise, he elsewhere articulates a distinction between voluntary and necessary human action that implies a similar notion. While he never in so many words observes the insufficiency of human willing absent God's aid, he does underline the need for God's grace if any good end is to be achieved, thereby implicitly endorsing such an assessment of the limits of human will. Finally, Cyprian does speak of the need for the operation of the "divine will"

---

[6] See Gregory of Nyssa's *Catechetical Oration* 29–31.

[7] Contrary to the suggestions of some recent literature, Augustine cites Cyprian by name more frequently than he does any other church father, excepting Paul. For the precise statistics, see Han-luen Kantzer Komline, "Grace, Free Will, and the Lord's Prayer: Cyprian's Importance for the 'Augustinian' Doctrine of Grace," *AS* 45, no. 2 (2014): 252–254.

(*uoluntas Dei*) "in us" (*in nobis*), though he does not pinpoint this operation as occurring on the level of human will. In these respects, Cyprian was on the cusp of the Augustinian notions of the fallen and redeemed wills; he had put nearly all of the theological conceptual framework in place upon which Augustine's articulation of these types of human willing would depend. Augustine's crucial addition to Cyprian's description of the impact of grace upon the human person was to pair language about a "divine will" with language of "human will." Augustine's view of the matter, however, was that Cyprian's precedent on related issues implied his own conclusions about God's gracious operation on the human will.[8]

Augustine finds in Ambrose of Milan not only an emphasis on the decisive role of God's will in transforming human beings similar to the one he finds in Cyprian but also allusions to the "human will." In *Contra Iulianum opus imperfectum* (*c. Iul. imp.*), Augustine quotes Ambrose as stating that "God calls those whom he pleases and makes religious whom he wills."[9] While this statement falls short of referring to the human will, one can see how such statements push to the brink of such a notion. The idea of the human will serves the purpose of explaining how God can make people religious, regardless of their disposition to religion, without violating their freedom. Subjecting Ambrose's writings to these kinds of synthetic interpretive moves did not always prove necessary, however, for Augustine had noticed texts where Ambrose himself took up biblical language of human willing. In one Ambrosian passage that Augustine quotes to support his view of predestination, Ambrose alludes to one of Augustine's favorite texts, Proverbs 8:35, "The will is prepared by the Lord," in conjunction with a reference to human will. Interpreting Luke 1:3, Ambrose writes, "For it did not seem good only by reason of the human will (*uoluntate tantum humana*), but as it was pleasing to Christ who speaks in me. . . . And when he says this he does not deny that it seemed good to God, for the will of human beings is prepared by God."[10] Here we see Ambrose functioning as a precedent not only for an explicit notion of the human will but also for the connection of

---

[8] For further details on Augustine's appeal to Cyprian's authority on the issue of the limits of human willing as well as claims Augustine lays to Cyprian's support for other aspects of his teaching on grace, see Kantzer Komline, "Grace, Free Will, and the Lord's Prayer," 255–279.

[9] See *c. Iul. imp.* 1.93 (CSEL 85.1:106).

[10] See *perseu.* 19.49 (PL 45:1024). On how Augustine both appropriated and went beyond Ambrose's teaching in his *Commentary on Luke,* see Han-luen Kantzer Komline, "From Building Blocks to Blueprints: Augustine's Reception of Ambrose's Commentary on Luke," in *Studia Patristica* 84, vol. 10, ed. Markus Vinzent (Leuven: Peeters, 2017), 153–166.

this notion with Proverbs 8:35, a pivotal text in Augustine's account of the human will. Augustine utilized both Cyprian and Ambrose, then, to bolster his mature views on the predicament of the fallen will and on the redeemed will's need for grace. The broader theological framework of Cyprian's thinking, Augustine was convinced, already entailed such notions implicitly, while Ambrose provided a precedent in terms of specific terminology.

A third crucial source for Augustine's thinking on the human will is the Christian scriptures. Specific verses and pericopes from the Old Testament as diverse as Proverbs 8:35, references in the *Enarrationes* to having a "right heart" before God, and tales of radical conversion from the historical books, proved decisive in leading Augustine to his distinctive articulation of the notion of human willing. As far as the New Testament is concerned, the single most important influence on Augustine's thinking on will was Paul. It was struggling with Paul that prompted the watershed developments of *Simpl.*, which were later reprised as Augustine's conception of human willing continued to develop over decades of controversy and constant ministry. He drew repeatedly on such texts as Romans 9, 1 Corinthians 4:7, Galatians 5:17, and Romans 7:19 to explain and justify his views of how human willing functions in its fallen state and what it requires to be healed. Augustine's involvement in polemical debates, rather than functioning as a competing explanation for the development of his views on the will, only further highlights the importance of the Pauline corpus for his thought.[11] His struggles with both the Manichees and his Pelagian opponents were, not least of all, struggles over Paul's legacy. His battles with these opponents took place on the field of Pauline interpretation. Examining the impact of these controversies upon Augustine's thinking has only further underlined the decisive role that Paul played in the development of his views.

As has been shown in successive chapters of this book treating each face of Augustine's multifaceted account of the human will, Augustine presents

---

[11] Manlio Simonetti has pointed out the contribution of Manicheism to prompting the Pauline renaissance of the late fourth and early fifth centuries. The Manichean dispute and the spread of asceticism in this period, Simonetti argues, revived the issue of the basis of justification and salvation. Were they due to free will or to some external cause? These two movements thus gave rise to a doctrinal impetus to study Paul. Pelagius, moreover, the author of an early Pauline commentary, played an active role in this Pauline renaissance, as did Theodore of Mopsuestia, Julian of Eclanum's host when he came under fire from Augustine. Thus both Augustine's Manichean and Pelagian polemical foes had personal ties to and promoted the renaissance in Pauline interpretation of Augustine's day. See Manlio Simonetti, *Biblical Interpretation in the Early Church: An Historical Introduction to Patristic Exegesis*, trans. John A. Hughes (New York: T. & T. Clark, 1994), 94. On the importance of Paul within Manicheism, see chapter 2.

his views on the topic not as introducing a new theory foreign to the biblical text but rather as emerging organically from the pronouncements of scripture. He derives many of his assessments of the concrete functioning of the human will from the biblical text, but he also draws his broader account of how these various contexts fit together in the larger arc of humanity's creation, fall, redemption, and final glorification from the overall narrative trajectory of the Bible. On both a micro and a macro level, Augustine developed an account of human will sourced from the story of scripture.

Augustine's attempts to inform his analysis of human willing with scripture fit his convictions about the subject matter in question: human willing itself, not just human efforts to theorize about this willing, he thought, should flow from God's word. Avowed methodology matched preferred ontology. In *Confessiones* (*conf.*) Augustine writes, "Your best servant is the person who does not attend so much to hearing what he himself wants (*audire quod ipse uoluerit*) as to willing what he has heard from you (*uelle quod a te audierit*)."[12] Serving God meant willing in a way that corresponded to the word from God that one had already received.[13] Our hearing is not to be conformed to what we already want; rather, what we want must be brought in line with what we have heard from God. This conviction served as a prescription for Augustine's vision of what the substantive source of human willing should be in addition to representing the ideal for the whole process by which he came to his mature understanding of the will.[14] At first, as he tells us so memorably in the *Retractationes*, he wanted free will to win out, and he struggled mightily to preserve it.

---

[12] *Conf.* 10.26.37 (CCL 27:175).

[13] As James O'Donnell observes in his commentary on *conf.*, "Hearing the Word is antecedent to right willing." See James Joseph O'Donnell, *Confessions* (New York: Oxford University Press, 1992), vol. 3, 196. O'Donnell's observation applies also to *conf.* 10.27.38, where the word precedes the reorientation of Augustine's desire and will: "You called and cried aloud and shattered my deafness."

[14] For Augustine, then, willing is not only the exercise of intellectual vision, though "vision" is certainly another important metaphor in his toolkit for thinking about the will (see chapter 5 of this book, where Augustine's portrayal of will as eye of the soul is discussed). For Phillip Cary, Augustine's distinctive psychology, including his notion of will, which is to be distinguished from that of the Stoics, is the product of an attempt to press his Platonist inheritance of the notion of intellectual vision into the service of a Christian doctrine of grace. See Phillip Cary, *Inner Grace: Augustine in the Traditions of Plato and Paul* (New York: Oxford University Press, 2008). His thinking on will is thus associated with all the problems attendant upon Platonist intellectual vision, one of which is a privileging of the visual over the auditory. Against this kind of privileging, Cary insists, "no mere seeing is enough. We walk by faith, not by sight," and faith has to do with being able to "hear" the gospel of Christ and believing it (128–129). Thus, in Cary's view, the Augustinian will is part of a matrix of thinking about grace that compromises the "Protestant" commitment to *fides ex auditu* (129). My view is that the Augustinian will depends methodologically and substantively upon the commitment to hearing the word of God as recorded in scripture.

But eventually, he recounts, he had to adjust his views to comport with what he was hearing from scripture. In terms of both method and matter, the banner over Augustine's notion of will reads *uoluntas ex auditu*. In this sense, the Christian scriptures anticipate Augustine's thinking on will, though few others, if any, anticipate him in at once adhering so closely to scripture when thinking through this topic and dedicating so much time and energy to it.

We should not conceive of philosophy, Christian precedent, and the biblical text as having provided input into Augustine's thinking as so many separate tributaries, coming together only in the reservoir of his own thought. Rather, these influences were mutually reinforcing from the outset. We have already observed how the Manichean and Pelagian polemical debates in which Augustine was embroiled encouraged his engagement with Paul. Likewise it is probable that Stoic and Pauline influences worked upon him in tandem. Though Augustine's view of will is sometimes portrayed as Stoic rather than biblical,[15] such a presentation of the matter dismisses the possibility of Stoic elements in the biblical corpus itself.[16] Just as some Stoic notions likely found their way

---

[15] Describing Augustine's statements about *uoluntas,* Byers presumes a dichotomy between "biblical" and "Stoic" qualities in Augustine's conception of will. She writes, "We might be tempted to assume that the puzzling sound of these statements is owing to a mysteriously Augustinian, biblical, Christian, or protomodern quality in the concept of 'will' itself." Instead, she contends, "across multiple texts we see that Augustine rather consistently uses the word *uoluntas* when he is speaking of motivation and using Stoic epistemological categories like impression and assent, and that he, like his Latin Stoic sources, uses *voluntas* for impulse (*hormē*) toward action" (*Perception, Sensibility, and Moral Motivation in Augustine*, 88–89).

[16] Since Abraham J. Malherbe's discussion of the role of popular philosophy in Paul's thought, New Testament scholars have tended to agree that the philosophies of Paul's intellectual milieu were operative in some form in his work, though opinions on the exact quantity and quality of these elements, and their relative weight with respect to other strands in his thinking, differ. See Abraham J. Malherbe, *Paul and the Popular Philosophers* (Minneapolis, MN: Fortress Press, 1989). For studies that seek to highlight significant Stoic strands in Paul's thinking, see Troels Engberg-Pedersen, *Cosmology and Self in the Apostle Paul: The Material Spirit* (New York: Oxford University Press, 2010), particularly chapter 4, which observes parallels between Paul's understanding of the relationship of divine and human agency and that of Epictetus; Troels Engberg-Pedersen, *Paul and the Stoics* (Louisville, KY: Westminster John Knox Press, 2000); and Tuomas Rasimus, Troels Engberg-Pedersen, and Ismo Dunderberg, eds., *Stoicism in Early Christianity* (Grand Rapids, MI: Baker Academic, 2010), which also addresses Stoicism in the New Testament more broadly speaking and in other early Christian texts. On the Hellenistic context of Paul's writings, see Troels Engberg-Pedersen, ed., *Paul beyond the Judaism/Hellenism Divide* (Louisville, KY: Westminster John Knox Press, 2001) and Troels Engberg-Pedersen, ed., *Paul in His Hellenistic Context* (Minneapolis, MN: Fortress Press, 1995). For essays treating the importance of a wide variety of aspects of Paul's context for his thinking on divine and human agency, see John M. G. Barclay and Simon J. Gathercole, eds., *Divine and Human Agency in Paul and His Cultural Environment*, Library of New Testament Studies 335 (London: T. & T. Clark, 2006).

into Augustine's views on will through scripture, in addition to flowing into his thought by more direct streams, scripture reached his conception of will through the conduit of earlier Christian writers. Though examples abound, we may note how Augustine points to Ambrose's use of Proverbs 8:35 and Cyprian using 1 Corinthians 4:7 as particularly important instances of this trend, as these verses served as linchpins for the Augustinian conception of will.[17] And, of course, ancient philosophy was part of the common idiom of the Christian tradition.

Precisely through a careful analysis of Augustine's thinking on will we have better equipped ourselves to see that his notion of *uoluntas* does not emerge in a vacuum. It draws on a number of overlapping streams of thought, though the relative importance, complexity, or even existence of each of these streams has not always been recognized. Here, as with Augustine's conception of will in general, familiarity may breed contempt. As observed in the introduction, it is easy to miss what is original about Augustine's thinking because many aspects of this thinking have become stock features of common Western intellectual perspectives. Likewise it is easy to miss the crucial role scripture and Christian traditions play in Augustine's thinking because we take so many features of these traditions, mediated to us not least of all by Augustine himself, for granted.

For an analysis and critique of the theoretical assumptions underlying the work of Malherbe and Engberg-Pedersen, see C. Kavin Rowe, *One True Life: The Stoics and Early Christians as Rival Traditions* (New Haven, CT: Yale University Press, 2016), 185–191. Rowe's criticism targets epistemology and the extent to which terms from differing traditions may be assumed to function univocally. He does not, however, deny that even rival traditions, which he takes Stoicism and Christianity to be, reflect overlapping assumptions. Nor does he intend to deny that Christians use terms found in Stoic texts. But he does deny that the meaning of these terms can be flatly equated, since this depends on the larger grammatical and linguistic context of the larger traditions and texts in which they are embedded. See objections 2 and 4 in his appendix, 259–261.

Rowe's overarching argument, as well as his specific critiques, pertains to this study insofar as Augustine's theological account of the human will illustrates both some of Rowe's general arguments about how Christianity and other traditions work, and the particular case he makes for the incommensurability of Christian and Stoic approaches to anthropology. See 199–201 and 228–230, where Rowe observes, "There is no such thing as 'the human' in abstraction from the story that runs from Adam to Jesus" (229). The same is true of the will as Augustine depicts it.

[17] As Gerald Bonner observes, "In the *Retractationes* 1.1.1 [28/29], he speaks as if it were St. Cyprian's *Three Books of Testimonies to Quirinus* III,4 which drew his attention to the significance of the Corinthians quotation." See Gerald Bonner, *Freedom and Necessity: St. Augustine's Teaching on Divine Power and Human Freedom* (Washington, DC: Catholic University of America Press, 2007), 44. Though Bonner ultimately concludes that this verse exercised its impact on Augustine gradually rather than at a single decisive moment, he observes the central role this text went on to play for Augustine, citing Hombert (see Bonner, 43–44). The influence of the story of the rich young ruler on Augustine and later readers through *The Life of Anthony* is another example of the pattern. See Gregory W. Lee, *Today When You Hear His Voice: Scripture, the Covenants, and the People of God* (Grand Rapids, MI: Eerdmans, 2016), 205.

Innovations in Augustine's Thinking on Will

This reflection brings us back to the question of novelty. What, if anything, was new about the Augustinian will? At least three features of Augustine's account of will deserve mention in this regard: theological differentiation, divine action, and the connection of the will with the heart.

First, Augustine introduced what I have been calling a "theologically differentiated" notion of the human will. As noted in the previous section, Augustine modeled his four-stage account of the human will after the basic narrative arc he identified in scripture, an arc moving from creation to fall to redemption and then to final consummation. This arc was, and is, familiar as could be. But the idea that the will functions in a drastically different way in each of these four periods of the Christian story of human salvation emerged with unprecedented clarity in Augustine's mature thought.[18] In terms more bold, stark, and direct than any had used before him, excepting only, perhaps, the biblical writers themselves, Augustine squarely acknowledged the contrast between the will in its original created integrity, the will in its fallen bondage, the will in its redeemed goodness, and the will in perfect freedom. The will in these various phases changed so radically that Augustine used entirely different imagery to describe each iteration. Moreover, the differences between the versions of will associated with each period were not limited to his use of contrasting metaphors. The concrete constraints, capabilities, and other characteristics of the will shifted from period to period. Augustine was the first person to observe that quite a number of important statements one might make about the human will are not "universally true."[19] Everything depended, he claimed, on context.

For Augustine the crucial question was a specific kind of context: theological context. For at the center of his account of the human will stood not

---

[18] Richard Sorabji has observed that Plotinus anticipated Augustine by connecting pride (*tolma*) and willing (*boulēthēnai* or *thelein*), and seeing these at the source of evil. See Richard Sorabji, *Emotion and Peace of Mind: From Stoic Agitation to Christian Temptation* (New York: Oxford University Press, 2000), 334. But Neal Gilbert also touches on a crucial point when he observes that what distinguished Augustine from earlier Latin writers was not the introduction of a concept of will *simpliciter*—indeed, the term *uoluntas* was already in use before Augustine to describe reasonable desire. What was new with Augustine was the idea that the will could be evil as well as good. See Neal Gilbert, "The Concept of Will in Early Latin Philosophy," *Journal of the History of Philosophy* 1 (1963): 18 and 32. As argued in this book, Augustine's statements justify extending this insight further.

[19] See *c. Iul. imp.* 5.53: "If, then, you say that the will cannot be attributed to necessity, even this is not universally true." CSEL 85.2: 259: *si ergo dicas: uoluntas necessitate non potest admoueri, ne hoc quidem uniuersaliter uerum est.*

the human agent but God. What God was doing to the human will turned out to be the decisive factor. The fallen will was the only unilateral contribution of the human race; all other types of willing were initiated by God. This was a second distinctive, and disorienting, feature of Augustine's account of the human will. God brought the created human will into existence, gifting it with extraordinary power and freedom. God rescued the fallen will from its imprisonment to sin, setting it free to seek the good. Again, God poured out grace upon the redeemed human will, enabling it to persevere in goodness and to enact the good at which it now aimed. Finally, God exalted the human will by grace to enjoy an unprecedented freedom, a God-like freedom from all possibility of sin, the freedom to delight endlessly in joyful, just praise. In all cases save sin, God's action rather than human action established the context that determined the characteristics of human willing. God's action began the story of the human will, and God's action brought it to its goal. What Augustine had said in *conf.* about beauty might as well be applied to his views on the will: "The hinge of this great subject lies in your creative act (*in arte tua*), almighty one: you alone do marvelous things."[20] Everything, in Augustine's mature account of human willing, turned on what God was doing. Augustine had developed a theocentric notion of the human will. Because, moreover, on Augustine's account, the God who transformed human willing was not merely the "unknown God" of the philosophers but also the God who became incarnate in Jesus Christ and touched human hearts by the power of the Holy Spirit, Augustine's theocentric notion of the human will was a distinctively Christian notion of the human will. The triune God stood at its center.

The theocentric character of Augustine's view of will led him to forge a connection that was definitive for his thinking on the topic: he linked together the notions of will (*uoluntas*) and heart (*cor*). Commenting on Augustine's originality in the epilogue to his classic work, *Augustine the Bishop*, Frederick van der Meer calls attention to Augustine's sensitivity to matters of the heart:

> He was an *homme de coeur,* blessed with the *esprit de finesse.* He is the
> father of Western piety, and, despite his intellectualism, the teacher of all
> who are unable to live by argument alone. In this connection one can only

---

[20] *Conf.* 4.15.24 (CCL 27:52).

repeat, once again, that passage from the *Pensées*: "Jesus Christ and St. Paul exist in the order of love, not in the intellectual order, for they aimed to bring fire, not to teach. Likewise St. Augustine . . ." Although his "heart" is to be understood not as a symbol of the will but as the seat of knowledge, and his "contemplation" is to be taken in the intellectualist sense, nevertheless, no-one can doubt for a moment that he did not simply approach divine truth with the surface of the personality, with the cold intellect, as a concept, but also experienced it as a profound reality in the furthest depths of his soul.[21]

Van der Meer's assessment requires qualification, but our investigation of Augustine's view of will can help us see how Augustine does elevate the heart vis-à-vis the intellect in a way that was unprecedented. Van der Meer is onto something when he endorses Pascal's idea that Augustine belongs in the order of love even more than he does in the intellectual order. But by associating Augustine's "heart" with knowledge as opposed to will, van der Meer understates his case. Specifying how these two terms are related, as the analysis of preceding chapters has equipped us to do, enables us to clarify why the intuition van der Meer is expressing is actually confirmed rather than qualified by Augustine's own Latin terminology. As we have seen in our discussion of the redeemed will, Augustine did not believe that "will" and "love" are always distinct entities. In fact, he identified a "good will" as "love" (*caritas*). Furthermore, just as he identifies a good will with love, so he identifies the seat of good willing, the will, with the seat of loving, the heart.

To reverse van der Meer's contrast by arguing that for Augustine "heart" is the symbol of will and not the seat of knowledge would only replace van der Meer's dilemma of the heart with another set of false alternatives. Instead it is vital to see that Augustine, in terminology as well as in general tenor, saw the will as just as much a matter of love and the heart as it was of the intellect. Van der Meer's impressionistic claims to Augustine's originality can be made more precise. There is, indeed, a way in which Augustine unseats the intellect from its throne in common understandings of human identity. He accomplished this by linking the will (*uoluntas*) and loving and the heart more closely than anyone had before him. His view of will shows us that a

[21] Frederick van der Meer, *Augustine the Bishop: The Life and Work of a Father of the Church* (New York: Sheed and Ward, 1962), 567.

person's heart, what a person loves, is at the core of who she is.[22] He does this by relating love to the Latin term *uoluntas* in a new way.

All three of the innovative features of Augustine's account of will here discussed—theological differentiation, theocentrism, and the connection to love—come into play in *conf.*, the remarkable account of Augustine's own story and the story of what it means to be a human being, a tiny piece of God's creation made and remade for eternal fellowship with the Creator. Augustine tells the story of creation, the fall, and redemption and holds out the hope of final restoration, not least of all through the lens of events in his own life.[23] The varying scenes of this story correspond to differences in what and how Augustine wills at any given time. God is the director of the events in the story. Augustine's journey to God happens because God is at work, constantly drawing Augustine toward his Maker. Finally, as any casual reader will see, the *conf.* is shot through with love; the outpouring of God's love in Augustine's heart transforms him to will rightly, and this love comes to palpable expression in the text. At one place in the work, Augustine confesses why he has bothered to recount the whole story of his former condition and his liberation: "See, I have narrated many things to you. I was able (*potui*) and wanted (*uolui*) to do this because you wanted first (*tu prior uoluisti*) that I confess to you my Lord God, because you are good, because your mercy endures forever."[24] Only because God first willed his confession does Augustine now will to make it. Augustine's story of the human will, like the story of his life, involves narrating many things: creation, fall, redemption, and eschaton, as well as their consequences for

[22] As we have seen, Augustine describes the human will as the site of God's direct intervention in human life; it is the first and crucial receptacle for the outpouring of the divine love that is grace. Given Augustine's identification of will with heart, such characterizations of the will reinforce the centrality of the heart for human identity. Observations of the importance of the heart likewise may be read as shedding light on the significance of will in his thought. See, for example, John Cavadini, "The Darkest Enigma: Reconsidering the Self in Augustine's Thought," *AS* 38, no. 1 (2007): 129, where Cavadini points out that Augustine uses "heart language . . . to describe one's most intimate identity." In speaking of the heart in this way, Augustine does not intend to suggest that the heart is something inherently "stable, settled, and solitary." Rather, the heart is at the core of human identity because it is the locus of human relationship to God, the place Christ is present and active through faith. Augustine's identification of will and heart means that what is true of the Augustinian heart also holds true for the will. To describe heart and will in the terms Augustine uses is to say that how God relates to the human being by grace is at the center of human identity.

[23] For an example of how Augustine's descriptions of events in his life point to larger patterns in the human condition and to the biblical narrative's capacity to illuminate these patterns, as far as they can be illuminated, see John Cavadini, "Book Two: Augustine's Book of Shadows," in *A Reader's Companion to Augustine's Confessions*, ed. Kim Paffenroth and Robert Peter Kennedy (Louisville, KY: Westminster John Knox Press, 2003), 25–34.

[24] *Conf.* 11.1.1 (CCL 27:194).

human existence. But, as this quotation suggests, none of this narration would have been possible without God. Just as, according to Augustine's account of the will, God's prior willing makes our good willing possible, so, he suggests here, the actual narration of his whole story derives from God's good and merciful initiative. The telling of the story depends on the same reality that it proclaims. Augustine's story of the will would be impossible to tell, and would fail to hold together, without a central dynamic: we will, just as we love, because God first willed and loved us.

Bibliography

I. Primary Sources

A. Latin Editions
1. CCL (Turnhout: Brepols)
Acad. CCL 29, 3–61. Ed. W. M. Green (1970).
ciu. CCL 47, 1–314; 48, 321–866. Ed. B. Dombart and A. Kalb (1955).
conf. CCL 27, 1–273. Ed. L. Verheijen (1981).
diu. qu. CCL 44A, 11–249. Ed. A. Mutzenbecher (1975).
en. Ps. CCL 38, 1–616; 39, 623–1417; 40, 1425–2196. Ed. E. Dekkers and J. Fraipont (1956).
ench. CCL 46, 49–114. Ed. M. Evans (1969).
haer. CCL 46, 283–351. Ed. R. Vander Plaetse and C. Beukers (1969).
Io. eu. tr. CCL 36, 1–688. Ed. R. Willems (1954).
c. Max. CCL 87A, 491–692. Ed. P.-M. Hombert (2009).
retr. CCL 57, 5–143. Ed. A. Mutzenbecher (1984).
c. s. Ar. CCL 87A, 183–256. Ed. P.-M. Hombert (2009).
Simpl. CCL 44, 7–91. Ed. A. Mutzenbecher (1970).
trin. CCL 50, 25–380; 50A, 381–535. Ed. W. J. Mountain and F. Glorie (1968).
uera rel. CCL 32, 187–260. Ed. K. D. Daur and J. Martin (1962).

2. CSEL (Vienna)
an. et or. CSEL 60, 303–419. Ed. C. F. Vrba and J. Zycha. F. Tempsky, 1913.
corrept. CSEL 92, 219–280. Ed. G. Folliet. Verlag der Österreichischen Akademie der Wissenschaften, 2000.
duab. an. CSEL 25.1, 51–80. Ed. J. Zycha. F. Tempsky, 1891/1892.
ep. 21 CSEL 34.1, 49–54. Ed. A. Goldbacher. F. Tempsky, 1895.
ep. 130 CSEL 44, 40–77. Ed. A. Goldbacher. F. Tempsky, 1904.
ep. 215 CSEL 57, 387–396. Ed. A. Goldbacher. F. Tempsky, 1911.
ep. 217 CSEL 57, 403–425. Ed. A. Goldbacher. F. Tempsky, 1911.
ep. 226 CSEL 57, 468–481. Ed. A. Goldbacher. F. Tempsky, 1911.
c. ep. Pel. CSEL 60, 423–570. Ed. C. F. Vrba and J. Zycha. F. Tempsky, 1913.
f. et symb. CSEL 41, 3–32. Ed. J. Zycha. F. Tempsky, 1900.
c. Fort. CSEL 25.1, 83–112. Ed. J. Zycha. F. Tempsky, 1891/1892.
gest. Pel. CSEL 42, 51–122. Ed. C. F. Vrba and J. Zycha. F. Tempsky, 1902.
Gn. litt. CSEL 28.1, 3–435. Ed. J. Zycha. F. Tempsky, 1894.
Gn. adu. Man. CSEL 91, 67–172. Ed. D. Weber. Verlag der Österreichischen Akademie der Wissenschaften, 1998.
gr. et pecc. or. CSEL 42, 125–206. Ed. C. F. Vrba and J. Zycha. F. Tempsky, 1902.

c. Iul. imp. 1–3 CSEL 85.1, 3–506. Ed. M. Zelzer. Hölder-Pichler-Tempsky, 1974.
c. Iul. imp. 4–6 CSEL 85.2, 3–464. Ed. M. Zelzer. Verlag der Österreichischen Akademie der Wissenschaften, 2004.
lib. arb. CSEL 74, 3–154. Ed. W. M. Green. Hölder-Pichler-Tempsky, 1956.
mor. CSEL 90, 3–156. Ed. J. B. Bauer. Hölder-Pichler-Tempsky, 1992.
nat. et gr. CSEL 60, 233–299. Ed. C. F. Vrba and J. Zycha. F. Tempsky, 1913.
nupt. et conc. CSEL 42, 211–319. Ed. C. F. Vrba and J. Zycha. F. Tempsky, 1902.
orig. an. CSEL 44, 545–585. Ed. A. Goldbacher. F. Tempsky, 1904.
pecc. mer. CSEL 60, 3–151. Ed. C. F. Vrba and J. Zycha. F. Tempsky, 1913.
perf. iust. CSEL 42, 3–48. Ed. C. F. Vrba and J. Zycha. F. Tempsky, 1902.
sol. CSEL 89, 3–98. Ed. W. Hörmann. Hölder-Pichler-Tempsky, 1986.
spir. et litt. CSEL 60, 155–229. Ed. C. F. Vrba and J. Zycha. F. Tempsky, 1913.

3. PL, ed. J. P. Migne (Paris, 1844–1864)
ep. Io. tr. PL 35, 1977–2062.
gr. et lib. arb. PL 44, 881–912.
c. Iul. PL 44, 641–874.
perseu. PL 45, 993–1034.
praed. sanct. PL 44, 959–992.
serm. 154 PL 38, 833–340.

4. Other Series
serm. 296 Miscellanea Agostiniana 1, 401–412. Rome: Tipografia Poliglotta Vaticana, 1930–1931.
serm. 54 Analecta Bollandiana 100, 265–269. Bruxelles: Société des Bollandistes, 1982.

B. English Translations
Augustine. *Against the Academicians and The Teacher.* Translated by Peter King. Indianapolis, IN: Hackett, 1995.
Augustine. "Answer to Julian." In *Answer to the Pelagians, II*, translated by Roland Teske, WSA I/24. Hyde Park, NY: New City Press, 1998.
Augustine. "Answer to Maximinus the Arian." In *Arianism and Other Heresies*, translated by Roland Teske, WSA I/18. Hyde Park, NY: New City Press, 1995.
Augustine. "Answer to the Arian Sermon." In *Arianism and Other Heresies*, translated by Roland Teske, WSA I/18. Hyde Park, NY: New City Press, 1995.
Augustine. *Answer to the Pelagians, IV: To the Monks of Hadrumetum and Provence.* Translated by Roland Teske, WSA I/26. Hyde Park, NY: New City Press, 1999.
Augustine. "Answer to the Two Letters of the Pelagians." In *Answer to the Pelagians, II*, translated by Roland Teske, WSA I/24. Hyde Park, NY: New City Press, 1998.
Augustine. *Arianism and Other Heresies.* Translated by Roland Teske, WSA I/18. Hyde Park, NY: New City Press, 1995.
Augustine. *Augustine: Earlier Writings.* Edited and translated by J. H. S. Burleigh. Philadelphia: Westminster Press, 1953.
Augustine. "The Catholic Way of Life and the Manichean Way of Life." In *The Manichean Debate*, translated by Roland Teske, WSA I/19. Hyde Park, NY: New City Press, 2006.
Augustine. *City of God.* Translated by Henry Bettenson. London: Penguin, 2003.
Augustine. *Confessions.* Translated by Henry Chadwick. New York: Oxford University Press, 1998.

Augustine. "A Debate with Fortunatus, a Manichean." In *The Manichean Debate*, translated by Roland Teske, WSA I/19. Hyde Park, NY: New City Press, 2006.

Augustine. "The Deeds of Pelagius." In *Answer to the Pelagians, I*, translated by Roland Teske, WSA I/23. Hyde Park, NY: New City Press, 1997.

Augustine. *Expositions of the Psalms*. Translated by Maria Boulding, WSA III/15–III/20. Hyde Park, NY: New City Press, 2000.

Augustine. "The Gift of Perseverance." In *Answer to the Pelagians, IV: To the Monks of Hadrumetum and Provence*, translated by Roland Teske, WSA I/26. Hyde Park, NY: New City Press, 1999.

Augustine. "Grace and Free Choice." In *Answer to the Pelagians, IV: To the Monks of Hadrumetum and Provence*, translated by Roland Teske, WSA I/26. Hyde Park, NY: New City Press, 1999.

Augustine. "The Grace of Christ and Original Sin." In *Answer to the Pelagians, I*, translated by Roland Teske, WSA I/23. Hyde Park, NY: New City Press, 1997.

Augustine. *Homilies on the First Epistle of John*. Translated by Boniface Ramsey, WSA I/14. Hyde Park, NY: New City Press, 2008.

Augustine. *Letters*. Translated by Roland Teske, WSA II/1–II/4. Hyde Park, NY: New City Press, 2001–2005.

Augustine. "Marriage and Desire." In *Answer to the Pelagians, II*, translated by Roland Teske, WSA I/24. Hyde Park, NY: New City Press, 1998.

Augustine. "The Miscellany of Eighty-Three Questions." In *Responses to Miscellaneous Questions*, translated by Boniface Ramsey, WSA I/12. Hyde Park, NY: New City Press, 2008.

Augustine. "Nature and Grace." In *Answer to the Pelagians, I*, translated by Roland Teske, WSA I/23. Hyde Park, NY: New City Press, 1997.

Augustine. "The Nature and Origin of the Soul." In *Answer to the Pelagians, I*, translated by Roland Teske, WSA I/23. Hyde Park, NY: New City Press, 1997.

Augustine. *On Free Choice of the Will*. Indianapolis, IN: Hackett, 1993.

Augustine. "On Free Will." In *Augustine: Earlier Writings*, edited by John H. S. Burleigh, 23–63. Philadelphia: Westminster Press, 1953.

Augustine. *On Genesis*. Edited by John E. Rotelle. Translated by Edmund Hill, WSA I/13. Hyde Park, NY: New City Press, 1995.

Augustine. "On Genesis: A Refutation of the Manichees." In *On Genesis*, translated by Edmund Hill, WSA I/13. Hyde Park, NY: New City Press, 2002.

Augustine. "On the Predestination of the Saints." In *Answer to the Pelagians, IV: To the Monks of Hadrumetum and Provence*, edited by John E. Rotelle, translated by Roland Teske, WSA I/26. Hyde Park, NY: New City Press, 1999.

Augustine. "The Perfection of Human Righteousness." In *Answer to the Pelagians, I*, translated by Roland Teske, WSA I/23. Hyde Park, NY: New City Press, 1997.

Augustine. "The Punishment and Forgiveness of Sins and the Baptism of Little Ones." In *Answer to the Pelagians, I*, translated by Roland Teske, WSA I/23. Hyde Park, NY: New City Press, 1997.

Augustine. "Rebuke and Grace." In *Answer to the Pelagians, IV: To the Monks of Hadrumetum and Provence*, translated by Roland Teske, WSA I/26. Hyde Park, NY: New City Press, 1999.

Augustine. *Responses to Miscellaneous Questions*. Translated by Boniface Ramsey, WSA I/12. Hyde Park, NY: New City Press, 2008.

Augustine. *Revisions*. Translated by Boniface Ramsey, WSA I/2. Hyde Park, NY: New City Press, 2006.

Augustine. *Sermons*. Translated by Edmund Hill, WSA III/1–III/11. Hyde Park, NY: New City Press, 1990.

Augustine. "The Soliloquies." In *Augustine: Earlier Writings*, translated by John H. S. Burleigh, 23–63. Philadelphia: Westminster Press, 1953.

Augustine. "The Spirit and the Letter." In *Answer to the Pelagians, I*, translated by Roland Teske, WSA I/23. Hyde Park, NY: New City Press, 1997.

Augustine. "To Simplician." In *Augustine: Earlier Writings*, translated by John H. S. Burleigh, 372–406. Philadelphia: The Westminster Press, 1953.

Augustine. *The Trinity*. Translated by Edmund Hill, WSA I/5. Hyde Park, NY: New City Press, 1991.

Augustine. "The Two Souls." In *The Manichean Debate*, translated by Roland Teske, WSA I/19. Hyde Park, NY: New City Press, 2006.

Augustine. "Unfinished Work in Answer to Julian." In *Answer to the Pelagians, III*, translated by Roland Teske, WSA I/25. Hyde Park, NY: New City Press, 1999.

Cyprian. "On the Lord's Prayer." In *On the Lord's Prayer: Tertullian, Cyprian, Origen*, translated by Alistair Stewart-Sykes, 65–93. Crestwood, NY: St. Vladimir's Seminary Press, 2004.

Erasmus, Desiderius, and Martin Luther. *Erasmus-Luther: Discourse on Free Will*. Translated by Martin F. Winter. New York: Frederick Ungar, 1961.

Origen. *On First Principles: Being Koetschau's Text of the* De Principiis. Translated by G. W. Butterworth. New York: Harper & Row, 1966.

II. Secondary Sources

Adams, Robert Merrihew. "Involuntary Sins." *Philosophical Review* 94 (1985): 3–31.

Arendt, Hannah. *The Life of the Mind: Volume Two, Willing*. New York: Harcourt Brace Jovanovich, 1978.

Ayres, Lewis. *Augustine and the Trinity*. New York: Cambridge University Press, 2010.

———. *Nicaea and Its Legacy: An Approach to Fourth-Century Trinitarian Theology*. New York: Oxford University Press, 2004.

Babcock, William. "Augustine and Paul: The Case of Romans IX." *Studia Patristica* 16 (1985): 473–479.

———. "Augustine on Sin and Moral Agency." *Journal of Religious Ethics* 16 (1988): 28–55.

———. "Augustine's Interpretation of Romans (A.D. 394–396)." *Augustinian Studies* 10 (1979): 55–74.

Ball, J. "Les développements de la doctrine de la liberté chez saint Augustin." *Revue philosophique de Louvain* 55 (1957): 404–413.

Barclay, John M. G., and Simon J. Gathercole, eds. *Divine and Human Agency in Paul and His Cultural Environment*. Library of New Testament Studies 335. London: T. & T. Clark, 2006.

Barnes, Michel. "Contra Sermonem Arianorum." In *Augustine through the Ages: An Encyclopedia*, edited by Allan D. Fitzgerald, 772–773. Grand Rapids, MI: Eerdmans, 1999.

Bathrellos, Demetrios. *The Byzantine Christ: Person, Nature, and Will in the Christology of Saint Maximus the Confessor*. Oxford Early Christian Studies. New York: Oxford University Press, 2004.

Berthold, Fred, Jr. "Free Will and Theodicy in Augustine: An Exposition and Critique." *Religious Studies* 17 (1981): 525–535.

Berthold, George C. "Did Maximus the Confessor Know Augustine?" *Studia Patristica* 17 (1982): 14–17.

———. "Dyothelite Language in Augustine's Christology." *Studia Patristica* 70 (2013): 357–364.

Bochet, Isabelle. *Saint Augustin et le désir de Dieu*. Paris: Études Augustiniennes, 1982.

Bonner, Gerald. *Freedom and Necessity: St. Augustine's Teaching on Divine Power and Human Freedom*. Washington, DC: Catholic University of America Press, 2007.

———. "Rufinus the Syrian and African Pelagianism." *Augustinian Studies* 1 (1970): 31–47.

Börjesson, Johannes. "Maximus the Confessor's Knowledge of Augustine: An Exploration of Evidence Derived from the Acta of the Lateran Council of 649." *Studia Patristica* 68 (2013): 325–336.

Boston, Thomas. *Human Nature in Its Fourfold State*. Falkirk: Patrick Mair, 1787.

Brown, Peter. *Augustine of Hippo: A Biography*. Berkeley: University of California Press, 2000.

———. "St. Augustine's Attitude to Religious Coercion." In *Religion and Society in the Age of Augustine*, 260–278. London: Faber and Faber, 1972.

Burnaby, John. *Amor Dei: A Study of the Religion of St. Augustine. The Hulsean Lectures for 1938*. London: Hodder & Stoughton, 1938.

Burns, J. Patout. *The Development of Augustine's Doctrine of Operative Grace*. Paris: Études Augustiniennes, 1980.

Byers, Sarah Catherine. *Perception, Sensibility, and Moral Motivation in Augustine: A Stoic-Platonic Synthesis*. New York: Cambridge University Press, 2013.

Cameron, Michael. *Christ Meets Me Everywhere: Augustine's Early Figurative Exegesis*. New York: Oxford University Press, 2012.

Cary, Phillip. *Augustine's Invention of the Inner Self: The Legacy of a Christian Platonist*. New York: Oxford University Press, 2000.

———. *Inner Grace: Augustine in the Traditions of Plato and Paul*. New York: Oxford University Press, 2008.

———. *Outward Signs: The Powerlessness of External Things in Augustine's Thought*. New York: Oxford University Press, 2008.

Cavadini, John. "Book Two: Augustine's Book of Shadows." In *A Reader's Companion to Augustine's Confessions*, edited by Kim Paffenroth and Robert Peter Kennedy, 25–34. Louisville, KY: Westminster John Knox Press, 2003.

———. "The Darkest Enigma: Reconsidering the Self in Augustine's Thought." *Augustinian Studies* 38, no. 1 (2007): 119–132.

———. "Feeling Right: Augustine on the Passions and Sexual Desire." *Augustinian Studies* 36, no. 1 (2005): 195–217.

Chappell, T. D. J. *Aristotle and Augustine on Freedom: Two Theories of Freedom, Voluntary Action, and Akrasia*. New York: Macmillan, 1995.

Charry, Ellen T. *God and the Art of Happiness*. Grand Rapids, MI: Eerdmans, 2010.

Cipriani, Nello. *Lo Spirito Santo, Amore che unisce: pneumatologia e spiritualità in Agostino*. Roma: Città nuova, 2011.

Clark, Mary T. *Augustine, Philosopher of Freedom: A Study in Comparative Philosophy*. New York: Desclée, 1958.

Couenhoven, Jesse. "The Necessities of Perfect Freedom." *International Journal of Systematic Theology* 14, no. 4 (2012): 396–419.

———. *Stricken by Sin, Cured by Christ: Agency, Necessity, and Culpability in Augustinian Theology*. New York: Oxford University Press, 2013.

Craig, William L. "Augustine on Foreknowledge and Free Will." *Augustinian Studies* 15 (1986): 41–63.

Daley, Brian E. "Christology." In *Augustine through the Ages: An Encyclopedia*, edited by Allan D. Fitzgerald, 164–169. Grand Rapids, MI: Eerdmans, 1999.

———. "The Giant's Twin Substances: Ambrose and the Christology of Augustine's *Contra Sermonem Arianorum*." In *Augustine: Presbyter Factus Sum*, edited by J. T. Lienhard et al., 477–495. New York: Peter Lang, 1993.

———. "A Humble Mediator: The Distinctive Elements in Saint Augustine's Christology." *Word and Spirit* 9 (1987): 100–117.

———. "Making a Human Will Divine: Augustine and Maximus on Christ and Human Salvation." In *Orthodox Readings of Augustine*, edited by Aristotle Papanikolaou and George E. Demacopoulos, 101–126. Crestwood, NY: St. Vladimir's Seminary Press, 2008.

Decelles, D. "Divine Prescience and Human Freedom in Augustine." *Augustinian Studies* 8 (1977): 151–160.

den Bok, N. W. "Freedom of the Will: A Systematic and Biographical Sounding of Augustine's Thoughts on Human Will." *Augustiniana* 44 (1994): 237–270.

Dihle, Albrecht. *The Theory of Will in Classical Antiquity*. Berkeley: University of California Press, 1982.

Dodaro, Robert. "Augustine on the Roles of Christ and the Holy Spirit in the Mediation of the Virtues." *Augustinian Studies* 41, no. 1 (2010): 145–163.

———. *Christ and the Just Society in the Thought of Augustine*. New York: Cambridge University Press, 2004.

Drecoll, Volker Henning. *Die Entstehung der Gnadenlehre Augustins*. Tübingen: Mohr Siebeck, 1999.

———, and Mirjam Kudella. *Augustin und der Manichäismus*. Tübingen: Mohr Siebeck, 2011.

Dupont, Anthony, and Matthew Alan Gaumer. "Gratia Dei, Gratia Sacramenti: Grace in Augustine of Hippo's Anti-Donatist Writings." *Ephemerides Theologicae Lovanienses* 86, no. 4 (2010): 307–329.

Du Roy, Olivier. *L'intelligence de la foi en la Trinité selon saint Augustin, genèse de sa théologie trinitaire jusqu'en 391*. Paris: Études Augustiniennes, 1966.

Engberg-Pedersen, Troels. *Cosmology and Self in the Apostle Paul: The Material Spirit*. New York: Oxford University Press, 2010.

———. *Paul and the Stoics*. Louisville, KY: Westminster John Knox Press, 2000.

———. *Paul beyond the Judaism/Hellenism Divide*. Louisville, KY: Westminster John Knox Press, 2001.

———, ed. *Paul in His Hellenistic Context*. Minneapolis, MN: Fortress Press, 1995.

Feldmann, Erich. "Der junge Augustinus und Paulus: Ein Beitrag zur (manichäischen) Paulus-Rezeption." In *Atti del terzo Congresso Internazionale di studi "Manicheismo e Oriente Cristiano antico,"* 41–76. Manichaean Studies 3. Turnhout: Brepols, 1997.

Flasch, Kurt. *Logik des Schreckens: Augustinus von Hippo, De diversis quaestionibus ad Simplicianum I 2*. Mainz: Dieterich'sche Verlagsbuchhandlung, 1990.

Frede, Michael. *A Free Will: Origins of the Notion in Ancient Thought*. Edited by A. A. Long. Berkeley: University of California Press, 2011.

Gerber, Chad Tyler. *The Spirit of Augustine's Early Theology: Contextualizing Augustine's Pneumatology*. Ashgate Studies in Philosophy & Theology in Late Antiquity. Burlington, VT: Ashgate, 2012.

Gilbert, Neal W. "The Concept of Will in Early Latin Philosophy." *Journal of the History of Philosophy* 1 (1963): 17–35.

Gilson, Etienne. *Introduction à l'étude de saint Augustin*. Paris: Vrin, 1928.

Harnack, Adolph. *History of Dogma*. Translated by Neil Buchanan et al. From the 3rd German edition. Vol. 5. Boston: Little, Brown, 1910.

Harrison, Carol. *Rethinking Augustine's Early Theology: An Argument for Continuity*. New York: Oxford University Press, 2006.

Harrison, Simon. *Augustine's Way into the Will: The Theological and Philosophical Significance of* De libero arbitrio. New York: Oxford University Press, 2006.

Hefele, Charles Joseph. *A History of the Councils of the Church, from the Original Documents*. Translated by William R. Clark. Vol. 5. Edinburgh: T. & T. Clark, 1896.

Hombert, Pierre-Marie. *Gloria gratiae: Se glorifier en Dieu, principe et fin de la théologie augustinienne de la grâce*. Paris: Institut d'Études Augustiniennes, 1996.

Hopkins, Jasper. "Augustine on Foreknowledge and Free Will." *International Journal for Philosophy of Religion* 8, no. 2 (1977): 111–126.

———. *Philosophical Criticism: Essays and Reviews*. Minneapolis, MN: Arthur J. Banning Press, 1994.

Horn, Christoph. "Augustinus und die Entstehung des philosophischen Willensbegriffs." *Zeitschrift für philosophische Forschung* 50 (1996): 113–132.

Huftier, Maurice. "Libre arbitre." *Recherches de théologie ancienne et médiévale* 33 (1966): 187–281.

Hume, David. *An Enquiry concerning the Principles of Morals: A Critical Edition*. Edited by Tom L. Beauchamp. New York: Clarendon Press, 2006.

Irwin, T. H. "Who Discovered the Will?" *Philosophical Perspectives* 6 (1992): 453–473.

Kahn, C. H. "Discovering the Will: From Aristotle to Augustine." In *The Question of "Eclecticism": Studies in Later Greek Philosophy*, edited by J. M. Dillon and A. A. Long, 234–259. Berkeley: University of California Press, 1988.

Kantzer Komline, Han-luen. "From Building Blocks to Blueprints: Augustine's Reception of Ambrose's Commentary on Luke." In *Studia Patristica* 84, vol. 10, edited by Markus Vinzent, 153–166. Leuven: Peeters, 2017.

———. "Grace, Free Will, and the Lord's Prayer: Cyprian's Importance for the 'Augustinian' Doctrine of Grace." *Augustinian Studies* 45, no. 2 (2014): 247–279.

———. "The Second Adam in Gethsemane: Augustine on the Human Will of Christ." *Revue d'études augustiniennes et patristiques* 58 (2012): 41–56.

———. "'Ut in illo uiueremus': Augustine on the Two Wills of Christ." *Studia Patristica* 70 (2013): 347–355.

Karfíková, Lenka. *Grace and the Will According to Augustine*. Boston: Brill, 2012.

Kelsey, David H. *Eccentric Existence: A Theological Anthropology*. Louisville, KY: Westminster John Knox Press, 2009.

Kenny, Anthony. *Aristotle's Theory of the Will*. New Haven, CT: Yale University Press, 1979.

Kierkegaard, Søren. *The Sickness unto Death*. Translated by Walter Lowrie. Princeton, NJ: Princeton University Press, 1941.

Kirwan, Christopher. "Review of Albrecht Dihle's *The Theory of the Will in Classical Antiquity*." *Classical Review*, new series, 34, no. 2 (1984): 335–336.

Knuuttila, Simo. *Emotions in Ancient and Medieval Philosophy*. New York: Clarendon Press, 2004.

Kondoleon, Theodore J. "Augustine and the Problem of Divine Foreknowledge and Free Will." *Augustinian Studies* 18 (1987): 166–187.

La Bonnardière, Anne-Marie. *Le livre de la Sagesse*. Paris: Études Augustiniennes, 1970.

———. *Le livre des proverbes*. Paris: Études Augustiniennes, 1975.

Lee, Gregory W. *Today When You Hear His Voice: Scripture, the Covenants, and the People of God*. Grand Rapids, MI: Eerdmans, 2016.

Lekkerkerker, A. F. W. *Römer 7 und Römer 9 bei Augustin*. Amsterdam: H. J. Paris, 1942.

Léon-Dufour, Xavier. "Grâce et libre arbitre chez saint Augustin: A propos de '*consentire vocatione Dei . . . propriae voluntatis est*.'" *Recherches de Science Religieuse* 33 (1946): 129–163.

Lettieri, Gaetano. *L'altro Agostino: Ermeneutica e retorica della grazia dalla crisi alla metamorfosi del De doctrina christiana*. Brescia: Morcelliana, 2001.

Lewis, Charlton T. *A Latin Dictionary*. New York: Oxford University Press, 1879.

MacDonald, Scott. "Augustine and Platonism: The Rejection of Divided-Soul Accounts of Akrasia." In *Uses and Abuses of the Classics: Western Interpretations of Greek Philosophy*, edited by Jorge J. E. Gracia and Jiyuan Yu, 75–88. Burlington, VT: Ashgate, 2004.

MacQueen, D. J. "Augustine on Free Will and Predestination: A Critique of J. H. Rist." *Museum Africum* 3 (1974): 17–27.

Malherbe, Abraham J. *Paul and the Popular Philosophers*. Minneapolis, MN: Fortress Press, 1989.

Mansfeld, Japp. "The Idea of Will in Chrysippus, Posidonius, and Galen." *Proceedings of the Boston Area Colloquium in Ancient Philosophy* 7 (1991): 108–110.

Marion, Jean-Luc. *Au lieu de soi: L'approche de saint Augustin*. Paris: Presses universitaires de France, 2008.

Maschio, Giorgio. "La tristesse de Jésus à Gethsémani: L'exégèse d'Ambroise de Milan." *Communio: Revue Catholique Internationale* 35 (2010): 91–102.

Mausbach, J. *Die Ethik des Heiligen Augustinus. Zweiter Band: Die sittliche Befähigung des Menschen und ihre Verwirklichung*. Freiburg: Herder, 1909.

O'Daly, Gerard. *Augustine's Philosophy of Mind*. Berkeley: University of California Press, 1987.

———. "Predestination and Freedom in Augustine's Ethics." In *Philosophy in Christianity*, edited by Godfrey Norman Agmondisham Vesey, 85–97. New York: Cambridge University Press, 1989.

O'Donnell, James Joseph. *Confessions*. New York: Oxford University Press, 1992.

Ogliari, Donato. *Gratia et Certamen: The Relationship between Grace and Free Will in the Discussion of Augustine with the So-Called Semipelagians*. Vol. 169. Bibliotheca Ephemeridum Theologicarum Lovaniensium. Leuven: Leuven University Press, 2003.

Pagliacci, Donatella. *Volere e amare: Agostino e la conversione del desiderio*. Roma: Città Nuova, 2003.

Pang, A. A. "Augustine on Divine Foreknowledge and Human Free Will." *Revue des Études Augustiniennes* 40 (1994): 417–433.

Rasimus, Tuomas, Troels Engberg-Pedersen, and Ismo Dunderberg, eds. *Stoicism in Early Christianity*. Grand Rapids, MI: Baker Academic, 2010.

Rees, Brinley Roderick. *The Letters of Pelagius and His Followers*. Rochester, NY: Boydell Press, 1991.

———. *Pelagius: A Reluctant Heretic*. Wolfeboro, NH: Boydell Press, 1988.

———. *Pelagius: Life and Letters*. Rochester, NY: Boydell Press, 1998.

Refoulé, F. "Datation du premier concile de Carthage contre les Pélagiens et du *Libellus fidei* de Rufin." *Revue des Études Augustiniennes* 9 (1963): 41–49.

Ries, Julien. "La Bible chez saint Augustine et chez les Manichéens." *Revue des Études Augustiniennes* 7 (1961): 231–243.

Ring, Thomas G. *An Simplicianus zwei Bücher über verschiedene Fragen*. Würzburg: Augustinus Verlag, 1991.

———. "Römer 7 in den Enarrationes in Psalmos." In *Signum Pietatis: Festgabe für Cornelius Petrus Mayer OSA zum 60. Geburtstag*, edited by Adolar Zumkeller, 383–407. Würzburg: Augustinus-Verlag, 1989.

Rist, J. M. *Augustine: Ancient Thought Baptized*. New York: Cambridge University Press, 1994.

———. "Augustine on Free Will and Predestination." *Journal of Theological Studies* 20 (1969): 420–447.

Rowe, C. Kavin. *One True Life: The Stoics and Early Christians as Rival Traditions*. New Haven, CT: Yale University Press, 2016.

Rowe, William L. "Augustine on Foreknowledge and Free Will." *Review of Metaphysics* 18, no. 2 (1964): 356–363.

Rutzenhöfer, Elke. "*Contra Fortunatum Disputatio*: Die Debatte mit Fortunatus." *Augustiniana* 42 (1992): 5–72.

Sage, Athanase. "Péché originel: Naissance d'un dogme." *Revue des Études Augustiniennes* 13 (1967): 211–248.

———. "Praeparatur Voluntas a Domino." *Revue des Études Augustiniennes* 10 (1964): 1–20.

Schaff, Philip. *History of the Christian Church*. 8th ed. Vol. 3. New York: Charles Scribner's Sons, 1914.

Sedley, David. Foreword in *A Free Will: Origins of the Notion in Ancient Thought*, by Michael Frede, vii–ix. Berkeley: University of California Press, 2011.

Sieben, Hermann-Josef, ed. *Antiarianische Schriften*. Vol. 48. Augustinus Opera-Werke. Munich: Ferdinand Schöningh, 2008.

Simonetti, Manlio. *Biblical Interpretation in the Early Church: An Historical Introduction to Patristic Exegesis*. Translated by John A. Hughes. New York: T. & T. Clark, 1994.

Sorabji, Richard. "The Concept of the Will from Plato to Maximus the Confessor." In *The Will and Human Action: From Antiquity to the Present Day*, edited by Thomas Pink and M. W. F. Stone, 6–28. New York: Routledge, 2003.

———. *Emotion and Peace of Mind: From Stoic Agitation to Christian Temptation*. New York: Oxford University Press, 2000.

TeSelle, Eugene. *Augustine, the Theologian*. New York: Herder and Herder, 1970.

———. "Faith." In *Augustine through the Ages: An Encyclopedia*, edited by Allan D. Fitzgerald, 347–350. Grand Rapids, MI: Eerdmans, 1999.

van der Meer, Frederick. *Augustine the Bishop: The Life and Work of a Father of the Church*. New York: Sheed and Ward, 1962.

van Gerven, J. "Liberté humaine et prescience divine d'après Augustin." *Revue philosophique de Louvain* 55 (1957): 317–330.

Verhees, Jacques. *God in beweging: Een onderzoek naar de pneumatologie van Augustinus*. Wageningen: H. Veenman, 1968.

Voelke, André-Jean. *L'idée de volonté dans le Stoïcisme*. Paris: Presses universitaires de France, 1973.

Wetzel, James. *Augustine and the Limits of Virtue*. New York: Cambridge University Press, 1992.

———. "Augustine on the Will." In *A Companion to Augustine*, edited by Mark Vessey, 339–352. Blackwell Companions to the Ancient World. Oxford: Wiley-Blackwell, 2012.

Widdicombe, Peter. "Athanasius and the Making of the Doctrine of the Trinity." *Pro Ecclesia* 6, no. 4 (1997): 456–478.

Wilken, Robert Louis. "*Spiritus sanctus secundum scripturas sanctas*: Exegetical Considerations of Augustine on the Holy Spirit." *Augustinian Studies* 31, no. 1 (2000): 1–18.

Williams, Rowan. "*De Trinitate*." In *Augustine through the Ages: An Encyclopedia*, edited by Allan D. Fitzgerald, 845–851. Grand Rapids, MI: Eerdmans, 1999.

———. *On Augustine*. New York: Bloomsbury, 2016.

Index to Works of Augustine

For the benefit of digital users, indexed terms that span two pages (e.g., 52–53) may, on occasion, appear on only one of those pages.

Scripture Index

For the benefit of digital users, indexed terms that span two pages (e.g., 52–53) may, on occasion, appear on only one of those pages.

Subject and Name Index

For the benefit of digital users, indexed terms that span two pages (e.g., 52–53) may, on occasion, appear on only one of those pages.

ignorance, *see also* knowledge
  evil a problem of, 81–82, 87
  obedience possible despite, 39–40
  as obstacle to right willing, 132–33
  sin not merely a problem of, 90
  in *Soliloquies*, 18
imago dei (image of God), 2n.8, 10–11,
    36–37, 54, 361–62, 369–70, 373–
    74, 377–78, 401n.60
imitation
  of Christ not sufficient for
      righteousness, 333–34
  of Christ requires liberation of Christ,
      291, 306
impulse toward action, *see hormē*
incarnation, 278, 282, 283–84, 285, 299–
    302, 321, 416, 419, 427–28
infant(s)
  Augustine as, 15
  and baptism, 131, 137
  God's will irresistible for, 125–26,
      145, 414–15
  lack free choice of will, 145, 390–91
  lack wills, 265–66n.114
intellect
  Augustine replaces intellect with charity
      as Platonic charioteer, 349
  as distinguished from will, 39–49, 56,
      101–2n.126, 428–30
  and feeling, 101–2n.126
  and human psychology, 284, 361–62,
      366, 377–78
  as not automatically producing good
      will, 39
  and sin, 1n.2
intentio (intention), 4, 37n.66, 111n.164,
    154, 242–45, 363–64,
    366–69, 375–76
intercession, 175–76, 188–89, 314–17,
    320–21n.135, 322–23
Irenaeus, 420n.4
Irwin, T. H., 3–4n.15
Isaac, 95

Jacob, 89, 95, 96, 97, 137
Julian of Eclanum, 12, 22n.21, 126–28,
    131, 145–47, 158–59, 198–99,
    204–5, 218–19, 229–34, 241,

    247–48, 265–66n.114, 269–71,
    273, 280, 304–5, 311–12, 317,
    386–87n.12, 387–88n.17, 389–
    90n.27, 395n.41, 401–4, 423n.11
justice/just
  and Christ, 278, 299, 305–6, 325–26
  and delight, 341–42
  and the eschatological will, 404, 407,
      410–11, 417
  injustice, 320–21
  and judgment, 139–40n.50, 281
  and the Lord's Prayer, 171
  reasoning from God's justice, 29, 42–43,
      53, 54–55
  and sin, 64, 74–75, 91, 181–82
  and theodicy, 33, 211n.136, 215–17,
      269–70n.124
  and the will, 133–34
justification, 140–41, 155, 255–56, 279,
    281, 299–300, 333–34, 395–96,
    423n.11
Justin Martyr, *see* apologists

Kahn, C. H., 2–3, 4–5, 9–10, 84n.70
Kantzer Komline, Han-luen, 86n.75, 157–
    58n.111, 178n.29, 286–87n.35,
    317n.123, 421–22n.7, 421–
    22n.8, 422–23n.10
Karfíková, Lenka, 5n.22, 6–7, 123n.8,
    142n.60, 374n.125
Kelsey, David H., 11n.38
Kenny, Anthony, 3–4, 84n.70
Kierkegaard, Søren, 1, 10, 81–82n.64
Kirwan, Christopher, 3
knowledge
  aligned with willing in
      Soliloquies, 17–21
  and common sense, 69, 70–72, 74
  and the eschaton, 381–82, 408–9
  of God, 5, 48–49, 145, 208, 410–11
  as God's gift, 218–19, 222, 237, 241–42,
      338, 415
  of the good, 127, 132–33, 136, 170, 180–
      84, 190, 195, 338
  and human psychology, 284–85, 364–
      65, 366, 369–70, 428–30
  of the law, 188–89
  love as surpassing, 339–40